D1031625

DOCUMENTARY HISTORY OF THE FIRST FEDERAL CONGRESS OF THE UNITED STATES OF AMERICA

4 March 1789–3 March 1791

SPONSORED BY

THE NATIONAL HISTORICAL PUBLICATIONS AND RECORDS COMMISSION

AND

THE GEORGE WASHINGTON UNIVERSITY

PROJECT STAFF
    CHARLENE BANGS BICKFORD, *Editor*
    KENNETH R. BOWLING, *Associate Editor*
    HELEN E. VEIT, *Associate Editor*

ADMINISTRATIVE ADVISORY COMMITTEE
    ROBERT BYRD
    LINDA GRANT DEPAUW, *Chair*
    CHARLES MCC. MATHIAS
    THOMAS P. O'NEILL
    GEORGE S. WILLS

VOLUME IX

THE DIARY OF WILLIAM MACLAY AND OTHER NOTES ON SENATE DEBATES

Kenneth R. Bowling

and

Helen E. Veit

Editors

The Johns Hopkins University Press, Baltimore and London

© 1988 The Johns Hopkins University Press
All rights reserved
Printed in the United States of America

The Johns Hopkins University Press
701 West 40th Street
Baltimore, Maryland 21211
The Johns Hopkins Press Ltd., London

The paper used in this publication meets the minimum
requirements of American National Standard for
Information Sciences—Permanence of Paper
for Printed Library Materials,
ANSI Z39.48-1984

Library of Congress Cataloging-in-Publication Data
Maclay, William, 1737–1804.
The diary of William Maclay and other notes on Senate debates.

(Documentary history of the First Federal Congress of the United States of America,
4 March, 1789–3 March, 1791; v. 9)
Bibliography: p.
Includes index.
1. Legislative journals—United States.   2. United States. Congress.   Senate—History—
Sources.   3. United States—Politics and government—1789–1797—Sources.
4. Maclay, William, 1737–1804.   I. Bowling, Kenneth R.   II. Veit, Helen E.
III. Series: Documentary history of the First Federal Congress of the United States of America,
March 4, 1789–March 3, 1791; v. 9.
KF350.D63 1972 vol. 9   328.73'09 s   87-22793
[KF45]   [328.73'01]
ISBN 0-8018-3535-6 (alk. paper)
ISBN 0-8018-3683-2 (pbk.; alk. paper)

To
Julian P. Boyd
(1903–1980),
who recognized the need
for a new edition of William Maclay's diary
and long hoped to complete it himself

CONTENTS

ILLUSTRATIONS

INTRODUCTION

When Vice President John Adams looked around the Senate chamber from the crimson-canopied chair in which he presided, he commonly observed several senators making notes. This was particularly true during such important debates as those concerning the location of the capital, the judiciary and funding acts, and the president's power to remove his appointees from office without the consent of the Senate. Senators made notes of their colleagues' remarks for the purposes of keeping track of arguments, knowing how and to whom they wished to respond, and maintaining a more complete record of Senate proceedings than that contained in its journals. Sometimes they drafted or completed copies of speeches they intended to deliver.

Adams's remark in his own notes, referring to William Maclay's "minutes," implies that no one was as diligent at note taking as the senator from Pennsylvania. Certainly no other senator valued his notes enough to transfer and expand upon them in a diary—Maclay called it a diary rather than a journal—like that which comprises Part I of this volume. Most of the senators probably discarded their notes soon after making them, while descendants destroyed others. What is probably only a small portion of the notes made by Pierce Butler of South Carolina, William Samuel Johnson of Connecticut, Rufus King of New York, William Paterson of New Jersey, and Paine Wingate of New Hampshire has survived. These, along with John Adams's notes, make up Part II. Unlike the diary of William Maclay, which can be read on its own with little introduction, some of the notes in Part II are barely intelligible without some knowledge of eighteenth century American political thought. But given this knowledge, they, especially those of William Samuel Johnson and William Paterson, are a fascinating source for the assumptions and general intellectual milieu of the members of the First Congress.

Historians have long sought documentary evidence of what occurred on the floor of the United States Senate during the six years when it met in secret. J. Franklin Jameson (1859–1937), who devoted a major part of his professional career to the location, preservation, and publication of manuscripts relating to the early national history of the United States, was one of these. His motivation came in part from his attitude toward the "full and in some respects valuable" record kept by William Maclay. Jameson considered Maclay "a man of a distinctly small, envious and suspicious character, and his diary record . . . so tinged with these qualities that I have always thought it a great pity that we have no better source." To a scholar he more candidly deplored the dependence of American historians on Maclay, whom he described variously as "a poor mean creature," a "contemptible creature," and an "atrabilious and parvanimus creature" whose diary is "poisoned and distorted by his mean malignancy."[1] The search proved frustrating for, although Jameson came close to discovering the notes of both William Paterson and Pierce Butler, he saw only the brief notes of John Adams and Rufus King, which descendants had published, and the speech of William S. Johnson.[2]

On 30 September 1788 William Maclay and Robert Morris of Pennsylvania became the first members elected to the First Federal Congress. Both men were Federalists who had worked for the adoption of the new United States Constitution. Morris, a Philadelphia merchant, had earned a national reputation by his service to Congress as superintendent of finance from 1781 to 1784, whereas virtually no one outside of Pennsylvania had heard of Maclay. Within his own state, however, Maclay was both well known and had sufficient political credentials to win the votes of all but one of the sixty-seven members of the politically divided assembly that elected the senators. The fundamental issue dividing the state's political parties was the governmental structure created by the state constitution of 1776. That document placed tremendous power in a unicameral assembly. The Supreme Executive Council and its president—the state had no governor—lacked independence and exercised little responsibility other than implementing the decisions of the assembly. Maclay had long supported the Anti-Constitutionalist or Republican party's campaign for basic constitutional change. Even so, Constitutionalist party legislators accepted Maclay as the best candidate because of his ties to land and agriculture and his residence west of the area of the state dominated by Philadelphia. The Anti-Constitutionalists, who controlled the assembly, considered Maclay an ideal choice, for he provided a western and agrarian balance while at the same time holding attitudes toward both the state and federal constitutions which were atypical of his section of the state. In addition, his personal and business ties to Philadelphians made him familiar with and often sympathetic to the city's needs and interests.[3]

His election to the federal legislature placed Maclay in a new political arena, among men who were, on the whole, better educated, better known, and more experienced in national politics than he. His Philadelphia friends did their best to recommend him to their New England and Southern correspondents. Political gadfly Benjamin Rush informed the Boston clergyman and

---

[1]To Walter Izard, 17 Oct. 1929, LC Archives, DLC; to George H. Haynes, 14 Dec. 1920, J. Franklin Jameson Papers, DLC; *American Historical Review* 1:375.

[2]Edmund C. Burnett to Jameson, 7 Oct. 1936, William S. Johnson Papers, DLC; Emily King Paterson to Jameson, [1902?], Jameson Papers, DLC; Owen Wister to Jameson, Pierce Butler Case File, DLC; Charles F. Adams, ed., *The Works of John Adams . . .*, 10 vols. (Boston, 1850–56); Charles R. King, ed., *The Life and Correspondence of Rufus King . . .*, 6 vols. (New York, 1894–1900).

[3]*DHFFE* 1:293–96. For more detail on WM's election, see Appendix E. For details about the political struggle between the Constitutionalists and Republicans in Pennsylvania from 1776 to 1790, see *Counter Revolution*.

historian Jeremy Belknap that "Mr. Maclay possesses great talents for government. . . . He is alike independent in fortune and spirit. In his manners he is a perfect republican." James Madison, soon to be a leader in the first United States House of Representatives, learned from Federalist publicist Tench Coxe that "Mr. Maclay, our Agricultural Senator is a decided federalist, of a neat clear landed property, with a law Education, a very straight head, of much more reading than the country Gentlemen in the middle states usually are, a man of fair character and great assiduity in Business."[4]

Abigail Adams reported to her husband John that a passing acquaintance "did not like pensilvana's chusing a man who had never been heard of before, he might be a good man, but he wanted those men in office whose fame had resounded throughout all the States." Adams was soon to hear more of Maclay from their mutual friend Benjamin Rush, who described him as "a scholar, a philosopher, and a statesman. Few men unite such great speculative with such accurate practical talents." When Vice President Adams and Maclay met, they took an immediate dislike to one another, in part because they shared more personality traits and values than either recognized. Adams considered Maclay to be a perfect specimen of the pedestrian type of person who should fill the powerless office of vice president.[5] Maclay had written for the newspapers in support of the election of Adams, but soon regretted his efforts. When provoked, it was Maclay's nature to put his ideas, observations, and frustrations on paper. Adams's preoccupation with ceremony so disturbed Maclay's republican sensibilities that it became a great spur to his decision to begin a daily record of what occurred in the Senate.

Thus did a man "who had never been heard of before" come to have a greater influence over what has been written about the First Federal Congress than any of his colleagues. The often caustic, sometimes witty, and generally accurate self-analytical diary that Senator Maclay kept stands just behind James Madison's notes from the Federal Convention as the most important journal in American political and constitutional history. It is the preeminent unofficial document of the First Congress and fundamental to the historical record of the United States Senate. A valuable source of information about both the work of the first Senate and the social life at the seat of government, it establishes without question that the founding fathers practiced the art of legislative politics much as their descendants do today. The diary illustrates the effects of personality and public opinion on the performance of a politician while providing insight into human nature.[6]

The first extant entry in the manuscript diary is that of 24 April 1789, but it is

---

[4]Coxe to Madison, 22 Oct. 1788, Madison Papers, DLC; *PBR*, p. 490.

[5]*DHFFE* 2:29; *PBR*, p. 499; John Adams to James Lovell, 16 July 1789, Adams Family Papers, MHi.

[6]Another analysis of WM's diary is Philip S. Klein, "Senator William Maclay," *Pennsylvania History* 10:83–93.

probable that Maclay began his endeavor at least one day earlier. The first signature of volume one of the manuscript is loose, and several of its ten pages are missing. Maclay used two of the pages for the rules he suggested for the Senate, which are printed here in Appendix A. His diary entries for 24 and 25 April fill two other pages. Six pages are unaccounted for, but, since Maclay numbered the first extant diary page as "3," it can be assumed that only two pages of dated diary entries are missing. The four other pages may have contained the Senate rules as adopted or perhaps something else Maclay considered important, since it is unlikely that such a frugal man left any pages blank. The abrupt beginning of the text further suggests that something is lacking because it was uncharacteristic of Maclay to undertake such a commitment without an explanation of motive. He later mentioned that his purpose was to provide information and justify himself to his constituents, particularly the Pennsylvania Assembly that elected him and to which he held himself accountable. The first time Maclay justified his behavior was in mid-May 1789, when he defended himself to Rush against charges that he had been opposing Adams in the Senate.

The point at which Maclay switched from being a supporter to an opponent of Adams can be dated precisely to the day prior to the first extant diary entry. On the morning of 23 April 1789 residents of New York City were "on tiptoe" about the arrival of George Washington, first president of the United States, due at the federal capital within hours. So Senator Maclay wrote Rush, adding that Adams, who had arrived two days earlier, manifested "every disposition to make himself acceptable to the Senate."[7] Later in the day, the Senate, six weeks after Maclay's arrival at New York and two weeks after achieving the quorum necessary to commence its business, debated the proper method of communication between the two houses of Congress and appointed a committee to determine what titles, if any, should be given to the president and vice president. The formality of these proposed ceremonies, which appeared to ape the British, and Adams's role in the proceedings incited Maclay to take notes of the debate.

The random and inconsistent punctuation in the early entries suggests that Maclay wrote them directly from his memory without thought to their style. Soon, however, he began the practice of making notes on loose sheets of paper during Senate debate. To give them style and permanence, he carefully rewrote them in narrative form in a blank book. As he did so, he added analysis of the debate and details about off-the-floor politics and his personal life at the federal capital, as well as comments on the character, motives, and morality of those with whom he associated. After making his daily entries, he regularly destroyed the notes, and only those for 23 September 1789 have survived. In April 1789, lacking a clean blank book, Maclay turned his "Letter Book 1789"

---

[7] To Rush, 23 April, 18 May 1789, Rush Papers, DLC.

upside down and began the narration in the back of it. The length of his early entries soon convinced the senator to retain copies of his letters elsewhere. Throughout his two-year term Maclay seldom failed to make an entry each day, and he was quick to scold himself if he delayed too long in transferring the notes to the bound volume. By the end of the First Federal Congress, he had filled two folio blank books and begun a third.

From the start, Maclay found himself at odds with most of his colleagues on such issues as the Senate rules, the adoption of British precedents in form or substance, the structure and procedures of the federal judiciary, the size and salaries of the federal bureaucracy, and the relationship between the executive and legislative branches. His displeasure with Congress and its decisions probably contributed to the poor health about which he so often complained. He saw the death of Pennsylvania Surveyor General John Lukens at the close of the first session of Congress as an opportunity to escape. Eminently qualified to fill the vacancy, Maclay argued to friends that he could serve Pennsylvania better as surveyor general than as senator. Maclay did not secure the appointment, and the second and third sessions of Congress proved no happier for him, despite the satisfaction of seeing Congress move to Philadelphia. Secretary of State Thomas Jefferson's foreign policy, Secretary of War Henry Knox's plan for a military establishment, and most particularly, Secretary of the Treasury Alexander Hamilton's recommendations for funding the debts of the federal and state governments all earned his opposition, while George Washington's support for them gradually diminished the revolutionary hero in his mind. Finally, the failure of two attempts to open the Senate debates to the public dismayed the democratic Maclay.[8]

The pain Maclay remembered when reflecting on his Senate career arose not only from his situation as a tenacious minority critic but also from a personality, a calvinistic morality, and an attitude about a legislator's role which he shared more with John Adams than with his other colleagues.[9] A sense of rectitude and a pessimistic view of human nature dominated Maclay's world view. While he believed that he almost always lived up to his high expectations for human behavior, he felt that most others did not, and he judged especially harshly those who, having once earned his respect, later fell from favor. Analytical and introspective by nature, Maclay was self-assured, proud, self-conscious, sensitive to neglect, and quick to take offense. He believed in temperance, frugality, seriousness, industry, integrity, fair play, and loyalty to the

[8]WM to Tench Coxe, 18 Oct. 1789, Coxe Papers, to Benjamin Rush, 18 Oct. 1789, Rush Papers, PHi; David Stuart to George Washington, 2 June 1790, GWP.

[9]On Adams's personality, see Paul Nagel, *Descent from Glory* (New York, 1983), chaps. 1–3. Contemporary comments on WM's personality are rare, but see Charles Lukens to Samuel Wallis, 15 Aug. 1773, Wallis Papers, PHarH, and Henry Wynkoop to Reading Beattie, 9 March 1789, *PMHB* 38:47. The analysis presented here is based on WM's diary and letters and on the insights Julian Boyd shared with the editors.

interests of locality and state. All of this combined to produce an unpretentious legislator, driven by a high-minded sense of self-sacrifice and duty to the public interest, who was economy minded, democratic, uncompromising, suspicious of motive, incapable of placing party loyalty first, and deeply concerned for—and defensive of—his reputation and that of the state he represented. Few of his Senate colleagues had the patience to look beneath his reserved and seemingly aloof manner, and Maclay was doomed to be an isolated, lonely, and usually ineffective outsider in the social and political life of the new government.

Maclay knew almost from the start of his Senate term that he would soon be judged by the Pennsylvania legislature which had elected him, for he had drawn a two year term when the Senate divided its members into two, four, and six year classes. His independence lost him the crucial support of the Philadelphia Federalists, and it became clear by the end of the second session that his reelection was in jeopardy. Despite his complaints about life as a senator, Maclay desired a second term primarily because he craved such a vote of confidence. In his analysis, he deserved and had earned reelection, and if the assembly did not willingly bestow it, he would not campaign for it. Occasionally, however, he made an effort. In late August 1790 he traveled to Philadelphia, where most of Pennsylvania's political leaders had gathered for the state constitutional convention and the final session of the state assembly under the Constitution of 1776. In his saddlebags he carried the diary he had so dutifully kept as a means of refreshing his memory so that he could justify his behavior to his constituents. Apparently, no one asked him to explain anything, much less to justify himself, and his diary provided instead a convenient place to record what he learned about the machinations over who should fill his Senate seat.[10]

When the assembly did not reelect Maclay to a second term, he returned home in the spring of 1791, mortified and deeply disturbed over the future of the United States. Occasionally he opened his Senate diary to reflect on that historic body. Indeed, some of the analysis that seems so insightful in the context of the date under which it appears was actually written days, months, and occasionally years later.

Some time after Maclay died in 1804, the senator's nephew, George Washington Harris (1798–1882), found the three volumes. He recognized their importance and, by the time of the Civil War, had shown excerpts to various members of Congress including Senators Simon Cameron of Pennsylvania and William Seward of New York. Harris, like J. Franklin Jameson, attempted to learn more about other surviving accounts of the debates of the first Senate.

---

[10]For information on the attempt to replace WM in the Senate, in addition to that in WM's diary, see Thomas Fitzsimons to Coxe, 20 Aug. 1790, Rush to Coxe, 13 Sept. 1790, Coxe Papers, PHi; and WM to Rush, 10 July 1790, Rush Papers, DLC.

From Alexander Hamilton's son, Harris sought the source for a quotation from a Senate debate which varied slightly from that in Maclay's journal. He read his uncle's 1789 and 1790 letters to Tench Coxe. Gales and Seaton, the editors of the debates of the early federal congresses, reported that not a particle of Senate debate was known beyond the little they had published in the *Annals of Congress*. They added that "the notes preserved by a senator in that early period must be very interesting, as shedding light on a portion of our public history so important and so little known."

By 1860 Harris had become convinced that portions of the diary should be printed at public expense. The joint library committee of Congress did not agree. Undaunted, Harris continued to seek congressional patronage for more than twenty years but with no success. When the committee rejected his request in 1866, it gave as one of its reasons the opinion that Congress should not pay to publish any manuscript that it did not own in a "complete and unmitigated" form. The diary was not "complete" because the second volume, which Harris had loaned to Jeremiah S. Black, later President James Buchanan's attorney general, could not be located. By June 1867, when Harris lined out Maclay's description of George Washington on 15 July 1790 as a dishcloth in the hands of Hamilton, he had retrieved the volume from Black. Someone had used it for a scrapbook, pasting newspaper clippings dated at Bedford, Pennsylvania, between 1850 and 1860 or later over several of the diary entries. To pressure the joint library committee, Harris secured a letter of support from Librarian of Congress A. R. Spofford in 1869. On 24 February 1870 the Senate adopted a resolution subsidizing the printing of the diary by offering Harris one thousand dollars and the promise to purchase some copies of the work when published. Harris's counteroffers were so outrageous that negotiations broke down. Six years later, Senator Cameron told Harris firmly that the library committee would reject any arrangement for publication unless it included purchase of the manuscript for the Library of Congress.[11]

After this rebuff Harris proceeded on his own and in 1880 his abbreviated and expurgated edition of the diary was published by a Harrisburg firm,[12] both Harper Brothers and Appleton having refused it. The dozens of pencil transcriptions and the sections marked to be omitted from the edition bear witness to both Harris's method of editing and his cavalier attitude toward the manu-

---

[11]Gales and Seaton to Simon Cameron, 7 Jan. 1859, G. W. Harris to James Hamilton, 13 May 1861, G. W. Harris receipt to Shippen B. Coxe, Nov. 1863, Harris Papers, PHi; John Killinger to G. W. Harris, 11 June 1860, Harris-Fisher Papers, PHarH; Letterbook of the Librarian of Congress, 1865–69, pp. 65, 92; Extracts from the Minutes of the Joint Committee on the Library, 1861–98, p. 12, LC Archives, DLC; A. R. Spofford to G. W. Harris, March 1869, G. W. Harris, ed., *Sketches of Debate in the First Senate . . .* (Harrisburg, Pa., 1880); S. Cameron to G. W. Harris, 29 May 1876, Society Small Collections, PHi.

[12]George W. Harris, ed., *Sketches of Debate in the First Senate of the United States in 1789–90–91 by William Maclay, A Senator from Pennsylvania* (Harrisburg, Pa.: Lane S. Hart, [1880]). A reprint was issued by Burt Franklin Editions of New York in 1969.

script. The joint library committee refused Harris's request in 1882 that Congress purchase a large number of copies of the book to help him recover his costs. Still not ready to give up, Harris next attempted to bypass the sacrosanct congressional committee process by having an appropriation for the purchase of the books inserted into the federal budget from the House floor. This unsuccessful effort came shortly before his death.[13]

In 1890, a "complete" edition of the diary was published by D. Appleton and Co. The editor was Edgar S. Maclay (1863–1919), a naval historian and distant cousin of the senator. He criticized the Harris edition because "many passages . . . were suppressed, as being too caustic in their strictures on eminent personages whom we are accustomed to regard with the highest veneration. This, however, in a great measure, destroyed the complexion of the context and the value of the work."[14] Far superior to most nineteenth-century documentary editing, Edgar Maclay's edition nevertheless corrected spelling, grammar, and punctuation, created paragraphs, omitted words that could not be transcribed or substituted others for them, and left out significant, though not extensive, portions of the text. In addition, there was no annotation to help the reader understand the document. Impressed with the diary as evidence for his interpretation of American political history, the historian Charles Beard reissued the 1890 edition verbatim in 1927, adding a second introduction and a handful of footnotes while retaining the 1890 index, despite changed pagination.[15]

In 1907 a descendant of William Maclay's daughter Esther, realizing the value of the diary, placed it on deposit at the Library of Congress. In 1924 he considered withdrawing the manuscript and asked the Library if its possession of the document was of any real consequence to the nation. The Library replied that, because the diary was a national manuscript, its withdrawal would be highly regrettable. In 1937, after the depositor's death, his family secured the support of Pennsylvania Senator Joseph Guffy for its effort to persuade Congress to purchase the deposited manuscript, threatening at the same time to withdraw it if the committee refused. Finally, in 1941, Congress paid the descendants $750 and secured the treasure for its library. The cost was about fifteen percent of what Harris had asked Congress to pay in 1870 to underwrite publication of a partial text of the document.[16]

---

[13]Harper & Brothers to G. W. Harris, 23, 27 July 1889, Appleton to G. W. Harris, 17 Aug., 17 Sept. 1880, Harris-Fisher Papers, PHarH; Samuel Randall to G. W. Harris, 26 June 1882, John Mitchell to G. W. Harris, Samuel Barr to G. W. Harris, 18 July 1882, Harris Collection, PHi.

[14]Edgar S. Maclay, *The Journal of William Maclay, United States Senator from Pennsylvania, 1789–1791* (New York: D. Appleton and Co., 1890).

[15]*The Journal of William Maclay, United States Senator from Pennsylvania, 1789–1791*, introduction by Charles A. Beard (New York: A & C Boni, 1927). In 1965 the Frederick Ungar Publishing Company of New York reprinted the Beard edition.

[16]Maclay Diary Case File, Manuscript Division, Memo, folder 339, Thomas Martin to Senator Joseph Guffey, 14 Dec. 1937, Manuscript Division Records, DLC.

Volume IX of the *Documentary History of the First Federal Congress* is the first of several volumes of the debates, correspondence, and other unofficial records of that body. It serves in particular as a supplement to volumes I and II, the Senate Legislative and Executive Journals, since it contains all known accounts of Senate debates. The bills and other official records to which the senators refer can be found in volumes IV through VIII of this series.

Transcription

Previous editions of these documents often not only modernized spelling and capitalization but also created words, sentences, and paragraphs. In contrast, our aim in transcription has been to alter the text as little as possible. We have preserved the writers' punctuation, capitalization, spelling, and paragraphing. On those occasions when the author's intent is unclear, we have attempted to base our decision on his usual practice; when such methodology provides no clue, we have followed modern form. An exception is the dateline or heading, to which we have given standard forms.

For the sake of comprehension and ease in reading, we have added spacing at what appears to be the end of a thought or sentence, whether or not it ends with a period. Similarly, we have retained the period and closed space when it comes within what appears to be an incomplete thought or sentence.

Symbols

{ } These braces indicate substantive additions to the diary of William Maclay which, as far as can be determined, were made on a date later than the original entry. No attempt has been made to date these additions although the reader may safely assume that most were made within several days.

⟨ ⟩ Angle brackets are employed to expand difficult or possibly ambiguous abbreviations, to add commas to separate proper names in lists, and to supply missing letters or words, for example, Am⟨eric⟩a, ⟨New⟩ York, and d⟨o⟩. Contractions with tildes are silently expanded.

[ ] Square brackets enclosing italics indicate information supplied by the editors. Words now missing from the Maclay diary which were there when Edgar S. Maclay published his edition in 1890 appear in Roman type inside square brackets. In Part II, Roman type in square brackets is also used in headings where the date is supplied by the editors.

Annotation

The annotation has been designed to enhance understanding of the First Federal Congress and the personal life of William Maclay. Subjects annotated in this volume will not be identified in future volumes of this documentary history unless additional information is required or is newly available.

References to Senate and House actions and documents that are clearly described in the *SLJ*, *SEJ*, or *HJ* on the date on which Maclay referred to them are not annotated. All references to towns and counties can be assumed to be in the colony or state of Pennsylvania unless otherwise indicated. The locations for all extant letters mentioned by William Maclay are footnoted or listed in Appendix D. They will appear in later volumes of the *Documentary History of the First Federal Congress*.

Population figures are from the 1790 census, and addresses are from contemporary New York and Philadelphia city directories. Geographical and biographical information without citation comes from Jedidiah Morse's *American Geography* or his *American Gazetteer, The Dictionary of American Biography, The Biographical Dictionary of Congress*, and *The Dictionary of National Biography*. Terms of office for Pennsylvania legislators are from the *Pennsylvania Manual, 1947–48*. Definitions or archaic words considered important enough to note are from the *Oxford English Dictionary*.

ACKNOWLEDGMENTS

The editors are grateful for the continued and long-term financial support that has been provided to this project by its two co-sponsors, the George Washington University and the National Historical Publications and Records Commission. Without the encouragement and commitment of these two institutions, publication of this volume would not have been possible. The AT&T Foundation also assisted us through a grant, and we wish to recognize publicly the importance of this contribution.

Several staff members of the First Congress project assisted the editors with this volume. Karen Hillerich Treeger committed a transcription to the word processor. She, Donna Cassell, and Wendy Wolff assisted with proofreading the transcription against the manuscript. In addition, Wendy Wolff lent her skilled editorial eye to the footnotes and improved them considerably. Allida Black did a content analysis of possible newspaper pieces by William Maclay. Most important was the contribution of Charlene Bickford. In addition to performing all of the administrative functions of a principal investigator, without which no volumes would appear, she made her well-honed editorial skills available to us whenever we sought them. In particular, she made valuable suggestions about the annotation and made decisions about how the volume, the first containing unofficial records of the First Congress, could and could not differ from its predecessors.

Members of the Maclay family have been supportive: Elizabeth Maclay Means, Margaret Maclay Paterson, and Lucy Maclay Koser of Gaithersburg, Maryland; Marjorie Maclay Heckler of Chambersburg, Pennsylvania; Margo Hykes of Haverford, Pennsylvania; and in particular Katherine Maclay of Gettysburg, Pennsylvania, and John and Joyce Maclay of Baltimore, Maryland, who provided access to family papers and other documents.

Various librarians and scholars have assisted the editors: Kenneth Coleman of the Department of History, University of Georgia; David Kimball and David Deutcher of Independence National Historical Park; Thomas Schaefer and Warren Wirebach of the Dauphin County Historical Society; Bonita Craft Grant and Maxine Lurie of the Rutgers University Library; Anne Ciliberti, Robert Lopresti, and Glen Bencivengo of William Paterson College; Roland Baumann of the Pennsylvania Historical and Museum Commission; Gordon Marshall of the Library Company of Philadelphia; Maxine Brennan of the Historical Society of Pennsylvania; William Casto of Texas Tech University; Gerald Shannon of Bethany College; Van Beck Hall of the Department of History, University of Pittsburgh; Dorothy Twohig of the Papers of George Washington; Kim E. Baer of the Pennsylvania Bar Association; James Perry of the Documentary History of the Supreme Court; Celeste Walker of the Adams Family Papers; Richard Sheldon and Don Singer of the National Historical

Publications and Records Commission; Margaret Christman of the National Portrait Gallery; Robert Haslack of the Embassy of the Netherlands; Jane Kaufman of Madison, Wisconsin; Richard B. Morris of the John Jay Papers; Dick Baker and Don Ritchie of the Senate History Office; and John Catanzariti of the Papers of Robert Morris.

The editors have often relied on the expertise of University of Wisconsin staff members, Eric Rothstein of the Department of English, Ken Sacks, Suzanne Desan, and Audrey Altstadt-Mirhadi of the Department of History, Mary Schil and William Cudlipp of the Department of Spanish and Portuguese, Gordon DenBoer and Lucy Brown of the First Federal Election Project, and Dorothy Whitcomb of the Medical Library. Our close association with the Documentary History of the Ratification of the Constitution at the University of Wisconsin has saved us months in the production schedule of this volume. Its staff, John Kaminski, Gaspare J. Saladino, Richard Leffler, and Charles Hagermann, provided the editors with space to work and access to their research collection. Especially useful was the extensive biographical research file compiled primarily by former staff member, Douglas Clanin. In particular, Saladino gave the biographical sketch a critical reading and Hagermann patiently assisted the editors in the use of computers. Another former staff member, Leonard Rapport, provided us with the initial information about the Maclay manuscripts within the then virtually unknown John Nicholson Papers at the Pennsylvania Historical and Museum Commission. Ernest Harper of Washington, D.C., deserves special mention for his support and encouragement.

The Library of Congress Manuscript Division frequently retrieved the Maclay manuscript so that we could access physical evidence and debate matters of transcription and afforded us the luxury of a private room in which we could proofread our transcription against the manuscript itself. Gary Kohn, Mary Wolfskill, Chuck Kelly, Janice Ruth, and James Hutson have each patiently honored our many requests. Jackie Goggin and Morey Rothberg of the division's J. Franklin Jameson Papers provided leads to valuable information about the history of the diary and the notes of William Paterson and Pierce Butler. Karen Garlic in the Library's Conservation Division, Lee Avdoyan in the Reference Room, and Carol Armbrewster in the European Division also assisted.

The editors wish to express special thanks to the late Julian Boyd, first editor of *The Papers of Thomas Jefferson*, Ruth Lester, his longtime associate, and Charles Cullen, his successor as editor. Boyd believed that Maclay's astute, penetrating insight into the motives of men, his candor, and his mastery of a trenchant pen produced a diary that was an American political classic. When Boyd died before he could complete his edition of Maclay's diary, Lester and Cullen provided us with Boyd's transcript (made by Joan Richardson, a former staff member) and his insightful notes about Maclay as a person and politician. Their generosity saved us much. In addition, Eugene Sheridan of the project undertook some important last-minute research for us at Princeton.

The editors are grateful to Jack Goellner, Director of the Johns Hopkins University Press, who enthusiastically endorsed our proposal to issue a paperback edition of this volume simultaneously with the hardback. In addition, Roger Bruns and Mary Giunta of the National Historical Publications and Records Commission encouraged this venture. We thank Jim Johnston, Henry Tom, and George Thompson of the Press and Charlie Mock of BG Composition, Inc. for assisting with our transition to computer typesetting, and Nancy West, who served as our competent and cheerful production editor.

CRP	T. Finn, ed., *Colonial Records of Pennsylvania*, 16 vols. (Harrisburg, Pa., 1851–53)
Counter Revolution	Robert L. Brunhouse, *The Counter-Revolution in Pennsylvania, 1776–1790* (Harrisburg, Pa., 1942)
DGW	Donald Jackson and Dorothy Twohig, eds., *The Diaries of George Washington*, 6 vols. (Charlottesville, Va., 1976–79)
DHFFC 4–6	*Legislative Histories*, volumes IV–VI of this series
DHFFE	*The Documentary History of the First Federal Elections, 1788–1790* (Merrill Jensen and Robert Becker, eds., vol. 1, Madison, Wis., 1976; Gordon DenBoer and Lucy Brown, eds., vols. 2–3, Madison, Wis., 1984–86)
DHROC	*The Documentary History of the Ratification of the Constitution* (Merrill Jensen, ed., vols. 1–3, Madison, Wis., 1976–78; John Kaminski, Gaspare Saladino, and Richard Leffler, eds., vols. 13–16, Madison, Wis., 1976–86)
DLC	Library of Congress, Washington, D.C.
DNA	United States National Archives, Washington, D.C.
DSI	Smithsonian Institution, Washington, D.C.
FFC	First Federal Congress
FG	[Philadelphia] *Federal Gazette*
GUS	*Gazette of the United States*, New York, N.Y., 15 April 1789–13 October 1790; Philadelphia, Pa., beginning with 3 November 1790 issue
GW	George Washington
GWP	George Washington Papers, Library of Congress, Washington, D.C.
Harvard Graduates	John Sibley and Clifford Shipton, *Biographical Sketches of Graduates of Harvard University in Cambridge, Massachusetts*, 17 vols. (Cambridge, Mass., 1873–1975)
Heitman	Francis Heitman, *Historical Register of Officers of the Continental Army . . .* (Washington, D.C., 1914)
HJ	*House Journal*, volume III of this series
ICHi	Chicago Historical Society, Chicago, Ill.
Iconography	I. N. Phelps Stokes, *The Iconography of Manhattan Island, 1498–1909*, 6 vols. (New York, 1915–28)
JCC	Worthington Ford et al., eds., *Journals of the Continental Congress, 1774–1789*, 34 vols. (Washington, D.C., 1904–37)
MHi	Massachusetts Historical Society, Boston, Mass.
NcD	Duke University, Durham, N.C.
NCHSP	*Northumberland County Historical Society Proceedings*

New York	Thomas E. V. Smith, *The City of New York in the Year of Washington's Inauguration 1789* (New York, 1889)
NhD	Dartmouth College, Hanover, N.H.
NHi	New York Historical Society, New York, N.Y.
NjP	Princeton University, Princeton, N.J.
NjR	Rutgers—The State University, New Brunswick, N.J.
NN	New York Public Library, New York, N.Y.
NNC	Columbia University, New York, N.Y.
NQ	William Egle, *Notes and Queries, Historical and Genealogical, Relating Chiefly to Interior Pennsylvania*, 4 ser. + 5 annual volumes (Harrisburg, Pa., 1894–1900)
NYDA	*The* [New York] *Daily Advertiser*
NYDG	*The New York Daily Gazette*
NYJ	*The New-York Journal*
OMC	Marietta College, Marietta, Ohio
PAH	Harold Syrett and Jacob Cooke et al., eds., *The Papers of Alexander Hamilton*, 26 vols. (New York, 1961–79)
PaAr	Samuel Hazard, John Linn, William Egle et al., eds., *Pennsylvania Archives*, (9 Series, Harrisburg, Pa., 1852–1935)
PBR	Lyman Butterfield, *Letters of Benjamin Rush*, 2 vols. (Princeton, N.J., 1951)
PCC	Papers of the Continental Congress, United States National Archives, Washington, D.C.
PHarH	Pennsylvania Historical and Museum Commission, Harrisburg, Pa.
PHi	Historical Society of Pennsylvania, Philadelphia, Pa.
Philadelphia Families	John W. Jordan, *Colonial Families of Philadelphia*, 2 vols. (New York, 1911)
PJM	*The Papers of James Madison* (William Hutchinson and William Rachal, eds., vols. 1–7, Chicago, 1962–71; Robert Rutland and William Rachal, eds., vols. 8–9, Chicago, 1973–75; Robert Rutland and Charles Hobson, eds., vols. 10–13, Charlottesville, Va., 1977–81)
PMHB	*Pennsylvania Magazine of History and Biography*
PP	[Philadelphia] *Pennsylvania Packet*
PPAmP	American Philosophical Society, Philadelphia, Pa.
PPIn	Independence National Historical Park, Philadelphia, Pa.
PPL	Library Company of Philadelphia, Philadelphia, Pa.
Princetonians	James McLachlan, *Princetonians, 1748–1768, A Biographical Dictionary* (Princeton, 1976); Richard A. Harrison, *Princetonians, 1769–1775, A Biographical Dictionary* (Princeton,

	1980); ibid., *Princetonians, 1776–1783*, A Biographical Dictionary (Princeton, 1981)
PRM	*The Papers of Robert Morris* (E. James Ferguson and John Catanzariti, eds., vols. 1–5, Pittsburgh, Pa., 1973–82)
PTJ	Julian Boyd et al., eds., *The Papers of Thomas Jefferson*, 20 vols. (Princeton, N.J., 1950–82)
SEJ	*Senate Executive Journal*, volume II of this series
SLJ	*Senate Legislative Journal*, volume I of this series
SR	Senate Records, RG 46, United States National Archives, Washington, D.C.
St. Patrick	John H. Campbell, *History of the Friendly Sons of St. Patrick and of the Hibernian Society for the Relief of Emigrants from Ireland* (Philadelphia, 1892)
Vi	Virginia State Library, Richmond, Va.
ViW	William and Mary College, Williamsburg, Va.
WGW	John C. Fitzpatrick, ed., *The Writings of George Washington*, 37 vols. (Washington, D.C., 1931–40)
Wilkes Barre	Oscar Harvey and Ernest Smith, *A History of Wilkes Barre*, 6 vols. (Wilkes Barre, Pa., 1909–30)
WM	William Maclay
Yale Graduates	Franklin Dexter, *Biographical Sketches of the Graduates of Yale College . . .*, 6 vols. (New York, 1885–1912)

Bassett, Richard	Delaware
Butler, Pierce	South Carolina
Carroll, Charles	Maryland
Dalton, Tristram	Massachusetts
Dickinson, Philemon	New Jersey
(took his seat on 6 December 1790, after being elected to fill the vacancy caused by the resignation of William Paterson)	
Ellsworth, Oliver	Connecticut
Elmer, Jonathan	New Jersey
Few, William	Georgia
Foster, Theodore	Rhode Island
Grayson, William	Virginia
(died 12 March 1790)	
Gunn, James	Georgia
Hawkins, Benjamin	North Carolina
Henry, John	Maryland
Izard, Ralph	South Carolina
Johnson, William Samuel	Connecticut
Johnston, Samuel	North Carolina
King, Rufus	New York
Langdon, John	New Hampshire
Lee, Richard Henry	Virginia
Maclay, William	Pennsylvania
Monroe, James	Virginia
(took his seat on 6 December 1790, after being elected to fill the vacancy caused by the death of William Grayson)	
Morris, Robert	Pennsylvania
Paterson, William	New Jersey
(resigned on 13 November 1790, after being elected governor of New Jersey)	
Read, George	Delaware
Schuyler, Philip	New York
Stanton, Joseph, Jr.	Rhode Island
Strong, Caleb	Massachusetts
Walker, John	Virginia
(appointed to fill the vacancy caused by the death of William Grayson; served from 31 March through 9 November 1790)	
Wingate, Paine	New Hampshire

Ames, Fisher	Massachusetts
Ashe, John Baptista	North Carolina
Baldwin, Abraham	Georgia
Benson, Egbert	New York
Bland, Theodorick	Virginia
(died 1 June 1790)	
Bloodworth, Timothy	North Carolina
Boudinot, Elias	New Jersey
Bourn, Benjamin	Rhode Island
Brown, John	Virginia
Burke, Aedanus	South Carolina
Cadwalader, Lambert	New Jersey
Carroll, Daniel	Maryland
Clymer, George	Pennsylvania
Coles, Isaac	Virginia
Contee, Benjamin	Maryland
Fitzsimons, Thomas	Pennsylvania
Floyd, William	New York
Foster, Abiel	New Hampshire
Gale, George	Maryland
Gerry, Elbridge	Massachusetts
Giles, William B.	Virginia
(took his seat on 7 December 1790, after being elected to fill the vacancy caused by the death of Theodorick Bland)	
Gilman, Nicholas	New Hampshire
Goodhue, Benjamin	Massachusetts
Griffin, Samuel	Virginia
Grout, Jonathan	Massachusetts
Hartley, Thomas	Pennsylvania
Hathorn, John	New York
Hiester, Daniel, Jr.	Pennsylvania
Huger, Daniel	South Carolina
Huntington, Benjamin	Connecticut
Jackson, James	Georgia
Laurance, John	New York
Lee, Richard Bland	Virginia
Leonard, George	Massachusetts
Livermore, Samuel	New Hampshire
Madison, James, Jr.	Virginia
Mathews, George	Georgia

Moore, Andrew	Virginia
Muhlenberg, Frederick A.	Pennsylvania
Muhlenberg, Peter	Pennsylvania
Page, John	Virginia
Parker, Josiah	Virginia
Partridge, George	Massachusetts
Schureman, James	New Jersey
Scott, Thomas	Pennsylvania
Sedgwick, Theodore	Massachusetts
Seney, Joshua	Maryland
Sevier, John	North Carolina
Sherman, Roger	Connecticut
Silvester, Peter	New York
Sinnickson, Thomas	New Jersey
Smith, William	Maryland
Smith, William	South Carolina
Steele, John	North Carolina
Stone, Michael Jenifer	Maryland
Sturges, Jonathan	Connecticut
Sumter, Thomas	South Carolina
Thatcher, George	Massachusetts
Trumbull, Jonathan	Connecticut
Tucker, Thomas Tudor	South Carolina
Van Rensselaer, Jeremiah	New York
Vining, John	Delaware
Wadsworth, Jeremiah	Connecticut
White, Alexander	Virginia
Williamson, Hugh	North Carolina
Wynkoop, Henry	Pennsylvania

PART I

THE DIARY OF WILLIAM MACLAY

FIRST SESSION

April 1789

New York   Friday, 24 April 1789

I understood that it was agreed among the Senators Yesterday, that they would meet at the Hall[1] this morning and go in a Body to pay their respects to

---

[1]Federal Hall, the building at Wall and Nassau streets in which the FFC met, was constructed between 1699 and 1704 and remodeled in 1763. Although it served primarily as New York's City Hall, the facility had been used by other official bodies, including the court that tried John Peter Zenger in 1735, the Stamp Act Congress in 1765, and the Confederation Congress from 1785 to 1789. Immediately after the decision by Congress on 13 September 1788 that the FFC would convene at New York, the city's Common Council chose Pierre L'Enfant to superintend the conversion of the building into an elegant meeting place for Congress. He made rapid progress and only minor work remained to be done when the FFC met in April 1789. Financed by lotteries and a special local tax, the conversion cost about $65,000, excluding interest on private loans.

As reconstructed by L'Enfant, Federal Hall measured 95 feet in width and 145 feet at its deepest point. A plainly appointed hall and four smaller rooms, two of which served as the caretaker's apartment, were situated on the Wall Street side of the first floor off a covered walk on the street. From the hall one entered the central three-story vestibule, which had a marble floor and an ornamented skylight under a cupola. Off this vestibule stood the House of Representatives chamber, a two-story, richly decorated octagonal room. An office for the Clerk of the House and one or more committee rooms were connected to the chamber. Access to the upper floors was gained by two stairways in the vestibule, one of them reserved for congressmen. The Wall Street side of the second floor consisted of the forty by thirty foot, two-story Senate chamber and several smaller rooms connected to it, including the "machinery room," used to display models of inventions, the Senate secretary's office, and the Senate committee room or rooms. Also on this side was the balcony on which Washington took the oath of office, located above the covered walk along Wall Street. Two lobbies surrounded the staircases; the one at the head of the public staircase displayed paintings, some by John Trumbull, while the other probably served as an audience area. At the back of the second floor were the two public galleries overhanging the House chamber. Little is known about the third story except that it contained several small rooms, one of which housed the New York Society Library.

In 1812 the building was torn down and the four lots on which it stood were bought by individuals. The United States government later purchased three of the lots and constructed the Greek Revival building that served successively after 1842 as the New York Custom House, the Sub-Treasury, and the Federal Reserve Bank of New York. In 1939 the building was designated a National Historic Site and in 1955, a National Memorial. (Louis Torres, "Federal Hall Revisited," *Journal of the Society of Architectural Historians* 29:327–38; *New*

3

Genl. Washington.[2] I went about 10 O'Clock to the Hall accordingly. there was however no person there, after staying some time Elsworth came in, I suspected how it was, I repeated the Conversation of last night & asked him, Whether he had been to wait on the General. *Yes he had been, and a number more with him, some went last night and some this Morning.* What a perfidious wretch it is. I however whipped down Stairs and joined The Speaker and a number more of the Pennsylvanians, who were collecting for that purpose. went paid my respects &ca. Mind this, not to resent it, but to keep myself ever out of his power. Mr. Izard had Yesterday, been very anxious to get a report adopted, respectg. the communications between the Houses. it was so, but now we hear the House below laugh at it. Mr. Izard moved to have the adoption taken from the Minutes, no this could not be done. But now a curious scene opened, Mr. Lee, being of the *Title* committee of Yesterday, produced a Copy of the resolution for appointing that committee and moved, that the House[3] should pass a Vote for the transmitting it down to the other House. this was truly ridiculous. but mind, this base business, had been went into solely Yesterday on the Motion of our President,[4] this was bare faced indeed— but now Lee wanted to bring it on again, when the President would not appear in it. I likewise suspect Lee's integrity in this Business he knows the giving of Titles would hurt Us. I showed the Absurdity of his motion plain enough. but it occurr'd to me, that by getting a division of the Resolution, I could perhaps thro'w out the part about Titles altogether. Mr. Carrol of Maryland showed he was against Titles, I wrought it so far, that I got a question whether, we should throw out the part about Titles altogether, we lost the question on the Throwing out

York, pp. 40–50; *Federal Hall National Memorial*, U.S. Department of the Interior [Washington, D.C., 1966])

[2]George Washington (1732–99), a planter, politician, and land speculator from Alexandria, Virginia, became a national hero because of his role as commander in chief of the Continental army. His unanimous election as president of the United States was announced on 6 April at the first joint session of Congress. He arrived at the seat of government on 23 April and took up residence at 3 Cherry Street, opposite Saint George's (now Franklin) Square. This house, built in 1770 and owned in 1789 by Samuel Osgood, had been the residence of the presidents of the Confederation Congress. The FFC requested it for Washington's use on 15 April. It was small and inconveniently located, and on 23 February 1790 Washington moved to the mansion at 39–41 Broad Way that Alexander Macomb had built in 1787. For Washington's residence in Philadelphia, see December 1790, n. 1. (*New York*, p. 19; *DGW* 5:448n–449n, 6:26n; Stephen Decatur, Jr., *Private Affairs of George Washington* [Boston, 1933], pp. 117–18)

[3]WM, throughout his diary, uses "House" to refer to the Senate as one branch or "house" of a bicameral legislature as well as to refer to the House of Representatives.

[4]WM, throughout his diary, often uses "president" or "our president" to refer to John Adams (1735–1826) of Braintree, Massachusetts, president of the Senate by virtue of his election as vice president of the United States. A Harvard-educated lawyer and officeholder, and a leading figure in the revolutionary movement, Adams represented American interests in Europe for a decade before 1788. He arrived in New York on 20 April and took the oath of office the next day. (*NYDA*, 21 April 1789)

that part.   however I could plainly see that we had gained Ground with the House.   Now a most curious question arose   the President knew not how to direct the letter to the Speaker.   he called on the House to Know how it should be directed.   the House shewed a manifest disinclination to interfere,   the president Urged. and ceased not untill a question was pointedly put whether the Speaker should be stiled *honorable*   it passed [*page torn*] in the negative.   And from this Omen, I think our P[resi]dent may go and dream about Titles.   for none wi[ll he get.]

Saturday, 25 April 1789

attended the House   Ceremonies endless ceremonies the whole business of the day.   I did not embark warmly this day.   Otis our Secretary[5] makes a most miserable hand of it,   the grossest Mistakes made on our minutes and it cost Us an hour or Two to rectify them.   I was up as often I believe as was necessary and certainly threw so much light on Two Subjects, that the debate ended on each.   The President as usual made us two or three Speeches from the Chair.   I will endeavour to recollect one of them.   It was on the reading of a Report. Which mentioned that the President should be received in the Senate Chamber and proceed thence to the House of Representatives to be Sworn—   Gentlemen I do not know whether the framers of the Constitution had in View the Two Kings of Sparta or the Two Consuls of rome[6] when they

[5]Samuel Allyne Otis (1740–1814), a graduate of Harvard in 1759, was a Boston merchant active in local politics prior to the Revolutionary War. Like his more famous siblings, the patriot James and the historian Mercy, he readily committed himself to the American cause. A major supplier of clothes to the army, he served briefly as deputy quartermaster general of the Continental army. After the war, Otis represented Boston in the state House of Representatives, where he was chosen speaker, and Massachusetts in Congress from late 1787 through 1788. He ran unsuccessfully for a seat in the first United States House of Representatives and then launched an aggressive letter-writing campaign to members of the FFC, suggesting himself for secretary of either house. On 8 April he was elected secretary of the Senate, a position he retained until his death. Despite WM's caustic criticism of his abilities and relationship with Adams, Otis proved to be a meticulous preserver of the Senate's archival record; it is primarily because of his efforts that the legislative history of the FFC can be reconstructed. For further details on the campaign for the secretaryship of the Senate, see *PMHB* 100: 317–20. (*Harvard Graduates* 14:471–80; *DHFFE* 1:545–69)

[6]John C. Hamilton, *History of the Republic . . .*, 7 vols. (Philadelphia, 1864–65), 3:560, quotes Adams as saying "Are we the two Kings of Sparta, the two Consuls of Rome, or the two Suffetes of Carthage." The source of this version is unknown, and attempts by George W. Harris, the first editor of WM's diary, to obtain it from Hamilton were unsuccessful. (Harris to James A. Hamilton, 13 May 1861, Harris Papers, PHi)

Details of what went on behind the closed doors of the Senate were occasionally reported in contemporary letters. St. George Tucker, the brother of Representative Tucker, became so outraged by the accounts he had seen that he composed a farce to ridicule the Senate proceedings and to expose the character of John Adams. The third scene of act one focuses on the question of titles and on the closed doors of the Senate. The words that Jonathan Goosequill uses to support titles, and the backing he receives from Mr. Leeshore are close to what WM reports about the positions and comments of Adams and Richard Henry Lee. (St.

~~foarmed~~ formed it.   one to have all the power while he held it, and the other to be nothing; nor do I know whether the Architect that formed our room, and the wide Chair in it, (to hold two I suppose) had the Constitution before him,   Gentlemen I feel great difficulty how to act,   I am possesed of two seperate powers, the one in esse, and the other in posse.   I am Vice President, in this I am nothing, but I may be everything,   but I am President also of the Senate.   When the President comes into the Senate, what shall I be, I cannot be then, no Gentlemen I cannot, I cannot—   I wish Gentlemen to think what I shall be;   here as if oppressed with a Sense of his distressed situation, he threw himself back in his Chair.   A Solemn Silence ensued.   God forgive me, for it was involuntary, but the profane Muscles of my face, were in Tune for laughter, in spite of my indisposition   Elsworth thumbed over the Sheet constitution, and turned it for some time;   at length he rose, and addressed the Chair with the most profound gravity.   Mr. President I have looked over the Constitution (paused) and I find Sir, it is evident & Clear Sir, that wherever ~~you~~ the Senate is to be, then Sir you must be at the head of them.   but further Sir, (here he looked agast, as if some tremendous Gulph had Yaned before him) I, shall, not, pretend, to, say.   Thursday next is appointed for Swearing in the President   I am worse of my rheumatism, but perhaps it is owing to the [cha]nge of Weather. for the Wind is at North West and Cold—   [Gav]e Mr. Vandalsen an half Johannes,[7]   he is to sell it and give me Credit for the amount,   his Bill 41/ 3∂.

Sunday, 26 April 1789

Went out half after 9 O'Clock   visited Governor St. Clair⟨,⟩ Genl. Butler⟨,⟩ Delany⟨,⟩ McPherson at Elsworth's,[8]   called on Mr. Clymer & Mr.

George Tucker to Thomas Tudor Tucker, 3 June 1789, "Up and Ride, or the Borough of Brooklyne," Tucker-Coleman Papers, ViW)

[7]William Vandalsem, a grocer, resided at the corner of Greenwich and Partition streets. He was apparently associated with the Bear Market, situated on the west side of Greenwich between Vesey and Partition. WM and Representative Wynkoop rented rooms from Vandalsem during the first session of the FFC. Today the World Trade Center towers above the site of both the Bear Market and the house in which WM composed the majority of his diary. (*New York*, p. 92)

A Johannes was a Portuguese gold coin worth $8.

[8]WM visited Vandine and Dorothy Elsworth's boarding house at 19 Maiden Lane. Several of the Virginia and Pennsylvania representatives resided there.

Arthur St. Clair (1734–1818), governor of the Northwest Territory from 1787 to 1802, left his native Scotland to serve with the British army in America during the French and Indian War. By the time of the War for Independence, in which he rose to the rank of major general, St. Clair was the owner of a substantial amount of western Pennsylvania land, held several local offices, and acted as agent for the Penns. A member of Congress from 1785 to 1787, he served as its president during the latter year. The governor spent nearly the entire first session of the FFC at New York conferring with Secretary of War Henry Knox and President Washington on territorial and Indian affairs and lobbying Congress for appropriate legisla-

Fitzsimons.   Mr. Clymer in the *exceptionables*, or peevish and fretting at every thing.   I know not how it is, but I cannot get into these Men.   There is a Kind of guarded distance on their parts, that seems to preclude sociability. I believe I had best be guarded too.   the very End of this Visit was to try to concert some Measures with them. for the removal of Congress, but they Kept me off.   I mentioned a favourable disposition in some of the Maryland Gentlemen. to be in unison with the Pennsylvania delegation.   they seemed not to credit me.   Mr. Obrien and Mr. Heally[9] came in and I took my leave. came home and as the day was blustering and cold staid all day in my room. wrote some letters.   Mr. Wynkoop dined out so I saw nobody.

Monday, 27 April 1789

Tryed me knee and walked a good deal   attended the Hall,   We had prayers this day by the Chaplain Docr. Prevost[10]—   a new Arrangement was reported from the Joint Committee of Ceremonies—   this is an Endless busi-

---

tion. An unsuccessful candidate for governor of Pennsylvania in 1790, St. Clair spent most of the second session of the FFC in the Northwest Territory. The third session found him at Philadelphia conferring with federal officials. See also *SEJ*, p. 536.

Richard Butler (1743–91), superintendent of Indian affairs for the northern department, 1786–88, was a native of Ireland. Prior to the War for Independence, in which he achieved the rank of general, Butler served as a soldier on the 1764 Bouquet Expedition and an Indian trader and agent. He helped to negotiate the Treaty of Fort Stanwix between Congress and the Six Nations in 1784, concurrently supervising the efforts of WM and other Pennsylvania commissioners to negotiate a state treaty. Butler moved from Carlisle to western Pennsylvania at the end of the 1780s and represented Allegheny and Westmoreland counties in the 1790–91 session of the state Senate. (*Historical Register . . . Interior Pennsylvania* 1:5–7; *Counter Revolution*, pp. 149–50)

Sharp Delany (c. 1739–99), collector of the port of Philadelphia from 1784 to 1799, was an emigrant from northern Ireland who established himself as an apothecary in Philadelphia about 1764. He became active in the revolutionary cause, serving in provincial conventions and as a colonel in the state militia. Knowledgeable in financial matters, Delany was an associate of Robert Morris. (*St. Patrick*, p. 108; *PMHB* 48:359)

William Macpherson (1756–1813), member of the Pennsylvania Assembly in 1788–89, was born at Philadelphia. He resigned a commission in the British army in 1778 and served as an aide to Generals Lafayette and St. Clair during the War for Independence. He was a Federalist delegate to the state ratification convention, and in 1789 Washington appointed him surveyor of customs at Philadelphia. See also *SEJ*, pp. 535–36. (*PMHB* 11:250–52)

[9]Michael Morgan O'Brien and William Heally were Philadelphians. Heally was a silver plater. O'Brien, a merchant, sought a federal post. He had participated in the small mob of Philadelphia Federalists who forcibly escorted two Antifederalist assemblymen to the State House in September 1787 so that the legislature could have a quorum and call a ratification convention. (Series 7, GWP, DLC; *1790 Pennsylvania Census*, p. 237; *DHROC* 2:110; *St. Patrick*, p. 129)

[10]Bishop Samuel Provoost (1742–1815), one of two congressional chaplains in 1789 and 1790, was a native of New York who graduated from Kings College in 1758. After receiving his divinity degree at Cambridge, England, in 1765, he returned to New York where he encountered difficulties with loyalist members of his congregation because of his patriot sympathies. Provoost became bishop of New York in 1786 and traveled to England for consecration in 1787. (*New York*, p. 139)

ness Lee offered a Motion to the Chair that after the President was Sworn. (which now is to be in the Gallery opposite the Senate Chamber) the Congress should ~~attend~~ accompany him to Saint Paul's Church[11] and attend divine Service. This had been agitated in the Joint Committee, But Lee said expressly, *That They would not agree to it.* I opposed. it as an improper Business, after it had been in the hands of the Joint committee and rejected, as I thought this a certain Method of creating a dissention ~~in~~ between the Houses. Izard got up in great wrath and stuttered that *the fact was not so,* he however could say nothing more I made an effort to rise the president hurried the question and it was put. and carried by the Churchmen hollow.[12] Mr. Carrol, tho' he had been the first to speak against it, Yet was silent on the Vote; this proves him not the Man of firmness which I once thought him. I went after this to hear the debates in the House of Representatives.[13] The duty of '6' Cents had been reported by the Committee on Molasses. The partiality of the New England members to this favourite Article was now manifest. all from their quarter was an universal Cry against it. three O'Clock came and an adjourment, was called for, before the Matter was settled. I took a long Walk after dinner, with the Speaker & Genl. Muhlenberg and my Knee, stood it very well— hope I shall be perfectly well in a few days— God grant it.

Tuesday, 28 April 1789

This day I ought to note with some extraordinary Mark. I had dressed and was about to set out. when General Washington the greatest Man in the World, paid me a Visit. I met him at the foot of the Stairs Mr. Wynkoop Just came in. we asked him to take a seat, he excused himself on Acct. of the number of his Visits. We accompanyed him to the door, he made Us complaisant Bows, one before he mounted and the other as he went away on Horseback— Attended at the Hall, just nothing at all done, I however paid my formal Visit to the Vice President, this Morning, being nearly recovered of my lameness— quitted the Hall about 12. called on Mr. Langdon, Who has been sick. some time it began to rain and I came home.

I may as well minute a remark here as anywhere else, & Indeed I wish it were otherwise {not for what we have, but for what others want}. But we have

---

[11]Saint Paul's Church, still standing at Broad Way and Vesey Street, was built between 1763 and 1766. Washington attended Episcopal services there while a resident of New York, sitting in a pew set apart for his use. (*New York*, p. 138)

[12]WM used "hollow" in its colloquial meaning of "completely." The Episcopal members of the Senate, or "Churchmen," included Johnson, Dalton, Morris, Lee, Izard, Read, and Henry.

[13]The House was considering the report of the committee of the whole House, out of which came the impost resolutions adopted on 28 April.

really more republican plainess, and sincere openess of behaviour in Pennsylvania, than in any other place I have ever been.   I was impressed with a different Opinion, untill I have had full opportunity of observing the Gentlemen of New England.   and sorry indeed am I to say it, But no People in the Union dwell more on trivial distinctions, and Matters of Mere form.   They really seem to show, a readiness to stand on ~~form~~ punctilio and ceremony.   a little learning is a dangerous thing. (tis said)   may not the same be said of Breeding.   It is certainly true. that People little used with Company are more apt to take Offense, and are less easy, than ~~well bred~~ Men much versant in public life—   They are an unmixed people in New England, & used only to see ~~people~~ Neighbours like themselves, and when once an Error of behaviour is crept in among them, there is small chance of it's being cured.   for should they ever go abroad, being early used to a ceremonious and reserved behaviour, and believing that good Manners consist intirely in punctilios. they only add a few more stiffened Airs to their deportment, excluding Good humor affability of ~~temper~~ conversation, and accomodation of temper and sentiment, as qualities too vulgar, for a Gentleman.   Mr. Strong gave us this Morning a Story. which with many others of a similar nature (which I have heard) places this in a clear point of light.   By the Constitution of Massachusetts the Senate have a right of communicating Bills to ~~their~~ lower house. some singular Business made them ~~lower House~~ shut the doors.   at this time called Sam. Adams of the Senate to communicate a Bill.   the door keeper told him his Orders; back returned the enraged Senator.   The Whole Senate took flame, and blazed forth in furious memorial against the lower House, for breach of privildge.   [a violent] contest ensued and the Whole State was convulsed with Litigation.[14]

Wednesday, 29 April 1789

Attended the Hall this day,   a Bill was read the 2d time respecting the administring the Oath for the support of the new Government.   a diversity of Opinion arose. Whether the law should be extended so as to oblige the Officers of the State Governments to take the oaths—   the power of Congress to do this was asserted by some and denied by others, in pointed Terms.   I did not enter into the Merits of either side.   But before the question was put, gave my opinion. That as the first Step towards doing good was to be sure of doing

---

[14]Samuel Adams (1722–1803), lieutenant governor of Massachusetts, had held public office almost continuously since 1765 but ran unsuccessfully as an Antifederalist candidate for the United States House of Representatives from Boston. The incident WM mentions is apparently a garbled version of an event in 1781 which is recounted in William V. Wells, *The Life and Public Services of Samuel Adams*, 3 vols. (Boston, 1866), 3:154. (*DHFFE* 1:742)

no harm.   Gentlemen had been very pointed for and against this power.   if we were divided here, what must we expect, the people out of doors to be. that in the exercise of the powers given Us by Congress, we should deal in no uncertainties.   that While we had the Constitution *plainly* before Us, all was safe and certain.   but if we took on us to deal in doubtful Matters, we trod on hollow Ground, and might be charged with an assumption of powers not delegated.   I therefore on this Ground was against the Commitment.   The Bill however was committed. and with it closed the Business of the day.

I have observed ever since we began to do Business that a Jehu like Spirit has prevailed with a number of ~~Members~~ Gentlemen, and with none more than with the Member from the Antient dominion, who is said to be a notorious ~~ant~~ Antifederalist.[15]   a most expensive and enormous Machine of a Federal Judiciary, pompous Titles, strong efforts after religious distinctions coercive laws for taking the Oaths &ca. &ca.   I have uniformly opposed as far as I was able every thing of this Kind.   and I believe have sacrificed every chance of being popular, and every grain of influence in the Senate, by so doing.   but be it so.   I have the testimony of my own conscience that I am right.   high handed Measures are at no time Justifiable, but now they are highly impolitic.   never will I consent to straining the Constitution, nor never will I consent to the exercise of a doubtful power.   we come here the Servants not the Lords, of our Constituents.   the New Government, instead of being a powerful Machine whose Authority would support any Measure, needs helps and props on all sides, and must be supported by the ablest names and the most shining Characters which we can select.   the Presidents amiable deportment, however smoths and sweetens every thing.   Charles Thomson[16] has however been ill used, by the Committee of Arrangement of the Ceremonial.   This is Wrong.   his name has been left out, of the arrangement, for tomorrow.

---

[15]It was to Lee of Virginia that WM attributed the heavy-handed and fast-paced tactics of Jehu, king of ancient Israel.

[16]Charles Thomson (1729–1824), secretary of the Continental and Confederation Congresses from 1774 to 1789, was a ten-year-old orphan when he arrived in America from northern Ireland. By the time of the Revolutionary War he had established himself as a Philadelphia merchant and a spokesman for the American cause. Thomson's commmitment to a strong central government gained him both friends and enemies during his long tenure with Congress. His supporters mentioned him as a candidate for the vice presidency. Among his enemies were Lee, Dalton, and Izard, the senators on the joint committee for the inaugural ceremony, Vice President Adams, and Representative Gerry, all of whom in 1789 combined their influence to prevent Thomson's election as secretary of the Senate, to deny him a seat at Washington's inauguration, and to block the creation of the domestic or home department. Some considered that department necessary for carrying out functions not assigned to the departments of foreign affairs, treasury, and war and advocated it as a place for Thomson. In July 1789 Washington accepted Thomson's resignation as secretary to Congress. In 1790 WM noted rumors promoting Thomson as a possible candidate for governor of Pennsylvania or his own seat in the Senate. (*PMHB* 100: 314–15)

Thursday, 30 April 1789

This is the great important day.   Goddess of Etiquette assist me while I describe it.   The Senate stood adjourned to half after 11 O'Clock,   about 10 dressed in my best Cloaths; went for Mr. Morris Lodgings, but met his Son[17] who told me, that his father would not be in Town untill Saturday.   turned into the Hall.   the Croud already great.   the Senate met.   The President rose in the most solemn Manner, never son of *Adam* seemed impressed with deeper gravity.   Yet what shall I think of him,   he often in the midst of his most important Airs, I believe when he is at a loss for expressions, (and this he often is, wrapped up I suppose in the Contemplation of his own importance) suffers an unmeaning kind of vacant ~~smile~~ laugh to escape him.   This was the Case today, and really to me bore the Air of ridiculing the Farce he was acting.   "Gentlemen I wish for the direction of the Senate   the President will I suppose address the Congress   how shall I behave,   how shall we receive it   shall it be standing or sitting,"   here follow~~ing~~ed a considerable deal of talk from him, which I could make nothing of,   Mr. Lee began with the House of Commons (as is usual with him) then the House of Lords then the King & then back again.   the result of his information was that the Lords sat and the Commons Stood. on the delivery of ~~the delivery of~~ the Kings Speach.   [*lined out*] Mr. Izard got up and told how often he had been in the Houses of ~~Commons~~ Parliament.   he said a great deal of what he had seen there.   made however this sagacious discovery, that the Commons stood because they had no seats to sit on. being arrived at the Bar of the House of lords.   it was discovered after some time that the King sat too, and had his robes and crown on.   Mr. President got up again & said he had been very often indeed, at the Parliament on those Occasions, but there always was such a Croud, and *ladies along*, that for his part he could not say how it was.   Mr. Carrol got up to declare that he thought it of no consequence how it was in great Britain,   they were no rule to us &ca.   But all at once the Secretary who had been out, wispered to the Chair that the Clerk from the Representatives[18] was at the door with a Communication.   and Gentlemen of the Senate how

---

[17]Thomas Morris (1771–1849) was frequently with his father during the first and second sessions of the FFC. (*PRM* 3:58n; Eleanor Young, *Forgotten Patriot, Robert Morris* [New York, 1950], p. 184)

[18]John Beckley (1757–1807), who came to Virginia from England as a child, had already been clerk to several official bodies, including the Virginia Senate, when he graduated from William and Mary in 1779. During the following decade he was clerk to the Virginia House of Delegates, the High Court of Chancery, and the ratification convention and served as mayor of Richmond. The United States House of Representatives elected him as its clerk on 1 April 1789. Beckley allied himself with the emerging Democratic-Republican Party and retained his office until his death, except between 1797 and 1800, when the Federalists controlled the House. Unlike the Senate's secretary, Samuel A. Otis, Beckley routinely destroyed all but the final version of the House's legislative records. For an analysis of his archival methods see *HJ*,

shall he be received?   a Silly kind of Resolution of the Committee on that Business,[19] had been laid on the Table some days ago,   the amount of it was that each house should communicate to the other what and how they choose.   it concluded however something in this way, that everything should be done with all the *propriety* that was *proper*.   the question was shall this be adopted, that we may know how to receive the Clk.   it was objected. this will throw no light on the Subject, it will leave you where you are.   Mr. Lee brought the House of Commons before Us again.   he reprobated the Rule declared that the Clerk should not come within the Bar of the House, That the proper mode was for the Sergeant at Arms with the Mace on his shoulder should to meet the Clerk at the door and receive his Communications   we are not however provided for this ceremonious way of doing business, having neither Mace nor Sergeant, nor masters in chancery, who carry down Bills— from the English Lords.

Mr. Izard got up, and labored unintelligibly to show the great distinction, between a Communication and a delivery of a thing.   but he was not minded.   Mr. Elsworth shewed plainly enough that if The Clerk was not permitted to deliver the Communication, the Speaker might as well send it inclosed.   repeated accounts came   the Speaker and representatives were at the door.   confusion insued.   the members left their Seats.   Mr. Read rose and called the attention of the Senate to the neglect that had been shewed to Mr. Thomson late Secretary.   Mr. Lee rose to answer him, but I could not hear one word he said.   the Speaker was introduced followed by the Representatives.   here we sat an hour and ten minutes, before the President arrived— this delay was owing to Lee⟨,⟩ Izard and Dalton, who had staid with us untill the Speaker came in, instead of going to attend the President.   the President advanced between the Senate and Representatives bowing to each.   he was placed in the Chair by the President of the Senate.   the Senate with their President on the right the Speaker and Representatives on his left.   the President of the Senate rose and address'd a short Sentence to him.   The import of it was that he should now take the Oath of Office as President.   he seemed to have forgot half of what he was to say for he made a dead pause and stood for some time, to appearance, in a vacant mood.   he finished with a formal bow.   and the President was conducted out of the middle Window into the Gallery and the Oath administered by the Chancellor.[20]   Notice of that the

pp. x–xv. (*PMHB* 72:54–59; E. Griffith Dodson, ed., *Speakers and Clerks of the Virginia House of Delegates, 1776–1955* [Richmond, 1955], pp. 19–20)

[19]The resolution of the joint committee on communication between the Houses was tabled on 28 April.

[20]Robert R. Livingston (1746–1813) held the post of Chancellor of New York from 1777 to 1801 and for that reason was asked to administer the oath of office to Washington. A member of a wealthy, landed, and politically influential New York family, Livingston graduated from Kings College in 1765. Admitted to the bar in 1770, he served as a member of various New York revolutionary bodies, as a delegate to Congress for several terms between 1775 and

Business was done, was communicated to the Croud by Proclamation &ca., who gave three Cheers, and repeated it on the Presidents bowing to them— as the Company returned into the Senate Chamber, the President took the Chair, and the Senate and Representatives their Seats, he rose & all arose also. and addressed them (see the address) this great Man was agitated and embarrassed more than ever he was by the levelled Cannon or pointed Musket. he trembled, and several times could scarce make out to read, tho it must be supposed he had often read it before. he put the part of the fingers of his left hand, into the side, of what I think the Taylors call the fall, of his Breetches. changing the paper into his left hand, after some time, he then did the same with some of the fingers of his left right hand. When he came to the Words *all the World*, he made a flourish with his right hand, which had left rather an ungainly impression. I sin I sincerely, for my part, wished all set ceremony in the hands of the dancing Masters. and that this first of Men, had read off, his address, in the plainest Manner without ever taking his Eyes off From, the paper. for I felt hurt, that he was not first in every thing. he was dressed in deep brown, with Metal buttons, with an Eagle on them, White Stockings a Bag and Sword— from the Hall there was a grand Procession to St. Pauls Church where prayers were said by the Bishop.[21] the Procession was well conducted and without accident, as far as I have heard, the Militias were all under Arms. lined the Street near the Church, made a good figure and behaved well The Senate returned to their Chamber after Service, formed & took up the Address. Our President called it *his most gracious Speech*. I cannot approve of this. a Committee was appointd on it, Johnson, Carrol, Patterson. adjourned. in the Evening there were grand fire Works. The Spanish Ambassadors House was adorned with Transparent paintings, The French Ministers House was illuminated, and had some transparent pieces[22] the Hall was grandly illuminated. and after all this the People went to bed.

1785, as secretary for foreign affairs between 1781 and 1783, and as a Federalist member of his state's ratification convention.

[21]Samuel Provoost.

[22]Don Diego de Gardoqui (1735–98), who resided at No. 1 Broad Way, had represented Spanish interests in the United States since 1785. Much of this time was spent in unsuccessful negotiations over a boundary treaty between Spain and the United States. Gardoqui left the United States at the end of the first session of the FFC. (*DGW* 5:184n; *New York*, pp. 19, 85)

Eleanor François Elie, Comte de Moustier (1751–1817), who resided near the Bowling Green at the foot of Broad Way, served as French Minister during 1788 and 1789. He was unsocial, proud, and did little to conceal his "illicit connection" with his sister-in-law, with whom he lived. The United States successfully urged his recall. (*New York*, pp. 26, 85–86; *DGW* 5:417n; *PTJ* 14:291, 340–41)

Transparencies were a popular art form at times of celebration and had been employed in America at least since the 1760s. Color was applied to window shades, to canvas, or to thin paper pasted on a framework behind which a candle or other source of light provided illumination. (Kenneth Silverman, *A Cultural History of the American Revolution* [New York, 1976], p. 96)

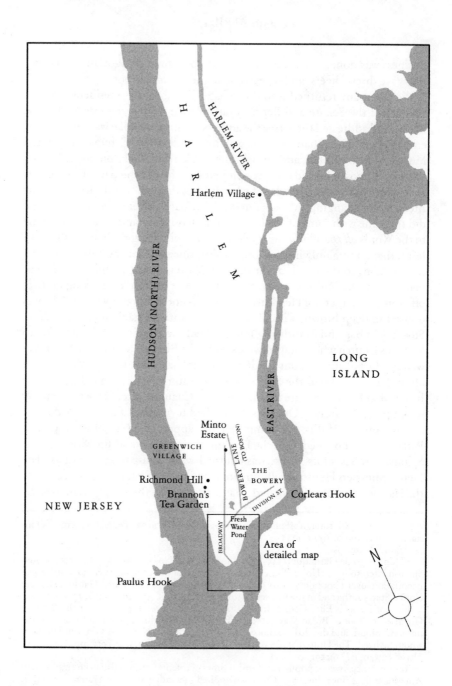

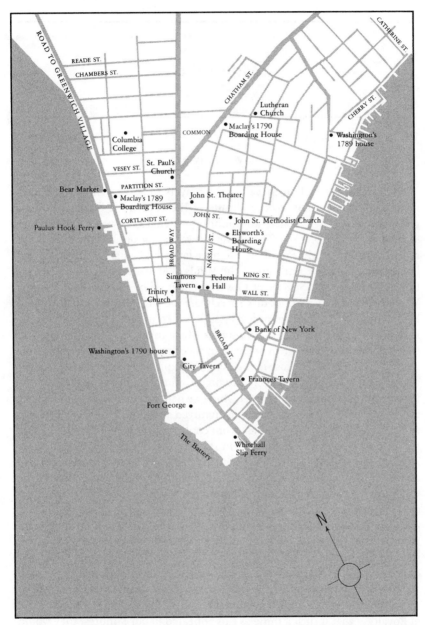

New York City and the surrounding area about 1789. (Graphics by Stephen Kraft.)

May 1789

Friday, 1 May 1789

attended at the Hall at Eleven, the prayers were over and the Minutes reading, When we came to the Minute of the Speech it Stood, *His Most gracious Speech*. I looked all round the Senate, every Countenance seemed to wear a blank. The Secretary was going on. I must speak, or nobody would. "Mr. President, we have lately had a hard struggle for our liberty against Kingly Authority the Minds of Men are still heated, everything related to that Species of Government is odious to the People. the Words prefixed to the President's Speech, are the same that are usually placed before the Speech of his Britannic Majesty— I know they will give offense. I consider them as improper I therefore Move that they be struck out, and that it stand simply ~~Speech or~~ address, or speech as may be Judged most suitable"— Mr. President rose in his chair and expressed the greatest Surprize, that any thing should be objected to on account of its being taken from the Practise of that Government under which we had lived so long and so happily formerly, that ~~for his part~~ he was for a dignifyed and respectable Government, and as far as he knew the sentiments of People they thought as he did. That for his part he was one of the first in the late Contest and *if he could have thought of ~~such a thing~~ this, he never would have drawn his Sword.* painful as it was I had to contend with the Chair, I admitted that the People of the Colonies (now States) had enjoyed formerly great happiness under that Species of Government, but the abuses of that Government, under which they had smarted had taught them what they had to fear from that kind of Government. That there had been a Revolution in the Sentiments of People, respecting Government, equally great as that which had happened in the Government itself. That even the modes of it were now abhorred. that the enemies of the Constitution, had objected to it, the facility there would be of transition from it to Kingly Government, and all the trappings and Splendor of Royalty. that if such a thing as this appeared in our Minutes, they would not fail to represent it as the first Step of the Ladder in the Assent to royalty. The President rose a second time and declared that he had mentioned it to the Secretary, that he could not possibly conceive that any Person could take offense at it. I had to get up again and declare that altho' I Knew of it being mentioned from the Chair. yet my opposition did not proceed from any motive of contempt, that altho' it was a painful task, it was solely a Sense of duty that raised me. the President stood during this time, said he had been long abroad, and did not know how the tempers of People might be now. up now rose Mr. Read, and declared for the paragraph. he saw no reason to object to it, because the British Speeches were stiled *most gracious* if we chose to object to Words because they had been used in the same sense in Britain we should soon be at a loss to d⟨o⟩ Business. I had to reply. "it is time enough to submit to necessity when it exists, at present, we are at no loss for words the Words Speech or address without any addition will suit Us well enough, ~~at present.~~" the ~~2d~~. 1st time I was up Mr. Lee followed me with a Word or two by way of seconding me. but When the President on being last up declared that he was the Person from Whom the words were taken, Mr. Lee got up and informed the Chair that he did not know that Circumstance, as he had been absent. When it happened. The question was put and carried for erazing the Words without a division. after the House adjourned the President took Me to one side declared how much he was for an efficient Government. how much he respected Genl. Washington & much of that Kind, I told him I would yield to no person in respect to Genl. Washington. that our Common Friends[1] would perhaps one day inform him that I was not wanting in respect to himself; that my Wishes for an efficient Government were as high as any Man's and begged him to believe that I did myself great Violence When I opposed him in the Chair; and nothing but a Sense of duty could force me to it— he got on the Subject of Checks to Government—and the Balances of Power— his Tale was long he seemed to expect some answer I caught the last Word, and said undoubtedly without a balance there can be no equilibrium, & so left him hanging in *Geometry*.

Let me not remember it to his disadvantage. But on Thursday soon after I came to the Hall, ~~the~~ our President stepped up to me said he had called at my lodgings, but found I was abroad. I thanked him for the honor he did me, and expressed my Sorrow, in the usual way, for being abroad. ~~I~~ I was however a little surprized considering the Hurry of the Day, and more especially as I had but just left home. at night I asked Vandalsen whether any Cards had been left for me. No. did nobody call. Nobody. Are you sure the Vice President did not. I am very sure. I know Mr. Adams the V.P. as well as I know any ~~Body~~ Man. I have been at home the whole day, he did not call. From the drift of dust and feathers, one finds how the Winds blow. I did not minute this ~~not when it happened~~ on Thursday, thinking that perhaps some mistake had happened which would explain itself. per-

---

[1] WM had already written Benjamin Rush, a friend and correspondent of both himself and Adams, suggesting that Rush inform Adams "in decent and distant Manner" that WM had been active on behalf of Adams's candidacy for vice president. See WM's entry for 22 June 1789. (WM to Rush, 23 April 1789, DLC)

haps it may still do so— Memorandum. The President's Speech is now in the hands of every one. and is received with merited applause. a thought as to the Composition of it. But first I will lay down my own rule for Judging in Cases of this Kind. When every word conveys an Idea, and Sentiment follows expression. the composition is good. But when the the words and expressions are so happily arranged, that every corresponding Idea and sentiment, brings a Kindred Group in it's Train. the Composition rises to Excellent, grand, Sublime, now for the sinking scale. When Ideas follow slowly, with difficulty, or not at all, the Composition may be termed heavy, dull, Stupid. I will read it again, but I declare I am inclined to place it under the *heavy head*.

{The unequivocal declaration—That he would never have drawn his Sword &ca. has drawn my Mind to the following rema[rk] That the Motives of the Actors in the late revolution were various cannot be doubted. The abolishing of Royalty [the] extinguishment of servility patronage and dependance attached to that form of government. Were among the Exalted Motives of Many Revolutionists. and these were the improvements Meant by them to be made of the War which was forced on Us by British Agression. In fin[e] the Amelioration of Government and bettering the Condit[ion] of mankind. These Ends and none other were publick[ly] avowed, and All our Constitutions and publick Acts were framed in this Spirit. Yet there were n[ot] wanting a party Whose Motives were different. The[y] wished for the Loaves and Fishes of Government and cared for nothing Else but a Translation of the diadem and Sceptre from London to Boston N. Yor[k] or Philada. or in [*lined out*] other Words the erection of a Ne[w] Monarchy in America. and to form ~~nott~~ Nitches for themselves in the Temple of Royalty— This Spirit Manifested itself Strongly among the officers at the clo[se] of the War. And I have been assured the Army wou[*ld*] not have been dissolved, if the Common Soldiers *would* have been kept together. This Spirit then corpora[ted] in the order of the Cincinnati[2] Where I trust it wi[ll] spend itself in an harmless flame, and soon beco[me] extinguished. That Mr. Adams should however so Unequivocally avow this Motive at a Time When a Republican form of Gov-

---

[2]The Society of the Cincinnati is a hereditary organization founded at the Newburgh, New York, army encampment in May 1783. Its purposes were to secure economic justice for the Continental army officers, perpetuate wartime friendships, and support the Union. The Society was immediately attacked by those, including Representative Burke, who considered it to be anti-republican and unamerican. Original members of the order who served in the FFC were Senators Grayson, Gunn, Hawkins, Monroe, and Schuyler, and Representatives Ashe, Baldwin, Bland, Boudinot, Bourn, Cadwalader, Gilman, Hartley, Laurance, Mathews, P. Muhlenberg, Parker, Trumbull, Tucker, Van Rensselaer, and Wadsworth. Several other members of the FFC were given honorary membership in the order prior to 1789: Senator Morris and Representatives Floyd, Jackson, and Sevier. (William S. Thomas, *Members of the Society of Cincinnati* [New York, 1929])

ernment is secured to Every State in the Union, Appears to me a Mark of extreme Folly.}

{I however Will endeavour (as I have hitherto done) to Use the Resentment of the Representatives, to defeat Mr. Adams &ca. on the Subject of Titles; The pompous & Lordly distinctions which the Senate have Manifested a disposition to establish between the Two Houses has, has nettled the Representatives.   And this Business of Titles May be considered As part of the same Tune.   While We are debating on Titles, I will thro' the Speaker Muhlenberg And other Friends get the Idea Suggested of Answering the Presidents Address Without Any Title, in contempt of Our deliberations on that Subject Which Still continue on on that Subject.   This Once effected Will confound them compleatly.   And establish a precedent they will not dare to Violate.}

{1790. It is Worthy of Remark that about this Time a Spirit of reformation broke out in France which finally abolished all Titles and every Trace of the Feudal system.   Strange indeed That it in that very Country Where the Flame of Freedom had been kindled an attempt should be made to introduce those absurdities and humiliating distinctions which the hand of reason aided by our example was prostrating in the Heart of Europe.

Note   15th June 1789 Abbe Seyes's Motion & National Assembly instituted   on the 19th Titles abolished in France.}[3]

Saturday, 2 May 1789

attended Senate   this a day of no Business Whatever.   Langdon came and shaked hands very heartily with me—   some of the other New England Men shy—   Patterson only was at the Senate Chamber before me,   he passed Censure on the Conduct of the President, said he made himself too busy— he hinted as if some of the Senate would have taken notice of the *gracious* affair if I had not.   I told him I was no Courtier, and had no occasion to trim.   But said it was a most disagreeable thing to contend with the Chair.   and I had alone held that disagreeable post more than once.   after Senate adjourned I saw the President standing disengaged,   I stepped up to him, asked for his health, and fell into common place chat,   he is not well furnished with common place chat small Talk, more than myself, and has a very silly Kind of laugh.   I have often looked with the utmost attention at him, to see if his Aspect Air &ca. could inspire me with an opinion of his being a Man of Genius.   But it was like repeating Tristram, Tristram. .[4]   No.   the thing

---

[3]Emmanuel Joseph Siéyès (1748–1836) was a leading member of the National Assembly, 1789–91. On 15 June 1789 he moved that the Estates General convert itself into what became known as the National Assembly.
[4]The allusion is to the impossibility of reviving the dead.

seems impossible—   It is a silly Opinion of mine, but I cannot get rid of it,
That every Man like a labelled bottle, has his Contents, marked in his visage.

Sunday, 3 May 1789

I did not feel very well this day   determined to try the Warm bath.   went
and bespoke it to be ready at eleven—   Went   continued in the Water near
half an Hour.   had a most profuse Sweat, but found a little of an head ach.   I
wet my head as well as the rest of me—   I can recollect, that bathing or
Swiming used to give me the head ach.   will see how it will affect me,   this
day the first that seems genial and Warm   It is now 4 O'Clock and I will take a
Walk.

In my Walk I fell in with Mr. Sturges⟨,⟩ Mr. Wyngate⟨,⟩ Mr. Goodhue
We took a circuit on the Island. and came into Town   on the way we talked of
the permanent residence.   they all allowed, That New York was not the
place,   One of them said it ought to be in Pennsylvania.   I said little, but
remarked that altho, we could be better accomodated in Philada. I thought we
should think of the permanent residence, where Houses should be built for the
Members from each State, where they would not be degraded to the humiliating necessity of begging for lodgings from House to House.   I however remarked cooly, that Virginia affected a quiesence in this place, expecting the
Pennsylvanians would be fretted into an acceptance of their Measures for the
potowmac.   That the Potowmac was convenient for a great part of Pennsylvania.   That by our Joining our Votes to those of Virginia and Maryland and the
More southerly States, we could go to the Potowmac any time.   one of them
remarked that in Senate the numerous Votes of Virginia would not avail.   I
did not get time to answer. for another reply'd that we had numbers on our
side in the Senate also.   they asked me to go to their lodging to drink Tea.   I
did so   there we found Mr. Thatcher and Mr. Grout.   I sat a good while.
Mr. Thatcher talked most, but a good deal wildly.   there was a good deal said
about the different New Countries.   I recommended the Genissio and the
Heads of the Susquehanah.[5]   I really think deservedly,   I however had no
objection to draw their attention to the Susquehannah.

---

[5]The Genesee Country was that part of New York lying west of Seneca Lake. In 1786
Massachusetts and New York agreed to resolve their conflicting claims to the area by ac-
knowledging that New York had jurisdiction but Massachusetts owned the land. Nathaniel
Gorham and Oliver Phelps, with Representative Wadsworth as a minor investor, purchased
its six million acres two years later. In 1790 Senator Morris, John Nicholson, and James
Greenleaf purchased all but 700,000 acres from them. See WM's diary entry for 16 August
1789. (Shaw Livermore, *Early American Land Companies* . . . [New York, 1962], pp. 196–
203)

   The 450-mile-long Susquehanna River, which flows into the Chesapeake Bay in Maryland, was a major transportation route in Pennsylvania. The East Branch originates at Otsego
Lake in central New York and flows south to meet the West Branch at Sunbury, WM's home

Monday, 4 May 1789

Went pretty early to the Post Office to deliver letters[6]   as I came back met General St. Clair.   he seemd desirous of speaking with me, said he had been at my lodgings, and asked me what I thought of the Presidents new arrangements.   it was the first I had heard of ~~it~~ them.   The President is neither to entertain nor receive invitations, he is to have Levee days on Tuesdays and Fridays.   when only he is to be seen.[7]   I told the General, That General Washington stood on as difficult Ground, as he ever had done in his life. That to suffer himself to be run down on the one hand by a Croud of Visitants so as to engross his time would never do, as it would render the doing of Business impracticable.   but on the other hand for him to be seen only in public on Stated times like an Eastern Lama would be equally offensive   if he was not to be seen but in public when nothing confidential could pass between him and any individual. the Business would to all appearance be done without him. and he could not escape the Charge of favouritism.   all Court would be paid to the supposed favourite.   weakness & insignificance would be considered as characteristic of the President and he would not escape contempt. That it was not thus the General gained the universal plaudits of his admiring Fellow Citizens.   I reiterated these Ideas in every shape, and in every different light I could place them ~~in~~ for near half an hour that we walked in the Front of St. Pauls Church.   the General said he wished to collect Men's Sentiments, and the design was to communicate them to the General.   I told him my late conduct in the Senate had been such, as would render any opinion of mine very ungraccious at Court, and perhaps he had best never make any mention of my name.   much more was said but not worth ~~reporting~~ committing to paper.   Attended Senate soon after,   the Bill prescribing the Oath &ca. was taken up. & the amendments.   the first amendment was on the enacting Clause.   it stood *be it enacted by the Congress of the United States*.   The amendment by the *Senate and Representatives*.   It was openly avowed by Mr.

---

from 1772 to 1791. The headwaters to which WM refers are those of the West Branch in Northumberland and Huntingdon counties, Pennsylvania, of which he had intimate knowledge because of his experience as a surveyor, Northumberland County official, and land speculator.

   [6]During the first session of the FFC the post office was located at 8 Wall Street. In October 1789 it was moved to 62 Broad Way. (*Iconography* 5:1255, 1280)

   [7]In May 1789 Washington began a practice of receiving visitors on Tuesday and Friday afternoons. He continued to hold a levee on Tuesday at three o'clock throughout the FFC, while the Friday levee became an evening affair beginning at eight and lasting about three hours, with Martha Washington as hostess. At the Cherry Street residence the formal dinners and levees were held in a large dining room at the front of the house. At the Broad Way house these functions were held in the public rooms on either side of the first floor hall. In Philadelphia levees were held in the first floor dining room at the rear of the house. (*GUS*, 2, 27 May 1789; *DGW* 5:451n, 6:26n; Decatur, *Private Affairs*, p. 118; *Address of Nathaniel Burt . . . on the Washington Mansion* [Philadelphia, 1875], p. 20)

Izard that the dignity and preeminence of the Senate was the object aimed at
by the amendment, but the Words of the Constitution are, all legislative
power herein granted shall be vested in a *Congress* of the United States, ~~again~~
again Sect. 8 the Congress shall have power.   The amount of all I said resolv'd
itself into this, the *legislative Authority* the *power* (of making laws in certain
Cases) is given to *Congress* but Congress execute this trust under the same
name.   in other words it is under the *Firm* of Congress that we have received
our *Authority* & *power*, let Us execute it under the same *firm*.   Elsworth who
is a Vastly better speaker than me was in Sentiment with me this time.   he
placed the Subject in various lights, and said enough I thought to convince any
one who was not determined to be otherwise.   But the fact with Us, is, that
the point sought after is to find what will be most agreeable. or in other Words
Where will the Majority be.   for never was a Text more practised on. than that
in a Multitude of Counsellors (say Senators) there is safety.   indeed it seems
the Governing Principle.   Mr. Izard gave Us a Kind of dissenting speech from
both original and amendment   he wanted the Presidents name in it.   ~~the~~
our President rose in the Chair to deliver Sentiments to the same Purpose. and
upon this Principle he was rather against the Amendment because it did not
mention the President.   the amendment carried.   The next amendment,
was a Clause obliging the officers of the State legislatures to take the Oath
within a Month after the first of August.   Mr. Elsworth argued on the inaccu-
racy of the language of the Amendment, That it was doubful as to the intent of
it every way   I though he nearly exhausted the Subject.   before the Vote was
put I chose to say something.   It amounted to this   that the Subject was a
doubtful one every way.   that the power of Congress at any time, or the
propriety of exercising it at this time, if admitted, the Words of the amendment were also doubtful, and doubted of.   I would therefore deal in no
doubtful Matters.   Izard rose in a flame.   declared he know not what Gentlemen meant by talking of doubts, he never heard of any.   he was very
angry.   Mr. Langdon followed him   read the Constitution that all *officers*
both of the *United States* and *several States* shall be bound by Oath—&ca.   I
had to get up in my own defence.   I observed the Gentleman mistook the
point.   the question was not whether the Officers should take the Oath. but
was it our business to interfere in it.   It was equally clear that Senators Representatives and Electors were to be chosen by the States, but who ever thought
of a law to oblige them to do these things,   the adopting States, by the Terms
of their adoption had pledged themselves to conform to the constitution
which contained these things among it's fundamental rules.   that among the
powers delegated to congress this was not mentioned, nor was it necessary,
being already provided for in the Constitution.   That as to doubts Individuals had doubted and States had doubted,   Massachusetts it appeared considered the power of making a law to be with Congress,   Connecticut thought

so differently that they had passed a State law for the purpose.   that for my part I greatly doubted at least of the propriety of medling with it, unless the States should be guilty of neglect.   But That I was not so uncharitable as to damn him that doubted not.   Up rose Lee   he was for the Amendment, but had more doubts than any body.   the rage of speaking caught hold of half the Senate at least.   some sensible things were said, but a great many follish ones.   Elsworth rose a second time,   he took nearly the Tract I had been on, but he explained everything with a clearness and perspicuity, which I was quite incapable of.   I was highly pleased with him.   how readily do the sentimental Strings sound unisons when both are touched by the same agreeable Motive.   but enough   the Amendment was carried against Us.   I learn'd this day that the Title selected from all the Potentates of the Earth for our own President. was to have been taken from Poland Viz. *Elective Majesty*,   What a royal Escape!   dined this day with the French Minister the first place I have been at since my illness.   but I have minuted enough for this day so stop.

Tuesday, 5 May 1789

The Bill of Yesterday had a 3d Reading.   But now how is it to be sent to the other House.   a Motion was made & seconded that it go by the Secretary. from ~~the M~~ half after 11 to half after ~~Two~~ One was this important question agitated.   the other House had affronted the Senate by sending up the Bill in a letter.   and now we would not send it down by a Member.   The dignity of the House was much insisted on.   we were plagued again with the Houses of Lords and commons, and parliamentary was the supplementary Word to every Sentence.   I doubted much Whether I should rise or not.   however When every body had something to say, I scorned to be silent.   I remarked that I rose with reluctance on a Subject, where I had not been able to draw any information from Experience. as the State I had the honor of representing had but One House.   Yet from What I could learn the States which had 2 Houses in the Union, carried on their Communications by the Members,   that this I considered as the most cordial and Friendly Mode of ~~Business~~ intercourse—and that I would much rather take example from our own States than from Great Britain.   that this intercourse therefore was the one which I most sincerely wished, and thought the sooner it was adopted the better, that if our Members should be ill treated below, as had been alledged by some Gentlemen, the fault would not be ours.   and then we would be fully justifyed in, adopting some other mode.   That a Communication by our Secretary was a bad one— that it interrupted business. as we could not proceed ~~in Business~~ without him.   if we meant it by way of returning the ~~neglect~~ affront that had been offered to Us this was wrong.   we should send the Bill by letter.   and this would be treating them in Kind— I was answered, or at least an attempt was made. But I was not convinced. Mr. Langdon got up soon after and seemed to adopt all I had said. but the Motion was carried against Us. Elsworth was with Us and so was Mr. Carrol, but he concluded with saying he would this time vote for the Secretary to go down with the Bill— gave my land lord another half Johannes he now owes me 2:1:10 paid him for some more wood.

2:1:10

paid Bo.   15:4

due—   1:6:6

I forgot to minute a very long Speech of Mr. Elsworth when the Bill was on the third reading He prefaced his discourse by saying he would make no Motion, but Gentlemen, might do as they pleased after he had delivered his sentiments.   The Whole amounted to this, that the great and dignified Station of the President, and the conspicuous part which he would act in the Field of Legislation, as all Laws must pass in review before him, and were subject to his revision and correction &ca. &ca. intitled him to have his name or place marked in the enacting Clause of the Bill all laws. or at least he should be brought into View among the Component parts of Congress.   Ideas of the above kind were dwelt on and varied with agreeable enough diction for near a Quarter of an Hour.   I am confident Elsworth neither wished nor expected to have any serious motion made on such untenable Ground.   What then could be his motive? solely to play the Courtier. something of this Kind had been hinted from the Chair.   Mr. Izard had been explicit on the Subject.
Mr. Elsworth now plays a middle game. he knows the thing cannot take place. but he will bring it fully in view, so that he can say. It was not my fault. and thus secure his Interest with the high Toned Courtiers.   Quere is such a Man to be trusted?   No Motion was made.   indeed the Spirit of his address was reduceable to this, I will make no motion, if any of you are foolish enough to do it, you May.

Wednesday, 6 May 1789

No Senate this day.   there was a Commencement at St. Paul's Church, the Senate were served with Tickets,   Dr. Johnson, the Principal of the College, could not attend with Us.[8]   I had heard that Mr. Morris was come to

---

[8]Members of both the Senate and the House attended the Columbia College commencement. The degree of bachelor of arts was conferred on ten graduates, including Henry Izard, son of the senator from South Carolina. Six received the degree of master of arts, including Senator Johnson's son-in-law, Roger Alden, deputy secretary of the Confederation Congress, and son, Samuel William Johnson. The degree of Doctor of Divinity was conferred on Rev. William Linn, one of the congressional chaplains. Senator Johnson, president of the

Town.   I went for his lodging.   this another Useless Journey for he is not
come.   I would have been very glad of Mr. Morris's Company,   it has happened otherwise.   I have been a bird alone.   I have had to bear the Chilling
cold of the North, and the intemperate Warmth of the South.   Neither of
which are favourable to the Middle State from which I come.   Lee & Izard hot
as the burning Sands of Carolina hate Us.   Adams with all his frigid Friends
cool and wary, bear Us no good Will.   I could not find a confidant, in one of
them, or say to my heart, here is the Man I can trust.   What has been my
conduct then.   Spirit of rectitude bear Witness for me.   have I trimmed to
one of them?   or have I withheld a single Sentiment, That my Judgment
approved of?   I trust I have not.   regardless of Consequences, with no Eye to
emolument, without a wish desire for reappointment. I wish mean to act as if I
were immortal.   And Yet I wish satisfaction to give Satisfaction and Content
to the State that sent me here,   never however will I purchase that with
discontent in my own bosom.   nor does my dear Country demand such a
Sacrifice at my hand.

Thursday, 7 May 1789

The Bill for taking the Oath for the Support of the Constitution came up
the Amendments all agreed to, and a small one added which was concurr'd
with.   the Committee Reported an answer to the Presidents Speech.   it was
read.   One part was objected to, which Stated, the United States to have been
in *Anarchy & Confusion* and the President Stepping in and *rescuing* them.   a
very long debate.   the Words were struck out   Mr. Lee offered part of the A
Sentence which I thought filled the Sentence with propriety,   it was however
lost—   Mr. Patterson offered a Clause.   rescued Us from evils *impending
over* Us—   this was carried, but half the Senate nearly made sour faces at it—
Mr. Elsworth said it was tautological.   but seemed at a loss as to mending
it.   I rose more in Consequence of a kind of determination, that I have
adopted of saying something every day, than from any fondness of the
Subject.   I admitted that there appeared something tautological in the
Words, and it was not easy to Mend them consistent with elegant diction.
but if the first syllable was taken from the Word *im*pending, it would then
stand evils pending over Us, the objection would be obviated but I would not
say the language would be eloquent.   but since I was up I could not help
remarking that I thought the Whole Clause improper, that to state the Whole
Union as being in Anarchy or under impending ruin. was sanctifying the

college, presided over the ceremony and concluded it "with an affectionate, pertinent, and
elegant Address to the Graduates—and a fervent Prayer to the source of all Wisdom and
Felicity, for their future prosperity and usefulness in life." (*NYDA*, 7 May 1789)

calumnies of our Enemies, who had long laboured in the foreign Gazettes to represent Us as a people void of Government. it was fixing a Stain on the Annals of America—for future Historians would appeal to the transactions of this very day, as a proof of our disordered ~~State. should~~ circumstances I therefore was against the Whole Clause. Mr. Wyngate followed me. and was for having the Clause struck, this could not well be done consistent, with Order. I mentioned that if a reconsideration was moved I would second it, it was reconsidered & amended. and afterwards recommitted, to the same Committee. they retired for the Purpose of dressing it. Now the President rose to draw the Attention of the Senate to the Manner of delivering the Answer to the President. A Committee was appointed to confer on this and other Subjects with a Committee of the Representatives. there are three ways Gentlemen (said our President) by which the President may communicate with Us. one is personally, If he comes here we must have a Seat for him, in England it is called a Throne, to be sure it is behind that Seat we must seek for Shelter and Protection. the second is by a Minister of State the third is by his Chamberlain, or one of his Aid De Camps I had almost said, But that is a Military Phrase. it may become a great constitutional question. seeing the House look blank, he said I throw these things out for Gentlemen to think of them. Mr. Lee got up & said, something on the Propriety of having a Seat with a Canopy for the President. Mr. Langdon said something, but he did not seem well collected & spoke so low I did not hear him. The time was triffled till near 3 O'Clock, the day was cold and the Members collected near the fire leaving their seats. The Committee returned with the Message. and it really read vastly better and was altered in the exceptionable places. in one place speaking of the Government. it mentioned dignity and *Splendor*. I submitted it to the Gentlemen who had the amending of it whether respectability, was not better than *Splendor*. Mr. Carrol of the Committee did not defend the Word Splendor, but said respectability had been used before, if he recollected right. Mr. Patterson said it sounded much better than respectability, and rounded the period. Doctor Johnson said Splendor signifyed, in this place, the highest perfection of Government, these were the three Members of the Committee. I mentioned, that if the Word respectability had been used immediately before, It would be improper. that dignity alone I thought expressed all that was wanted. as to the seeking of sounding names and pompous expressions, I thought them exceptionable on that very Account. and that no Argument was necessary to show it— That different Men had a train of different Ideas raised by the same Word, that Splendor when applied to Government brought into my mind, instead of the highest perfection, all the faulty finery brilliant scenes and expensive Trappings of Royal Government. and impressed my mind with an Idea quite the reverse of republican respectability which I thought consisted in form and prudent

Councils frugality and Oeconomy, I found I was not seconded. and concluded, that my motion went to recommend a reconsideration of the Word Splendor to the Committee. they did not alter it, & the Answer was agreed to. the President rose in the Chair & repeated twice, with more Joy in his face than I had ever seen him assume before, he hoped the Government would be supported with *dignity and Splendor.* I thought he did it by way of Triumph over me. for a former defeat I gave him. but may be I was mistaken.

Friday, 8 May 1789

attended a joint Committee on the removing the papers of the old Congress, made progress in the Business, agreed to meet half after ten on Monday, and report,[9] Senate formed the Secretary as Usual had made some Mistakes which were rectifyed. & now Mr. Elsworth moved for the report of the Joint Committee to be taken up on the Subject of Titles. It was accordingly done Mr. Lee lead the Business, he took his old Ground, all the World civilized and Savage called for titles, that there must be something, in human Nature that Occasioned this general Consent, that therefore he conceived it was right. here he began to enumerate the name⟨s⟩ of many nations, who gave Titles such as Venice Genoa &c. the Greeks and Romans, it was said had no Titles, but making a profound bow to the Chair, you were pleased to set us right in this with respect to the Conscript Fathers[10] the other Day here he repeated the Presidents Speech of 23d Ulto. almost verbatim all over.

Elsworth rose. he had a Paper in his Hat, which he looked constantly at, he repeated almost all that Mr. Lee had said but got on the Subject of Kings. declared that the Sentence in the Primer of *Fear God and honor the King*[11] was of great importance that Kings were of divine appointment, that Saul the head & shoulders taller than the rest of the People was elected by God and anointed by ~~him~~ his appointment. I̶h̶a̶ I sat after he had done for a considerable time, to see if anybody would rise. at last I got Up. and first answered Lee as well as, I could withe nearly the same arguments drawn from the Constitution as I had used on the 23d ulto. I mentioned that within a Space of 20 Years back, more light had been thrown on the Subject of Government, and on human affairs in General than for several Generations before. That this light of Knowledge had diminished the veneration for Titles. and that Mankind now considered themselves as little bound to imitate the follies of

---

[9]On 13 April the Senate appointed a committee to confer with a committee from the House on the disposition of the papers of the Continental and Confederation Congresses. The House appointed members on 28 April.

[10]The Senate of the Roman Republic.

[11]This instruction, from the New Testament, 1 Peter 2:17, was common in primers.

civilized Nations, as the Brutality of Savages,   that the Abuse of Power, and the fear of bloody Monsters, had extorted Titles, as well as adoration in some instances from the Trembling croud.   That the impression now on the Minds of the Citizens of these States was that of horror for Kingly authority.   Izard got up   he dwelt almost entirely on the Antiquity of Kingly Government he could not however well get farther back than Phillip of Macedon   he seemed to have forgot both Homer and the Bible—   he Urged for something equivalent to Nobility having been common among the Romans for they had 3 names which seemed to answer to Honorable. or something like it before, and something behind—he did not say Esqr.   Mr. Carrol rose and took my side of the question,   he followed nearly the Tract I had been in, and dwelt much on the information was that was now abroad in the World,   he spoke against Kings.   Mr. Lee & Mr. Izard were both up again   Elsworth was up again Langdon was up several times but Spoke Short each time.   Patterson was up.   But there was no knowing which side he was of.   Mr. Lee considered him, as against him and answered him, but Patterson finally voted with Lee. The President repeatedly helped the speakers for Titles.   Elsworth was enumerating how common the appellation of President was, the President put him in mind, That there were Presidents of Fire Companies & of a Cricket Club,   Mr. Lee at another time was saying he believed some of the States, authorized Titles by their Constitutions.   the President from the Chair told him that Connecticut did it.   at Sundry other times he interfered in a like Manner,   I had been frequently up to answer new points during the debate.   I collected myself for a last effort   I read the Clause of the Constitution against Titles of Nobility, showed that the Spirit of it was against not only granting Titles by Congress but against the permission of Foreign Potentates granting *any Titles Whatever*—that as to kingly Government it was equally out of the question, as a republican Government was guaranteed to every State in the Union that they were both equally the forbidden fruit of the Constitution.   I called the attention of the House to the Consequences that were like to follow.   that Gentlemen seemed to Court a rupture with the other House.   the Representatives had adopted the report and were this day acting on it, or according to the Spirit of the report.   we were proposing a Title. our Conduct would mark us to the World as marked actuated with the Spirit of dissention.   and the Characters of the Houses, would be as aristocratical and democratical.   The Report was however rejected.   Excellency was moved for as a Title by Mr. Izard, it was withdrawn by Mr. Hi Izard. and Highness with some prefatory word proposed by Mr. Lee.   now long Harrangues were made in favour of this Title   Elective was placed before.   it was insisted that such a dignifyed Title would add greatly to the weight and authority of the Government both at home and abroad.   I declared myself totally of a different Opinion.   That at present it was impossible to add to the

respect entertained for General Washington.   That if you gave him the Title
of any P foreign Prince or Potentate. a belief would follow. that the Manners of
that Prince and his modes of Government would be adopted by the
President.   (Mr. Lee had just before I got up read over a list of the Titles of all
the Princes and Potentates of the Earth, marking where the Word Highness
occured.   the Grand Turk had it all   the Princes of Germany had, Sons and
Daughters of Crowned heads &ca.)   that particular Elective highness, which
sounded nearly like electoral Highness, would have a most ungrateful sound to
Many thousands of industrious Citizens who had fled from German Oppression.   That Highness was part of the Title of a Prince of or Princess of the
blood and was often given to Dukes.   that it was degrading our President to
place him on a par, with any Prince of of any Blood in europe.   nor was there
one of them, that could enter the lists of true glory with him.   but I will
minute no more   the debate lasted till half after 3 O'Clock and it ended in
appointing a Committee to consider of a Title to be given to the President—
this Whole silly Business is the Work of Mr. Adams and Mr. Lee,   Izard
follows Lee, and the New England Men who always herd together follow Mr.
Adams.   Mr. Thomson says. this used to be the Case in the old Congress.   I
had to be sure the greatest Share in this debate & must now have compleatly
sold, (no, sold is a bad word for I have got nothing for it) every particle of Court
favour   for a Court our House seem determined on, and to run into all the
foolerries fopperies finerries and pomp of Royal etiquette   and all this for Mr.
Adams.

Saturday, 9 May 1789

attended the Hall at 10 O'Clock to go on the Judicial Committee.   Met
many of the Members,   I know not the Motive but I never was received, with
more familiarity, nor quite so much, before by the Members   Elsworth in
particular seemed to show a kind of fondness.   the Judicial Committee did no
business.   Senate formed   it took a long time to correct the minutes.   Otis
keeps them miserably.   at length the Committee came in and reported a
Title.   *His Highness the President of the United States of America and Protector of the rights of the same.*   Mr. Few had spoke a Word or Two with me
and signifyed his unwillingness to do anything hastily—   he got up and spoke
a good deal against hasty Measures.   he did not pointedly move for Postponement—but it amounted nearly to it.   The Clerk of the other House in the
mean time appeared at the bar and announced the adoption of the Report of
the Joint Committee (rejecting Titles)   I got up and expressed my opinion
that what had fell from the H⟨onorable⟩. G⟨entleman⟩. from Georgia
amounted to a Motion for Postponement. and asked leave to second him.   I

then pointed out. the rupture that was likely to ensue with the other House that this was Matter of very serious import. and I thought it our indispensible duty to avoid any inconvenience of that kind. that by the Arrangement between the Houses in case of disagreement. a Conferrence might be requested that my intention was if the Postponement was carried to move immediately for a Committee of Conferrence to be appointed on the difference between the Houses and I had hopes that by these Means, all Subject of debate would be done away. Mr. Read got up and moved, that the Report might be adopted. he was not seconded but the Motion was in itself Idle. Mr. Strong Spoke in favour of the Postponement, and was interruptd from the Chair. Mr. Dalton after some time, spoke in favour of it. I could now see a visible anxiety in the Chair. I had a fine slack & easy time of it today, Friends seemed to rise in Succession Lee went over his old Ground twice, but owned at last that there was great difficulty every way. but said plainly the best mode was for the House to adopt the Report and then the other House would follow. he found however the current begin to turn against him, and he laid his head on his hand as if he would have slept. Mr. Strong was up again, he said among many things that he thought, the other House would follow. but there was a risk in it— Mr. Izard got up at last he too was for postponement. I could see the President kindled at him. Mr. I. said we knew the other House had adopted the report. the President interruptd him, and said No we had no right to know it. nor could we know it. Untill after the Clk. had this morning given Official information. the Members lined themselves. and the question was called for. Up now got the President and for 40 minutes did he harrange Us from the Chair. he began first on the Subject of Order & found fault, with everything almost. but down he came to particulars, and pointedly blamed a Member for disorderly behavior. the Member had mentioned, the appearance of a Captious disposition in the other House, this was disorderly, and spoke with asperity, the Man he meant was Mr. Izard. all this was only prefatory. on he got on his favourite topick of Titles, and over the old Ground of the immense advantage, of the absolute necessity of them. When he had exhausted this Subject, He turned a new leaf, I believe on a conviction that the postponement would be carried, and perhaps the business lost by an Attention to the other House. Gentlemen I must tell you, that it is You and the President that have the making of Titles suppose the President to have the appointment of Mr. Jefferson at the Court of France.[12] Mr. Jefferson is in Virtue of that appointment, the most illustrious

---

[12]Thomas Jefferson (1743–1826), author of the Declaration of Independence and minister to France since 1785, was educated at William and Mary and trained in the law. He served in Congress and as governor of Virginia during the Revolutionary War. Jefferson reluctantly relinquished his ministerial post to become the first secretary of state. He assumed the duties of that office on 21 March 1790 and took up residence in New York at 57 Maiden Lane on 1 May. See also *SEJ*, pp. 550–51. (*PTJ* 16:279)

the most powerful and what not— But the President must be himself,
something that includes all the dignities of of the diplomatic Corps, and
something greater still.   what will the Common People of Foreign Countries,
what will the Sailors and Soldiers say, George Washington President of the
United States,   they will despise him *to all eternity*.   this is all nonsense to
the Philosopher but so is all Government Whatever.   the above I recollect
with great Precision.   but he said fifty things more equally injudicious, which
I do not think worth minuting.

{Having experienced relief by the interference of sundry Members, I had
determined not to say another word but his new leaf appeared so Absurd I
could not help some animadversions on it.

The Constitution of the U.S., has designated our chief Magistrate by the
Appellation ~~of the~~ of *The President of the U.S. of America*   This is his Title of
Office, nor can We alter add to or diminish it, without infringing the Constitution,   in like Manner Persons authorized to transact Business with Foreign
powers are stiled *Ambassadors public Ministers* &ca.   to give them any other
appellation, would be an equal infringement,   As to Grades of Orders or
Titles of Nobility, nothing of that kind can be established by Congress.

Can then the President & senate ~~declare~~ do that which is prohibited to the
United States at large.   certainly not.   let Us read the Constitution— *No*
Title of Nobility shall be granted by the United States—   the Constitution
goes further,   the Servants of the public are prohibited from accepting them
from any foreign State King or Prince, so that the appellations & Terms given
to Nobility in the old World Are contraband language in The U.S. nor can we
apply them to our Citizens consistent with the Constitution.   As to What the
common People Soldiers & Sailors of foreign Contries may think of Us. I do not
think it imports Us Much—   perhaps the less they think or have occasion to
think of Us the better.   But suppose this a desirable point   how is it to be
gained.   the english excepted, Foreigners do not understand our language
We must Use Hohen Mogende to a Dutchman Beylerbey to a Turk or Algerine,
and so of the rest,   from the English indeed we may borrow ~~Titles~~ Terms that
would not be wholly Unintellig⟨ib⟩le to our own Citizens but will they thank
Us for the Compliment,   would not the plagiarism be more likely to be
attended with contempt, than respect, among all of them.   it has been admitted that all this is nonsense to the Philosopher.   I am ready to admit that
every high sounding pompous appellation descriptive of Qualities Which the
Object does not possess, must appear Bombastic nonsense in the Eye of every
wise Man.   But I cannot admit such an Idea with respect to Government
itself.   Philosophers have admitted not only the Utility but necessity of it.
and their labors have been directed to correct the vices and expose the follies
which have been engrafted upon it, and to reduce the practice of it to the
principles of common Sense, such as we see exemplified by the Merchant the

Mechanic and the farmer, when every Act or Operation tends to a productive or beneficial Effect. And above all to illustrate this fact, That Government was instituted for the Benefit of the People and That no Act of Government is Justifiable That has not this for it's object.   Such has been ~~the Subject of~~ the labours of Philosophers with respect to Government, and sorry indeed would I be, if their labors should be in vain.}

It is evident, that he begins to despair of getting the Article of Titles thro' the House of Representatives.   and he has turned his Eye, to get it done solely by the Senate.   after all this he had to put the Question, and the Postponement was carried.   I kept my Word and offered the resolution for a Conference ~~of~~ on the difference &ca.   it was carried.   and the Committee appointd.   Elsworth the most conceited Man in the World, drew up a new resolution.   it was to keep the difference out of sight and was to proceed, de novo, on a Title for the President   I did not care to enter into debate, but expressed my fear that the House of R. would be irritated, and would not meet Us on that Ground.   and as if they meant to provoke the other House. they insisted that the minute of rejection should go down with the appointment of the Committee—   little good can come of it thus circumstanced. more especially as the Old Committee were reappointed.

Sunday, 10 May 1789

being Sunday. bathed and staid at home all the day after as it was rainy, and I was afraid to go out for fear of catching cold.   Wrote to my family as usual. A Philada. Mercht.[13] was in with Mr. Wynkoop   he alledged that Mr. Fitzsimons delayed the impost Bill untill his own India Men should arrive for it seems he has more than one.[14]   on Friday Evening Mr. Fitzsimons owned that he had set Gerry on to bring in the temporary Bill.[15]   now it seems the temporary bill must be rejected again.   I asked Mr. Fitzsimons what could be the Means of the Bill hanging so long in the hands of the Committee.   he blamed Gerry, said it was left with Gerry last Saturday. that he had called this evening (Friday) and he found it still lying on Mr. Gerry's Table untouched. I asked if he did not expect blame.   he said he was afraid they would say of

---

[13]Herman Joseph Lombaert (c. 1756–93), a native of Flanders and Wynkoop's son-in-law, was in partnership with James Vanuxem at 79 Water Street, Philadelphia. (Clement Biddle, *The Philadelphia Directory, 1791* [Philadelphia, 1791], p. 78; *A Collection of Papers Read before the Bucks County Historical Society* 3:214)

[14]American merchants began a profitable trade with Asia in 1784. At least five vessels, or India Men, had left Canton, China, for the United States earlier in 1789. (*PP,* 20 May, 5, 6, 19 June 1789; *Columbian Centinel,* 4 Aug. 1789)

[15]The temporary or interim Collection Bill [HR-3], introduced by Gerry on 8 May and tabled on 18 May, was replaced by a permanent Collection Bill [HR-6] on 27 May; this was in turn replaced by another permanent Collection Act [HR-11], which Washington signed into law on 31 July.

him as he was a Merchant, that he delayed, it untill his own Vessels would arrive from the East Indies, *they do indeed say so*. And I say the Bill is delayed by some Means to the great loss of the Revenue. Mr. Wynkoop remarked, that Mr. Fitzsimons acted in a double Capacity as a Merchant, & as a Representative. the Man reply'd Shrewdly. *You will always find the Merchant Uppermost.*

Monday, 11 May 1789

I have actually delayed making up my Journal for this day untill the Morning of the 12th. I feel how very wrong this is. There is a bluntness over my Memory already. The first thing I did in the Morning, was delivering my letters at the Post Office,   called to see if Mr. Morris was come to Town,   he was not.   Met two Committees, at the Hall.   first on the affairs of the Old Congress Papers,   this Business disposed ~~off~~ of.   the second on the Judiciary department.   Senate met   Mr. Lee moved to put off, the Order of the day, on the Subject of Titles. untill tomorrow   agreed to.   he then moved to consider of appointing a Serjeant at Arms   this lost.   Mr. Izard and sundry Gentlemen of the Senate dissatisfy'd with our President.   he takes on him to school the Members from the Chair.   his grasping after Titles ~~has~~ h a s b e e n observed by every body.   Mr. Izard after describing his air Manner deportment and personal figure in the Chair, concluded with applying the Title of *Rotundity* to him.   I have really often looked at him with surprize mingled with contempt when ~~I have seen~~ he is in the Chair and no Business before the Senate.   instead of that sedate easy air which I would have him possess, he will look on one side then on the other then down the Knees of his Breetches, then dimple his visage with the most silly kind of half smile. which I cannot well express in English.   the Scotch Irish have a word that hits it exactly, *smudging*.   God forgive me for the Vile thought, but I cannot help thinking of a Monkey just put into Breeches when I see him betray such evident marks of Self conceit.   He made Us a Speech this day also.   but as I did not minute the heads of it, when he spoke I will not attempt to recollect it.   Senate adjourned.   and the Judicial Committee met, sat till near three O'Clock.   appointed a Subcommittee to draught a Bill.[16]   I do not like it in any part.   or rather I generally dislike it.   but we will see how it looks in form of a Bill.   after dinner we were called on by the Speaker and his Brother and asked to eat a Pennsylvania dinner, tomorrow.   took a Walk.   I received a Ticket from the President U.S. to ~~attend~~ Use his Box this Evening at the Theatre. being the first of his Appearance at the Play House since his entering on his Office.   Went.   The President⟨,⟩ Governor of the State. Foreign Ministers⟨,⟩ Sena-

---

[16]Ellsworth and Paterson, and perhaps others including Strong, composed the drafting subcommittee.

tors. from N⟨ew⟩. H⟨ampshire⟩. C⟨onnecticut⟩. P⟨ennsylvania⟩. M⟨assachusetts⟩. and S⟨outh⟩. C⟨arolina⟩. and some ladies in the same Box.   I am old and notices or attentions are lost on me.   I could have wished some of my dear Children in my place.   they are Young and would have enjoyed it. long might one of them live to boast, of their having been seated in the same Box with the first Character in the World.   the Play was the School for scandal,   I never liked it, Indeed I think it an indecent Representation before ladies of Character and Virtue.   Farce the old Soldier.   The House greatly crouded, and I thought the Players acted well.   But I wish we had ~~had~~ seen the *conscious Lovers*, or some one that inculcated, more prudential manners.[17]

Tuesday, 12 May 1789

Went early this morning to wait on Mr. Fitzsimons   was informed that Mr. Morris had called to see him this Morning.   took no Notice of this but went in quest of ~~him~~ Mr. Morris   found him at the door where he kept his office. took a long walk with him, and gave him a detail of all that had happened in the Senate since He left it, as exactly as I could,   he seemed to listen to me in a friendly way.   Came to the Hall at Eleven,   Senate met, but there really was nothing happened worth minuting,   the Business of considering the Title which was laid on the Table, was postponed, to see what would be the result, of the Conference of the Joint Committee on that Business.   adjourned. went to hear the debates of the H. of R. from the Gallery,   from thence went With Mr. Morris to the President's Levee.   staid untill the Company began to withdraw,   felt I believe a little awkward, for my Knee pained me ~~a Lot~~ and this Business of standing was not very agreeable to me.   left Mr. Morris at the Levee   came home. staid till 4 OClock. and went and dined with the Speaker.   This day the President gave Us no set speech from the Chair.   But I know not Whether it was want of Memory or design but a Motion made ~~and~~ by me and seconded by Lee, was passed by, by him, and a second Motion put,   he however seemed confused.   The Speech which he made Yesterday, was on the Subject of our having a Serjeant at Arms,   he seemed to Wish that the Officer should be *Usher of the black rod*.[18]   He described this office as appurtenant to the House of Lords.   and concluded by telling Us, that Sir

---

[17]Richard Sheridan's *School for Scandal*, first produced in 1777, was performed by the Old American Company at the John Street Theatre. Built in 1767, the theatre was located on the north side of the street, halfway between Broad Way and Nassau Street. The farce or comic opera performed that evening was John O'Keeffe's *The Poor Soldier*, first produced in 1783. (Charles Beecher Hogan, *The London Stage 1660–1800 . . . Part 5: 1776–1800*, 3 vols. [Carbondale, Ill., 1968], 1:8, 2:639; *NYDA*, 13 May 1789; *New York*, p. 167) First produced in 1722, *The Conscious Lovers* was written by Richard Steele. (Emmett L. Avery, *The London Stage 1660–1800. . . Part 2: 1700–1729*, 2 vols. [Carbondale, Ill., 1960], 2:694)

[18]The gentleman usher of the black rod carried a black wand surmounted by a golden lion as a symbol of office. Among his functions was to act as usher to the House of Lords.

Francis Mollinaux, was the officer, *and that he had the Honor of being intro-duced by him, to the House of Lords.*

{My Business with Mr. Fitzsimons this morning was to inform him how much I feared the caballing of the New England Members in the Senate. and that if they were not gratifyed in some measure on their favourite Article of Molasses, they would join with every Member who objected to any single Article and promise him gratification, in his particular humor, if he would join them. by these means all the discontents being united, and ~~gratification~~ in-dulgence given even to caprice and whim the Bill would be lost. he laughed at my fears— the Molasses affair was to be called up again. I asked him if he was sure of Majority, in the House for continuing the duty at 6 Cents. very confident of it. Yet he was mistaken and it was reduced to 5— I felt great Joy on the coming of Mr. Morris to Town. for now I shall have one in whom I can confide.}

Wednesday, 13 May 1789

Paid some Visits this Morning. Senate Met. the President put Us in mind. That the Report, for the President's Title lay on the Table. Mr. Lee informed the House that the Committee on that business had met but being in the Senate Chamber were dispersed on the meeting of the Senate, and had agreed to meet tomorrow Morning. Report for classing the Senate presented to lie on the Table.[19] Moved, and a Committee appointed to confer—on the Subject of News Papers. A Committee of 8 appointed for the penal Federal Laws. I can observe a total change of Behaviour, or at least a Considerable one in our President, instead of directing Two Senators, to read the ballots for Committee Men. as he did heretofore. he this day read them aloud from the Chair, and the Clk. tallied this is the first Step towards reformation, and I hope it will be *progressive*.

Thursday, 14 May 1789

this a most Stormy day with rain. went to the Hall half after nine, met Mr. Ellicott and took him with me to the Board of Treasury. he left his Papers.[20] I met the Committee for the dividing of the rooms. I told Few and the Committee in General That I had heard there were designs on foot, to

---

[19]This report recommended a method for implementing the second clause of Article I, Section 3, of the Constitution, requiring the senators to be divided into three classes, to serve respectively for two, four, and six years. WM, who drew a two year term, refers to Morris and the other senators who drew the longest term as six-year men. He believed them to be less accountable for their conduct in office.

[20]Andrew Ellicott (1754–1820), a surveyor, resided in Bucks County, Pennsylvania, until 1775 when his family founded Ellicott City, Maryland, a milling and foundry center. After

saddle Congress, with the Expence of the City Hall.   He did not give a Word of Answer.   L enfant,[21] was with Us, and like most Frenchmen, was so talkative, that scarce a word could be said.   adjourned to meet tomorrow at 10 'O'Clock   Senate met.   the President reminded Us of the Title report. The Committee were out on that business.   classing report adopted.   a Motion of Yesterday was on the Table for the regulating Joint Committees, Elsworth, according to his custom drew another one.   Mr. Langdon withdrew his in complaisance to Elsworth.   Lee moved to strike out the later part of Elsworth's.   Elsworth in Complaisance to Lee seconded him.   this spoild the Motion and all complaisance being at an end.   the rest was rejected by the House.   It was here the President made Us his Speech for the day.   he said parliamentary Customs, when found convenient should be followed as good Examples (this is the first time ever I heard him guard his parliamentary lessons, but I observed Yesterday there was a change) that Conferrences were very seldom used by the Houses in great Britain that little benefit was obtained from them.   that there could be but little Use only in Case of difference of Opinion with respect to Bills,   the whole seemed to aim at lessining the intercourse between the Two Houses.   I could not help thinking of his speech of the 9th instant   it seemed, the second part of it.   Now rose Mr. Lee to report on Titles. from the joint Committee.   He reported that the Commit-

---

militia service in the War for Independence, he became an almanac maker and surveyor, spending considerable time in the West, conducting boundary surveys for Virginia and Pennsylvania. In 1791 Washington chose him to run the four lines of the District of Columbia. Ellicott's papers were related to the congressional resolution of 6 June 1788 instructing the geographer, Thomas Hutchins, or someone else duly appointed, to survey the western boundary between New York and Pennsylvania, known as the Erie Triangle. Hutchins requested Ellicott to undertake the survey, and Ellicott sought an advance for expenses. The board of treasury refused, and in April 1789 Ellicott appealed to WM, who suggested that if Ellicott sent him a memorial and the original instructions from Hutchins, it would perhaps not be necessary for him to come to New York to argue his case. The matter was resolved in August when Congress adopted a joint resolution on the survey of the western boundary of New York in response to a petition from Ellicott. Washington then appointed Ellicott, who conducted the survey between the first and second sessions of the FFC. It was on this mission that he made the first topographical survey of the Niagara River and its falls. See also *DHFFC* 6:2118–23. (WM to Ellicott, 6 May 1789, Maclay Diary Manuscript, DLC)

The board of treasury was located in Fraunces Tavern at Broad and Pearl streets. Its establishment in 1784 removed management of the financial affairs of the United States from a single executive, the superintendant of finance, a post previously held by Robert Morris. The three members of the board were Samuel Osgood, Walter Livingston, and Arthur Lee. The treasury department took over its functions in September 1789.

[21]Pierre Charles L'Enfant (1754–1825), born in Paris and trained in architecture and engineering, rose to the rank of major in the American army. He was a member of the Society of the Cincinnati and designed its insignia. A variety of artistic endeavors during the 1780s brought him to the attention of civic leaders, particularly in New York where he resided. In 1788–89 he superintended the conversion of New York City Hall into Federal Hall. L'Enfant was recommended as architect to prepare a building for Congress when it moved to Philadelphia in 1790 but did not get the job. In 1791 Washington chose him to survey and design the Federal City within the District of Columbia. (Fitzsimons to Miers Fisher, 16 July 1790, Fisher Papers, PHi)

tee from the other house had adhered in the Strictest Manner, to their former resolution.   he moved that the report which had been laid on the Table in favour of Titles, should be entered on the files of the House. and that a Motion which he had in his hand should be adopted.   the Spirit of the ~~report~~ motion was, that to keep up a proper respect for our Chief Magistrate attention should be paid to the customs of civilized nations. that the appearance of the affectation of simplicity, would be injurious, that the Senate had decided in favour of Titles from these Motives, but that in conformity to the Practice of the other House, for the present they resolv'd to address the President without Title ☞

{☞ ~~Mr. Muh~~ Yesterday G⟨eneral⟩. M.(Muhlenberg) accosted me with ~~the with~~, *Your highness of the Senate*. on my pausing he said Wynkoop had been Christened by them his highness of the ~~R~~ Lower House, and he thought I was intitled to the same distinction in the Senate   As we shall have ~~it~~ had the Business all over again ~~this day let me see~~ I determined to try What Ridicule could do.   if all Men Were of one ~~height~~ Stature, there would be neither high nor low.   Highness When apply'd to ~~Man~~ An Individual, must naturally denote the *[lined out]* excess of Stature Which he possesses over other Men.   An Honorable Member told Us the other day of a certain King Who was the Head & shoulders taller than any Body Else.   this more especially When he was gloriously greased with a great Horn of Oyl. must render him *highly* conspicuous.   History too, if I mistake not, will furnish Us with an Example When a great Thracian obtained the Empire of the World from no other Circumstance;[22]   But if this antiquated principle is to be adopted, give Us fair play, let America be searched, and it is most probable that the Honor will be found to belong to some Hughe Patagonian.   ~~It may be said this~~ This indeed is putting one Jockey over the Head of another.   true, but Nature has done it, And Men should see where she leads, before they adopt her as a Guide.   It may be said That ~~the~~ This business is Metaphorical, And the high Station of the President intitled him to it.   Nothing can be true Metaphorically which is not so naturally, And Under this View of the proposed ~~tittle~~ Title, it belongs with more propriety to the Man in the Moon than Any body Else. as his Station (when we have the Honor of seeing him) is certainly the most exalted of any that we know of.   Gentlemen may say this is fanciful.   Would they wish to see the Subject ~~in the Subject~~ in the most serious point of View that it is possible to place it.   Rome after being benighted for Ages, in the darkest Gloom of ~~Ell~~ Ecclesiastick & Aristocratick Tyranny, beheld a Reformer in the 14th Century who preaching from Stocks & Stones, And the busts & fragments of Antient Heroes, lighted up the lamp of Liberty to Meridian Splendor,   intoxicated with Success, he assumed a String of Titles, none of which, in my recollection, was ~~as~~ equally Absurd ~~as~~ with the one before You.   In Conse-

---

[22]Apparently Alexander the Great.

quence of Which and of his apeing some other Symbols of Nobility & Royalty, he fell & pulled down the Whole Republican Structure along with him. marking particularly the Subject of Titles as one of the principal Rocks on Which he was ~~principally~~ Shipwrecked.}

{Mem. The Fall of Rienzi the roman reformer,[23] who split on the Rock of Titles was compleatly in point.}

{As to the later part of the Titles, I would only observe, That the power of War, is the Organ of Protection. This is placed in Congress by the Constitution. Any attempt to divest them, of it, And place it elsewhere, even with Geo. Washington is Treason against the United States, or at least a Violation of the Constitution.}

Mr. Carrol rose and opposed the imperfect resolution being put on the files by Order of the House. ~~as such a Vote would~~ I seconded him in opposing this, as putting such a thing on the files by special Order of the House was giving it an auth~~or~~ority, which no postponed paper should have, and carried the Air of an adoption. papers were never specially ordered on the files, but with a view of perpetuating information, a special order for putting on the files, would hereafter be considered as an adoption. this part of ~~Mr. Lee's~~ the Motion ~~was~~ being lost, by a general postponement of the ~~resolution~~ Report.

Mr. Morris rose after the question had been carried & expressed his dislike of title Viz. *Highness* and the *Protector of the rights of America.* he said the protection lay with the Whole Congress. ~~I thought him~~ he was right in his remarks, but he was told the question was carried— Mr. Carrol expressed great dislike at the forepart of the Motion, which Stated the Acts of the Senate to be in favour of Titles, when in fact, no such resolution Ever had passed the Senate. I rose and moved a division of the Motion was immediately seconded by Mr. Carrol. now a long debate ensued. Mr. Else. traversed the Field of Titles over again. Dtr. Johnson spoke much more to the point. Mr. Patterson after reading over the Motion was of Opinion that a division should take place at the Word Senate. I was also with Mr. Morris of opinion that the division would stand best at this place. I withdrew my motion and seconded his for the division From the Word Senate. the division was full enough to answer all the purposes which they avowed. taking it at this place. but it is evident they have not given up the Idea of Titles, and seem insultingly to say so, to the House of Representatives. Affectation of simplicity is directly charged on the other House. this they amended by putting in the Word *appearance*. I endeavoured to draw my principal Argument when last up, from the unfairness of the forepart it expressly recited a determination of the Senate to grant Titles. no such resolution had ever passed. it might be

---

[23]Niccolo Gabrini, Cola di Rienzi (1313–54), led the revolution in Rome in 1347 which overthrew the aristocratic government. Assuming the old title of tribune, he antagonized the people by his arbitrary policies, and they drove him out of Rome a year later. He returned as dictator in 1354, only to be murdered.

imply'd that the Senate were in favour of Titles, but why refer to a resolution that did not exist.   Accomodation was the principle held out.   but was ever thing done with so ill a grace!   it was saying we meet you on the principles of accomodation, but you are compleatly wrong, and we are perfectly right. can any good come of such accomodation?   Mr. Carrol declared that the Idea, held forth, was that the Senate were for Titles.   But it was well known they were not all for Titles.   he was opposed and so were sundry other Gentlemen.   he wished only for a fair question that it might be seen who were for them, and who were not.   he wished the Yeas and Nays. and let the World Judge.   Mr. Few declared the Gentleman had missed the Opportunity of the Yeas and Nays.   they should have been called when the report against Titles was rejected.   Mr. Few was much out in this for there were but 3 of Us. and he need not have made his remarks.   it was evident that they wished to prevent the Yeas and Nays.   the Question was put   the House divided   8 with Us 10 against Us   Mr. Carrol called for the Yeas and Nays.   none rose with him but Mr. Henry and myself.   and for ~~want~~ want of another Man we lost them.
The Committee was now ordered to wait on the President to Know the time When he will be pleased to receive the Address of the Senate.   the Report of the Joint Committee on the inrolment of papers was read.   and the House adjourned.   and now I hope we have disposed of a Business which in one shape or other has engaged almost the Whole time of the Senate from the 23d of April the day that ~~the~~ our President began it.   Had it not been for Mr. Lee, I am firmly convinced, no other man would have ventured, to have followed our President.   but Lee lead   Elsworth seconded him. the New England Men followed & Izard Joined them.   but really haud equis passibus,[24] for he was only for the Title of Excellency which had been sanctifyed by Use.   This Lee has a cultivated understanding, great Practice in public business, with a factious restless disposition.   He has acted as high Priest thro' the Whole of this Idolatrous Business.   It is easy to see What his aim is,   by flattering the President of the Senate he hopes to govern all the Members from New England, and with a little assistance from Carolina or Georgia, to be absolute in the Senate.   Elsworth and some more of the New England Men flatter him in turn, expecting he will be with them on the question of Residence.   Had it not been for our President and Lee I am convinced the Senate would have been as averse to titles as the House of Representatives   The Game that our President & Mr. Lee appear to have now in View is to seperate the Senate as much as possible from the House of Representatives.   ~~The~~ our President's doctrine is that all honors & Titles should flow from the President and Senate only.   But once more Subject of Titles farewell.   may I never hear Motion or debate on thee More.
{In Order to get out of the kind of puzzle which Lee had engaged Us in, we

---

[24]Not with equal steps.

moved a general postponement of the Report on the Title, hoping this would cut up the Whole Matter by the Roots.   It was carried.   And even after this Lee hung with obstinacy to the Idea of putting it on the files of the House.}

{Thro' the Whole of this ~~Idolatrous~~ base business I have endeavoured to Mark the Conduct of Genl. Washington.   I have no Clue that Will lead me fairly to any Just conclusion as to his sentiments.   I think it Scarce possible but he Must have dropped Something, On a Subject Which has excited so much Warmth.   if he did it was not on our side, or I would have heard of it.   But no Matter, I have by plowing with the Heifers of the other House compleatly defeated them.}

Friday, 15 May 1789

called early this Morning on Mr. Scot.   I know not where he was but I did not find him untill the 4th time of my calling—   it was to guard him on the Subject of appropriating the rooms of the City-Hall.   this is a deceitful Business.   I put into his hands a form of a Report.   But he does not seem to be the right Stuff to Work with.   but I have got the Business in a good train.   and Mr. White of Virginia is to draw a report.   Senate Met.   on the reading of the Minutes, Mr. Few got up and moved Warmly that the Minute of Yesterday on the division of Mr. Lee's Motion should be struck out—   Lee was for it in a Moment.   by these Means the Vote of Yesterday which respected Titles would ~~be Struck out~~ have the appearance of Unanimity,   It was opposed by Mr. Carrol⟨,⟩ Elsworth and Myself; the minute however remained   The Committee reported that the President of the States would receive our address a Quarter after 12 on Monday.   It was said we should go in Carriages.   The classing Report was called for   the Ballots were drawn   I fell in the first Class, with Mr. Dalton⟨,⟩ Mr. Elsworth⟨,⟩ Mr. Elmer⟨,⟩ Mr. Carrol and Mr. Grayson.   The President now informed the Senate that a letter had come to his hands which he supposed was intended for him, but it was most improperly directed,   It was directed to his Excellency the Vice President.   he asked the Opinion of the Senate laughingly. and concluded that it was against all Rule.   I said that untill we had a rule obliging People to be regular, we must submit to their irregularities, more especially of this kind.   Mr. Morris, said the Majesty of the People would do as they pleased.   all this ~~was in my opinion~~ I considered as sportive.   But he put a Serious question should the letter so directed be read.   Langdon and Sundry other said, Yes and read it was   from Loudon the Printer[25] offering to print for Us—   adjourned—

[25]Samuel Loudon (1727–1813), newspaper editor and book store owner, immigrated to New York City about 1753, probably from northern Ireland. After pursuing a variety of occupations, he founded the *New York Packet* in 1776. It was the city's oldest newspaper in 1789. As a Federalist editor, Loudon requested help from Alexander Hamilton in support of his letter. (*PAH* 5:341–42)

William Maclay. Photograph of oil painting by Nick Ruggieri.
(Courtesy of Kim E. Baer, Pennsylvania Bar Association, Harrisburg, Pa.)

{I cannot help here noting a Trait of insolence in Lee⟨,⟩ Elsworth and Johnson. This Committee take on them to inform the Committee of the Representatives. *That the Senate would for the present address the President under the same Stile and Title as the House of Representatives had given him.* This in fact was saying the Senate will do what we please. Insolence indeed. but the fact Justifies it—} {But with all their Art I have Jockeyed them for Once.}

Saturday, 16 May 1789

settled all accounts with Mr. Vandolsen and he owes me Twelve Shillings and Sixpence 12/6— Visited Mr. Dalton & Mr. Langdon. attended the Committee on the dividing the rooms delivered my Sentiments plainly with respect to the Residence of Congress, it was brought in View, by talking of this buildg. Viz. that from here we would go. that I scorned all private trick and Cabal about it, and would openly at all times declare for a departure from this place. Committee to meet on Monday at 10— Senate met. A Message came from the ~~Senate~~ H. of R. it was on the affair of a Joint Committee on News papers and employing Printers. Sundry Petitions had come in from different Printers, One was Just now read from one Fenno.[26] I moved that Fenno's and all Petitions of a similar nature should be referred for information to the Committee on the News papers and the employing printers, it was seconded. Elsworth rose in great warmth and opposed it violently, some more of the New England Men joined him. It really seemed to me as if. he wished to try whether he could not carry any thing. he was however disappointed. a report of a Committee for revising the Minutes was read.[27] the Petition of one Duncan Campbell[28] was read and occasioned Sundry remarks, laid on the Table. The address was now produced engrossed.[29] the Word, To, disobliged Elsworth, and a long debate insued about it, I did

---

[26]John Fenno (1751–98) was a Bostonian whose career as a merchant had failed. In 1789 he moved to New York City where he planned to establish a newspaper and obtain a share of the federal government's printing. His *Gazette of the United States* had as its purpose the dissemination of favorable sentiments about the new Constitution and its administration. Soon after the beginning of the second session of the FFC, the Senate employed Fenno to print its committee reports, bills, and journal. He retained the contract when he moved his office and newspaper to Philadelphia just prior to the third session. (Fenno to Joseph Ward, 23 Feb. 1789, Ward Papers, ICHi)

[27]This was the report of the committee appointed on 14 April to consider the method of keeping and publishing the Senate journal.

[28]Duncan Campbell (d. 1807), a British-born Nova Scotian who served as a lieutenant with James Livingston's First Canadian Regiment, petitioned for reimbursement of advances in supplies and money that he made to encourage Canadians to enlist in the American army. He resided in New York City. See also the petition volumes. (Heitman; *JCC* 31:660; *Journal of the House of Representatives of the United States*, 31 Jan. 1800)

[29]The address was the Senate's response to Washington's inaugural speech.

not touch this trite Subject. but it was to be signed and here a Mighty difficulty was signified from the Chair and the Wisdom of the House called on to determine if the Chair had done right. every act had been signed, J. A. Vice President. the President gave this information in such a way, as left no body in doubt. That his opinion Went with the Practice. Mr. Carrol got up said he thought it a Matter of indifference, & concluded that he agreed it should be signed, Vice President. His looks I thought betrayed dissent. But the Goddess of good nature will apologize for this slight Aberation from sentimental rectitude. he has ~~total~~ for some time past been equally with myself opposed to the Opinions of the Chair. and this was his peace offering. About ~~ten days~~ Two weeks ago I was with Mr. Read of the Delaware State. in the upper Gallery of H. of R. A Message came from the Senate. the Signature was read aloud John Adams Vice President. Mr. Read turned to me and said that is Wrong. Yet Mr. Read now made a very long Speech declaring there was no impropriety in it. Mr. Lee hinted very diffidently his disapprobation of it, Mr. Morris, said our Acts should be signed by our own President. Mr. Elsworth. shewed ~~m~~ some inconveniencies that would attend this practice I rose, said the Very Term Vice President, carried on the face of it, the Idea of holding the Place of the President in his Absence. that every Act done by the Vice President as such. implyd that when so acting he held the place of the President. in this point of View nothing could be more improper than the Vice President signing an address to the President. It was like a Man signing an Address to himself. that the Business of the Vice President, was When he acted exactly the same with that of President. and could not mix itself with Us as a Senate. Here the President Tryed very hard to raise a laugh. seeing him willing to bear on down I continued. Sir we know You not as Vice President within this House. as President of the Senate only do we know you, as President of the Senate only can You sign or authenticate any Act of that body. He said after I sat down that he believed, he need not put the question a Majority of those who had spoke seemed to be in favour of his signing as President of the Senate. Mr. Carrol said he need not put the Question and none was put— adjourned.

Sunday, 17 May 1789

Staid at home this day and bathed, wrote letters to Sundry Persons. did not go out untill 4 O'Clock, when I thought it Warm enough— called at the Lodgings of Mr. Fitzsimons and Clymer they had gone to Brunswick. walked to the Speakers, we walked to Cuylers Hook,[30] the East wind blew

---

[30]New Brunswick, New Jersey, is situated on the Raritan River, thirty-five miles southwest of New York City. It could be reached by ferrying across the Hudson River to Paulus Hook

raw and cold I left them and came home. found myself rather indisposed. caught some cold, in my Walk, and was the worse for it. I never
have been in a place remarkable for such a variable weather. set out When
one will with ever such agreeable Sunshine, I never have been able to go two
miles and return without a change of Air, the wind which crosses the north
river,[31] is cold. but there is a rawness, in the East Winds that with me, seems
to clog the Springs of life. Mr. Scott however from Washington County has
experienced a favourable revolution in his health, since he came here.

Monday, 18 May 1789

attended the Hall at 10 O'Clock on what was called the Arrangement
committee,[32] but they did not meet. and nothing was done, General discourse only obtained among, principally, on the necessity of our removal to a
permanent Residence. White⟨,⟩ Sturges and Scott, were with me. Senate
met, the address was read over. and we proceeded in Carriages to the President's. to present it. having no part to act, but that of a mute, I had nothing
to embarrass me. we were received in an Anti Chamber, had some little
difficulty about Seats. Fro as there were several wanting from whence may be
inferred, that the Presidents Major Domo.[33] is not the most provident, as our
numbers were well enough known. We had not been seated more than three
Minutes, When it was signifyed to Us, to wait on the President in his Levee
Room. Our President, went foremost and the Senators followed, without
any particular Order. we made our bows as we entered, and our President,
having made a bow began to read our address, he was much confused, the
Paper trembled in his hand, tho' he had the aid of both by resting it, on his hat
which he held in his left hand. he read very badly all that was on the front

(present-day Jersey City), from which a daily stagecoach service operated. On weekends
there was direct boat service. (*New York*, pp. 102, 105)

Corlears Hook, or Crown Point, was situated on the lower east side of Manhattan Island,
just south of the present site of the Williamsburg Bridge.

[31]Hudson River.

[32]The committee to confer with a House committee for the purpose of dividing, arranging, or appropriating space in Federal Hall was appointed on 9 May. House members were
appointed on 10 May.

[33]Washington's house steward was Samuel Fraunces (c. 1722–95), a West Indian probably
of French and African extraction. He became a New York tavern keeper as early as 1759 and
had been proprietor of Fraunces Tavern in 1770. During the revolutionary war he helped to
foil an attempt to assassinate Washington and apparently acted as a spy for him. Beginning
in 1785, in return for these services and for his aid to American prisoners during the war,
Congress rewarded him financially and leased the tavern as offices for the departments of
foreign affairs and war and the board of treasury. Fraunces accompanied Washington when
the seat of government moved to Philadelphia. (*JCC* 28:207–8)

pages   the turning of the Page seemed to restore him. and he read the rest with more propriety.   This agitation was the more remarkable ~~to me~~. as there were but 22 Persons present and none of them Strangers.   The President took his reply out of his Coat Pocket,   he had his Spectacles in his Jacket Pocket, having his hat in his left hand, & the paper in his right, he had too Many Objects for his hands,   he shifted his hat between his forearm and the left side of his breast, but taking his Spectacles from the Case, embarrased him,   he got rid of this, small distress, by laying the Spectacle Case on the Chimney Piece.   Col. Humphreys stood on his right and Mr. Lear on his left.[34]   having adjusted his Spectacles which was not very easy considering the engagements on his hands, he read the reply with tolerable exactness and without much emotion.   I thought he should have received Us with his Spectacles on, which would have saved the making of some uncouth Motions, Yet on the Whole he did nearly as well as any Body els⟨e⟩ could have done the same Motions. could the Laws of Etiquette have permitted him to have been disencumbered of his Hat it would have relieved him much.   after having read his reply he delivered the paper to our President, with an easy inclination, bowed round to the Company and desired them to be seated.   This Politeness seems founded in reason, for Men after standing quite still some time, want to sit, if it were for only a Minute or Two.   Our President, did not comply, nor did he ~~not~~ refuse, but stood so long, that the President repeated the request,   he declined it by making a low bow & retired   we made our bows, came out to the ~~dood~~ door and waited till our Carriages took Us up.   Col. Humphreys waited on Us to the door.   returned   Senate formed   the address and reply were ordered in the Minutes—   Clk. of the H. of R. brought up the impost Bill,   Thursday was assigned for it.   some Petitions were read and the House adjourned.

---

[34]David Humphreys (1752–1818), presidential aide and member of Washington's official family, was born in Derby, Connecticut, and graduated from Yale in 1771. During the War for Independence he served as an aide to Washington and rose to the rank of lieutenant colonel. In 1784 Congress appointed him secretary to the commission for negotiating commercial treaties in Europe. Upon his return to the United States two years later, he turned his literary talents and conservative political philosophy to an attack on democracy as one of the authors of the "Anarchiad." Humphreys drafted a long inaugural address for Washington, which asserted a philosophy of strong presidential leadership, but it was discarded at the urging of Madison. Between 1789 and 1791, Washington appointed Humphreys as a commissioner to negotiate with the Creek Indians, a secret agent of the United States in Europe, and the first American minister to Portugal. Nathaniel E. Stein, "Washington's Discarded Inaugural Address," *Manuscripts* 10:2–17, contains the extant portions of Humphreys's draft, the manuscript of which was cut into pieces and distributed to collectors and others by Jared Sparks. See also *SEJ*, p. 485. (*Harvard Graduates* 17:527–45; Herbert B. Adams, *Life and Writings of Jared Sparks*, 2 vols. [Boston, 1893], 2:211–13)

Tobias Lear (1762–1816), Washington's secretary and a member of his official family, was born in Portsmouth, New Hampshire, and graduated from Harvard in 1783. He went to Mount Vernon in 1786 to become Washington's private secretary. During the FFC Lear carried messages and documents from the president to Congress. (*DGW* 4:337)

Tuesday, 19 May 1789

paid Visits to 10 O'Clock   attended at the City hall but the arranging
Committee did not meet,   Senate met at 11—   a Report was taken up,
regulating the mode of keeping the Journals, and directing them to be published Monthly.   agreed to and the Committee appointed, to prepare them
for the Press.   adjourned,   I was not of any committee, so went into the
House of Representatives to hear the debates,   the House was in Committee
of the Whole, on the Establishment of the great departments.   staid untill
after 2 O'Clock.   had agreed with Sundry of our Pennsylvania Friends, to go
to the Levee.   Genl. Muhlenberg. came to me and told me they would meet
me in the Committee room.   We did so and went to the Levee.   I went
foremost and left them to follow & do as well as they could,   indeed they had
no great thing of a Pattern, for I am but a poor Courtier.   The Company was
large for the Room   the foreign Ministers were there, Van Berkel the Dutch
Minister[35] (for the first time I suppose) Guady as a Peacock.   our Pennsylvanians withdrew before me.   the President honored me with a particular Tete a
Tete,   how will this Weather suit your farming?   poorly Sir, the Season is the
most backward I have ever known.   It is remarkably so here, but by letters
from Pennsylvania, Vegetation is slow in proportion there—   The Fruit it is to
be expected will be safe, backward seasons are in favour of it.   but in Virginia
it was lost before I left that place.—   much depends on the exposure of the
Orchard,   those with a northern aspect, have been found by Us, to be the
most certain in producing fruit.—   Yes that is a good Observation and should
be attended to.   Made my bow and retired.

Wednesday, 20 May 1789

I attended at the Hall about half after 10 O'Clock   ~~the~~ the Committee did
not meet me.[36]   Senate met, but there was no business done.   adjourned
that the Committees might go to Work,   I thought I caught cold, yesterday in
the House of Representatives, and set off to come home   Col. Few, overtook
me, and we took a long Walk to View the Gardens of a Dutchman who lives,
beyond the Bowery.[37]   spent, some time with a ~~go~~ degree of satisfaction

[35]Franco Petrus Van Berckel (bap. 1760), minister from the Netherlands, arrived at New
York on 10 May 1789. He served until 1795. (*New York*, p. 86)

[36]This was probably the committee on the appropriation of space in Federal Hall.

[37]The Dutchman was probably the German Baron Poellnitz. See n. 45.
Bowery Lane or Road began at Division Street on the northern edge of the city and
connected with the road to New England. It was approximately the western boundary of the
Bowery, an area of southern Manhattan Island which extended along the East River from
Division Steet on the south to present-day 21st Street on the north. The name originated
with the bouweries, or farms, established by the Dutch on Manhattan Island in the seventeenth century. (*Iconography* 5:1231, 6:67–68)

viewing his harmless, and silent litle beauties of the Garden.   On the road Mr. Few threw out many generous sentiments on the Subject of the temporary residence.   the general belief is however, that he is friendly to this place.   returned & felt nothing the better for my walk,   staid at home the residue of the day,   Mr. Clymer and Fitzsimons called to see Us.   nothing remarkable.

Thursday, 21 May 1789

Went about half after nine to Mr. Morris's lodgings,   he was out, but expected in.   staid untill 10, then went to the Hall. and staid untill the Senate met.   ~~The~~ Our President is progressive in reformation   he used to Keep Us, untill half after Eleven, or a quarter at least   he was here this day 8 or 10 Minutes before Eleven. and Strange to tell, he was without a Sword—   The impost Bill being the order of the day was taken up. and postponed untill Monday.   a Resolution was handed to the Chair by Elsworth.   It was for the Senate forming something like a Committee of the Whole.   however it seemed to amount to nothing more than a Suspension of our Rules. for the time mentioned or alluded to in it.   adjourned and I returned home to write letters—   An Idea is gone abroad, That the Merchantile Interest has been exerted to delay this Bill.   the Merchants have undoubtedly regulated the Prices of their goods agreeable to the proposed duties. so that the consumers of dutied Articles really now pay the Whole of the impost.   and Whatever the proposed duties exceed the State duties now paid, is clear gain to the Merchant,   some of them indeed dispute the payment of the State impost.   The Interim Collection Bill, is rejected in the lower House, and the reason given, is the mos⟨t⟩ loose I ever heard assigned Viz. It was said a better one was framing.   surely this was no parliamentary reason.   had any new bill been offered to the House, had any been in the hands of a Committee. the reason would have justifyed the Measure, But because it is said Mr. Williams of Baltimore[38] is making One, of his own Motion, and without any order of the House, is not so proper.   perhaps it may turn out best.

---

[38]Otho Holland Williams (1749–94), naval officer for the port of Baltimore since 1783, was the son-in-law of its representative, William Smith. Born to a Welsh family in Prince George's County, Maryland, Williams moved with them to Frederick County, where he lived until about 1767 when he settled in Baltimore. He was a government clerk before the War for Independence, in which he achieved the rank of brigadier general in the Continental army. Active in state politics, he wrote newspaper articles in support of ratification of the Constitution. In 1787 he platted Williamsport on family land at the junction of the Potomac River and Conococheague Creek, but his hopes that the site would be selected as the capital of the United States came to naught. In August 1789 the Senate confirmed his appointment as collector of the port of Baltimore. Williams spent most of May 1789 in New York and may have contributed to the drafting of the Collection Bill [HR-6]. See also *SEJ*, p. 499. (*DGW* 4:84n; *DHROC* 15:13n)

Friday, 22 May 1789

attended at the Hall at 10 O'Clock and waited a whole hour for the Committee for arranging the rooms.   they did not meet.   the Senate met.   soon after the Clerk of the lower House attended with the Bill for taking the Oaths, which was presented to the Chair.   the President rose, and addressed the House.   I am placed have since the other day, when the Matter of my signing was talked of, in the Senate, examined the Constitution,   I am placed here by the People, to part with the Stile given to me is a dereliction of of my right, it is being false to my Trust.   Vice President is my Title and I will It is a point I will insist upon.   he said several other things then paused and looked over the Bill—   he then addressed the Senate again. and with great positiveness told them that he would sign it as Vice President of the United States and president of the Senate.   he asked Mr. Lee if it had been compared, and handed it to Mr. Lee,   I cannot say Whether he signed it before he spoke to Mr. Lee or after, but it was not read, nor was any question Whatever put upon it, Whether it should be read? Whether it should be signed? or any other Motion whatever.   Mr. Elsworth got up and declared himself satisfyed with that way of signing.   Mr. Strong got up and thought it should be Vice President Alone.   this is certainly a most egregious insult to any deliberative body. but as Patterson told me a day or Two after the *gracious affair*, that if I had not opposed that measure somebody else would.[39] I determined to see who would oppose this, and all was Silence.

adjourned till Monday 11 O'Clock.   called on Mr. Morris this afternoon told him, that Murmurs were abroad would were abroad against the Conduct of the Congress.   That altho' the duty was not collected for the Use of the public. Yet as the rates were in the Possession of every body, the Merchants had raised their goods in proportion, that the public was now in the act of paying. & the Merchants Gainers.   for the public got Treas Treasury got nothing. that commercial influence was blamed for the delay.   he replyd I suppose they blame me   I answered these things were said before he came to town.   I desired him to appoint some time, when I would wait on him, in Order to examine the impost bill that we might be prepared with any amendments which we would offer.   he appointed Sunday at 9 A.M.   I asked his Opinion as to the hight of the duties.   generally, he said he wished, to see the bill for Collection, and to know under What penalties Smugling would be prohibited, that from them he could form an Opinion Whether they were too high or not.   I reply'd that they would not be too high with regard to the amount of the revenue raised.   and I would have the penalties, and prohibitions against

---

[39]WM referred to the Senate debate on 1 May during which he succeeded in erasing from the minutes the phrase "His most gracious Speech," which Adams had used to describe Washington's inaugural address of 30 April.

smugling as severe as possible— and if under these Circumstances the de-
pravity and Villany of People would render the ~~Revenue~~ Impost unproductive. it would at least demonstrate the necessity of adopting some other mode
of supplying the treasury.

Saturday, 23 May 1789

this a fine day and all the World are ~~runing~~ a gadding. A Mr. Dennis
called this Morning he says the Ship Cheasapeake from Bengal, is unloading
at Amboy[40]— the duties on this Ship would by his acct. have been about
£80,000. some say 10'— I am much distressed with the delays of
Congress. the reputation of our Administration will be ruined— the Merchants have actually added the amount of the duties to the price of goods in
this point of View the impost is levyed but not a farthing goes into the
Trea⟨s⟩ury of the United States, and all the difference between the State
duties levyed and the proposed duties is clear gain to the Merchants. in the
Jerseys it is all clear gain for they have no duties, and Vessels are daily crouding
them to Store their goods untill the impost takes place— Delany's Estimate
of the impost for Pennsyla. for a Year was 863,623 dols. = 323,858:12:6 half
of this taken for the Spring importation is 161,929:6:6 as Pennsylvania is
supposed 1/8 of the Union if we were all ~~conse~~ adopting States, the loss would
be 1,295,434:10:0 and the devil of it is, that this Sum will actually be paid by
the Consumers— I could not bear my own thoughts on this Subject any
longer, I considered it as my duty to go and rouse our Pennsylvania Members— I called on the Speaker and his Brother first they admitted all I
said, from there I went to Mr. Scott, he said it was undeniable. I endeavoured to rouse all of them from here I went to the lodgings of Fitzsimons &
Clymer found Mr. Fitzsimons. delivered my mind with great freedom &
he heard me with more patience, than ever I remember. he said he wished he
had Stuck to this business from the begining. That he had brought the
draught of a bill which was committed to Gerry⟨,⟩ Lawrence and himself,
he left it with Lawrence, being an Official Man, to correct. That Lawrance
kept it 3 weeks and did nothing. that then Gerry took it and Kept it 2 Weeks

---

[40]Patrick Dennis, merchant, New York harbor pilot and ship captain, performed a variety
of marine services for New York and the Continental army during the War for Independence.
In 1790 he declared bankruptcy, and Washington appointed him to command the port's
federal revenue cutter. (Richard Murphy, *History of the Society of the Friendly Sons of Saint
Patrick* [New York, 1962], pp. 25, 49, 78; *PAH* 7:97; *NYDG*, 26 Feb. 1790)

The *Chesapeake*, owned and mastered by John O'Donnell of Baltimore, arrived from the
Ganges River in Bengal after a voyage of two and a half years. (E. Thornton Cook, comp.,
John O'Donnell of Baltimore [London, 1934], pp. 43-46; *PP*, 20 May 1789)

Perth Amboy, between the Raritan River and Arthur Kull Sound in New Jersey, was an
excellent harbor with easy access from Sandy Hook.

and put it into the hands of Mr. Williams of Baltimore Who had kept it, untill within these 4 days— That it came from Williams a most voluminous thing of more than 40 pages that he would now stick to it untill it was finished.
there could not have been selected within the Walls of the House two such improper Characters as Gerry & Lawrence, Gerry highly Antifederal married and intimately connected with the Trade of this place.[41] Lawrence of New York a mere tool for British Agents & factors. nothing else could have been expected. the foregoing calculation is certainly founded on Delany's estimate is certainly much too high. but if we suppose the Port of Philada. to receive one fifth only of the importations, and throw off one half for Errors and accidents. Yet still the loss sustained will be near a Million and an half of Dollars. and the greater part of this Sum actually remains, as profit to the Merchant. Mr. Fitzsimons has promised that the bill shall be reported on Monday. the Speaker has promised to go among the Members and rouse them all in his power for my part. think what they will of me. I will not be silent.

Sunday, 24 May 1789

being Sunday. I attended Mr. Morris agreeable to appointment. we did not perfectly agree about the preamble of the Bill,[42] but there was no difference of Consequence it was verbal only. we came to the discrimination between Nations in Treaty and those not. here we differed, he was totally against it. he used Arguments I made some reply. but each retained his opinion, more Mr. Morris said the Teas would bear More. he said double and I agreed to it. I alledged that all $7^1/_2$ ad Valorem Articles should be raised at least to 10 ℔ ct. Mr. Morris seemed, of the same way of thinking. Mr. Morris however suddenly exclaimed, let Us go to Fitzsimons, he knows all about it, he has been thinking on the Subject, I want to go and take a Strool Strole somewhere; I thought, by this he did not like close thinking I have been of this Opinion before now. He has however a Strong and vigorous Mind, When it does act. to Fitzsimons we went, and found him very busy at the bill. Mr. Carrol, of the Representatives came in, we got on the discrimination. we were all of a different Opinion from Mr. Morris, we asked Mr. Fitzsimons the reason of so many Articles being at $7^1/_2$ Which we thought should be 10 along with glass and China; he said there really was no reason for it, but the House would not agree to it. Mr. Morris proposed a Jaunt to the Narrows but no boat could be got, we then walked up the North river to one

---

[41] In 1786 Gerry married Ann Thompson, daughter of the New York City merchant James Thompson. (George Billias, *Elbridge Gerry* [New York, 1976], p. 147)
[42] Impost Act [HR-2].

Branon's who has the Green House and Gardens,[43] here we dined. Mr.
Morris often touched me on the Subject of my dislike of the Vice President
we got on the Subject of their Salaries, Mr. Morris mentioned 20,000 Doll.
for the President, and 8,000 for the Vice President. I opposed both but it was
in the funny way all of it. at one time however when Mr. Morris was absent I
spoke seriously to Fitzsimons, saying, the old Proverb must be reversed, no
Penny no Paternoster. here it must be no Service no Salary. Mr. Morris had
alledged that the Vice President must see the foreign Ministers &ca. as the
President could not. and the Salary was to enable him to do so. And What
Obligation is he under to do so? some of the Presidents of Pennsylvania have
had 1,250 ℔ an. to enable them to see Strangers, some have not spent £10 ℔
an. but in that ~~Subject~~ way. they had hinted so often at my dislike of the Vice
President that after dinner I gave them one of his Speeches in Senate. Was
this prudent? No, but I never was a prudent Man. Strolled after dinner,
about the House taken by the Vice President[44] sat in the Shade. crossed
thro' the Fields, and came at length to Baron Polnitz's.[45] this Man we found
sensible and well informed. he has studied agriculture and has more Machines in that way than I have seen before. I have heard him spoke rather
disrespectfully of. this however I suppose flowed, from the force of our old
habits derived from the English who seldom ever speak well of a foreigner I
will see him again. it is said he has moved in the higher Stations of life and
seen much, but I intend to hear from him, and perhaps will hear more of him
in the mean while.

Monday, 25 May 1789

Went early this morning to the Hall wrote letters to my family, the
Senate met. The impost bill was taken up. and according to Elsworth's
resolution, we were to act as if in a Committee of the Whole. But the

[43]The Narrows is the passage from the Atlantic Ocean between Long and Staten islands,
nine miles south of Manhattan.
   Charles F. Brannon's tea garden was located off Greenwich Road at the intersection of
present-day Spring and Hudson streets. Its greenhouse contained citrus trees, geraniums,
aloes, and other plants. (*Iconography* 5:1319; Frank Monaghan and Marvin Lowenthal, *This
Was New York, The Nation's Capital in 1789* [New York, 1943], p. 44)
   [44]John Adams's New York residence, Richmond Hill mansion, built in 1767, was situated
on the road to Greenwich Village, at the present Varick and Charlton streets. Its location on a
hill near the Hudson River provided a view not only of New York City but also of New Jersey
and Long Island. (*New York*, pp. 51, 217; Stewart Mitchell, *New Letters of Abigail Adams*
[Boston, 1947], pp. 7, 17)
   [45]Baron Frederick Carl Poellnitz (1734–1801) resided on the 22.5-acre Minto Estate, located north of the city in the vicinity of present 9th Street and Broad Way. He was a landed
German nobleman who had married into the British aristocracy before settling in 1784 in
New York, where he conducted agricultural experiments and promoted a newly invented
threshing machine. (*DGW* 6:12n–13n; *New York Genealogical and Biographical Record*
80:130–41)

President kept the Chair.   and I thought it M Made Mr. Elsworth look foolish.   a Message was anounced from the President by General Knox.[46]   according to the Resolution we were in Committee, but the President kept the
Chair and the General advanced and laid the Papers being very bulky, on the
Table.   Our President had given Us a speech before the Minutes were read on
the Subject of receiving a Message from the President,   his supreme delight
seems to be in etiquette.   But I really believe he had a farther View in it.   the
Entry on the Minutes for Friday did not appear to me to correspond with the
facts,   there was something that imported the Bill being reported by a the
Committee that compared it, and the minute read that the *Vice President*
signed it.   I determined I would not imp imbroil myself with him, if possible.   and nobody made any Observation   {by making his Observation at
this time he directed the attention of the Senate from the Minutes.}   We sat
on the Impost bill and debated long on the Stile of the enacting clause   it was
an old Field.   and the same arguments were used which had formerly been
advanced.   but the Stile of the Law which had already passed was adopted.
now came the first duty of 12 Cents on Spirits of Jamaca proof.   we debated
untill a quarter past 3 and it was reduced to 8—   adjourned—   When I came
home in the Evening, I told Mr. Wynkoop the business of the day,   he said
thereat things of this kind made him think whether our single Government in
Pennsylvania was not best.[47]   certain it is that a Government, with so many
Branches affords a larger field for caballing.   first in the lower house.   and
the Moment a party finds, a Measure lost or likely to be lost. all engines are set
to Work in the Upper House.   if they are likely to fail here, the last attempt is
made with the President.   and as most pains are always taken by bad Men and
to Support bad Measures, the calculation seems in favour of the exertions and
endeavours that are used, more than in the Justness of the Measure.   on the
other hand a fuller field is opened for investigation.   but unfortunately intrigue and cabal takes place of fair inquiry.   here an Observation forces itself
on me. That in general the farther any Measure is carried from the People the
less their Interests are attended to.   I fear that our impost bill will be lost rendered in a great measure unproductive.   this Business is the Work of the New
England Men.   they want the Article of Molasses quite struck out or at least

---

[46]Henry Knox (1750–1806), secretary of war, 1785–94, was a Bostonian who began his
career as a bookseller. He served in the Continental army throughout the War for Independence, rising to the rank of major general. He and his wife, Lucy Flucker Knox, were
prominent figures in the social life of the federal government at New York and Philadelphia.
See also *SEJ*, p. 507.
    Washington's message brought the Senate its first executive business; the related docu-
ments are printed in the *SEJ*, pp. 137–63. During the FFC the *SLJ* does not indicate the points
at which the Senate took up executive business: confirmation of presidential appointments
and relations with other nations including Indian tribes. In his diary, WM does not distinguish between executive and legislative business.
    [47]For a description of the government of Pennsylvania under the state Constitution of
1776, see the Introduction.

greatly reduced, therefore they will [*lined out*] Strike at every thing   or to place it in a different point of view, almost every part of it will be proscribed. either by one or other of those who chuse to take opponents, for every conspirator must be indulged in the Sacrifice of his particular enemy.

I called on Mr. Fitzsimons, some time ago to express my fears on this very head and I wished him to ~~re~~ consent to a reduction of the Molasses duty to 4 Cents. to avoid a thing of this kind.   but I was not attended to—   Indeed I thought he had the best right to know.   I felt too much confidence about that time in the return of Mr. Morris.

Tuesday, 26 May 1789

attended the Hall early   was the first.   Mr. Morris came next   the President next.   I made an Apology to the President for the Absence of our Chaplain Mr. Linn.[48]   There had been some conversation Yesterday in the Senate about the Stile of the bishop[49]   it had been entered on the minutes *right reverend.*   the President revived this discourse and got at me about Titles   I really never had opened my mouth on the affair of [*lined out*] Yesterday.   he however addressed all he said concluding You are against Titles.   But there are no People in the World so much in favour of Titles as the People of America and the Government never will be properly administered, untill they are adopted in the fullest Manner.   We think differently indeed on the same Subject.   I am convinced that were we to adopt them in fashion of Europe we would ruin all.   You have told Us Sir that they are idle in a philosophic point of View.   Governments have long been at odds with common Sense.   I hope the Conduct of America will reconcile them,   instead of adding respect to Government I consider that they would bring the personages who assumed them into contempt and Ridicule.

Senate met   after some Motions as to the Business which should be taken up, and the appointment of a Committee of Conferrence, on the mode of receiving communications from the President the impost was taken up. there was a discrimination of five Cents in favour of Nations having commercial Treaties with Us, ⅌ Gall. on ℞ Jamaica Spirits.   Then rose against ~~this~~ all discrimination, Mr. Lee⟨,⟩ Mr. Dalton⟨,⟩ Mr. Izard, Mr. Morris⟨,⟩ Mr.

[48]William Linn (1752–1808), one of two congressional chaplains, held the position in 1789 and 1790. He graduated from the College of New Jersey in 1772 and was ordained a Presbyterian minister in 1776. Linn had served pastorates in Cumberland County, Pennsylvania, and Elizabethtown, New Jersey, and as president of Washington Academy in Somerset County, Maryland, before the end of 1786, when he became one of the ministers of the Collegiate Reformed Protestant Dutch Church, New York City's largest congregation. Born near the Maclay family homestead in Lurgan Township, Linn was a longtime friend of WM's. (*New York*, p. 125; *Princetonians, 1769–1775*, pp. 231–35)

[49]Samuel Provoost.

Wingate⟨,⟩ Mr. Strong.   At first they rather gave opinions than any Arguments.   I declared for the discrimination, that if Commercial Treaties were of
any Use at all, Nations in Treaty should stand on better Terms than those Who
had kept at a Sulky distance.   But if we now treated all alike, we need never
hereafter propose a Commercial Treaty.   I asked if we were not called on by
Gratitude to treat with discrimination, those Nations who had given Us the
helping hand in the time of distress—   Mr. Carrol rose on the same side with
me,   I was however answered from all sides.   All commercial Treaties, were
condemned.   it was echoed from all parts of the House that nothing but
interest governed all Nations.   my very Words were repeated, and contradicted in the most pointed Terms   I never had delivered any thing in the
speaking way on which I was so hard run   Strong, who is but a poor Speaker
shewed ill nature. said nothing like reason or argument had been offered.   It
was insisted that this discrimination was showing an inimical disposition to
great Britain, it was declaring commercial War with ~~them~~ her.   I had to reply
as well as I could.   I alledged that these Arguments went against the Whole
System of Administration under the old Congress. and in some Measure
against the engagements entered in to by that body, altho these engagements
were sanctifyed by the Constitution.   That Great Britain had nothing to do in
this business, that Nations in Treaty were on Terms of Friendship.   that
Strangers had no right to be offended at acts of kindness between friends.
she might be a friend if she pleased, and enjoy these favours.   on the contrary
I thought our Friends were the people who had a right to be offended if no
discrimination took place.   It had been asserted That interest solely governed
Nations,   I was sorry it was so much the Case.   but I hoped we would not in
every point be governed by that Principle.   The Conduct of France to Us in
our distress, I thought was founded in part on more generous principles.   had
the principles of interest solely governed, she would have taken advantage of
our distress, when we were in abject circumstances, and would have imposed
hard Terms on Us.   instead of Treating on the Terms of Mutual reciprocity—   she likewise remitted large Sums of Money,   was this from the principal of Interest only?   What had been the Conduct of the Two nations since
the peace?   Civility on the part of the French, and a very different treatment
by the British, our News papers teemed with these Accounts—   (Elsworth
had said "it has been asked if we are not called on by gratitude &ca."   "I
answer No"—)   The answer No has been, given to the Calls of gratitude on
this Business, But ~~I declared~~ the great Voice of the People at large would give a
very different answer.   so far as my sphere of knowledge extended, I had a
right to say so, but the Sense of the people at large expressed by their Representatives in the ~~other~~ Clause before Us holds a different language.   Mr.
Langdon spoke and seemed to be of our Opinion.   I did not hear a no
however on the question but Mr. Carrol's and my own.   All ran smoth now,

till we came to the Molasses— till quarter after 3 did the New England beat this ground even to the baiting of the Hook that catched the fish that went to buy the Molasses. the Motion was to reduce it to ~~five~~ four Cents from 5— I had prepared notes but there was such an eagerness to speak and finding we should carry it, I let them fight it out— the vote for 4 carried— all the Arguments of the other house were repeated over and over.

Wednesday, 27 May 1789

I spent this morning in writing letters to my family, to go by General Butler who sets off this day and will pass by Harrisburgh.[50]   Attended Senate, the Minutes were read   I was astonished to hear Strong immediately get up & begin a long Harrangue on the Subject of Molasses— One looked at another.   Mr. Carrol had taken his Seat next to me   several ~~several~~ of the Gentlemen murmured.   at last Mr. Carrol rose and asked pardon for interrupting any Gentleman but said, that Matter had been determined Yesterday.   Mr. President said the question had been taken on four Cents being put instead of 5 but no question had been taken on the paragraph, after it was amended.   the Whole Sentence was "on Molasses ℔ gallon 4 Cents"— that a second question should be put on it, was idle.   but it was plain That this matter had been agreed on between the President and the New England Men.   and in all probability they have got some People who voted for 4 Yesterday to promise to Vote for less today.   Dalton however got up and made a long speech that some of the Gentlemen were absent & particularly the Gentleman who moved for the 4 Cents. and desired it might be put off untill tomorrow.   I must declare this the most uncandid piece of proceeding that I have seen in the Senate.   now came wine of madeira   all the Arguments of Yesterday were had over again, and it was voted at 18 Cents— when we came to loaf Sugar it was postponed.   When we came to Cables. the New England Men moved to postpone every thing of that kind Mr. Langdon being absent, untill we came to Steel.   I then moved ~~that~~ an adjournment as it was near the time. for I wished Mr. Morris to be here. as I expect a pointed opposition on that business—and as he has all the information on the most of Subjects.   I have been as attentive as possible to get information as far as my Sphere of

---

[50]Located at the site of Harris's Ferry, on the east bank of the Susquehanna River, 107 miles west of Philadelphia, Harrisburg was the creation of WM's father-in-law, John Harris, Jr. WM surveyed the town in 1785, and within four years one-half its lots were developed, and it boasted almost 900 residents and a newspaper. In 1788 it had been chosen by Antifederalists as the site of the first statewide political convention in American history which met to discuss amendments to the United States Constitution and candidates for the FFC. WM had considerable economic interest in the town, including several lots, an island in the river, an adjacent 200-acre farm that he developed into Maclaysburg, and a ferry. He advocated Harrisburg as an ideal location for either the state or federal seat of government. (*NCHSP* 2:67-71; *Counter Revolution*, p. 115)

influence extended.   But the private communications of the Citizens of Philada. have generally been by letter to Mr. Morris⟨,⟩ Mr. Fitzsimons or Mr.
Clymer.   I regret, that they furnish me with none of this information,   I
must however serve my Country as well as I can.   The Collection bill is at last
reported,[51]   I~cannot~ I cannot think but that there has been studied delay in
this Business   the Bill itself is said to be a Volume.   it is ordered to be
printed.

Thursday, 28 May 1789

having found the Opposition to run hard Yesterday against the impost, I
determined, to ~run~ go this Morning among all my Pennsylvania Friends and
call on them, for any information, which they could give me in the way of their
private letters or otherwise,   I got an Account of all the Sugar Houses in
Philada. from the Speaker.   called on Mr. Morris   told him the War of Molasses was to be waged again.   called on Mr. Clymer and Fitzsimons.   got
from Mr. Fitzsimons a list of the Pennsylvania protecting duties.   then went
to the Hall.   I was here near an hour before any Person came   Langdon,
Carrol, and the President came.   The discourse was general on the Subject of
Government,   if our New government does well (said our President) I shall be
more surprized than ever I was in my life.   Mr. Carrol said he hoped well of it,
it would be sufficiently powerful.   if it is said he, I know not from Whence, it
is to arise   It cannot have energy, it has neither rewards nor punishments,
Mr. Carrol reply'd the People of America were enlightened, information and
Knowlege would be the Support of it.   Mr. Adams reply'd information and
Knowlege were not the Sources of Obedience, That Ignorance was a much
better source.   somebody reply'd, that it had formerly been considered as the
Mother of devotion—but the doctrine of late was considered as rather
Stale—   I began now to think of what Mr. Morris had told me.   That it was
necessary to make Mr. Adams Vice President. to keep him quiet.   he is
antifederal, but one of a very different turn from the general Cast,   a mark
may be missed as well above as below, and he is an high flyer.   Senate met.
Cables Cordage &ca. came up.   they stood at .75.   Mr. Langdon spoke
warmly against this   Mr. Morris moved a reduction to .50.   I urged him so
much that he said .60.   this was seconded.   I had to show some pointed
reason why I urged .60.   indeed it was much against my will that any reduction took place.   the protecting duties of Pennsylvania, were 4/2 about 56
Cents.   to place the Manufacturers of Pennsylvania who had a claim on the
faith of ~Pennsylvania~ the State. on worse ground than they stood before,
would be injurious, in a degree to their Private property, and break the engagement the State had made with them.   this Argument went to all the protect-

---

[51]Fitzsimons reported the Collection Bill [HR-6] to the House on 27 May.

ing duties of Pennsylvania— Gentlemen had complained, that they had no hemp in the eastern States. this was the Case of Pennsylvania, at the Close of the War the protecting duties on Cordage called for the manufacturing of it. the manufacture called for the hemp. it was in fact a bounty on the raising of that Article. the effect of the protecting duty in Pennsylvania, was at first felt by the importers it was for a time an unproductive Expence. it is thus almost with every distant prospect he that plants an Orchard cannot immediately eat the fruit of it. But the fruit had already ripened in Pennsylvania—and so it would in other places— I was up 4 times in all. we Carried it however at .60. we passed on with little interruption untill we got to twine Mr. Lee kept Us an hour and a quarter on this Business, because the Virginians, had hitherto imported their nets from Britain. Once for all however I may remark of him that he has given opposition to every Article. especially the protecting duties he declares openly against the Principle of them. Grayson declares against all impost, as the most unjust and oppressive mode of taxation. It was in Vain Lee was told he could be supplied with all the Nets Virginia wanted from any part of New England. that what could be supplied from any one part of the union, should be protected by duties on the Importations of the same Articles from foreign parts. it was lowered to 150 Cents. And now for the Article of Molasses. Lee who is a perfect Ishmael, declared the second question totally out of Order. It is true parliamentary precedent might be alledged in favour of such second question but in the present case it was evidently a trick. and I guessed some parties had changed sides. from the discourse it appeared to me that Few of Georgia had changed. the President made an harrangue on the Subject of Order. the facts were all agreed to, Viz. That it was agreed to to strike out five Cents— That the first motion seconded was to insert 2—Cents, the 2d Motion seconded was for 3 Cents. the 3d Motion seconded was for 4 Cents. that a very long & tedious discussion took place with all the three Motions before the Chair. That an adjournment had been called for and negatived, expressly on the avowed reason that the ~~Senate~~ Committee would first get rid of the Article. That the President mentioned from the Chair that he would put the question on four first, that being the highest Sum. the question was put and carried. and the Senate afterwards adjourned— The President made a Speech, which really was to me unintelligible, he seemed willing to perswade the Members, That the above was a very unfair mode of doing business & that they had not an opportunity of declaring their sentiments freely in the above way. he concluded however, *that after the four had been carried it was in Order for to move for any lower Sum.* Somebody whispered that he ought to get his Wig dressed— Mr. Morris rose and declared it was with reluctance that he differed with the Chair on a question of Order. as was begining to argue on the Subject. But the New England Men seeing their

darling President likely to be involved in embarrassment for the ungarded
Steps he had taken in their favour, with one consent declared they were
satisfyed to pass the Article at present, and take it up in the Senate.[52]   Now
came the postponed Article of Loaf Sugar.   Lee laboured with with Spite and
acrimony, in this business.   he said the loaf Sugar of America was bad   it was
lime and other vile composition,   he had broke a Spoon in trying to dissolve
and seperate it.   and so I must go on breaking my spoons, and three Millions
of People must be taxed to support half a Dozen People in Philada.   he
pronounced this Sentence especially the part about the spoon, with so tremu-
lous an accent, and so forlorn an aspect, as would have excited even Stoics on to
laughter.   there was a laugh, but no retort on him.   I supported the Motion
by Showing that the Sugar baking business was of importance. as it gave
employment to many other artificers the Mason Brick Maker Layer Carpenter
and all the Artificers employ'd in building, for they had to build largely.   the
Coppersmith Potter and Cooper was in much employ with them.   the Business was in a declining State and some Sugar Houses discontinued.   that in
Pennsylvania the old protecting duty was 9/10∂. ℔ Cwt. and the raw Sugar was
1/ ℔ Cwt.   That now there was no protecting duty Whatever.   for one Cent
on the lb. of brown was in proportion to 3 on the loaf.   that the Sugar baker of
Pennsylvania was therefore undeniably on a Worse footing than formerly at
least by the Whole amount of the Pennsylvania protecting duty, and as he paid
6/6 ℔ Cwt. more on the importation of raw Material, the British too aimed at a
Monopoly of this business and gave a bounty of 26/ Sterling on Exportation.
so that it became Us to counteract them or loose the Manufacture.   Mr. Morris
and Mr. Dalton. satisfyd some Gentlemen as to the Manner of importing
Sugars.   I thought this as plain a Subject as could come before the House. and
Yet we divided. and the president gave Us the Casting Vote.   he desired leave
to give Us the reasons of his Vote.   this seemed to imply a degree of Vanity, as
if among Us all we had not placed the Matter in a right point of View   for my
part I was *satisfyd* with his Vote.   It was now near 4 OClock.   adjourned.

Friday, 29 May 1789

The Senate met   the Article of Steel was passed over with little difficulty,
and here I confess, I expected a considerable Opposition—   Nails and Spikes
came next   here an Opposition from the Carolina and Georgia Members to an
increase of the duty.   Now came Salt.   Up rose Lee of the Antient Dominion.   he gave Us an Acct. of the great Revenue derived from Salt in France
England and all the World.   Condemned the General System of the Bill
said this was almost the only Article in it that would reach the interior parts of

[52]The Senate at this time was acting as a committee of the whole under the rule proposed
by Ellsworth and adopted on 21 May.

the State.   that the interior parts of the Country with their New lands, could much better afford to pay high taxes than the settlers of the exhausted lands. that the carriage of it was nothing for they had all teams and fine Horses.   he concluded a lengthy harrangue with a Motion for 12 Cents which in his opinion was vastly too low.   he was seconded by Mr. Carrol of Maryland.   Elsworth rose for an Augmentation but said if 12 was lost he would move for 9.   Lee, Carrol, Elsworth and Morris Speakers in favour of the Augmentation.   any Reduction seemed out of the question with every body. against the Augmentation.   Speakers Izard⟨,⟩ Few and Self.   I thought my Friends on our side of the question were rather Warm. and used some Arguments that did not apply well.   They perhaps with equal Justice thought the same of me.   I advocated the New Settlers, endeavoured to show that their Superior Crops were Justly due to superior labour   that every Acre of new land cost from 5 to 10 dollars ⅌ Ann. clearing and fencing,   that the Expences of the New buildings were immense.   that Men spent an Active life often on a farm, and died with the farm in debt to them.   That New Settlers laboured for Posterity for the public.   that they were the real Benefactors to the Community and deserved exemption if any.   It had been said. it was their Choice.   no.   M̶ Necessity dire necessity compelled many.   But were they exempted—from the Effects of the other part of the Bill.   No.   They could raise no Sheep   of Course had no Wooll,   Coarse duffelds, Blankets Swanskins, in a Word all their Wollens, were imported.   and they would of Course pay the impost on these Articles from *Necessity* which was not the Case in general with other Citizens who might either manufacture or buy, as they had the Materials. But over and above this luxuries would find their way among them,   all People d̶o̶w̶n̶ down to the Savage were fond of finery, the rudest the most so and I was convinced that the poor. the amount of their several Stocks taken into Consideration, spent more in superfluities than the rich.   That all these Arguments apart. the Article of Salt, was the most necessary of any in the bill, and in proportion to the Original Cost was the highest, taxed.   That it was a new and an untried Source of Revenue in Many of the States, that it ought therefore to be touched with a gentle hand, if at all.   That I knew not Whether the discontents would follow that had been predicted, and hoped they would not.   But wished we could g̶i̶v̶e̶ avoid giving Occasion for any. That for these reasons I should at present be for leaving it w⟨h⟩ere the wisdom of the other house had placed it.

the question was put.   the House divided.   and the President gave it in our favour.   In the Course of this debate it came out that Mr. Fitzsimons had furnished Mr. Carrol with all his remarks and the documents, which he had collected on the Subject of Revenue, as well respecting Pennsylvania, as the Union in General.   I do think that as an Individual, I have taken as much pains to collect information as any of them.   But I am much less known.

and of Course information by letter, from individuals has generally fallen to the Share of Mr. Fitzsimons⟨,⟩ Mr. Morris and Mr. Clymer. The information from the Collectors Office I never could get. tho' Mr. Fitzsimons told me in Philada. that Delany had furnished him (*but reluctantly*) with it. Mr. Morris has a State of the Custom House of Philada. or some such paper he used it this day as he sat beside me. I asked him to let me see the Article of Salt in it. he said it was not there. What shall I think of Lee, this Ishmael of the House. he laboured the Article of Subject of titles with a diligence worthy of a better cause. he seemed disposed to destroy the Whole effect of the impost bill. on every other Article the Tax on Salt he knows must be odious—and this he is for doubling at the first Word. he is a great advocate for an Excise. if I really wished to destroy the New Constitution. or to injure it to the utmost of my power. I would follow exactly the line of Conduct which he has pursued. Far be it however from me to say this of him. People employ the same Means for very different Ends. and such is the Variety of human Opinion, that the same Object is often aimed at by directly contrary Measures directly con opposite— adjourned to Monday.

Saturday, 30 May 1789

the Speaker called. he dined Yesterday, with the President. a number of the Senators were present. the Pennsylvanians had agreed to call on Mrs. Morris[53] between 10 & 11— Mr. Morris had Yesterday mentioned that time as a convenient time to her. The Gentlemen of Congress have it seems, called on Mrs. Washington[54] & all the Congressional ladies. Speaker⟨,⟩ Wh Wynkoop and self, called on Mrs. Morris half after 10, not at home left our Cards. being in the lady Way We called to See Mrs. Langdon and Mrs. Dalton.[55] found Mr. Langdon—the Ladies abroad. this finished the visit-

[53]Mary White (1749–1827), daughter of Esther Hewlings Newman and Thomas White, a wealthy Maryland landowner who resided in Philadelphia, and sister of William White, first bishop of the American Episcopal Church, married Robert Morris in 1769. She raised seven children and maintained an interest in her husband's political activities. She spent a month in New York in 1789. (*Account of the Meeting of the Descendants of Colonel Thomas White* . . . [Philadelphia, 1879], pp. 49–76)

[54]Martha Dandridge Custis (1731–1802) was a wealthy widow when she married George Washington in 1759. She arrived at New York on 27 May, accompanied by her nephew Robert Lewis, her grandchildren, Eleanor Custis and George Washington Parke Custis, and Mrs. Robert Morris, and remained with her husband during all three sessions of the FFC. (*DGW* 1:211n; *New York*, p. 239)

[55]Elizabeth Sherburne (c. 1760–1813), daughter of John Sherburne of Portsmouth, New Hampshire, married John Langdon in 1777. She resided with her husband during most of the first session of the FFC. (Lawrence Mayo, *John Langdon of New Hampshire* [Concord, N.H., 1937], pp. 47, 140–41, 231–32, 285)

Ruth Hooper (1739–post 1817), daughter of the wealthy and prominent "King Robert" Hooper of Marblehead, Massachusetts, married Tristram Dalton in 1758. She thrived in the social life at the seat of government and lived there with her husband during the first and

ing tour. came home felt uncommonly heavy this day. it was warm never wished so much for home. think I must absolutely set off for home about this day Week. the Collection bill is reported—and I will do all I can to inspire my Acqua⟨i⟩ntances with a Spirit of Expedition in both Houses.

Sunday, 31 May 1789

being Sunday was called on this Morning by General St. Clair, he desired my Commands for Philada. Wrote by him to Mr. Peters and Mr. Harris[56] I find going out hurts me. I come home almost from every Walk with a Sore Throat, complaint in my breast or something of that kind. I therefore determined to Stay at home more. read and kept my room.

---

second sessions of the FFC. (Charles Pope and Thomas Hooper, *Hooper Genealogy* [Boston, 1908], p. 109; *Harvard Graduates* 13:569–78)

[56]Richard Peters (1744–1828), speaker of the Pennsylvania Assembly, 1788–90, and first speaker of the state Senate, 1790–91, was a witty, wealthy lawyer who resided his entire life at Belmont, an estate adjacent to Philadelphia. He graduated from the College of Philadelphia in 1761 and served as secretary of the board of war from 1776 to 1781 and as a member of Congress in 1783.

John Harris, Jr., (1726–91) WM's father-in-law, founded and promoted Harrisburg on land he owned there. He was raised on the Susquehanna River, where his father had established Harris's Ferry. In 1785 he persuaded the assembly to create Dauphin County, in which Harrisburg is located, by separating it from Lancaster County. See Appendix C.

June 1789

Monday, 1 June 1789

called this Morning on Mr. Clymer and Fitzsimons, I wished for a general Abstract of the trade of the United States Mr. Fitzsimons had such a paper. for he one day gave Us some Accounts from it he however put Sheffield's Pamphlets[1] into my hand. I had never read Sheffield's Work and therefore received it with pleasure. came to the Hall and was soon delighted with the Reception of letters from my family. who were all well and my dear little Son Billy[2] recovered of the small Pox for which he has been innoculated. the impost Bill was taken up and a number of Articles passed over. When we came to Tea. the impost proceeded on a discrimination in favour of our own Ships. here a Motion was made by Elsworth seconded by Lee. that Went against all discrimination in favour of our own Shipping, or in other Words against any protecting duty for the East India Trade, and indeed the Arguments went against the East India Trade altogether. I got up early in the Business. I laid it down that the Use of Tea was now so general, that any interdiction of it was impossible. That have it the People would if this then was the Case, common prudence told Us to get it from the first hand. That it was evident Teas were now obtained Vastly cheaper, than before our Merchants traded to China. this difference had been stated at 50 ℔ Cent on some Teas. it had been alledged against this Trade, That it destroyed the lives of Seamen. the fact had been represented different to me by those Who had made the Voyage. That it was the practice of all Nations to encourage their own trade, but our permitting the British to supplant Us in this Trade, was suffering them to encourage their Trade at our Expence. it had been said the British would take raw Materials from Us and give Us Teas. that I was well informed the Chinese took many Articles from Us and some that no other

---

[1]John Baker Holroyd, Earl of Sheffield, (1735–1821) published his treatise, *Observations on the Commerce of the American States . . .*, at London in 1783. An edition appeared in Philadelphia the same year. He opposed Adam Smith's free trade theories and argued against a commercial treaty between Britain and the United States. In response, William Bingham published *A Letter from an American . . . to a Member of Parliament* at London and Philadelphia in 1784. By 1789 Holroyd had also published pamphlets on the economy of Ireland and on the Corn Laws. (*PJM* 7:296–97n)

[2]William Maclay (1787–1813) was WM's youngest son. See Appendix C.

People would take. a detail of these Articles I had no doubt would be more fully entered into by some of the Gentlemen Who would follow me. to talk of not protecting a trade sought after by all the World, was a new Phenomenon in a National Council. I therefore was clearly for the Discrimination.

Mr. Morris followed, he went most minutely into the india Trade— shewed that Ginseng was a considerable article in that Trade. Anchors Iron Masts Spars. naval Stores of all kinds he in fact made it clear that a dollar sent to Europe for East india Goods would not import more than half a Dollar sent to the East Indies— the debate was amazing lengthy. both Few ~~of~~ & Elsworth. said the Trade had been represented as flourishing, this it had obtained without any protecting duties why then give any now. I rose to information and mentioned that the protecting duty of Pennsylvania was 2∂ ℔ lb. and the protecting duty of the State of N. York 2∂ and that the ill policy of withdrawing these duties now When the Trade to the East was threatned with combinations against it, was evident— we got the discrimination carried by 9 votes against 8— now for the duty Mr. Morris moved to raise all the Tea duties, this was lost But I wish we had uniformly moved to raise for by this means. we secured it at the rate in the bill. When we came to the real discrimination now a great debate arose. 4 Cents was the difference on Boheas and so nearly in proportion. Mr. Lee moved for eight. avowedly on this Principle. that the 4 Cents were more than the old protecting duty, under which the Trade had flourished. this debate was mostly conducted ~~on~~ on our side by Mr. Morris. I only shewed that tho' the difference Between 6 & 10 Cents was more than the old protecting duties. that the difference between 6 & 8 was less—and that the Gentlemen on their own Principle should have moved for more than 8— but in the critical Situation of the Trade to the east, with combinations in India. Contracts and Ships fitted out at Ostend and the encreasing endeavour of the English to ingross the Whole Trade of the East— the discrimination of 4 was not too much. carried it at 4 OClock 9 to 8— {In the first Argument. I mentioned that if there had been any exclusive Company engrossing the india Trade there might be something, in the Arguments— this however was not the Case nor could it be.}

Tuesday, 2 June 1789

had an excellent opportunity of writing home by the Person who brought my letters Yesterday. this employd me to near 11 O'Clock attended at the Hall after some preliminary Business proceed on the impost bill without much opposition till we came to an enumeration of 15 or 16 Articles which all stood at 7¹/₂ ℔ Ct. the most of these Articles stood in the old protecting duties of Pennsylvania at 12¹/₂ ℔ Ct. I feared much the Spirit of reduction would get into the opposers of the impost & that they would be for lowering everything. From this sole motive I would have moved an Augmentation by way of securing the duty where it was. however here I had better ground. I set out with naming over the greater part of the Articles, on which the protecting duties in Pennsylvania were 12¹/₂ ℔ Ct. and 13 ℔ Ct. in New York. I reasoned from the effect of these duties on the promoting the manufacture but by the present duties the Manufacturers would stand on worse ground by 5 ℔ Ct. than they had done under the States laws. that altho' the united States were not absolutely obliged to make good the engagements of the State to individuals. yet as individuals had imbarked their property in those Manufactures, depending on the State laws I thought it wrong to Violate those laws, without absolute necessity. I was as usual opposed by the Southern People. before I rose I spoke to Mr. Morris to rise and move an Augmentation he said *no, come day we do it.* Mr. Few of Georgia asserted that the Manufacturers of Pennsylvania would be better of⟨f⟩, under the 7¹/₂ than they had been under the 12¹/₂ ℔ Ct. Mr. Morris got up and asserted the same thing. I declare I could not believe either of them. Mr. Morris however stated the Manufacture of Papers to be in the most flourishing condition imaginable in Pennsylvania— said he was afraid to mention the amount of paper that had been imported last Year least he would not be believed—That it had been stated to him at not less than £80,000— he went thro' the business down to the gathering the rags in the Street. after this it was in vain to say anything more—but the effect was that it stood at 7¹/₂— a number of Articles were now raised to 10 ℔ Ct.— but what surprized me was that Mr. Morris was against raising leather & leather Manufactures Canes Walking Stiks Whips ready made cloathing Brushes, Gold Silver and plated Ware Jewellry & paste Work—wrought tin and pewter Ware— he gave no reason for this which is not Usual with him— some of the Articles were notwithstanding placed at 10 without him— his Weight in our Senate is great on commercial Subjects— Mr. Morris moved at my request to have Cotton exempted for some time from duty. this carried by a Kind of Compromise— we proceeded smothly till we came to the draw back on fish &ca. & New England rum[3]— long Conversations on this Subject, but agreed to— we expected a Sharp debate on the drawback on or discount on american Vessells—but it passed Nem. Con. the last Clause Mr. Morris moved hard to expunge—but it was carried & I heard not a *No* but his own— it was now late and adjourned.

---

[3] The Impost Act [HR-2] provided a five-cent-per-gallon drawback or refund of the duty on imported molasses that was subsequently exported in the form of rum. It also provided, in lieu of a drawback on salt, a five-cent-per-barrel allowance on exported pickled fish and salted provisions and a five-cent allowance per one hundred pounds of exported dried fish.

I omitted to mention in its proper place that Mr. Morris moved for 10 ℔ Cent—on a long list of Scythes Sickles Axes Spades Shovels locks hinges &ca. &ca. down to plow Irons, but none of them were carried, & of Course they stood in the Mass of 5 ℔ Cent.

Wednesday, 3 June 1789

In rather a disagreeable situation with my Swelled Knee.   This Vile Rheumatism seems determined to torment me while I stay here.   attended at the Hall at 10   read the News paper.   at 11 the Senate met,   the Clerk from the House of Representatives came with a Message and brought up the Law about the Oaths.   the Impost was taken Up—   the Title and preamble debated and altered a little, and now a lengthy debate took place on a Motion of Mr. Lee. to put off the Consideration of the Bill untill Monday next.   I spoke first against this Motion   I was for proceeding immediately.   The Bill had been very long under Consideration.   The public Expectation had been tired, A Million of dollars had been lost to the Treasury, and what was still worse the People had paid the Money, for the Merchants had raised their goods. and the impost was in actual collection on all the Spring importations   That I wished the New Government might stand fair with the public and give them no just cause of Censure at so early a period—   after very considerable debate Mr. Morris moved that tomorrow be assigned for the ~~consideration th~~ 2d reading in the Senate—   this was agreed to—   now a long debate took place about the News papers[4]—   all the Printers of the City croud their papers into the hands of the Members—   the bulk of the Papers consist of ~~News~~ advertisements—   Useful information ought not be excluded, but this is overdone—   the real Mean appeared to me to be the taking of one or Two papers—by each Member—   But one part of the House strugled for taking all the other for taking none—   no Vote could be carried for either, and of Course the Printers will continue their old practice of sending and expect payment—   Mr. Morris some time ago promised the London Prices current,   his Words were I will give You—one—   they are of no Use in the World to anybody further than all the duties are marked in them And on the Business of the impost, they may be useful—   I thought he was long in performing his promise and this day asked him for it,   he said he had one and would let me see it, But he had it not here—   perhaps I was mistaken in this business.

---

[4]On 2 June the Senate postponed consideration of the resolution, passed by the House on 28 May, regarding which newspapers should be received by members of Congress at public expense. The Senate took no action on 3 June, and the *SLJ* does not mention the debate.

Thursday, 4 June 1789

went to the Hall at 10 but found the Chamber occupied by Two committees[5] sauntered about, till 11 rather disagreeably. Senate ~~were~~ was formed the Minutes were read— they Stood ~~thus~~ Mr. Langdon administered the Oath to the *Vice President*[6]— the *Vice President* administered &ca. the Law is the Oath. &ca. shall be administered *by any* One Member of the Senate *To the President of the Senate* and by him to all the Members, and again—*The President of the Senate for the time being.* The Minutes are totally under the direction of our President or rather Otis is his Creature— I told Patterson that I would not get up let them be as they would but now a discourse was raised again whether the Members should be stiled Honorable on the Minutes. The President declared from the Chair that it was a most serious affair and a Vote of the House should be taken on it. he gave Us a touch again on the Subject, was against using the Word Unless. Right was added to it. he said a good deal to this purpose. Lee was up in a moment for it. The President made 2d Speech he said it was of great importance, if we took the Title Honorable it was a colonial appellation and we should disgrace Ourselves for ever by it, that it was apply'd to the Justices of every Court— Up now rose Grayson of Virginia and gave Us Volley after Volley against all kinds of Titles Whatever— louder and louder did he inveigh against them, Lee looked like Madness. Carrol and myself exchanged looks and laughs of Congratulation Even the President himself seemed Struck in an heap. Izard, would have said *rotundity*. Grayson mentioned the Doge of Venice in his harrange as he was mustering all the great names in the World— pray do you know his Title said the President from the Chair— No says Grayson smartly I am not ~~so~~ very well acquainted with him— We now took up the Impost Bill and proceeded smothly till we came to the Article of Molasses— it was the Wish of a Majority of the Senate to have the question without any debate but now Mr. Dalton rose—and we were obliged to hear every thing over again which had been formerly advanced. it was long and tedious some observations were just & pertinent. but many quite foreign to the purpose. Dr. Johnson rose on the same side, Dalton was for lowering to three Cents. but Doctor Johnson said, he had been convinced that it ought to be but Two—~~the drift~~ or rather none at all. the drift of the Doctor⟨'s⟩ Arguments ~~were~~ was—Molasses imported, is either distilled, and then as a raw Material it ought not to be taxed, or it is consumed by the poor as food and so ought not to be taxed, so it ought not to be taxed at all— up rose Strong and facing himself to the right where—Mr. Morris &

---

[5]The two committees were apparently those considering the mode of communicating the acts of Congress to the states and the Punishment of Crimes Bill [S-2].

[6]Prior to the arrival of Adams, the Senate elected Langdon to serve as its temporary president, and it was because of this that he administered the oath to Adams.

The three volumes of Maclay's diary. (Courtesy of the Library of Congress.)

myself sat, fell Violently on the Members from Pennsylvania, with insinuations that seemed to import, that we wished to overcharge New England with an undue proportion of the impost— What was the most remarkable Mr. Morris had wispered to me, that he would not get up on the Business. But would attend with the Utmost attention to all their Arguments fully determined, to give them their utmost Weight. But when this attack was begun, I could see his Nostrils Widen, and his nose flatten like the head of a Viper. Elsworth however got up before U̶s̶ him—and this gave him time to recollect himself. he rose after E⟨ll⟩sworth, and charmingly did he unravel all their Windings— it is too long to set down. but he was clear strong and conclusive. I in the mean While busied myself in exam⟨in⟩ing the Abstract of the importations into Philada. given me by Delany. In this place I cannot help remarking. that there is something of a singularity in my disposition. altho' I was equally concerned, I really felt Joy on this attack, and the more so, when I saw Mr. Morris moved the buffitings that I used to get from some of these People in his absence, and the sentimental insults that I received seemed now to say, take you too n̶o̶w̶ a part. When he had done, I rose and repeated from their own Observations that the Whole of the Molasses imported into Massachusets, was 3 Millions of Gallons— Two Million they distilled, and had the draw back if they chose to export it—so that this was totally out of the present question— that consumed in the State in Substance was the remaining

Million— but we imported last Year so much Molasses into Pennsylvania, that making sufficient Allowance for Two distilleries that were worked, the remainder for consumption in Substance was half a Million— was this the object to make such a Stir about? It was said that some of the New England rum was drunk, in the State be it so, take any given quantity, be it What it may, it is consumed under a duty of 4 Cents ℔ Gall. for the Gallon of Molasses Ye Yeilds in distillation rather a larger than a less quantity of Rum. than Gallon for Gallon— but we import near One Million of Gallons of Spirits into Pennsylvania and this is consumed under a duty of from 8 to 10 Cents ℔ Gall. We imported also 5 Million of raw Sugar, above One Million of Coffee, which was said to be half of the Coffee used in the united States—besides a full proportion of all other goods That I spoke not at random, or without book here was the Abstract in the hand Writing of Sharp Delany the Collector. were we then the People for imposing unequal Burthens No. We were imposing no burthens, of which we were not about to bear a Share, a great, perhaps the greatest Share. Dalton rose and remarked on the great uncertainty of all Calculations. he was however modest. a variety of People Spoke some heat seemed at one time to arise between Lee and Langdon— There was a considerable shifting about the question— it was at last settled that the question should be. to reduce the duty to three Cents, expressly on the Condition of taking away the Drawback. Mr. Morris and myself both Voted against it. Izard⟨,⟩ Gun and some others voted expressly on the Condition of the drawback being taken away. the others joined but with a design of retaining the Drawback— so stands this curious affair untill tomorrow— past 3 and a⟨d⟩journed— I must not omit that Carrol got up, and Spoke well on our side, he stated the inequality of duty on Molasses and Sugar as Sweets—that a Gallon of Molasses was equal as a Sweet to 7 lbs. of good brown Sugar— 7 Cents on one 4 on the other.

Friday, 5 June 1789

Came with my swelled knee, called this Morning, on Mr. Fitzsimons, and got from him a list of the V imports into Pennsylvania and into Virginia, went to the Hall and waited untill the Meeting of the Senate. we now fell to the impost and proceeded to the Article of Loaf Sugar. and here they directly moved a reduction of a Cent— Lee & Elsworth spoke against it as formerly— I rose & repeated the Sum of the Old Arguments. Doctr. Johnson who was with Us before now fell off Dalton changed and it was reduced to 3— We swam on smothly to the Teas imported from any other Country than China this clause admitted admitted all foreigners to come directly to China America from China & India Dalton Moved an amendment that should confine the

direct Trade from India and China to ~~Ameri~~ the U.S. to our our own
Vessels. Mr. Morris got up, and said that altho he was in Sentiment with the
Gentleman, Yet as he believed it would not meet the Approbation of Gentlemen he would not second the Motion, but leave the Matter until experience
would fully show the necessity of it. Mr. Carrol got up said if the Matter
was right, it should be tryed now, and not wait for experiment, which might be
attended with detriment and, seconded the Motion— and now strange to
tell both Lee and Elsworth rose and supported the Motion. I listened with
astonishment. When I recollected the debates on this very Subject on ~~the~~
Monday last— the Whole Trade to india was then inveighed against—condemn'd and almost execrated. and now the very Men declared for it, and for
securing it exclusively to Ourselves— this change I cannot account for, if
there was any preconcerted Measure Mr. Morris certainly knew nothing of it.
One inference however follows clearly from the Conduct of Lee & Elsworth.
That they are governed by conveniency or cabal. had Judgment ~~have~~ been
the rule of their conduct, their behavior on Monday would not have been so
inconsistent with that of this day— I was contented with the bill as it
stood, the difference of duty, and the discount of ten ℔ Cent, in favour of our
own Vessels, I thought pretty well, for protecting our Trade, without absolutely excluding all the World. But I had another reason I doubt much
Whether the House of Representatives will agree to our amendments. every
new One will, ~~be~~, or may be, a Source of dissention or delay— I have laboured with all the diligence in my power, to hasten on the impost, but I am
counteracted, for what can one Man do it now seems evident, that a merchantile influence is exerted to delay the impost, untill they get—in all their
Summer goods— this is detestable. This is. — but I have not a name for
it. I wish we were out of this base bad, place. Yesterday was the ~~Birthday~~
anniversary of his Britannic Majesty⟨'s⟩ Birth— It was an high day, and
celebrated with great festivity on that Account; The old leaven of Antirevo-
lutionism has leavened the Whole lump. nor can we keep the congress free
from the influence of it. People may act as they think proper in their Elections, and they will still do so. Lawyers and Merchants are generally their
Choice— But it seems as difficult to restrain a Merchant from striking at
~~Game~~ Gain, as to prevent the keen spaniel from Springing at Game, that he
has been bread to pursue. habit with them is become a Second nature. indeed the Strongest propensities of nature are often postponed to it. Lawyers
have keeness and a fondness for disputation. Wrangling is their business,
but long Practice in supporting any cause that offers, has obliterated all regard
to right or wrong, the question only is, which is my side? and this the
Slightest Circumstance, a Word a hint, a nod, a Whim or silly conceit, often
determines, even with them Who are ~~im~~ above ~~mercenary~~ pecuniary influence. Treats dinners attentions &c. &ca. are all his— and When Once the

elegit is made, when once the part is chosen, all that follows is a Contest for Victory.   O, Candor and integrity, Jewels of the human soul, where are Ye to be found?   seldom in professional Men.   often in the plain and sober Countryman.   never however in the sordid Clown.

About 2 O'Clock the Word Levee and adjourn was repeated from Sundry quarters of the House.   adjourn to Monday,   the President caught hold of the last.   is it the pleasure of the House that the adjournment be to Monday?   a single No could not be heard among the prevailing Ayes— here are most important bills before Us, and Yet we shall throw all by for empty Ceremony, for attending the Levee is little more.   nothing is regarded or valued at such Meetings but the qualifications that flow from the Taylor Barber or dancing Master, to be clean shaved Shirted and powdered, to make Your bows with grace and be master of small chat on the Weather play or news paper anecdote of the day, are the highest qualifications necessary—   Levees may be extreamely Useful, in old Countries w⟨h⟩ere Men of great fortunes are collected, as it may keep the Idle from being much worse employ'd   But here I think they are hurtful,   they interfere with the Business of the public, and instead of employing only the Idle, have a Tendency to make Men Idle, who should be better employ'd.   Indeed from these small beginings I fear we shall follow on, nor cease till we have reached the summit of Court Etiquette, and all the frivolities fopperies and Expence practised in european Governments.   I grieve to think that Many individuals among Us are aiming at these Objects with unceasing diligence—   settled with Mr. Vandolsen & he owes me 0:11:6.

Saturday, 6 June 1789

it was half past 10 when Mr. Bell called on me   he represented Mrs. Baxters Situation to be so low, That I might never see her, if I did not do it soon,[7]   he seemed so earnest that I should go with him, That I agreed to meet him in half an hour at the Ferry house and accompany him home.   the wind was high and direct a head,   it was five when we reached Elizabeth town point.[8]   here was Governor Livingston[9] and a dining party,   they had eat their fish ~~and fish~~

[7]William Bell of Elizabethtown, New Jersey, was the husband of Isabella Plunket Bell (1760–1843), daughter of WM's longtime friend William Plunket. Isabella's sister, Esther Plunket Baxter, died of consumption soon after WM's visit. See Appendix C. (John Blair Linn, *Annals of Buffalo Valley, Pennsylvania, 1755–1855* [Harrisburg, Pa., 1877], pp. 271–72; *NQ*[4], 3:289–90)

[8]Elizabethtown is in Essex County, New Jersey, fifteen miles southwest of New York. One of the oldest towns in the state, it claimed a newspaper and about 150 houses. Representative Boudinot resided there. The Point is about two and a half miles northeast of town, at the lower end of Newark Bay. Regular ferry service ran from the Point to the foot of Whitehall Street in New York City. (*New York*, p. 105)

[9]William Livingston (1723–90), governor of New Jersey from 1776 until his death, resided

and were sauntring in a porch. Mr. Bell, introduced me to the Governor, a Man plain & rather rustic in his dress & appearance. I had often heard of his being a Man of uncommon Abilities, & was all attention. but the Occasion afforded nothing but remarks of the convivial kind. let me Comment that the old Gentleman in returning late was overturned in his Chair and much bruised— twas near night when We came to Mr. Bell's— Poor Mrs. Baxter lay a Skeleton indeed, I cannot say but she may recover, but much indeed does it seem against her. She too was gay, and she Yet is Young, Useful lesson to the fluttering Females, of the Neighbourhood, if lessons were of any Service in these giddy times. I soon found I was not the only Member of Congress, in this Quarter. most of the Representation from South-Carolina wasere floating in this Neighbourhood. this Evening, and all Sunday, the House was— filled with decent Visitants, mostly however females, and charmingly did they talk chat it. The almost only Subject, was the Measures that were pursued to detain Congress in New York. There is in this Vicinity a Mrs. Rickets,[10] this Lady leads the Business in this Quarter, she enters into it, with a Spirit that risks reputation and sets all censure at defyance; indeed the Volumes of Conversation, poured out on this Subject might be stiled, with propriety, the Campaigns of Mrs. Rickets. But while she is characterized as the Mere flash of frivolity, her Husband is represented as a Pattern of Industry and Œconomy, and That he indulges his Cara Sposa, in the her Utmost extravagance, not from a Sheepish or sneaking disposition, but from the purest motives of Benevolence, and a sincere desire of making her happy. This Character made a deep impression on my milky temper. and I sincerely wished to have seen him somewhere in a field by himself, that I might have chatted with and learned something more of him.

Monday, 8 June 1789

wrote letters to my Family & Mr. Harris. set off in a frail Chair for the point, with a lady but the Chair had like to have broke down and I quitted it to her. came to the point, a few minutes too late for the first boat, left it a quarter after 10 in a second boat, but it was half after two before I reached New York, Sweated and almost broiled in a burning Sun. upon the Whole the jaunt was a disagreeable One, but it was right to see the poor the languid perhaps dying Mrs. Baxter. how lately was she gay as the Summer insect and

---

near Elizabethtown. Born at Albany, New York, he graduated from Yale in 1741 and became a member of the New York bar in 1748. He was active in the politics of that colony until he moved in 1772 to New Jersey, which he represented in Congress from 1774 to 1776 and at the Federal Convention.

[10]Sarah Ricketts (d.c. 1826) was the "dear wife" of James Ricketts (1754–c. 1825). (*Genealogical Magazine of New Jersey* 3:18; State of New Jersey, *Index of Wills . . .*, 3 vols. [n.p., 1912–13], 1:462)

how soon may any of Us be as she is— heard on my coming to my lodging of the Arrival of Two India Men at Philada. under Command of Barry & Truxon.[11] who report all the rest to be on their way. and now perhaps we shall get the impost ~~Bill~~ and collection bills passed.

Tuesday, 9 June 1789

Altho' I was not present Yesterday, nevertheless they were busy at the impost. The affair of confining the East India Trade to the Citizens of America, had been negatived. and a Committee had been appointed to report on this Business. the Report came in with very high duties amounting to a prohibition. But a new Phenomenon had made its appearance in the House since Friday a Pierce Butler from Carolina had taken his Seat and flamed like a Meteor, he arraigned the Whole impost law. and then Charged (indirectly) the Whole Congress with a design of oppressing South Carolina. he cryed out for encouraging the danes and Swedes, and foreigners of every kind to come & take away our produce, in fact he was for a Navagation Act reversed— Elsworth⟨,⟩ Morris⟨,⟩ Carrol⟨,⟩ Dalton⟨,⟩ Langdon for the Report, Few⟨,⟩ Izard⟨,⟩ Butler⟨,⟩ Lee against it; and untill 4 O'Clock was it battled, with less order less sense and less decency too, than any question I have ever Yet heard debated in the Senate, I did not like the report well, but concluded to vote for it all things considered. rather than by rejecting it to have all ~~things~~ set afloat on that Subject again. Butlers party had conducted themselves with so little decorum, that any effect their Arguments might have had, was lost by their Manner. and nobody rose but themselves— this was really the most misspent day that I remember in Congress. I did not rise Once. but often called for the question. Tomorrow is assigned for the third reading of the Bill and I hope We will finish it, or at least send it down to the other House. {if I had stood in need of any proof of the instability of Lee's Political Character this day gave me a fresh instance of it, now again he vilifyed and traduced the India Trade.}

---

[11]Capt. John Barry (1745–1803), a ship owner and shipmaster, had been one of America's naval heroes during the War for Independence. He came to Philadelphia from Ireland about 1760. An ardent Federalist, he led the small mob that escorted two Antifederal assemblymen to the State House in September 1787 when they had stayed away in order to prevent a quorum and the calling of a convention to ratify the Constitution of the United States. Soon thereafter, Barry left for China, and the state's attorney general declined to prosecute him. He commanded Senator Morris's ship, the *Asia*, which arrived at Philadelphia on 4 June. (*DHROC* 2:111n; *PP*, 5 June 1789)

Capt. Thomas Truxtun (1755–1822), who was born near Hempstead, New York, went to sea at age twelve. He experienced great success as a privateer during the War for Independence and returned to merchant shipping afterward. He commanded the *Canton*, which arrived at Philadelphia on 5 June. (*Websters American Military Biographies* [Springfield, Mass., 1978], p. 442; *PP*, 6 June 1789)

Wednesday, 10 June 1789

attended at the Hall at the usual time, and the Impost Bill was taken up for a third reading— I will not enter into any detail, of the Speeches & Arguments entered into. We once believed that Lee was the Worst of Men, But I think we have a much worse than he, in our lately arrived Mr. Butler. this is the most excentric of Creatures, he moved to strike out the Article of Indigo, Carolina Was not obliged to Us for taking Notice of her affairs. ever and anon crying out against local Views and partial proceedings. and the most local and partial Creature I ever heard open a mouth. all the impost Bill was calculated to ruin South Carolina, he has Words at Will, but scatters them the most at random of any Man I ever heard pretend to speak. he seems to have a particular antipathy to ~~Mrs.~~ Mr. Morris, Izard has often manifested, something of a similar disposition— we sat untill 4 O'Clock but did not get quite thro it.

Thursday, 11 June 1789

attended the Hall as usual— Mr. Izard & Mr. Butler opposed the Whole of the Drawbacks in every Shape Whatever Mr. Grayson of Virginia Warm on this Subject said we were not ripe for such a thing we were a New nation and had no business for any such regulation, a Nation Sui Generis— Mr. Lee said Drawbacks were right, but would be so much abused, he could not think of admitting them. Mr. Elsworth said New England Rum would be exported in Stead of West India to obtain the Drawback— I thought it best to say a few Words in reply to each. We were a New Nation it was true. but we were not a new People we were composed of individuals of like Manners habits and Customs, with the european Nations what therefore had been found Useful among them came well recommended, by Experience to Us; Drawbacks, stood as an example in this point of View to Us— That if the Thing was right in itself, there could be no just argument drawn against the Use of a thing from the abuse of it; it would be the duty of Government to guard against abuses, by prudent appointments, and Watchful attention to officers. That as to changing the kind of rum, I thought the collection bill would provide for this. by limiting the exportation to the original Casks and packages. I said a good deal more but really did not feel much interested either way. But the debates were very lengthy Butler flamed away and threatned a dissolution of the Union with regard to his State—*as sure as God was in the firmament.* he scattered his remarks over the Whole impost bill calling it partial oppressive &ca. and solely calculated to oppress S. Carolina and Yet ever and anon declaring how clear of local Views how candid and dispassionate he was. he

degenerated into one declamation   his State would live free or die glorious
&ca. &ca.—   We however got thro by. 3 O'Clock.   I will now memorandum
one remark.   the Senators from Jersey Pennsylvania Delaware and Maryland,
in every Act seemed desirous of making the impost productive, both as to
revenue, and effective for the encouragement of Manufactures. Thro and
seemed to consider the Whole of the imposts (salt excepted) much too low.
Articles of luxury many of them would have raised one half.   But the Members both from the north and still more particularly from the South, were ever
in a flame, When any Articles were brought forward that were in any considerable Use among them.

dined this day with Mr. Morris.   Mr. Fitzsimons and Mr. Clymer all the
Company, except Mrs. Morris & 3 Children.[12]   Mrs. Morris talked a good deal
after dinner   she did it gracefully enough. This being a gayer place and she
being here considered as at least the 2d female Character at Court.   as to taste
etiquette &ca. she is certainly the first.   I thought she discovered a predilection for New York.   but perhaps she was only doing it Justice While my
extreme dislike aversion like a Jealous centinal, is for giving no quarter.   I
however happened to mention that they were ill supply'd with the Article of
Cream.   Mrs. Morris had much to say on this Subject   declared, they had
done all they could and even sent to the Country all about, but that she could
not be supply'd.   she told many anecdotes on this Subject. particularly how
two days ago she dined at the Presidents   A large and fine looking Triffle was
brought to Table. and looked appeared exceeding well indeed—   she was
helped by the President, but on taking some of it, she had to pass her handker-
chief by her mouth, and rid herself of the Morsel, on which she wispered the
President—the Cream of which it is made, has been miserably Stale and
rancid, on Which the General Changed his plate immediately   But But she
added with a titter, Mrs. Washington eat a Whole heap of it.   but Where in
the World has this Triffle lead me.   I have ever been very attentive to discover
if possible General Washingtons private Opinions on the pompous part of
Government.   His address of fellow Citizens, to the Two Houses of Congress
seems quite Republican.   Mrs. Morris however gave Us something on this
Subject;   Gen. Washington in a Visit to her *had declared himself in the most
pointed Manner for large Generous Salaries, and added that without large
Salaries proper Persons, never could be got to fill the offices of Government
with propriety.*   he might deliver something of this kind with propriety
enough without using the Word large.   however if he lives with the Pompous
People of New York he must be something more than human, if their high
toned Manners have not some effect on him.   On going first among Indians I

---

[12]WM apparently referred to the three youngest children of Senator and Mrs. Morris,
Charles (b. 1777), Maria (1779–1852), and Henry (1784–1842). (*Descendants of Colonel
Thomas White*, pp. 178–84)

have observed decent White People view them with a kind of disgust, but where the Indians were by far the most numerous, the disgust would by degrees wear off, indifference followed and by degrees attachment and even fondness,   how much more likely are the Arts of Attention and obsequiousness, ~~likely~~ to make an imitative Impression.

Friday, 12 June 1789

Attended the judicial Committee and had the Bill read over.   it was long and somewhat confused,   I was called out,   they however reported it, soon after the Senate met.   and a number of Copies were ordered to be Struck off; Monday Se'night appointed for it.   The Indian Treaties were now taken up and referred to a Committee of 3 to report—   Mr. Butler made a most flaming Speech ~~from~~ against the Judicial bill   he was called to Order from the Chair and was not a little angry about it.   The french Convention was called up and read respecting the privilidges of Consuls Vice-Consuls &ca. but was postponed.[13]   We now adjourned and I went to the levee.   I was rather late, Most of the Company were coming away.   I felt easier than I used to do and I believe I had better attend every day untill I finish the affair of Davy Harris.[14]   I spoke to Coll. Humphreys and desired to know when I should call on him,   he said nine O'Clock, and I believe I will go at that Hour tomorrow.

In the Evening Mr. White of Virginia called on me,   we walked after Tea.   had much discourse on the Subject of removing Congress.   I have not been mistaken in my Opinion of the Virginians,   he declared for Staying here rather than agree to the Falls of Delaware—   as we came home the Speaker overtook Us on Horseback.

Saturday, 13 June 1789

being Saturday, and having no party made to go any where, went to the House of Representatives to hear the Debates,   they were on the Collection

---

[13]Consideration of both the Treaties of Fort Harmar and the 1788 Consular Convention with France are recorded in the *SEJ*. The treaties are printed in the *SEJ*, pp. 152–63, and documents related to the consular convention are printed in the *SEJ*, pp. 251–351.

[14]David Harris (1754–1809), a favorite brother-in-law of WM's, obtained the senator's assistance in his attempts to secure a federal job between 1789 and 1791. He was born at Harris's Ferry and served in the Pennsylvania line of the Continental army from 1775 to 1777. His career as a merchant at Baltimore, Maryland, failed late in the 1780s despite a trip to France in 1786 to secure business. In 1789 Harris desired the position of comptroller or surveyor of the port of Baltimore, and in 1790 he sought to be named commissioner of loans for Maryland. Because of the opposition of at least one Maryland representative, neither application succeeded. See Appendix C. (David Harris to GW, [1789], 24 July 1790; WM to GW, 20 July 1789, GWP, DLC; Harris to Tench Coxe, 14 March 1791, Coxe Papers, PHi; *PTJ*

Bill. I staid Two Hours they were in Committee, and really made but small Progress— There was not one debate worth committing to paper— settled with my landlord he owes me £1:10:2.

Sunday, 14 June 1789

Wrote this day Two sets of letters home—one to Mr. Harris inclosing one to Mrs. Maclay to go by a Mrs. Ossay[15] of Harrisburgh. the other set to go by the Post. Oh this was a tedious tedious day, I think I shall long remember it— I was ill with my sore knee went to the Bathing House and bathed, did not go to any place of Worship. could not engage myself to reading— had indeed no book of an engaging nature. I will leave a blank here which I can fill up at my leasure if I chuse. {My Mind revolts in Many instances against the Constitution of the United States, Indeed I am afraid it will turn out the Vilest of all Traps that ever was set to ensnare the freedom of an unsuspecting People.

Treaties formed by the executive of the United States Are to be the Laws of the Land. to cloath the Executive with legislative ~~Power~~ authority, is setting aside our modern & much boasted ~~discoveries~~ distribution of Power into legislative Judicial and Executive. discoveries unknown to Locke & Montesquieu and all the antient writers. It certainly contradicts all the Modern Theory of Government. And in practice must be Tyranny.

Mdm. Get if I can the Federalist,[16] without buying, it is not worth it. but being a Cast[17] book Izard or somebody else will give it to me. It certainly was instrumental in procuring the adoption of the Constitution. This is merely a point of Curiosity and Amusement. to see how Wide of his Explanations and Conjectures the Stream of Business has taken it's Course.}

Monday, 15 June 1789

attended at the Hall, and the Tonnage Act was taken up. we got about half way ~~thro' it~~ the first clause of it by 4 OClock. A Clause stood on all ships or Vessels within the united States, *and belonging Wholly to a Citizen or*

10:325; *Commemorative Biographical Encyclopedia of Dauphin . . .* [Chambersburg, Pa., 1896], p. 81)

[15]WM married Mary Harris (1750–1819) in 1769. See Appendix C. Mrs. Ossay may have been the wife of either George or Frederick Youse. (*1790 Pennsylvania Census*, p. 86)

[16]The *Federalist* is a series of eighty-four essays in support of the adoption of the Constitution, written by Alexander Hamilton, James Madison, and John Jay over the signature "Publius." Most of the essays had appeared in newspapers before publication of a two-volume set by John and Archibald McLean at New York in the spring of 1788. (*DHROC* 13:490n)

[17]One of the meanings of the Scottism "cast" is "ingenious."

Citizens thereof. Izard moved to have the latter part ~~of~~ Struck out the Effect of which would have been, that no discrimination would have been made between our own Citizens and foreigners— Lee⟨,⟩ Butler⟨,⟩ Grayson⟨,⟩ Izard and Few argued in the most unceasing Manner and I thought most Absurdly on this Business. The first time I made a short remark that the foreigner and Citizen must both, build their Ships in America, and then evidently for everything that followed they stood alike— That the Superior Capital of the Foreigners would enable them to build more Ships lower than Us, and would in time give them the Whole of our Trade. that the Bill bore on the face of it a discrimination in favour of our merchants but the fact would turn out otherwise and therefore I was for continuing the Clause as it Stood— A little before the question was put I rose a second time. said no former transaction was so likely to throw light on this Subject, as a Short History of the British Navigation Act.[18] Cromwell originated it, in Spleen against the Dutch. But the Effects of it were seen before the restoration and it was then reenacted. great Murmurs arose the Scotch thought themselves ruined, and sent their peers up to remonstrate against it. The Tonnage of great Britain then Stood at 95,266— in 15 Years it was 190,533— in 20 Years more it was 273,693 the Present Tonnage of Massachusets alone is now 180,000, it had been urged That it would be time enough half a Century hence to talk of Measures for a navy, a single State was in a better condition now, in point of Shipping, than the British nations were at the restoration. therefore delay was the worst of policy. it was generally allowed, that the Spirit of the navigation Act was to give a Monopoly of the Trade of the British nations to their own Shipping & sailors in View solely Mercantile this was perhaps wrong as by these Means our foreign Articles would be dearer and our home produce cheaper, but the Object was a National One. Shipping and Sailors were the Objects and tho the ~~Merchants were~~ landed part of the Community was not perhaps so rich Yet the nation was safe—for national Power is of more consequence than individual Wealth. the Suspension of the Navigation Act, as was believed would be productive of a great flow of Wealth, to the British ~~Merchants~~, Nation, or at least the manufacturing & Agricultural parts of it. but the purchase would cost them their Shipping and Sailors— and finally the foreigners would have a Monopoly, of the Whole Traffick one of the Wo⟨r⟩st of evils provided they conducted their Navigation on Terms of more Œconomy, as was generally believed of the Dutch. But what were we doing were we passing a Navigation Act, no, a slight discrimination was all that was aimed at, and if this Motion was adopted, the discrimination would

---

[18]The Navigation Act of 1696, which consolidated earlier navigation acts of Parliament, required that no goods or commodities could be imported into or out of any English colony except in English-owned ships, of which the master and three-fourths of the crew were English. It also stipulated that certain enumerated colonial exports, including sugar and tobacco, could be shipped only to England or her colonies.

operate against Us— the question was put & the clause remained— near 4 & adjourned.

Tuesday, 16 June 1789

this day passed the Residue of the Tonnage Bill with ~~out~~ much debate. broke up early and went to hear the debates in the House of Representatives, after dinner went and Walked, a considerable time to try to gain Strength for my knee. some observations having called me up this day, I endeavoured to comprize all I had to say in as little bounds as possible, by observing that there were Two extremes in commercial regulations equally to to be avoided. The principle of the Navigation Act, might be carried so far as to exclude all foreigners from our ports. the consequence would be a Monopoly in favor of the Mercantile Interest. the other was an unlimited licence in favor of foreigners. the Consequence of which would be a Monopoly in favor of the cheapest Carriers, and in time a total dependence on them. both extremes ought to be avoided, by giving certain indulgencies to our own trade, & that of our Friends, in such degree as will secure them the Ascendancy, without hazarding the expulsion of foreigners from our ports.

Wednesday, 17 June 1789

Inclosed Copies of the Judicial Bill. to Lewis⟨,⟩ Peters⟨,⟩ Tench Coxe and Myers Fisher.[19] called on Mr. Morris & signed jointly with him. letters to the

---

[19]William Lewis (1751–1819), a prominent Philadelphia lawyer, was a member of the Pennsylvania Assembly from 1787 to 1789 and the state constitutional convention, 1789–90. He was born in Chester County and, as a Quaker, became an influential force in the state antislavery movement. In 1789 Washington appointed him United States attorney for Pennsylvania. See also *SEJ*, p. 535. (*DHROC* 2:729)

Tench Coxe (1755–1824), a lifelong resident of Philadelphia, was a political economist and international merchant whose writings on behalf of the adoption of the United States Constitution gained him national prominence. He openly supported the British during the early years of the War for Independence and held no political offices until the late 1780s, when he served in the Annapolis Convention of 1786 and in the Confederation Congress during its last months. In 1790 Alexander Hamilton chose him to serve as assistant secretary of the treasury. Coxe, an expert on manufacturing and internal improvements, drafted Hamilton's 1791 report on manufactures. WM and other members of the FFC corresponded with Coxe regularly, and his papers contain a wealth of information about Congress. (Jacob E. Cooke, *Tench Coxe and the Early Republic* [Chapel Hill, N.C., 1978], pp. 182–86)

Miers Fisher (1748–1819), a native Philadelphian, was a lawyer, Quaker, and member of the city council at the time of the FFC. He became a leader in Pennsylvania's antislavery movement, was a director of the Bank of North America, and was active in preparing for the arrival of the federal government when Congress chose Philadelphia as the temporary seat of government in 1790. (*Philadelphia Families* 1:668–69; 1790 folder, Miers Fisher Papers, PHi)

President and the Chief Justice enclosing Copies.[20]   from here called on Mr. Scott.   told him of the request of the Arrangement Committee[21]   met and made a Short report.   the Senate formed   passed the Residue of the impost Bill. without much debate.   In now came Mr. Jay, to give information respecting Mr. Short, who was nominated to supply the Place of Mr. Jefferson at the Court of France, while Mr. Jefferson returned home.[22]   and now the President rose to give us a discourse, on the Subject of form   how we should give our *Advice* and *consent*   I rose perhaps more early than might have been wished by some and stated, That this Business was in the ~~way~~ nature of Election, that the Spirit of the Constitution was clearly in favour of ballot, that this mode could be applied without difficulty, that When the Person was put up in

---

[20]The president of Pennsylvania from 1788 to 1790 and governor from 1790 to 1799 was Thomas Mifflin (1744–1800), a lifelong resident of Philadelphia. He graduated from the College of Philadelphia in 1760 and began a career as a merchant before entering politics. An ardent advocate of the American cause against England, he served in the assembly from 1772 to 1776 and in the Continental Congress from 1774 to 1776. From 1775 to 1779, when he resigned his commission as a major general, he served as an aide to Washington and as quartermaster general. His military career estranged him from his Quaker heritage, and his attempts to undermine Washington politically made him one of the general's most prominent enemies. Mifflin served as president of the Confederation Congress in 1783–84, signed the Constitution as a delegate to the Federal Convention, and was the only member of the assembly not to vote for WM for the Senate. (*DHROC* 2:730; *DHFFE* 1:295)

The chief justice of Pennsylvania from 1777 to 1799, Thomas McKean (1734–1817), was one of a group of revolutionary leaders active in the politics of both Delaware and Pennsylvania. Born in Chester County, Pennsylvania, and a resident of Philadelphia from 1774, he signed the Declaration of Independence on behalf of Delaware, completed seventeen years as a member of the Delaware Assembly in 1779, and represented Delaware in Congress almost continuously from 1774 to 1783. A Federalist, McKean served in both the Pennsylvania Ratification Convention of 1788 and the state constitutional convention of 1789–90. His application to Washington in 1789 for a federal judicial appointment was unsuccessful. (*DHROC* 2:730; Series 7, GWP)

[21]The committee was the one appointed on 9 May to consider the appropriation of space in Federal Hall.

[22]John Jay (1745–1829), secretary for foreign affairs from 1784 to 1789 and chief justice of the United States from 1789 to 1795, acted as secretary of state until March 1790. A native of New York City, Jay graduated from King's College in 1764, was accepted to the bar in 1768, and served as a member of the Continental Congress from 1774 to 1777 and as its president from 1778 to 1779. Jay represented American interests in Spain from 1780 to 1782 and acted as a peace commissioner in France with John Adams and Benjamin Franklin from 1782 to 1784. He was a member of the New York Ratification Convention and authored some of the *Federalist* essays. See also *SEJ*, pp. 523–24.

William Short (1759–1849), private secretary in France to American minister Thomas Jefferson, 1785–89, and American chargé d'affaires there, 1789–92, was born in Surry County, Virginia. In 1779 he graduated from William and Mary and qualified to practice law two years later. Prior to embarking for France in 1784, he served for a year on the Virginia Executive Council. See also *SEJ*, pp. 554–55.

On 16 June Jay delivered a message from Washington nominating Short as chargé d'affaires, and the Senate ordered Jay to bring to the Senate the papers mentioned in the message. Most of WM's diary for 17 June covers the debate, which is recorded in the *SEJ*, over whether the Senate, which found itself establishing precedent in the consideration of its first presidential nomination, should advise and consent by voice or by secret ballot. The document that Jay brought to the Senate on 17 June is printed in the *SEJ*, pp. 353–57.

Nomination, The the favourable Tickets should have a Yea—and the others should be blanks— Few of Georgia rose & seconded me. Izard made a long Speech against it Mr. Carrol spoke against it Mr. Langdon and Mr. Morris— But Lee⟨,⟩ Elsworth and Butler were for it. Mr. Morris speech principally turned on it's being below the dignity of the Senate who should be open bold and unawed by any Consideration Whatever. I rose at last and spoke perhaps longer than I had done on any former Occasion— It had been considered as unworthy of a Senator to conceal any Vote, the Good of the public however required Secrecy in many things, but the Ballot did not take away the right of open Conduct, on the Contrary it was the duty of every Senator, to disclose the defects of any Candidate. where they were great or at might be attended the with danger to the public. But as the Nominations came from the President, it [*lined out*] was not to be expected Characters notoriously flagitious would ever be put in nomination. every Senator when voting openly would feel inconvenience from Two Quarters, or at least he was subjected to it. I would not say, in european language that there would be Court favour and Court resentment, but there would be about the President a kind of Sunshine, that people in general would be well pleased to enjoy the Warmth of, openly Voting against the nominations of the President, would be the sure mode of loosing this Sunshine. But there was this was applicable to all Senators in all Cases— But there was more, a Senator like another Man, would have the interest of his friends to promote. the Cause of a Son or a Brother might be lodged in his hands, will such a one in such a Case wish openly to oppose the Presidents Judgt.? in no But there are other Inconveniencies the disappointed Candidate will retaliate the injury which he feels, against the Senator— it may be said the Senators Station will protect him— this can extend only to the time of his being in office, and he too must return to private life, Where as a private Man, he must answer for the offences given by the Senator. The Ballot left the Judgment equally free, and none of the above inconveniencies followed when these equal advantages flowed, without any of the disadvantages, the mode least Subject to inconvenience was preferable. Many Gentlemen had declared how perfectly indifferent it was to them. I believed the same thing of every Senator in the Present House, But was this always to continue. no we must expect Men of every class and every description within these Walls, the Present Character of our President was no Security, that we should always have men equally eminent. That in those places where elections were conducted Viva Voce. the hopes and fears of Electors were so wrought on by the Wealthy Powerful and bold, that few Votes were f given intirely free from influence. unless it was by the happy few who were independant in Spirit as well as in fortune. that we need not expect the Senate would always be composed of such desirable Characters. That it had been clearly stated and admitted, that the Business could be equally well

~~done by Ballot, in the present Case, as by Viva Voce—and~~ the Mode by Ballot was equally applicable to the present Case, as that of Viva Voce. and being free from many inconveniencies, that the other was subject to ought undoubtedly to be adopted.

{The balloting Business prevented my Minuting in Order the More important debate on the Tonnage Act— The Villanous amendments, (for Which We may thank the influence of this City,) for doing away the discrimination between Foreigners in and out of Treaty with Us have been carried. It was in vain That I gave them every Opposition in my power. I laid down a Marked difference between impost & Tonnage the former imposition is paid by the Consumer of the Goods the later rests on the Owner of the Ship at least in the first instance. That sound policy dictated the principle of encouraging the Shipping of Our Friends. That Nations not in Treaty could not be considered as the Most Friendly. I read the 5th Article of the Commercial Treaty with France And deny'd that We had any power of imposing Any Tonnage on her Shipping save an equivalent to the 100 Sols On Coasters,[23] I gave my Unequivocal Opinion That a want of discrimination in her favour was contrary to the Spirit of the Treaty, and expressed fears of her Resentment. Elsworth Answered me, but the most That he said was that Our interest called for it, and he pledged himself that we would never hear from France about it. but speaking was in vain I never saw the Senate more listless or inattentive nor more determined.}

Thursday, 18 June 1789

and now the mode of approving or disapproving of the nomination— I did not minute it Yesterday. But our President rose in the Chair, and delivered his Opinion how the Business ought to be done— he read the constitution argued and concluded, I would rise in the Chair and put the question individually to the Senators, do you advise and consent, that Mr. Short be appointed Charge des Affaires, at the Court of France—do you and do you— Mr. Carrol spoke long for the Viva Voce mode— he said ballot was productive of caballing and bargaining for Votes he then wandered so wide of the Subject, as to need no attention. Mr. Elsworth made a most elaborate harrangue. a great part of it was however about the duty of our President. and inventing a mode how he might also ballot in Case of a division. he however towards the close of it made a strange distinction, that voting by

---

[23]France and the United States signed a treaty of amity and commerce in 1778 under which each nation granted the other most favored nation status. Article 5 exempted the United States from payment of the duty of one hundred sols or sous per ton on foreign ships, except when American ships transported French merchandise to another French port, and recognized the right of the United States to enact a duty on French ships carrying American merchandise between U.S. ports. (*SEJ*, p. 400)

ballot suited bashful Men best, but was the worst way for bad and unprinci-
pled Men.   I wished to repeat nothing of what had been said Yesterday but
reply'd, That so far from balloting being productive of cabaling, it was the very
bane and antidote against it.   that Men made bargains for certainties, but it
was in vain to purchase or bargain for a Vote by ballot which there was no
certainty of the party ever obtaining, as he had no method of securing the
performance of a promise or of knowing whether he was deceived or not.
that as to the distinction of balloting being the Worst way for bad Men, I
thought different.   The wo⟨r⟩st of Men were known to respect Virtue.   the
ballot removed all external force or obligation,   it was the only chance of
making a bad Man act Justly,   the Matter was left to his own Conscience
there were no Witnesses,   if he did wrong it was because he loved Vice more
than Virtue, which I believed, even among bad Men, was not the fact, in one
Case out of ten.   The question was at last taken and carried by 11 Votes   7
against it.   is Z[24] was so crooked he voted against Us, tho he had spoken for
Us, and quoted Harrington to show his reading—   The People who lost this
question manifested much uneasiness, particularly the President and Mr.
Langdon—   Langdon was even fretful   the President threw difficulties in
our way;   The Senate had decreed, their advice and Consent by ballot.
{Nothing like this in History or ever heard of before—}   But What Rank was
Mr. Short to hold in the diplomatic Corps?   what Kind of Commission was he
to have?   this must be settled by ballot—   he set Us afloat by those kind of
queries, and an Hour and a quarter was lost in the most idle and desultory
discourse imaginable.   he seemed willing to entangle the Senate—or rather
some of them really were entangled, about the Secretary of the Legation and
the Charge des affairs, not knowing a distinction   we however got thro' it by a
Resolution declaring our advice and consent in favour of Mr. Short[25]—   took
up the impost and talked Idly to past the usual time of adjournment—   and
adjournment called for and took place—   {After having again explained the
Manner of concurring or rejecting a Nomination by ballot in a Manner so plain
as did not admit of Contradiction I replyd to the Observation "That no
Example of any thing of the Kind could by be found in History"—That the
Old Kingdom of Arragon Where, Tho' the Execu[tive] Was Monarchical, Yet
that republican Provision had been attended to with Unexampled
Attention   The Court pp appointed to by the Justiza gave their Sentence by
Ballot—and offered to produce History to the point—but was not contradicted—}
    {I have ever been as attentive as I possibly could be, to discover the real
disposition of the President U.S.   he has been very cautious hitherto, or
rather inactive, or shall I say like a Pupil in the hands of his Governor, or a

---

[24]Ralph Izard.
[25]Senate actions on the Short nomination and the decision to proceed by secret ballot are
recorded in the *SEJ*.

Child in the Arms of his Nurse. the Message about Mr. Short, couches a Matter that may be drawn into Precedent. it states the desire of Mr. Jefferson to return for some time. and nominates Mr. Short to supply his place during such Absence. the leave for return &ca. is not laid before the Senate— granting this power to be solely with the President, the power of dismissing ambassadors seems to follow—and some of the Courtiers in Senate fairly admitted it. I chose to give the matter a different turn—and delivered my Opinion That, our ~~appointing Mr. Short~~. concurring in the appointment of Mr. Short fully imply'd the Consent of the return of Mr. Jefferson— That if we chose to prevent the return of Mr. Jefferson it was only to negative the Nomination of Mr. Short or any other one to fill his place— It is the fault of the best Governors when they are placed over a people to endeavour to enlarge their powers, by applying to public Stations what would be laudable in private individuals. a desire of bettering their Stations. thus the farmer acts well who by industry adds Field to Field—and so would the Governor who would add to the public, ~~but a desire~~ Wealth or happiness, but adding to the personality, if I may so speak, or to the personal power of the Governor, is a faulty industry.

A question has been agitated with great Warmth in the House of Representatives, Whether the Sole power of displacing Officers, or to speak Strictly. the Secretary for foreign affairs, shall remain with the President. from the small begining in the Case of Mr. Short, it is easy to see What the Court Opinion, will be with respect to this point— Indeed I entertain not a doubt, but many People are aiming, with all their force to establish a Splendid Court, with all the Pomp of Majesty. Alas Poor Washington if You are taken in this Snare, how will the Gold become dim? how will the fine Gold be changed? how will all your Glory fade?}

{Neutrality the point of profit, the Grand desideratum of of a Wise Nation, among contending powers—

Multiplied Engagements, & contradictory Treaties. go to prevent this blessing, & involve a Nation in Foreign Quarrels.

China Geographically Speaking may be called the Counterpart to our American World   O, that We could make her policy the political Model of Our Conduct with respect to other nations, ready to dispose of her Superfluities to all the World.   She stands committed by no Engagement to any foreign part of it.   dealing with every comer she seems to say, We trade with You and You with Us, While common interest sanctifies the Connection, but that dissolved we know no other engagement.}

Friday, 19 June 1789

and now the impost Bill as sent back from the House of Representatives, with an almost total rejection of our amendments was taken.   There was but

little Speaking.   Mr. Lee made a distinction in his parliamentary Way between the Word insist & adhere.   and it was carried to Use the Word *insist*—   after the Two first Articles were insisted On Mr. Morris moved that
One Question should be taken on all the other disagreements; saving time was
his Object, but we only lost by it.   he did not seem to have been well understood,   I rose and explained his motion, & to his Satisfaction as he said—
the Result of the Whole Was that we nearly insisted on all our amendments,
and I suppose they will adhere to the original bill—   This really seems like
playing at cross purposes—or differing for the sake of the Sport.   I voted on
the principles of Accomodation throughout the Whole—   indeed this was
but repeating my former Vote.   Indeed there then was nothing to differ
about   only Opinion founded on Conjecture—   One imagined a thing was
too high, another thought it too low—   my Opinion was that they were all
too low to raise the Money which we wanted—   others wished them low on
purpose that the defficiency might be so t great that we would be forced into
an Excise   I abhorred this Principle, tho my Colleague is fond of it.   adjourned over to 11 OClock on Monday.   and now I will endeavour to Use this
interval in riding to try to drive this Vile Rheumatism out of my Knee.   I have
never been perfectly recovered of it, and my right Knee is still much swelled—
    went to hire an Horse after dinner   could not get a very indifferent one with
saddle & Briddle under 2/ ℔ hour—   thought this such abandoned extravagance would not give it—   spent tonight to get an Horse   Van Dalsen hired
one for me at a Dollar ℔ day or half D. for half a day.

Saturday, 20 June 1789

    was in Horseback at 5 O'Clock   rode to near 8   came home breakfasted
rested one hour and half, & rode to 12.   asked what I had to pay, and was
obliged to pay 6/—   the Horse would not have sold for £ more 6 or 7
pounds—   was exceedingly fatagued.   lolled on bed to near 4 and Joined
the Speaker and a party to drink Tea at one Lephers, where we were civilly
treated.   think my Knee is not Worse of the riding   the day excessive hot.

Sunday, 21 June 1789

    rode till 8 O'Clock   very warm,   think I never felt the Heat more oppres-
sive in my life,   staid at home & wrote to my family,   in the Evening Clymer
and Fitzsimons passed by   a Walked a Short way with them,   I gave my
Opinion in plain language that the Confidence of the People was departing
from Us, owing to our unreasonable delays,   asked them, have you received

any letters, shewing signs of such a Temper,   Fitzsimons said No, But the thing told for itself, and could not be otherwise—   1:7:8 due by my Landlord.

Monday, 22 June 1789

Attended the Senate.   The Bill for settling the new Judiciary was taken up.   Much discourse about the mode of doing business.   We were in Committee   the first & 2d clauses postponed.   a Question taken whether there should be district Courts,   much wrangling about Words—   this was carried,   But now Mr. Lee brought forward a Motion nearly in the Words of the Virginia amendment, Viz. that The Jurisdiction of the Federal Courts should be confined, to cases of admiralty and Maritime Jurisdiction.[26]   Lee and Grayson—Supported this position, Elsworth answered them. and the ball was kept up untill past three O'Clock.   The question was going to be put.   I rose and begged to make a remark or Two,   The Effect of the Motion was to exclude the Federal Jurisdiction, from each of the States, except in cases of admiralty and maritime Cases.   But the Constitution expressly extended it to all cases of in law and equity under the Constitution the Laws of the united States, Treaties made or to be made. &ca.   we already had existing Treaties and were about making many laws.   These must be executed by the federal Judiciary.   the Arguments which had been used would apply well, if amendments to the Constitution were under Consideration. but certainly were inapplicable here.   I sat down   some called for the Question and some for an adjournment—   the adjournment carried—   Strong this day in Conversation, mentioned that *the President would continue no longer in office, Than he saw Matters fairly set a going*—and then Mr. Adams will begin his reighnn this no doubt is a desirable [*lined out*] Æra for the new England Men.   {The very Principle Which Actuated Doctor Rush[27] And myself When We puffed

---

[26]On 27 June 1788 the Virginia Ratification Convention proposed twenty amendments to the Constitution in addition to a bill of rights; the text of the amendment WM mentioned can be found in *DHFFC* 4:18–19.

[27]Benjamin Rush (1745–1813), Philadelphia physician, reformer, and political activist, was born in Philadelphia County. He had known WM since the two met in the 1750s as students at West Nottingham Academy in Cecil County, Maryland. Rush graduated from the College of New Jersey in 1760 and received his medical education at the University of Edinburgh. He wrote anonymous and often hyperbolic newspaper articles on a variety of subjects, including the American cause in the early 1770s and the movement for new federal and state constitutions at the end of the 1780s. Rush served in Congress during 1776 and 1777, signing the Declaration of Independence, and as a surgeon general in the Continental army. He was a Federalist member of the state ratification convention. From 1783 to 1789 Rush and WM cooperated in a variety of projects including the establishment of Dickinson College, the first federal elections, the effort to call a state constitutional convention, and some minor land speculation. Rush maintained a correspondence with several members of the Pennsylvania delegation in the FFC, including WM. The letters are rich in detail about the politics of Congress prior to its removal to Philadelphia, when the correspondence

John Adams in the papers and brought him forward for Vice President, will probably make him President— We knew his Vanity, and hoped by laying hold of it to render him Useful Among the New England Men In Our Scheme of bringing Congress to Pennsylvania.[28] But his Pride Obstinacy And Folly Are equal to his Vanity. And Altho' it is A common Observation That fools are the Tools of Knaves, and I am certain Weak Men are Often brought forward with such Views—Yet John Adams has served to illustrate Two points at least with me, Viz. That a fool is the most Unmanageable of All Brutes—and That Flattery is the Most Irksome of All Service.}

Tuesday, 23 June 1789

Attended at the Hall, a little after Ten, came into the Senate Chamber, there was nobody here but Mr. Adams, he was in the great Chair, When I came in but he left it. came and sat near me untill he read a News paper shifted to the Chair next to me began a discourse on the Subject of Pennsylvania. said they were the best republicans in the Union, Their adoption was unequivocal. this could not be said of Boston New York or Virginia. *Surely* there was a meaning in this. I reply'd that We had no doubt our Faults but certainly the Virtues of Plainess industry and Frugality would be allowed to Us in some degree, That Federalism was General, but there was a general Abhorrence of the Pomp and Splendid Expence of Government, especially everything which bordered on royalty— several Members came in and joined Us— Senate formed and the Business of Yesterday, was taken up. just w⟨h⟩ere we left it. The discourses of Yesterday were all repeated— Mr. Lee endeavoured to give the Whole Business a new Turn to elude the force of What I had said Yesterday, according to his explanation of admiralty and maritime Jurisdiction he would have taken in a Vast Field. I rose and read over from the Constitution a number of the powers of Congress—Viz. collecting Taxes duties imposts, ~~reg~~ naturalization of Foreigners. Laws respecting the Coinage, punishing. the counterfeiting of the Coin. Treason against the united States &ca. declared that no force of Construction. could bring these Cases within Admiralty or maritime Jurisdiction—and Yet all these Cases, were most expressly the Province of the Federal Judiciary. so that the ques-

---

ceased. (WM to Benjamin Rush, 2 March 1783, Gratz Collection, PHi; *Princetonians, 1748–68*, pp. 318–25)

[28]When Adams returned from England in 1788, Rush informed him that Pennsylvania would assist in obtaining a prominent position for him in the new government, if the southern and eastern states would gratify Pennsylvania by placing the seat of the federal government on the Delaware River. On 6 August 1788, a widely reprinted article in the *Pennsylvania Gazette* stated the same idea without naming Adams. *Gazette* articles on 8 October and 31 December 1788, also widely reprinted, named Adams as the best choice for vice president and described his qualifications. It is not clear which articles were authored or coauthored by WM. (*PBR*, p. 469)

tion expressly turned on this point. shall we follow the Constitution or not.   I said a good deal more but this was the Substance.   Mr. Lee after some time opposed me with a very singular argument,   He rose and Urged that the State Judges would be all Sworn to support the Constitution.   That they must obey their Oath, and of course execute the Federal laws—   he varied this Idea in sundry Shapes.   I rose and opposed to this. that ~~the very Effect of~~ the Oath taken by the State Judges, would produce quite a contrary effect.   that they would swear to support the Constitution.   That the Constitution placed the Judicial power of the Union in One Supreme Court and such inferior Courts as should be appointed.   & of Course the State Judges in Virtue of their Oaths, would ~~asbs~~ abstain from every Judicial Act under the federal laws. and would refer all such Business to the federal Courts.   that if any Matter made cognizable in a federal Court, should be agitated in a State Court, a plea to the Jurisdiction would immediately be put in, and proceedings would be stayed.   no reply was made.   the question was soon taken and the Motion was rejected.

The first clause of the Bill was now called for.   Grayson made a long harrangue.   I mentioned that I thought, this an improper time to decide absolutely on this part of the Bill.   If the Bill stood in its present form and the Circuit courts were continued, Six Judges appeared to be too few.   If the Circuit Courts were Struck out. they were too Many.   That it would have pleased me better.   But as we were in Committee. I would not consider myself as absolutely bound, by anything that happened now.   but would reserve myself untill the second reading in the Senate.   Mr. Elsworth rose and made a most elaborate harrangue, on the necessity of a numerous bench of Judges.   he enlarged on the importance of the Causes that would come before them, of the dignity it was necessary to Support, and The Twelve Judges of England in the Exchecquer Chamber were held up to View during the Whole harrangue.   and he seemed to draw Conclusions, that 12 were few enough—   I readily admitted, that the information respecting the English Courts, was fairly Stated; But in England the Whole Mass of litigation in the Kingdom came before these Judges, the Whole Suits arising from 8 or 9 Million of People.   here it was totally different.   the Mass of Causes would remain with the State Judges, those only arising from federal laws, would come before the federal Judges.   and these would comparatively be few indeed. When they became numerous it would be time enough to encrease the Judges—   Mr. Grayson rose again and repeated his Opinion That numbers were necessary, to procure respectable decisions.   I reply'd, that in my Opinion the Way to secure respectable decisions, was to chuse Eminent Characters for Judges.   that numbers rather lessend responsibility &c. and unless they were all eminent, tended to obscure the decisions—   the Clause however was passed—   adjourned at the usual hour.

Wednesday, 24 June 1789

rode out early this morning but returned before 8, attended at the Usual time. The Bill for the Judiciary was taken up. the first debate that arose was whether there should be Circuit Courts or courts of Nisi Prius.[29] this distinction was started by Mr. Johnson from Connecticut was adopted and spoke long to, by Mr. Butler. This kept Us the most of the day. I did not give a Vote either way. indeed I do not like the bill. the Vote was for district Courts. We proceeded to the Clause about Quakers taking an affirmation. I moved an amendment, that all persons conscientiously scrupulous of taking an Oath, should take the affirmation great opposition to this, the Quakers abused by Izard. Mr. Mr. Morris and myself defended them. I read the Constitution by which the affirmation is left open to every one. and called this Whole Clause unconstitutional. the President himself may qualify by affirmation. the constitution does not narrow the Ground of Conscience. I was up and down often on this Business. But the Grand procession of the Free Masons[30] came by, with much noise of Musick &ca. a little after three. and the House adjourned— Had a very long Walk this afternoon with Mr. Contee and Mr. Seney of Maryland— they seem agreeable and accomodating Men. they are very willing to remove Congress from this place. they named Harrisburgh, I believe to try me, I said little in favour of it. But assured them That of 200 Acres which I had adjoining that Town they should have One, if they went there. My Memory certainly fails me of late I had this day some Conversation of importance with some Person, which I had determined to note down but it has escaped from my Memory. and I can Neither recollect Person place nor Subject, only that I had determined to minute it.

Thursday, 25 June 1789

Mr. Winkoop came to Town last night I went this Morning with him to Visit Mr. Patridge and Mr. Sedgwick Who had been polite enough to leave Cards at my lodging found their lodging with some difficulty, this Business over, attended at the Hall. First Business was to take up the impost Bill. concurred with the lower House about the Stile of the enacting Clause. But a Spirit of great Obstinacy manifested with regard to the 4th &

---

[29]*Nisi prius* here refers to the manner in which the English superior courts of common law heard and decided cases originating outside of London. The judges rode on circuit to preside singly at jury trials of factual issues. After the jury verdict, the judgment was rendered by the court as a whole at London.

[30]The Freemasons celebrated the feast of St. John the Baptist with a sermon at St. Paul's Church and a parade. (*NYJ*, 25 June 1789)

5th Clauses   Mr. Morris most pointedly against discrimination &ca. between nations in Treaty, & others.   Lee & Elsworth same.   the Tonnage Bill was read   the same difference occurr'd—   Managers of Conferrence chosen on both Bills, Mr. Morris⟨,⟩ Mr. Lee⟨,⟩ Mr. Elsworth.   read the Bill for the department of foreign affairs   laid on the Table.   and now took up the Judiciary. and the affair of the affirmations—   ran Elsworth so hard & the other Antiaffirmants, on the Anticonstitutionalism of the Clause. that they at last consented to have a Question taken Whether, the Clause should not be expunged—and expunged it was—   laboured in the Judiciary 'till 3 and adjourned.

Friday, 26 June 1789

attended the Hall at the usual time,   the Managers were met and the Conferrence begun.[31]   the Senate formed but the Managers were Absent.
at the Conferrence some were for proceeding and others were for waiting, the Members stragled to and from the Conferrence Chamber—   an adjournment was often spoken of, at last moved and carried—   Well may it be said That Men are but Children of a larger Growth. for on this Question being carried there was the same flutter of Joy among the Members. that I have seen among Children in a School on giving leave.   and away all hurried except a few that remained a little to see if the Conferrence would finish.   among these I was one Who Wished to know the result of the Conferrence.

Saturday, 27 June 1789

went a little before 10 to deliver a letter to Mr. Morris, in favour of Mr. Harris from a Mr. Ridley[32]—   Mr. M. read the letter and only remarked Mr. Harris's Friends are much in earnest.   I mentioned the Petition which I held in my hand from Mr. Harris[33]   the point I wished to bring Matters to, was for him to deliver it in—   he was guarded and threw out such Sentiments as shewed me he would not move in the Matter.   said the Petition had best be enclosed in a Cover and directed to the President.   I held it up, said it was directed

---

[31]The attempt to resolve House and Senate differences on the Impost [HR-2] and Tonnage [HR-5] acts was the first use of a conference committee and accordingly generated great interest in Congress.

[32]Matthew Ridley (1749–89), an English-born Baltimore merchant, who had served in Europe as an agent for his firm and for the state of Maryland during the War for Independence, had also written to his brother-in-law, John Jay, on behalf of Harris. (Matthew Ridley to John Jay, 22 April 1789, Ridley Papers, MHi; *PRM* 2:33n)

[33]Harris's undated petition for a federal job is in Series 7, GWP.

already. that Mr. Harris wished it might be put into the hands of Col.
Humphrey's. That I thought I had best follow his directions. I went with
my lame knees, the d first to Visit Col. Butler—Who had been thrown from a
Chair with Mr. Huger and was hurt. Mr. Morris went with me. he has never
asked me to his House save once & I shall not go much. from Visiting Mr.
Butler I went. to the President's, the day was now hot the Walk was long
I was lame, and the Streets were ripped up a great part of the Way, to be new
paved. all these things made the Journey one of Consequence. some Years
ago ten times as far would have been nothing. I saw Col. Humphreys inquired for the Presidents health, and delivered Mr. Harris's Petition. Hum-
phrys was cold. I cannot say what will come of it. but my hopes are not
high, I am an ill Courtier, the part I have taken in Senate, has marked me
as no Courtier, and I fear will mark poor Davy as a man not to be brought
forward— returned to the Hall and was very much fatagued.

The Senate met, and the Managers of the Conferrence reported, an Agreement of a number of Articles. But the Bills were not in the Senate. it seems
when the conference was agreed to, by the Senate. and notice of such Concurrence sent down to the H. of R. our wise Secretary sent down the Bills—along
with with the Communication— I was for insisting That in parliamentary
language the Bills, were still before, the Senate, they had been there when
the Conferrence was appointed— no Vote of the Senate had been passed to
send them down. the Conferrence was appointed only on the disagreement. there was a great deal said—the amount of which resolved itself into
this that a Mistake had been committed. Mr. Morris said if the Bills had been
fairly in his possession, he would have brought them back to the Senate. he
actually went to try to get them from the Managers on the part of the House of
Representatives there seemed to be a Jealousy between the Two Houses, who
should act first. as the one which acted last would reject the Bill, or at least have
the blame of rejection, if the Bill was lost. Gentlemen could not reconcile
themselves to act without the Bills. (for there were two of them, one on impost
and the other the Tonnage Act) some moved to act on the report of the
Managers— after however much desultory conversation it was agreed to take
up the Bill for the Judiciary. we Were proceeding on this When a Message was
anounced— Sundry communications were brought by the Clerk. and the
Amendments of the Senate were all adopted on the impost Bill, save on the
Articles of Porter and Coal— such was the Haste of the President, that he put
One Question on both these Articles at Once, and both agreed to, but the
Tonnage Bill was retained, and the Principle of discrimination between Na-
tions in Treaty and those not, was still adhered to by the H. of R. on this Bill—

made some further progress in the Judiciary and adjourned about 2
O'Clock.

Sunday, 28 June 1789

Spent this day except a small ride in the Morning, at home. and wrote to my dear family. how can I answer it to myself, That I stay so long from them. how happy will my return make all their little hearts, and Yet I stay here wrangling vile politicks, in a Contentious Senate, where there is no harmony of Soul. no wish to communicate a happy Sensation. where all is Snip Snap, and Contradiction Short. Where it is a Source of Joy, to place the Speech of of a fellow Senator, in a distorted or ridiculous point of View. Where you may Search the Whole Union, and cannot say, That you can find the Man of your Heart. But away with them, and let me think of my dear Family. sent a set of letters by Dr. Ruston[34] for my Family.

Monday, 29 June 1789

attended at the Hall early sent my letters to the post Office. and now for the Judiciary. I made a remark where Elsworth in his diction had varied from the Constitution. this Vile Bill is a child of his, and he defends it with the Care of a parent. even with wrath and anger. he kindled as he always does When it was medled with, Lee however after some time joined me, altho' the President shewed himself against Us. We carried the amendment; We got on to the clause Where, *a Defendant, was required on Oath to disclose his or her knowledge on Oath in the Cause &ca.* I rose and declar'd that I wished not to take up the time of the Committee, as perhaps few would think with me (this I said in allusion to what had happened in the Committee, where I had exerted myself in Vain against this Clause) But that I could not pass, in Silence, a Clause which carried such inquisitorial powers with it, and which was so contrary to the Sentiments of my Constituents. That extorting evidence from any Person was a species of Torture and inconsistent with the Spirit of freedom. put [*but*] perhaps I should say something more pointed. When the Matter came before the House in Senate.[35] (my reason, of acting thus was, I had spoke to Mr. Morris, and found he would not second me in it, as

---

[34]Thomas Ruston (c. 1740–1804), an independently wealthy Philadelphian, was born in Chester County. He graduated from the College of New Jersey in 1762 and received his medical degree from the University of Edinburgh in 1765. He remained in England throughout the War for Independence as an open supporter of the American cause, but returned to Philadelphia in 1785 with the wealthy English heiress he had married. Ruston did not practice medicine but instead devoted himself to personal business and a variety of intellectual pursuits. His unpublished thoughts on American finance, written while he was in England, brought him to the attention of Robert Morris. (*Princetonians, 1748–68*, pp. 402–7)

[35]The Senate was considering the Judiciary Act [S-1] as a committee of the whole at this time, and thus WM meant that he might say more in debate in the full Senate.

Miers Fisher had not, taken notice of this Matter in his letter). Patterson however of the Jerseys sprung up   declared, he disliked the Clause and having spoke a While moved to Strike it out.   I then rose and declared since One Man was found in the Senate for Striking it out I would second him.   Up now rose Elsworth, and in a most elaborate harrangue supported the Clause.   now in Chancery now in common law and now common law again with a Chancery side—   ~~Patt~~ he brought forward Judge Blackstone, and read much out of him.   Patterson rose in reply, and followed him thro' these ~~thort~~ thorny paths, as I thought with good Success.   he shewed Justly enough, that Blackstone cut both ways & nothing could be inferred from him, but his ridiculing the diversity of practice between Chancery Practice and that at common law. Elsworth heard him with apparent composure; he rose with an Air of Triumph, on Patterson's sitting down.   Now said he, everything is said that can possibly be said to support this Motion   the very most is made of it that ingenuity can perform.   and he entered again the Thorny thicket of law forms. and seemed to batter down all his Antagonist had said, by referring all that was advanced to the forms of law, with which every thing had been Shackled under the British Government,   he really displayed ingenuity in his defense,   he made repeated Use of of the Term shackled, and how we were now free and he hoped, how we would continue so.   I determind to have a Word or Two at the Subject.   Said I was happy to hear that the World was unshackled from the Customs of Antient Tyrany,   that there was a time, When Evidence in criminal Cases was extorted from the Carcass of the Wretched Culprit, by Torture happily we were unshackled from this, but here was an attempt to exercise a Tyranny of the same kind over the Mind,   the Conscience was to be put on the ~~Wrack~~ rack,   that forcing Oaths or Evidence from Men I considered, as equally tyrannical as, extorting evidence by Torture, and the consequence, had only the difference between excusable lies and Wilful perjury.   That I hoped never to see shackles of this kind imposed.   That Chancery had been quoted common law had been quoted as practised in England, but neither would apply to the present, Case,   the party was to answer in Chancery, but it was to the Judge. and his questions were in Writing—   but here by the Clause he must be examined in open Court, before the Bench and Jury, and cross examined and tortured by all the address and Malice of the Bar.   I had further to add that by the Bill of rights of the State that I had the honor to represent, no *Person could be compelled to give Evidence against himself.*   That I knew this Clause would give offence. to my Constituents.   Elsworth rose and admitted that three new points had been started.   he aimed a reply but I thought he missed the Mark in every one.   the rage of speaking now seemed. to catch the House   Basset was up   Read   Strong.   and at it we sat till half after 3—and ~~th~~ an adjournment was called before the Question was put—

Elsworth moved an amendment, That the Plaintiff too should Swear, at the request of the Defendant, Just before the House adjourned.

Tuesday, 30 June 1789

I am still miserably lamed with the rheumatism   attended at the Hall at the Usual, time.   The Clause with Elsworth's amendment, was taken up.[36]   I rose first, said that instead of the Clause being amended I thought it, much worse.   That it was alledged with justice against the Clause as it stood before, that great Opportunities and Temptations to perjury were held out, but this was setting the door fairly open,   The Contest now would be who could swear most home to the point.   That if I was against it before I was much more so now.   Mr. Lee rose and seemed to misstate the the Matter,   I rose and endeavoured to do the business Justice—   Up rose Elsworth and threw the common law back alltthe way to the Wager of Law which he asserted was still in force.   Strong rose and took the other side.   in a long harrangue, he went back to the Antient B Tryal by Battle which he said was yet unrepealed—but said repeatedly there was no such Case as the present.   Elsworth's Temper forsook him   he contradicted Strong with rudeness, said what the Gentleman asserted was not fact, that defendants were admitted as Witnesses, That all Might be Witnesses against themselves   got Blackstone, But nothing could be inferred from Blackstone, but such a thing by Consent.   Patterson got up and back he went to the feudal System.   He pointedly deny'd Elsworths positions,   Basset rose   Read rose and we had to listen to them all.   the Questions were however put first on Elsworth's Amendment, and ~~next on S~~ was lost.   next on striking out—and it was carried—   The Tonnage Bill was taken,   we concurr'd in one Clause but adhered in the rest.   and now back to the Judiciary   Mr. Lee moved, that the postponed Clause about the Ambassadors Consuls &ca. should be taken up,   it was so,   I saw Mr. Adams begin to fidget with a kind of eagerness or restlessness, as if a nettle had been in his Breeches.   he could not restrain himself long, and up he got to tell Us all about Ambassadors other Ministers and Consuls, and what he did with his Majesty here and his Majesty there, and how he got an answer in this Case and how he never got an answer in that.   and how he had with Mr. Jefferson appointed Mr. Barclay[37] to the Emperor of Morocco & how the Parliament of

---

[36]Section 15 of the Judiciary Act [S-1] was under debate.

[37]Thomas Barclay (1728–93) was a Philadelphia merchant who performed a variety of diplomatic services for the United States between 1781 and 1787. In 1785 Jefferson and Adams named him as their agent for carrying out the commission of Congress to negotiate a treaty of amity and commerce with the emperor of Morocco. He returned to Philadelphia in 1787 and attempted unsuccessfully to obtain a federal appointment during the FFC. (*PTJ* 11:493n; *PJM* 4:291n)

Bourdeaux mistook the Matter & dismissed Mr. Barclay from an arrest, &ca. &ca.   I could not help admiring the happiness of the Man.   When he had occasion to refer to something said by Elsworth, he called him the *right* Honorable Gentleman.

July 1789

Wednesday, 1 July 1789

very lame particularly in my right Knee. attended at the Hall, at the usual time— the Clause was taken up of the Judiciary, "That Suits in equity shall not be sustained in either of the Courts of the united States in any Case Where a remedy may be had at law," Doctr. Johnson rose first against the Clause, Elsworth answered him and the following Gentlemen all in Turn, Lee⟨,⟩ Read⟨,⟩ Basset ~~and~~ Patterson & Grayson, Strong spoke in favour of the Clause. the Lawyers were in a rage for speaking— many things were said in favour of Chancery, that I knew to be wrong. never was there a field more beaten, from the first Chancellor down, the Lawyers seemed all prepared— to Show their intensive reading. It was near three and I determined to say something, a Case was often put of a Man covenanting to convey land and dying, before performance, that there was no relief without Chancery I however rose, said much information had been been given, on this important Subject, but I wished for a great deal more, for instance I desired to know the Number of Attorneys and persons employed in the Law department in England, and the ~~Sum~~ millions (for it was said to amount to several) annually extorted, by the law departments from that nation, particularly Whether the Sum so extracted did not exceed the agregate of the Sums in dispute before the Courts, Whether any nation in the World ~~could~~ besides the English could pay their Taxes and Support such an expensive Judiciary, that these points being settled, would afford matter of important advice to Us, Whether it was prudent to imitate the famous English Jurisprudence in all its parts. That the advantages of Chancery were to my certain Knowledge overrated, that the famous Case of the Bond of performance, gave little Trouble in Pennsylvania—that the Person having paid his bond brought his Suit, and the parties generally consented to a Judgt. and sale of the Lands and the Sheriff made Title— That I thought the Clause a good one, and wished for it to be more effectual to prevent the flowing of Causes into that tedious Court. up rose George Read in Angry Mood said he had a Cause of the kind in Pennsylvania that he had consulted the ablest Men there and received for answer there was no remedy in Pennsylvania. and asserted that the People of Pennsylvania wished for a Chancery, and many of them lamented the want of it.   I got up, declared as far as I knew the Sentiments of the People of Pennsylvania they disliked a Chancery, but that Many of them knew not even the name,   I never had heard any People speak ~~of~~ in favour of it but some Gentlemen of the Bar, and even among them some doubted Whether it would do most harm or good,   that in general it was considered by those who knew anything of the Matter as the Field even the Gentlemen of the Bar would reap the fullest harvest, and it was considered that they enjoyed a plentiful crop as Matters now stood,   I stated the affair of the Bond over again, so plainly that Read called out, in Case of Consent I grant it,   I had only to add in Case they do not consent, 12 honest Jurors are good Chancellors, if not to give the land at least to give the Value of *it*.   the Clause stood on the Question.   The Gentlemen of the Bar in the House, seemed to have made a common cause of it, to push the powers of Chancery as far as possible,   Mr. Morris seemed almost disposed to join them   as we rose he said, if I had spoke, I believe I should have differed with You about Chancery.   ~~Mmdd.~~ I know not what put it there, but it was in my head in a Moment that he has 2 Sons[1] Studying the law.   This day the discrimination, between the Ships of nations in Treaty and those not, on the Tonnage Bill, was rejected in in the House of Representatives also, and of Course the Tonnage Bill now passes.   When this doctrine was first broached in in the House of R. of no discrimination it was called toryism, and there were but 8 Votes for it on a division.   but Mark the influence of the City of New York or let me call it British influence   to Work they set in the Senate. and before the impost Bill got up, they had secured a Majority to reject the discrimination—   But some Pretext was necessary, even in the Senate,   the discriminations in the impost and Tonnage Bills were said to be arrant Triffles.   no Compensation for the injuries our Trade received,   that a deeper mode of Retaliation should be entered on such as would effectually cure all disadvantages, & carry the remedy to every particular disease, and retaliate on every Nation exactly in kind.   and Where a disadvantage was imposed, a corresponding one should be imposed by Us, and not Chastise all Nations out of Treaty with the same punishment.   as to gratitude or national Friendship, they were held not to exist. and all that was to be done with nations in Treaty, was to observe the Terms of those Treaties.   a Committee therefore of Mr. Morris⟨,⟩ Mr. Langdon[2] were appointed to examine the State of our commerce, and to bring in a Bill, for the protection of our Commerce, but the ~~lm~~ discriminations, are now Struck out of both bills and I do not expect to hear any thing more about the protecting of our Commerce, unless it should be taken up in the House of Representatives.

Maddison too, is charged with having laboured the Whole Business of

---

[1]Robert Morris, Jr. (1769–1804), and Thomas Morris (1771–1849) were Senator Morris's oldest sons. (*Philadelphia Families* 1:741)

[2]The other members of the committee appointed on 17 June were Butler, Dalton, and Lee. The committee reported on 13 July.

discrimination, in Order to pay Court, to the French Nation thro Mr. Jefferson our Minister at Paris— I feel much readier to believe him Guilty of another Charge. Viz. his Urging the Doctrine of taking away the right of removals of Officers from the Senate. in Order to pay his Court, to the President, whom I am told he already affects to Govern— Time will however throw light on both these Subjects— {It has done so in a rema⟨rka⟩ble. Manner in one of them Vid. diay. of 14th Feby. 1791.}

Thursday, 2 July 1789

went this day to the Hall at the usual time   The bill was taken up for the Judiciary,   I really dislike the Whole of this bill, but ~~of it~~ I endeavoured to mend it in several places; and make it as perfect as possible, if it is to be the law of the Land—   But it was fabricated by a knot of Lawyers who Join hue and cry to run down any Person, who will venture to say one Word about it.   This I have repeatedly experienced, and when I am certain (for a Man may sometimes be certain of his being right) of having moved obvious & proper amendments, I have been pushed at from both right and left by them, and not a Man to second me.   be it so however this is no reason that I should be silent.   I ran Elsworth hard on the Uselessness of part of this Bill today, and thought I had the advantage in some of the Answer⟨s⟩ I gave.   But it was of little avail. Grayson tho' a Lawyer told me Yesterday, That it was in Vain to attempt anything,   the People who were not Lawyers, on a Supposition that Lawyers knew best, would follow the Lawyers, and a party were determined to push it.   I needed no information from him on this head.   we however came to a clause   the import was that on bonds, Articles of Agreement Convenants &ca. The Jury should find the Breech. and the Judges assess the damages.   I attacked this Mixed, half common law half Chancery proceeding   accused the Bill of inconsistency   that A Clause had already been adopted, which excluded Chancery Where common law would afford a remedy.   here we had a Jury & common law, acting with the Cause and we flew from it to Chancery Powers.   this was inconsistency.   The Jury were the proper Chancellors in such a Case to assess the damages, & I liked them much better than the Judges,   they were from the Vicinity and best Acq⟨u⟩ainted with the parties and their Circumstances,   When the Judgt. was by default or ~~conf~~ entered up a Jury of inquiry of damages, should ascertain the Sum.   Strong made a long Speech how this could not be done on the Principles of Common Law and Chancery Principles, & seemed willing to show his Accurate reading on these points.   and concluded by saying either he or the Gentleman last up did not understand the Principles of those Courts for the Gentleman was for doing what could not he thought be done.   I rose quick to reply.   said the Clause

John Adams. Oil painting by John Singleton Copley, 1783.
(Courtesy of The Harvard University Collection, Bequest—Ward Nicholas Boyleston, 1828.)

was before Us   the Clause was in our power,   what I wanted done was clearly expressed,   I hoped we were not always to be tramelled with the fetters of English Jurisprudence.   That we would shew we had Judgt. and would act for ourselves, independent of any forms.   and concluded with a question Whether we were always to be considered as empty bottles That could contain nothing But what was poured into them?   several Gentlemen now rose and agreed, with me in objecting to the Clause, but there seemed some difficulty in amending. & it was postponed, for amendment.

Friday, 3 July 1789

This was warm quite as much so I thought as any day I remember in Pennsylvania,   attended at the Hall and business went on at the usual time,   it was the Judiciary which we were upon.   light and very Triffling debates in general   Mr. Read got up & kept *hammering* for a long time (as Mr. Morris termed it,) and really it was difficult to say what he would be at.   I did not embark in any debate, untill we came to the Clause impowering the Judges, either on their own knowledge, or complaint of others, to apprehend bail commit &ca.   I alledged, the Judges would be men of like passions and resentments as other Men, that they should not be both Witnesses and Judges accusers and all   that the complaint also should be on Oath,   I moved therefore to strike out those Words and insert "upon Oath or affirmation made and reduced to writing & signed by the party stating sufficient reason in Law."
Lee of Virginia seconded me this time, But according to custom I had Elswo⟨r⟩th and the Gentlemen of the bar up against it,   It was insisted that this was agreeable to the laws of England, that the Oath of the Judge would bind him to all this.   That a Judge had a right to Use his private Judgt. just as a Juryman had a right to act on his private knowledge.   Elsworth⟨,⟩ Strong⟨,⟩ Basset⟨,⟩ Grayson and others all up. and Volumes did they pour out.   I could not get speaking for a long time,   I however made. a Short reply.   said We were now framing the law which would be the rule of Conduct for the Judges.   That practice such as the Gentlemen insisted on, had been Used by Judges, and from Experience we had learned the danger of it,   cases were known ~~where~~ where the resentment of a Judge was the Accusing Spirit and Prejudice pronounced Judgt.   every part of English Jurisprudence was not unexceptionable. nor would I blindly follow them in every thing.   That the Case adduced of a Juryman using private Knowledge would not apply   a Juryman, legally speaking had no private Knowledge, or at least none that he ought to keep private,   if he knew anything pertinent to the issue he ought to disclose it upon Oath to his fellows, in Court, and this was the Law, and daily practice upon it.   if A Judge happened to be the only person having knowl-

edge of the Commission of a Crime, let him apply to some other Justice   this I had known done.   the Case of a forcable entry did not apply, ~~this~~ to common practice.   and Yet in this Case the Justices would generally bind over Witnesses to prosecute   I hinted at some other parts of the Clause as imperfect & said much more before I sat down, particularly as to the dangerous ground on which we trod considering the interference ~~of~~ or the very propable interference of the Federal and State Legislatures.   and the giving more power over the liberty of the Citizen to the former than ~~the later would~~, was usually practised by the later, would not fail to sow the seeds of dissention.   ~~it~~ I had shewed this Clause to Mr. Morris before I ~~spoke~~ moved for the alteration.   he approved of it.   but he went out and staid away untill all was over.   he asked when He came in. if his presence would have altered the Vote,   I told him ~~No, we had los~~ I supposed not   we had lost it.   I know nothing of the reason of his absence.   Charity and good humor will say, it was accidental.   He has been, at least I thought so, rather distant with me,   he has shewed me none of the communications which he has received respecting the Judiciary   This has not been my conduct with regard to him.   and I know he has shewed our Atty. Genls.[3] remarks to Lee⟨,⟩ Carrol and Elsworth.   I likewise know he has, rema⟨r⟩ks from Judge Hopkinson[4]—   nothing shall be wanting on my part to act in Harmony with him   I wispered him at a leisure time, We should have a Meeting, and compare all the remarks we have received and make up our Minds as to the amendments which we will move.   I paused   he did not reply,   continued, I am quite disengaged. I will call on you at any time— When it is convenient.   Reply'd, it must be here, I have all the papers here, agreed, I will meet you at any time.   nothing more—   Settled with my landlord   he owes me £1:15:8   {Mr. Morris had a Set of Remarks from Wilson and a Set drawn up by Chew⟨,⟩ Rawle & Wallace which I never saw.}[5]

---

[3] William Bradford, Jr. (1755–95), attorney general of Pennsylvania since 1780, graduated from the College of New Jersey in 1772. He served in the army from 1776 to 1779 and then completed his legal training. Bradford, a lifelong resident of Philadelphia, married Representative Boudinot's daughter, Susan. (*Princetonians, 1769–1775*, pp. 185–91)

[4] Francis Hopkinson (1737–91), judge of the admiralty for Pennsylvania since 1779, was a publicist as well as a musician, poet, and essayist. Born in Philadelphia, he graduated from the College of Philadelphia in 1757 and became a member of the bar in 1761. He represented New Jersey in the Continental Congress in 1776, signed the Declaration of Independence, and was chairman of the navy board and treasurer of loans between 1776 and 1781. A Federalist, he served in the Pennsylvania Ratification Convention and in 1788 directed the spectacular grand Federal parade in Philadelphia. Washington appointed him judge of the United States District Court for Eastern Pennsylvania in 1789. See also *SEJ*, p. 534.

[5] James Wilson (1742–98) was appointed associate justice of the Supreme Court in 1789, having been unsuccessful in securing the position of chief justice. Raised and educated in Scotland and admitted to the Pennsylvania bar in 1767, he established a successful practice in Carlisle before settling at Philadelphia in 1778. Wilson signed the Declaration of Independence, and in the 1780s he returned to Congress to advocate a strong central government. He was an influential Federalist at the Federal Convention and the Pennsylvania Ratification Convention. Many members of the FFC attended his lectures on law and government at the University of Pennsylvania during the third session. See also *SEJ*, p. 537.

Saturday, 4 July 1789

this the Anniversary of American Independance   the day was el celebrated
with much pomp[6]—   the Cincinati assembled at St. Pauls Church, where an
Oration was pronounced by Col. Hamilton in Honor of General Green.[7]   the
Church was crouded   the Cincinnati had seats allotted for themselves wore
their Eagle at their Button Holes—and were preceeded by a flag.   The oration
was well delivered, the Composition appeared good, But I thought he should
have given Us some acct. of his Virtues as a Citizen as well as a Warrior.   for I
suppose he possessed them, and he lived sometime after the War. and I believe

Benjamin Chew (1722–1810), prominent jurist and member of the Philadelphia Common
Council during the FFC, was born in Maryland. He received his legal training in Philadelphia and London. Admitted to the Pennsylvania bar in 1746, he held a variety of appointive
offices in Delaware and Pennsylvania prior to the War for Independence, including attorney
general of Pennsylvania, 1755–69, and member of the Pennsylvania Council, 1755–75.
Unwilling to give active support to the Revolution, Chew lost his public offices. (*Counter
Revolution*, p. 221)

William Rawle (1759–1836), a native Philadelphian and one of its assemblymen, 1789–90,
was a loyalist who pursued his legal studies in British-occupied New York City during the
War for Independence and in London. After the war he returned to Philadelphia, where he
was admitted to the bar in 1783.

Joshua M. Wallace (1752–1819), judge of the Burlington County, New Jersey, Court of
Common Pleas since 1784, was a Federalist delegate to the New Jersey Ratification Convention. Born at Philadelphia, he graduated from the College of Philadelphia in 1767 and
settled at Burlington in 1784. Wallace was the brother-in-law of Pennsylvania attorney
general William Bradford, Jr., and an intimate of many Philadelphians. (Robert B. Beath,
Historical Catalogue of the St. Andrew's Society of Philadelphia, 2 vols. [n.p., 1907–13],
2:166–67; Evan M. Woodward and John F. Hageman, *History of Burlington and Mercer
Counties* . . . [Philadelphia, 1883], pp. 67, 128)

[6]The day's ceremonies included a military parade from the Battery along Broad Way. The
New York chapter of the Society of the Cincinnati met at City Tavern in the morning and
appointed a committee to deliver congratulations of the day to the president, the vice
president, and the speaker of the House. The committee failed to locate the speaker. (*GUS*, 8
July 1789)

[7]Alexander Hamilton (1757–1804), secretary of the treasury, 1789–95, and son-in-law of
Senator Schuyler, left his birthplace, the Island of Nevis in the Caribbean, in 1772. He made
his way to Elizabethtown, New Jersey, where he was befriended by Elias Boudinot. In 1773 he
moved to New York City and came to prominence as a patriot pamphleteer while still a
student at King's College. From 1777 to 1781 he served as Washington's aide-de-camp with
the rank of colonel. An articulate spokesman for a strong central government, Hamilton
supported that cause in the Confederation Congress in 1782–83, the Annapolis Convention,
the Federal Convention, and the New York Ratification Convention as well as in the *Federalist* essays. WM opposed Hamilton's political and economic program during the FFC and
believed him to be the force behind those congressmen who wished to use the United States
Constitution to strengthen the federal government at the expense of the states. See also *SEJ*,
p. 523. (*PAH* 1:44)

Nathanael Greene (1742–86) of Rhode Island achieved fame as a major general com-
manding the Continental Army in the South at the end of the War for Independence. His
widow, Catherine, petitioned the FFC to honor his claims against the United States.
Hamilton's description of the militia as "the mimicry of soldiership" in his eulogy to
Greene caused Representative Burke to attack him during a House debate on 31 March 1790.
A duel between the two men was barely averted. (*PAH* 6:333–58)

commenced farmer— except my attendance at St. Pauls, I kept House all day as I find going out only hurts my Knees both of which are still affected by the Rheumatism.

Sunday, 5 July 1789

was a rainy day staid at home all day my thoughts chiefly employd about my family, how much of the Sweats of life do I loose in being seperated from them. after however having staid so long, I had better give my Attendance a Week or Two longer.

Monday, 6 July 1789

came early to the Hall, in Order to send my letters to the Post Office. Doctor Johnson, and some other Members came in familiar Chat to the time of the Meeting of the Senate. the Judiciary was taken up, and the Residue of it passed without any interesting debate— Our President called for the Sense of the House When it should be read a third time the Members shewed plainly, that they considered, it as not having been touched, *in Senate* on second reading all that had passed having only been in Committee The President, insisted that the Bill had been Twice read, so it certainly had, but the 2d reading was in a Committee of the Whole Senate, he said former bills had been treated just as he wanted this one Treated— We knew, or at least I knew, that this was not, the Case. he shewed a peevish Obstinacy, as I thought, he does not like the doctrine of a Committee of the Senate, nor has he ever submitted to it—for he ought to leave the Chair—

Tomorrow however was assigned for a third reading, with a kind of saving priviledge to make amendments— Mr. Morris came in, a little before we broke up he put into my hands the letter & remarks of our Chief Justice[8] on the Judiciary, directed to Us Jointly. But the Atty. General's remarks and Judge Hopkinson's I have not Yet had the opportunity of perusing—
Thursday assigned for the Bill for foreign affairs
Friday for the department of War.
and Monday next for the Treasury Department—

Tuesday, 7 July 1789

attended the Hall at the usual time the Judiciary was taken up for a third reading. I can scarce account for my dislike to this Bill. but I really fear it

---

[8]Thomas McKean.

will be the Gunpowder plot[9] of the Constitution, so confused, and so obscure it will not fail to give a general Alarm.   Elsworth has lead this business backed with Strong⟨,⟩ Patterson⟨,⟩ Reed often, Basset seldom.   We came to the Clause which allowed, the district Judges to sit on the hearing of appeals from themselves,   I did not rise to oppose this,   Grayson however got hold of it. and hammered hard at it,   Basset rose & took partly the same side,   now I thought the Matter in an hopeful Way.   Elsworth immediately drew an amendment, as he said to cure their Objections tho it was nothing like the Matter.   I drew a Clause nearly in these Words—   Provided that no district Judge shall Sit on the rehearing of any Cause formerly adjudged by him.   We got Elswo⟨r⟩th⟨'s⟩ Motion postponed to put a Question on it.   It was agreed that the Sense of the House should be taken on this,   We carried it.   and I rose and said since the Sense of the House was declared on this Subject, I wished some of the Gentlemen of the Bar to frame a Clause in the Spirit of the determination.   That the Effect of the determination would reach farther than the present Clause, for it would prevent, the Circuit Judge, from sit-⟨t⟩ing in the Supreme Court on an appeal When he had given original Judgt.   this was agreed to, and so we killed Two birds with One Stone.   the most Triffling Word catching employd Us untill after 3 O'Clock.   I cannot help observing under this days head. that Mr. Phile the late Naval officer of Philada.[10] brought this Morning most ample Extracts of the Trade of that port for the last Year.   he said these were Copies sent him for his own Use. but that at an early period he made out a set and delivered them to the President of the State to be forwarded to Congress, and he said they were actually forwarded; I could only say I never saw them, altho' I used all diligence to possess myself of every paper that could give me the smallest information.   received letters this day from Harrisburgh and from Baltimore,   all Well.

Wednesday, 8 July 1789

attended as usual this day at the Hall,   The Judiciary was taken up, Elsworth by far more accomodating this day, than I ever knew him,   We sat the Usual time, but the debates were very triffling indeed. and not one worth committing to paper.   The Chief Justice of Pennsylvania⟨,⟩[11] Mr. Wilson⟨,⟩

[9]The gunpowder plot was the foiled project of a group of English Roman Catholics, led by Guy Fawkes, who planned to blow up Parliament when James I came for opening ceremonies on 5 November 1605.
[10]Frederick Phile (d. 1793), naval officer of the port of Philadelphia since 1777, maintained the position when it became a federal appointment in 1789. He had been deputy naval officer from about 1755. Phile was a doctor but ceased practice about the time he became naval officer. See also *SEJ*, p. 536. (Phile to John Henry, 23 March 1789, Madison Papers, DLC)
[11]Thomas McKean.

Miers Fisher, the Speaker Mr. Peters, Tench Cox, and Sundry others, have in their letters approved of the General Outlines of the Bill,   any amendments which they have offered have been of a lesser nature.   I own The approbation of so many Men of Character for abilities has lessened my dislike of it, Yet I cannot think of the Expence attending it, which I now consider as Useless, without a kind of sickly Qualm overshadowing me.   Bradford's and Judge Hopkinsons remarks I have not Yet seen.   nor need I now care about them, as we will probably finish it tomorrow;   would that I had finished business so far as to be able to return home tomorrow.   I find however I must stay Yet a little longer.   this is painful but all things considered I cannot help it.

Warm Plaster

for obstinate fixed rheumatic pains—made by melting over a Gentle fire an Ounce of Gum Plaster, and Two drams of blistering Plaster—spread on soft leather and applied to the part affected   taken off and wiped once in three or four days & wiped—and renewed once a fortnight.

Thursday, 9 July 1789

Still much afflicted with the Rheumatism   attended this day the usual time at the Hall,   a great part of this day was taken up with light debates chiefly conducted by the lawyers on both sides, and the Object seemed to be the encreasing the powers of Chancery,   Mr. Read a Man of Obstructed Elocution was excessively tedious.   Elsworth has Credit with me,   I know not however whether it be the Effect of Judgt. Whim or Caprice, but he is generally for limiting the Chancery powers.   Mr. Morris and myself differed in every Vote this day.   We always have differed on the Subject of Chancery.   This day I got Copies of the 3 Bills for the great departments.[12]   Besides being calculated on a Scale of great Expence. Two Grand Objections offer themselves on these bills—the lessining the power of the Senate, taking away from them any Vote in the removal of Officers, and the power of advising and consenting, in one Case of the first Consequence.   and the other the placing the President above business and beyond the power of responsibility—placing putting into the hands of his officers the duties required of him by the Constitution,   Indeed these appear to me to have been the moving Reasons for bringing forward the bill at all.   nor do I see the necessity of having made this business a Subject of legislation.   the point of View in which it presented itself to me was. That the President should signify to the Senate. his desire of appointing a Minister of foreign affairs, and nominate the Man   and so of the other necessary departments.   if the Senate agreed to the necessity of the office and the Man they would concur,   if not, they would negative. &ca.   the House would get the

---

[12]The War Department Act [HR-7], the Foreign Affairs Act [HR-8], and the Treasury Act [HR-9].

Business before them when Salaries came to be appointed, and could then, give their Opinion by providing for the officer or not.   I see this mode might be abused.   But for the House of Representatives, by a side Wind, to exalt the President above the Constitution and depress the Senate below it, is.   but I will leave it without a name.   they know the Veneration entertained for General Washington. and believe the People will be ready to Join, in the Cry against the Senate. in his favour, when they endeavour to make him a party. they think they have fast hold of Us. and that we dare not, refuse our Assent to these bills, & so several of them have not failed to declare.

Friday, 10 July 1789

this day the Lawyers shewed plainly the Cloven foot of their Intentions in the House.   Read⟨,⟩ Basset⟨,⟩ Patterson⟨,⟩ Johnson⟨,⟩ Grayson and other had got a Hasty kind of amendment passed late Yesterday; the Amount of it Was that in the Circuit ~~Courts~~ Courts, under the name of equity they should have all the depositions copied, and sent up on an Appeal as Evidence to the Supreme Court. on the rehearsing of facts or Words to that import,   I had some Conversation with Elsworth. in the Morning about it, and offered to him to move for a reconsideration of the Matter   he wished to reserve this ~~Matter~~ Business for himself however; he accordingly moved the reconsideration, in a lengthy Speech And was seconded by Strong,   at it now they Went, and untill after three Scarce a Word could be got in edgewise for the Lawyers.   Butler tho' lame bounced up Twice.   I wished to speak but could not get leave   the President got up in the Chair.   I rose and told him I wished to say a Word or Two.   Sir I am no professed admirer of the Judicial System before You, but the best part of it is the Circuit Courts,   these sir the amendment ~~before Y~~ of Yesterday will render abortive   the seeds of appeal and the Materials too, are provided for every cause,   the System of delay is so firmly established, and the certainty of procrastination such, that Justice never can be obtained in it—   let Us follow the Scheme a moment.   The depositions are taken and carried up Six or seven hundred miles to a federal Court,   But by the law they cannot be used, if the party is able to attend.   the Witness is subpoena'd but does not attend,   an Attachment issues—   but the party will kill the Messenger run to the Woods, fly to the Indians rather than attend,   Well but the Court, can issue a dedimus potestatem[13] and Commissioners may be appointed. and in three or four Years the Testimony may be collected.   Well and What now,   is the fact to be tryed by Chancery Powers.   I am bold to say no Issue of fact ever was tryed or found for or against in Chancery.   facts often were carried into Chancery, as evidence but if they were doubted of, issue was

---

[13]This writ empowered the named persons to perform certain acts such as administering oaths or taking testimony.

joined on them, and directed to be tryed by a Jury.   But now the ~~fact~~ Business unfolds itself,   now we see what Gentlemen would be at,   it is to try Facts on civil law principles, without the aid of a Jury, and this I promise You never will be submitted to.   The question was put and we carried it.   But the House seemed rather to break up in a Storm.[14]

Saturday, 11 July 1789

should go to the nearest Stack of Wheat Rye Straw Hay or such like Material, and draw out Two stems.   One in the name of each party, and the longest should win the Cause.   he shewed it to me   I gave him an hearty laugh of approbation.   not indeed that I admired either the Wit or Novelty of it. but I considered it as the index of a Sure Vote.   But I was mistaken   He voted against Us and the Clause was lost.

I could see an Air of Triumph, in the visages of Gentlemen of the Bar, Elsworth excepted.   who has really credit with me, on the Whole of this Business,   the part he has acted in it, I consider as candid {(bating his caballing with Johnson)} and disinterested   Mr. Lee of Virginia, was for the Clause and spoke well.

As we came down the Stairs Docr. Johnson was by my side.   Doctor (said I) I wish you would leave off, using these side Winds, and boldly at once bring in a Clause for deciding all Causes on civil law principles without the aid of a Jury.   No No said he the Civil law is a name I am not very fond of.   I reply'd, you need not care about the name, since you have got the thing.

Sunday, 12 July 1789

I was ill last night,   my swelld knee gave me great pain and prevented my rest,   put on Flannels and staid at home all day,   had no book but Buchan's family Physician[15]   read a good deal in it,   What a Lazar House[16] the World is—   Surely the pleasures of life, are as chaff in the Ballance against ponderous Lead, compared with the ills ~~of~~ and dolors of the human race.   infinite Wisdom surely shows Us but a small part of her Works.   There must be a Ballance some Where.   or shall we View it in an other light, that the only good we enjoy is the Effect of prudence,   Alas! she does not always command

---

[14]One page, of which only a sliver containing isolated words remains, has been lost from the manuscript at this point. It was already missing in 1880 when George W. Harris published his edition of the journal.

[15]William Buchan, *Buchan's Family Physician* (Philadelphia, 1787).

[16]A Lazar House was a home for destitute people with contagious diseases.

it. It is in Vain however to attempt to rend the impenetrable Vail that conceals, the mysterious Ways of Providence.

my dear family I wish I were with you.

Monday, 13 July 1789

I forgot to minute Yesterday, that late in the afternoon Charles Thomson visited me. We had much chat of the political kind, he shewed a great disposition to go into the Field of the President's power; he was clearly of Opinion that the President ought to remove all Officers. &ca. indeed he said so much on this Subject that I had like to have entertained a Suspicion That he came on purpose to sound or rather prepare me, on the Subject, I agreed to Sundry of his Observations at the same time dissented in plain but not pointed terms from some other things. perhaps this is the best way on the Whole for an independant Man to Act. Honesty on the Whole is the best policy. I really feel for Mr. Thomson's situation. a Man who has been the graphic faculty of the old Congress the hand & Pen of that Body from their first organization, and who, I feel a kind of certainty of the fact, wished to die in an eminent office. would not suffer his Friends to continue him Secretary of the Senate, and his Enemies have taken advantage of it, and declared him out of Office, and mean to keep him so. It was certainly bad policy of him to refuse the offers of his Friends. the political door is harder to be opened than any other, if once it is thrown in One's a Man's face.

The Senate met, and Mr. Bassets Motion with respect, to the Effect of a Writ of Error, as a Supersedeas to an execution. was taken up. Mr. Reed speak spoke long, in support of the Motion. Mr. Elsworth equally long against it. I rose and made sundry remarks. and the amendment was carried, It was not a Material one however in the Bill. While the Minutes were reading, I Stepped to Elsworth, & asked, if he would not Join me in an attempt to regain the Clause, we had lost on Saturday, he paused a little and said he would.

Mr. Elsworth rose and spoke long on the Subject of the necessity, of a discrimination. or some boundary line between the Courts of Chancery & Common law. he concluded with a Motion nearly in the Words of the Clause we had lost. Mr. Lee and myself both rose to second the Motion Mr. Lee however sat down, and left me Up. I therefore determined to avail myself of my situation and say something. declared my concurrence of Sentiment for limiting Chancery Strictly, as the bill stood, Chancery was open to receive every thing; in England, Where by the letter of the law, no suit could be brought in Chancery, if the Common law afforded a remedy, Yet such was the nature of that Court, and so advantageous had it been found to the Practitioners, That it had encroached greatly on the Common Law, Gentlemen, would not consider this as an inconvenience. so high were their Ideas of English Jurisprudence, they said all the World admired it, and every Member of this House must admire it, (this was Docr. Johnson's language on Saturday) I was ready to admire it too, but I would first endeavour to describe it. It consisted of a great number of Grades of Courts rising in ~~gradation~~ Succession over each other Common pleas Kings Bench Exchecquer, Chancery &ca. so admirably organized and connected, that the One was generally ready to begin where the other Ended, and so formed, that as long as ever a Client had Money he might, purchase delay, or in other Words get law for it. That in England at this time it was rather a Tryal of the depth of purse than of right, and accordingly nothing was more common, than for a Man who was going to law, to calculate and compare his pecuniary resources, with his adversary. The Cost however being fairly counted, and neither party afraid, at it the Angry Men go, as they are are eager & bleed freely, they mount perhaps with tolerable rapidity untill they arrive at the regions of Chancery. but here their bills ~~and~~ are filed, and all their facts collected, and in some half dozen of Years, maybe a Judgt. is given, but mark the first Judgt. is seldom ever final— here then a new number of facts must be adjusted & some ten or Twenty issues ~~of~~ or feigned Wagers must be tryed in Kings bench. in some three or four Years a new Cargo of facts are furnished. the Examiner goes to Work and he spends some Two or three Years, the Chancellor too perhaps must have the Opinion of the Judges of Kings bench, here is a new Tryal but at last he gives a Judgt. But Two of the Council sign a petition for a rehearing, and the Whole Business must be gone over again, but is the Business done no such thing. another petition comes in for a Review and the Whole Business must be gone over a third time, here I was interrupted by the President, who said there was an instance of a Cause being finished, by the present Chancellor, in his life time. I answered quick, One Swallow does not make a Summer Mr. President. and went on. but are they done Yet. no such thing the House of Lords is before them, and ~~before~~ by the time they get out of the far End of ~~that~~ it, one if not both are compleatly ruined. this is the progress of your Wealthy parties w⟨h⟩ere plum is matched to plum. But what of your unequal Matches, Your poor and rich parties? Why sir if the relative Wealth of One is to that of the other as 4 to 1 the poor Man will get about one fourth part of the way, if as 2 to 1 half way if as 3 to 4 three fourths of the way before the Exhausted party drops off into ruin. here By way of illustration, I repeated the Annesly Cause[17]— Sir never was so admirable a Machine contrived by the Art of Man. to Use Mens passions, for the picking of their pockets & to lengthen Justice into Trade. The present bill before you, has been consid-

---

[17]This notorious Chancery case, finally resolved by the House of Lords in 1741 after decades of contention, concerned rival claims to an inherited estate in Ireland. (*The English Reports, Volume I, The House of Lords* [London, 1900], pp. 573–80)

ered, as enjoying perfection in proportion, as it approaches the British System Sir, I have given you the Opinion which I know Many sensible Americans entertain of the System of English Jurisprudence, with such people English features will be no recommendation of the bill. Sir I cannot boast, a general knowledge of the Sentiments of Men in the Union, from what I know of my own State I am confident a great Majority abhor abhor a Chancery. Those Whom I have generally heard advocate the S a Chancery were professional Men. I really believed this was the case generally, over the Union, I knew many People complained of Chancery in the Jerseys £126:0:0 had been paid lately, for taking the Testimony only in a Chan Chancery suit in that State. Suits had been pending thirty Years. in their Chancery and had cost thousands. That I was clearly of Opinion that every thing after the Verdict of a Jury was a mere Trap to catch fees. and might be stiled the Toils of law added to perplex the Truth. The Bill however before you sir, as it now stands, is not chancery. it is something much worse, the barr between Chancery and Common law is broken down. it all actions may now be tryed in the federal Courts by the Judges, without the intervention of a Jury. The Tryal by Jury is considered as the Birth right of every american, it is a priviledge they are fond of, and let me add it is a priviledge they will not part with.

This day the report of our Committee for considering our Commercial Injuries reported, I do not like it, the End is answered. perhaps for which the Stir was made, when this Committee was appointed & now the Business Ends in a Bubble. I will however get a Copy of the report before I pronounce on it.

Tuesday, 14 July 1789

The Senate met, and One of the Bills for organizing one of the public departments, That of foreign affairs was taken up. after being read. I begged leave of the Chair to Submit, some general Observations which tho apparently diffuse. I considered as pertinent to the bill before Us, the first Clause of which was there shall be an executive department &ca. there are a number of such bills, and may be many more, giving tending to direct the most minute particle of the Presidents Conduct. if he is to be directed how he shall do every thing it follows, he must do nothing without direction, to What purpose then, is the executive power lodged in the President, if he can do nothing without a law directing the mode Manner and of Course, the thing to be done. May not the Two Houses of Congress on this principle pass a law depriving him of all power. you may say it will [*lined out*] not get his approbation. but Two thirds of both Houses will make it a law without. him. and the Constitution is undone at Once. Gentlemen may say how is

~~this~~ the Government then to proceed on these points.   the simplest in the World,   the President communicates to the Senate that he finds, such & such officers necessary in the Execution of the Government. and nominates the Men.   if the Senate approve they will concur in the Measure.   if not refuse their Consent &ca.   When the appointments are made, the President in like Manner communicates to the H. of R. that such appointments have taken place & requires adequate Salaries.   then the House of Representatives might shew their concurrence or disapprobation by providing for the Officer or not.   I thought it my duty to mention these things, tho' I had not the Vanity to think, I would make any prosalites in this Stage of the business, and perhaps the best apology I could make was not to detain them long.   ~~a long desultory~~ I likewise said That if the Senate were generally of my mind, a Conferrence between the Houses should take place.   But the Sense of the House would appear on taking the ~~Sense of the House~~ Question on the first Clause.   The first Clause was carried,   now came the second Clause,   it was for the Appointment of a Chief Clerk by the Secretary, who in fact was to be principal *Whenever the said principal Officer shall be removed from Office by the President of the United States.*   There was a blank pause at the End of it.   I was not in haste but rose first.   Mr. President—Whoever attends Strictly to the Constitution of the United States will readily observe that the part assigned to the Senate was an important one, no less than that of being the great Check, the regulator & Corrector, or, if I may so speak, the Balance of the Government.   In their legislative Capacity, they not only have the Correction of all bills Orders Votes or resolutions but may originate any of them, save Money bills,   in the executive branch they have likewise power to check and regulate the proceedings of the President,   Thus Treaties the highest and most important part of the Executive department, must have a Concurrence of Two thirds of them.   All appointments under the President and Vice President. must be by their advice and Consent, unless they concur in passing a law divesting themselves of this power.   by the Checks which are intrusted with them upon both the executive and the other branch of the legislature, the Stability of the Government is evidently placed in their hands.   The approbation of the Senate was certainly meant. to guard against the Mistakes of the President in his appointments of officers.   I do not admit the Doctrine of holding Commissions during pleasure as constitutional, and shall speak to that point presently.   but supposing for a moment, that to be the Case.   is not the same guard equally necessary to prevent ~~removals~~ improper steps in removals as in appointments, certainly ~~the Spirit of the Constitution~~ common inference or induction can mean nothing Short of this.   It is a maxim in legislation as well as reason, and applies well in the present Case, that it requires the same power to ~~enact~~ repeal as to enact   the depriving power should then be the same as the appointg. power.   But was this a point left at large by the Constitution?

clearly otherwise.   five or Six times in our Short constitution is the tryal by impeachment mentioned—in One place, the H. of R. shall have the sole power of impeachment—in another the Senate shall have the sole power to try impeachments.   in a third Judgt. shall not extend further than to removal from Office and disqualification to hold or enjoy Offices &ca.   the President shall not pardon in Cases of impeachment.   the President Vice President and *all civil officers* of the United States shall be removed from Office on impeachment &ca.   no part of the Constitution is so fully guarded or more clearly expressed than this part of it.   and most justly too, for every ~~just~~ good Government guards the reputation of her Citizens as well as their life and property.   ~~for~~ every turning out of Office, is attended with reproach & the person so turned out is Stigmatized with infamy.   by means of impeachment a fair hearing and Tryal is secured to the party.   without this What Man of an independent Spirit would accept of such an Office,   of What Service can his Abilities be to the Community if afraid of the nod or beck of a Superior, he must consult ~~hims~~ will in every Matter.   Abject Servility is most likely to mark the line of his Conduct, & this on the One hand will not fail to be productive of despotism and Tyranny on the other.   for I consider mankind as composed nearly of the same Materials in America as in Asia, in the United States as in the East Indias.   The Constitution certainly never contemplated any other mode of removing from Office.   the Case is not omitted here   the most ample provision is made.   if Gentlemen do not like it, let them obtain an alteration of the Constitution, but this cannot be done by law.   if the Virtues of the present Chief Magistrate are brought forward, as a reason for vesting him with extraordinary powers. No nation ever trod more dangerous ground.   his Virtues will depart with him.   but the powers which You give him will remain, and if not properly guarded will be abused by future Presidents; if they are Men.   This however is not the Whole of the Objection I have to the Clause   a Chief Clerk is to be appointed, ~~and When~~ and this without any advice or Consent of the Senate.   This Chief Clerk, on the removal of the Secretary will become the principal in the Office, and so may remain during the Presidency.   for the Senate cannot force the President into a nomination, for a new Officer.   This is a direct Stroke at the power of the Senate.   Sir I consider the Clause as exceptionable every way, and therefore move You to Strike it out.

Langdon Jumped up in haste   hoped the Whole would not be Struck out. but moved, that the clause only, of the President ~~appoint~~ removing, should be Struck out.   up rose Elsworth & a most elaborate Speech indeed did he make, but it was all drawn from Writers on the distribution of Government. the President was the Executive officer   he was interfered with in the appointment it was true, but not in the removal.   the constitution had taken one but not the other from him.   therefore removal remained to him intire—   he carefully avoided the Subject of impeachment—   he absolutely used the following Expressions with regard to the President.   *"It is Sacrilege to touch an Hair of his head, and, we may as well lay the President's head on a block and strike it off, with one blow"*   the way he came to Use these Words was, after having asserted, that removing from offices was his priviledge.   We might as well do this, as deprive him of it.   he had sore Eyes and a green silk over ~~his eyes~~ them,   on pronouncing the last of the Two Sentences, he paused put his hand kerchief to his face and either shed tears or affected to do so.   When he sat down, both Butler and Izard sprung up.   Butler however continued up.   he began with a declaration, that he came into the House in the most perfect State of indifference, & rather disposed to give the power in question to the President   But the arguments of the H⟨onorable⟩. G⟨entleman⟩. from Connecticut had, in endeavouring to support the Clause, convinced him in the clearest Manner, that the clause was highly improper and he would vote against it—   Izard now got at it. and spoke very long against the clause. Strong got up for the clause and a most confused speech he made indeed—   I have notes of it, but think it really not worth answering, unless to shew the folly of some things which he said—   Docr. Johnson rose and told Us twice before he proceeded far, that he would not give an Opinion on the power of the President,   This Man's conscience will not let him be a thorough paced Courtier—Yet he wished not to loose his interest with the President.   however his Whole argument went against the Clause.   and at last he declared he was against the Whole of it—   Mr. Lee rose   he spoke long and pointedly against the clause   he repeated many of my Arguments, but always was polite enough, to acknowledge the Mention I had made of them.   he spoke from a paper which he held in his hand.   he continued untill it was past 3 O'Clock and an adjournment was called for and took place—   in looking over my notes I find I omitted to set down Sundry arguments which I used, but no matter.   I will not do it now.

Wednesday, 15 July 1789

Senate met.   Mr. Carrol shewed impatience to be up first.   he got up and spoke a considerable length of time   the burthen of his discourse seemed to be want of power in the President and a desire of increasing it,   great complaints of what he called the *Atrocious assumption of power in the States.* Many allusions to the power of the british kings,   *the king can do no Wrong,*   if anything improper is done, it should be the Ministers that should answer.   How strangely this Man is changed.   (The Collection bill was called for and read for the first time).   now Elsworth rose with a most lengthy debate.   The first Words that he said, were, in this case the Constitution is our only rule for we are sworn to Support it. but neither quoted it nor ever named it afterwards except as follows   by allusion. He said I buy a Square Acre of land   I buy the Trees. Waters & every thing belonging to it.   the executive power belongs to the president.   the removing of officers is a Tree on this Acre.   the power of removing is therefore his,   it is in him,   it is no where else.   thus we are under the necessity of ascertaining by implication where the power is,   he called Docr. Johnson Thomas Aquinas, by implication too, & said things rather uncivil of some other of his opponents.   most carefully did he avoid entering on the Subject of impeachment.   after some time however he got fairly on new ground   lamented the want of power in the President. asked did we *ever quarrel* with the power of the Crown of Great Britain?   No, We contended with the power of the parliament.   no one ever thought the power of the Crown too great.   said he was growing infirm   should die and should not see it, but the Government would fail for want of power in the President.   he would have power as far as he would be seen in his Coach and Six,   ~~W~~ *We must extend the executive Arm.*   Mr. Lee Yesterday had said something about the Dutch.   if we must have examples said he let Us draw them from the People Whom we used always to imitate, from the nation Who have made all others bow before them. and not from the dutch who are divided & factious.   He said a Vast deal more but the above was all I minuted down at the time—   Mr. Izard rose and answered.   Mr. Butler rose and spoke.   it was after 3   Mr. Lee rose   said he had much to say, but would now only move ~~and~~ an adjournment.   as it was late the House accordingly adjourned.   I have seen more caballing and meeting of the Members in knots this day, than I ever observed before,   as I came up Stairs Elsworth⟨,⟩ Ames and Mr. Morris stood in a knot.   up stairs soon after, Elsworth⟨,⟩ Carrol & Strong got together,   as soon as the house adjourned Carrol took Patterson aside.   and there seemed a General hunt and Bustle, among the Members, I see plainly public speaking on this Subject is now ~~lost~~ Useless.   and we may put the question when we please,   it seems as if a Court party was forming, indeed I believe it was formed long ago.

Thursday, 16 July 1789

Attended pretty early this Morning   many were however there before ~~Us~~ me.   it was all hudling away in small parties   our President was very busy indeed.   running to every one, he openly attacked Mr. Lee before me on the Subject in debate.   and they were even loud on the business   I began to Suspect. That the Court party had prevailed,   Senate however met and at it they went   Mr. Lee began, but I really believe the Altercation tho' not a Violent One, which he had with the president, had hurt him, for he was languid, and much shorter than ever I had heard him on almost any Subject.

Mr. Patterson got up,   for a long time you could not know what he would be at,   after however he had warmed himself with his own discourse, as the Indians do with their War Song, he said he was for the Clause continuing,   he had no sooner said so than he assumed a bolder Tone of Voice.   Flew over to England   extolled its Government   wished in the most unequivocal language, that our President had the same powers,   said let Us take a 2d View of England, repeating nearly the same thing,   let Us take a 3d View of it said he and he then abused the Parliament for having made themselves first Trennial and lastly Septennial.   Speaking of the Constitution he used expressly these Words. speaking of the removing of Officers. *There is not a Word of Removability in it.*   his Argument ~~of course~~ was that the Executive held this Matter of Course—   Mr. Wyngate got up and said something for Striking out.   Mr. Read rose, and was swinging on his legs for an Hour,   he had to talk a great deal before he could bring himself, to declare against the ~~Clause~~ Motion, but now a most curious Scene opened—   Dalton rose, and said a number of things in the most hesitating, and embarrassed Manner,   it was his recantation   had just now altered his mind from What had been said by the Honorable Gentleman from Jersey.   he was now for the Clause   Mr. Izard was so provoked. That he jumped up   declared nothing had fell from that Gentleman that possibly could convince any Man—   that Man might pretend so, but the thing was impossible,   Mr. Morris's face had reddened for some time   he rose hastily.   he threw Censure on Mr. Izard   declared that the recanting Man behaved like a Man of honor.   that Mr. Patterson's Arguments were good and sufficient to convince any man.   the Truth however was that every body believed that John Adams was the great Converter, but now Recantation was in fashion.   Mr. Basset, recanted, too. tho' he said he had prepared himself on the other side   We now saw how it would go.   and I could not help admiring the frugality of the Court party in procuring Recantations or Votes, which you please.   After all the Arguments were ended & the ~~Votes~~ Question taken the Senate was 10 to 10 and The president with great Joy cryed out *it is not a Vote*, without giving himself time to declare the division of the House, and give his Vote in Order.   Every Man of our side in giving their Sentiments, spoke with great freedom. and seemed willing to avow their Own Opinion in the openest Manner.   Not a Man of the others who made any speech to the Merits of the Matter, but went about it and about it,   I called this singing the War Song and told ~~him~~ Mr. Morris I would give him every One Who I heard Sing the War Song, or in other Words those who could not avow the Vote they were fully minded to give, untill they had raised Spirits enough, by their own Talk, to enable them to do it.   Grayson made a Speech   it was not long.   But he had in it this remarkable Sentence.   "The Matter predicted by Mr. Henry,[18] is now coming to pass, consolidation is the object of the

---

[18]Patrick Henry (1736–99), member of the state House of Delegates, 1740–84 and 1787–

New Government, and the first ~~Object~~ attempt will be to destroy the Senate, as they are the Representatives of the State legislatures.''

It has long been a Maxim with me, That no frame of Government Whatever, would secure liberty or equal administration of Justice to a People, unless Virtuous Citizens, were the legislators & Governors.   I live not a day, without finding new reason to Subscribe to this Doctrine.   What avowed & repeated attempts have I seen to place the President above the powers stipulated for him by the Constitution.

For Striking out	Against Striking out	
Butler	Reed	
Izard	Basset	
Langdon	Elsworth	
Johnson	Strong	
Wyngate	Dalton	President
Few	Patterson	
Gun	Elmer	
Grayson	Morris	
Lee	Henry	
Maclay 10	Carrol 11[19]	

{I reply'd to a number of their Arguments, and the Substance of them is on the adjoining Loose Sheet[20]—}   {of All the Members of our House the Conduct of Patterson surprises me most.   he has been characterized to me as a Staunch Revolution Man & Genuine Whig.   Yet he has in every republican Question deserted and in some instances betrayed Us.   I know not that there is such a thing as buying Members, but if there is he is certainly sold.

I never was treated with less respect than this day,   Adams behaved with Studied ~~neglect~~ inattention   He was snuffling up his Nose, kicking his heels or talking & Sniggering with Otis, the Whole time, I was up.   Butler, tho' no Man bears a thing of this kind with less temper, engaged Wingate⟨,⟩ Izard & his End of the Table in Earnest conversation.   Elsworth⟨,⟩ Basset⟨,⟩ Reed

---

90, was a major force in Virginia and national politics. He was born in Hanover County, Virginia. After 1779 he resided in Henry County, which had been named for him in 1776. His elected offices included member of the House of Burgesses, 1765–75; delegate to Congress, 1774–75; governor of Virginia, 1776–79 and 1784–86; and presidential elector, 1789. He refused to attend the Federal Convention in 1787 and led the opposition to the Constitution in the Virginia Ratification Convention a year later. Henry secured the election of Antifederalists as the first senators from Virginia, almost prevented the election of James Madison to the House, and was a candidate for both president and vice president, at least in the minds of the Federalists, who had reason to fear his influence. (*DHFFE* 2:166, 181, 193, 415; *FG*, 3 Jan. 1789)

[19] This vote is not recorded in the *SLJ*. On 18 July the vote was taken again and the slightly different tabulation is in the *SLJ*, p. 86.

[20] The loose sheet is no longer with the manuscript diary, although remnants of the wafer that held it are visible.

formed another knot.   Mr. Morris went out.   The Door Keeper[21] was kept
on a continual trot, calling out Strong⟨,⟩ Patterson⟨,⟩ Henry⟨,⟩ Carrol
&ca.—   I might he have said more, but it was Useless.}

Friday, 17 July 1789

attended at the Hall half after 9 O'Clock—   we read and corrected the long
Judiciary   the Senate Met at the usual time.   This same Judiciary was taken
up and went over.   and Now Mr. Butler rose against it.   Mr. Grayson spoke
against it, and Mr. Lee was more pointed than any of them.   had Mr. Lee
joined in my Objections against it at an early period, perhaps we might have
now had it, in better form.   Mr. Butler offered a Motion, for leave for any
Member to enter his dissent on the Minutes.   This proved a most lengthy
debate,   it was 4 O'Clock before it was decided.   he lost his Motion tho'   I
thought it, and right.   and now Mr. Lee⟨,⟩ Mr. Grayson⟨,⟩ Mr. Butler⟨,⟩
Mr. Izard Wingate rose for the Yeas and Nays on the Judiciary bill   they were
given,   I was in the negative.   I opposed this bill from the begining.   It
certainly is a Vile law System, calculated for Expence, and with a design to draw
by degrees all law business into the federal Courts.   The Constitution is
meant to swallow up all the State Constitutions by degrees and this to Swallow
by degrees all the State Judiciaries—   This at least is the design some Gentlemen seem driving at.   Oh Sweet Candor when wilt thou quit the Cottage,
and the lisping infants lip, and shed thy Glory round the Statesman's head.
is it inscribed on human fate, that Man must seem grow wicked to seem
wise.   and must the path of politicks, be for ever incumbered with briars and
Thorns—
I had been much pressed to dine with the Speaker in a Company of Pennsylvanians   I went there and sat till Six,   I am a poor String in a convivial
Concert,   my lame Knee will neither let me eat nor drink—   I am old and
ought to know it,   I came away quite tired of the volatile Tattle of the
Table,   I never had much but now much less taste, for convivial Joy.   some of
the Company grew very talkative before I left them—{particularly the Governor of the Western Territory.[22]   he must soon sink in the publick Opinion, if
he Conducts himself as he did this Evening,   he was Tediously talkative &

---

[21]James Mathers (1750–1811) was born in Dublin, Ireland, and came to New York City
before the War for Independence. After serving in the war, he became doorkeeper for
Congress in 1788, having been the assistant since 1785. Mathers was recommended by several
members of Congress for a congressional position, and the Senate chose him as its doorkeeper on 7 April 1789. He served in this position until his death. (*JCC* 34:153; *National
Intelligencer*, 5 Sept. 1811; *DAR Lineage Book* 147:137; Testimonial, 4 March 1789, Petitions
and Memorials: Applications for jobs, SR, DNA)
[22]Arthur St. Clair.

dwelt much on the fooleries of scottish antiquity; and what was worse shewed ill nature when he was laughed at.}

Saturday, 18 July 1789

We had some debate Yesterday about the adjournment.   it was agreed to sit this day expressly, with a design to take up the Collection Bill.   as soon as the Minutes were read Mr. Morris called for it and I seconded it.   But Elsworth called for the bill on foreign affairs (as he was sick and wanted a few days Absence and Basset Who had staid over the time he expected. was likewise going out of Town.)   We had now much curious conversation   Mr. Grayson made some remarks, on our mode of doing business   our doors were shut, and a Member was debarred the priviledge of a protest   we were shut up in conclave.   we however have often had this business before Us.   the President however took Occasion. to get up and gave Us his History of Protests.   he said the House of Lords only had that right,   they had it in a feudal right; they were originally, an armed Militia for the defense of the Country, and were supposed possessed of every thing honorable.   but as to the Scotch peers that was a peice of patch Work   the Senate were an elective body and their Motives, would be to preserve their popularity—in Order to secure their Elections, and therefore they ought not to have any power of protesting.   Elseworth made a second motion that the Bill for foreign affairs should be postponed to Wednesday fortnight.   Langdon seconded this.   Sundry Gentlemen called however for the Bill.   Mr. President put the Question on the Bill and it was taken up.   The Gentlemen against the Bill Mr. Izard⟨,⟩ Langdon and Johnson declared all they wished was the Yeas and Nays in the same form. as they had passed Yesterday. the President giving the Casting Vote.   Elsworth proposed that Basset should withdraw. & then there would be a Tie.   Basset did not like it.   Elsworth proposed to withdraw and actually did so.   all this was occasioned by the Absence of Butler,   and now the Yeas and Nays were taken on the Words. *by the President*.   Our President gave the Casting Vote.   Mr. Lee moved an amendment in the fore part of the Bill which did not seem well digested,   it was lost of Course.   the amount of it was that the Officer should be responsible.   I rose and said I could not consent to it, for by the ~~later~~ 3d Clause of the bill the officer was made such an abject Creature so dependent on the Nod of a Superior, I thought it cruel to make him in any ~~Measure~~ degree responsible for Measures in which he could have no free agency.   he had been called Servant,   he was more   he was the Creature of the President.   The President was a responsible Officer by the Constitution,   it had been said, no Use Would ever be made of this.   I hoped there

never would be any Occasion but respondeat Superior,[23] was a Maxim in
Law, and I supposed We would have to trust to it— Mr. Langdon moved to
Strike *to be appointed by the said Principal Officer.* I could not see What he
aimed at. Doctor Johnson got up and complained of the Approbation of the
President in the last part of the Clause as reflecting on the Senate to Whom the
Constitution had given the power of approving. I doubted whether I should
rise or no, thinking all opposition Vain I determined however to speak.
Mr. P. this Clause calls the Chief Clerk an inferior Officer I think differently
of him. This sir will be ~~ther~~ the Man Who will do the business, in England
Sir that Country from which we are so fond of taking Examples. the Chief
Clerks do the Business. so much so that on an Eminent Character being told by
a person who seemed in Concern on the Occasion, That the Ministry were
changed. Asked gravely if the Clerks in the Office were changed. being
answered No. give yourself no further uneasiness then, the business will
meet with no interruption. so will it be here. the calling him an inferior
Officer however paves the Way for his appointment by the Head of the Department, but What is the Use of the Clause here? I think freely and freely will
I speak. the Secretary appoints his Clerk of Course, and the Clerk of Course
will take care of the Office records book and papers, even if the Principal
should be removed. they are to be under Oath or affirmation, faithfully to
execute the trust committed to them, it is not to be presumed that they will
abandon the papers to the Winds. What then is the Use of the Clause?
clearly to put it into the power of a President, if so minded, to exercise this
office without the advice or consent of the Senate as to the Officer. the
consent of the President at at the End of the Clause points out this Clearly.
this is a kind of Consent unwarranted, by the Constitution. ~~I therefore~~ The
President removes the Principal, the Clerk pleases him well, being, the Man
of his approbation. The Senate cannot force him to a nomination. and the
business may proceed, during his Presidency. The objects ostensibly held out
by the bill are nugatory, the design is but illy concealed, it was for these
reasons I formerly moved to strike out ~~this a similar~~ this Clause. and I am
still averse to the Whole of it. Patterson got up. said the later part of the
Clause perhaps was exceptionable and he would have no objection to strike it
out. Mr. Morris rose and said something to the same import, but as Doctor
Johnson had glanced something at the Conduct of the other House. and as
What I said leaned the same way. Mr. Morris said Whatever the particular View
might be of the Member who brought in this clause. he acquitted the House in
general of any design against the Senate. Mr. Elsworth. rose and said much
more on the same Subject. I rose said I thought nothing on this Subject
which I would not avow. The House of Representatives had debated 4 days,
on a direct Clause for vesting the President with this power. and after having

---

[23]The legal doctrine that a superior is liable for the actions of a subordinate.

carried it with an open face. they dropped and threw out the Clause and here produced the same thing cloaked and modifyed in a different Manner by a side Wind. I liked for my part plain dealing. and there was something that bore a very different aspect in this business.

Sunday, 19 July 1789

determined to set off, home come what would   Went for Mr. Morris lodgings, he was out of Town   visited Mr. Butler who, lives just by him.   visited Mr. Clymer who was just returned from Philada.   called on Mr. Izard on my way home   he was most Violent, on the subject of our late Measures   he abhors our President.   came home.   read mostly in the afternoon   visited by the Speaker⟨,⟩ Genl. St. Clair⟨,⟩ Delany⟨,⟩ MacPherson & Sundry other Gentlemen   my health requires a Journey home.   But I this day read the Story of Father Nicholas in the Lounger.   I am no St. Hubert no Sinner know no Delaserres or Trenvilles.[24]   But this Story had an effect on me.   I will go and see my family.

Monday, 20 July 1789

Asked leave of absence for Three Weeks on Acct. of my health,   obtained it without difficulty.   ~~on my Journey and set off at 4 Clock for Philada.~~

{I remained some time in my place after Business was over to give An Opportunity to Any of the Members, Who choose it, to Wish me A Good Journey, or Speak to me on Business, if they had Any.   Henry of Maryland And a Group soon gathered about me.   They seemed to think that my going was owing to dissaffection to public Measures, As Much As to indisposition. This I would not Own, but in qualifyed sense.   "That my disappointment with respect to public Measures, And, conseq⟨u⟩ent Vexation, had perhaps aggravated my Indisposition."

Fun now let loose her frolicks Upon Me.   And Who of all the human Race will thank You for that?   not One in a 1000 will believe a Word of it.   And if Any do, they will call You Fool for Your Pains.   Gratitude no Governing principle Among the humanum Pecus, ~~the Herd of Mankind~~.   Fear, Fear, Only the Parent of Obedience Among the Herd of Mankind.   The Hangman in this World and the Devil in the Next.   Republican theories well enough, in times of publick Commotion or at Elections.   But all Sensible Men, Once in

---

[24]*The Lounger* was a periodical journal of essays published at Edinburgh from 1785 through 1787. "The power of corrupt society and false shame over the natural feelings of virtue. Story of Father Nicholas" comprised numbers 82–84 and appeared on 26 August, 2 and 9 September 1786. Henry Mackenzie, who edited *The Lounger*, apparently wrote the story, which included the characters St. Hubert, Delaserre, and Trenville.

power, know that Force is the only effectual Means to Secure Obedience.
Hence has flowed, and for ever Will flow the failure of Republican Govern-
ments.   Oligarchies And Aristocracies follow, till Monarchy tops the System,
And will continue, till some Unskilful Driver overloads the Ass, And then The
restive Beast throws both itself And the Rider in the Mire, And the Old process
begins Again—   A Senator will be elected, in Your State before long said
One,   Your Patriotism will be of great Service to You then!   A Single dinner
Given by a Speculator (People Who do not like You) will procure 10 Votes
Where Your disinterestedness has not secured You One, And You must intreague and cabal as deep And deeper too, than Your Adversaries, or we Will
not see You here Again.   Is there a Single One of the Majestic Mob Who Will
not belie defraud deceive And cheat You for the Smallest interest.   Health is
too great a Sacrifice for Such An herd.   The Whole was delivered with so
comic An Air, that a Serious Answer seemed improper, And Yet I wished to say
something, And for the Sake of Harmony, if possible in the same Key.

Gentlemen I have at home Good Neighbors Good} [25]

---

[25]One page was cut out of the manuscript at this point prior to the 1880 edition of the
journal.

August 1789

Sunday, 16 August 1789

came to New York at 10 OClock last night greatly fatagued with my Journey.[1] went after breakfast to Mr. Morris's lodgings   he was abroad.   called on Mr. Clymer at his lodgings and left his & Mr. Fitzsimons' letters.   called to see Scot and Ellicot,   both abroad.   called on Mr. Izard.   he gave me a short History of the Court party[2] which (as might be expected) is gaining Ground. A Conference has been held with the President,[3] in which Mr. Izard declared, that the President owned he had consulted, the Members of the House of Representatives as to his ~~appointments~~ nominations.   but likewise said he had not acted so with the Senators.   as they would have an Opportunity, of giving their advice & consent afterwards.   this small annecdote serves to develop his Conduct.   or rather to fix my Opinion of his Conduct, for some time past.   to wit a Courtship of, and Attention to the house of Representatives, That by their Weight he may depress the Senate.   and exalt Prerogatives on their ruin.   Mr. Izard was clearly of Opinion, That all the late Measures flowed from the President's.   Mr. Madison in his Opinion was deep in this business.   The President, shewed great want of temper, (as ~~he~~ Mr. Z said) when One of his Nominations was rejected.[4]   The President may however be considered, as in a great measure passive in the Business.   The Creatures that surround him, would place a crown on his head, that they may have the handling of its Jewels.

---

[1]WM spent at least a day in Philadelphia on his return to Congress. On 14 August Benjamin Rush recorded the following in his commonplace book:

> Mr. Maclay (of the Senate of the United States) drank tea with me. He observed that half the Senate were lawyers—that he never knew one of them retract or Alter an opinion After the fullest discussion of it—which he ascribed to their habits of contending for *victory* instead of *truth* at the Bar. He added further that he had heard Jno. Adams, say in a private company, "the more ignorant people, Are, the more easily they will be governed." (Rush Papers, PHi)

[2]WM's reference here is to those members of Congress who supported the concept of a strong independent executive and/or sought to curry favor with the president.

[3]The conference between the president and a Senate committee, chaired by Izard, was for the purpose of agreeing to a mutually acceptable mode of communication between the president and the Senate in the formation of treaties and in making appointments. Actions regarding the matter are recorded in the *SEJ*, pp. 17, 24, 28–30.

[4]On 5 August the Senate rejected the nomination of Benjamin Fishburn to be naval officer for the port of Savannah. Actions regarding the matter are recorded in the *SEJ* on 3, 5, 7, and 10 August. For more on Fishbourn see *SEJ*, pp. 23–26, 491.

{Mr. Izard informed me of the attempt of Gorham to get the land commonly called the Triangle from Pennsylvania, or at least to delay the Business untill he could get a number of New England men settled on it so as to hold it by force and make a second Wyoming of it.[5]   He said Mr. Morris had got the business put off untill Wednesday expecting my coming to Town.   by his Acct. a Strong party is forming by Gorham. and they expect to carry it against Pennsylvania.   I immediately left him Sunday as it was. to call on Scot and Ellicot to prepare for this business   could find none of them.}

{My Haste & Agitation On hearing of Gorham's Affair prevented My Noting all Mr. Izard's Communications.   he said all your Measures are rebrobated & rejected Yo & will be rejected   Your voting by Ballot in Agreeing to Nominations and so on—   We have All been to dine With the Great Man It's all disagreeable to him And Will be Altered &c.   He Gave me clear hints of my loss of Character at Court &c. And of the direct Influence of the President with the Members of the Congress. &c.   For Some time past (as the Indian said) I could see how the Watches Went, But I did not know before the Way they Were Wound Up.

It was to counteract a Growing influence Which observed to gain Ground daily that I moved the Consent to appointments &ca. to be Given by ballot, the having carried this Motion was passing the Rubicon in transgression As It Went to cut pluck Up patronage by the Roots, And to Undo this is, it seems, a knot Worthy of Presidential Interference.

A thought here on the Subject of *Influence*   Strip it of it's Courtly coloring And is it either More or less than *Corruption*?   When Walpole debauched the British Senate Was it M either Morally or politically different Whether he did it by Court favor loans Jobs lottery Tickets Contracts Offices or expectancy of them or With the Chinking Guinea,   The Motive And effect Was certainly

---

[5]Nathaniel Gorham (1738–96) of Charlestown, Massachusetts, was a merchant and politician. He had been speaker of the state House of Representatives, president of the Confederation Congress, presiding officer of the committee of the whole at the Federal Convention, and Federalist delegate to the Massachusetts Ratification Convention during the 1780s. Gorham was a member of the partnership that held title to the six-million-acre Genesee Tract in western New York. See also *SEJ*, p. 504.

Pennsylvania, desirous of access to the Great Lakes, disputed New York's claim of jurisdiction over the southwest corner of the Genesee Tract, known as the triangle or Erie Triangle. Congress had ordered a survey on 6 June 1788 to resolve the dispute. Gorham petitioned the FFC to delay implementation of the order because his title to the land would be invalid if Pennsylvania were awarded jurisdiction. Today, the disputed land forms that portion of Erie County, Pennsylvania, which lies north of the forty-second parallel, east of Lake Erie, and west of the western boundary of New York. See May 1789, n. 5, for more on the Genesee Tract and *DHFFC* 6:2123–24 for Gorham's petition.

The Wyoming Valley, on the East Branch of the Susquehanna River above present-day Wilkes-Barre, gave its name to a lengthy and sometimes violent controversy between Pennsylvania and Connecticut over conflicting jurisdiction and land titles in a large section of east central Pennsylvania. The Wyoming question, one of the major interstate issues to come before the Confederation Congress, was resolved in favor of Pennsylvania. See Appendix E for more information on the controversy and WM's involvement in it.

the Same.   But Walpole Was A Villain.   What then must the Man be that follows his Footsteps?}

Monday, 17 August 1789

went out altho I was not very well.   It was near 9 OClock before I could see Mr. Scot. and he was then in bed— I saw Mr. Morris who had just received all the papers from Mr. Ellicot, about the Triangle.   not one of them had ever thought, that Pennsylvania had actually purchased this land of the Indians   I called on Genl. St. Clair who will set this in ~~an~~ a clear point of View, if they will not give Us time to send to Philada. for the deed &ca.

Attended the Senate at the Usual Hour,   the Business agitated this day in the Senate was the bill for regulating the Coasting Trade.   some progress was made in it. When it was postponed and the Affairs of Georgia taken up with respect to the Indians,[6]   some Warmth on this Business   sat untill after 4 and adjourned.

Tuesday, 18 August 1789

busy preparing for the debate on the Triangle which is to come on tomorrow.   Senate met at the usual time.   the Bill for the indian Treaties was taken up. and considerable debate.   I asked for information, for some estimate of the Expense but it seems none had been furnished.   a Motion was made for reducing the Sum appropriated from 40 to 20 M. of doll. but no estimate appeared for either.   I lamented my want of information. but declared I hoped the H. of R. had some just Grounds to go on when they voted the 40.   that I would for once trust to them. since I must vote in the dark. but the 20 was carried.   We then read over the penal law[7] for the 2d time & debated on it untill the Hour of Adjournment.

Wednesday, 19 August 1789

Senate met and Went on the Appointment of an Officer to run the Line of the Triangle.   I will not attempt a detail of the Arguments.   Maps Resolves of Congress Contracts &ca. were produced by Us, which those who voted for Us, declared carried demonstration with them.   We had every Man East of the Hudson against Us. and the most of them speakers.   Dr. Johnson in particular, was very uncandid,   Elsworth voted against Us but spoke but little, King & Schyler managed the debate principally,   Langdon was very often

---

[6]Indian Treaties Act [HR-20].
[7]Punishment of Crimes Bill [S-2].

up.   every point on the paper annexed was canvassed, and a Vast many more.

{Act of Cession by the State of New York. to the united States. on the 1st March 1781.[8]   Accepted by Congress on the 29th October 1782.

(Here show'd that the cession was made on Geographick principles, by the Map. and explain, how the north West Corner of Pennsylvania, came to be placed 50 say 54$\frac{1}{2}$ miles farther West. and how the Company & State of New York wish to avail themselves of that Circumstance—)

On the 18th April 1785 a cession of the same Territory was accepted by Congress, from the State of Massachusetts, in the same Words.[9] only the Pennsylvania line is not mentioned, on a Supposition that there was a Vacancy of 2 minutes of a degree between them.

A Meridian passing thro', the westerly bend of lake Erie, or thro' a point 20 miles West of the most westerly bend of Niagara River.   one or the other must be the Western limit of the State of New York. as the boundary is to be a meridian and must pass thro' one or other of these points.

On the 6th of June 1788, Congress ordered the Geographer of the U.S.[10] to run the boundary line giving notice to the Executives of the States of New York and Massachusetts. and to make an Accurate Survey of the land lying West of the Meridian between lake Erie and the state of Pennsylvania. that the same might be sold—(read the Resolution.)[11]

On the 16th of June 1788 the Geographer, instructed Andw. Ellicot Esqr. to perform this Service (read the instructions).[12]

---

[8]The act of cession is printed in *JCC* 19:211–13.

[9]The act of cession is printed in *JCC* 28:271–73.

[10]Thomas Hutchins (1730–89), geographer to the United States, 1781–89, was born in Monmouth County, New Jersey. He served in the West during the French and Indian War as an officer in both the Pennsylvania and the British armies. After refusing to bear arms against his countrymen, he was imprisoned in England in 1779. When he was released in 1780, he joined the Continental army. Hutchins applied his engineering skills and geographical knowledge to a variety of military works, surveys, and publications. In 1785, Congress placed him in charge of surveying the territory northwest of the Ohio River, and he died on his way there to complete his survey of the first seven ranges.

[11]*Resolved* That the geographer of the United States be and he is hereby directed to ascertain, by himself or by a deputy duly appointed for the purpose, the boundary line between the United States and the States of New York and Massachusetts agreeably to the deeds of cession of the said States.

That the said geographer ~~or his deputy having~~ inform the executives of the states of New York and Massachusetts of the time of running the said line in Order that they or either of them may if they think proper have persons attending at the time.

That the said geographer or his deputy having run the meridian between lake Erie and the state of Pensylvania and marked and noted down in his field book proper land marks for perpetuating the same shall proceed to make a survey of the Land lying west of the said line between lake Erie and the state of Pensylvania ~~so as to ascertain the quantity thereof and~~ make return of such survey to the board of treasury, who are hereby authorised and empowered at any time before or after such survey to sell the said tract in whole at private sale for a price not less than three fourths of a dollar per acre in specie or public securities drawing interest. (*JCC* 34:203)

[12]Ellicott had supplied WM with a copy of his instructions. See May 1789, n. 20.

On the 7th of July 1788 the State of Pennsylvania offered, by Wm. Bingham and James Reed 3/4 of a Doll. ℔ Acre—for this Land—(read the offer)[13]

On the 28th August 1788. the Pennsylvania proposals were accepted and the bargain closed.

By the Board of Treasury—(read the acceptance)[14]

On the 4th of September 1788 Congress vested the right of Jurisdiction over the said Tract in the State of Pennsylvania—(read the Resolution)[15]

Pennsylvania thus vested with the right both to soil and Jurisdiction, pursued her usual System, with regard to New Lands; and altho' it was said That

---

[13]We the Delegates of the State of Pennsylvania, in compliance with instructions, and in virtue of powers, received from the said State, do hereby offer to contract (in behalf of the said State,) with the Honble. Board of Treasury, for a tract of land belonging to the United States, contained in the interval betwixt a Meridian Line, run between Lake Erie and the state of Pennsylvania, and the Boundaries of the States of New York and Massachusetts, at the rate of three-fourth of a dollar per acre; payable in Gold or Silver, or in public securities of the United States, bearing interest; when the quantity ascertained by actual survey, in the manner prescribed by a Resolution of Congress, of the 7th of June, 1788. (*PaAr* [1], II:383)

William Bingham (1752–1804), banker and speculator in land and public securities, was born in Philadelphia. After graduating from the College of Philadelphia in 1768, he served as British consul on Martinique from 1770 to 1776 and as American agent in the West Indies from 1777 to 1780. His public duties and private business ventures there brought him tremendous wealth. Upon his return to Philadelphia he married Anne Willing, daughter of Anne McCall and Thomas Willing, and, along with his father-in-law and Robert Morris, founded the Bank of North America. Bingham served in Congress from 1786 to 1788 and led the unsuccessful effort to seat the FFC at Philadelphia. See also January 1791, n. 11. (*DHFFE* 1:413)

James Randolph Reid (1750–89) of Cumberland County and Bingham were the only Pennsylvanians attending on 7 July 1788 and therefore presented the state's offer. (*Princetonians, 1769–1775*, pp. 514–17)

[14]The United States in Congress, having by their act of the 20th Instant, determined that no Reservations are in their judgment, necessary to be made on account of the United States, in a certain Tract of Land, contained in the interval betwixt a meridian Line, run between Lake Erie and the State of Pensylvania; and the Boundaries of the State of New York and Massachusetts. We beg leave to acquaint you that we accept your Proposal for the purchase of the said tract, on behalf of the state of Pennsilvania, as expressed in your letter of the 7th July, 1788. (*PaAr* [1] II:382)

[15]Whereas it appears that the board of treasury in conformity to the Act of Congress of the 6th. June last have entered into a contract with the Delegates of the state of Pennsylvania in behalf of the said State, for the tract of land bounded East, agreeably to the cession of western territory by the States of Massachusetts and New York, south, by Pensylvania, North and West, by lake Erie, and whereas the said tract is entirely separated from the other lands of the western territory, over which the jurisdiction of the United States extends; and whereas under these circumstances it will be expedient for the State of Pensylvania to hold and exercise jurisdiction over the tract aforesaid, therefore,

Resolved, that the United States do hereby relinquish, and transfer all their right, title and claim to the Government and Jurisdiction of the said tract of land, to the State of Pennsylvania forever; and it is hereby declared and made known that the laws and public Acts of the said State shall extend over every part of the same tract to all intents and purposes as if the same had been originally within the charter bounds of the said State; provided that the Inhabitants of the said tract shall be maintained in all the rights and priveleges which other citizens of the said State of Pensylvania are now or may hereafter be constitutionally entitled to enjoy. (*JCC* 34:499–500)

the Congress ought to quiet the Claims of the indians with respect to lands sold by them. she chose in conformity to antient Usage, to purchase of the Natives.   Genl. Butler and Col. Gibson were appointed Agents at the Treaty at Muskingum.[16] and the Purchase of these Lands was made.   We have not the Deeds. and other documents to produce,   if they are required we will send for them.   But General St. Clair now in Town. was present at making the Contract. present at obtaining the Deed, and present at the Payment of ~~the purchase M of~~ the Consideration at Fort Pitt.   The delay of making the Survey keeps out of the Treasury of the United States about 625,000 Dolls. the interest on which is about 9,000 doll. Specie ℔ ann. and the State of Pennsylvania is retarded in the Settlement of the Country.   if Mr. Gorham or any individual is injured, a federal Court will soon be opened.   But the delays are attended with national as well as State disadvantages, and ought not to be protracted.}

{Mr. Morris will vote with and support me, But it is Strange That Gorham, should be so often calling him out & holding conversations with him.}

I cannot pretend to say how often I was up, but my Throat was really sore with speaking.   so plain a Case I never before saw cost so much trouble.   under my present impression. I am ready to vote every Man Void of Principle who voted against this Measure.   at a quarter past three we got the resolve passed.   I cannot help writing that Senatorial Honor dwells not east of the Hudson.   Strong was most uncandid & selfish, and often up.   I wish I may soon have Occasion to retract my above Opinion.   it is painful to think so badly of one's fellow Members.

Thursday, 20 August 1789

this was a dull day in Senate & might be said to make amends for the Bustle of Yesterday   the Coasting bill engaged Us all day. in a round of dullness not one Member seemed to understand the Whole of it, so much had it been patched & mended.   It really rather seems a System for tolerating and countenancing Smugling than otherwise,   I told them so. tho I did not chuse to embark much in it.   Mr. Lear has for Two days past been introduced quite up to ~~the~~ our President's Table, to deliver Messages.   Mr. Izard rose to know the reason of this.   our President said he had directed it to be so, & alledged in a Silly kind of Manner, that he understood, the House so.   there was some talk about it, a few days ago, but I understood the Sense of the Senate to be, that

---

[16]John Gibson (1740–1822), an Indian trader and linguist, had been a resident of the Pittsburgh area since the capture of Fort Pitt from the French in 1758. He served in the Continental army during the War for Independence, primarily in the West.

The Treaty at Muskingum, or Treaty of Fort Harmar with the Six Nations, concluded 9 January 1789, confirmed the Indian cessions of the 1784 Treaty at Fort Stanwix. It is printed in the *SEJ*, pp. 160–63.

the Head of a department, if he came to deliver a Message from the President should be admitted to the Table. but a private Secretary received at the Bar. It is not one farthing Matter. but the Clerk of ~~of~~ the Representatives is received at the bar, and I think him a more respectable Character. than any domestic of the President. Our President however never seems pleased, but when he is concerned in some triffling affair of Etiquette or Ceremony. Triffles seem his favourite object, and his whole desire to be, totas in illis.[17]

Friday, 21 August 1789

The report of the Committee that had conferred with the President was taken up. The most of it was where the President should sit on his being introduced into our Chamber, and where our President should sit &c. &ca. a second resolution was added declaring that the Senate should give their Advice and consent in all Cases by Viva Voce Vote. this being directly contrary. to a former resolution which I had moved for I rose and remarked that this matter had been solemnly debated formerly and decided in favour of a ballot When it, came to the single point of consenting to a Man nominated. That I was still of the same Opinion. And would vote against the present Resolution. Z[18] rose said it was true that the present Resolution would repeal the former one and it was so intended. as he apprehended there was a change in the sentiments of the Senate on that—Subject. Mr. Morris rose said there was a change in the Sentiments of the Senate. and he hoped his H⟨onorable⟩. Colleague would change his Sentiments for *his own Sake*— I rose, said it was a Matter in which I was not in any degree personally concerned, and if I ever were nothing should make me *for my own sake* change my Vote while my Judgment remained unaltered. It could not as far as I knew affect me personally. but even if it did, it should make no odds. On the Question I gave my No in a Voice sufficiently audible. One other faint no only issued from the ~~other~~ opposite side of the House. so that now the Court party triump⟨h⟩s at large. The Words for *his own sake* were not without a Meaning. I have never been at the Table of the President or Vice President. or taken the least notice of for a considerable time by the diplomatic Corps. or the People of Ton in the City. but I care not a fig for it. Davy Harris too has lost his nomination for an Office in Baltimore. But be it so I have done what is right, I followed, my Judgt. & rejoice in it.

Notice was given just before we broke up that the President would be in the Senate Chamber at half after 11 tomorrow to take the advice and consent of the Senate on some matters of consequence but nothing communicated.[19]

---

[17]Immersed in them.
[18]Ralph Izard.
[19]All the Senate proceedings mentioned by WM on this date are recorded in the *SEJ*.

Saturday, 22 August 1789

Senate met and went on the Coasting bill,   the Door Keeper soon told Us of the Arrival of the President.   The President was introduced and took our President's Chair—   he rose and told us bluntly that he had called on Us for our advice and consent to some propositions respecting the Treaties to be held with the Southern Indians[20]—said he had brought Genl. Knox with him who was well acquainted with the business.   He then turned to Genl. Knox Who was seated ~~at his~~ on the left of the Chair.   Genl. Knox handed him a paper which he handed to the President of the Senate, who was seated on a Chair on the floor to his right.   our President hurried over the Paper.   Carriages were driving past and such a Noise   I could tell it was something about indians, but was not master of one Sentence of it.   Signs were made to the door Keeper to shut down the Sashes.   Seven heads (as we since learn) were stated at the End of the Paper which the Senate were to give their advice and consent to.   they were so framed that this could be done by Aye or No.   ~~Our Presid.~~ The President told Us a paper from an Agent of the Cherokees[21] was given to him just as he was coming to the Hall.   he motioned to General Knox for it, and handed it to the President of the Senate.   it was read,   it complained hard of the unjust Treatment of the People of North Carolina &ca. their Violation of Treaties &ca.   Our President now read off, the first article to which our advice and consent was requested.   it referred back principally to some statements in the body of the Writing which had been read.   Mr. Morris rose   said the Noise of carriages had been so great that he really could not say that he had heard the body of the paper which was read and prayed it might be read again.   it was so.   It was no sooner read than our President. immediately read the first head over and put the Question do you advise and consent &ca. There was a dead pause.   Mr. Morris wispered me, we will see who will venture to break silence first.   ~~Our Presi—~~   Our President was proceeding As Many As—   I rose reluctantly indeed, and from the length of the pause, the hint given by Mr. Morris, and the proceding of our President, it appeared to me, that if I did not, no other one would. and we should have these advices and consents ravish'd in a degree from Us.   Mr. President. The paper which you have now read to Us appears to have for it's basis Sundry Treaties and public Transactions, between the southern Indians and the United States &and the States of Georgia North and south Carolina.   The business is new to the Senate, it is of importance, it is our duty to inform ourselves as well as possible on the Subject.   I therefore call for the reading of the Treaties and

---

[20]Documents related to treaties with the southern Indians are printed in the *SEJ*, pp. 165–250.

[21]The paper is printed in the *SEJ*, pp. 199–201. Bennet Ballew, a trader of Scottish origin, accompanied the Cherokee delegation to New York, acting as their agent, interpreter, and negotiator. (*Virginia Independent Chronicle*, 21 April 1790)

other documents alluded to in the paper now before Us.[22]   I cast an Eye at the President of the United States,   I saw he wore an aspect of Stern displeasure.   General Knox turned up some of the Acts of Congress, and the Protests of One Blount Agent for North Carolina[23]—   Mr. Lee rose and named a particular Treaty which he wished read.   the Business laboured with the Senate,   there appeared an evident reluctance to proceed.   The first Article was about the Cherokees,   it was hinted that the Person just come from them, might have more information.   The President ~~of~~ U.S. rose said he had no objection to that article being postponed and in the mean time he could see the Messenger.   the 2d Article which was about the Chickasaws and Choctaws was likewise postponed.   the 3d Article more immediately concerned Georgia and the Creeks.[24]   Mr. Gun from Georgia moved this to be postponed to Monday   he was seconded by Few   Genl. Knox was asked, when Genl. Lincoln[25] would be here on his way to Georgia.   he answered, *not untill Saturday next*   the Whole House seemed against Gun and Few.   I rose & said When I considered the Newness and the importance of the Subject, that One Article had already been postponed, That Genl. Lincoln the first named of the ~~Trustees had~~ Commissioners would not be here for a Week. The deep interest Georgia had in this affair, I could not think it improper that the Senators from that State should be indulged in a postponement untill monday. more especially as I had not heard any inconvenience pointed out that could possibly flow from it.   the Question was put and actually carried.   But Elsworth immediately began a long discourse on the Merits of the Business. he was answered by Mr. Lee Who appeald to the Consti⟨tu⟩tion with regard to

---

[22]These documents are printed in the *SEJ*, pp. 165–99.

[23]William Blount (1749–1800), governor and superintendent of Indian affairs for the Territory South of the River Ohio, 1790–96, was born on Pamlico Sound, North Carolina. A Martinsborough merchant and land speculator, he served during the 1780s in both houses of the state legislature, Congress, the Federal Convention, and as a Federalist at the November 1789 ratification convention. Benjamin Hawkins defeated him for election to the first United States Senate. See also *SEJ*, p. 526. Blount's protest of 28 November 1785 against the Treaty of Hopewell asserted that several of its stipulations violated the rights of North Carolina. His objection was included among other documents submitted to Congress by the president on 7 August 1789 and is printed in *DHFFC* 5:1091.

[24]A map of the Cherokee lands, south of what is now Tennessee and North Carolina, and those of the Chickasaws, Choctaws, and Creeks is printed in the *SEJ*, p. 242.

[25]Benjamin Lincoln (1733–1810) was appointed in 1789 as one of three commissioners to negotiate a treaty with the southern Indians and also as collector for the ports of Boston and Charlestown, Massachusetts. Born into a farming family in Hingham, Massachusetts, he served the town as clerk, justice of the peace, and in the provincial congresses. Massachusetts appointed Lincoln a general in 1776, Congress bestowed on him the rank of major general in the Continental army a year later, and in 1778 he achieved command of the southern army. General Lincoln was appointed the first secretary at war and served in that office during 1781–83. Returning home in 1783, he engaged in farming and land speculation in Maine, commanded the Massachusetts troops sent to suppress Shays's Rebellion early in 1787, and served as lieutenant governor. At the state ratification convention in 1788, he voted as a Federalist. See also *SEJ*, pp. 507–8.

the powers of making War.   Butler & Izard answered &ca.   Mr. Morris at last informed the disputants that they were debating on a Subject that was actually postponed.   Mr. Adams denyed in the face of the House that it had been postponed.   this very Trick has been played by him and his New England Men more than Once.   the Question was however put a 2d time and carried.   I had at an early stage of the business wispered Mr. Morris that I thought the best way to conduct the business was to have all the papers committed—   my reasons were that I saw no chance of a fair investigation of subjects while the President of the U.S. sat there with his Secretary at War, to support his Opinions and over awe the timid and neutral part of the Senate—   Mr. Morris hastily rose and moved that the papers communicated to the Senate by the P. of the U.S. should be referred to a committee of 5, to report ~~immediately~~ as soon as might be, on them.   he was seconded by Mr. Gun.   several Members Grumbled some Objections.   Mr. Butler rose made a lengthy speech against committment.   said we were acting as a Council   no Councils ever committed anything,   Committees were an improper mode of doing business,   it threw business out of the hands of the Many into the hands of the few. &ca. &ca.   I rose and supported the mode of doing business by Committees, asserted that Executive Councils did make use of ~~Councils~~ommittees, that Committees were used in all public deliberative bodies &c. &ca.   I thought I did the Subject Justice. but concluded, the Commitment cannot be attended with any possible inconvenience,   some articles are already postponed untill Monday,   Whoever the Committee are (if committed) they must make their report on Monday morning.   I spoke thro' the Whole in a low tone of Voice.   Peevishness itself I think could not have taken offence at anything I said.   as I sat down the President of the U.S. started up in a Violent fret.   *This defeats every purpose of my coming here,* were the first words that he said,   he then went on that he had brought his Secretary at War with him to give every necessary information, that the Secretary knew all about the Business—and yet he was delayed and could not go on with the Matter—   he cooled however by degrees   said he had no Objection to putting off the Matter untill Monday, but declared he did not understand the Matter of Commitment,   he might be delayed he could not tell how long,   he rose a 2d time and said he had no Objection to postponement untill Monday at 10 O'Clock.   by the looks of the Senate this seemed agreed to.   a pause for some time ensued.   We waited for him to withdraw,   he did so with a discontented Air.   had it been any other, than the Man who I wish to regard as the first Character in the World, I would have said with sullen dignity.   I cannot now be mistaken   the President wishes to tread on the Necks of the Senate.   Committment will bring this matter to discussion, at least in the Committee when he is not present.   he wishes Us to see with the Eyes and hear with the ears of his Secretary only, the Secretary to advance the

Premisses the President to draw Conclusions. and to bear down our deliberations with his personal Authority & Presence,   form only will be left for
Us—   This will not do with Americans.   but let the Matter Work   it will
soon cure itself.[26]

Monday, 24 August 1789

the Senate met, the President of the U.S. soon took his Seat and the Business
began.   The President wore a different aspect from What he did ~~Yesterday~~
Saturday   he was placid and Serene. and manifested a Spirit of Accomodation,   declared his consent, That his questions should be amended,   a tedious debate took place on the 3d Article,   I was called on by Mr. Lee of Virginia
to State something respecting the Treaty held by Pennsylvania,[27]   this
brought me up.   I did not speak long, but endeavoured to be as pointed as
possible,   the 3d Article consisted of Two questions   the first I was for   I
disliked the 2d but both were carried—   the 4th Article consisted of sundry
questions,   I moved pointedly for a division   got it voted for the first, and
opposed the 2d part,   a long debate ensued, which was likely to end only in
Words.   I moved to have the Words, *or in failure thereof by the United States*
struck out. and altho Elsworth⟨,⟩ Wyngate and Dalton had spoke on the same
side with me Yet I was not seconded,   my Colleague had in private declared
himself of my opinion also.   It was an engagement that the United States
would pay the stipulated purchase Money for Georgia in case Georgia did
not.   the Arguments I used on this Subject were so plain I need not ~~not~~ set
them down—   Yet a shamefacedness, or I know not what flowing from the
presence of the President kept every body silent.   The next clause was for a
free port on the Alatahama or St. Mary's River.[28]   This produced some debate
and the President proposed *Secure port* in place of free port.   agreed to.
now followed something of giving the Indians Commissions on their taking
the Oaths to Government.   It was a Silly affair but it was carried without any
debate.   now followed a Clause whether the cession of Lands should be made
an Ultimatum with the Creeks.   there was an alternative in case this should be
negatived. but Strange to tell the Senate negatived both. When it was plain
one only should have been so.   a boundary was named, by a following clause
which the Commissioners were to adhere to.   Money & Honorary Commissions to be given to the Indians.   The old Treaties with the Creeks Choctaws &

---

[26]The events of this date, except for the action on the coasting bill, are recorded in the *SEJ*.
[27]The 1784 Treaty of Fort Stanwix, at which WM was a commissioner, purchased from the
Six Nations all remaining Indian land claims within Pennsylvania. The Treaty at Fort Harmar
with the Six Nations, or Treaty at Muskingum, confirmed the cessions.
[28]The Altamaha River flows into the Atlantic about halfway between South Carolina's
southern border and the St. Mary's River, which separated Georgia and Florida.

Chickasaws made the basis of the future Treaty,[29] [*lined out*] tho' none of them were read to Us. nor a single Principle of them explained. (but it was late) the 20,000 dollars applied to this Treaty, if necessary. This closed the business   the President of U.S. withdrew & the Senate adjourned[30]—   I told Mr. Morris on Saturday that I would get a Copy of the queries or articles to be answered to and call on him that we might make up our minds.   he appointed this morning, and I called accordingly,   we talked and talked but concluded nothing.   I have several times called on him for similar purposes, and thus always the Matter has ended.   just as the Senate had fairly entered on business, I was called out by the Door keeper to speak to col. Humphreys—   It was to invite me to dinner with the President on Thursday next at 4 OClock. I really was surprized at the invitation.   it will be my duty to go.   however I will make no inferences Whatever.   I am convinced all the dinners he can now give or ever could, will make no difference in my Conduct.   perhaps he knew not of my being in Town.   perhaps he has changed his mind of me.   I was long enough in Town however before my going home.   It is a thing of Course and of no Consequence.   nor shall it have any with me.

Tuesday, 25 August 1789

attended at the Usual hour,   on Saturday I had proposed to Mr. Morris, to bring forward all the places which had been mentioned for the permanent Residence of Congress at One time.   he answered rather roughly, *let those that are fond of them, bring them forward,   I will bring forward the falls of Delaware*   accordingly altho the President was every moment looked for, he presented the Draught of the falls[31] to the Chair.   Yesterday I could do nothing for the attendance of the President   this Morning however I took the first Opportunity & presented the Draught with the description of Lancaster,   I nominated Wright's Ferry, York Town, Carlisle⟨,⟩ Harrisburgh⟨,⟩ Reading and Germantown, giving a Short description of each.[32]

---

[29]The old treaties referred to, the Treaties of Hopewell, were with the Chickasaws, Cherokees, and Choctaws and are printed in the *SEJ*, pp. 169–80.

[30]WM's entry to this point describes events that are recorded in the *SEJ*.

[31]The lowest falls of the Delaware River at Trenton, New Jersey, stood out among several locations vying to become the permanent capital of the United States. Congress voted in 1784 to establish its federal town there, but Southerners led by William Grayson struck appropriations for the town from the budget. The draught or sketch of the proposed location presented to the Senate included land on both sides of the Delaware, approximately between Bordentown, New Jersey, on the south and Washington Crossing, New Jersey and Pennsylvania, on the north. This sketch, which is no longer extant, accompanied a petition from the Citizens of New Jersey and Pennsylvania, dated 24 July 1789. This petition is printed in *DHFFC* 6:1856–58. For Senator Morris's investment in land at the site, see *A Collection of Papers Read before the Bucks County Historical Society* 3:343–55)

[32]Because of his support for a national capital situated on the Susquehanna River, prefera-

after this the Coasting bill was taken up and read the third time.   Then the
Resolution for adjourning the 22d. 7ber   a debate ensued but was carried.
{a Residence [*resolution*] was carried by J.A.'s Vote on the favorite point of
removability vid. tomorrow's diary—}   after this the Amendments.   they
were treated contemptuously by Z,[33] Langdon and Mr. Morris.   Z moved they
should be postponed to next Session   Langdon seconded & Mr. Morris got up
and spoke angrily but not well.   they however lost their Motion and Monday
was assigned. for the taking ~~it~~ them up.   ~~now came the~~ I could not help observing the Six Year Class hung together on this business or the most of
them.   now came the Compensation Bill.   I moved the Wages to be five
dollars ⅌ day.   I was seconded by Elmer, but on the Question, only Wingate
him and myself rose.   Mr. Morris almost raged, and in his Reply to me said he
cared not for the Arts people Used to ingratiate themselves with the
public—   In Reply I answered, that I had avowed all my motives.   I knew

bly at Harrisburg, where he and his in-laws owned two ferries and hundreds of acres of land,
WM felt obliged to encourage rival locations in Pennsylvania to promote themselves. Shortly
after his election to the Senate he had written to prominent citizens in several of the state's
towns urging them to provide him with information about their towns' qualifications.
(Minutes of the Committee, 11-21 November 1788, Historical Society of York County; WM
to Jasper Yeates, 13 March 1789, *Historical Register . . . Pennsylvania* 2:306)
    Lancaster, in 1789 the most populous interior town in the United States, was a thriving
trade center and the seat of Lancaster County. WM and Morris had been holding the sketch of
a ten-mile square around Lancaster and the accompanying petition, dated 17 March 1789,
waiting for the appropriate time to present it. The petition is printed in *DHFFC* 6:1859-61.
(WM and Morris to Edward Hand, 3 April 1789, Maclay Diary Manuscript, DLC)
    Wright's Ferry, established in the 1720s, was located on the Susquehanna River in Lancas-
ter County on the road between Philadelphia and York. In 1788 Samuel Wright platted a
town at the site and changed its name to Columbia in hopes of enticing Congress to it. To
many New Englanders the location seemed an ideal compromise between the falls of the
Delaware and the falls of the Potomac. When the House voted on 7 September 1789 to locate
the national capital on the Susquehanna, Wright's Ferry was the expected site. (*Papers Read
before the Lancaster County Historical Society* 18:37-38)
    York, the seat of York County, was the residence of the Continental Congress for eight
months in 1777-78. Its citizens petitioned the House on 22 August 1789, asking that the
national capital be located there, but the document is not extant. Representative Hartley, a
resident of York and the author of *Observations on the Propriety of Fixing upon a Central
and Inland Situation for the Permanent Residence of Congress* (New York, 1789), was the
site's leading advocate.
    Carlisle, the seat of frontier Cumberland County, is situated in the Great Valley, seven-
teen miles west of the Susquehanna River. The petition of its citizens, presented to the
House on 27 August 1789 but not recorded in the journal, is not extant. (*NYJ*, 3 Sept. 1789)
    Harrisburg was proposed as a location for the capital in the House on 3 September 1789,
but the motion failed. (*NYDA*, 5 Sept. 1789)
    Reading, the seat of Berks County, is located on the Schuylkill River at the head of the
Great Valley. Its citizens' nonjournalized petition to the House, presented by Hiester on 27
August 1789, is not extant. A poem signed "P.Q." and published in the *GUS* of 29 August
1789 was based on the petition. (*NYJ*, 3 Sept. 1789)
    Germantown was tied intimately to Philadelphia, seven miles to the southeast. Many
prominent Philadelphians had large country homes there. The town's nonjournalized petition, presented to the House on 27 August 1789, is not extant. (*NYJ*, 3 Sept. 1789)
    [33]Ralph Izard.

the public mind was discontented,   I thought it our duty to attend to the
Voice of the public.   I had been informed that the average of the Wages of the
Old Members of Congress, was a little better than 5 dollars ℔ diem.   I wished
to establish this as a Principle   I would then have data to ~~establish~~ fix a price
on. as the old Wages never were complained off.   Morris⟨,⟩ Z & Butler were
in a Violent Chaff.   Mr. Morris moved that the pay of the Senators should be 8
doll. ℔ day   up now rose Z   said that members of the Senate went to boarding Houses lodged in holes and Corners, associated with improper Company,
and conversed improperly, so as to lower their dignity and Character   that the
Delegates from South Carolina Used to have £600 Sterg. ℔ Year and could live
like Gentlemen. &c. &ca.   Butler rose   said a great deal of Stuff of the same
kind, That a Member of the Senate should not only have a handsome income
but should spend it all.   he was happy enough to look down on these
things,   he could despise them.   but it was scandalous for a member of
Congress to take any of his Wages home.   he should rather give it to the poor.
&ca. &ca.   Mr. Morris likewise paid himself some Compliments on his manner & Conduct in life ~~and~~ his disregard of money; and the little respect he paid
to the common Opinions of People.   Mr. King got up   said the Matter
seemed of a delicate nature, and moved a Committee to Whom the bill might
be referred   this obtained. and a Committee of 5 were appointed.   by the
Complexion of the Committee it would seem. the Senate want their wages
enlarged   {I answered Mr. Morris in a way that gave him a bone to chew but I
believe it is as well forgot.}

Wednesday, 26 August 1789

attended the Senate   the minutes were lengthy but I was surprized to find
no notice taken, of my presenting the Draught of Lancaster the letter, and my
nomination of the other places in Pennsylvania, altho I had put in Writing, the
Whole Matter and given it to the Secretary.   When he had read about half
way of his Minutes, I rose and called on him to know Why he had not inserted
them.   he said he was not come to them but seemed much confused.   he
however got the letter and handed it to the President. to read it and it was
read.   after this the nomination was read, and Butler opposed their being put
on the minutes   I however had a Vote for their going on.   Mr. Morris was all
this While out.   he was of the Committee on the Compensation bill.[34]
When he came in Otis the Secretary came to him and wispered something to
him   God forgive me if I heard wrong or apprehended Wrong, but I thought
he said *Maclay has got that put on the minutes*   Mr. Morris, went out and
staid out untill Senate adjourned leaving his hat & Stick (perhaps he was

---

[34]Salaries–Legislative Act [HR-19].

writing letters in the adjoining room)   he called in as the Senate rose and
seemed unwilling to leave me in the room with Otis.   I went with him to the
Door but returned and spoke to Otis.   all this is perhaps the Effect of over
observation.   I however care not.   the penal Law was taken up.   Elsworth
had a String of Amendments   for a While he was listened to, but he wraught
himself so deep in his niceties and distinctions as to be absolutely incompre-
hensible   he fairly tired the Senate and was laughed at.   I think he may be
well stiled the *Endless Elsworth*.   I forgot to minute Yesterday that the Treasury bill was taken up.   a number of the Senate had recanted again on this
Bill, and were against the power of the President's removing, and had
amended accordingly.   the H. of R. sent us up and Adherence.   and now
Mr. Morris proposed to me to leave the House   I would neither do this nor
change my mind and he was angry.   this was before we had the difference on
the Compensation Bill.   last night there was a meeting of the Pennsylvania
delegation. on the Subject of fixing the permanent Residence,   there was
little of Consequence said.   they ~~agreed however~~ mentioned their former
agreement to Vote for every place that should be nominated in Pennsylvania.   Clymer said some things that savoured more of independence than
any of them.   Scot declared he would put himself intirely in their hands and
move anything that should be agreed on.   Mr. Clymer declared for the Potowmac,[35] rather than stay here.   I understood him that he thought this
politically right.   Fitzsimons and the Speaker seemed to second everything
that Mr. Morris said.   Hartley was for Susquehannah and York Town.   But
indeed I think the Whole Measure likely to be abortive.   They have brought
the Matter forward but have no System.   {I saw this but did not hazard a
single sentiment on the Subject, indeed I could not without implying some
kind of Censure.   I called this morning and indeavoured to put Mr. Scott on
tenable ground in the affair of removal, & left him in a proper way of
thinking.   at least if he should be defeated, to advance nothing but what is
defensible.}

Thursday, 27 August 1789

the Business in the Senate was the 3d reading of the penal Bill.   we had but
little debate untill we came to a clause making it highly criminal to defame a

---

[35]Most congressmen understood the Potomac to mean the environs of Georgetown,
Maryland, a tobacco-exporting town at the head of navigation on the river and the seat of
Montgomery County. In 1783 Congress voted to locate one of its dual residences at or near
Georgetown or the lower falls of the Potomac. Residents of Georgetown petitioned the
House on 7 September 1789 and the Senate on 28 June 1790 to become the seat of government, but neither petition is extant. In 1789 and 1790 some congressmen advocated locating
the capital as far up the Potomac as Conococheague Creek. The Residence Act [S-12] named
the creek and the Anacostia River below Georgetown as the part of the Potomac on which the
capital should be placed. (*JCC* 25:714)

foreign Minister.   here Izard⟨,⟩ King and Johnson made a great Noise for the
paragraph.   Mr. Adams could not sit still in his chair   it was a Subject of
Etiquette & Ceremony   Two or three times did his impatience raise him to
talk in a most triffling manner.   however it did not avail   the paragraph was
lost.   Mr. Morris could not sit one Moment with Us.   the Subject of the
permanent residence was in agitation in the other House.   to tell the Truth
Mr. Morris's Whole Attention seems bent to one Object.   to get the federal
Residence to Trenton.   Mr. Scott brought in a Motion to the following Effect
{agreeable to what had been settled this Morning,—} "That a place ought to
be fixed for the permanent Residence, of the General Government, as near the
center of Population Wealth and extent of Territory, as is consistent with the
convenience of the Atlantic navigation, *having also a due regard to the Western Territory.*" and concluded that Thursday next be assigned for taking it
up.   This was carried   Senate adjourned early. at a little after 4   I called on
Mr. Basset of the Delaware State,   We went to the President's to dinner.   the
Company were President & Mrs. Washington, Vice President and Mrs. Adams.
the Governor and his Wife⟨,⟩ Mr. Jay and Wife⟨,⟩ Mr. Langdon & Wife⟨,⟩
Mr. Dalton and a Lady perhaps his Wife {and a Mr. Smith.} Basset⟨,⟩ myself,
Lear & Lewis ~~his~~ The President's 2 Secretaries.[36]   the President and Mrs.
Washington sat opposite each other in the Middle of the Table.   the Two
Secretaries one at each end.   It was a great dinner & the best of the kind ever I
was at.   the room however was disagreeably warm.   first was soup   Fish
roasted & boiled meats, Gammon Fowls &ca.   this was the dinner.   the
middle of the Table was garnished in the usual tasty way. with small Images
flowers (artificial) &ca.   the dessert was, first Apple pies puddings &ca. then

---

[36]Abigail Smith (1744–1818) married John Adams in 1764. After having been separated by
the demands of his political and diplomatic career during the greater part of the decade
following 1774, John and Abigail resided in Paris and London from 1784 until their return to
the United States in 1788. When he became vice president, she joined him at New York on 25
June 1789. (*New York*, p. 217)
   George Clinton (1739–1812), governor of New York from 1777 to 1795, represented his
native Ulster County in the state assembly from 1768 to 1775. As a legislator, he supported
the patriot position in opposition to Philip Schuyler and his allies. From 1775 to 1777 Clinton
served in Congress and in the army. A leading opponent of ratifying the federal Constitution, he was also an Antifederal candidate for the vice presidency. (*DHFFE* 2:182, 233, 367)
   Cornelia Tappan (1744–1800) of Ulster County, New York, married George Clinton in
1770. In 1789 and 1790 she and the governor resided at 10 Queen Street in New York City.
(*New York Genealogical and Biographical Record* 98:208; *DGW* 5:499n, 6:78n)
   Sarah Livingston (1756–1802), daughter of Susannah French and William Livingston,
revolutionary governor of New Jersey, married John Jay in 1774. They resided in Europe from
1779 to 1784, after which they made their home in New York City. (Richard B. Morris, ed.,
John Jay, Unpublished Papers, 3 + vols. [New York, 1975–], 1:123, 680, 2:723)
   Robert Lewis (1769–1829), who acted as a copyist in the president's official family, was the
son of Fielding Lewis and George Washington's sister, Betty. He accompanied Martha
Washington to New York in May 1789 and often attended her on her trips about New York
City. (*DGW* 6:4n–5n; Douglas S. Freeman, *George Washington*, 7 vols. [New York, 1949–
57], 6:204; Decatur, *Private Affairs*, p. 57)

iced creams Jellies &ca. then Water Melons Musk Melons apples peaches nuts. it was the most solemn dinner ever I eat at, not an health drank scarce a Word said. untill the Cloath was taken away. then the President filling a Glass of Wine with great formality drank the health of every individual by name round the Table. every body imitated him changed glasses and such a buz of health sir and health Madam, & thank You sir and thank You Madam. never had I heard before   indeed I had like to have been thrown out in the Hurry but I got a little Wine in my Glass, & passed the Ceremony. the Ladies sat a good While and the Bottles passed about. but there was a dead Silence almost. Mrs. Washington at last withdrew with the Ladies. I expected the Men would now begin. but the same Stillness remained   the President told of a new England clergyman who had lost an hat and Wig in passing a River called the Brunks. he smiled And every body else laughed. he now and then said a Sentence or two on some common Subject. and What he said was not amiss. Mr. Jay tried to make a laugh by mentioning the Consatina of the Duchess of Devonshire leaving no *Stone* unturned, to carry Fox's Election[37] there was a Mr. Smith[38] here who mentioned, how *Homer* described Æneas leaving his Wife and carrying his father out of flaming Troy, he had heard somebody, (I suppose) witty on the Occasion—but if he had ever read it he would have said *Virgil*. The President. kept a fork in his hand when the Cloath was taken away I thought for the purpose of picking nuts. he eat no nuts but played with the Fork striking on the Edge of the Table with it. We did not sit long after the Ladies retired   the President rose and, went up Stairs to drink Coffee. the Company followed. I took my hat and came home.

Friday, 28 August 1789

There was a meeting of ~~some~~ the Pennsylvania delegation at the lodgings of Clymer and Fitzsimons. I did not hear of it untill I came to the Hall but I hastened there. The Chief Justice of Pennsylvania and Mr. Petit [*lined out*] attended. with a Memorial from the public Creditors.[39] Their business was

---

[37]Georgiana Cavendish, Duchess of Devonshire (1757–1806), a Whig partisan, canvassed heavily for the reelection of Charles James Fox in 1784. Jay's "Consatina" (little conceit) about her is based on the general belief that she gave kisses in exchange for votes. His pun on the word "stone" is based on its vulgar usage.

[38]Perhaps William Stephens Smith (1755–1816), son-in-law of John and Abigail Adams.

[39]The memorial of the public creditors was presented to the House on 28 August and to the Senate on 31 August.

Charles Pettit (1736–1806), Philadelphia-born authority on financial matters and debt speculator, moved to New Jersey after his marriage in 1758. There he was admitted to the bar and held several important appointive offices. From 1778 to 1781 he acted as assistant quartermaster general of the Continental army. At the end of the war, Pettit returned to Philadelphia and engaged in the importing business. In 1784 and 1785, he served in the assembly, where he authored the state's funding system. Pettit attended Congress during

soon done, as we promised to present it in both Houses. but it seems their was a further design in the Meeting.   Mr. Morris attended to deliver proposals from Mr. Hamilton on the part of the New England Men &ca. &ca.   now after the Eastern Members have in the basest manner ~~deceived~~ deserted the Pennsylvanians, they would come forward with proposals thro' Mr. Hamilton.   This same Mr. Morris is as easily duped as another.   I spoke early and declared that now the New England Men find their deceitfulness has not availed them. and Yet they wish to try their Arts a second time.   That their only view was to get a negotiation on foot between them and the Pennsylvanians. That they might break the Connection that is begun between the Pennsylvanians and the southern People.   I was extremely happy to find this Sentiment pervade the Pennsylvanians.   Mr. Morris laboured in vain, and his Chagrin was visible. We came for the Hall.   in coming up ~~the~~ broad Street Mr. Morris declared he would oppose the Susquehannah as the permanent Residence, for it was unfavourable to commerce.   he observed me and added. as far as he could consistent with the engagements he had come under to the delegation.   I needed no such declaration of his. to fix my Opinion of his Conduct.   he has had no other Object {but the falls of delaware} in View since he has been a Senator.   at least this has been his Governing Object.

Attended at the Hall and now the Report of the Committee on the Compensation bill was taken up.[40]   as I knew there was a dead Majority against every thing I could propose I had determined not to say a Word but flesh and blood could not bear them.   The doctrine seemed to be that all worth was wealth, and all dignity of Character, consisted in expensive living.   Z⟨,⟩[41] Butler⟨,⟩ King⟨,⟩ Morris led boldly   they were followed by the bulk of the Senate at least in the way of voting.   Mr. Carrol of Maryland, 'tho' the richest Man in the Union was not with them.   I did not speak long.   and enraged ~~at Such Doctrines~~, as I was, at such doctrines, I am sure I did not speak well.   I endeavoured to shew What the True dignity of Character of Individuals consisted in, as well as of the Assembled Senate.   and then turning shewed that extravagant Expense haughty and distant Carriage with contemptuous behaviour to the Mass of mankind. had a direct contrary effect.   that in short Mankind were not esteemed in the ratio of their Wealth.   and that it was in Vain for the Senate to attempt acquiring dignity or consequence in that way. That I was totally against all discrimination.   That we were all equally ser-

1785–87. In 1787 and 1789, he was an unsuccessful Antifederalist candidate for the Federal Convention, the Pennsylvania Ratification Convention, and the first United States House of Representatives. For more on the Pennsylvania funding system, see Miscellaneous Notes, n. 2. (*DHFFE* 1:424–25; E. James Ferguson, *The Power of the Purse* [Chapel Hill, N.C., 1961], pp. 278, 280)

[40]Salaries–Legislative Act [HR-19].

[41]Ralph Izard.

vants of the public. That if there really was any difference in dignity, as some
had contended, it could not be encreased by any act, or Assumption of ours,
it must be derived from the Constitution, which afforded, in my Opinion, no
Authority for such distinction. Elsworth seemed to aim at a kind of Middle
Course said he agreed there was a difference in dignity &ca. but at present
was against any difference in pay Mr. Adams was too impatient to keep his
seat dignities distinctions Titles &ca. Are his Hobby Horses and the Creature
must ride. Three times did he interrupt Elsworth. he asked him if the
dignity of Senate was to be settled by the People? if the Old Congress had
not degenerated for want of sufficient pay? When Elsworth said the House
of Lords in Britain had no pay, he hastily rose and said a Seat in the House of
Lords was worth £60,000 Ster. ⅌ Ann. Elsworth laid a Trap for himself. up
rose Z⟨,⟩ Lee and others and called for the Sense of the House on the Principle.
Whether there should be a discrimination or not. It was in vain to urge that
this was out of Order. Lee said it was a division of the Clause. I mentioned
that if they must have such a ~~clause~~ Question they should move a postponement. It was in Vain, either way they would have this Question. which was
a leading one Elsworth and Sundry others who had ~~voted~~ occasionally
hinted something of the Superior standing of the Senate. Voted with it. ~~No~~
The Yeas and nays were called. Mr. Elsworth now took the back seat he had
voted for a discrimination, but had repeatedly in his former Arguments mentioned, 6 dollars as enough for the Senate. to be consistent he moved the pay
of the Representatives should be 5 doll. & mentioned my Principle of an
Average of the pay, which he said applied well to the Representatives. I rose
and mentioned that this was the Sum I aimed at for both Houses. but if this
was carried and the Senate stood at 6, we who had voted Against a discrimination. if there was no division of the House might stand in an odd light on the
Minutes. there really was nothing of Consequence in the last observation,
and it was not very well founded. but when the question on the 5 doll. was
taken and lost. King & sundry others called for the Yeas and nays with an
avidity, That I had never observed before. I voted against the Clause as I did
against every other Clause of the bill. When the pay of the Senators came
forward in the next Clause at 6 doll. I rose & declared I did not wish to detain
the Senate. But I had voted against a discrimination When the Yeas and nays
were taken. I had voted a pay of 5 doll. ⅌ day to the Representatives. this In
my Opinion was sufficient pay for the members of either House. the Yeas
and nays were likewise taken on this question. I therefore moved that 6 doll.
should be struck out and 5 inserted. and concluded that then there would be
consistency in my Votes. I had voted no discrimination. I had voted for 5
doll. to the Representatives. I now wished to have my vote for 5 doll. to the
Senators ~~and~~ on the Minutes— such a Storm of Abuse never fell perhaps on

any Member. It was nonsense   Stupidity,   it was a Misfortune to have men void of Understanding in the House.   Z⟨,⟩ King and Mr. Morris, said every rude thing they could.   I did not retort their abuse, but still explained the consistency of my motion   I stood the rage and insult of the bulk of the House for what appeared to me an hour and an half but it was not half so much perhaps.   Z. was most vehement that no such ~~question~~ motion should be admitted.   it was foolish   it was nonsense   it was against all rule &ca.   and all this, altho' there never was a fairer ~~questi~~ or plainer motion before the House,   it was in vain that I declared I did not begin the business of Yeas and nays.   it was in vain that I offered to withdraw the present motion. if all the Yeas and Nays were taken off.   Z raved for the previous question,   he was reply'd to, that this would not smother the Motion.   when abuse and insult would not do then followed intreaty.   we adhered to the Motion. and had the Yeas and nays.   Genl. Schyler joined Us so that We had 4—   now, some other Business was done,   it was past 4 OClock & we adjourned.

It is the Agreement of all the World. That Dreams are perfectly Idle.   But I cannot help ~~help~~ remembering that all last night I was perplexed ~~with Angry~~ in my sleep with Angry Ideas and fretful Occurrences.   unluckily, these pre-admonitions, if they are such, never act as preventatives with me.

Saturday, 29 August 1789

The House having adjourned over untill Monday. I had nothing to do   I felt myself worse of my complaints   both Knees swelled with the Rheumatism.   I however wished to see the Pennsylvania ~~deleg~~ Representatives. and Went to the Hall.   I saw Hartley and exhorted him against entering into any Cabal with regard to the Residence.   that the line now marked out and the principles laid down for fixing the federal Residence, were broad open and honorable, and such as any Man might avow. and above all cautioned him to beware of the Arts and devices of the New England Men.   He took it kindly, but did not seem to stand in need of any Such caution.   a moment after I met Mr. Smith of Maryland.   He had a Terrible Story, and *from the most undoubted authority*.   A contract was entered into by the Virginians and Pennsylvanians. to fix the permanent Residence on the Potowmac, right or Wrong.   and the temporary residence was to be in Philada. and Clymer and Fitzsimons were gone to Philadelphia to reconcile the Citizens of that place to it.   I answered I know nothing of all this, I doubt it, I really do not believe it,   so far as respects myself. if I am considered as included, I know it to be false.   He adhered to it with a firmness that surprized me.   I called on almost all the Pennsylvanians, during the Course of the day. and informed them of the Tale.   they all disowned every communication Whatever in the way of

Contract with the Representation of any State. I called on Mr. Smith in the Evening told him he must be misinformed he declared he had it thro' one person only from One of the Pennsylvanians themselves. he however would give no names. I told him be that as it might I believed the Matter to be groundless. he seemed afraid that I would suspect Mr. Morris but did not acquit him of it. I left him, having paid more Attention to this business than perhaps it merited— I know What a Wretch Otis is, I therefore called on him to see how he had made up the Minutes of Yesterday, on the 3 sets of Yeas and Nays, all was right. This I thought necessary.

I am not well in health, but this is not all, I feel a heavy kind of melancholy hang on me as if I were disgusted with the World, I do not know that; with the Senate I certainly am disgusted. I came here expecting every man to act the part of a God. That the most delicate Honor the most exalted ~~honor~~ Wisdom, the most refined Generosity was to govern every Act and be seen in every deed. What must my feelings be on finding rough and rude manners Glaring folly, and the basest selfishness, apparent in almost every public Transaction. they are not always successful it is true. but is it not dreadful to find them in such a place.

Sunday, 30 August 1789

being Sunday found myself really ill and a fever on me. was ill all last night. I had an invitation to ride with the Speaker but was obliged to decline it. Staid at home all day, and wrote letters to my dear family. was not able to venture out. was worse after dinner and had to go to bed. had a Sleep and a Gentle Sweat & found myself, something better after it.

Monday, 31 August 1789

found myself very ill this Morning a most Acute pain settled in my left hip. I however dressed & went to the Hall. after What had passed with Otis notwithstanding I before knew him to be a Villain, I scarce could suspect him of practising anything now. when he came to the Motion however he read it, That the pay of the Senators should be 5 dollars and that the pay of the Representatives should be six. I heard him with Astonishment. but there was no time to be lost. I moved the necessary Alteration and had it inserted. Z[42] attempted to Support the Secretary. I staid a While. but found myself too sick to attend. I came out of a Window and found Otis in the Corner room, I called on him to explain this business. he hum'd haw'd

---

[42]Ralph Izard.

said his Memory was bad,   I put him in mind of my having called on him on Saturday, and that then it stood right.   I made him however copy it on a Peice of paper.   Vid. M.[43]   He said it was, so in the other book   went to fetch it but did not return—   Sick & came home.

---

[43]WM wafered the paper Otis wrote out for him into his diary at this point. It read:
> On motion to amend the report as it regards the pay of the Senators by striking out Six dollars & inserting five dollars.
>
> passed in the Negative.

On the reverse of the paper WM wrote:
> Had a Card to dine with the Vice President on Friday   excused myself on acct. of my Health.

September 1789

Tuesday, 1 September 1789

exceeding ill with a settled and acute pain in my loins particularly on my left side or hip. dressed however and went to the Hall. the Salary Bill[1] was taken up, there seemed a disposition in a Number of the Senators to give Princely incomes to all the federal Officers. I really was astonished. can it be that they wish to surround the President, with a set of lordly & pompous Officers, and thus having provided the furniture of a Court, nothing but the name of Majesty highness or some such Title will be wanted to step into all the Forms of Royalty. My honorable Colleague seemed particularly attached to all the Officers of the Treasury, he either moved or seconded Motions for augmenting the Salaries of every One of them. I however cannot blame him in particular, he was more decent than Many of them. The avowed object of these proposed Augmentations, was to enable the Officers to live in Stile keep public Tables &ca. I was not able to rise, against this Principle, but Elsworth and others did the Subject Justice.

I found the parties so nearly balanced, that my Vote generally decided in favour of the lowest Sum. This made me sit in extreme pain untill we got over the bill, I then withdrew, and it was really with difficulty, That I got to my lodging. almost every Motion for encreasing the Salaries was accompanyed, with a declaration, how vastly the Salary was below the dignity of the office, and that they moved such small additions despairing of obtaining greater from the House— The Citizens of New York, Where it is expected these Salaries will be spent, and I really believe the Candidates themselves are busy & perhaps others too who expect favours from the Offices.

Wednesday, 2 September 1789

It is in vain, pain and Sickness is my lot I cannot attend the Hall. Mr. Morris called late in the evening. by him I find advantage was taken of my Absence, and a reconsideration was moved & an addition carried to some of the Salaries, Bonny Johney Adams giving the Casting Vote. the moderate part of the House exclaimed violently against the taking this advantage of my

[1]Salaries–Executive Act [HR-21].

absence, and obtained a postponement of the bill untill to morrow.   but
Alas! I cannot attend if the Whole union were at Stake.   I feel transfixed with
so acute a pain thro' my loins, that I cannot move more than if I were
impaled.   to give me any information on this Subject was not however Mr.
Morris's object.   There has been a Violent Schism between him and the
Pennsylvania delegation, or at least a part of them.   he begged leave to give
me the Whole detail of it.   It was long, containing the first engagements at
the City Tavern.[2]   Viz.   That Whatever place in Pennsylvania, the New England Men should name, the Pennsylvanians would vote for it.   that every
place named in Pennsylvania, should be voted for by the Whole delegation.
These things I knew not they having been transacted while I was absent.   But
what I well knew, was that when Mr. Scot's motion came forward. the New
England Men instead of naming the falls of delaware, as Mr. Morris expected,
this being the point to which all his Negotiations with Jay⟨,⟩ Hamilton &ca.
tended. they came prepared the to expose the Pennsylvanians and ridicule the
whole   in this critical moment the Virginians stepped in to the support of
Scot's Motion. rescued the Pennsylvanians from ridicule and gave the Whole a
Serious face.   In this State were matters on the 28th Ulto. and I thought then
that all negotiation with the New England Men was at an End.   indeed I was
not for entering into any private engagements with any of them.   my constant language to the delegation was. You are on tenable ground now   keep
yourselves there.   something was however said as we parted on the 28th.   if
the New England Men have anything to say, it must come from them.   Mr.
Morris catched this and opened a negotiation with them. and carried Matters
so far that a Meeting, was appointed by Mr. Morris of the Pennsylvania delegation at Clymer and Fitzsimons lodging at 5 O'Clock yesterday Evening.   Mr.
Morris wispered me in Senate the Whole business is settled, and you must
come to C⟨lymer⟩. & F⟨itzsimons⟩.'s lodgings at 5 OClock.   on quitting the
Senate Chamber I called Scot out of the Representative Chamber to tell him to
apologize to the Meeting for my absence, as I found myself scarce able to move
one Step.   all was new to him he said   if any Agreement was made it must be
with the Virginians   I saw a cloud of mystery in the business, wished to
attend. and parted with Scot telling him. if I cannot attend. I will send an
Apology, by Mr. Wynkoop.   I could not attend.   but so nobly was this
Matter managed. that While Mr. Morris was introducing Mr. Goodhue and
Mr. King on the part of the eastern States. Mr. Madison was introduced on the
part of Virginia or introduced himself   there however he was, and occupied a
room down Stairs, while Goodhue and King Sat with Mr. Morris—up

---

[2]City Tavern stood at No. 18 Broad Way, just below Little Queen Street. A tavern estab-
lished in 1754 and the principal hotel of the city, it was managed by Edward Bardin. The
Pennsylvania delegation held dinner meetings there, and on 31 July and 5 August, when
WM was at home in Sunbury, the "first engagements" took place. (*New York*, pp. 18–19;
Daniel Hiester Account Book, 1789–92, Berks County Historical Society)

Stairs— Messages were exchanged, the Result was that Clymer⟨,⟩ Fitz-
simons⟨,⟩ Hiester⟨,⟩ Scott, and the Speaker declared totally against any
Treaty with the New England Men. Hartley & Wynkoop declared themselves
disengaged, and all parties departed. What Mr. Morris complains most bitterly of, is, That Fitzsimons should permit him to bring the New England Men
to his lodging on the Terms of treaty, when he was determined against treating
with them. and that there should be any Terms of Communication with
Madison to which he was a Stranger.

Mr. Morris however has not quitted the Game, he told me all the New
England Men and ⟨New⟩ York delegation, were now met and they would on
the Terms of the original proposals. name a place in Pennsylvania, for they had
actually agreed on one, which he had no doubt was the falls of Delaware (by
the by I doubt it) and then we would see how the Delegation would answer it to
their Constituents to negative a place in Pennsylvania. he then said something to me, as to our Conduct in the Senate. I said I thought we had better
come under no ~~further~~ engagements to any of them. but regulate our conduct
on the principles of the interest of our State subordinate to the great good of
the Union. he agreed to this, and took his leave. and now we shall see
What a day will bring forth. The Virginia Terms seem to be, give Us the
permanent Residence. and we will give Philada. the temporary residence— Mr. Morris declared, a Vote could not be obtained in the Senate for
an adjournment, to Philadelphia.

Thursday, 3 September 1789

Mr. Wyncoop went early to a meeting of the Pennsylvania delegation.
they were staggered at the thoughts of voting in the first instance for a place out
of the State. The Business came on in the House of Representatives,
Goodhue took the lead, and, and; here I could give an advantageous lecture
on scheming. the Mariners Compass has 32 points the political one perhaps
as many hundreds, and the Schemers an indefinite number. and yet there is
but one of them that will answer— it is true there were not so many points in
the present case but the Wind came from an unexpected Quarter. all Mr.
Morris Expectations were blasted in a Moment. for Goodhue moved a Resolution for the Susquehannah. as the Sense of ~~the Eastern dele~~ of the eastern
States exclusive of New York. the debate was long and tedious. and the
Business of this day ended with carrying Scotts Motion. Goodhue's Stands
untill tomorrow Elsworth popped in this morning to see if I could possibly
attend on the Salary bill,[3] but I could not. Mr. ~~Morris~~ Elmer called in the
evening. [*lined out*] I know not in the Senate a Man, if I were to chuse a

---

[3]Salaries–Executive Act [HR-21].

friend, on whom I would cast the Eyes of Confidence so soon as on, this little Doctor.   He does not always vote right. and so I think of every Man who differs from me. but I never yet saw him give a Vote, but I thought I could observe disinterestedness in his Countenance,   if such an one errs, it is the Sin of Ignorance. and I think heaven has pardons ready sealed for every one of them.   Behold O God, can such an one say the machine which thou hast given me to work with.   faithfully have I plyed it's powers.   if the result has been Error, intentional criminality was not with me.   He was very urgent for my attendance on the Salary bill, But on seeing the State of my Knee readily admitted, there could be no expectation of it.   He told me Mr. Morris was exerting his utmost address in engaging Votes against the Susquehannah.   he had influence with the Jersey Members.   The Argument was that they had been treated with disrespect, in not being bare consulted. When the York & eastern Members fixed on the Susquehannah.   If Mr. Morris really expects to obtain a Vote for the delaware, after what has happened, it is a proof how far interest will blind a Man.   But I do not believe he has any such expectation. his design must be to ruin the Susquehannah Scheme. and in fact keep Congress in New York.   I have heard him declare it ought never to be any Where but in Philada. or New York.   these places suit his plans of Commerce.   nor do I believe he ever will consent to its being any where else, unless it be on his own Grounds at the falls of Delaware.

Friday, 4 September 1789

Goodhue's motion was carried,   Mr. Morris called in the Evening   he sat a long time,   I never saw Chagrin more visible on the human Countenance. Well said he I suppose You are gratifyed.   I really was vexed to see him so deeply affected,   I said coolly, I could not be dissatisfyed.   he repeatedly declared he would vote for the Susquehannah, because he had said, so,   But he would do every thing in his power against it.   This he called candor, but I think he cannot call it consistency.   it has long been alledged in this place that Mr. Morris governed the Pennsylvania delegation & I believe, this Idea has procured Mr. Morris uncommon attention.   this delusion must now vanish.   he made a long Visit   Mr. Winekoop and myself said every thing in our power to soften him, and we seemed to gain upon him.   he mentioned with apparent regret, some rich lands in the Conestoga Manner which he had exchanged with John Musser for lands on the delaware.[4]   still confined and in a miserable way with my swelled knee.

---

[4]Conestoga Manor in Lancaster County was surveyed for William Penn in 1717. It consisted of approximately 16,000 acres north of Conestoga Creek between the present township of Lancaster and the Susquehanna River. The exchange probably involved Morris's 435-acre Indian Town tract on Conestoga Manor and Musser land in Pennsylvania near the falls of the

Saturday, 5 September 1789

worse, confined mostly to bed.   visited by sundry Gentlemen   Scot⟨,⟩
Hiester⟨,⟩ Fitzsimons called in the Evening.   ~~Ifi~~ the Susquehannah Potowmac & delaware in every mouth   I find Mr. Wynkoop has revived his hopes of
the Delaware.   he said if we loose the Susquehannah. then it will be fixed at
the Delaware.   I looked hard at him, and asked if he had seen Mr. Morris.
he answered no hesitatingly.   I can find by several hints this day that there is
some new scheme on foot.   Mr. Wyncoop tiezed me so incessantly about a
Doctor, that I unfortunately said Yes.   he asked who I Knew   I ⟨s⟩aid Docr.
Treat.   he was gone in a moment.   & soon after Treat & Rodgers[5] called. very
well dressed.   the Sole point I wished them to attend to was my left Knee.   I
could hardly get them to look at it,   they said it was immaterial.   An't you a
good hand to take Medicine.   (No, faintly)   you are all over indisposed you
must undergo a Course of Physick.   You must take a Course of Antimonials
to alter your blood.   a Vomit said the other to clean your. Stomack.   I
begged leave to observe that I was well circumstanced in my body both as to
Urine & feces.   had not an high fever   my Knee Gentlemen my Knee   and I
shewed it to them flayed as it was with blistering.   here is my great pain.
Poultice with Indian Mush, and we will send you some Stuff to put on the
Poultice. and the antimonial Wine & the drops and the laudanum &ca.
&ca.   they seemed to me like Store Keepers with their Country Customers,
wont you take this and this & this.   you must take this & this &ca.

Sunday, 6 September 1789

very ill and close confined   Izard called to see me.   the moment I saw him
I considered that he came on a scrutinizing Errand.   I made no mystery of
anything I knew,   told him that the certain effect of any new Scheme in the
Yorkers or New England Men would most infallibly place us at the
Potowmac.   he repeatedly mentioned a new scheme being on foot, but I

Delaware River where Morris was speculating in 1789. (*Historical Papers and Addresses of the Lancaster County Historical Society* 28:143, 42:22)

[5] Dr. Malachi Treat (c. 1735–95), born at Abington, Pennsylvania, began his practice in New York City prior to the War for Independence. During the war he served as physician general of the hospital for the northern department and afterward as one of three chief hospital physicians and surgeons of the medical department of the Continental army. (John H. Treat, *The Treat Family* [Salem, Mass., 1893], p. 208)

Dr. John Richardson Bayard Rodgers (1757–1833), son of the New York City Presbyterian minister, John Rodgers, and a 1775 graduate of the College of New Jersey, studied medicine under Benjamin Rush and at the universities of Pennsylvania and Edinburgh. He settled in New York and opened a practice with Dr. Treat at 18 Little Queen Street shortly before the FFC convened. (*Princetonians, 1769–1775*, pp. 518–20; *New York*, p. 94)

could not learn what it was. Mr. Morris is in close connection with the Yorkers & communicates every thing to them.

Mr. Clymer called on me he spoke highly in favour of the Susquehannah as being the most favourable position in the State for the benefit of Pennsylvania. blamed Mr. Morris much. said, *he would yet ruin all.* in the Evening the Speaker called he speaks more confidently of the Susquehannah ~~not~~ than any of them. I told him I did not like the adjournment when the question was ready to be put Yesterday. he endeavoured to account for this. but I think it bodes ill.

{The Doctor's Stuff on the Blister spoiled all. it Stopped the discharge and I was much worse. they called to perswade me to take the antimony &ca. &ca.}

Monday, 7 September 1789

I am still very ill, this day was the Tryal of Shift evasion and subterfuge in the House of Representatives but the Susquehannah Vote was carried by a Majority of 7 & Ames⟨,⟩ Lawrence and Clymer appointed a Committee to bring in a bill. close confined and very ill, unable to get information, or to minute it down if I had it. I am still ill. this day the Doctors called & vexed me again.

Tuesday, 8 September 1789

still close confined, and in very bad health the speaker called and gave Us an anecdote of Mr. Madison. which seems to discover some Traits of the less amiable in his Character. While the Salary of the Governor of the Western Territory had been before the House in the first Stage of the Business. Madison had supported it at 2,500 doll. but during the Susquehannah debate Mr. Clymer seeing Governor St. Clair in the Gallery addressed a Note to him for information. The Governor sent back an answer in writing, which contradicted the position of the Friends of the Potowmack. this day Madison Moved a reduction of 500 doll. from his Salary.

The Doctors did not call this day and it seems like relieving me from half of my ailment.

Wednesday, Thursday, Friday, Saturday,
9–12 September 1789

confined, but find myself much better, and now begin to think confidently of seeing my family in health on my part, the Relief which I have experi-

enced, has been from the application of Blisters and Cupping.   This Week
has been one of hard Jockeying between the Senate and House of Representatives.   The Senate insisted and adhered too, for a mark of Superiority in their
pay.   It was a tryal who would hold longest out   the House of R. gave way
more especially after the Senators told them if you want your pay send Us a bill,
for yourselves only. and we will pass it.   I really wonder in the temper the
House is in, that they had not done it.   but they were aware that the Majority
of the Senate would fly from this proposal. as I believe Many of them need
Money as much as any of the Representatives can do.   It was a Tryal of Skill in
the way of Starvation.   and the dignity or precedence or call it what you will,
which could not be gained from the Understandings of the House of Representatives, was extorted from their purses.   I have been visited this Week by all
the Pennsylvanians. and by Docr. Elmer and Mr. Wyngate of the Senate.   I
will venture but one remark on the Business of the permanent Residence.   it
will however be rather a series of remarks   Neither New England Men nor
Yorkers, are sincere about moving from this place. and they firmly believe the
Whole will end in Vapor.   Mr. Morris is to destroy the Susquehannah
Scheme, in the Senate if not sooner, in Order to bring forward the delaware.
this he will do with small Assistance, from the Yorkers by engaging the Senators of Jersey and Delaware,   & this being done. the delaware destroys itself
for the New England Men fall to pieces, their engagement having only been
for the Susquehannah.   These arts are likely enough to succeed.

Sunday, 13 September 1789

Wrote my letters for home   sat up a good deal and found myself, much
better.   in the Evening Mr. Morris Mr. Clymer & Mr. Fitzsimons called on
me.   I thought that the Susquehannah had not got Justice done in the Arguments.   spoke long on the Subject to possess them of my Ideas of it.   all the
talk & Speculation about the Western Country is Visionary,   nothing will
come into the Atlantic Rivers from the Western Waters   if it should the
Susquehannah has the advantage in the double Connection by Juniata and the
West Branch[6]   I was listened to with I thought apathy.   However—

---

[6]The Juniata River flows eastward from the Allegheny Mountains, joining the Susquehanna about fifteen miles above Harrisburg. It was an important link in the chain of rivers
which some Pennsylvanians thought could provide a water route to the West. WM owned
275 acres on the river at what is now Mifflintown and lived there from 1767 to 1771. The site of
"Maclays" is prominently and accurately displayed on William Scull's 1770 map of Pennsylvania, but a 1788 map, produced for the *Columbian Magazine* and based on Scull, shows
WM's property in an incorrect location.
For the West Branch of the Susquehanna see May 1789, n. 5.

Monday, 14 September 1789

about 12 Mr. Clymer called in,   said he had a letter from Reading Howell[7]
with important information,   he read part of it, and desired I would draw up
the thoughts which I had expressed last night That a publication might be
prepared against the time of taking up the Bill.   Doctor Johnson & Mr. Carrol
of Carrolton called while he was in, and interrupted Us a little.   he staid a
Moment after them. and said he would call early tomorrow Morning That we
might settle on something for publication.   I expressed plainly to him the
same thoughts which I minuted on Saturday but he said Mr. Morris was now
contented.   I was so unwell. That I had to go to bed, and here leaning om on
my elbow I arranged something, but was greatly at a loss for Maps. and for the
distances on the Susquehannah & Potowmack begin⟨nin⟩g. at Tide Water to
Fort Pitt.[8]   I sent Mr. Wynkoop to call on Mr. Smith of Maryland for them
was abroad.   I sent a note to Mr. Smith begging he would call on me with
them, but he did not. so that what I composed was with blanks.

Tuesday, 15 September 1789

between 10 & 11 Mr. Clymer⟨,⟩ Mr. Fitzsimons & Governor St. Clair
called,   I read what I had prepared, and it seemed to give satisfaction.   but I
took notes of Sundry Matters, from them to be inserted.   the Blanks were
however still open.   they promised to furnish these distances from Mr.
Ames.   this was done after I had arranged the Composition and the putting
them in could not be done but clumsily.   I hastened to get over the Business,
expecting they would call soon but night came, without my hearing from
them.   I cannot go out, and there is a listlessness, in all our Pennsylvanians on
this Subject.   I can think of Many things, which I would have done, could I go
about, which must now remain undone.

Wednesday, 16 September 1789

Tomorrow the Bill for the permanent Residence is to be taken up.   and Yet
all is quiet, on our parts.   Mr. Wynkoop told me he had Walked a long time

---

[7]Reading Howell (1743–1827), Philadelphia surveyor and map maker, was engaged in
producing a detailed map of the state, which he published in 1792. He had been a state
commissioner to study the navigability of the Delaware River in 1789. (*PMHB* 59:281; *CRP*
16:178)

[8]Fort Pitt was situated at the strategic confluence of the Allegheny and Monongahela
rivers in Westmoreland County. The Penns planned the town of Pittsburgh for the site in
1765.

⟨opposite Trinity Church[9] with Mr. C⟨lymer⟩. & F⟨itzsimons⟩. and that they had spoke of me & nothing more.   he offered to do anything.   I thought of Hartley   he is active and will be in earnest.   Mr. Wynkoop went for him   he came, and I put the paper[10] in his hands.   Mr. Winekoop returned in before the House met   told me Childs[11] was to print, it and they were to send the proof sheet to me for correction.

about 2 OClock Mr. Morris⟨,⟩ Mr. King & Mr. Butler called on me.   the talk was only about the Judiciary.   Mr. Morris said he had followed Elsworth in every thing,   if it was wrong he would blame Elsworth.   King said he had never had an Opportunity of Judging of it.   I censured it as freely as ever. There was a meeting of the Pennsylvania delegation this Evening to regulate their Conduct respecting the part they would act about the opening of the Susquehannah.   They agreed to wait on Smith and Seney in the Morning.   I had begged Mr. Wynkoop, that they should get the Proof sheet and correct it.   but it is like they would not ~~touch it~~ send for it.   the Printer's Boy however called on me. and I corrected it.   I can find, that Germantown is the place that is to be played against the Susquehannah.   I had hopes this Opposition was dropped.   I believe they are not as active as some days ago, but lie by fully bent to take all advantages.   We will see What they will do.   But I have laid it down as the only sure Ground to adhere to the Susquehannah.

Thursday, 17 September 1789

some People are so hardy as to deny that the Susquehannah affords any navigation at all.   Boudinot is one of them.   It would really be of Service to him if he could be made to blush.   I wrote to Mr. Burrell[12] to furnish an extract of the Stores forwarded up the Susquehannah in the year 1779. & the usual load of ~~of~~ a river Boat.   Mr. Wynkoop went to him with the letter.   he said he would do what he could but rather excused himself.   I sent some

[9]Trinity Church, located at Broad Way and Wall Street, was in the process of reconstruction during the tenure of the FFC at New York, having been destroyed by the fire of 1776. Established in the late seventeenth century, it was the oldest Episcopal congregation in the city. (*New York*, pp. 136–37)

[10]WM's unsigned piece, which can be found in Appendix B(1), was published in the *NYDA* of 17 September 1789.

[11]Francis Childs (1763–1830), a Philadelphia-born printer, established himself at New York with the assistance of his patron, John Jay, and edited the New York *Daily Advertiser* between 1785 and 1796. He took John Swaine as a partner in July 1789. Childs and Swaine secured a lucrative printing contract with the House of Representatives and moved to Philadelphia with Congress in 1790, although they continued to edit their New York newspaper. (*New York*, pp. 209–10)

[12]Jonathan Burrall (1753–1834) of Connecticut had served the Confederation Congress as commissioner for adjusting the accounts of the commissary and quartermaster's departments of the Continental army. For WM's involvement with these supplies in 1779, see Appendix E. (*PRM* 4:253n; Francis S. Drake, *Dictionary of American Biography* . . . [Boston, 1872], p. 145)

information to Mr. Ames by Mr. Wynkoop.   and now we must see What they will do.

The day is rainy, and nobody has called.   about dark Parson Lynn came in.   Joy was in his Countenance.   he told me the Maryland condition[13] was carried, and of Course there would be Schism among the Pennsylvanians, that Gerry had moved for the Falls of Delaware instead of ~~Fa~~ Susquehannah.   the Whole of What he said convinced me that I was not in the least mistaken as to the Measures that are carrying on.   the Pennsylvanians will divide the New England Men and Yorkers   both will come off with apparent Honor. and congress remain Where it is.   late at night in comes Mr. Wynkoop in higher spirits than ever I saw him.   It is all over with the Susquehannah.   We must vote against it now.   I have just come from Clymer's & Fitszimons lodgings they are of the same Opinion.   and now for the Falls of Delaware.   The Marylanders have carried a clause that ~~the Pennsylvanians~~ Pennsylvania & Maryland shall consent, to the Satisfaction of the President, that the navigation of the Susquehannah be cleared but not at their Expense.   We never can consent to lay our State under any restrictions.   the only reply I made was. so then rather than consent that the Navigation of the Susquehannah should be opened, you will drive Congress away from its Banks.   this is the point of View in which it will be considered, and in which you must expect to answer for it.

Friday, 18 September 1789

I wished to see some of our Pennsylvanians.   Clymer & Fitzsimons had called a meeting last night in Order to make them change their ground and Vote for the falls. of Delaware.   this was the intention of the Meeting from What Mr. Wynkoop clearly enough expressed.   I wrote a note to Hartley, but he just came in as I was sealing of it.   he was in an high rage at the Philadelphians, and declared they had been insincere from the Beg⟨innin⟩g.   he seemed to want my Opinion.   I gave it freely to adhere firmly to the Ground that had been taken, and support the Bill at all Events.   I had wrote a Note to the Speaker.   But he came in, immediately after I had sent it away,   he seemed clearly in Sentiment with Hartley. and gave substantial reasons for it.   he said an absolute agreement had been made between the Pennsylvanians on one part and Smith & Seney of Maryland on the other.   That the Maryland Condition should be that ''Pennsylvania would ~~take to no Measures~~

---

[13]The Maryland Condition, also known as the Proviso Clause, was inserted into the Seat of Government Bill [HR-25] by the House in the committee of the whole. First proposed on 7 September, it declared that land could not be purchased at the site on the Susquehanna River selected for the seat of government until Maryland and Pennsylvania had satisfied the president of the United States that they had made provision for the removal of all obstacles to navigation between the mouth of the river and the seat of government.

~~to prevent the~~ throw no impediment in the way of Clearing ~~of~~ the Susquehannah" This gave intire Satisfaction to Smith & Seney, was to have been brought forward by the Friends of Susquehannah & Smith and Seney by voting for it, would have carried this & rejected the other Maryland Condition. But Mr. Fitzsimons broke the agreement & flew off, ~~and would have nothing~~ Yesterday Morning this of Course fixed Smith & Seney to the exceptionable condition which was carried by Means of their Votes. so that it seems as if Mr. Fitzsimons wished some Vote to be carried that would furnish him and others with a Pretext of breaking off from the Susquehannah. For they could have prevented this Maryland Condition if they had chose so to do. He further said That Mr. Clymer began to read a letter from the Speaker of Pennsylvania,[14] which Fitzsimons prevented him going thro' with! further That his Partner in Philada. mixes with all classes of People. "That the Common People were well satisfyed with Congress being on the Susquehannah, but of late he could hear among the leading Men about the Bank &ca. many Opinions and predictions That it never would be on the Susquehannah." &ca. I think it ~~not~~ no unfair Conclusion to say, Philada. Spite hath done this. altho' it be the Act of but a few individuals in that place. I can now clearly account for the listlessness and Apathy of some Persons respecting the Susquehannah, indeed it is questionable whether the late application to me was anything more than a blind, to cover their intended defection.

By this and Yesterday's Papers, France seems traveling in the Birth of Freedom, her Throws and pangs of labour are Violent. God give her an happy delivery. Royalty Nobility and the Vile pageantry, by which a few of the human Race lorded it over, and trod on the Necks of their fellow Mortals, seem likely to be demolished with their kindred Bastile, which is said to be laid in Ashes. Gods! with what indignation do I review the late attempts of some [*lined out*] Creatures among Us, to revive the Vile Machinery. Oh Adams Adams what a Wretch art thou! This Evening the Speaker called he repeated over the Whole of What he had told me in the Morning, in the Presence of Mr. Wynkoop, said he did not know what to make of Men who agreed to a thing over nigh⟨t⟩ & deny'd it in the Morning; Fitzsimons and Clymer were tired of the Susquehannah &ca. &ca.

Saturday, 19 September 1789

This morning Col. Hartley's Servt. called on me with a note & shewed me the Copy of letter which the Col. had wrote to Clymer & Fitzsimons. he called on them for an adherence to their former tenor of Conduct respecting

[14]Richard Peters.

the Susquehannah. and plainly declared that their defection now, would be considered as a proof of their insincerity from the Begin⟨nin⟩g.   I am unwilling there should be any Schism, among the Pennsylvania Representatives. perhaps this letter may lay the foundation of it.   perhaps it may have a contrary effect at the Present Moment,   it is however done. without the advice of any Person. and we are left to attend to the Event.

   I have wished much to have seen Clymer and Fitzsimons for some days past.   I dropped distant hints of this often to Mr. Wynkoop.   this had no effect.   I could not Justify myself in sending for them.   however I know not, if I could have any influence with them.   and I know that Wynkoop carries faithfully every Word which I say, to them.   Doctor Franklin[15] says *the World will do it's own Business.*   I must let do so on this Occasion, for my lame Knees, will not let me help it.   Mr. Wynkoop left the House, came home and went on a party of Pleasure,   had a note from Col. Hartley,   the permanent Business is put off untill Wednesday next, on Acct. of the indisposition of some Members.   the House by joint resolution with the Senate, are to break up on Tuesday.   {(Hartley was mistaken when he wrote this note)}   appointing Wednesday seems like the Oblivion Committee in the British parliament on the American Petitions before the Revolution.   But we will see What will come of it—   In the Evening Mr. Dalton called to see me   soon after Mr. Morris and Mr. Fitzsimons came in,   soon after Mr. Scott, and Parson Linn. the Parson went away   Mr. Dalton went away.   Mr. Scott said What shall we do with the Residence   I believe we must vote for it.   I don't know said Mr. Fitzsimons   if the Condition had only been *that we should not prevent the clearing of the Susquehannah.* I should not have cared,   Scott said in fact it amounts to no more now.   I don't know said Fitzsimons.   Mr. Morris said abruptly, the Contract is broke,   we were to have this thing free of any Condition,   I have however a letter from Peters on this Subject   he got out the letter but did not read it.   Mr. Scott was on his feet and went away.   The others soon followed—   when Mr. Morris talked of the Contract being broke, I asked have any of the eastern People given way   have any of them voted against the Susquehannah.   Mr. Fitzsimons said No—   I can readily guess What Mr. Morris means by saying the Contract is broke.   Ne⟨e⟩d his Vote be expected?

Sunday, 20 September 1789

   being Sunday wrote letters to my family   the day was fine.   I got an Hackney Coach. and rode out about an hour and an half.   felt the Worse for

---

[15]Benjamin Franklin (1706–90), a Boston-born Philadelphia printer, writer, diplomat, and scientist, closed a lengthy political career in the fall of 1788 when he completed his final term as president of Pennsylvania. His last public acts involved the FFC. He signed the

it   perhaps it was only the fatague.   Col. Hartley called in the Morning
says the Business of the permanent Residence will come on tomorrow.   Mr.
Wyngate and Genl. Irwin[16] called to see me.   Mr. Wynkoop went Yesterday
Evening to New Ark.[17]   came home late.   he soon asked me What of the
federal Residence.   I had no News on the Subject.   he talked himself a good
deal on the Subject.   I thought I could clearly gather from What he said. that
the Effort would be to throw off the Whole Business for this Session.   for from
What I can learn they are not able to d engage the New England Men for the
Delaware—   therefore postpone and ~~take Chance of~~ & wait for—the Chapter of Chances.[18]

Monday, 21 September 1789

dressed myself this day   weak & languid but went to the Hall.   thought I
would not be able to stay long, but when the business began I seemed amused
and grew better   I staid it out untill after 3 OClock,   The Judges Salaries
were taken up.   That of the Chief Justice had been settled before at 4,000
doll.   That of the puisne Judges was put at 3,000   Mr. Morris moved for 500
more   seconded by Izard.   a division 9 & 9   Mr. President had to give the
Casting Vote and had the Yeas & Nays called on him.   he however made a
Speech,   somebody had said Judges could be had for less.   "That People
must be abandoned and forsaken by God. who could speak of buying a Judge
as you would an horse.   Judges should portion their Children bring them up
provide for them &ca. &ca.   Many families in New England had suffered by
the head of it being a Judge."   Motions were made for encreasing every thing
almost,   none however carried, untill they came to the Atty. Genl.   Mr.
Morris moved it should be 2,000 doll.   King seconded,   a division 9 & 9 and
the President voted for it.   Wyngate ~~voted for it~~ called for the Yeas and
Nays.   Adams looked pitiful   said he would be made the ~~Skape~~ Scape Goat
for every thing   a number got up to have the Yeas and Nays retracted.   Grayson who had been with Us before spoke against having them now, so they were
not called.   the H. of R. however threw out this amendment, and it was
reduced to 1500.

petition of the Pennsylvania Society for the Abolition of Slavery and anonymously attacked
Representative Jackson in the press for his speech on slavery in the House. ("Historicus,"
FG, 25 March 1790)
    [16]William Irvine (1741–1804), a commissioner for settling accounts between the United
States and the individual states from 1788 to 1793, was born in northern Ireland. After
serving as a British naval surgeon during the French and Indian War, he practiced medicine at
Carlisle, Pennsylvania. He served throughout the War for Independence, holding the rank
of brigadier general from 1779 to 1783. He encouraged Pennsylvania to purchase the Erie
Triangle and represented that state in Congress from 1786 to 1788. See also *SEJ*, p. 534.
    [17]Newark, seat of Essex County, New Jersey, is situated nine miles west of New York City.
    [18]Unforeseen events.

Hartley called me out to tell me That the Susquehannah Bill was carried. Mr. Morris was all day calling out Members.   Grayson⟨,⟩ Gun⟨,⟩ King⟨,⟩ Reed & Butler were some of them that I saw him take aside.   the Citizens and Wynkoop dared not vote against it.   It would have had no effect if they had,   Mr. Morris being a Six Years Man, considers himself as independent. and he is to destroy it in the Senate.   He has always expressed his contempt for the Opinions of the People.   the others think to escape censure by this pitiful Shift.   But we know them.   When I consider how agreeable it will be to the eastern Members and to the Yorkers to destroy all this business, I really fear Mr. Morris.   it is so easy perswading men to do what they wish for.   we must however wait the Event.

Tuesday, 22 September 1789

dressed and went to the Hall,   resolution came up from the other House, for rescinding the Resolution of adjournment of this day, and for adjourning on Saturday   concurr'd.   Bill for the permanent Residence read the first time   Butler moved to postpone to next Session   seconded by Grayson. Lee⟨,⟩ Butler and Grayson spent above an hour,   they had only Z[19] & Gun to join them on this Business   5 in all.   from hence I think we may prognosticate that the Bill will pass in some shape or other.   Mr. Morris in the deepest Chagrin. did not speak to me in the Morning   left his usual seat to avoid me.   first went and sat beside Mr. Dalton.   then rose and took out Mr. Reed.   came in again and went and took a seat beside Grayson.   Bland called out Grayson   Mr. Morris followed.   came in again and went and took a seat beside Elsworth.   never spoke untill we were coming out of the Senate Chamber,   he then asked if I continued to grow better,   I answered in the affirmative, but he could not talk to me.

I met Governor St. Clair at the Hall.   if I had no other Clue, I could tell how the Philadelphians stood by him   he was all full of doubts,   the bill would never do.   the President would never act on it,   the River might not admit of Navigation &ca. &ca.   The Bill however passed 31 to 17 in the House of Representatives—   Wynkoop cannot sit with me this Evening   he is chatting down Stairs.   Mr. Linn called   told me the design of the Virginians and a Carolina Gentleman was to talk away the time, so that we could not get the bill passed.

Wednesday, 23 September 1789

went to the Hall early   Mr. Carrol came in.   told me Mr. Morris was against the Bill and wanted to bring forward Germantown and the Falls of

---

[19]Ralph Izard.

Delaware.   The Senate Met and every endeavour was used to waste time.
Lee⟨,⟩ Butler⟨,⟩ Grayson refused to go on the Business as Gun was absent.
Gun came & then they wanted to go and see the Ballon[20] let off.   But at last
the Bill was read over,   I was called out,   there was Mr. Morris⟨,⟩ Mr. Fitzsimons and Col. Hartley,   Fitzsimons began telling me What the Pennsylvanians, had agreed to do.   first strike out the Proviso Clause,   if this could be
done. then agree to the Bill.   But if this could not be done, then abandon the
Susquehannah and Try for the falls of the Delaware and Germantown.   as he
stated it to me I understood that all the Pennsylvanians but myself had agreed
to this.   I told him it was a late moment to call on me When the Bill had
actually been read over and the first Clause taken up.   That the Proviso had
nothing so terrible in it as to make me ~~loose~~ abandon the Bill rather than consent to it.   That I saw no safety in any thing but adhering to the Bill and if we
lost this Bill we must go to the Potowmack.   Mr. Morris raged out something
against the Proviso as to the advantage the State would loose, by such a proviso
being adopted, and concluded with a tremendous Oath by *God* I never will
Vote for the Bill, unless the Proviso is thrown out.   I said slowly he would act
as he pleased.   He knows as well as I do, that the ~~House~~ Senate never will reject the Proviso;   Fitzsimons & Morris however said, let Us call King out.
King came.   Fitzsimons said. ~~five out of~~ the ~~8~~ Pennsylvania Delegates. were
against the Proviso, and in case the Proviso was continued 5 were for trying the
Falls of Delaware and Germantown.   Col. Hartley corrected him and told
him only four.   as I had nothing to do with their bargain I turned on my heel
and left them.   I thought it strange Conduct of our Delegates after they had
all voted for the bill to be making such offers.   if the Proviso is struck out, the
2 Marylanders will Vote against Us.   if in, Mr. Morris has Sworn he will Vote
against it.   I have expected nothing else of him for some time.   Mr. Morris
moved that the first & 2d clauses should be postponed. so as to come at the
Proviso,   This brought on a lengthy debate,   Butler was severe on Mr. Morris,   said his Views were totally local   let Us keep the federal Town on the
Susquehannah, & let there be no navigation out of it, and then you must come
to Philada.   but rather than have the Susquehannah opened, which will take
some of our Trade away we will not let You put the federal Town there,   Morris reply'd with apparent heat,   the other retorted,   Grayson and Lee were
both up   Z[21] was up.   and long speeches were made.   the question was
however put, and carried.   and now Mr. Morris moved to strike out the
Proviso,   I forgot who seconded him.   The reason he gave was that the State
of Pennsylvania, had a bargain on hand with Maryland about this Matter, and
Commissioners were appointed to negotiate it.   Pennsylvania would suffer

---

[20]The well-advertised ascension of Joseph Decker in a balloon that was 100 feet in circum-
ference followed two August flights of smaller unmanned balloons. The balloon caught fire,
and the experiment ended in failure. (*New York*, p. 184)

[21]Ralph Izard.

the Susquehannah to be opened, if Maryland would suffer a Canal to be dug
between the Bays of Chesapeak and Delaware.[22]   That he would be betraying
the Interest of the State in so eminent a degree, that he dared not go home to
Pennsylvania, if such a clause was in the Bill.   I had hinted to Mr. Morris that
the last law for clearing the Susquehannah, had no Condition.   but he answered the Marylanders thought it had.   It was now that the most unbounded abuse was thrown on the State of Pennsylvania   Lee⟨,⟩ Grayson⟨,⟩
Butler & Izard struggled who should be up to rail at the Government.   Mr.
Carrol. got up and answered Mr. Morris mildly.   I whipped out & sent for Col.
Hartley and got from him the ~~bill~~ late law for clearing the Susquehannah.   so
great was the rage for speaking that I could scarce get a Word said.   I endeavoured to be up first on the sitting down of Butler.   but Lee was up with me   I
begged for indulgence as I had information to give which I thought very
material.   I stated the importance of the Question and declared it my duty to
give all the information in my power.   That the State of Pennsylvania deserved none of the illiberal abuse that had been bestowed on it.   That no such
design as shutting up the Susquehannah could be charged on ~~them~~ Government.   I then read several clauses of the Act. declaring the Susquehannah
and its Branches high Ways to the Maryland line.[23]   I declared I did not think
there was a single Pennsylvanian of Character that would be so base as to Wish
the shutting up the Mouth of that River.   That for my part I considered the
Proviso as harmless, and if it tended to give Satisfaction to the public at large or
any individuals, I had no Objection to it.   That I thought the Business on the
part of ~~Susquehannah~~ Pennsylvania done already, but if any thing more was
wanted, I had no doubt of their doing it.   I could for my part apprehend no
danger from the Proviso.   much it was said was put, by it, in the Presidents
power.   But he had his honor to support,   I was convinced he would neither
triffle with his own Character, nor the public Expectation and I was convinced
no defeat would be experienced on the part of the State of Penn-

---

[22]This interstate conflict was due to competition for commerce between the ports of
Baltimore and Philadelphia. Situated near the head of the Chesapeake Bay, Baltimore would
be the natural outlet for water-borne trade from the Susquehanna watershed unless a canal
were cut across the Delmarva Peninsula to Delaware Bay and the Delaware River, making
Philadelphia more accessible. Maryland had recently agreed to discuss such a canal with
Pennsylvania.

[23]In 1771 the Pennsylvania Assembly passed an act declaring the Susquehanna River a
public highway above Wright's Ferry and authorizing a commission to supervise its clearing.
WM was one of the commissioners appointed. The act was rewritten in 1785 to declare the
river a public highway to the Maryland line. WM read portions of the 1785 act to the Senate.
In September 1789 the Pennsylvania Assembly appointed commissioners, including WM's
brother Samuel, to undertake a serious survey of the Susquehanna and other rivers in the
state for the purpose of determining where locks and canals were necessary. On 28 September
1789, the assembly appropriated money for clearing the Susquehanna, but only above
Wright's Ferry. (James T. Mitchell and Henry Flanders, eds., *The Statutes at Large of
Pennsylvania, from 1682 to 1815*, 18 vols. [Harrisburg, Pa., 1896–1915], 11:540–42, 13:355)

sylvania— The rage for speaking did not subside, but it took a different turn   Mr. Morris said he did not know of that Law.   the Question however was put, and 5 only rose for rejecting the Proviso   Morris⟨,⟩ King⟨,⟩ Schyler⟨,⟩ Johnson & Dalton.   There was now a cry for adjournment to see the Balloon. & the Senate Rose.

Mr. Clymer called about 8 OClock, began to speak against the Susquehannah.   Said there was an old interest and a New interest starting up to destroy it in Pennsyl. by sending the Trade into the New interest,   That he would not for 1000 Guinneas the law would pass,   that the old Commercial interest, had nourished Philada.   it was an Ornament to the State.   he seemed willing to perswade me that I should vote against the Bill,   I asked him how he thought it would look for me to vote against it, when they had all Voted for it on Monday last?   he said he was induced to do so expecting a Change in the Senate.   That he would not for half his Estate he had done so.   That he was duped into it.   I told him that was not my case, for I had followed my Judgt. hitherto and would continue to do so.   That if we changed our ground in the Senate, and could insert any other place, than the Susquehannah, we lost our hold of the Eastern People, and the Whole fell to the ground, agreeable to What I had told him on Monday Week.   and that the next session Virginia would come forward with 5 members from N. Carolina and be joined by 2 or 3 from Pennsylvania and we should infallibly go to the Potowmack and for my part I would rather stay on the Susquehannah.   he declared for his part he would not.   Mr. Clymer used to extol the advantages of the Susquehannah, and declared as he sat on my bedside about a fortnight ago, that no position in Pennsylvania was equal to Susquehannah.   all this change has taken place since Genl. Irwin came to Town, and declared there was a Contract on foot for clearing the Conewago falls[24] for £4000—   {now what am I to think of the Citizens of Philada. and some other of the Pennsylvania Delegation,   can I help concluding, on the most undeniable data as well from What I have heard, as from Circumstances & their own declarations, That they ever have been opposed to the Susquehannah. and voted for it purely to save their popularity in the State. and ~~trust~~ trusted to Morris Who is a Six-Year Man ~~to~~ & who on all occasions despises the Voice of the People, to destroy the bill in the Senate. have I a name for such Conduct?   thus barefacedly to drive away Congress from the State rather than, a few Barrels of flour should pass by the Philada. Market in descending the Susquehannah, and rather than the Inhabitants of that River should enjoy the natural advantages, of opening the navigation of it.   I think it probable these vile Arts will prevail.}

---

[24]Conewago Falls blocked the Susquehanna River at Middletown, north of Wright's Ferry. It was the first of a series of falls and rapids impeding navigation on the lower fifty miles of the river. Meetings were held in 1789 to discuss the best method of bypassing the falls, and a canal and locks were completed in 1797. (James W. Livingood, *The Philadelphia-Baltimore Trade Rivalry, 1780–1860* [Harrisburg, Pa., 1947], pp. 28–32)

Maclay diary entry for 24 September 1789. (Courtesy of the Library of Congress.)

A page of Maclay's rough notes for 24 September 1789. (Courtesy of the Library of Congress.)

Thursday, 24 September 1789

This day marked the Perfidy of Mr. Morris in the most glaring Colors, notwithstanding his engagement entered into at the City Tavern notwithstanding his promise repeated in Many companies afterwards, he openly voted against the Susquehan⟨nah⟩ King⟨,⟩ Schyler and all the New England Men except Doctor Johnson Voted against it. Mr. Morris's Vote alone would have fixed

Us on the Susquehannah for ever.   The affair has taken the very turn I predicted,   our ruin ~~in~~ is plotted contrived and carried on by Mr. Morris—in
conjunction with the ⟨New⟩ Yorkers—   I gave an Account of the Center of
Population being in Pennsylvania, the Center of Wealth, and geographical
center,   Went at large into all the detail of the Potowmack and the Susquehannah,   When the Potowmack was voted for, I was long on my legs, or I
should say my Knees and they grew weary.   We easly threw out the Potowmack—   but I well knew all this was in vain—   I will put in my rough notes
in my book[25]—   this Whole Morning and for an hour after the Senate Met,
the York Senators and Representatives were in the Committee room, and Mr.
Morris running backwards & forwards like a Boy, taking out one Senator after
another to them. & Adams delaying business for them.   No business was ever
treated, with more barefaced partiality.   Mr. Morris moved, that the Words
~~on the~~ at some convenient place on the Banks of the Susquehannah &ca.
should be struck out, and that it might remain a blank, for any Gentleman
that pleased to name a place.   I objected to this as unfair, for by this Means
the Banks of the Susquehannah would be thrown out, When in fact that place
might, have more friends than any other individual place.   for all those Who
wished a different place, would unite in this Vote however different their
Views might otherwise be, and thus the place rejected in the first instance
would be laid under ~~a~~ an unfavourable impression.   That I saw no reason to
deviate from the Common mode, Which had always been. to move to strike
out certain Words in Order to insert certain other Words, and thus Men would
plainly see their way clear, and the intention of the Mover,   Mr. Adams
answered me from the Chair,   said it was all fair.   it was in Vain to argue,
the question was put, and seven only rose.   Up got Mr. Morris   said the
Question was not understood.   ☛ Vid. annex'd rough Paper   and began his
explanations.   {Mr. Morris Said he had often wished to explain himself on
the Subject of the Residence but was always prevented.   That Pennsylvania,
was averse to the Susquehannah and would give 100,000. dollars to place it at
Germantown.   I rose to the point of Order ~~declared~~, declared that no motion
or application for reconsideration could be received from a Member in the
Minority. quoted parliamentary practice, and appealed to the Chair.   Mr.
Adams now made One of his Speeches,   unfortunately it seems none of our
Rules at the time re⟨a⟩ched the point,   new Matter had been alledged in
Argument &ca.   it was in vain that I alledged, that no business ever could
have a decision, if Minority Members, were permitted to move reconsidera-
tions, Under every pretense of new Argument.   Adams gave it against me,
Mr. Morris now Assumed a bolder tone   flamed away in favor of
Germantown   repeated his offers in the name of the State &ca.   I declared I

---

[25]WM wafered his rough notes into the journal. They are printed at the close of this day's
entry.

considered myself to enjoy the Confidence of Pennsylvania in as unlimited a
Manner as my Honorable Colleague, that I firmly believed the General Sense
of the State, was more in favour of the Susquehannah than Germantown, and
that if Money was to be given, the Susquehannah was most likely to obtain
it,   I however deny'd that any M State Money was appropriated to any such
purpose, and called on my Colleague to produce the Authority on Which he
made the offer.   He now came forward the Great Man & the Mercht. and
pledged himself that if the State would not He would find the Money.   a
Vacant Stare, on this, seemed to occupy the faces of the Senate.   But [*lined
out*] the New England Men helped him out.   It was proposed that the Valid-
ity of the law should depend on the payment of the money & that a clause for
this purpose should be now inserted in the Bill.   And to work some of them
went in fabricating such a clause.   Mr. Morris had not Yet been regularly
seconded.   but I began to see, When it was too late, that I had committed a
Mistake in not appealing to the House from the Decision of the Chair—}
Basset got up and recanted,   said he had not understood the Question,   this
is usual with him.   (This Man has repeatedly of his own Accord told me that
the Susquehannah was the only proper place)   It was in vain that we Urged
that the question was fairly put,   a Reconsideration was called for.   there is
really such a thing as Worrying weak or indifferent Men into a Vote.   Urging
that the Matter had not been sufficiently explained understood, &ca. how fair
and inoffensive the Measure &ca.   all these Arts were plaid off, with the
utmost address upon this Occasion, and with the weight of John Adams
Succeeded.   it was reconsidered and 11 voted for this fair and inoffensive
Measure,   in a moment by way of fixing them, against the Susquehannah,
altho' it was still called up out we will take a Vote on the Susquehannah, the
Yeas and Nays were called.   and now Grayson and Lee moved for the Potowmack.   (note they had moved for striking out the Word Pennsylvania, so as to
leave the Whole banks of the Susquehannah open, and lost it)   now was a
lengthy debate in which I supported the Susquehannah.   but it is too lengthy
much to insert what I said.   the annexed papers were the basis of it.[26]   the
Potowmack lost it, and the Blank now remained.   Mr. Butler now rose and
Moved to fill the blank with the Words banks of Susquehannah &ca. the same
Words which had been struck out.   I seconded the Motion.   up got Mr.
Morris and opposed this with warmth,   he allowed That there might be a
question taken on the Susquehannah   But he had [*lined out*] would have a
Vote taken on his plan first.   Butler insisted that as his Motion was fairly
before the House and seconded. it must be disposed of,   Morris reply'd
without any reason on his side indeed, but he had no need of reason when he
had in this Votes enough at hand,   King got up and said he had no objection

---

[26]These papers are no longer here; they probably were inserted into the manuscript at the
beginning of the day's entry, where a trace of wafer remains.

to a Vote being taken on the Susquehannah, but it ought to be the last place.   however for the sake of Order they had to move a postponement of our M the Motion on the Susquehannah.   the postponement was carried.
Mr. Morris then came forward with an amendment for locating ten Miles Square Ad⟨joinin⟩g. the N City of Philada. in the Counties of Philada. Chester and Bucks including Germantown. with a Proviso that the Act should not be in force untill the 100,000 dollars should be secured to the United States, by Pennsylvania. &ca.   I could not abandon the Susquehannah at any rate in the Present Stage of the Business, but for me to enter into a an Proviso, which would operate as an Engagement on the State was without the least Authority for so doing, appeared to me highly improper.   I therefore under every View of the Matter concluded in a Moment to vote against his Motion.   the Susquehannah Bill. placed the federal town in the heart of Pennsylvania, provided for purchasing the Land erecting the buildings &ca. without one farthing expense to the State. to say nothing of the most important Object of clearing the Susquehannah. which in would be done by federal and Maryland Money in case of Congress being placed on its banks.   I therefore reserved my vote for the Susquehannah—   the House divided on Mr. Morris's Motion 9 & 9.   the President rose to give the casting Vote,   he spoke well of the Potowmack, (to gratify the Virginians) Slightly of the Susquehannah (which had has but few Friends.) highly of Philada. and New York, in each of which places he said the Congress ought to stay alternately, four Years at a time, in each.
said if the question were to reject the Whole business he could have no doubt.   But as Pennsylvania had offered the Money he would vote for Germantown.   Thus fell our hopes.   this unwarranted offer of the Money knocked down the Susquehannah.   it was now near 4 OClock and an adjournment was called for. and took place.[27]
    Mane ad Aulam   Vide Wy....e & W......rth.   in confabulation, noluerunt ad me loqui—Malum Omen—habem opportunitatem loquandi illi, inimicus est, Patt Patris felices inimicus—(casus omissus)—unus Quo. dup Con. in C.R. absent, the Y. Senators, &ca.—[28]
    Message—Bill for meeting of Congress 1st Monday of Jany. next—
explanatory Act, respecting Coasting Trade—Schyler came in and sent out Mr. Morris to the grand Committee[29]   Grayson called out—Grayson smiling

---

[27]The following are WM's rough notes taken during debate on this date. They are the only ones to survive.

[28]Stayed at the Hall   Saw Wyngate and Wadsworth in conversation,   they did not want to talk to me—   Bad sign—   Having opportunity to talk to them,   they are my personal enemies, enemies of a happy country—(the reason for such being omitted)—   a quorum gathered in Committee Room absent, the New York Senators &ca.

[29]The grand committee refers to a meeting in the committee room at which the New York delegation discussed with individual senators the agreement it and the Pennsylvania delegation had reached on the temporary residence of Congress.

horridly a Gastly Grin came in.   We—at near 12 the Committee of Consul. broke up. and the Members came in.

Baron Glaubeck[30] papers read—a question of Postponement taken on them—non potest sed erratimus Momentum.[31]   had all that he ~~sent~~ sought for.

no appropriation but by Law.   6.   Elsworth spoke well on the Subject of Glaubeck—carried for Glaubeck   to bring in a Bill—Izard⟨,⟩ Grayson⟨,⟩ Carrol.

Order of the day—Grayson, an amendment, to strike out, "in the State of Pennsylvania"   8 for it, lost.

Butler long Winded calling for reasons, no Combination   Reed, answered, and recurred to Butlers language of Yesterday giving all the delay possible— Butler, again. in answer to Reed.

agai.	Dalton	Bassett	for
Reed	Elsworth	Butler	
Schyler	Johnson	Carrol	
Wyngate	King	Grayson	
	Maclay	Gun	
	Morris	Henry	
	Patterson	Izard	
		Lee	

Mr. Morris—Motion. Joins in the hope that no Citizen of Pennsylvania wishes to—strike out, *at some convenient place on the Banks of the River Susquehannah in the State of Pennsylvania,* be Struck out.   7.   Bassett changed, seconded by Patterson, carried—

for

-11-
Basset
Butler
Dalton
Elsworth
Gunn
Lee
Morris
Aye
Wyngate

Grayson, moved for the northern Banks of the Potowmack—seconded by Lee   Lee on population—Climate Extent Fertility—Rose and went ~~in~~ at large

---

[30]P. W. J. Ludwig, Baron de Glaubeck (d. 1790/91) served during 1781–82 as a volunteer aide-de-camp to General Daniel Morgan. He petitioned the House in 1789, and the FFC granted him one-year's pay at the rank of captain. See also the petition volumes. (Heitman; *New Hampshire Gazetteer*, 13 March 1790)

[31]It cannot be done for we erred in the motion.

into the Business—Grayson rose in opposition—Opinion of the President—.7 for it—lost—quote the Governor of the Western Territory, and Mr. Brown—in favor of the Susquehannah—relative Quantity of Navigation—40 miles a day Grayson says has been poled against the Stream—

Butler moved to replace the Words struck out   I, seconded—never entered into any combination   never tryed to get Votes out of Doors—

Mr. Morris moved to postpone our motion to bring forward Germantown—seconded by Reed.   Division—the Ayes have it.   President against it. New York or Philada. the proper place—said Mr. Morris—Speak strongly—Kensington[32] extolled—the soil &ca. well spoken of—and Justly— would not give reasons for fixing on the Susquehannah—because it was a secondary spot—Butler opposed Mr. Morris—complained of the uncentral Position of Philada.   Read ~~attended~~ called ~~on~~ & delivered Mr. Morris—a Paper—Elsworth gone from Us—and we shall ~~U~~ loose it— interrupted by President—Center in Pennsylvania—Elsworth decide⟨d⟩ly for Germantown—Carrol against Mr. Morris—certain of a Separation if it is fixed at Philada.   Dalton for Philada.   extolls the eastern Country, Main,[33] Grows like the Kentucky[34]—Grayson, cannot consider the proposal of Germantown as serious—Mr. Morris, in answer to Carrol, Philada. will draw the Trade to Philada. in spite of the efforts to clear the Susquehannah—confines the offer to the Money now, but hopes the land will also be given—Chester & Bucks[35]— King has amended Mr. Morris Resolution—

Contents		non Contents—	
Yorkers 9	Basset	9	more favorable
Connecticut	Dalton	Butler	to the Potomac
Wyngate	Elsworth	Carrol	than Susquehan⟨nah⟩
President gave	[*lined out*]	Grayson	
the Casting Vote	King	Gunn	
Delaware	Morris	Henry	
	Patterson	Lee	
	Reed	Maclay	
	Schyler	Izard	
	Wyngate	Johnson	

[32]Kensington was a suburb of Philadelphia, located just northeast of the city in the Philadelphia County township of Northern Liberties. It lay approximately between what is now Kensington Avenue in Philadelphia and the Delaware River. Laid out after 1730, it was a growing manufacturing and port town by the late 1780s. (Joseph Jackson, *Encyclopedia of Philadelphia*, 4 vols. [Harrisburg, Pa., 1931–33], 3:809–10)

[33]Maine in 1789 was a district consisting of the five most northerly counties of Massachusetts. Its 96,000 inhabitants were represented in the House by Thatcher.

[34]Kentucky was a district of Virginia consisting of the seven most westerly counties of the state. Brown represented its 73,000 residents in the House. During its third session, the FFC adopted the Kentucky Statehood Act [S-16], which consented to the separation of the area from Virginia and its admission to the Union as a new state.

[35]Chester and Bucks counties bordered Philadelphia County, and portions of them were

Friday, 25 September 1789

a good deal unwell but attended the Hall.   the ~~Clerk~~ Secretary had omitted the first question on the Striking out of the Susquehannah, and the Reconsideration.   he however corrected it himself afterwards with the leave of the House.   The Affair of One Baron Glaubeck took up some time. but was postponed.   Carrol now moved to strike out the Residence being in New York untill the federal buildings should be erected.   I determined to leave myself free from any Obligation to stay in New York and voted with him. more especially as I was free from all Obligation Whatever.   Mr. Morris began now to dress the Bill, but seemed Slack about the 100,000 doll.   he was called on from the Chair however and Sundry parts of the House to bring it forward   I was very unwell, and left him to dress his own Child as he pleased and came home.

This Evening Mr. Scott called to see me.   he said Mr. Morris⟨,⟩ Mr. Clymer and Mr. Fitzsimons assured him. That the Yorkers and New England Men would pass the bill, and that they ~~had~~ the Pennsylvanians M⟨orris⟩. C⟨lymer⟩. & F⟨itzsimons⟩. had promised that Congress should stay three years in New York.   Mr. Wynkoop then said that they had made such a bargain.   I told them that was the first Acct. I had heard of the Matter.   I expressed my doubts of their Sincerity.   Wynkoop was sure of them & that he could depend on them. &c. &ca.

Saturday, 26 September 1789

very unwell this day but dressed and went to the hall   sat some time.   the Appropriation bill[36] was taken up, and Now Col. Schyler brought forward an Acct. of 8,000 doll. expended by Mr. Osgood[37] in repairing and furnishing at the House which the President lives in,   this was a great Surprize to me for, Altho a Vote had originated in the House of Representatives, for furnishing

included by Morris in his motion to locate the permanent seat of government in the environs of Germantown.

[36]The Appropriations Act [HR-32] evolved from an estimate of supplies presented to the House on 9 July and ordered printed the next day. WM cut a copy of the report out of the *NYDA* of 16 July. It was pasted into volume 1 of the manuscript diary. The report is printed in *DHFFC* 4:55–58.

[37]Samuel Osgood (1748–1813), member of the board of treasury from 1785 to 1789, Antifederalist, and postmaster general from 1789 to 1790, was born in Andover, Massachusetts, and graduated from Harvard in 1770. He served as an aide to Massachusetts General Artemas Ward in 1775 and early 1776. Osgood was a member of several legislative bodies, including the Massachusetts Senate in 1780 and Congress from 1781 to 1784. In the latter body, he opposed Robert Morris's centralist philosophy. In 1786 Osgood married the widow of the wealthy New York City merchant, Walter Franklin, and became owner of the house in which Washington lived during the first session. See also *SEJ*, p. 509. (*Harvard Graduates* 17:412–19)

the House Yet I considered that Allowance for all this had been made in the President's Salary.   I was however taken so unwell that I had to come home.

When I first went into the Senate Chamber this Morning the Vice President⟨,⟩ Elsworth and Ames Stood together, railing against the Vote of Adherence in the H. of R. on throwing out the Words, *the President of,* in the Begin⟨nin⟩g. of the federal Writs.   I really thought them Wrong, but as they seemed very opinionated, I did not contradict them.   This is only a part of, their old System of giving the President as far as possible every apendage of Royalty. The original reason of the English Writs running in the Kings name was his being personally in Court. and English Jurisprudence still supposes him to be so.   but with Us it seems rather confounding the Executive and Judicial Branches.   Ames left them and they seemed rather to advance afterwards, said the President personally was not ~~not~~ subject to any process whatever, could have no action Whatever brought against him ~~Whatever~~.   was above the power of all Judges Justices &ca.   For What said they would You put it in the power of a common Justice to exercise any Authority over him and Stop the Whole Machine of Government.   I said that altho, President he was not above the laws.   both of them declared You could only impeach him. and no other process Whatever lay against him.   I put the Case   suppose the President commits Murder in Streets.   impeach him.   But You can only remove him from Office on impeachment.   Why When he is no longer President, You can indict him.   but in the Mean While he runs away.   but I will put an other case suppose he continues his Murders daily, and neither houses are sitting to impeach him.   Oh! the People would rise and restrain him.   very well You will allow the Mob to do what the legal Justice must abstain from. Mr. Adams said I was arguing from Cases nearly impossible.   there had been some hundreds of crowned heads, within these 2 Centuries in Europe. and there was no instance of any of them having committed Murder.   very true in the retail way, {Charles the IX of France excepted,} they generally do these things on the great Scale.   I am however certainly, within the bounds of possibility, tho' it may be very improbable.   Genl. Schyler joined Us.   What think You Genl. said I by way of giving the Matter a different turn.   I am not a good Civilian but I think the President a kind of Sacred Person.   Bravo, my Jure divino,[38] Man.   not a Word of the above is worth minuting, but it Shows clearly how amazingly fond of the old leven many People are   I needed no index however of this kind with Respect to John Adams.

Sunday, 27 September 1789

being Sunday and a very stormy day, I staid at home all day.   did nothing but wrote letters to my family   exceedingly tired of this place.   but the day

---

[38]Divine Right.

of my departure draweth nigh.   And I am much better than I have been. and hope I shall be able to travel well enough.   Saw no Person Whatever save Mr. Winekoop Who returned from an Excursion he made over the River.

Monday, 28 September 1789

felt pretty well in the morning   dressed and went to the Hall.   sat a little While but had to get up and walk in the Machinery room.   Viewed the pendulum Mill, a Model of which stands here.   it really seems adapted to do Business,   returned and sat a While with the Senate but retired and came home to my lodgings.   sincerely hope an adjournment will take place tomorrow.   the pay list is making Out. which seems likely to finish the business—   left the old Acts of Congress in 13 Vols.[39] with Mr. Vandalsen— and one small Writing Desk—   Mr. Wynkoop came in in the highest Joy   all was well   Germantown happy Germantown has got the Congress,   he ravished up his dinner got his Trunk and boots and away with him, to tell the glorious News—   I cannot help having a despicable Opinion of this Man,   It would not be easy to find a more Useless ~~man~~ member.   he never speaks never acts in Congress. but implicitly follows the Two City Members   he does not seem formed to act alone even the most Triffling affair.   well for him is it that he is not a Woman & handsome. or every fellow would debauch him.   I have been just thinking how impossible it is for the Yorkers to be so blind as to let Congress go away. in the Manner Wynkoop says they have done.   if the lower House have really passed the bill, the Yorkers have no Resource but in the President.   I am greatly surprized at this days Work.   I have opened the book and taken up my Pen. to wipe away all the Surprize above mentioned. Parson Linn has just told me that some Triffling amendment was tacked to the Bill just sufficient to send it up to the Senate. and the Senate have thrown it out. and with the Consent of the Philadelphians too, I suppose.

just as I was leaving the Hall. Izard took me aside   asked me to stay.   said a Triffling amendment will be made in the lower house just enough to bring it up here & we will throw it out,   I told him I wished nothing so much as to see an End of the Business.   I was not able to attend. but if I was I could not be with him on this question.   Well then You must not tell Morris, of this   I was just going away and said I will not.

Tuesday, 29 September 1789

came to the Hall   saw Mr. Morris   I did not envy him his feelings,   I might be mistaken   he looked as if he feared me.   I determined not to say a

---

[39]The official thirteen volume edition of the Journals of Congress, 1774-1788, had been

Word to him, save the Salutation of Good Morning, which passed mutually between Us.   to praise his ~~Conduct~~ Management was impossible, and I really felt such contempt for his Conduct, as placed me far above the thoughts of any Reproaches.   He came to me after some time and desired me to walk into the Committee room.   he then told me That Grayson would be Absent on Acct. of his health.   That Docr. Johnson had said he would be Absent.   and now let Us play the Yorkers a Trick, let Us call a reconsideration & perhaps we may carry it.   I objected to that mode of doing business. and besides counted the Votes & shewed him that the Attempt was vain even if John Adams ~~were~~ was in favour of the Bill, which we well knew he was not.   in the mean While Docr. Johnson came in.   by way of concluding the business of the Tete a Tete I said there was no better method than leaving the Business with a philosophic face.   we returned to the Senate and I have my doubts, whether he meant any thing more than an essay to talk me into good humor on a Supposition, That I was soured at his Conduct.   I could not sit in the Senate   came out and reclined as well as I could in the little committee room.   Elsworth came out in a little time,   I asked him if the Business was got thro' in Senate   he said Yes.   I then went to the Treasury drew my pay, discharged my lodgings took a place in the Stage and set off for Philada.

---

published over the previous decade, usually by the Philadelphia firm of Dunlap and Clay-poole. WM received a set under the terms of a joint resolution of Congress adopted on 8 June 1789. (PCC, Item 187:43)

Miscellaneous Notes

24th May 1785 the Governor of Virginia,[1] wrote to Governor Dickinson of Pennsylvania, stating the improvements of the Western Navigation, and desiring leave to cut roads thro' Pennsylvania from Fort Cumberland to the navigable part of Youghiogeny.

Vid. the Reasons of the Pennsylva. Council against the funding Law of Feby. 1785—among my Papers—[2]

Cheyne on the Sciatica.[3]   take one Two or 3 drams to half an Ounce, according to the Strength of the Patients Stomach, of the etherial Oil of Turpentine, which is that which comes off between the Spirit and the Oil, in drawing off the common Oil of Turpentine; This is to be taken in Triple the quantity of Virgin honey, in a Morning fasting for 4, 5, 6, or 8 days at farthest, intermitting a day now and then, as the Patients Occasion require, or his Stomach suffers by it.   large draughts of Sack Whey[4] must be drank after it, to settle it on the Stomach or carry it into the blood.   likewise every night must be taken, a proper dose of Mathew's pills[5] (or half a simple of pil. Sopononacea (soap pills)[6] that is if the Oil has been taken in the Morning—

---

[1]Virginia Governor Patrick Henry's letter, dated 9 May 1785 and enclosing a resolution of the legislature adopted in January, was received by the Supreme Executive Council of Pennsylvania on 24 May. Neither the resolution nor the letter gives any more detail on the proposal than WM reports. (*Journal of the Virginia House of Delegates* (1784–85), p. 95; *CRP* 14:467; Executive Letterbooks, Vi)

[2]By the Pennsylvania funding law of 1785, the state assumed all debts owed to its citizens by either Congress or the state and provided a combination of revenue sources, including the sale of public lands, to pay the interest on the debt. Authored for the most part by Charles Pettit, it allowed for no discrimination between original holders of the certificates of debt and those who had purchased them. The debate over the act provided the Pennsylvania delegation with a rehearsal of many of the issues raised by Hamilton's funding plan in 1790. The Supreme Executive Council detailed its opposition to the law in a message dated 1 February 1785. (*Counter Revolution*, pp. 170–71; *CRP* 14:328–42)

[3]Dr. George Cheyne (1671–1743) was a prolific English medical writer. WM referred to his *Essay of the True Nature and Due Method of Treating the Gout*, 10th ed. (London, 1753).

[4]Sack Whey was a medicinal drink composed of a dry white wine and whey.

[5]Mathew's Pills, which consisted of soap of tartar, black hellebore, and opium, acted as a cathartic and diuretic and were known as the universal medicine. (George Motherby, *A New Medical Dictionary* [London, 1791], pp. 502–3)

[6]Soap pills consisted of two parts soap to one part white birch sap. They were a source of ascorbic acid, acted as a diuretic, and were sometimes used as a vehicle for ingesting opium, laxatives, or other prescribed medicines. (William Lewis, *Edinburgh New Dispensatory* [Philadelphia, 1791], pp. 147, 199–200, 578)

a dram or Two of flour of Brimstone[7] Twice a day in a Cup of Milk to confirm the Cure.   to be repeated in Case of a relapse.   Calibeate Waters[8] and bitter Volatiles good to strengthen & confirm the Cure—

Memorandum.   the memorable Motion which I made on the 25th August 1789 for placing the Wages of Members of Congress at 5 doll. ∰ day. in which I was seconded by Dr. Elmer and joined in the Vote by ~~Schyler~~ & Wingate, is left out intirely in the Minutes—vid. the Journals—

William Antis,[9] has bought the first improvement on the Big Spring, on the East side of the Cayuga lake, about 8 or nine miles up the Lake.   he wishes permission from the Government of New York, to settle, he being a Gun-smith, and the right of preemption for said land, he likewise intends building a Mills &ca.

1789 Decemr. 22d	Cash in Doll. reced. of Wm. Dewart[10]	300.
	Do. in a seperate bag reced. from Hurley[11] in Doll.	150
	Do. in a Purse old Pillar doll.	20
	Do. Gold in same Purse 2 Joes = 32 Doll.	32
		502 doll.
	Household Book for expences	22 Do.

Philada. Jany. 3d left with Mr. Adlum[12] forty five pounds Seven and Six pence State Money of 1785.   a Certificate in my own name for 146:17:0 No. 18845 bearing interest from the first april 1780 and a Militia one to Robert Cham-

---

[7]Flour of Brimstone is powdered sulphur.

[8]Chalybeate Waters are those heavily infused with iron.

[9]William Antes (1731–1810) had been Northumberland County Commissioner in 1781–82. He moved to western New York in 1795. (NQ[1898], p. 225; On the Frontier with Colonel Antes. . . [Camden, N.J., 1900], pp. 488–89)

[10]William Dewart (1740–1814), a prominent merchant in Sunbury since 1775, had immigrated to Pennsylvania from northern Ireland in 1765. (NCHSP 8:182)

[11]A Daniel Hurley resided in Northumberland County at the time of the 1790 census.

[12]John Adlum (1759–1836), a private surveyor born at York, had a brief military career in 1776 which ended with his imprisonment and parole. He settled near Sunbury in 1784 and met WM, who recommended him for state employment. Between 1787 and 1790 he surveyed the northern boundary of Pennsylvania and the reserved tracts in the Erie Triangle. He also examined the navigability of the Schuylkill and, with WM's brother Samuel, several of the state's western rivers. Adlum knew the territory and leaders of the Six Nations well but was unsuccessful in 1791 in securing appointment as agent for Indian affairs in the Northern Department. (PMHB 84:271–76; Journal of Samuel Maclay [Williamsport, Pa., 1887], p. 11; Series 7, GWP)

bers[13] for 9:10:0 No. 4530 interest from 1st July 1783—five years paid—To take out a patent for Richd. Malone.[14]   for a Tract on Chillesqua [*Chillesquaque*] a Patent for Jacob Myer in The Dutch Valley[15] and One for myself and the Heirs of Col. Hunter[16] deceased he to keep an exact Account—I likewise left in his hands a Note on Charles Stewart[17] of the Jersey's for £4:10:0   Mr. Adlum has received £4:10:0 from Mr. Stewart

Sent off Jonas on New Year's Morning, with the Horses   gave him 3 Crowns and some small change amounting to about 5 Shill. more.   I gave him a Crown for his own Use—

Reced. the followg. Acct. from Mr. Adlum.   Expense of patenting a Tract of land for Wm. Maclay & the Heirs of Col. Hunter.   S⟨urveyor⟩. G⟨eneral⟩. 15/   Secretary 1:11:0,   Receiver Genl.[18] fees 1:0:0   purchase 1:10:9:   certifi-

---

[13]Robert Chambers, a prominent neighbor of the Maclay family at Middle Springs in Lurgan Township, emigrated from northern Ireland. (*PMHB* 24:42, 29:164)

[14]Richard Malone may have been the man of that name who in 1790 resided in Mifflin County.

[15]Dutch Valley, where WM owned land on Holland Run, is in Augusta Township south of Sunbury.

[16]Samuel Hunter (1732–84), who came from northern Ireland about 1750, made his reputation as a military leader. He served in the French and Indian War and on the Bouquet expedition and was stationed at Fort Augusta and Sunbury from at least 1768 until his death. Colonel Hunter received important land grants on the West Branch of the Susquehanna as a result of his military service and was one of the founders of Sunbury. (*NCHSP* 4:36–43)

[17]Charles Stewart (1729–1800), a resident of Hunterdon County, New Jersey, since 1755, had immigrated to Pennsylvania from northern Ireland in 1750. Pennsylvania appointed him a deputy surveyor in 1769, and he held title from the colony to land in the Wyoming Valley. Like WM, he was deeply involved in the controversy with the Connecticut settlers there. He was commissary general of issues for the Continental army from 1777 to 1783. Stewart owned much land in both Pennsylvania and New Jersey and represented New Jersey in Congress in 1784 and 1785. (*New York History* 60:250; *NCHSP* 9:25)

[18]Daniel Brodhead (1736–1809), surveyor general of Pennsylvania from November 1789 until his removal from office in 1800, was a resident of Northampton County. He became a deputy surveyor in 1773 but soon joined the Continental army. Commandant at Fort Pitt during 1779 and 1780, he retired in 1783 with the rank of brigadier general. His tenure as surveyor general was marked by poor record keeping and cooperation with large land speculators. Brodhead replaced John Lukens (1729–89), who had held the job since 1761. WM's entire career as a deputy land surveyor had been under Lukens's direction and he long dreamed of obtaining the office for himself. As soon as he learned of the death of Lukens, WM wrote to Benjamin Rush and Tench Coxe, seeking their support, insisting to Coxe that he could serve the state better as surveyor general than as senator and that he dreaded returning to New York. Brodhead got the appointment, with the support of Governor Thomas Mifflin, whose brother's widow he had married. For more on Lukens, see Appendix E. (Norman B. Wilkinson, *Land Policy and Speculation in Pennsylvania, 1779–1800* [New York, 1979], pp. 137–38; *PMHB* 16:88; To Coxe, 18 Oct. 89, Coxe Papers, PHi; To Rush, 18 Oct. 89, Rush Papers, PHi)

David Kennedy (c. 1735–96), secretary of the Pennsylvania land office from 1781 until his death, had served previously for three years as a Philadelphia County justice of the peace.

cates 4:12:3   recording Specie 7/6—the other Money State—

patenting Jacob Meyer's land   S.G. 15/   Secretary 1:8:1   R.G. 1:0:0   purchase 9/6   certificate: 1:8:6   Recorder Specie 7/6.   the certificates cost him 2:14:0 Specie—

(*CRP* 11:559, 689, 14:444, 16:350; Heber Gearhart Collection, Genealogical Society of Pennsylvania, PHi)

Francis Johnston (1748–1815), who came to prominence as a patriot leader in his native Chester County, held the position of receiver general of the land office from 1781, when he retired from the army, until 1800. In 1784 Johnston and WM were two of the commissioners sent by Pennsylvania to negotiate a treaty with the Six Nations at Fort Stanwix. (*PMHB*, 29:361; *Wilkes Barre*, 3:1453–54)

SECOND SESSION

December 1789–January 1790

[Wednesday, 30?] December 1789

came to [*Philad*]a.   Find the Whole City in [*com*]m[o]tion with regard to the New Constitution[1]   The Lawyers all determind On a Chancery.   And the whole City Lawyers bent Upon An Upper House.   My old School Fellow Doctor Rush full of these Views.   I Asked him Whether Finley, Smilie[2] & others to Whom the Country Members looked Up, would not Thwart their Expectations.   He said As to Finley We have him in Management, *And can do just What we please with him   As to Smilie he is so incorrigi⟨b⟩le a Savage and withall so giddy and man⟨a⟩geable, That every attention would be lost on him.*   I determined to find Smilie as I hoped Something from his rustic Virtue.   I did so and brought him to my lodging at Ogdon's.[3]   I stated to him briefly the City Views ⟨to⟩ conform the new Constitution to the British

---

[1]The convention to prepare a new Pennsylvania constitution met at Philadelphia from 24 November 1789 to 26 February 1790 and from 9 August to 2 September 1790. (*Counter Revolution*, pp. 225–27; *PBR*, p. 509)

[2]William Findley (1741–1821) of Westmoreland County was a member of the Pennsylvania Supreme Executive Council and state constitutional convention during the second session of the FFC and of the state house of representatives during the third session of the FFC. He emigrated from northern Ireland in 1763 and served in various military and civilian posts during the War for Independence. After the war Findley was a member of the Council of Censors, the assembly, and the ratification convention. An Antifederalist candidate for the first United States House of Representatives, Findley attributed his defeat to rains in western Pennsylvania on election day. Like WM, he advocated moving the state capital from Philadelphia to Harrisburg. (*Western Pennsylvania Magazine of History* 20:31–40; *PMHB* 5:445; *DHFFE* 1:415)

John Smilie (1742–1813) of Fayette County served on the Pennsylvania Supreme Executive Council during the first session of the FFC, the state constitutional convention during the second, and the state senate during the third. He came from northern Ireland in 1760. During the 1780s he was a member of the Council of Censors, the assembly, the ratification convention, and the Harrisburg Convention. He was an unsuccessful Antifederalist candidate for presidential elector in 1788. (*Western Pennsylvania Magazine of History* 33:77; *DHFFE* 1:261, 391, 426–27)

[3]William Ogden kept a tavern at 222 South Second Street in Philadelphia. WM lived there during the third session of the FFC. (*The Philadelphia Directory*, 1791)

Broad Street and Federal Hall, New York City. 1797 watercolor, probably by John Joseph Holland. (I. N. Phelps Stokes Collection, Miriam & Ira D. Wallace Division of Art, Prints & Photographs, The New York Public Library, Astor, Lenox, and Tilden Foundations.)

176

Standard of Two houses and a Single Executive. I stated in the Strongest Terms that I could the folly of imitating a Constitution which had been framed on the principles of Necessity. The King Nobility & dignifyed Clergy were Materials Already provided, Men Were familiarized with them they were Materials provided, with such Strong prejudices in their favor that there was no erecting the building without them Happily we were without them & the Prejudices attendant upon them. first principles Ought to be examined as to grades and distinctions in Government. perhaps We should neither retain the British form nor Shadow of it. I saw he heard me with some degree of impatience And Spoke of An Engagement. I told him I had Much to say. and particularly something On the Subject of Chancery. He begged I would write to him from New York and furnish him with my Sentiments. nor did he cease till he laid me Under a promise to do so. I wished to interest him After he was on his feet to leave me. I add⟨ressed⟩ him As follows The Eyes of the Republican, the revolutionary & agricultural Interest of Pennsylvania Are Upon You Finley and those that Are with You, give them a Specimen of Your firmness and Convince them that they have not misplaced their Confidence. *He said He did not know how that Was.* Spoke Strongly of his Republicanism. Urged a Communication of my Sentiments and left me.

Friday, 1 January 1790

[*dine?*]d this day with the Revd. Doctor Smith Provost of the College of Philada.[4] he ratled out before [*dinn?*]er. The People [*sa*]y that Robt. Morris prevented Congress coming to the Susquehanna. and that you prevented their coming to Germantown. (directing his discourse to me) pray how do they make out that Charge? Why you were not there When the Vote on Germantown was last taken & if you had it might have been carried. I was not there it is true that having left the House thro indisposition, but if I had been there and voted for Germantown it could not have altered the Case as the division was seven & eleven. and the fault was their's who brought on the Question without me, if they expected my Assistance. pray Sir who is the Author of this pretty Story, I wish to call on him about it? it has *nae* Author the People say ~~say~~ *sae*. it was in his own house and I was obliged to let him get off with this pitiful Shift. I did not ~~need~~ stand in need of this anecdote to convince me of the disposition of sundry Philadelphians towards, nor is This the only lie they will tell of me.

---

[4]William Smith (1727–1803) held the office of provost of the College of Philadelphia from 1755 until 1791, except for the decade, 1779–89, when the Pennsylvania Assembly revoked the College's charter. Born in Scotland, Smith graduated from the University of Aberdeen in 1747 and arrived in America in 1751. He was an Episcopal minister who devoted his life to the cause of education and became a major figure in Philadelphia intellectual circles.

Saturday, 2 January 1790

Spent the day untill half after 3 in Private affairs   went to dine with the President of the State.[5]   The company was large   mostly country Members of the Convention.   I [*did?*] not need to be told That it was an electioneering decision   he wishes to be future Governor of the State under the new constitution.   I was seated near Arthur Lee of Virginia.[6]   He got on the subject of classing the Senate of the United States. & did not hesitate to pronounce that there had been management in it.   declared one Man concerned in it was capable of anything.   I did not chuse to tell him What I thought of the Business. nor the impression it made on me at the time,   these Matters are as well [*illegible*]ated.   I find however that he is no friend of [*Mr.*] Morris's.   I took the Opportunity When Mifflin was using the Urinal, and of Course could not see [*me?*] to [*step?*] off. for he pushes his Bottle hard [*illegible*] person, noted for Sobriety, drinks if he can.

Sunday, 3 January 1790

dined this day with Mr. Morris,   the Company was not large.   I did not expect convivial Joy or the flow of Soul.   indeed I never was on Terms of intire confidence with him   to be so, would be, to deliver myself intirely into his hands. and this I trust I never shall do with any man.   as the lights were brought in, I came away and prepared my affairs for setting off in the Morning.

Monday, Tuesday,
4–5 January 1790

on my Journey to New York   arrived late on the 5th and went to lodge with the Speaker of the House of Representatives and his Brother Genl. Muhlenberg. at Doctor Kuntz's.[7]

---

[5]Thomas Mifflin.

[6]Arthur Lee (1740–92) of Virginia, younger brother of Senator Lee, was without political or appointive office in 1790 for the first time in twenty years. His Antifederal politics contributed to his defeat for the FFC by John Page, and because of his controversial reputation, Washington refused to appoint him to the Supreme Court. Born at Stratford in Westmoreland County, Virginia, and trained in Great Britain as a doctor and later as a lawyer, Lee preferred politics. In 1776 he was appointed American agent to France with Benjamin Franklin and Silas Deane. Deane's activities and relationship with Congressman Robert Morris earned Lee's censure, and he forced Deane's recall in 1777. Lee was recalled two years later. Lee was a member of Congress from 1781 to 1784 and a member of the board of treasury, from which he continued his attack on Morris, from 1785 to 1789. Lee's political career ended in 1790 when he failed to unseat his second cousin, Richard Bland Lee, in the second congressional election. (*PJM* 12:390–91; *Harvard Graduates* 13:245–60)

[7]Dr. John Christopher Kunze (1744–1807), pastor of Trinity and Christ Lutheran churches

New York   Wednesday, 6 January 1790

attended at the Hall and my presence compleated a quorum.   A Letter from the President of the United States was read, desiring to be informed of the time a quorum would be formed &ca.   was committed to Izard and Strong.   nothing else of any consequence.   adjourned.

Thursday, 7 January 1790

attended as usual.   When the Minutes were read Mr. King rose and made a Motion to amend the Journals of Yesterday with respect to the Presidents letter. by striking out all that part and inserting a clause which he held in his hand.   I saw the thing was preconcerted & therefore did not chuse to Waste time.   the thing was done tho' contrary to all rule.   Strong and Dalton moved to have the word honorable struck out from before the names of the Members.   lost it.   Motion for leave to protest by Butler not seconded. Strong & Izard reported, That the President would attend in the Senate Chamber at 11 OClock tomorrow.   a Resolution of the Representatives for appointing Chaplains was concurr'd, & the Bishop[8] appointed on the part of the Senate.   This day at & after Dinner I thought uncommon pains were taken to draw from me some information as to the part I would act respecting the federal residence   The Whole World is a shell and we tread on hollow ground every step.   I repeatedly said. I have mark'd out no ground for myself   my object shall be the Interest of Pennsylvania subordinate to the good of the Union.   Mr. Wynkoop called in the Evening.   he was directly on the Subject of the permanent Residence   Susquehannah must never be thought of.   he repeated this Sentiment more than once.   to have been silent would have imply'd consent to it.   I said for my part I would think of Susquehannah, and I considered Mr. Morris's conduct in destroying the Bill for that place as the greatest political Misfortune that ever befell that State.

Friday, 8 January 1790

all this Morning nothing but Bustle about the Senate Chamber in hauling Chairs and removing Tables.   he The President was dressed in a second

---

in New York, resided at 24 Chatham Street. He had come to America from Saxony in 1770. Kunze was the husband of Margaretha Henrietta Muhlenberg, sister of the Pennsylvania representatives. WM and the two brothers resided in the Kunze home during the second session of the FFC. Frederick Muhlenberg found WM's company there "entertaining & useful." (*New York*, pp. 144–45; F. Muhlenberg to Rush, 9 Jan. 1790, Berol Collection, NNC)

[8]Samuel Provoost.

Mourning, and ~~del~~ read his speech well.   the senate headed by their President were on his right   The House of Representatives ~~on~~ with their Speaker were on his left.   his Family[9] with the heads of Departments attended.   the business was soon over and the Senate were left alone   the Speech was committed rather too hastily as Mr. Butler thought, who made some remarks on it, and was called to order by the Chair.   he resented the call, and some Altercation ensued.   adjourned untill monday.

Saturday, 9 January 1790

  spent this forenoon in paying Visits & in the afternoon wrote letters to my Family.

Sunday, 10 January 1790

  being Sunday staid at home all day as it was very cold,   read &ca.   The Speaker told me this day what I have been no stranger to for a considerable time past.   That a certain set in Philada. were determined to have me out of the Senate   That Armstrong[10] was brought forward for that purpose &ca. &ca.   {A Small concern indeed, and I am happy that it did not hurt me.}

Monday, 11 January 1790

  The Senate received from General Knox The Proceedings of the Commissioners on the Embassy to the Southern Indians,[11]   a considerable part of the day spent in reading them.   Tis a spoiled peice of business; and by way of Justification of their conduct in not having made peace, they seem disposed to precipitate the United States into War.   The not uncommon fruits of employing military Men.   this however is but my first Idea on the Business.   Wish I may find Occasion to alter it.   Mr. Lear brought in a Ratification from the

---

  [9]At this time GW's official family consisted of David Humphreys, Tobias Lear, William Jackson, Thomas Nelson, and Robert Lewis. (*DGW* 6:4)

  [10]John Armstrong, Jr. (1758–1843), WM's strongest opponent for election to the Senate, left Pennsylvania for New York after marrying into the Livingston family early in 1789. The son of General John Armstrong of Carlisle, John, Jr., withdrew from the College of New Jersey in 1775 to join the Continental army. He served throughout the war, achieving his greatest fame in 1783 when, while a major and an aide to General Horatio Gates, he penned the Newburgh Addresses denouncing Congress. Armstrong served as secretary to the Supreme Executive Council from 1783 to 1787, as commander of the militia sent to restore order to the conflict ridden Wyoming Valley in 1784, and as a member of Congress during 1787–88. See also *SEJ*, p. 532. (*Princetonians, 1771–83*, pp. 4–14; *DHFFE* 1:238, 293–95)

  [11]Receipt of the president's message is recorded in the *SEJ*. The related documents are printed in the *SEJ*, pp. 202–41.

State of North Carolina, or rather a Copy of it, from the President.   And now the Committee reported an Answer to the President's Speech, the most Servile Echo ever I heard.[12]   there was however no mending it.   One part of it seemed like pledging the Senate to pay the Whole amount, of the public debt.   this was however altered.   Many of the Clauses were passed without either Aye or No in silent disapprobation.   I told both King and Patterson that I had never heard so good an Echo, for it repeated all the Words intire. they both denyed that they had anything to do with it. and said it was Izard's Work.

Tuesday, 12 January 1790

visited from Breakfast time to Eleven with the Speaker and Genl. Muhlenberg.   on reading the minutes it was plain That our Secretary had neither System nor Integrity in keeping the Journal.   It is not however worth while to blot paper with his blunders.   In now came Genl. Knox with a bundle of Communications.   I thought the Act a mad one, when a Secretary of War was appointed in time of Peace.   I cannot blame him,   the Man wants to labour in his Vocation.   here is a fine scheme on paper to raise 5,040 Officers non commissioned Officers & Privates at the Charge of 1,152,000 doll. for a Year to go to War with the Creeks, because the Commissioners being ignorant of indian affairs failed of making a Treaty, after having spent 15,000 dollars to no Manner of purpose.   But we will see What will come of it.

I made an unsuccessful Motion, ~~when~~ when it was proposed that the Whole Senate should wait on the President with the answer to the Speech.   first I wished for delay that we might see the Conduct adopted by the House of Representatives,   I thought it likely they would do the Business by a Committee.   in that Case I wished to imitate them, and as a Committee with Us had done all the Business so far I wished it to continue in their hands, that they might have exclusively all the *Honors attendant on the performance*.   That I as a Republican Was however opposed to the whole business of echoing Speeches,   It was a Stale ministerial Trick in Britain, to get the Houses of parliament to chime in with the speech, and then consider them as pledged to support any Measure which could be grafted on the Speech.   It was the Socratic mode of Argument introduced into politicks, to entrap men into Measures they were not aware of.   I wished to treat the speech in quite a different Manner.   I would commit it for the purposes of examining, whether the Subjects recommended in it, were proper for the Senate to act upon,   if they were found to be so, I would have committees appointed to bring forward

---

[12]The remnants of wafer on the page of the diary on which WM made his entries for 7–10 January indicate a missing insert. It may have been a copy of the president's speech or perhaps the Objections printed in Appendix A.

the necessary bills.   But we seem to neglect the Useful, and content ~~ourself~~
ourselves with compliments only, and dangerous ones too.   But for my part I
would not consider myself as committed, by anything contained in the answer.

Wednesday, 13 January 1790

This was a day of small importance in the Senate.   Mr. Hawkins a Senator
from North Carolina took his seat.   The silliest kind of Application came
from our President. That the Senate should direct him to sign some Bill for
furniture got for Mr. Otis,   I opposed it. as I know Otis.   There is in all
probability some roguery in it.   It was however dropped and the Senate after
setting Idle for a considerable time adjourned.

Thursday, 14 January 1790

This was the day devoted to Ceremony by both Houses of ~~Ho~~ Congress   at
11 O'Clock ~~both~~ the Senate attended at the President's to deliver their
answer,   at 12 the House of Representatives attended.   It is not worth while
minuting a Word about it   We went in Coaches got our answer which was
contemptuously short, returned in Coaches, sauntered an hour in the Senate
Chamber and adjourned.   Every Error in Government will work its own
remedy among a free People,   I think both Senate and Representatives are
tired of making themselves the gazing Stock of the croud, and the Subject of
remark to the Sycophantic Circle that surround the President. in Stringing to
~~the President's~~ his Quarters, and I trust the next Session, will either do without
this business altogether, or do it by a small Committee, that need not interrupt
the Business of either house.   I have aimed at this point all along.   It is
Evident from the President's speech That he wishes, everything to fall into the
British mode of Business.   *I have directed the proper officers to lay* before you
&ca.   Compliments for him, and business for them.   he is but a Man but
really a good one.   and we can have nothing to fear from him, but much from
the Precedent he may establish.
　　I dined this day with the President,   It was a great dinner, all in the Taste,
of high life.   I considered it as part of my duty as a Senator, to submit to it,
and am glad it is over.   The President is a cold formal Man, but I must declare
he treated me with great attention,   I was the first Person with Whom he
drank a glass of Wine,   I was often spoken to by him, Yet he knows well how
rigid a republican I am.   I cannot think that he considers it worth while to
soften me.   It is not worth his While,   I am not an Object if he should gain
me, and I trust he cannot do it by any improper means—   This day the

budget as it was called was opened in the House of Representatives.   An extraordinary rise of Certificates has been rema⟨r⟩ked for some time past.[13] This could not be accounted for neither in Philada. nor elsewhere.   But the Report from the Treasury explains all.   he recommends, indiscriminate funding.[14] and in the Stile of a british Minister has sent down his bill.   Tis said a Committee of Speculators in certificates could not have formed it more for their advantage.   It has occasioned many serious faces,   ~~We~~ I feel so struck of an heap. I can make no remark on the Matter.

Friday, 15 January 1790

attended at the Hall,   a Committee was appointed to bring in a bill for extending the Judiciary of the United States to No. Carolina. and the Senate adjourned.   The Business of Yesterday will I think in all probability damn the Character of Hamilton as a Minister for ever.   It appears that a System of Speculation for the engrossing Certificates has been carrying on for some time.   Whispers of this kind come from every quarter.   Dr. Elmer told me that Mr. ~~Constable~~ Morris must be deep in it, for his Partner Mr. constable[15] of this place, had one contract for 40,000 doll. Worth.   The Speaker hinted to me that Genl. Hiester had brought over a Sum of Money from Mr. Morris for this Business,   he said the Boston People were concerned ⟨in⟩ it.   and indeed there is no room to doubt but a Commotion is spread over the Whole continent on this Villanous business.   I pray God, they may not prosper.   I walked out this Evening,   I call not at a single house, ~~but~~ or go into any company, but traces of Speculation in certificates appear.   Mr. Langdon the Old

[13]Between April and November 1789 the value of United States public securities rose from about twenty-five to thirty-three cents on the dollar, and by the end of the year they had climbed to as high as fifty cents. State securities, even the highest, were significantly less valuable during the same period. Securities fluctuated during the spring of 1790 as the FFC debated the details of a funding plan, rose to about sixty-five cents at the time that the Funding Act [HR-63] was approved, and reached eighty cents by the end of the year. (Ferguson, *Purse*, pp. 257, 270, 328–29)

[14]Many original holders of public certificates had parted with them at a price well below their face value. In purchasing back its certificates, the government planned to pay face value, but some people believed it would be more just to pay only the market value to those holders of certificates who had purchased them from the original owners and give the difference between that price and the face value to the original owner. On 22 February the committee of the whole House decided against making such a discrimination.

[15]William Constable (1752–1803), business partner of Robert and Gouverneur Morris, was a prominent New York City merchant and speculator in land and public securities. Born in Dublin, Ireland, and educated there at Trinity College, he came to the colonies in the 1760s and served during the Revolutionary War as an aide to Lafayette. After the war he established himself at Philadelphia but moved to New York in 1784. He claimed to Gouverneur that Senator Morris had promised him advance information as to the best time to profit from federal funding of the debt. (*St. Patrick*, pp. 105–7; Ferguson, *Purse*, p. 328)

and intimate Friend of Mr. Morris lodges with Mr. Hazard.[16]   Mr. Hazard, has followed buying Certificates for some time past,   he told me he had made a business of it.   it is easy to guess for Whom.   I told him You are then among the happy few, who have been let into the Secret.   he seemed abashed, and I checked by my forwardness, much more information which he seemed disposed to give.   The Speaker gave me his Opinion this day that Mr. Fitzsimons, was concerned in this Business as well as Mr. Morris. and That they stayed away for the double purpose of pursuing the Speculation, and remaining unsuspected.   I have One criterion with respect to Mr. Fitzsimons.   I have heretofore heard him declare himself, in the most unequivocal Manner in favour of a discrimination.   mark the Event.

Saturday, 16 January 1790

as the Senate stood adjourned over to Monday I had nothing to do, and staid at home all day   wrote letters to my family,   the Speculations in certificates in the Mouth of every one.

Sunday, 17 January 1790

being Sunday staid at home all day   have a return of the Rheumatism. am afraid that the cold bath has hurt me.   believe I had better abstain from it, for a While.   I have attended in the Minutest manner to the Motions of Hamilton & the Yorkers   sincerity is not with them.   they never will consent to part with Congress.   Advances to them are vain.   one session or Two more here will fix Us immoveably.   We can move from here only by Means of the Virginians.   the Fact is indubitable.   I could write a little Volume to illustrate it.   Buckley is very intimate with the speaker on one hand and Madison on the other.   I can, thro this Channel communicate What I please to Madison.   and I think I know him.   But if he is lead it must be without letting him know that he is so.   in other Words he must not see the String.

Monday, 18 January 1790

attended at the Hall   at the usual time the Senate Met.   but there was no business before them and adjourned.   Hawkins of North Carolina said as he eam came up he passed Tw⟨o⟩ expresses with very large Sums of Money on

---

[16]Ebenezer Hazard (1744–1817), postmaster general of the United States from 1782 to 1789, was the son of a Philadelphia merchant. After studies at Samuel Finley's academy at West Nottingham, Maryland, and the College of New Jersey, where he graduated in 1762, Hazard became a publisher in New York City. His decision to limit the free circulation of newspapers, which was made during the debate over the ratification of the Constitution, may have been the reason that Washington refused to reappoint him in 1789. Hazard moved

their way for North Carolina, for the purpose of Speculation in certificates. Wadsworth has sent off Two small Vessels for the Southern States, on the Errand of buying up certificates. I really fear the Members of Congress are deeper in this business than any others. Nobody doubts but all ~~these Communication~~ this commotion originated from the Treasury. but the fault is laid on Duer.[17] but respondeat Superior.[18]

Paid the Speaker ¹/₃ of 5 Cords Wood sawg. & handg.	3:2:0
¹/₃ of the Price a Bar Candles 45 lb.	0:13:9
for a pair silk stockings advanced for me	1:2:6
	£4:18:3

Tuesday, 19 January 1790

Senate met at the Usual Hour I had observed Elsworth busy for some time, there had been some. Intercourse between him and Izard. he rose with a Motion in his hand which he read in his place. the amount of it was, that a Committee should be appointed. to bring in a bill defining Crimes and punishments under, the Federal Judiciary. he did not affect to conceal that ~~the~~ a bill of this nature had been left pending before the Representatives, at the End of the last. Session. but declared he wished to settle an important point in Practice. Whether all Business should not originate de novo,[19] with

to Philadelphia in 1790 and became an editor of historical documents. (*Princetonians, 1748–1768*, pp. 338–84; *WGW* 30:16–17; *DHROC* 15:308n)

[17]William Duer (1747–99), a New York City merchant and a major speculator in land and public securities, was assistant secretary of the treasury from September 1789 through April 1790, when questions about conflict of interest caused his resignation. Born and educated in England, Duer came to New York in 1768. He served in various revolutionary bodies, including Congress from 1777 to 1779, and was secretary to the board of treasury from 1786 to 1789. During his tenure at the treasury department, he and William Constable formed a partnership for the purpose of purchasing the state debts of North and South Carolina. (*PTJ* 18:653n–654n; Irving Brant, *James Madison, Father of the Constitution, 1787–1800* [Indianapolis, 1950], p. 302)

Although there is no evidence that Hamilton leaked his plan prior to its delivery to Congress, his close relationship with speculators such as Andrew Craigie and William Constable and, in particular, his friend and assistant, William Duer, allowed some outsiders to acquire advance knowledge of his intentions. (Ferguson, *Purse*, pp. 271–72)

[18]"Respondeat superior" is the legal doctrine that a superior is liable for the actions of a subordinate.

[19]The *de novo* issue arose because the rules of neither house of Congress mentioned the status of unfinished business at the end of a session and because the Seat of Government Bill [HR-25], which located the permanent residence of the federal government at Germantown near Philadelphia, had been postponed to the second session of the FFC. New England and Southern congressmen, who opposed the bill, argued that all business should begin *de novo*, while Pennsylvanians insisted that legislation should carry over from one session to the next. The *de novo* approach, they argued, would cost Congress valuable time every session and would establish a permanent precedent merely to kill a particular bill. WM found himself in a distinct minority on the joint committee to decide the question, and it recommended that all business die at the end of each session. Both houses concurred in the committee's report.

every new session.   he then laboured long to show that this was a New Session. and concluded as the session was New Everything else should be new, Mr. Izard seconded him in a Speech which I thought contained nothing new.   Basset got up, and declared that he had but Just taken his Seat. that every thing was new to him, that he could not determine in such haste and moved a Postponement.   I rose Seconded Basset and gave as additional Reasons, That the Matter had been acknowleged to be of great importance That I therefore trusted it would not be gone into with so thin a representation of the Southern States.   that the most respectable State was not represented at all.   That it I thought it improper to attempt deciding on a Matter which would go to regulate the future Proceedings of Congress in both Houses, as it would be fixing a Precedent. without some Communication with the Cham-⟨ber⟩ of Representatives.   that they had appointed a Committee to bring forward the Unfinished Business, which had a very different appearance from Begining de novo.   Gentlemen had argued much to show this was a new session but granting this. I could not see that the inferences they wished to draw from it would follow.   They need not fear a defficiency of business, there would be enough to do without rejecting the progress we had made in the former session.   &ca. &ca.   for I was up a good While—   King got up.   he laboured to support Elsworth, and to show from parliamentary proceedings, that New Sessions originated New Business after every prorogation of parliament.   he was long.   I rose however & took him on his own ground with regard to the prorogation of parliaments.   shewed that it was a prerogative of the Crown to prorougue the parliament.   that the British Crown generally exercised this power. When the parliament went on what was considered as forbidden ground,   that the parliaments were forced into this mode of procedure.   for When any parliament had been prorougued, for trans handling disagreeable Subjects to attempt to take them up in the same stage would inevitably be followed by the same fate.   they were therefore obliged to begin de novo at least with every Subject the least disagreeable to the Court.   and indeed it was the best policy to begin all de novo. and thus affecting to conceal their Knowledge of the offensive Subjects.   But these were reasons of conduct which had no existence here.   The President had no prorouging power   he could not check our deliberations.   I had no objection to adopt Rules similar to those of the parliament of great Britain, where they would apply, not because they were in Use there but on the principle of their Utility.   but when a direct inconvenience attended them. as in the present Case when the deliberations of the former session on the subject before Us would be lost, they ought to be rejected with Scorn.

Elsworth found it would go against him.   he then moved the postponement should be untill tomorrow—   it was lost.   Moved it should be to monday.   it was lost.   general Postponement took place.   Wyngate now

rose and made a singular motion   it was that. the bill formerly before the
Senate for regulating the Process in the federal Courts should be taken up.   a
pause ensued, as this was certainly unfinished business of the former Session
the bill in question, having been postponed on the bringing forward a Temporary law.[20]   Langdon said he would have seconded the Gentleman but he
considered this ~~Matter~~ Bill as involved in the Matter which had just been
postponed.   Elsworth, who sometimes contradicts Langdon, for the sake of
contradiction. said it was not involved in it, and seconded Wingate for bringing it on.   and on it was brought.   the Secretary served the Members of
Senate with Copies of it.   Wingate put it into the hands of the President.
and he read it all over. and was returning to the first paragraph. When
Elsworth finding where he was. got up   said his intention was to second the
Gentleman to have a Committee appointed to bring in a bill for regulating
Processes &ca.   Adams attended to him, and without any question how to get
rid of the bill Adams, put a Question for a Committee and A Committee was
accordingly appointed.   and now we will see What for a figure Otis will make
of the Minutes. in the Morning.   I do not want to be captious but. I must not
let them draw this into Precedent.

Wednesday, 20 January 1790

I am not disappointed in Otis,   every Word respecting the Bill was suppressed in ~~this day's~~ Journals read this Morning,   the Entry stood Ordered
that Mr. King⟨,⟩ Mr. Strong &ca. be a Committee to report a bill to regulate
Processes &ca.   It would have been considered as manifesting a Spirit of
Contention, if I had attacked the Minutes, and I let it pass.   but if they
endeavour to make any Use of it. I will then be at liberty to act, and make the
most of Circumstances.   I came early to the Senate Chamber but found our
President and Elsworth both there before me.   I concluded that they had
come on the Errand of making or correcting the Journals. so as to cover
Elsworth⟨'s⟩ hair Breadth escape of Yesterday.   They were in close consulta-
tion,   I passed them. and took no further notice.   Izard⟨,⟩ Few and Schyler
were all in Conferrence with Elsworth.   the Minutes were no sooner finished
than Elsworth rose and called for the Motion of Yesterday. & made a Speech in
support of his Motion,   it could not be said to be very long, tho' he said a
great deal.   to do business to prevent Idleness, to satisfy our Constituents,
prevent loss of time &ca. &ca. were the subjects of it.   I began with declaring
that the Gentleman's Ardor to do Business was highly laudable.   but there
was such a thing as making more haste, than good speed.   that if œconomy
and to prevent loss of time were his objects I thought he missed the Mark by

---

[20]The Courts Act [S-4] was revised into a temporary law during its second Senate reading
on 18 September 1789.

attempting to take up every thing de novo, for thus all the time spent on the unfinished business in the former session would be lost.   that I thought the present motion Scarce in Order,   it had been moved Yesterday, that the Motion should be taken up this day and negatived.   Monday next had also been negatived.   but there was a reason of much more Consequence, which tho' it had occurred to me Yesterday I had forbore to mention.   but had since inquired of sundry Members of the House of Representatives. and was assured that the very bill in question, was reported by the Committee for unfinished business. and the report, remained On the Speaker's Table, unacted upon. that for Us to decide on a Business actually before the Representatives, I considered as highly improper. and would not fail of giving offense.   after I had done speaking I left the Senate Chamber, came down Stairs   called out General Muhlenberg, gave notice by him ~~by~~ to the Speaker how much I wanted. the Report of the Committee.   Mr. Beckley was good enough to send up by the door keeper the original report.   I got it   found the Bill reported as I had mentioned.   returned and read in my place the part I had alluded to. The affair took now a new turn. and a Motion was made to appoint a Committee to confer on the Subject with a Committee of the other House.   I rose and enforced this with all the energy I was master of.   It was carried and the Committee were Langdon⟨,⟩ ~~Mr.~~ Henry and myself.   The Yorkers lost Countenance when they saw the Committee.   but now the⟨y⟩ brought forward a Curious Motion   it was to take the Sense of the Senate ~~to~~ in Order that it might stand as a Rule of Conduct for the Committee.   I rose against this with all my might,   I have not time to set down my Arguments   they are Obvious,   several followed me.   I had however concluded with a Motion for postponement which was seconded.   they saw how it would go and withdrew their motion.   I consider Mr. Morris as highly blame worthy, in his non Attendance.   he expects that the bill will be destroyed. and he wishes it may be done in his Absence that the blame may be laid on me by the Citizens of Philada.   I wish that I could believe him incapable of this kind of Conduct. I have however kept it's head above Water so far.

Thursday, 21 January 1790

I am disappointed (Strange but cannot help it.), in the Committee   it is Elsworth⟨,⟩ Myself and Henry   and Henry has recanted, told me he would be of the same Opinion with Elsworth.   Mr. Morris took his Seat this day.   he took pains pointedly to be against me. on a Motion which offered to the Chair—that we should take only Two of the Many Papers which are published here.   It is in Vain   all confidence between him and me is at an End.   there indeed never was any between me and any of the Philadelphians.   I must look to myself & do my own Conscience Justice. and Act independent. The Muhlenbergs are Friendly and they will be my Company. The Members of the Committee on the part of the Representatives are Sherman⟨,⟩ Thatcher⟨,⟩ Hartley⟨,⟩ Jackson & White.   to Meet tomorrow at 10 O'Clock.

Friday, 22 January 1790

I met the Committee a few minutes after ten. Elsworth began a long discourse and concluded for all business which had passed between the Houses to begin de novo. He⟨,⟩ Jackson and White had much parliamentary Stuff. but Hartley had some Books and the Precedents were undoubtedly against them. Elsworth made room for Henry to speak, by desiring him in plain Words to do so. from Which it was plain enough, that they had communicated. he seemed Willing I should not speak. I however made way for myself. and reprobated Every Idea of Precedent drawn from England, tho I declared if notices were to be taken of them I thought they made for Us. I read from the Journals, the postponement, of the Bill which I told them plainly had given rise to the Present Contest, "On Motion that the further Consideration of the bill be postponed, *to the next Session of Congress,*" it passed in the Affirmative   By the Minute on the Journals, the Bill must be taken up in the present session. any proceeding of a contrary nature must depend on an ex post facto principle. We may enter into Rules for the future Government of our conduct. but the past is out of our power, constitutionally speaking. The general Practice of all the legislatures are in favour of taking up the unfinished business in the State they were left. so far is this from being considered as improper. That the Constitutions of some of the States, enjoin it is a principle that no bill, unless in Case of necessity, shall be enacted into a law in the same Session, in which it originated. it is the common practice in all the Arrangements of life, it stands highly recommended by œconomy, which is certainly a republican Virtue. I considered it as undeniably certain, That a particular fact had given rise to this Whole business. here then to controul a single incident, We are attempting to establish a general Rule; This is inverting the Order of business, with a Witness. and to get rid of a particular bill, must involve ourselves in perpetual inconvenience. Mr. White alledged the Opinion was not new. I appealed to the Minutes of both houses when bills had been postponed, to this session in the Senate the bill for the permanent Residence   in Chamber of Representatives, the bill on Crimes and punishments. It was in Vain to Argue, the Vote went against Us. and a report agreed to, that the bills which had been in passage between the Two houses should be regarded as if nothing had passed in either respecting them or words to that amount. after the report was made

in the Senate. our President, wanted Us to proceed immediately on it.   I
moved some delay, and it was postponed to Monday.

Saturday, 23 January 1790

this a most delightful day.   there was no Senate. and as the Triffling business of visiting must be got over, set about it. in good earnest.   the
Speaker⟨,⟩ Genl. Muhlenberg, and Genl. Hiester, were the party with myself.   We run off, most of the business. and of Course have nearly done with
it.   There was something happened. to me lately which I will not minute.
but let it serve as a caution to me to observe as much as possible, independence
of Character, and Conduct.   This is a Vile World Where a Man must Walk
among his Friends and Fellow Mortals as if they were Briars and Thorns, afraid
to touch, or be touched by them.   and Yet the older I grow the More I see the
necessity of it.

Sunday, 24 January 1790

this was a dull day every way.   a small Snow fell all day, and melted as it fell
in the forenoon.   the Ground Whitened towards evening.   'Twas such a day
as I have seen early in April When the Robins first come. and the S.W. Winds
labour to push back the Chilling Air of the N.E.   I staid at home all day and
wrote letters to my family.   I now proposed the Scheme of their Writing to me
every Sunday that thus each party might act under the Sentiment ~~that~~ of
Reciprocity, ~~While~~ and enjoy the pleasing Sensation, while they were writing
to and thinking of the Object of their most tender affections the beloved
Object was employed, in the same sympathetic correspondence. and That our
kindred hearts and affections, beat Unisons, at the same instant, tho' ~~tho~~ separated as far as New York & Sunbury.[21]

Monday, 25 January 1790

The Senate met, and the President informed, the House of the Order of the
day to take up the report of the Joint Committee.   I rose and observed that I
saw many empty Seats,   the Senate was thin.   I therefore wished for a little
delay, untill the Members were collected.   after the House filled, the Business
was entered on.   Mr. Morris shewed a disinclination to rise.   Mr. Basset was
up and after he sat down. I hinted to Mr. Morris a point that I thought might be

---

[21]Sunbury, seat of Northumberland County and WM's residence from 1772 to 1791, is
located near the confluence of the east and west branches of the Susquehanna River, about
fifty miles below the Wyoming Valley.

proper in Support of Basset. said he had better rise. if he did not, I would. he said he thought *I had better not*. I thought his Conduct misterious. tho' perhaps I was wrong. I rose however & one Word brought on ~~at~~ another. all the Arguments ~~in~~ of the Committee were had over again much enlarged and amplyfyed. I was four times up in all. for the Two last times I asked leave. I really thought I had the advantage over both Elsworth & Henry. but When is it that I do not think well of my own Arguments? I found I had made some impression on Izard. he was up and concluded with saying something that seemed like a wish for further time to deliberate. I rose said I considered What the Honorable Gentleman had said as amounting to a Motion for postponement, and I begged leave to second him. he said he wished it postponed. but now Patterson rose on our side. but he displeased Izard. and the Question on the postponement was put. but we lost it. after I had been twice up. but it was all in Vain Cicero with all the powers of Apollo could not have turned the Vote in our Favour. I had a small scheme in protracting the time untill the other House would break up, that the Example of our House might not add any weight to their Scale of deliberation and I hoped. that in the mean time they might perhaps pass on the business. Mr. Morris stuck fast to his Seat, nor did he rise or say a Word during the Whole time. eight voted for Us and 10 against Us the Yeas and Nays were called. the Vote was hurried down into the Chamber of the Representatives, and they adopted it almost without a division.

Tuesday, 26 January 1790

This a most unimportant day in the Senate. A Committee was moved for to bring in a bill for ascertaining Crimes and punishments under the federal legislature, the Committee were appointed withdrew for a few Moments into the Secretary's Office ~~with the old bill~~ returned with the old bill which had been before Us last session, & reported it. ~~Butler desired~~ this was really ridiculous, but the Vote of Yesterday seemed to call for it. Butler moved that a letter from some foreigner[22] should be sent to the Chamber of Representatives. The letter had been read formerly but in so low a Voice, That I could not tell a Word of it. it was not read now. Mr. Morris left his seat and Went & looked at it. came back and said nothing about it. I was ~~sent~~ silent on Butler's Motion. But When I came home the Speaker immediately attacked me for the Absurdity of our Conduct in sending them a letter of much importance, touching Proposals of a Treaty with the Republick of Genoa. I really

---

[22]Gaetan Drago de Dominico, a member of a large and influential merchant family of Genoa, had earlier asked Congress to appoint him American consul at Genoa. His letter of 21 September 1789 is printed in *SLJ*, p. 228. (PCC; Giovanni B. Boero, *Le Famiglie Mazzini e Drago* [Genoa, 1970])

knew nothing of the letter, but it was my own Fault.   and it really ought to be a lesson to me and every Senator. to attend well to What is done at our Chair.   there is really no dependance to be placed neither on our President nor Secretary.

Wednesday, 27 January 1790

The bill of yesterday,[23] was read, by paragraphs.   it was curious to see the Whole Senate sitting silent. and smiling at each other and not a word of remark made or making on the bill.   Elsworth rose to inform the Senate that it was the same bill which had gone thro' all the forms, in the last Session. Strong, moved an amendment, however. that the Judges should issue the Warrants, for Execution. of Criminals   I rose and shewed, from the Constitution, That the President of the United States. had the power of granting Pardon in all Cases, except those of impeachment, that by the Judges taking on them, to issue the Warrants the Opportunity of his granting pardon was taken away.   Elsworth according to custom, supported his bill thro' thick and thin.   There was a great deal said and I was up 3 or 4 times.   I moved a postponement of the clause and it was carried.   Hawkins the New Member from N.C. rose and objected to the Clause respecting the benefit of Clergy. he was not very clear.   I however rose, really from motives of friendship,   I will not say compassion for a Stranger.   I stated that as far as I could collect the Sentiments of the H⟨onorable⟩. G⟨entleman⟩. he was opposed to our Copying the law language of Great ~~Brit~~ Britain,   That for my part I wished to see a Code of criminal law for the Continent, and I wished to see a tone of Originality running thro' the Whole of it.   I was tired of the servility of imitating English forms.   That I could not say Whether the bill would not be Materially, injured, by leaving out the Clause.   I wished it should be left out, but I thought at any rate. it had better be postponed.   It was postponed.   Received Sundry letters this day from Philada.   I told Mr. Morris that the Chancery was rejected.   he said he was sorry for it.   I said frankly that is not my case.   he asked is there anything further   I told him a sharp debate, had taken place. whether persons holding federal Appointments could act under State Commissions, which had been determined in the negative.[24]   he reply'd that ~~was~~ is levelled at me and Wilson.   my friends ~~had~~ have named me for Governor.[25] and Wilson for Chief Justice. but I will save them the trouble by declaring off.

---

[23]Punishment of Crimes Act [S-6].

[24]The events that WM reported to Morris occurred in the Pennsylvania Constitutional Convention.

[25]Politicking for the October 1790 election for the first governor began at least as early as January, even before the convention completed its business. The Pennsylvania delegation to the FFC was involved in seeking a proper candidate, and WM commented on it several times

Thursday, 28 January 1790

attended at the Senate Chamber, and reced. letters from home. more agreeable to me than all the wrangling of the Senate.   the bill for crimes & punishments was taken up.   Strong's Amendment was rejected & I offered one which was likewise rejected.   and the bill passed.   Basset moved something like an amendment.   however he went to Elsworth, and it between them was really altered for the better.   The Carolina bill was now taken up and Specially committed to Hawkins⟨,⟩ Elsworth & Butler.   Mr. Lear from the President communicated the Act of Rhode Island, appointing a Convention. there was a request, also from some public Characters of the State requesting a Suspension of the Effects of the funding law respecting that State.[26] Elsworth moved that the same committee might bring in a Clause for the Rhode Islanders.   I voted against this and gave as a reason that as it respected the Revenue, altho' not *raising* Yet it should be left to the other house.

If I needed proof of the Business of Hamilton I have it in the fullest Manner, this day.   his Peice was communicated. in Manuscript as far as Philada. Thos. Willing[27] in a letter to the Speaker of the Representatives. after passing many Eulogiums on Hamilton's Plan concludes, "for I have seen in manuscript his Whole peice."   and it has been used as the basis of the most abandoned System of Speculation ever broatched in a free Country.   Mr. Morris, this day as he sat beside me in our places in Senate. whispered to me, That he would not be as regular in his Attendance as he used to be, that he was engaged in settling his public Accounts. which would engage him for a great part of his time.   I remarked, that cannot be helped, the Business is a necessary one.   Indeed I think it highly so to him, if he regards his Reputation. and in my Opinion he has left, it too long at Stake already.

Friday, 29 January 1790

Samuel Johnson one of the Senators from North Carolina attended was Sworn and he and his Colleague were classed.   a letter was received from The

---

in his diary. Frederick A. Muhlenberg and Robert Morris were leading possibilities. In September both men joined Clymer and Fitzsimons in declaring their support for Arthur St. Clair. Thomas Mifflin, however, won reelection with 90 percent of the vote. (Harry Tinkcom, *Republicans and Federalists in Philadelphia, 1790–1801* [Harrisburg, Pa., 1950], pp. 33–40)

[26] The request was for a further suspension of provisions in the revenue acts which treated Rhode Island as a foreign state because it had not yet ratified the Constitution.

[27] Thomas Willing (1731–1821), president of the Bank of North America, was a lifelong Philadelphian. Educated in England, Willing had an active political career prior to the War for Independence, serving as mayor of Philadelphia and in the assembly. As a member of Congress in 1776, he voted against the Declaration of Independence and thereafter held no political office; however, his mercantile firm, to which he had admitted Robert Morris as a partner in 1757, was active in supporting the American cause. (*PRM* 3:121n)

Treasurer of the U.S.[28] with his Accounts.   they were read by the Secretary.
and Attended to with great listlessness by the Senate.   the amount was
350,207 Doll. 24 cents. and may generally speaking be ~~said~~ called Civil list
disbursements. and said to be expended in New York.   Mr. Morris wispered
something to me about his Accounts & concluded "I find him damned sharp,
he has an Eye as keen as a   "   stopped.   I thought it very strange that
he should speak to me at all in this way.   perhaps it was, that he wishes to
return to some kind of familiarity with me.   But I cannot tell what brought a
Strange flash of Suspicion over me   Why should he say anything tending to
inspire me with a belief that he had difficulty in settling his Accounts,   Men
do not commonly own things of this kind.

Saturday, 30 January 1790

as my complaints in the Rheumatic way still continued, I staid at home all
day.   Wrote to Mr. Nicholson and inclosed The Budget Opened[29]—of Which
I can remark the fate.   wrote likewise to Doctor Ruston   Vid. the Copies.

Sunday, 31 January 1790

Staid at home all day   wrote to my family according to Custom.   amused
myself in Writing a peice ~~in~~ under the Character of an Old Soldier and Irishman.   {this enclosed also some days After to Mr. Nicholson.[30]}
{In is in vain to think of submitting to the insolent injustice of New England
& the Yorkers.   but the point now is to reconcile the southern men. particularly those of Virginia.   Madison & Buckley govern them.   Madison's mark
is the Treasury.   to be our Secretary is Buckley's bait.   the changes would be
great political amendments.   Memdm.}

---

[28]Samuel Meredith (1741–1817), treasurer of the United States from 1789 to 1801, was the
son of a Philadelphia merchant. He was an active patriot before the War for Independence,
and during the war he rose to the rank of brigadier general of the Pennsylvania militia.
Meredith served in the assembly from 1781 to 1783 and in Congress from 1786 to 1788.

[29]John Nicholson (1757–1800), comptroller general of Pennsylvania from 1782 to 1794 and
Antifederal leader, was the conduit through which WM submitted most of his anonymous
newspaper pieces. He immigrated to central Pennsylvania from Wales prior to the War for
Independence. Nicholson opposed the financial programs of both Robert Morris during the
1780s and Alexander Hamilton during the FFC, in part because of the negative impact they
would have on his extensive land speculations. WM relied on him for information during the
debate over Hamilton's funding plan, much to the dismay of Pennsylvania Federalists, who
were attempting to remove him from office. (Robert Arbuckle, *Pennsylvania Speculator...
John Nicholson, 1757–1800* [University Park, Pa., 1975])
"The Budget Opened," which can be found in Appendix B(2), was printed in the
Independent Gazetteer on 6 February.

[30]The piece, which can be found in Appendix B(3), was printed in the *Independent
Gazetteer* on 20 February.

February 1790

Monday, 1 February 1790

this was an unimportant day in Senate   The North Carolina Members produced an Act of session which was committed.   but Mr. Ellicott sent in for me and I chatted with him in the Committee room untill the Senate were about to adjourn which was early.   Mr. Hamilton. is very uneasy as far as I can learn about his funding System.   he was here early to wait on the speaker. and I believe spends most of his time in runing from place to place among the Members.   Mr. Ellicot's Acct. of the falls of Niagara are amazing indeed,   I communicated to him my scheme of an attempt to account for the Age of the World. ~~he do~~ or at least to fix the period When the Water began to cut the ledge of Rock over which it falls.   the distance from the Present pitch. to Where the fall originally was. is now 7 miles   for this Space a Stupendous Channel is cut. in a Solid limestone Rock in all parts 150 feet deep. but near 250 at the Mouth or part Where the Attrition began.   People who have known the place since Sir Wm. Johnson took Posession of it about 30 Years ago give out that there is an Attrition of 20 feet in that time   now if 20 feet = 30 Y. = 7 miles or 36,960 feet—amt. 55,440 years.

Tuesday, 2 February 1790

This an unimportant day and remarkable for nothing so much as the Submission of Mr. A. Brown of Philada. Printer,[1] to the Secretary of the Treasury. who acknowledges the receipt of Sundry pieces against the Secretary's Report.

---

[1] Andrew Brown (c. 1744–97), Philadelphia Federalist editor and publicist, came to Massachusetts from northern Ireland as a British officer in 1773. He sided with the colonists and served as deputy muster master general for the Eastern Department of the Continental army from 1777 until the end of the War for Independence. For most of the time between 1783 and 1788, he ran a school for girls, first at Lancaster and then at Philadelphia. During 1785 he had a brief stint as a newspaper editor in New York. In 1788 Brown founded the *Federal Gazette*, which he continued to publish under various names until his death. During the third session of the FFC, Brown petitioned Congress to be named its official printer. (J. Thomas Scharf and Thomas Westcott, *History of Philadelphia, 1609–1884*, 3 vols. [Philadelphia, 1884], 3:1977; Heitman)

Brown's "submission," printed in the *NYDG* of 2 February, first appeared in the *FG* on 26 January.

but *conceives* the Secretary has refuted every Argument &ca. and will publish nothing against him.   this Wretch is here looking for an Office and the Public will certainly believe that Hamilton has bought him.   these acknowledgements appeared in McLean's paper.[2]   hard to say which is the baser Creature the Buyer or Seller.

Wednesday, 3 February 1790

This day nothing of importance was transacted in Senate, and the House adjourned early.   The Speaker and Genl. Muhlenberg. made a point of my going with them. to dine with Mr. Fitzsimons and Clymer.   I would not go. untill they declared, that they had authority to invite me.   I went.   The Company were Pennsylvanians.   No discourse happened untill after the Bottle had circulated pretty freely.   Mr. Scott joined Us.   He declared, it was in vain to think of any place but the Potowmack   Mr. Wynkoop declared the utmost readiness to go to the Potowmack.   Mr. Fitzsimons seemed to hark in for some time.   Clymer declared over & over he was ready to go to the Potowmack.   After some time I spoke most decidedly and plainly.   I will not go to the Potowmack.   if we once vote for the Potowmack the Die is Cast. Pennsylvania has lost it & we never can return.   I will bear with the Inconveniencies of New York much longer rather than do it.   Fitzsimons is an errant Fox,   I could feel him trim round.   upon the Whole I am quite as well pleased that I went to this dinner.   And Yet they liked my Company but little. if I was not much mistaken.   at one time when they were regreting the influence of New York in keeping Us here. I said Gentlemen We had it once in our power to fix Ourselves elsewhere.   "As the ~~Set~~ Scotchman said in his prayers, We were left to the freedom of our own will, and a pretty hand we made of it."

Thursday, 4 February 1790

This a most unimportant day in the Senate.   the bill for extending the impost to North Carolina was brought in to be signed[3]   the President got up and had a good deal to say.   that a question was put in the House of Representatives. and if Gentlemen wished any other Method they should say so.

---

[2]Archibald McLean (d. 1798), a book dealer and Federalist printer who was born in Scotland, published the *New York Daily Gazette* throughout the FFC's tenure at New York. McLean's *Independent Journal*, a predecessor to the *Gazette*, had been the first newspaper to carry the *Federalist* essays. (William M. MacBean, *Biographical Registry of Saint Andrew's Society of the State of New York*, 2 vols. [New York, 1922–25], 1:212)
[3]North Carolina Act [HR-36].

Elsworth was immediately up, said all was perfectly right. the House had passed the Bill they had nothing more to do with it. Strong got up had some sleeveless thing to say about the Practice of Parliament, but concluded all was right. I got up and declared, since Gentlemen were speaking their minds, I would declare that I thought the business Wrong. that after Gentlem both Houses had elaborately argued and passed a bill it was referred to a Committee of One from the Senate & two from the House of Representatives. That it was then in their power to alter the bill if they were bad Men there was no check on them, if even a Member knew a bill to be vitiated. he could not correct it. an if, or an and, might most materially affect a bill. the Change of the Tense of a Verb. might alter a Whole Sentence. I was clearly of Opinion every bill ought to be compared at the Table. and as the President when he signed a bill, did it for and in the name of the Senate the Question should be put. shall it be signed or no? It was however of no avail. nor indeed did I conclude with any motion. but meant my Observations to open the Way for taking up the Business some other time. This was a public day with the Speaker. all the Company were Pennsylvanians except Judge Livermore. he soon went away. We had a great Many clever things from Mr. Morris and Clymer on the good of the State. the clearing the Susquehannah the Tulpachocking Canal[4] &ca. I will vote for the Susquehannah *now* says Morris. Even Clymer was condescending but it was like grin⟨n⟩ing a Smile. hints were thrown out about, uniting the delegation and much could be done by their Effort. I wonder if they are silly enough to think that their Arts cannot be seen thro? the Government of Pennsylvania is the Object. the Speaker mentioned Charles Thomson, as having been spoke of. Clymer said in such a tone of Voice, as he did not expect me to hear, *he will make a good Senator.* I know him Clymer well. and perhaps, if I were to consult my own feelings and general interest. I would wish Charles Thomson or any other person in my room. Mr. Morris threw a Paper on the Table before the Speaker. The Speaker looked at took it up, Clymer muttered something. Fitzsimons looked confused, and went away. I will know What this paper was. Mr. Morris said I am quite off with the ⟨New⟩ Yorkers. I will have nothing more to do with them. I cannot penetrate the Scheme of the Philada. Junto. as to the Person they contemplate for Governor. A Man Who will be their Tool, is the design. but they have not Yet fixed on their Man—particular Object.

---

[4]Since the seventeenth century, when William Penn dreamed of a sister city for Philadelphia on the Susquehanna River, Philadelphia's promoters had at various times seriously discussed the possibility of an all-water route to that city from the Susquehanna. One of the first efforts of the Society for Promoting the Improvement of Roads and Inland Navigation, founded in Pennsylvania in 1789 by such men as Robert Morris, George Clymer, and Tench Coxe, was the revival of the project. The plan was to construct a canal between the headwaters of Tulpehocken Creek, which flows into the Schuylkill River, and Swatara Creek, which flows into the Susquehanna. (Livengood, *Philadelphia-Baltimore*, pp. 9, 100–102)

Friday, 5 February 1790

this Morning at Breakfast. the Speaker told me What the Paper was.   the Yorkers had stipulated Under their hands to go to the Susquehannah.   and the Pennsylvania Delegation myself excepted. (who by the by was the moving Spring of the Business) had agreed under their hands to Stay Two Years in New York.   this engagement of the Pennsylvanians had been in the hands of the Yorkers untill now,   that Mr. Morris had possessed himself of it. had crossed the names and now shewed it, at the same time that he made the declaration against having any thing to do with the Yorkers.[5]   Well might I say a pretty hand we made of it.   Attended this day at the Hall   the Minutes were read and just nothing at all more done.

Saturday, 6 February 1790

The Senate stood adjourned over to Monday.   I had a card above a Week ago. to dine this day with Mr. Otto, the Chargé d'Affairs of France[6]   it was very cold and I sent an Excuse and staid at home.   amused myself in writing a paper. tend⟨in⟩g. to shew the Use of the State legislatures, maintaining their Consequence in the Arrangement of the Empire.[7]   It was an Idle day with me.   read the roman Antiquities in an old Author.[8]   I am really much better of my Rheumatism since I took to keeping myself Warm.   rest and Warmth. are perhaps the best ~~things~~ applications I can make   I have drunk Madeira Wine for three days past in Moderate quantities, and really think I feel better for it.

Sunday, 7 February 1790

This was a cold day, and I staid at home.   my employment the Writing of letters to my family.   Mr. Bingham called to see Us Yesterday.   he had much to say of the affairs of Pennsylvania.   upon some Person remarking that the

[5]A copy of the agreement, which was signed by all of the Pennsylvania delegation except WM, Hartley, and Hiester, is in the King Papers, NHi. It is dated 23 September 1789.

[6]Louis Guillaume Otto (1754–1817), French chargé d'affaires from 1785 to 1792 and ranking representative of France in the United States during the second and third sessions of the FFC, first came to the United States in 1779 as secretary to the French minister. The German-born diplomat sent many letters to his home government discussing the issues confronting the evolving federal government. In 1790 Otto married Fanny, daughter of Hector St. John de Crevecoeur. (Margaret M. O'Dwyer, "A French Diplomat's View of Congress, 1790," *William and Mary Quarterly*, 3rd series 21:408–44; *PMHB* 30:271)

[7]The unsigned piece, which can be found in Appendix B(4), was published in the *Independent Gazetteer* on 20 February.

[8]This was probably *Roman Antiquities* by Dionysius of Halicarnasus, written at the close of the first century B.C.

Parties of Republican and Constitutionalist would be done away, he said the party would but take a new name.   it would from henceforth be the Eastern and Western interest of the State.   I said had Congress been on the Susquehannah. such a Party would never have been known.   sent a peice to Mr. Nicholson for publication. with a design to spirit up the State Legislatures, to attend to their own importance and instruct ~~the Stat~~ their Senators on all important questions.

Monday, 8 February 1790

Attended Senate   the first business that presented it self. was a letter from R. Morris to the President inclosing a long memorial praying Commissioners to be appointed to inquire into his conduct while Financier. and mentioning his unsettled Accounts as a partner in the House of Willing & Morris, which were in train of settlement.   he requested the Memorial might stand on our Minutes.   some little objection was made.   no particular Vote was taken, and it went on of Course.   I am really puzzled with this Conduct of my Honorable Colleague.   the Charges against him are not as Financier. But as Chairman of the Secret Committee of Congress—and for Money received as a Mercht. in the begining of the business.   it seems admitted that he rendered important Service as Financier, and if I can penetrate his design it is to cloack his faults in the Secret committee, with his meretorious Conduct as Financier.   must mark the end of it.   This day the Report of the Secretary was taken up in the House of Representatives.   I have heard Fitzsimons reprobate the funding law of Pennsylvania, heard him condemn the Doctrine of an indiscriminate fund. &ca. &ca.   Yet this day he laid on the Speakers Table a String of Resolutions nearly echoed from the Secretary's report.

Tuesday, 9 February 1790

Mr. Morris's Memorial was committed this day to Izard⟨,⟩ Henry & Elsworth.   I am still more and more at a loss What he would be at.   It seems as if he wanted to make a noise, to get Commissioners appointed on that part of his conduct which he can defend, and thus mislead the public.   I find the old Resolve of Congress of the 20th June 1785[9] was brought in by a Committee appointed on a letter of his own.   he represented this Resolve of Congress to have been the Act of his malevolent Enemies and persecutors.

---

[9]Resolved, that three Commissioners be appointed to enquire into the receipts and expenditures of public Monies, during the Administration of the late Superintendent of finance, and to examine and adjust the accounts of the United States, with that department, during his Administration, and to report a state thereof to Congress. (*JCC* 28:568)

We had a Message from the House of Representatives by Buckly with the enumeration bill.

A Message also from the P. U. S. on the difference of limits between the U.S. & M Nova Scotia, with a number of Nominations.[10]

Hamilton literally speaking is moving heaven and Earth in favour of his System. The Revd. Doctor Rodgers[11] called on me and Genl. Muhlenberg this Evening   he owed no Visit for that he had pay'd a day or Two ago.   directly he began to extol Hamilton's System. and away with it as if he had been in the pulpit. I checked him.   he made the Visit Short.   The Cincinnati are another of his Machines. and the Whole City of New York.   he is attacked however in this days paper pretty smartly by Governor Clinton as I take it, for the Writer seems to aim personally at him.[12]

Wednesday, 10 February 1790

Attended the Hall but soon left the Senate to attend the debates in the Hall Representative Chamber.   staid with them untill near three O'Clock, but the debates were not interesting   it all turned on an Amendment offered by Mr. Scott the amount of Which was that. the debts should be ascertained before provision was made for them.   The Committee rose without any decision.

Thursday, 11 February 1790

attended the Senate.   the Committee reported Yesterday While I was out on Mr. Morris's Memorial. That the prayer of it should be granted.   There was no Order of the day.   I wished to hear the debates of the House of Representatives. and went down.   I found Madison up.   he had got thro' the introductory part of his speech, which was said to be elegant.   the Ground I found him on. was the equity power of Government. in regulating of property. which he admitted in the fullest manner with this exception,   When the State was no party, The United States Owe justly and fairly the whole amount of the federal debt.   The question then is to whom does [lined out] do they owe it.   in this question they are not interested, as the amount is the same. let who will receive

---

[10]Receipt of these messages is recorded in the *SEJ*. Documents related to the boundary dispute are printed in the *SEJ*, pp. 359–86.

[11]John Rodgers (1727–1811), minister of the Presbyterian churches at New York, had been a resident of the city since 1765. Born in Boston and raised and trained for the ministry at Philadelphia, he received an honorary D.D. from the University of Edinburgh in 1768. He was an active patriot during the war, serving as chaplain for both legislative and military bodies. By 1789 Rodgers was one of the leading Presbyterian ministers in the United States. His son was one of WM's doctors in 1789. (*New York*, p. 149)

[12]The attack on Hamilton may have appeared in an issue of the *New York Morning Post*, which is no longer extant.

it.   the case of the original holder admits of no doubt.   but what of the Speculator who paid only a Triffle for the Evidences of the Debt.   The end however of his Speech produced. a Resolution to the following effect.   That the Whole should be funded. but that in the hands of Speculators, at the highest market price only. and the Surplus to the Original holder who performed the Service.   The debate lasted to the Hour of adjournment. and they rose without deciding.   dined this day with General Knox,   the Company large & Splendid, consisting of the diplomatic Corps Members of Congress &ca.

{L̶e̶n̶t̶ Genl. Muhlenberg
T̶w̶o̶ h̶a̶l̶f̶ Joes, pd. g̶o̶l̶d̶ }

Friday, 12 February 1790

Attended the Hall   the Order of the day was to take up the enumeration bill.   I objected to the Whole of a lengthy Schedule. and moved a commitment.   I was seconded. but some Gentlemen wishing to proceed in the bill 'till they came to the clause I withdrew my motion.   Elsworth came forward with a Motion to strike out the Clause about the Marshall. and insert One to do it by a Commissioner.   I opposed him.   was joined by Patterson.   the debate was scarce worth minuting.   But it let me into the Character of Governor Johns⟨t⟩on   He had said something for the bill as it stood. but When Elsworth made his Motion, he got up to tell how convincing the Gentleman's Arguments were, and that they had fully convinced him.   this I considered as something in the Taste of Esprit de Corps. for he is a Lawyer.   but both h̶i̶m̶ he & his Colleague looked foolish when they lost it.   I got a hard hit at Elsworth.   he felt it, and did not reply.   the bill was immediately after committed. and the Senate adjourned   Elsworth came laughing to me, said he could have distinguished with respect to the point I brought forward.   I said Elsworth the Man must knit his net close that can catch You. but You trip sometimes.   so we had a laugh. and. parted,   went immediately into the Representative Chamber.   but the Whole day was spent on the Quaker Memorial for the Abolition of Slavery.

Saturday, 13 February 1790

This a Vacant day,   I went to the Hall to meet with Mr. R. Harris,[13]   he did not meet me   went to seek for him at Dr. McKnights[14]   could not find

[13]Robert Harris (1768–1851), WM's brother-in-law, had come to New York for an unspecified operation. See December 1790, n. 28, and Appendix C. (*NQ*[3] 1:354)

[14]Charles McKnight, Jr. (1750–91), born at Cranbury, New Jersey, graduated from the College of New Jersey in 1771. His medical studies with William Shippen at Philadelphia

him.   called on Mr. Scott, and endeavoured to give him every Argument in my power against Hamilton's Report.   I shall not minute them here.   I wish however to arm him and every friend to discrimination with every possible Argument as I fear if the business is lost with them.   there will be small chance with Us.   dined this day in an agreeable way with Doctor Johnson the principal of the College.   the Company was not large.   there were 3 Senators⟨,⟩ the Speaker of the R.s⟨,⟩ Genl. Muhlenberg and some Strangers.

Sunday, 14 February 1790

being sunday wrote home to my Family.   to my Brother and to Mr. Nicholson inclosing to him Strictures on the Conduct. of the Secretary and O....d [*Osgood*] respecting the 11,000 doll. paid for furniture, under the Resolve of 15th April last. in the Character of a distressed Woman, complaining of her Servants.[15]

Monday, 15 February 1790

attended in Senate.   our President. produced the Petitions and Memorials of the Abolition Society.   he did it rather with a Sneer. saying he had been honored with a Visit from a Society a self constituted one he supposed.   he proceeded to read the Petitions and memorials.   Izard & Butler had prepared themselves with Long Speeches on the Occasion.   Izard in particular railed at the Society   called them fanaticks &ca.   Butler made a personal attack on Dr. Franklin. and charged the Whole Proceeding to Antifederal Motives. That the Doctr. When Member of Convention had consented to the federal Compact.   here was he acting in direct Violation of it.   That the Whole business was designed to overturn the Constitution.   I was twice up   the first time I spoke generally as to the benevolent intentions of the Society. &c. &ca.   upon Butler's attack I requested Mr. Morris to rise & defend him. King was up speaking in favour of the Carolina Gentleman.   I remarked King is courting them.   Yes said he and I will be silent from the same motive that makes him speak.   the⟨y⟩ then bad⟨e⟩ me rise   I did so.   shewed that the Doctor was the head of a Society which was not as of Yesterday.   That he could not Strictly have the Acts of the Society charged to his personal Account.   that

---

were interrupted by the Revolution. He served as a surgeon throughout the war, holding the office of surgeon general of hospitals in the middle department of the Continental army from 1778 to 1780 and was one of three chief physicians and surgeons of the army, 1780–82. At the war's end he moved to New York City, where he became the physician for many of the city's most prominent families. (*Princetonians, 1769–1775*, pp. 156–60)

[15]On 15 April 1789 Congress had authorized Samuel Osgood to prepare, at its expense, the house he owned at 3 Cherry Street as a residence for the president. WM's piece on the subject was published in the *Independent Gazetteer* on 27 March 1790. See Appendix B(7).

the Society had persevered in the same line of Conduct. long before the Constitution was framed. that there was nothing noval in their Conduct &c. &ca. nothing was done nor moved to be done. as the Matter is in Commitment with the Representatives. where the Measure has many friends. adjourned and went to hear the debates in the lower House. Sedgwick, Lawrence, Smith & Ames took the Whole day. they seemed to aim all at One point to make Madison ridiculous. Ames, delivered, a long String of studied Sentences— But he did not use a single Argument, which seemed to leave an impression he had public faith public Credit, Honor & above all Justice, as often over as an Indian would the great Spirit, and if possible with less meaning. and to as little purpose. Hamilton at the head of the Speculators with all the Courtiers, are on one side these I call the party who are actuated by interest. The Opposition are governed by Principle. but I fear in this Case Interest, will outweigh Principle.

I drank this day at dinner Two Glasses of wine with the Speaker, I will continue this practice for a Week. and observe the effect.

Tuesday, 16 February 1790

this day not remarkable much either way in Senate except that Mr. Morris gave the clearest proof of a disposition always ready to abandon me on every motion which I make. The enumeration bill was before Us. the point at Which I aimed was to begin the enumeration in April that so. the Census might be taken. before our Election. and the Universal belief is That Pennsylvania, would be a gainer. Butler moved to have the time extended One Year from the first of August next. here I threw in the most pointed opposition, and laid down the Principles of the Amendment Which I proposed. Elsworth said he would be for extending the time to 9 months and Mr. Morris to my astonishment rose and supported Elsworth for the 9 months. so Butlers Motion was carried— The Arguments I used were that every Measure tending to give the People confidence in our Government, should be adopted. without delay. the Present Representation, was on a supposititious enumeration and was believed to be erroneous. a second Election therefore ought not to proceed, on such uncertain ground &ca. &ca.

Wednesday, 17 February 1790

The Business done this morning was receiving the report of the Committee to whom was recommitted the 6th Clause of the enumeration bill— It had been recommitted at the instant and urgent motion of Mr. Butler. and the Committee as if to insult him reported the Clause without ~~amendment~~ alteration.   the bill was passed. and ordered for a third reading tomorrow.   adjourned.   and Went to hear the debates in the Chamber of Representatives.   The Paper ~~called the~~ containing the publication called *the Budget opened* was given by Genl. Hiester to Wynkoop and never more heard of.   I asked him for it this day, but he deny'd his ~~w~~ knowing anything about it.   Boudinot took up the Whole time of the Committee 'till the ~~time~~ hour of Adjournment.   It was all dead loss for nobody minded him.   Wrote this evening to my Brother.   paid this day one half Joe ~~towards~~ for boarding half for the Week past. and half of it in advance for next Week.

Thursday, 18 February 1790

we had a message this day from the President of the United States respecting the Boundary between Nova Scotia and the State of Massachusetts   a committee was appointed some time ago, to Whom this Business was referred.[16] The report of the Committee on the cession from North Carolina, was called up   some time spent on it. and it was postponed to Monday next.   The Senate now adjourned.   and we went into the lower house to hear the debates on Mr. Madison's Motion.   Madison had been up most of the Morning. and was said to have spoke most ably   indeed he seemed rather Jaded, when I came in,   he had early in this business been called on to shew a single instance. When any thing like the present had been done.   he produced an Act of parliament in point, in the reighn of Queen Ann.   but now the Gentlemen quitted this ground, and cryed out for rigid right, on law Principles. Madison modestly put them in mind, that they had challenged him on this ground, and he had met them agreeable to their Wishes.   adjourned, without the Question.

Friday, 19 February 1790

attended at the Senate Chamber.   here I found a packet from Mr. Nicholson   it contained Two setts of his letters to me, cut out of the News papers.[17]   he appologizes for the delay of the Peices I sent him for publication, by the prior engagements of the Press meaning as I take it his letters to me.   I believe I ought not to blame him.   The Priest will christen his own Child first.   they are all to appear on Saturday, as he expects.   This day we

---

[16]The receipt of the message is recorded in the *SEJ*. The related documents are printed in the *SEJ*, pp. 386–87.

[17]The enclosure consisted of Nicholson's letters to WM dated [28] and 29 January and 8 February 1790, cut from the Philadelphia *Freeman's Journal* of 3, 10, and 17 February 1790. Nicholson also sent copies to Madison on 17 February, claiming they were published at WM's request. Partial drafts of the letters are in the Nicholson Papers, PHarH. (*PJM* 13:45)

did nothing in the Senate but read the minutes and adjourned over to Monday. went to hear the debates in the House of Representatives. but they were dull and uninteresting. and Yet the question was not put all parties seemed tired Yet unwilling to give out. I am vexed with them, the real good and care of the Country seems not to enter into all their thoughts. The very system of the Secretary's report, seems to be lay as much on the People as they can bear Madison's Yeilds no relief as to the burthen but affords some Alleviation, as to the design the Tax will be laid for. and is perhaps on that Account more dangerous. as it will be readier submitted to, {There is an Obstinacy a perverse peevishness, a selfishness, which shuts him up from all free communication. he will see Congress in no other light than as one party. he seems to prescribe for them to follow ~~already~~ laws already made. As if they were An Executive Body. Whereas the fact is. That the Mass of the People say three Millions (the Payers) and the Holders of Certificates a few thousands (the Receivers) are the ~~two~~ Parties and the Business of Congress is to legislate on the principles of Justice between them. A funding System will be the Consequence. That political Gout of Every Government which has adopted it. With all our Western Lands for Sale & Purchasers every day attending at the Hall begging for Contracts. What Villany to Cast the debt on Posterity. But pay the debt. or even put it in a Train of payment And you no longer furnish food for Speculation. The great object is by funding &ca. to raise the Certificates to par, & thus the Speculators Who now have them nearly all engrossed will clear above 300 ℔ Cent.}

Saturday, 20 February 1790

Staid at home all day. save the time I went to Bobey Harris, I do not like the Way I saw him in, it was near One O'Clock and he lay Stupifyed with Laudanum. I have not been without some Apprehensions ever since this Operation was performed on him. much indeed was it against my Will, but die or live the Business is done. Mr. Fitzsimons it is like called here this day. I was not called down. The Speaker mentioned at dinner how accomodating Fitzsimons had been. that he declared Mifflin must not be Governor, if he was they would be worse off, than if no new Constitution[18] had been made. they then mutually agreed that Mr. Morris's Memorial should be pushed in Congress. as the grand preparatory for his appointment to the Government.

M'd'm. Lancaster lesson.[19]

---

[18]The new constitution of Pennsylvania.

[19]During the second session of Congress, WM used the abbreviation "L. L." on several occasions. The editors believe this might refer to "Lancaster Lesson," an experience in which WM felt he had been betrayed politically. This may have occurred in conjunction with the

Sunday, 21 February 1790

having despatched the duties of the day that is written to my dear Family. Politicks the Business of the Week, obtruded themselves on me. I have observed a kind of Spirit of Uncertainty hover over the Representative body. a Want of Confidence either in the Secretary's Scheme or in Madison's Proposal. like a flight of Land Fowl at Sea, they seem bewildered, and Wish for a resting place. but distrust every Object, that offers. I think now would be the time to fix them on some moderate Measure. I drew the following Resolutions

Resolv'd That funds be immediately provided, sufficient to pay 3 ℀ Cent. on the domestic debt of the United States, which has been liquidated before the 4th of March last. and that the same be paid annually to the Persons holding the Evidences of such debt. upon their application for the same.

Resolv'd That a land Office be opened, for the sale of the Western Territory, in which Certificates of the domestic debt, only, shall be receivable. to operate as a sinking fund, for the extinguishment of the said debt. and the arrears of interest due on the same.

I went with these Resolutions to Mr. Scotts lodgings. But shame to tell it he a Man in Years, and burthened with complaints and infirmities had lodged out. & was not come home Yet. the Manner in which my inquiries for him were answered, sufficiently explained the Objects of his Absence. such Occultations are common with him. Pity that a good head should be lead astray, by the inordinate lust of it's concomitant Members. went and called at the city Tavern had the good fortune to find him Mr. Sterret.[20] chatted a long time with him. and went to see Bobey Harris, in the way I passed by Mr. Scotts lodgings, I asked a Servant who stood in the Door. if Mr. Scott was within, "he was just gone up to his room." I gave him my sentiments on the Trim of his House & read the Resolutions. explaining as a kind of Interim or passo tempo[21] or something that would perhaps take as nothing was committed, or decided finally on. The Child however was not his own. but he declared that if Madison would join they could be carried. I wished him to communicate with Madison. he was afraid of Madison's pride. he requested me to do it. after some time I agreed to do it. and to communicate

---

convention that met at Lancaster in November 1788 for the purpose of nominating Pennsylvania's representatives to the First Federal Congress. WM and many other Federalists from outside Philadelphia were upset that the Philadelphians at the Lancaster Convention opposed the nomination of Tench Coxe. (*DHFFE* 1:296–97, 313–29)

[20]Samuel Sterrett (1756–1833), a Baltimore merchant and Antifederalist who was defeated in the first congressional election, had been private secretary to Elias Boudinot in 1782 and 1783 when Boudinot was president of Congress. At New York City in May 1790, Sterrett married Rebecca, daughter of the revolutionary leader, Isaac Sears. (*DHFFE* 2:243; [Baltimore] *Maryland Journal*, 1 June 1790)

[21]Temporary step.

the result to him.   called but Madison was out—   Inclosed the Resolutions
this Evening to Mr. Scott.   and promised to call in the Morning on Madison.

Monday, 22 February 1790

called on Madison   he made me wait long.   he came down Stairs and
returned with me to his room.   I enlarged on the Business before the House as
much as I thought my time would allow.   Told him plainly there was no
chance of his Succeeding.   it hurt his *Littleness*   I do not think he believed
me.   I read the Resolutions.   I do not think he attended to one Word of
them. so much did he seem absorbed in his own Ideas,   I put them into his
hand.   he offered them back without reading them.   I did not readily hold
out my hand to take them,   he tendered them a second time   I took them.
and then by degrees wound up my discourse, so as to draw to the point of
wishing him a good Morning.   His pride seems of that kind which repels all
communication.   he ~~seemed~~ appears as if he could not bear the Condescen-
tion of it.   ~~Went to the Senate Chamber~~   a motion was made to adjourn
Izard objected.   expected some Resolution would be sent up, from the House
of Representatives to wait on the President with compliments on his Birth day
&ca.   I took my hat and came down stairs.   Those who staid were disappointed.   Madison's Matter was over before I came down, and a poor show his
party made.   the Obstinacy of this Man has ruined the Opposition.   the
Secretary's report will now pass through perhaps unaltered.   I could not help
observing that now both Fitzsimons and Clymer spoke.   they Were Secretary
all over.   Fitzsimons gave me notice of a Meeting of the Pennsylvania Delegation at his lodgings at Six O'Clock.   I went.   The Ostensible Reason was to
consult on the adoption of the State Debts.   But the fact to tell Us that they
were ~~d~~ predetermined to do it.   Morris Swore by G..... it must be done.
and Clymer Strange to tell! expatiated on the growing Grandeur of Pennsylvania if it was done.   Our Roads would be all made And our Communications
all opened by land and Water. &c. &ca.   These appeared Strange Words to me
coming from that Quarter.   Fitzsimons was much more argumentative.
but they were all predetermined. and only called on our complisance to Assent
to their better Judgt.   I choose to mention publickly That I thought we scarce
did Justice to the State we represented that we did not meet oftner, and consult
on her interest.   this met with an echo of applause.   Fitzsimons proposed his
lodgings as a Rendezvous Weekly.   Mr. Morris directly spoke of Wine &
Oysters.
{and it was agreed to meet every monday Evening at Simons's[22]—   I took
however care to bear my unequivocal Testimony against the adoption now

---

[22]Simmons's Tavern, at the corner of Wall and Nassau streets next to Federal Hall, was run
by John Simmons.

proposed, and in fact made the above proposal to obviate any Suspicion of Obstinacy or Unsociability.}

Tuesday, 23 February 1790

The Senate Sat more than an hour doing nothing at all, but looking at each other. Elsworth and Strong got together. ~~at~~ at a time when we had all got in chatting parties about the fires and Stoves, we were suddenly called to Order, and Elsworth was up. it was a most formal motion indeed which he made. and then read a Resolution stating that ~~the Resolution~~ a mistake had been made Yesterday in a Communication which had been sent to the House of Representatives. and desiring them to return the paper. it was about the North Carolina Cession. and I suspected all was not very right. but indeed as much thro' pastime as otherwise I opposed him. he grew Serious and solemn. and I grew rather sportive but with a grave face on, and we made noble debate of it. it would be Idle to blot an inch of paper with it. the question was at length put and Elsworth lost it. greatly was he mortifyed indeed. and sat down in a Visible Chagrin. Docr. Johnson Who had not spoke before now got up and said Angry things. He did not move absolutely for a reconsideration. But Elsworth followed him, and urged a reconsideration. it was seconded by Strong. I got up & opposed the reconsideration as out of Order. and another most important debate ensued. the Chair was called on. and he declared the question out of Order. Mirabile dictu![23] I turned to Mr. Morris. had he decided so in the Case of the Susquehannah bill (said I) we should have had Congress on the banks of that river. Mr. Morris said, Yes. Mr. Morris got on the Subject of the difficulties he laboured under in the Settlement of his Acct. told me, That he had to send again to Philada. for a Receipt book in Which were some Triffling Accounts for Money paid to Expresses of 40/ and such small Sums, but concluded I will have everything settled and the most ample receipt and Certificate of the Accounts being closed.

Wednesday, 24 February 1790

attended this day in Senate   no Business of any Consequence done.   was much afflicted with a Violent head Ache   came home and bathed my feet. but my head so bad I had to lay down. this was a day of Company at our House.   Madison was in the invitation and came early and asked for me, but I could not come down Stairs. I was sorry for this, but as the saying is there is no help for sickness. drank Tea and felt, better after it, but kept my bed.

---

[23]Wonderful to relate.

Thursday, 25 February 1790

feel almost well of my head Ache   but I thought best to stay at home more especially as I expected nothing of Consequence to be done in the Senate. was agreeably surprized with the arrival of Mr. Richardson[24] Who brought letters to me from my family   received also letters from Philada. containing some News Papers, in one of which ~~was~~. were Two Peices Which I forwarded some time ago for publication.[25]   Those from my family were however to me the most agreeable.   Wrote back letters by Mr. Richardson Who goes tomorrow.

Friday, 26 February 1790

attended at the Hall   shewed it to Mr. Richardson   then went with him to the bank[26] to get some money changed,   took leave of him   visited Bobey Harris.   attended at the Hall where no business was done.   received an Agreeable letter from Dr. Logan[27]   Went in the Evening, and drank Tea with Mr. Wynkoop, who has got, his Wife[28] with him.   finished the Evening in reading.

Saturday, 27 February 1790

No Senate this day,   went with the Speaker to buy books.   I bought. Peter Pindar.[29] Whose Sarcastic and satirical ~~Vain Vain~~ Vein will write Monarchy

---

[24]Isaac Richardson of Northumberland County married Margaret, daughter of WM's friend William Plunket. See Appendix C. (*Genealogical and Biographical Annals of Northumberland County, Pennsylvania* [Chicago, 1911], p. 488)

[25]WM's "Old Soldier and Irishman" and his piece on instructing United States senators, both of which were printed in the *Independent Gazetteer* on 20 February 1790, can be found in Appendixes B(3) and B(4).

[26]The Bank of New York, incorporated in 1784, was located at 11 Hanover Square. Alexander Hamilton was active in its creation. (*New York*, p. 110)

[27]George Logan (1753–1821), a Germantown agriculturalist, was a member of a prominent Pennsylvania Quaker family. He received his medical degree from the University of Edinburgh in 1779. He served in the assembly from 1785 to 1788 and on 10 September 1788 nominated WM for the Senate. Although Logan supported the adoption of the federal Constitution, he, like WM, quickly left the Federalist party. His wife, the historian Deborah Norris Logan (1761–1839), annotated one of WM's letters to her husband with the words, "a man of good sense and a firm Republican for whom my dear Husband always professed much regard." (Frederick B. Tolles, *George Logan of Philadelphia* [New York, 1953], p. 84; WM to George Logan, 25 April 1790, Logan Papers, PHi)

[28]Sarah Newkirk (1742–1813) of Pittsgrove, New Jersey, became Wynkoop's third wife in 1782. She spent the month of March 1790 with her husband at New York. (*A Collection of Papers Read before the Bucks County Historical Society* 3:212; *PMHB* 38:43, 48–49, 191)

[29][John Wolcut], *Instructions to a celebrated Laureat . . . by Peter Pindar* (New York, 1788).

into disrepute in Britain.   his Shafts are aimed personally at his present Majesty, but many of them hit the Throne, and will contribute to demolish the Absurdity of royal Government.   Thus even Peter, who I guess to be a Servile Creature paying Court to the Heir apparent, and the rising Royal Family. may be an Useful Instrument in opening the Eyes of ~~Government~~ Mankind to the Absurdity, of human Worship, and the Adulation ~~and~~ nay Almost Adoration, paid to Work of their own hands.   Kings and Governors originally were meant for the Use and Advantage of the Governed.   but the Folly of Men has puffed them out of their places. and made them not only Useless but Burthensome.   General Hiester called and sat this Evening   the Pennsylvania News papers Spoke of, particularly Oswald's[30] of the 20th.   it had been in the House of Representatives.   But the Speaker said Fitzsimons got his hands on it, and he saw no more of it.   I reminded him. That I had left one of those Papers in his and the Gen⟨eral⟩:s. room. and that also was mislaid.   I however got one of them for Hiester. as Two were inclosed to me.   Wrote this day to Geo. Logan   Vid. Letter book—

~~paid for the Speaker at the Book Store 2:0:0 York pd.~~

Sunday, 28 February 1790

being Sunday staid at home all day   read and wrote letters to my family.

~~Lent Genl. Muhlenberg 2 half Joes paid~~

---

[30]Eleazer Oswald (1755–95), controversial editor of the Philadelphia *Independent Gazetteer* from 1782 to 1795, published many of WM's newspaper pieces, including two on 20 February. He arrived in the colonies from England in 1770 and served in the army from 1775 through 1779, achieving the rank of lieutenant colonel. From 1779 to 1781 Oswald assisted in the publication of the Baltimore *Maryland Journal*. After Pennsylvania's ratification of the Constitution, he became an active, vocal Antifederalist. (*DHROC* 13:xxxv–xxxvi)

March 1790

Monday, 1 March 1790

visited Mr. Harris who I find mending fast. returned to the Hall. sat for some time nothing done. received a note to dine on Thursday with the President of the United States. went into the Chamber of the Representatives and heard the debates 'till 3 O'Clock, Which I thought unimportant. Ames however read in his place, a String of Resolutions, touching, the Manner in which the States, were to bring forward their Claims, which I thought alarming.

Tuesday, 2 March 1790

Just nothing done this day in Senate save receiving Baily's bill for certain Inventions in the from the Representatives. some Spiteful remarks made on it, tomorrow assigned for a second reading. Visited Mr. Harris who I find recovering fast. did not attend in the House of Representatives. Our President goes every day, and the Members spend their time, in lampooning him before his face. and in communicating the Abortions of their Muses, and Embrio Witlings. round the room. perhaps they may have got & dressed the buntlings of their brains, at their lodgings, in Order to pop them on the Company to the greater advantage.[1] A resolve passed the Representatives, this day that seems to show, that they begin to *think*. It is a call on the Secretary. to ascertain the Resources, that may be applied to the payment of the State debts, if they should be adopted. The Speaker was at the Levee today. When he came home, he said *The State debts must be adopted*, this I suppose is the language of the Court.

---

[1]Two such poems, exchanged by Page and Tucker, are included in Page's letter to St. George Tucker, 25 Feb. 1790. (Tucker–Coleman Collection, ViW) The poems were circulated around Virginia, and Washington learned that George Mason was so pleased by them that he made his own copies. (*The Papers of George Mason*, 1725–92 [Robert Rutland, ed., vols. 1–3, Chapel Hill, N.C., 1970], 3:1191n–1192n)

Wednesday, 3 March 1790

This day Baylie's bill taken up for a 2d reading. five Members rose to oppose it. I was up 3 times and I am convinced we should have carried it. Mr. Morris rose however. and proposed, That it should be committed to the very Men who opposed it. Langdon made a formal motion to this purpose and was seconded by Basset. such a Committee was accordingly appointed. It is a new Way, to commit a bill to it's enemies, We will see What will come of it.

Thursday, 4 March 1790

Visited Mr. Harris this Morning found him recovering fast. I have an Interest in every thing that hath happened to him. of Which he is little Aware. indeed nobody knows my feelings on this Subject, but myself. he will I trust be well in a few days. and if his complaint, should be compleatly removed. It may tempt me to advise a Person in Whose Wellfare I feel myself deeply interested, to submit to the same Operation. but of this hereafter.

My bodeings of Yesterday were not ill founded with respect to Baily's bill. A Man ought not to put his hand in a Dog's Mouth & trust to his generosity, not to bite it. commit the bill to its declared Enemies, and trust to their generosity to report in favour of it. my conjectures were right and they have reported dead against it. dined with the President of the United States. it was a dinner of dignity. all the Senators present, and the Vice President. I looked often round the Company, to find the happiest faces. Wisdom forgive me if I wrong thee. but I thought Folly & happiness, were the most nearly allyed. The President seemed to bear in his Countenance a settled Aspect of Melancholy. no chearing ray of Convivial Sunshine ~~seemed to break~~ brook thro' the cloudy Gloom of settled seriousness. at every interval of eating or drinking he played on the Table with a fork or knife like a drumstick. next to him on his ~~left~~ right sat bony Johny Adams. ever and anon mantling his Visage with the most unmeaning Simper that ever dimpled the face of folly. Goddess of nature forgive me, if I censure thee, for that thou madest him not a Taylor. so full of small attentions is he. & so well qualifyed does he seem to adjust the Etiquette of loops and buttons. but stay perhaps I wrong thee. so miserably doth he measure Politicks and so unmercifully & unskilfully would he play the Shears of Government, in cutting out royal robes & habiliments That it may Justly be doubted, Whether the Measure of his understanding be adequate to the adjusting the Proportions of the back belly and Breech of the human form. agreeable to the Rules of an experienced Habit Maker. Thus Goddess among the Savage Tribes, of the lazy lying lumpish

Indian who can neither hunt fish nor hoe Corn. makest thou, the dreaming smoking pretended Pro~~fit~~phet Priest & Politician.   Goddess We acknowledge thy power and Submit to thy Sway. but humbly pray we may never have another similar Example of it.

Friday, 5 March 1790

Just after I entered the Senate Chamber I received from my Brother[2] a letter which made me considerably uneasy about some rascally carryings on at the Pennsylvania land Office.   It has occasioned me to write Sundry letters. And really has fretted me a good deal.   but away with it.   This day gave a fresh instance of the Rascallity of Otis.   the Committee on Baily's bill. reported Yesterday and said not One Word more nor was another word said in the Senate, but Otis had on the Minutes Ordered that the Report be accepted.   I did not immediately observe it, but I called on him about it.   his Excuse was. Mr. Adams had Ordered him to do So.   Visited Mr. Harris   found him getting much better.

Saturday, 6 March 1790

Staid at home ~~all day~~,   in the Evening visited Mr. Harris, whom I found recovering.   I wrote this day to the S⟨urveyor⟩ G⟨eneral⟩ Secretary and Rec⟨ieve⟩r. Gen⟨eral⟩. of the Land office[3] respecting the Affair of which my Brother wrote to me.   read the Account of the Pelew Islands, by Keate, A catch penny thing.   perhaps true enough, but Stretched and Swelled as if it had been puffed by Hawksworth.[4]   ~~visited Mr. Harris in the Evening,~~   ~~he recovers fast.~~   paid my Barber for a 2d Month, and 1/6∂ for a Ribbon.

[2]WM had three brothers. The editors believe that his references to "my brother," here and throughout the diary, are to Samuel Maclay (1741–1811), with whom he shared similar interests and a parallel career. WM's other brothers were Charles Maclay (1739–1834), who farmed in Franklin County, and John Maclay (1734–1804), a local official and entrepreneur in Franklin County. Samuel, who had assisted WM on land surveys before the Revolution, owned a considerable amount of land in north central Pennsylvania and represented Northumberland County in the legislature from 1787 to 1791. In 1790 he served as one of three commissioners appointed to investigate the navigability of Pennsylvania's western waters. Samuel married Elizabeth, daughter of WM's friend, William Plunket. The two were so close that Samuel accompanied William as far as Elizabethtown, New Jersey, when he went to New York to assume his seat in the Senate. See Appendix C. (*NCHSP* 14:134–35; Samuel to John Maclay, 17 March 1789, in the possession of John B. Maclay, Jr., of Baltimore, Md.)

[3]The Pennsylvania Land Office, created in 1781 and composed of a secretary, a receiver general, and a surveyor general, supervised surveys and determined the conditions of land sales. In 1790 it was located in the west wing of the State House. (*Pennsylvania Statutes* 10:309–14)

[4]George Keate, *An Account of the Pelew Islands* (Philadelphia, 1789).

John Hawkesworth (c. 1715–73) was an English writer whose 1773 account of English voyages to the South Seas received widespread condemnation as inaccurate and indecent.

Sunday, 7 March 1790

devoted this day to writing to my family. wrote to every One even little
Billey. I however crouded the Girls into One letter. This hardly fair. but I
must be more liberal to them next time. called to see Mr. Harris & found him
quite chearful. he will be about in a few days, if nothing happens amiss to
him.

Monday, 8 March 1790

This the important Week & perhaps the important day, When the question
will be put on the Assumption of the State debts. I suspect this from the
randevouzing of the Crew of the Hamilton Galley. it seems all hands are
piped to Quarters. 4 O'Clock   I was either deceived or the adoption party do
not Yet consider themselves strong enough, to risk the putting of the question,
for it seems the day has passed, and nothing is done. The naturalization bill
was taken up. The debates were exceeding lengthy & a great number of
Amendments moved. Mr. Morris stood by me in one, that was to enable
Aliens to hold lands in the United States. Tis said he has an Agent in Europe
now, for selling lands.[5] I am wrong to minute this Circumstance. he is
however very seldom with me. I know not how it came but I was engaged on
one side or the other warmly on every question. the Truth of the Matter is, it
was a Vile bill. illiberal and Void of Philanthropy. and needed mending
much. We complained that such an ungenerous bill should be sent Us. to
the Representatives from Pennsylvania, (at least I did.) They answered
~~We You~~ we had little to do. and they sent Us employment. This night the
Pennsylvanians supped together at Simmons's. 'T'was freely talked of that
the question was to have been taken this day on the Assumption of the State
debts but Vining from the Delaware State is come in & it was put off, untill he
would be prepared (By the Secretary as I suppose) so that my Morning creed,
was a well founded belief. The language of the Philada. Gentlemen is still
for adoption. the great reason formerly Urged for it was. That Penna. would
draw a great revenue from the Union. I brought forward the Case of Amsterdam to Whom the United Provinces owed great balances which were not paid.
a Century after their revolution. Mr. Fitzsimons said they were not paid Yet
nor never would be, but then with one Voice all the the three Citizens said
little if anything would be due to Pennsylvania. and declared that settling old
Accounts was misspent time,   burn all old Accounts said Mr. Morris. and pay
only the People Who now hold certificates. I wished for harmony and declined argument. but said the Citizens of Penn. never would not abandon the

---

[5]Gouverneur Morris was Morris's agent.

State Securities.   this was admitted.   But Mr. Morris said the State might
Subscribe the amount of them.   This would be sinking Two ℔ Cent to the
State, as they would Subscribe in at 4 ℔ Cent. & pay 6 to their own Citizens.
but I forbore entering into Argument.   Col. Hartley Keept shuffling about,
still repeating all depends on the adoption of the State debts   if this is not
done. New England and Carolina will fly off. and the Secretary's System is
ruined—   We must, we must, adopt.   Heartly is Cocky, but this in fact, is
the Court Lesson.

Tuesday, 9 March 1790

In the Senate Chamber this Morning Butler said he heard a Man say he
would give Vining a 1,000 Guineas for his Vote. but added I question whether
he would do so in fact—   so do I too, for he might get it for a 10th part of the
Sum.   I do not know that pecuniary influence has actually been Used, but. I
am certain, That every other kind of management. has been practised, and
Every tool at Work that could be thought of.   Officers of Government, Clergy
Citizens Cincinnati, and every Person under the influence of the Treasury.
Bland and Huger carried to the Chamber of Representatives.   one lame, the
other sick.   ~~and at~~ Clymer stopped from going away tho' he had leave.   and
at length they risked the question. & carried it 31 Votes to 26.   and all this
after having tampered with the Members since the 22d of last. Month,   and
this only in Committee, with many doubts, that some will fly off. and great
fears that the North Carolina Members will be in before a bill can be matured
or the report gone thro'.   Mr. Morris received a note signed I. C. communicating the news,   he only said I am Sorry it is by so small a Majority.   Genl.
Muhlenberg & G⟨enl⟩. Hiester of the Pennsylvanians only were in the negative—   I had to Wrangle with the New England Men alone, on the Naturalization bill, till near One O'Clock   Johns⟨t⟩on of North Carolina took in
some degree part with me.   I held my own or at least I thought so, with
tolerable Success.   but such shuffling and want of candor—I really scarce ever
before was Witness to.   I certainly however gained greatly.   Twice Yesterday
did we attempt without Success to throw out the Two Years residence.   The
amendment, which I had offered, went to cure this defect with respect to the
power of holding lands.   numbers of Gentlemen now declared their dislike
of the Two Years and wished the bill to be committed for this purpose of
having this part rejected   I agreed, but We were very unluckey in our Committee.   We Pennsylvanians act as if we believed that God made of one blood
all families of the Earth.   but the Eastern People seem to think that he made
none but New England Folks—   it is strange that men born & educated
Under republican forms of Government, should be so contrasted, on the

Subject of General Philanthropy.   In Pennsylvania Used as we are to the
reception and adoption of Strangers. We receive no Class of Men with such
diffidence as the Eastern People.   they really have the Worst Characters of any
People Who offer themselves for Citizens, Yet these are the Men Who affect
the greatest fear of being contaminated with foreign Manners Customs or
Vices—   perhaps it is with Justice that they fear an adoption of any of the
later, for they surely have enough already.

Wednesday, 10 March 1790

Was the first at the Hall this Morning.   however it was not long before some
of the Secretary's Gladiators came in.   What an abject thing a Man becomes
When he makes himself a Tool to any ~~man~~ One.   I ventured to predict to one
of them, that the Secretary's System would fail.   Why but the Assumption of
the State debts is carried already.   I ventured to tell how.   frome me distant
as the room would let him, did he fly off.   Basset has this day declared in the
most unequivocal Manner against the adoption of the State debts.   says if
they are adopted—he will move for Two ⅌ Cent.   I asked him how Mr. Reed
would be on this Question.   he said against Assumption But both of them
acted a Weak part in the Affair of Residence.   The business of this day does
not merit a minute.   The Senate adjourned early and I came home. as I did
not feel very well—   We had Company this day.   the greater part were New
England Men Who soon went away.   Burke and Tucker both Voted for the
Assumption of the State debts.   Tucker declared his Views in the Most unequivocal Manner.   after the States were discharged by the federal Assumption to Spunge the Whole.   Burke reprobated the Whole of the Secretary's Report. and declared it would blow up.   he was not so explicit, but
seemed in Unison with Tucker—   What must come of the Report. if these
Men are sincere?   they have been among the Supporters of it—but Alas.
"What poor supple things Men are" bending down before even dinner. and
floated away by every flask of Liquor—   (paid my boarding off this day).

Thursday, 11 March 1790

Snowed all last night and a Snowey Morning.   attended at the Hall.   Two
bills came up from the Representatives.   the bill for Inventions[6] and One to
give additional Salaries to Clerks. read the first time,   a bill for the Mitigation
of fines and forfeitures ~~came~~ was taken up for a second reading   opposed by
Basset and Few,   a commitment was early moved. and seemed generally
agreed to.   but the Members popped up & down talking about it, and far

---

[6]Patents Act [HR-41].

about it. for above an hour.   something occurred to me which none of them touched. but I thought it Useless to rise.   besides I had been almost incessantly on my legs on the 8th & 9th. and a Man even a good speaker looses all Weight if he makes himself troublesome.   Patterson I find belongs to the Gladiatorial band.   I have ~~of~~ ever thought, since I knew him, That he was a loaf and Fish Man.   he talks of resigning, and I suppose we will hear of his being a Judge. or something better than a Senator.

Friday, 12 March 1790

Attended this day at the Hall   no Business of Consequence done.   The Committee on the Naturalization bill reported. But far Short of the Points which I wished established, in it.   There really seems a Spirit of Malevolence against Pennsylvania in this business,   We have been very liberal on the Subject of admiting Strangers to Citizenship,   we have benefited by it, & Still do benefit.   some Characters seem disposed to deprive Us of it.   I moved a postponement, of a day that we might consider of ~~it~~ the amendment.   It was easily carried.   But. Z[7] snapped, ill natured as a Cur, and said. No. alone.

Mr. Morris, turned towards me this day & seemed to invite a Tete a tete.   he said Mr. Wilson is coming over,   I asked if on any Court business   he did not know   believed not.   We spoke of Who would be Governor.   he declared in favour of St. Clair,   spoke against Mifflin & Bingham.   I said I had heard Miles[8] spoke of.   he objected to Miles as wanting knowledge.   I never made any mention of any of the Muhlenbergs.   He objected to Mifflin.   said ~~Vid.~~ see What sort of People he has put in Office   the S⟨urveyor⟩ G⟨eneral⟩ was mentioned.   he said You should have had that Office.   I went into some detail of the duties of that Office   shewed that it was one in which a drone might slumber, but if filled well was a most laborious Office. and pointed out how.

Saturday, 13 March 1790

being saturday the Senate did not meet.   I staid at home all day.   read and looked over the Journals of Congress.   a day perfectly unimportant.   The Streets were very sloppy with the melting of the Snow.

[7]Ralph Izard.

[8]Samuel Miles (1739–1805), a member of the Pennsylvania Supreme Executive Council from 1788 to 1790 and mayor of Philadelphia from April 1790 to April 1791, was born at Whitemarsh. He served as deputy quartermaster general for the state from 1778 to 1782. In 1783 he became one of the judges of the High Court of Errors and Appeals and was elected to the Council of Censors but resigned both positions after a bitter public dispute with John Nicholson over his accounts as quartermaster. (*American Historical Record* 2:117; *PRM* 1:122n)

Sunday, 14 March 1790

There was a considerable fire in the neighbourhood last night.[9] it of Course raised me by day light. after breakfast The day seemed so delightful, I could not help walking I went, to Mr. Scots lodgings. I got at him on the Subject of the Secretary's report. he declared to me altogether against it. I asked him if he had any correspondence with Pennsylvania he declared No. I put Nicholson's peice into his hand, I put Mr. Finley's letter into his hand. I told him. there were some People discontented in Pennsylvania I read Dr. Logan's letter to him on that S as a proof of it, he called it antifederalism. I took out Dr. Rush's. call him Antifederal if you Will. It was worse. he gave into the Allegations against Nicholson with regard to the State Accounts, to say all of him in One Word he has thrown himself into Fitzsimons's Work Wake, more from the Principles of Indolence than anything else. he will not give himself the Trouble of acting independently. I found a Woman in the room with him, with a Young Child in her Arms. he appeared to be fondling on the Child.

I called in the afternoon on a Mr. Ryerson[10] a Member of Assembly from Pennsylvania, at the City Tavern. I expected he had letters from my Brother but he had none. nor did my Brother know of his coming. I asked him what was doing in the Assembly of Pennsylvania, he said not much he had dined out with Mr. Morris. I spoke to him of the adoption of the State debts. O Yes he believed People were generally for it. on speaking a little further I found him absolutely Ignorant, of every ray of information about them. he owned it after some time and desired me to put some State of the Matter on Paper. & that he would pay particular Attention to it. When he returned.

Monday, 15 March 1790

I complied with Mr. Ryerson's request and furnished him with an Abstract of the State debt of Pennsylvania, and a number of remarks on it. I reead it very deliberately to him, and he seemed to Understand it.[11] The only debate of any consequence this day in Senate was on the Alienation Naturalization bill. the same illiberality as was apparent on other Occasions, possessed the New England Men. Migration is a Source of Population to Us. and they wish

---

[9]The violent fire occurred in the kiln and malt house of the Watson and Willet brewery on Catherine Street. (*NYDG*, 15 March)

[10]Thomas Ryerson (1753–1835) represented Washington County in the assembly in 1789–90 and in the Pennsylvania House of Representatives, 1790–91.

[11]The manuscript to which WM referred, and which he read to Ryerson on 15 March, was probably the basis for "A Pennsylvanian," *Independent Gazetteer*, 27 March 1790, if not the piece itself. It is printed in Appendix B(5).

to deprive Us of it.   I was up several times but always endeavoured to be concise, and to the point as much as I possibly could.   Mr. Morris was up once,   I thought he lost himself and by way of geting out. said he was of the same Opinion with the Member from New York—(Mr. King)   Mr. King is a⟨s⟩ much against Us as any of them. but he does it in an indirect Manner. We spent to 3 OClock on it.   I dined this day at Elsworth's ~~Mr.~~ by Invitation from Genl. Hiester.   Madison⟨,⟩ Bishop Provost. and a Considerable number at dinner   The Speaker & Genl. Muhlenberg   nothing remarkable.   I called on Ryerson & put into his hands, a number of remarks pointedly against the Assumption &ca.   he talked of great intimacy with my Brother.   my Brother had mentioned him to me, in Terms of respect, in some of his letters.   I therefore treated him with unbounded confidence.   This was imprudent & I ought not to have done it.   nor would I, had it not been for some of my Brothers letters, in which he mentions Ryerson, as connected with him on some political points.

Tuesday, 16 March 1790

Mr. Morris looked with a Strange degree of Shyness at me for some time after we met in the Hall.   I had heard that Ryerson came from Philada. to do business with Mr. Morris—   it occurred in a Moment to me, that he had betray'd to Mr. Morris all that had passed betweeen him and me, and likewise my remarks in manuscript on the Assumption of the State debts.   In this moment the Mens conscia recti,[12] was a Treasure to me.   I had told Ryerson. That there were no hopes of Mr. Morris being with me on this Question. but I had passed no Censure on him for it.   I determined to avow all I had done. as I did nothing with any View of concealment.   I had hinted to Ryerson that I rather wished than otherwise That the General Assembly should declare their Sense on the question of Assumption.   And the More so as Carolina had instructed their Members for it.[13]   Mr. Morris after sitting serious a good While, turned to me   began a familiar Chat.   at last asked me to Walk on one side from our Seats, and asked me if back lands could still be taken up.   I told him Yes.   he immediately proposed to me to Join him in a Speculation in lands. which he said he thought he from his Connections in Europe could sell at a dollar ℔ Acre.   I paused a Moment.   said, as our Waste Lands were totally unproductive such a thing might be beneficial to the public as well as ourselves.   That in those points of view, I saw no Objection   I stated some affairs of our Land Office briefly.   and he concluded we would make up our Estimates, the first leisure moment.   if he is in earnest in this Matter. he will

---

[12]A good or clear conscience.
[13]The South Carolina House of Representatives instructed its congressional delegation to vote for assumption on 19 January 1790.

be favourable to the lowering of the Terms of the land office.   I have however
the most Unequivocal Proof of the baseness of Ryerson. Who notwithstanding
his promises, has communicated every thing to Mr. Morris—   The principal
debates this day were on, the Naturalization bill, and were characterized with
the same illiberality, as those I before mentioned—   We had company this
day mostly Virginians—   Col. Bland was of the number.   he is an Assumer
on the Subject of the State debts.   he avowed his design to be. a demonstration to the World. that our present Constitu⟨ti⟩on aimed directly at consolidation. and the sooner every body knew it the better.   so that in fact he
supported the Secretary on Antifederal Principles   This I believe, is the design of Gerry & many More.   The New England Men however want to get
their State debts shook off before they declare themselves compleatly.   In
their former attempt to sink them they raised, Shays's Insurrection.[14]

After dark I received a letter from my brother calling Ryerson a *Scoundril* in
direct Terms.   he is a mere tool to the Philadelphians and has deceived my
Brother.

Wednesday, 17 March 1790

the Appropriation bill, was just, read.   and the President passed to & took
up the Mitigation bill   it was on the 3d reading and Elsworth offered an
Amendment. & the bill was committed.   now the Naturalization bill was
taken up. & all our old Arguments went over and over again   The fact is. the
adoption of Strangers has set Pennsylvania far a head of her Sister States   they
are Spiteful and envious, and wish to deprive her of this Source of population,
but it will scarcely do to avow openly so ungenerous Conduct.   It therefore
must be done Under various Pretences. and legal distinctions.   Two Years
Residence was insisted on in the bill.   We cared not for this but let the
Stranger hold Land the Moment he comes &ca. &ca.   Two law Opinions were
supported in the debates of this day.   One, that the power of holding lands
was a feature of Naturalization.   That lands &ca. could not be held without
it.   This doctrine was pushed so far by Elsworth, as to declare that the rights of
Electors being elected &ca. should attend. and be described in the Act of
Naturalization.   all that could be said would not support this doctrine
Elsworth was even so Absurd as to suppose, if a Man acquired the right of

---

[14]Late in the summer of 1786, farmers in central and western Massachusetts, burdened by
taxes and debts, formed armed groups known as "regulators" and closed the courts of five
counties. The state used the militia to crush the rebellion in January 1787, but the public
rejected harsh treatment for the insurgents and a new state government pardoned those who
had been condemned to death. Daniel Shays (c. 1747–1825) was one of several leaders.
(*DHROC* 13:92n)

suffrage in one State he had it in all &ca.   This Doctrine it was seen would not carry. and now One more conformable to the common Law, was set up.

It was alledged that the disability of an Alien to hold lands arose from the common law. & was seperable from the rights of Naturalization as in the Case of Denization, in England Where the Crown could confer the right of giving receiving and holding real property.   When an Alien therefore was enabled to hold real Estate. it was in reality by repealing part of the common law with respect to him. not by giving a power but taking away a disability.   It therefore strictly speaking rested, with the respective States whether they would repeal the common Law with respect to Aliens. touching the point of holding property.   and being a pure State concern had no Occasion to be made any mention of in the Naturalization Act. but must remain to be settled by the different States by Law, as well as the rights of Election &ca.   We of Pennsylvania contended hard to have a Clause for impowering them Aliens to hold &ca.   But the Above reasoning prevailed and we lost it.

Before Senate were m formed. this Morng. Mr. Carrol of Carrolton happened to be sitting next to me.   We were chatting on on some common Subject.   The President was in the Chair, which he had taken on the performance of Prayer.   he hastily descended, came and took the Chair next to Mr. Carrol.   he began abruptly, How have you arranged Your Empire on your departure. Your Revenues must suffer, in your absence,   What Kind of Administration have you Established for the Regulation of your Finances—   is Your Government intrusted to a Vice roy Nuncio Legate Plenipo. or Charge des affairs—   &c. &ca.   Carrol endeavoured to get him down from his imperial language by telling him. he had a Son in Law who Paid attention to his affairs &ca.   T'was in Vain   Adams would not dismount his Hobbey.   at it again   nor was their an Officer in the House hold civil or Military departments of Royal or imperial Government. that he had not an Allusion to.   I paired my nails—and thought he would soon have done.   But it is no such easy thing to go thro' the detail of an Empire.   Guardian Goddess of America canst thou not order it so, that when thy sons cross the Atlantic they may return with something else, beside european Forms and Follies.   but I found. this Prayer ruffled me a little so I left. them. before Adams had half settled the Empire.

Mr. Morris had some further chat on the proposal of Yesterday.   I told him if I thought it possible, that disadvantage could flow, either to the public or individuals I never would hear of it.   he said Advantage would probably flow to the public from it.   It would be the Means of bringing Us both Money and People.   I now touched him on the Subject of lowering the back Lands of Pennsylvania.   It was a cold scent.   I find he is for the Scheme of What the Speculators, call *dodging*—selling the lands in Europe before he buys it here.   he repeated that a dollar an Acre could be got for it.

Thursday, 18 March 1790

The Burthen of this days debate. was the Naturalization bill over again.
From the most accurate Observation I have been able to make the Conduct of
the Members, have been influenced by the following motives. as Pennsylvania is supposed likely to derive most benefit by Migrations. The Eastern Members are disposed to check it as much as they can. Jersey nearly indifferent.
Delaware absolutely so. Maryland. as Jersey. Virginia unrepresented.
North Carolina, favourable. South Carolina & Georgia want People much.
but they fear Migrations & will check them rather than run the Chance of
importing People who may be averse to Slavery. hence the Bill passed the
House nearly as it came up from the Representatives. The Governing Ideas
however seemed to be the following. That the holding property was separa-
ble from, and not absolutely connected with Naturalization. That Laws and
regulations relating to Property, not being among among the powers granted
to Congress remained with the different States. Therefore Congress would
be guilty of an Assumption of power if they touched it. That the holding
Property was a common Law Right. and the disability of Aliens to hold property arose from that quarter. King, Patterson, Basset⟨,⟩ Reed⟨,⟩ Henry,
G⟨overno⟩r. Johns⟨t⟩on all finally settled in this way. Elsworth dead against
this. the holding property (real). a feature inseperable from Naturalization
&ca. Strong rather inclined to Elsworth Dr. Johnson said about as much on
One side as the other, Few too, is said to be a Lawyer. but tho he spoke a great
deal, he did not seem to enter into the distinction. for our parts we wished
the naturalization bill to be in as exact conformity as possible to the existing
Laws relating to aliens, in Pennsylvania. and this I am convinced would have
been the case had it not been for that low spite which, contaminates public
Characters, as well as private life.

Friday, 19 March 1790

The Naturalization bill taken again now Butler too proud to have lent his
aid to any Motion that was not his own came forward with 2 Motions. they
were in fact nearly the same which had been negatived 3 or 4 times before. It
was alledged they were all out of Order. but he was indulged and lost them
both. Now Few must be a great Man and he must bring forward his Motion
Too, It was equally out of Order but he was indulged in the loss of it— It
appears that all over Europe where the Civil Law prevails Aliens hold
Property. It is the Common Law of England that deprives them, of holding
real Estates. The common law has been received by Us, and with it. this

Consequence. However since We cannot get the rights of Property fully acknowleged. it is best that the Naturalization bill say nothing about it—

Saturday, 20 March 1790

Mr. Morris got warmly at me this day about. the Affair of land repeated he thought even more than a dollar ℔ Acre could be got, and requested me to Write him An Account of the kind of Lands distance to market, &c. &ca. I wrote to him as follows. New York 20th March 1790 Sir

The lands concerning which you have made enquiry, are situated in the County of Northumberland,[15] on the heads of Lycoming Pine Creek & Tioga, branches of the River Susquehannah their distance from Philada. as the roads now go is from 130 to 200 miles, but it may be shortened by opening a more direct communication. the County of Northumberland in which the first settlements were made about the Year 1770, was totally desolated, by the incursions of the Indians during the Revolution. a misfortune it never can experience a second time, as the late Settlements of the State of New York, being extended north of it & Luzerne County form a compleat Barrier. And the Savages, now greatly diminished must soon, be, totally excluded, by the encreasing settlements, from the atlantic side of the great lakes Ontario and Erie. Northumberland County now contains between Two and three thousand families. Provisions of all kinds can be had in Abundance. the Average Price of Wheat Rye Indian Corn Barley Buckwheat & Speltz, when compounded, has seldom been equal to half a Spanish dollar ℔ Bushell. the present Year it is higher, not owing to any failure of Crops, but the uncommon demands for exportation. The Country in which these lands are situated. is mountainous. but the high ridges are never included in the Surveys. It is covered with an immense forest of timber. Maple Sugar Tree Beech Birch Oak of all kinds, Pine mostly of the White and Spruce kinds, White Walnut Wild Cherry, Hickory Ash &ca. These forests some time ago, seemed to set Husbandry at defyance but We now know, That independent of the advantage of clearing the ground. they can be converted to Useful purposes, in the Manufacture of Pot Ash. The different Streams of the Susquehannah, offer the means of conveying any produce whatever to market. This Country has been observed to be peculiarly favourable to Grass, and perhaps the raising of Cattle, may be the most profitable objects of Husbandry, as Stock carries itself to market. These parts enjoy in an eminent degree the advantage and security of double Crops. The snows which fall regularly, at their proper Season in Winter, insure a plentiful harvest of the fall Grain a Wheat and Rye with tol-

---

[15]Northumberland, the huge wilderness county that extended along the northern part of Pennsylvania from east of Sunbury to the Allegheny River, had 17,161 residents in 1790. WM was a leading citizen of the county and resided at Sunbury, the county seat.

erable husbandry seldom Yielding less than Twenty Bushels ℔ Acre. The length of the Summer is well adapted to Indian Corn Flax Oats Spring barley Summer Wheat Tobacco and Velables of all kinds. Buckwheat is often sowed, with success, in the same Summer on the ground from Whence Wheat Rye or Winter barley had been reaped. perhaps so far as respects Seasons the interests of Husbandry, are no where better secured than in Pennsylvania. the Abundant exports of flour Grain &ca. from the port of Philada. afford full prooff of this. It is certain that as You advance southward and diminish the rigors of Winter, You lessen the certainty of the Winter Crops. While ascending to the north the contracted and Chilly Season, seldom brings to Maturity the Summer produce, which is often blasted or pinched by early frosts. Yet such is the rage of Migration, that lands with all the advantages of Soil and Climate in the bosom of Society, are neglected. for fancied Elysiums in Yazoo or Kentucke.[16]

I cannot state with precision the quantity of these lands, having no actual Surveys before me. but know there are not less than 50,000 Acres. if I can render You any further information I shall be happy in doing so. and am Sir Yr. most &ca.

W.M.

Honorable R. Morris Esqr.

Writing the foregoing letter was all I did this forenoon. The Speaker took me in his carriage, and we rode in the after noon.

Sunday, 21 March 1790

wrote letters to my family this forenoon. dated a Peice of Intelligence from Hamiltonople &ca. after dinner walked alone up and down back and forward on the Island. The Speaker told me, The Report was not to be taken untill Fitzsimons came back which was to be on Thursday. he knows all the motions of the Janissaries and Gladiators &ca.[17]

---

[16]The Yazoo country consisted of twenty-five million acres of land sold by Georgia to several Yazoo land companies at the end of 1789. It included much of the present-day states of Mississippi and Alabama. (*DHFFC* 5:1371–83)

[17]WM's piece from Hamiltonople, which discusses the reason for the postponement of the debate on public credit, was printed in the *Independent Gazetteer* on 27 March. It can be found in Appendix B(6).

Hamilton submitted his Report on the Public Credit on 14 January 1790. The House did not discuss it during the two weeks between 15 and 29 March.

Janissaries were a class of fierce soldier-slaves of Turkey who accepted absolute obedience to their master, the sultan. By the mid-seventeenth century they had become politically powerful enough to overthrow and execute sultans.

Gladiators were professional combatants, chiefly slaves and criminals, at the command of wealthy Romans who owned or patronized them. WM and other writers used these terms, particularly the latter, to refer to supporters of Hamilton's financial program.

Monday, 22 March 1790

Visited Mr. Wilson's lodgings, with the Speaker. I then went with Mr. Wynkoop to visit Mr. Carrol of Carrolton. We got on the Subject of the State of Carolina having instructed their Representation. could any hints have gone from here. (said he) to set them on this Measure? He is a roman Catholick, and the intimate friend of Mr. Fitzsimons. this question raised the following train of Ideas in my mind. "Fitzsimons is gone to prevent a similar Measure in Pennsylvania, and I am suspected of having given hints to set such a Measure going. perhaps something of this kind may be alledged against me with Justice. The Doctrine of Instruction may certainly be carried so far, as to be in effect the Tribunitial Veto of the Romans. and reduce Us to the State of a Polish diet.[18] But it is introduced perhaps the best Way is for all the States to Use it. and the general Evil, if it really should be One. Will call for a Remedy. but here is a Subject Worthy of Inquiry. is it to be expected that a federal law passed, directly against the ~~Whole~~ Sense of a Whole State, will ever be executed in that State? if the answer is in the negative, it is clearly better to give the State an early legislative negative. than finally let her Use a practical One. Which would go to the dissolution of the Union."

A Memorial of One Tracy[19] was read, praying a Bankrupt law to be passed Under the Authority of the United States. A Motion for the Appointment of A Committee to bring in a bill for such purpose. there was a great deal of speaking On this Subject. & really I thought the Subject had not justice done to it. I got up and was listened to with Attention, While I explained the difference between the Common laws for the discharge of Insolvent Debtors & the laws respecting Commissions of Bankruptcy, and confind the later to its proper field, the Trading part of the community, and this part only belonged to the Congress to take up. & I doubted Whether they had done most harm or good &ca. I was lead into a detail of the laws of England on this head— much was said on all hands, but We negatived the Motion. The Appropriation Bill was now reported. with a very Triffling amendment indeed, to divide a Sum of about 190 dollars, between our door keeper and the Door keeper of the Representatives. The momentum of a Spittle would have been as effectual to stop the flowing of the Sea. As any Effort. to check this bill. The Appropriations were all in Gross, to the amount of Upwards of half

---

[18]Each Roman tribune had the power to veto any decision he opposed.

From the late seventeenth century until the passage of the Constitution of 1791 each member of the Polish Diet had the power to disagree to any action, thereby defeating it.

[19]Nathaniel Tracy (1751–96), a Newburyport merchant who declared bankruptcy in 1786, was unsuccessful in his quest for a national bankruptcy law. After graduating from Harvard in 1769, Tracy made a fortune in international trade and as the operator of a fleet of privateering vessels. Between 1779 and 1784 he represented his town in the state constitutional convention and in both houses of the legislature. See also the petition volumes. (*Harvard Graduates* 17:247–51)

a Million. I could not get a Copy of it. I wished to have Seen the particulars specifyed but such an hurry I never saw before. I did not see the bill in the hands of any of the Members. But they might have had it for ought I knew. I really fear the Committee gave themselves little Trouble about it. the Moment it was thro' Genl. Schyler & Mr. Morris called for it on the third and last reading. For they said the Secretary wanted to make remittances to Europe. they got What they wanted & thus We had done with it. This mode of Business cannot last long. All evils it is said cure themselves. here is a general appropriation, of above half a Million of dollars. the particulars are not mentioned the Estimate on which it was founded may be mislaid or changed, in fact it is giving him the Secretary the Money for him to account for as he pleases. This is certainly all Wrong the Estimate should have formed part of the bill or should have been recited in it.

Am I too sharp sighted, or have I observed. some Shyness. in some People. I believe it is the former. Mr. Morris this day asked me if I had prepared anything on the Subject, we had been conversing about. I put the letter into his hands. he received it with apparent satisfaction put it into his Pocket. he asked me if some kind of Houses could not be raised and covered with bark at a Small Expence on these lands, I told him they might if honest Men were employed Who would not make a Job of it— The Senate adjourned about 2 O'Clock. I was told there was warmth in the House of Representatives, on the Quaker memorial. and Went in. The house have certainly greatly debased their dignity. Using base invective indecorous language 3 or 4 up at a time. manifest signs of passion. the most disorderly Wandering, in their Speeches, telling Stories, private anecdotes &ca. &ca. I know not What may come of it. but there seems a General discontent among the Members. and many of them do not Hesitate to declare, that the Union Must fall to pieces, at the rate we go on. Indeed Many seem to Wish it.

Tuesday, 23 March 1790

Went with a party to wait on Mr. Jefferson. he was out left our names. sat a long time in the Senate without doing anything Whatever. At last up came the appropriation bill. the original bill gave Gifford Dally[20] the Door Keeper of the Representatives 192 Doll. for Services during the Vacancy. We divided this Sum and Gave 96 doll. to Dally and 96 to Mathers our Door keeper. this they would not agree to. continued the 192 Doll. to Dally and

---

[20]Gifford Dalley, House doorkeeper from 1789 until 1794, when he was removed for neglect of duty, had unsuccessfully sought the position of doorkeeper for Congress in 1788. He had been removed as deputy quartermaster of the New Jersey troops in 1778 for misbehavior and neglect of duty. Congress often used his services at City Tavern in Philadelphia to provision public gatherings and celebrations. (*JCC* 11:504, 14:984, 34:152n, 153)

put in 96 for Mathers.   Pretty amusement For the Governors of a great Empire to play at cross purposes.   King⟨,⟩ Elsworth⟨,⟩ Morris, were all up and adhere. Adhere was heard from Every Quarter of the House.   our President put some Questions. but Whether it was for Non Concurrence insisting or adhering I do not remember.   It was however carried no One thinking it Worth While to say No.

Mr. Morris chatted with great Freedom with me this day on his private Affairs.   explained some of the difficulties he has met with in the Settlement of his Accounts.   says the Balance will be in his favour.   declares he will soon have done. and put to silence his Adversaries.   Justice says plainly this ought to be the Case if he has been injured.   he is very full of the Affair between him and me.   his Countenance Speaks the Appearance of Sincerity and Candor.   Interest however the Grand Anchor to secure any man lies at the bottom.

Wednesday, 24 March 1790

This day little of Consequence done in the Senate.   the appropriation Bill was sent up   The Representatives withdrew their amendment after having shewed a Spirit of petulence to no purpose.   I was called out of the Senate, When I came in. The Report of the Committee on the difference of boundary between the United States & ~~Georgia~~ Nova Scotia was Under Consideration ~~When I came in.~~ I said a few Words Which appeared to be Well received on the Subject.[21]   Izard & Butler both Manifested a most insulting Spirit this day. When there was not the least Occasion for it. nor the smallest affront offered.   these Men have a most settled Antipathy to Pennsylvania, owing to the Doctrines patronized in that State, on the Subject of Slavery   Pride makes Fools of them. or rather compleats What nature began.   This day the Speaker entertained,   the Company was not numerous   the discourse Un⟨ent⟩ertaining—or at least nothing remarkable.

Thursday, 25 March 1790

The Speaker told me last night That Mr. Clymer, wished to see Us this Morning at his lodgings.   As I always embrace the smallest hint to meet the delegation, I was early ready, but the Friends Who had been in Town on the Abolition Business called in Two parties to take leave of Us.   I however hastened to Mr. Clymer's lodgings   found: Scot⟨,⟩ Hiester & Wynkoop at the Door.   I asked, What had happened   Scot with a great laugh said Clymer had read them a letter to the Speaker and was dreadfully afraid that all the

[21]Discussion of the committee report is recorded in the *SEJ*.

People would fly to the Western World.   I replyd. Scott I told You some time ago that all this would happen, if You taxed the Anlantic States too high. & You gave me a great Monongahela laugh in Answer.   Aye says he and I will give You Many More.   I went up Stairs and had a letter of Clymers composing, put into my hands.   the amount of it was that every Man was worth £200 Sterling.   That every Man Who went to the Western country, was lost to the United States, & therefore every Tract of land we sold to a settler would be attended with the loss of a Man or his equivalent £200. deducting the Triffle the U.S. would get for the Land.   All this fine Reason falls dead to the Ground. should it appear that the Man is not lost to the U.S.   It is however fact, that by an impolitic Oppression of Taxes. We may Detach the Whole Country from Us and connect them with New Orleans. & in that case. we will get nothing for the lands.   Clymer came in. and said on the Principle of that letter he would Vote against paying any of the public Debts with back lands. What a deal of Pains he has been at, to fish up some kind of reason, to accomodate his Vote to the Wish of the *public Creditors* alias Speculators they are a powerful body in Philada. & therefore not to be neglected.   I asked What our Friends in Philada. thought particularly on the Assumption of the State Debt.   he said they were divided But there were more *against it* than *for it*.   he now said some fine things on the improvements of the State &ca.   I walked with him & Col. Hartley   all the way to the Hall did his Tongue run on the Subject of going to the Potowmac.   I bore my Testimony in the plainest language against all this.   regretted our not having try'd an adjournment to Philada. a Year ago.   said if We could go to Philada. with a promise of the permanent Residence on the Potowmac, we could without it—   He was peevish and fretful.

No business of consequence done in the Senate   Two bills came up to be signed—   Our President. Used these Words from the Chair before he signed them.

Is there any ~~Obs~~ Objection, Gentlemen, to the signing of these Bills?   He seems a tone lower than he used to be.   The Amendment on the Mitigation bill was non concurred & Managers for a Conferrence appointed.

Friday, 26 March 1790

The bill for the augmenting the military to 1600 Men &ca. came up read and Monday. appointed for a second reading.   A Petition read from Capn. Barry and others, for Commutation &ca.   nothing done ~~of~~ Else in Senate   spent some time on the bill for the incouragement of Inventions &ca.[22]   The Speaker had company this day, all Pennsylvanians.   Mr. Morris took pains to

---

[22]Patents Act [HR-41].

make himself agreeable   The Speaker told him, they had determined to risk the Revenue Business, as they now found Williamson & Ash would be for the Assumption. As they had changed their Minds.   how true is the Observation made by Henry of Maryland. all great Governments resolve themselve into Cabal.   Our's is a mere System of Jockeying Opinions.   Vote this way for me, & i'll vote that way for you.

Saturday, 27 March 1790

being Saturday, read in my room.   after dinner walked and caught cold. in the Evening received a few Lines from Dr. Rush in which he tells me I am complained of for corresponding with the Comptroller General.[23]   This I well know comes from Fitzsimons   he would wish, that no man but himself should know any thing of the finances of Pennsylvania.   I have made advances to the Philadelphians repeatedly, but they shake Us off. and when meetings had been settled for the Communication of Knowledge they have ~~shook Us off~~. broop [*broke?*] them up.   but I am found to possess knowledge of the finances of Pennsylvania.   the presumption is that I correspond with Nicholson.   am become independent of them, & therefore criminal.   I had wrote to the Doctor but inclosed a note to him on this Subject for which. see my letter book.   Mr. Morris has made no agreement with me about lands.   he said he would draw up something, on this Subject, in Writing.   nothing of this has happened. & perhaps never Will.   I thought such a thing might happen. and was careful in my letter. but I will make no rash conclusions. Time will settle all Matters.   And we with all our little bustlings will soon be quiet as the Trodden sod.

Sunday, 28 March 1790

being Sunday was a day devoted to the thoughts of my family.   Wrote letters as usual.   I have been upwards of three Months from them.   this is really disagreeable   the time may come When I would give anything in my power to be one day with them, and now I am absent, with my own consent. I wish I was honorably off, with this same business of Senate.   if Congress continues to sit in New York I cannot pretend to continue a Member of it. Circumstances may direct me to What is best.   God has however given to every Man his Talent. for the express Purpose. of Making Use of it. or in other Words that he may conduct himself on the Principles of right reason.   May he enable me to keep my lamp Trimmed always.   ~~stat~~ staid at home all day.

---

[23]John Nicholson.

Monday, 29 March 1790

Committee on the bill for the progress of Arts &ca. reported.   3 other bills.
came up to Us.   one for Treating with Indians. for extending the Effect of the
State Inspection laws. and the north Carolina Cession bill.   the last amended
by striking out the Words Honorable from before the names of the Senators.
Butler bounced & Izard made frightful faces at it.   They were opposed by
King⟨,⟩ Elsworth & Patterson.   I was pleased to see the Eastern Yorkers &
southern People at it.   The Business was got rid off. by a new Clause altogether, in the begining of the bill. from Which a clear inference in Practice
follows   Viz. That the Whole of a bill is in the power of the Senate. notwithstanding their former agreement & the concurrence of the other house, to any
part or parts of it.   & their deliberations are not confined to the parts only
respecting Which the disagreement Subsists.   I have spoke to Otis. to copy all
the Papers. That I may plead this Precedent if necessary. for this Doctrine was
pointedly denied in the disputes respecting the permanent bill.[24]   (Vid. my
Papers. for the Copies made out by Otis.)   This day the H. of R. took up the
Report of the Committee of the Whole House on the Secretary's Report. and
after adopting the 3 first clauses recommitted the One on the Assumption of
the State debts 29 to 27. so that I hope This will be rejected at last.   The
Speaker has declared That he will vote against it, if there should be a Tie in the
House.   This was my Opinion which he early adopted, and Which He has so
often Subscribed to, That it will be impossible for him to recede from it. Upon
this Principle.   That a Matter of Moment. not absolutely necessary, had better be omitted than carried by so small M a Majority as One Vote.   This Opinion has met with much approbation from many Members of Senate & I have
taken care to let the Speaker know it.

Tuesday, 30 March 1790

The Bill for additional pay, to the Clerks of the Accounts between the
United States & individual States was called up & lost.   3d reading of the Bill
for the Progress of Useful Arts. produced a debate by the New England
members, in favour of a Man from their Country, but by being Joined by the
Southern Men, we defeated them.   Read the Law for giving Effect to the
Inspection Laws of the States.   Message from the Representatives with cession
bill agreed to.   Message from the President. with nominations to Vacant
Offices.[25]   The bille bill for the Military Establishment took up the rest of the
day, in desultory debate, and was finally committed to 7 Members.   This bill

---

[24]WM may have been referring to the Seat of Government Bill [HR-25].
[25]Receipt of the message is recorded in the *SEJ*.

seems laying the foundation of a Standing Army.   The justifiable Reasons for Using force, seem to be the enforcing of laws, quelling Insurrections, and repelling Invasions.   The constitution directs all these to be done by Militia.   should the United States unfortunately be involved in War an Army for the Annoyance of an Enemy in their own Country, (as the most effectual mode of keeping the Calamity at a distance and forcing an adversary to Terms) will be necessary.   This seems the Meaning of the Constitution. & that no Troops should be kept up in peace.   This Bill certainly aims at different Objects.   The first Error seems to have been the appointing a Secretary at War. When we were at Peace, & now we must find Troops. least his Office should ~~want~~ run out of employment.   dressed and attended the Levee.   I generally Used to leave this part of Duty to Mr. Morris.   but now he is gone and least, there should be any Complaints, I will discharge this Peice of Etiquette.   the day was fine & the Levee large.

Wednesday, 31 March 1790

A Call of the Gladiators this Morning   therefore expect it will be a day of some importance in the House of Representatives.

In Senate the bill for enforcing the inspection laws of the State had a third Reading.[26]   The appointments of Rufus Putnam a Judge of the Western Territory⟨,⟩ James Brown Atty. for Kentuckey & Henry Bogart Surv⟨eyo⟩r. for Albany were consented to[27]—   Senate adjourned early   went to hear the Event of this days debates in The house of Representatives.   Nothing remarkable save a Violent personal Attack on Hamilton by Judge Burk of South Carolina which the Men of the blade say must produce a duel.[28]   The Question was not taken on the Assumption.

---

[26] About 5 March, when the Senate adopted the resolution which led to this bill, WM had written to the Supreme Executive Council for information on state inspection laws. WM's failure to comment on the bill suggests that he considered it equitable to his state. (James Trimble to Peter Lloyd, 10 March 1790, RG 27, PHarH)

[27] Rufus Putnam (1738–1824), judge of the Northwest Territory from 1790 to 1796, was born at Sutton, Massachusetts. He served throughout the War for Independence as a military engineer, rising to the rank of brigadier general. He was an organizer of the Ohio Company, founded in Massachusetts in 1786. Two years later he became superintendent of Marietta, the company's settlement in the Northwest Territory. See also *SEJ*, p. 511.

James Brown (1776–1835), lawyer and younger brother of Representative Brown, was born in Staunton, Virginia, and moved to Lexington, Kentucky, from Virginia in 1789. He declined the appointment as a United States district attorney. See also *SEJ*, p. 494. (*Filson Club History Quarterly* 16:83)

Henry Bogart, appointed surveyor of the port of Albany, had served on the Albany committee of safety and correspondence in 1775 and as a second lieutenant in the Continental army in 1777. (*SEJ*, p. 521)

The confirmation of the appointments is recorded in the *SEJ*.

[28] See July 1789, n. 7.

Mr. Wynkoop, spoke to me in the Representative Chamber, to have a meeting of the Delegation   I supported this Idea. and we agreed to meet at the Speakers.   but I first Went and drank Tea with Mr. W̶ Winkoop & Mrs. Wynkoop.   There wa⟨s⟩ a great deal of desultory discourse at the Meeting Mr. Clymer took on him to Assert. That the State of Pennsylvania was in debt to the Union. and disbelieved all Mr. Nicholson's Statements. & declared unequivocally for burning all old Accounts.   I mentioned Nicholson's Statements as being made from Authority, and that they neither ought nor could be invalidated, on supposition.   That the old confederation had proceeded every Step, on the grounds of a final settlement,   that to annihilate the old Accounts was contrary to the new constitution which had sanctifyed every Act of the old Congress.   nor could I see how any State could call on the Union to assume any Debt of her's untill she shewed by a Settlement That she had exceeded her requisitions.   Both Clymer and Wynkoop are seeking for some Plausible excuse to change their ground   I have endeavoured to humor them. but their Pride & obstinacy are hard to Subdue.

April 1790

Thursday, 1 April 1790

This day in Senate Two bills were signed. The Carolina Cession Act, & the bill for giving effect, to the State Inspection Laws.

A Committee was also, appointed to settle the pay of the Senators Up to this Time.

The Senate adjourned & I went into the Chamber of Representatives to hear the Debates. It was a dull Scene Gerry took up the Time of the Committee to the hour of adjournment. he is a tedious & most disagreeable Speaker. the Committee rose & no Question was taken. Soon after I came in I took an Opportunity of Speaking to Mr. Wynkoop. I was pointing out some Inconveniencies of the Assumption. I found he seemed much embarrassed. Lawrence & Benson had got him away from his Usual seat, to near where they usually commonly sat. he paused a little, got up rather hastily, said, God bless You. Went out of the chamber and actually took his Wife & proceeded home to Pennsylvania. The way in Which this good Man, can best serve his country is in superintending his farm. perhaps there is no method more acceptable to nature. he certainly is wanting in political fortitude. Benson⟨,⟩ Lawrence⟨,⟩ The Secretary and others have paid attention to him. and he has not firmness of mind to refuse them his Vote. But he has done What equally offends them. & subjects himself to Ridicule. he has abandoned the Whole Business. & deserted the Cause of his Country at a time When an honest Vote, was is inestimable. Tomorrow being good Friday, we adjourned over to Saturday.

Friday, 2 April 1790

The House of Representatives met, but adjourned on Account of the Holliday. I conversed this day at the Hall with George Gray.[1] he declares. the

---

[1]George Gray (1725-1800), innkeeper and political leader, resided south of Philadelphia at the site of the lower Schuylkill River ferry. He represented Philadelphia County in the state assembly from 1772 to 1777 and from 1780 to 1784. He also served as a Federalist in the convention that ratified the Constitution and in the state constitutional convention of 1789-90. (*PMHB* 11:78-79; Norma Price, *From Meetinghouse to Statehouse, 1683-1783* [Wallingford, Pa., 1976], pp. 21-39)

People of Pennsylvania. are universally opposed to the Assumption.   now the Matter seems understood.   This is the effect of the publications. Which I have laboured hard indeed to get into the Prints.   The Speaker is now firm against the Assumption. & so is Scott.   Clymer is so too. ~~but~~ I believe.   but am not quite certain whether his Wish of Popularity has Yet been able to Subdue his pride & Obstinacy.   Hartley is too giddy and unsettled for any One to determine how he will Vote. and as his Judgment has no share in it the Presumption is that he will vote with Smith of Carolina and those whose company he always keeps.   I have put my Political life in my hand, in Starting this Opposition in the Teeth of the Philadelphians.   if I fail my Seat in Congress and disgrace in the public Eye will follow.   but I am conscious of Rectitude of intention. and hic Murus aheneus esto, nil conscire sibi, nulla pallescere culpa.[2]   I was this day to have dined with the Secretary.   but a Violent Storm of Wind & rain came on. and I could not get an Hackney.   The Speaker offered me his Carriage. but then his Servants were all gone to Church.

Saturday, 3 April 1790

Called in the morning at Mr. Hamilton's Office to make an Apology for not dining with him   could not see him   he was closetted with the Secretary at War.   was desired to stay untill he was disengaged.   The importance of my business I thought would not justify This.   gave my name & compliments to Col. Hamilton, and information that the badness of the Weather prevented my dining with him Yesterday. as I happened to be so unfortunate as not to be able to procure a Carriage.

And now this momentuous affair being settled went to the Hall.   The minutes were read.   a Message was received from the President of the United States   a report handed to the Chair.   We looked and laughed at each other for half an hour and adjourned.   The Report was the pay due to each Member.   Docr. Elmer & Mr. Basset. Whispered me after the Report was handed in, That King & Schyler were allowed full pay. notwithstanding they had not been much with Us.   And That Dr. Johnson was allowed full pay & mileage to Connecticut, tho' he lives here. While the Time Dr. Elmer was Absent was deducted.   Honesty thrives but badly East of the Hudson.   I went in the Representative Chamber expecting the Assumption would be taken up.   A listless Apathy seemed to pervade the Whole.   Two Motions were negatived, touching some appointment of a foreign nature.[3] That did not seem to have

---

[2] Be this your wall of brass, a guileless heart, a cheek no guilt turns pale. (Horace, *Epistles 1*)

[3] The House was debating authorization for a second chief clerk in the department of state who would concentrate on the foreign responsibilities of the department.

been well digested.   Somebody said Adjourn. and they adjourned Accordingly.   This really seems like the Mockery of Business.   The New England Men despair of being able to saddle Us with their Debts and now they care not whether, they do any Business or not.   Mr. Geo. Gray of the lower Ferry, Mr. Leiper, his Son in Law⟨,⟩[4] Col. Oswald and another Gentleman dined with Us.   We had much free conversation after dinner.   Mr. Leiper had waited on Fitzsimons before he came away.   Fitzsimons advised him not to come. & told him a Year hence would be time enough.   *That nothing would be done in the business untill he returned to New York.*   They sat till late   I was happy to have a Company of Pennsylvanians.

Sunday, 4 April 1790

I wrote my letters early,   the day was inviting & I could not avoid, the temptation of walking out.   I went to Scots lodgings. and he walked with me.   The Town is much agitated about a Duel between Burke & Hamilton,[5]   so many People concerned in the Business, may really make the fools fight.

When I was called down to dinner, the Speaker and Genl. were closetted with Clymer and Jackson.   all was profound mystery.   we had half finished our dinner, before they Joined Us.   I saw they were filled with thoughts of importance but I scorned to be inquisitive.   I retired to my chamber   the Speaker soon came to me. And unfolded the Mystery.   Clymer had a proposal. to barter away the Pennsylvania Votes for an Assumption. for the Carolina & Massachusetts Votes for an adjournment to Philada.   He & Fitzsimons are now Squirming like Eels in a Basket. to regain the Popularity which they have, or are likely, to, loose. On this Business. by bringing forward a plausable Pretext to Justify their late Vote.[6]   The Speaker however openly avowed to me the reason of the Vote for Assumption.   Viz. Consolidation, and Uniting in One Government.   I told him plainly Hamilton had no Abilities for such a Work—and the thing would miscarry in his or any other hands.   I determined to go and call on Clymer about this Business   I did so, but he had Jackson,[7] (of the Presidents Family) with him.   I sat till I was tired

---

[4]Thomas Leiper (1745–1825), a Philadelphia tobacco manufacturer since 1765, came to Maryland from Scotland in 1763. He married George Gray's daughter, Elizabeth, in 1778. See also the petition volumes. (John A. Leiper, *Thomas Leiper* [Wallingford, Pa., 1976])
[5]See July 1789, n. 7.
[6]Their 9 March votes in favor of assumption.
[7]William Jackson (1759–1828), presidential aide from September 1789 through December 1791, handled correspondence for the president and may also have acted as a bodyguard. Born in England and raised in South Carolina, he served as a soldier in the South Carolina Line of the Continental army from 1776 to 1780. From 1782 to 1783 he was assistant secretary at war under Benjamin Lincoln, whose aide he had been in the southern campaign. He engaged in commerce in Philadelphia during the 1780s and acted as secretary to the Federal

& rose with the first of the Company to come away   Clymer asked me to walk on the Battery. and ~~Walked~~ we ranged almost the whole length of the Town up the East river & back again, without his giving me an Opportunity of speaking with him,   I felt hurt at his distant Treatment.   I went with him home.   he called Jackson in.   Jackson made a Florid Harrangue. on the Golden Opportunity of bartering the Votes of Pennsylvania, with South Carolina and Massachusetts. to give the Assumption and get. the Residence of Congress   Whatever I might have done in other Company, I would not commit myself to Jackson.   I spoke my sentiments sincerely on the Villany of bartering Votes. declared my opinion that ~~Congress~~ Pennsylvania need make no sacrifice to obtain Congress,   That Matters were working as favourably as could be wished.   That I entertained no doubt of adjourning to Philada.   That assuming the State debts in the Manner proposed, was so radically wrong that nothing could Justify the Act.   & that the Postponement of it ought to take place at any rate.   Clymer said it would not be postponed   it would be carried.   I said the Pennsylvanians might see each other before that time   he said they could not.   I told him, if the Pennsylvanians were able to postpone it, after a Contract was made they were able to do it without any Contract. And if they really meant to sell their Votes it was Idle to talk of giving them without & before a contract was made.   make a present of a thing & you need not demand a Price afterwards.   I concluded with saying I would have time enough to make up my mind. before the Business appeared before the Senate.   But had no Objection to deliver my sentiments at any time, & had given them now with Freedom.

The cold distant stiff and let me add stinking Manner of this Man. is really painful to be submitted to.   I never will go into any Company with design to give offense. but I really think out of respect to myself I ought to avoid his Company.   at least I need not go into it without necessity.   Jackson's interferring in this Business is far from proper.   hence appears plainly, how much the Assumption of the State Debts Is made a point of, by the Court Party.   In fact the reduction of the State Governments. was the Object in Theory in framing both, the Constitution & Judiciary, & in as many Laws of the United States as were capable of taking a Tincture of that kind.   But it won't do.

Monday, 5 April 1790

The bill for the progress of Useful Arts. was concurr'd with after considerable debate.   The Report of the Senators from the joint Committee on the

---

Convention in 1787, but his attempt to be elected secretary of the Senate was unsuccessful. Skilled at dealing with people, Jackson acted in effect as a political aide for Washington. (Freeman, *Washington* 6:204, 362; Decatur, *Private Affairs*, p. 57)

Mitigation bill was, that the disagreement continued— a Communication from the President of the U.S. of three Acts of the legislature of New York. The Whole Papers were read. the act of Transmission from the Government of New York, was pomposity itself. they however often reitterated the Words *Free & Independent*, Which I thought done designedly. I had some discourse with Col. Hartley and he has promised to withhold his vote for the Assumption for some time at least. I went this ~~Even~~ afternoon to hear a Negro preach,[8] can only say it would be in favour of religion in General. if preacher's manifested the same fervor and sincerity that was apparent, in his Manner. he declared himself untuttored, but he seemed to have the Bible by hart. Tempora Mutantur, et nos mutamur in illis.[9] note the cause when I know it. received a number of letters from home, Philada. &ca. this day.

Tuesday, 6 April 1790

The Senate seemed likely to have no business before them this day, But all at Once up rose Few and offered a Report on the bill for the Military Establishment. some Triffling amendments were made in the Compensation to the Officers. But the Bill was materially the same. This is a Vile Ministerial Trick and I have no doubt Hamilton has been tampering with the Committee. It was generally agreed to as the Sense of the Senate. That no Report should be offered untill the Bill for regulating the intercourse with the Indians, & the Treaty bill should be put into the hands of the same Committee But Whatever is, is best. it is out of the hands of that committee & postponed, ~~an~~ I spoke against the Whole bill. as the egg from which a standing Army would be hatched. As ~~in fact~~ it is a standing Army in fact. for the Smallness of the number ~~did~~ does not diminish the Principle. but I foresee I will have much to say Under this Head. at a future day.

Carrol of Carrolton edged near me in the Senate Chamber. and asked me if I had seen the King of France's Speech and the Acts of the Tiers Etates. by which the distinctions of Nobility were broken down. I told him I had & I considered it by no means dishonorable to Us, that our Efforts against Titles & distinction were now seconded by the Representative Voice of 24 Millions. a flash of Joy lightnened from his Countenance. How fatal to our fame as lovers of liberty, would it have ~~been to Us~~ been had we adopted those Shackles of Servility which enlightened Nations are now rejecting with detestation.

---

[8]WM probably referred to "Black" Harry Hosier, an itinerant Methodist preacher who had been associated with Francis Asbury and was in the area at the time. The sermon probably took place at the John Street Methodist Church where many blacks worshipped and where Hosier had preached in 1786. (Elmer T. Clark, ed., *The Journals and Letters of Francis Asbury*, 3 vols. [Nashville, Tenn., 1958], 1:362n, 494n, 681n–682n)

[9]The times are changed, and we are changed with them.

Wednesday, 7 April 1790

A Committee was appointed in Senate for bringing in a bill, for the Government, of the Territory of the U.S. South of the Ohio.   I did not oppose the appointment of the Committee, but told some of them that they must make it stand alone. As I wished to avoid all Expence.   I had no notion of Salaries to the Governor Judges &ca.   I considered the Motion brought forward, by way of making some entry on the Journals, as much as any thing else.   A Short bill however came up & had a first reading.   The Speaker had Company this day,   I was wanting in Spirits & did not seem to enjoy it.   the Table was however filled well, And there was a good Flow of Conviviality.   After dinner the Speaker told me, That Fitzsimons & Clymer wanted to see the delegation at their Quarters.   I was not well, it was late, and a Tempest of Wind & very cold.   But I went.   if Fitzsimons had been hired to extol the political Merit of Massachusetts & South Carolina, and depreciate that of Pennsylvania.   It was in vain that I told him everything, in a pecuniary point of View, must remain in Doubt, untill the Accounts were settled.   That the Only Man Who had it in his power to give An Opinion on the subject (The Comptroller Genl.)[10] had taught Us to think differently.   said the State Navy & defense of the River Delaware had cost vast Sums.   I could not see That the defense of Delaware &ca. was any more a charge against Pennsylvania. than the Expence of the American Arms before Boston, was a demand against Massachusetts. or the Charges ~~agai~~ at York Town against Virginia.   if Pennsylvania advanced the Money it was in the General defense As well as her own.   And the Charge lay well against the Union.

The Business of this Meeting was to consult about an adjournment to Philada. & as the votes of Pennsylvania, would determine for or against the Assumption. Whether they could not be so managed as to effect that Measure.   I will only set down What I said on the Matter as Opinion.   That to barter Votes at any rate was unjustifiable.   That the risk of loosing Votes, was as great as the Chance of gaining by making a bargain with either side. For Philada. had Friends on both sides.   That the best mode was to postpone the Assumption. & push the adjournment for Philada. While both parties feared & both courted the Pennsylvania Votes.

Thursday, 8 April 1790

A bill which came up Yesterday for suspending part of the Revenue Law with respect to the Port of Ye⟨o⟩comico in Virginia[11] was read a second

---

[10]John Nicholson.

[11]The Collection Act [HR-50] related in part to Yeocomico, located near the mouth of the Potomac River, about ten miles from the Chesapeake Bay.

Time. Now Elsworth moved some Alteration of the Law with regard to some ports in Connecticut. Langdon wanted an Alteration for New Hampshire. & Dalton one for Massachusetts. It was committed to these three Members— God forgive me if I wrong them. but I fear they want to make loop holes in the impost Law to suit, their private Purposes. or rather the purposes of State Smuggling.

I never observed so drooping an Aspect, so turbid & forlorn an appearance, as overspread the Partizans of the Secretary in our House this forenoon. If I chose to Use the Language of political Scandal I would call them the Senatorial Gladiators Elsworth & Izard in particular ~~both~~ Walked almost all the Morning, back & forward Strong & Patterson seemed moved, but not so much agitated King looked like a Boy that had been Whipped & Genl. Schuyler's Hair stood on End, as if the Indians had fired at him. I accounted for the appeara⟨nce⟩ of King & Schyler, from the publications that have appeared against them in the Papers for Two days past.[12]

Just before Dinner Andw. Brown the Printer called. It seems there has been a Meeting of the Citizens of Philada. On Saturday last, to consider on the Subject of General Knox's report. & A Committee is appointed to draw up something.[13] Brown has refused to print for them, and has flew off to this place. For the double purpose of giving notice of the Event, and claiming his reward. & perhaps a third motive has had weight with him for I really never saw any Man have more the appearance of fright upon him. I know him to have been a Spy & tool for Hamilton for some time past. He told Us of some Man having offered some Violent Peices to him for publication, which he said were wrote well. but he refused to print them & the Author took them away. He said they were addressed to the Yeoma⟨n⟩ry of Pennsylvania I suspect this may be my friend Geo. Logan. he ought to beware of A. Brown he does not know him. Brown owned to Us. That Hamilton had wrote to Jefferson in his favour after publishing his Recantation, & refusal to print anything against the Secretary's Report.

Friday, 9 April 1790

the Committee of Yesterday reported the bill with Elsworth's amendment only. said Mr. Hamilton was of Opinion When the New Impost Law was enacted, the other Amendments could be introduced. this is Art in him. to

---

[12]The controversy about King and Schuyler in the press concerned the fact that the New York legislature had forbidden members of the New York delegation in Congress to hold seats in the legislature. In 1790 King was a member of the assembly, while Schuyler and Representative Laurance were members of the state senate. See "An Elector," *NYJ*, 8 April 1790, and "A Citizen," *NYDG*, 7 April 1790 (reprinted in *NYDA*, 8 April 1790).

[13]The Philadelphia meeting was announced in the *Independent Gazetteer* on 3 April. A week later the paper reported that a large number of people had gathered at the Statehouse

make friends to his new bill. And shows that he either is still confident of Success or affects it. There was no Objection & the bill had all its readings. Elsworth reported a bill for the Government South of the Ohio. It was to be the same, as the Government of the Western Territory, mutatis mutandis.[14] I had some Previous discourse with Elsworth on this Subject. I can with Truth pronounce him the most uncandid Man I ever knew possessing such Abilities. I am often lead to doubt Whether he has a particle of Integrity, perhaps such a Quality is Useless in Connecticut.

In Senate this day the Gladiators seemed more than commonly busy as I came out from the Hall. All The Presidents Family were there Humphreys⟨,⟩ Jackson⟨,⟩ Nelson[15] &ca. &ca. they had Vining with them. & as I took it were a standing Committee to catch the Members as they went in or came out. The Crisis is at hand. At dinner the Speaker told me, there had been a Call of the Secretary's party last night. Fitzsimons, he said, had been sent for. & they had determined to risk an Action tomorrow.

Saturday, 10 April 1790

busy to near Eleven writing letters to my Family, dressed and attended. to see the Event of the day. but it was put off. by. consent. The Treasurer[16] told me the Reason of it afterwards. Schurman who is against the Assumption is expected to go away, & thus the other party will be left strongest, or at least more so by One vote. The Secretarys People Scarce disguise their design. Which is to create a Mass of Debt, which will Justify them in seizing all the Sources of Government. thus annihilating the State legislatures, and erecting an Empire on the Basis of Consolidation.

Sunday, 11 April 1790

Staid at my lodgings almost all day, a few minutes excepted, when I went to the lodgings of General Irwin, who this day, is to set off on his Journey to

---

to discuss Secretary Knox's plan for regulating the militia and that, after voting their disapproval of it, they appointed a committee of seven to draft a memorial to present to the citizens, should Congress take up the plan.

[14]Necessary changes being made.

[15]Thomas Nelson (b. 1764), presidential aide and member of Washington's official family from October 1789 through 1790, was the son of Washington's friend and signer of the Declaration of Independence, Thomas Nelson, Jr. (1738–89). His duties were "to assist in writing, receiving and entertaining company, and in the discharge of such other matters as is not convenient or practicable for the President to attend to in person." When considering Nelson's appointment, Washington recorded the qualities he sought in an aide: "a good address, abilities above mediocrity—secresy and prudence—attention and industry—good temper—and a capacity and disposition to write correctly and well, and to do it obligingly." (*WGW* 30:367; *DGW* 5:448, 451n)

[16]Samuel Meredith.

Carlisle. wrote Sundry letters. read &ca. I charged General Irwin with letters for Harrisburgh & Sunbury. wrote a few lines to Eleazer Oswald Editor of the Independent Gazetteer to enclose his paper and forward it to my Son Johney to be left at Adam Zantzingers,[17] in Market Street Philada.

Monday, 12 April 1790

The business done in Senate this day was Triffling. A bill for establishing the Government of the North Carolina Cession was taken up,[18] I had Occasion to speak to it, & moved a postponement, untill the bill be printed & put into the Members hands, it was carried Elsworth was fretted & I cared not. Two amended bills came up from the other house & were postponed we adjourned between 12 & 1 O'Clock I went into the House of Representatives. to hear the Question of Assumption taken. Clymer got up said the Assumption was 2 millions & a Quarter against his State. More than she ought to pay. but for confirming the Government & for National Purposes he would vote for it. I could not hear all he said. but the above was the amount of it. Fitzsimons hoped to have a great many conditions obtained, such as that the Interest of the State Debt should be paid in the respective States. That no improper charges should be brought forward. But he would Vote for it now, in expectation, that these conditions would be obtained afterwards. certainly, this could not be called the Conduct of a Wise Man. he voted as well as Clymer for it formerly & took all the Pennsylvania delegates with him except Hiester & Genl. Muhlenberg. without any condition Whatever. Unless it might be private Ones ~~below~~ known only to himself & the Treasury. The question was however taken & lost. 31 against 29 for it. Fitzsimons⟨,⟩ Clymer & Hartley voted for it. Sedgwick from Boston pronounced a funeral Oration over it. he was called to Order, some Confusion ensued he took his hat & went out. When he returned his Visage to me bore the visible marks of Weeping. Fitzsimons reddened like Scarlet his Eyes were ~~bringm~~ full. Clymer's color always pale now verged to ~~cadaverous~~ a deadly Whiteness. his lips quavered, and his neither Jaw shook with convulsive Motions. His head neck & Breast consented to Gesticulations resembling those of a Turkey or ~~Fowl~~ Goose, nearly strangled in the Act of deglutition. Benson bungled like a Shoemaker who had lost his End. Ames's Aspect was truly hippocratic, a total change of face & feature. he sat torpid as if his faculties had been benumbed. Gerry exhibited the advantages of a cadaverous appearance. at all times palid, and far from pleasing, he ran no risk of deterioration. ~~with Hectic hems & consumptive~~ Thro' an interruption of Hectic hems and consumptive coughs. he delivered himself of a declaration,

---

[17] Adam Zantzinger was a Philadelphia merchant.
[18] Southern Territory Act [S-8].

That the Delegates of ~~his state~~ Massachusetts. would proceed no further, but write to their State for instructions.   happy Impudence sat enthroned on Lawrence's brow.   he rose in puffing pomp, and moved that the Committee should rise. And Assigned the agitation of the House as a Reason. Wadsworth hid his Grief Under the rim of a round hat.   Boudinot's wrinkles rose into ridges. and the Angles of his mouth were depressed, and their apperture assumed a curve resembling an horse Shoe—   Fitzsimons first recovered recollection. and endeavoured, to rally the discomfited & disheartened heroes.   He hoped the good Sense of the House would still predominate and lead them to reconsider the Vote which had been now taken.   and he doubted not but it would yet be adopted. Under proper Modifications.   The Secretary's Group pricked up their Ears and Speculation wiped the Tear from either Eye.   Goddess of Description paint the Gallery.   here's the paper find fancy quils or Crayons Yourself.

Tuesday, 13 April 1790

Nothing of moment done this day in the Senate.   the ~~North~~ bill for the Territory south of the Ohio. passed a 2d reading.   some Triffling debate on the Amendments of the bill defining Crimes & punishments.   The day was clear tho somewhat cold.   but I felt a desire of being abroad. and Walked out almost all day, with Mr. R. Harris who is now abroad again.

Wednesday, 14 April 1790

There was nothing of importance transacted this day in Senate.   no debate Worth minuting.   The Senate adjourned   We went or at least I went into the House of Representatives   But even there. everything seemed equally unimportant.   The House adjourned. and as I was to dine this day with Mr. Izard, the Speaker and Genl. ⟨Muhlenberg⟩ being likewise engaged at the same place. We had an hour on hand to Saunter away before dinner.   it began to rain as we got to Izards.   There was of the Company Old Van Berkel.[19] The Speaker of the New York House of Representatives[20] Members of Congress &ca.   among our Wine I mentioned the expected death of Dr. Franklin. Izard knew him as well as any Man in the World.   Docr. Johnson would Yield

---

[19]Pieter Johan Van Berckel (1725–1800), minister plenipotentiary to the United States from the Netherlands between 1783 and 1788, was frequently referred to as "Old Van Berckel." He remained in the United States after he was replaced in office by his son, Franco Petrus Van Berckel. (*DGW* 5:507n)

[20]Gulian Ver Planck (1751–99) was a New York City merchant and speaker of the state assembly. (William E. Ver Planck, *The History of Abraham Isaacse Ver Planck* [Fishkill Landing, N.Y., 1892], pp. 104, 162–68)

to no Man, in intimate acquaintance with his Character.   And at him they
both went.   I really never was much of an admirer of the Doctor. but I could
hardly find in my heart to paint the Devil so bad.   he had every fault of Vanity
ambition want of Sincerity. &c. &ca.   Lee's ~~want of~~ rascally Virtue of Prudence was all They would leave him.

I must note it down, That Clymer called me out of the Senate Chamber this
day   it was on no business of any Consequence.   he talked with me a Considerable time.   After I came into the Representative Chamber he came and
took a Chair beside me.   I must declare that be his Motives What they may, I
never saw him so condescending.   I will not baulk him in his advances to
me.   my heart tells me, That peace with all the World is the Most acceptable
and desirable object to be pursued.   I will not shun her but place my self in
her paths—   What is it that wispers in my Ear? That if any dirty trick is played
me, That has it's date about this time. That I need not be at a loss to guess the
Author.   No.   No.   I will give it, no such meaning.   I will not suppose
him to have worn a Cloack, but that he came cloathed in Candor.

Thursday, 15 April 1790

the Bill for regulating the military establishment was called up.   The
Friends of this bill seem Chiefly to be Butler⟨,⟩ King & Schyler. Who appear
to be arrant Tools in this as in every other business.   I have opposed this bill,
hitherto as often as it has been before the house, as the foundation, the Corner
Stone of a Standing Army.   The Troops are augmented one half.   The Reasons hitherto given, have been the distressed State of Georgia   Butler has
blazed away on this Subject at a great rate   declared over and over That
Georgia would seek protection elsewhere. if Troops were not sent to Support
her &c. &ca.   said fifty Indians had penetrated into that State of which he had
authentic information &ca.   Carrol Joined him⟨,⟩ King & Schyler,
Elsworth & Lee opposed them.   Lee made a Set Speech against standing
Armies.   he really spoke Well.   King at last got up and rather upbraided the
Georgia Members for their Silence on this Question.   This brought Up Col.
Gun.   He declared he knew nothing of 50 Indians making any inroad into
Georgia   he was just from there and had the latest Accounts.   Georgia was in
peace and never had a better prospect of continuing so.   there existed no
cause in Georgia for augmenting the Troops. and since that was the reason
assigned for it he should vote against it.   Infatuated People That we are the
first thing done under our new government, was the Creation of a Vast number
of Offices and Officers.   a Treasury dilated into as many branches, as invention could Frame.   A Secretary at War with an Host of Clerks,   And above all
a Secretary of State.   and all these Men labour in their several Vocations.

Richmond Hill, New York, residence of Vice President John Adams. (Courtesy of the Library of Congress.)

hence We must have a Mass of National Debt, to employ the Treasury.   an Army & Navy for fear the department of War should lack employment.   Foreign engagements too must soon be attended too, to keep Up the Consequence of that Secretary— the next Cry will be for an Admiralty,   give Knox his Army, and he will soon have a War on hand.   indeed I am clearly of Opinion That he is aiming, at all this even now.   and that few as the Troops are that he now has under his direction, he will have a War in less than 6 Months on hand, with the southern Indians.

Lent the Speaker 50 dollars.

Friday, 16 April 1790

And now again for the augmentation of the Troops   I took a minute View of all the Papers forwarded by Genl. Knox.   They were Copies of letters which he had received. from different places. and carried evidently Management on the face of them.   Thus for Instance Genl. Knox writes to Genl. Wayne[21] in Georgia. to inform him, Whether the Spaniards had not lately supplyd the Indians with Arms and Ammunition.   Genl. Wayne answers that his inquiries on this head resolve themselves in the Affirmative.   And adds his Opinion that it is highly probable, hostile Uses may be made of these Supplies by the savages.   In this Manner leading letters procure favourable answers from Men who expect to be employ'd in Case Troops are raised.   Before Col. Gun came the dangers and distress of Georgia were magnifyed, as far as fancy could form frightful Pictures.   Col. Gun contradicts all this.   New Phantoms for the day must be created.   Now a dreadful & dangerous conspiracy, is discovered to be carrying on between the People of Kentuke and the Spaniards.[22]

---

[21]Anthony Wayne (1745–96) resided on a plantation in Georgia presented to him by that state in recognition of his Revolutionary War service, from which he retired in 1783 with the rank of brevet major general. He was born in Chester County, Pennsylvania, and represented the county in the assembly, 1784–85. In 1785 WM gave him a lot in Maclaysburg in recognition of their friendship and of Wayne's motions in the assembly to create Dauphin County and to declare WM the victor in the disputed 1785 Northumberland County assembly election. Wayne was a Federalist delegate at the Pennsylvania Ratification Convention. In 1791 he defeated Representative Jackson, who was seeking reelection to the House of Representatives, but the seat was declared vacant when questions arose concerning Wayne's legal residence. (NCHSP 9:13)

[22]During the 1780s the political leaders of Virginia's Kentucky counties became increasingly discontented with their situation. They accused Virginia of postponing statehood for the district and Congress of supporting Spain's insistence on a twenty-five-year closure of the Mississippi River to American trade. In mid-1787 James Wilkinson of Kentucky met with the Spanish governor of Louisiana at New Orleans and informed him that Kentucky was on the verge of declaring its independence and seeking foreign protection for itself from the United States. In exchange for various promises, the Kentuckian took an oath of allegiance to Spain and agreed to work for the union of Kentucky with the Spanish colonies in America. John Brown, who represented the Kentucky counties in Congress from 1788 to 1791, was less committed to the intrigue than Wilkinson. Nevertheless, he held discussions about it in 1788

King unfolded this mysterious Business. adding he conceived his fears were well founded.   he firmly believed there was a Conspiracy.   That it was dangerous to put Arms into the hands of the Frontier People for their defense. least they should Use them against the United States.   I really could scarce keep my seat & hear such base Subterfuges made Use of, One after another.   I rose, demanded What right Gentlemen had to monopolize information,   if they had it. let them come forward, with it and give other People An Opportunity of Judging of the authenticity of the information as well of as the Persons in possession of it.   declared I could not, lamely sit and hear the Characters of the People on the Western Waters traduced by by the lump.   This day was the first ever, I heard of the Word Conspiracy being apply'd to the Inhabitants of the Western Waters I had a right to doubt it. Untill authentic Proof was brought forward of the fact.   I felt myself disposed to wipe King hard and certainly did so.   It was moved & seconded very fairly to reduce the number to one thousand and carried 11 to 9.   Elsworth tho' he had spoke for the Reduction. Voted against Us.   Mr. Morris desired to be excused from Voting. As he had Come but lately.   Elsworth said he voted—against 1,000 because he wanted 12,000 and tho it was certainly out of all Order. got a Question put on this number and carried it by one Vote.   No Man ever had a more compleat Knack of putting his foot in a Business than this same Elsworth.   at 1,000 We should have had but One Regiment.   now the Committee to Whom it is recommitted will try to continue them in Two.   & Yet œconomy, is all his Cry.   I gave notice that when the title of the Bill came to be considered I would move to strike out, "for regulating the military establishment of the United States." & mention particularly, What I took the intention of the Troops to be, agreeable to the old Acts of Congress.   Viz. *Protection of the Frontiers of the United States. facilitating the Surveying & selling the public lands, and preventing unwarrantable encroachments on the same.*   The Man must be blind who does not see, a most unwarrantable Management respecting our military affairs.   The Constitution certainly never contemplated a Standing Army in time of peace   A Well regulated Militia to execute the laws of the Union, quell insurrections and repel Invasions, is the very language of the Constitution.   General Knox offers a most exceptionable bill for a General Militia law. which excites (as it is most probable he expected) a general

---

with the Spanish minister to the United States, Diego de Gardoqui. Wilkinson took credit for Brown's election to the FFC and informed the governor of Louisiana that Brown would act as a spy for Spain in that body. Virginia's agreement to Kentucky's separation and the adoption of the Kentucky Statehood Act [S-16] by the FFC put an end to the conspiracy. Brown's involvement became a major issue in his successful campaign for reelection in 1790. Considering the amount of correspondence engendered by Wilkinson, Brown, and the Spanish officials, it is not surprising that the existence of the conspiracy was known to members of the FFC by April 1790. See also Patricia Watlington, "John Brown and the Spanish Conspiracy," *Virginia Magazine of History and Biography* 75:52–68. (Patricia Watlington, *The Partisan Spirit* [New York, 1972]; *DHFFE* 2:313–14)

Opposition.   Thus the Business of the Militia stands still. and the military establishment bill which encreases the standing Troops One half is pushed with all the Art & address of ministerial Management.

Saturday, 17 April 1790

being Saturday a party were formed to go to Haarlem.[23]   long cooped up in the City. I joyfully joined them.   but the Wind soon blew cold & raw from the East,   we could not stay out of doors,   like most other human expectations, Our ~~Plans W~~ hopes vanished in disappointment.   I got some cold, and felt slight complaints of the rheumatic kind.   The ramble has however had it's Uses. & may cure me on the Subject of Excursions for the future.

Sunday, 18 April 1790

this the most tempestuous day which I remember.   Snow Torrents of rain and high Winds.   kept House all day, read & wrote to my family.   The Speaker received letters by which it appears. The Philadelphians or at least the Aristocrats will support Mifflin rather than him for Governor.   he recapitulated the return they had always made to him for his engaging the Germans to support their Measures.   he had a Share of the Profits of the Vendue office, from Paton but it amounted to little.   they deserted him in the appointment. of Vendue Master, for the Northern liberties.   he got the office in Montgomery by a constitutional Vote, & it never paid him for the paper he spent for the Republican party.[24]

Monday, 19 April 1790

The Journals of the Senate can scarce designate a day of less importance than the Present.   The Yeas & Nays had been fairly taken on reducing the Troops

---

[23]Harlem was a seventeenth century civil division consisting of almost the entire northern half of Manhattan Island. Its southern boundary was a diagonal line running approximately from what is now 129th Street on the west to 74th Street on the east side of the island. The scenic rural area contained the 150-year-old village of Harlem. (*Iconography* 4:plate 36, 6:plates 84 B–F, p. 654)

[24]John Patton (1745–1804), auctioneer or vendue master for Philadelphia since 1787, emigrated there from Sligo, Ireland, in 1761. He was a prominent ironmaster who had married into the Bird family of Berks County. (*CRP* 15:322; *PRM* 3:448n; *St. Patrick*, p. 129; *PMHB* 31:48)

The Northern Liberties, a suburb of Philadelphia, was a Philadelphia County township on the Delaware River adjacent to the northern border of the city.

Montgomery County is contiguous to Philadelphia County on its northwest side. Muhlenberg, a leader of its large German community, became recorder of wills and deeds when the county was organized in 1784.

from 1,600 to 1,000, but the way the minutes read, the question was for Striking out every Man Viz. the Whole 1,600. Elsworth moved to Strike out the Whole of the Yeas & nays &ca. This certainly was against all rule, the reading of the minutes is for correcting not altering them. Wyngate & Langdon spoke a good deal but it was in Vain. they carried it. I bought two little Pocket Books for Betsey & Nelly.[25] to be sent home by Bobey Harris. On the Villum in One of them I wrote

> A Dady to a Daughter dear
> this little present sends
> May she to him, far off or near
> by duty make amends.

In the other One I wrote—the following

> A Father to a favourite Child
> presents this little Toy
> May she thro' life, a Sunshine mild
> and happiness enjoy—

Wretched Man that I am, who do not break loose from this disagreeable place, and Stay live & die with my family.

Tuesday, 20 April 1790

dressed this day to go with Bobey Harris to the Levee. But the President. had left Town & was gone to long Island. We sat a long time in the senate without doing any thing but at last the Committee, on the Military bill reported. The Report was a mere Matter of detail, only the clause limiting the bill to Two Years was Struck out. I had given notice that I would move to alter the Title of the bill so as to express the Use & intention of raising the Troops, but our President in order to Jockey me was for putting the Question on the bill without saying any thing about the Tittle at all. Elsworth who cannot bear that any body should move any thing but himself, and to Whom I had shewed the Title I proposed to offer. pushed himself before me. with a Title different & much shorter. He was not seconded. I offered mine & was seconded by Lee. A long debate ensued. Elsworth now gave all the Opposition in his power. It was really painful to hear the Servile Sentiments that were advanced. The Spirit of the Whole was. That we had nothing to do with the Troops. had no right to know What the President did with them or apply'd them to. It was interferring with his command. &ca. &ca. I thought they were well answered but what of that We lost it. Elsworth now showed plainly that he cared little about his Motion. & that he had only started his to draw off, the Senate from mine. Butler had declared he would

---

[25]Elizabeth (1772–94) and Eleanor (1774–1823) Maclay were WM's eldest daughters. See Appendix C.

second him, during the debate on mine.   I therefore called for it.   He now moved it different Viz. *An Act to raise Troops for the Service of the United States*.   his first Motion was *for the defense of the Frontiers & for other Purposes*.   all we could do was to get a question on it such as it was.   the Senate divided 10 & 10.   The President made a remarkable Speech   ~~he said.~~ He said to raise Troops for the Service of the United States was was as much A Standing Army, as a Military Establishment. & voted for the old Title.   I thought I confirmed every Argument I advanced either from the old or New Constitution of Pennsylvania or from the Constitution of the United States. But a Sentence from the Secretary is of more avail than all the Constitutions, in the United States. with many People.   The limiting clause at the End of the Bill, confining it to 2 Years being lost I moved that the T⟨h⟩ree Years in the first Clause should be Struck out, and Two inserted,   I brought forward the appropriation Clause of the Constitution.[26] to support me in this Motion. But as it was known where the Majority was I could not obtain a second—   We a Meeting last night of our delegation on the Subject of removing Congress. The avowed language of the Philadans. to make a Potowmac Contract.   I insisted we should loose, as much. on one hand as we could gain on the other. & infamy was certain.   that the business could be better done without it &ca.

Wednesday, 21 April 1790

The Bill for regulating the Military Establishment was taken. Up for a third reading being in Senate,   and of course in Order I moved to restore the 17th Sect. which had been struck out Yesterday. In the following Words, And be it further enacted That this Act shall continue and be in force Untill the 26th day of March 1792.   I went over the Constitutions of Pennsylvania Old & new ~~shewed~~ shewed that they were abhorrent of a Standing army in time of Peace.   inferred as I thought clearly the same Doctrine from the Constitution of the United States.   I then shewed that this bill established a standing Army.   it was for regulating the Military Establishment of the United States.   It carryed a permanent Establishment on the face of it. and as it was unlimited in point of time. it clearly carried with it a permanent Standing Army.   I compared it to the Mutiny bill of Great Britain.   All the World knew Great Britain had a Standing Army. And her Soldiers were enlisted generally for Life. & Yet the Yealousy of the Nation was such that the boldest Minister dared not propose the extending the Mutiny Bill to more than One Year.   In legislative Theory the English had no standing Army   It was but an annual one.   but if the bill passed in it's present form. We should not have even theory to oppose to a standing Army. &ca.   Elsworth got up and said the

---

[26]Article I, Section 8, paragraph 12.

reason the Clause was Struck out. was that it contradicted the Term of Enlistment, & he made a distinction between enlisting men for three Years &
appropriating pay for them for 3 Years   We could do One   We could not do
the other. without breaking the Constitution.   he wished they were enlisted
for seven or ten Years &ca.   I answered, That it seemed as if Men strained their
ingenuity to try how near they could approach an Infraction of the Constitution, without breaking it.   There could be no doubt, but the Clause limiting,
the appropriation to 2 Years was meant as a bar. against a Standing Army.
and Yet Gentlemen seemed to strain their faculties, to accomplish the very end
prohibited, without being chargeable with a direct breach of Command-
ment.   &c. &ca.   Elsworth declared both Yesterday & this day that Military
Establishment meant & could mean nothing short of a Standing Army.   Carrol Used the same Language. and expressly said that tho' the Constitution of
Pennsylvania might forbid it, we were not to be governed by any State constitution.   but of all the Flamers none blazed like Izard.   he wished for a
Standing Army of 10,000 men.   he feared nothing from them.   no nation
ever lost their liberty by a standing Army.   &c. &ca.   The Romans lost their
liberty.   but it was not by the Army Under Julius Ca⟨e⟩sar.   he was well
aswered by Lee.   But it was in Vain.   A standing Army was the avowed
Doctrine,   & on the Question Lee⟨,⟩ Wyngate & myself rose.   I openly
declared my regret, That there ~~was~~ were not enough of Us to call the Yeas &
Nays.   Mr. Morris was not in at taking the Question.

I find in some Conversation which I have had with the Speaker That Hartley
is very dependent in his circumstances.   a mere Borrower and Discounter of
Notes at the Philada. bank.   It is much against him in point of prudence, that
he should be the most extravagant, Member of the Pennsylvania Delegation.

Thursday, 22 April 1790

The morning looked so tempting I could not resist the impulse, I felt for
Walking out.   The Speaker Joined me at the Door.   We called on Mr.
Wynkoop who is confined with his sore leg.   We got on the Assumption of the
State debts.   I find the Speaker rather wavers of late.   Wynkoop seemed all
Secretary.   I embarked as I generally do. and I endeavoured to speak so plain,
That I scarce think it possible I could be misunderstood.   and I could not help
thinking. That to Understand, and ~~Yield~~ obtain consent, were inseparable.
he wa⟨i⟩ved What I said. As if he would push all by in the lump.   but if I had
talked to a mute Camel. or addressed myself to a dead Horse. my speech would
have had the same effect.   And Yet he seemed to have neither Opinion nor
System of his own.

Attended at the Hall   a Bill was committed   a Message received & Senate adjourned.

wrote short Peice against the Assumption of the State debts.   sent a Copy to Baily for Publication[27]   This day there were accounts published of the death of Doctor Franklin. & the House of Representatives resolv'd to crape their arms for a Month.[28]   When I consider how much the Doctor has been celebrated. and When I compare his public fame, with what I know of his private Character, I am tempted to doubt Whether ever any Man was perfect.   Yet perhaps it is for the good of Society that patterns of perfection should be held up, for Men to copy after.   I will therefore give him my vote of praise.   & if any Senator moves crape for his Memory I shall have no Objection to it, 'tho' we suffered Grayson to die, without any attention to his Memory, Tho' he belonged to our Body, and perhaps had some claim to a mark, of Sorrow.

Friday, 23 April 1790

Felt rheumatic pains over considerable parts of me. & really have some fear, that I shall have a fit of it.   A bill had been committed Yesterday *for the relief of a certain description of Officers.*   I believe it came from the Secretary at War.   It was absolutely Unintelli⟨gi⟩ble.   and it really struck me That it was meant as the Stock to engraft some Mischief on with respect to the Commutation Pensions and half pay of the Old Army, everything relating to which We had generally considered as settled.   I spoke freely of it Yesterday and this day tho' I was not of the Committee.   The Committee however reported against the Whole of it & it was rejected.   It really seems as if a listlessness or spirit of Laziness pervaded the house of Representatives.   anything ~~almost~~ which comes from a Secretary is adopted, almost without any Examination.   The Military Establishment bill came up   concurr'd to.   Strange that not a Penn-

[27]The piece was printed in the *NYDA* and *Freeman's Journal* on 28 April. It can be found in Appendix B(8).

Francis Bailey (c. 1735–1815) was editor of the Philadelphia *Freeman's Journal* from 1781 to 1792, probably the most partisan Antifederalist newspaper in the United States. He was born in Lancaster County and ran a print shop in Lancaster from 1772 to 1780. In February 1790 Bailey had petitioned Congress for an exclusive right to profit from an invention that would afford security against counterfeiting. The House adopted the Bailey Bill [HR-44] for this purpose, but the bill was defeated in the Senate. See also the petition volumes. (*DHROC* 13:xxxiv–xxxv).

[28]The badge of mourning, adopted by Congress in 1774, consisted of a black crepe or ribbon worn on the arm or hat. Women wore a black ribbon or necklace. The Senate, where Franklin's political enemies were dominant, refused to take notice of the death until forced to do so during the third session when the president of the commonalty of Paris transmitted a eulogy on Franklin to it. See March 1791, n. 1, and *PTJ* 19:78–115 for more about the FFC and the death of Franklin. (*JCC* 1:78)

sylvanian should Object to this bill.   as it now stands it flatly contradicts the Constitution of Pennsylvania both old & new.

Carrol, rose and made a Motion That the Senate should wear crape A month. ~~or~~ for the loss of Doctor Franklin.   before he was seconded Elsworth got up and opposed it.   said as it could not be carried in the Senate he trusted it would not be seconded.   I rose and seconded Carrol.   Izard & Butler hated Dr. Franklin, & I will know that this opposition of Elsworth aimed at their gratification,   perhaps my supporting Carrol had something of a tincture of the same kind.   King & Dr. Johnson joined Elsworth.   Elsworth addressed Carrol & told him (thro the Chair) that he might as well withdraw his motion as it would be lost.   This was really insulting.   But as the Matter strictly speaking, was not Senatorial. or such as belonged to Us, in our Capacity as a public body, and as it was opposed. Carrol looked at me & I nodded Assent & it was withdrawn.

Saturday, 24 April 1790

A party was formed by Genl. Muhlenberg to ~~gon~~ on Long Island but recollecting the disappointment of last Saturday, I declined going with them staid at home and spent the day rather in a lounging Manner.   wrote Some letters   the Speaker proposed a ride in his Carriage,   I was all passive.   Sed L. L.[29]   he took a Lady who was indisposed,   I went in the Evening and sat a While with Mr. Wynkoop.

In the afternoon, Henry, Stone, and some other Members of Congress called on me to go and see some Cattle of enormous Size.   I went.   Two Bullocks of great bulk indeed, were shewed to Us.   I was sorry for my Walk.   they were in the Yard of the slaughter house.   I now learned some Secrets of the Butcher's Business, which I never knew before.   The Ox is emptied by repeated bleedings of almost all his Juices before he is killed.   a place is fitted Up to w⟨h⟩ich their heads are drawn up by a rope & the Jugular Veins are opened.   the Blood ~~runs~~ falls down on Boards ~~paced~~ inclined so that it runs into a Trough, fixed in the Ground.   And Hogs are kept to feed on it.   all this preparation is to make the Beef White.   These great harmless Creatures had undergone several of these bleedings & were moving about faint & languid with looks of dumb despair.   Oh. Man what a Monster Art thou.   I cannot get rid of the impression this sight has left on me.

Sunday, 25 April 1790

I wrote letters as usual, this Morning, to my family   at 10 went to Mr. Wynkoop's lodgings in Order to go to Meeting,   it blew up cold and began to

rain.   The Clergyman we intended to hear (Doctor Lynn) was sick. so we did
not go out   but I sat with him a considerable time   our Chat was on various
and triffling subjects.   Wheather, home, farming and What not.   after a
pause he broke out with a laugh saying how fine & quietly we got over the
military Establishment   all smoth not a Word of opposition.   he expressed
great satisfaction, and seemed to manifest that kind of Triumph, which would
follow the performance of an arduous task with ~~much~~ unexpected facility.
surely the ministerial Gentry must have looked for opposition, and prepared
themselves accordingly. and my worthy friend must have been of their Council.   This seems an hard thought, but what am I to believe.   I however soon
undeceived him with regard to the part I had acted in the Senate and he looked
like a Man Who unexpectedly ~~found~~inds himself in Strange Company.

Monday, 26 April 1790

Attended at the Hall.   Mr. Walker from Virginia, the Gentleman elected
in the room of Mr. Grayson took his Seat.   the Progress [*Process*] bill[30] which
in fact consisted only of One Clause continuing the old One to another session
had a second Reading.   We did not continue in our Seats for more than 3/4ths
of an hour till King moved An adjournment   Modesty by degrees begins to
leave,   We Used to stay in the Senate Chamber till about 2 O'Clock Whether
we did any thing or not. by way of keeping up the Appearance of Business.
But even this We seem to be got over.   Doctor Elmer asked me to walk with
him.   I saw Cards handed round the Senate.   but this happens so often.
That I took no notice of it.   When we were in the Street the Doctor asked me if
I had not a Card to dine with the President.   I told him with all the indifference I could put on. No. & immediately took Up some other Subject which
entered ~~One~~ On with eagerness. As if I had hardly noticed his Question.
This is the second time the Docr. has asked this same question. so that the
President's neglect of me can be no Secret.   how Unworthy of a great Character, is such littleness?   He is not aware however that he is paying me a Compliment. That none of his Guests can claim.   he places me above the influence of
a dinner. even in his own Opinion.   perhaps he means it as a punishment, for
my opposition of Court Measures.   either way I care not a fig for it.   I
certainly feel a pride arising, from a consciousness, That the greatest Man In
the World, has not Credit enough with me to influence my conduct in the
least.   this Pride however or perhaps I should call it self approbation. is the
result of my conduct, and by no means the motive of it.   This I am clear in.

I am so very intent on getting Congress away from this place. That I went to
see the Philadelphians, and concert What farther was to be done.   I wished to
communicate to them the Result of my inquiries, and receive their Stock of

---

[30]Courts Act [S-9].

information on the Subject of removal.   I had sometime ago determined never to call on them any more, but my Anxiety on this point. made me break thro' this Rule.   But the result has made me reenact my former Resolution. I think it is best to respect myself.   let this Resolution be as a ring on my finger. or the Shirt on my back   let me never be without it.

This Morning we had a Snow near Two inches d deep—   it melted as it fell ~~and as the~~ during the forepart of the day. and turned at last to rain.

This day Mr. Clymer made his famous speech for throwing away the Western World.[31]   A noble Sacrifice tryly, to gratify the public Creditors of Philada. reject Territory the extent of an empire, so that it may be out of the power of Congress, to oblige the public Creditors to take any part of it.   {This added to the Confiscation of the 17/6 in every pound ~~which n~~ of the alienated Certificates, which virtually belong'd to the person who performed the Original Service, and bestowing it on base Speculation, compleats the Counterpart of Villany to the Meritorious Soldier on the One hand & the defrauded and betrayed Country on the other, Whose resources are rejected, that the Debt may become irredeemable and permanent.}

Tuesday, 27 April 1790

This a day of no Business in Senate   before the house formed Mr. Adams our President came to where I was sitting & told how many late pamphlets he had rec⟨e⟩ived from England how the Subject of the French Revolution agitated the English Politics.   That for his part he despised them all, but the production of Mr. Burke.[32]   and this same Mr. Burke despises the French Revolution   Bravo Mr. Adams, I did not need this Trait of Your Character to know You.   In the Evening I called at the Post Office on a Business of Mr. Zantzinger's.   Langdon who lodges nearly opposite called to me from a Window.   I went over and had a long discourse with him on the Subject of removing Congress   he wants to make the Assumption of the State Debts the Condition of it.   I was guarded as to any concessions on this Subject.   he avowed in the most unequivocal Manner, That *Consolidation* of the different Governments was his Object in the Matter, That perhaps it was against the Interest of his State in particular &ca. &ca.

This morning was Snowy and remarkably cold   ~~I have~~.   I have used the cold bath for Two Mornings past, & I think with good effect.   I certainly am

---

[31]Clymer's speech, in which he declared it romantic to suppose that the American West would remain part of the United States, was not well reported in the press. A year earlier he had detailed his thinking on the matter to Benjamin Rush. (*NYDG*, 3 May 1790; Clymer to Rush, 7 Aug. 1789, copy at PHi, courtesy of George M. Curtis III and Richard H. Kohn)

[32]Edmund Burke (1729–97), the English member of Parliament, published his *Reflections on the Revolution in France* in 1789.

better in health. and feel a very great increase of Appetite.   perhaps I must be guarded as to this point.   The flesh Brush I never omit.   The Party Who went on Long Island, Saturday Week have most of them repented of it.

Wednesday, 28 April 1790

This was really a Snowy day,   the distant hills in the Evening were still White.   even in the Town the houses were White till in the afternoon   three successive snowy days, at this time of the Year. appear extraordinary indeed. Childs this day published a piece which ~~was~~ I contrived to get into his hands.[33]   neither he nor any of the Printers here know me to be a Writer. nor will they know it, unless the Speaker or Genl. Muhlenberg should blow me.   but even they do not know me to be the Author of more than two or Three pieces.
As we had nothing to do in Senate. Carrol moved for a Committee to consider What was to be done about Rhode Island &ca.   One was accordingly appointed.   The Senate adjourned early on pretense of doing business in Committees.   I went, for a While, into the House of Representatives.   but finding the Debates unimportant I went to settle some private business and soon came home, Where I remained the rest of the day.   In the Evening had the Satisfaction to receive letters from home.   up to the 15th Instant. all well.

Thursday, 29 April 1790

called to see Col. Gun.   he was willing to talk and I had no mind to interrupt him.   he spoke freely relating to the bare faced Conduct of King & Elsworth in Supporting every Measure proposed, by the Secretarys.   Indeed their Toolism is sufficiently evident, to every Body.   He says the agitating the affair of Rhode Island, is only to furnish a Pretext to raise more Troops.   be this as it may. That Carrol was only a Tool, in bringing it forward Yesterday was sufficiently evident.   Gun is going to Philada. & I have arranged Matters so that he will be taken notice of there.   no Business was done in Senate but consenting to some Nomination sent down Yesterday.[34]   And the Senators from Virginia laid a Resolution on the Table, for opening the doors of the Senate, on the discussion of Legislative Subjects.[35]

---

[33]See Appendix B(8) for the piece, which Francis Childs published in the *NYDA*.

[34]Both the nomination and the Senate's consent to it are recorded in the *SEJ*.

[35]On 30 April WM was the only senator to join Lee and Walker of Virginia in voting for the resolution to open the Senate doors to allow public observation of the debates. (David Stuart to GW, 2 June 1790, GWP)

Friday, 30 April 1790

A Flood of Business came up this day from the Representatives. But none of it was acted Upon save the first Reading of Bills & appointing, A Committee to confer with them on some point of Order or etiquette. Mr. Morris spoke to me to repeal the Law on that part of the Judiciary about holding a District & Circuit Court at York Town. I gave it as my Opinion That it was best to let the other House do it, as they had introduced York town & I find Boudinot has this day carried in a bill for this purpose.[36] I hate the Whole of the Judiciary. & Indeed made no place at first but Philada. for holding the Courts. I shall not therefore give them any opposition if a place is hereafter appointed for holding any Circuit Court it perhaps should be Harris burgh. The Senate adjourned over to Monday.

---

[36] A committee on the subject was appointed at the instigation of Boudinot, but it never reported. The matter was resolved by the Circuit Courts Act [S-13].

May 1790

Saturday, 1 May 1790

This is a day of General moving in New York, being the day on which their leases chiefly expire.   It was a finer day than Yesterday.   I could not forbear the impulse of Walking out.   I went for Mr. Scot, but he had changed his lodging as was not to be found.   fell in with Walker & Parker of Virginia they were coming to visit our house   they pressed Us so hard for dinner that We consented.   I had not however walked enough. and Went to see Mr. Wynkoop.   We got again on the Subject of the State Debts.   I never saw a Man take so much pains *not* to see a Subject.   It is however now disposed of. at least for this Session.

I have a letter from Dr. Rush   he praises the Peice[1] I sent him, calls it sensible. owns himself convinced,   his Words. *I have erred thro' Ignorance on this Subject.* speaking of the State Debts.   with less prudence than integrity I attacked the Secretary's Report the Moment it appeared.   When that leading feature in it ~~was carried~~ the Assumption of the State Debts, was carried by a Majority of five in the Committee of the Whole Representatives, I redoubled my efforts against it.   & I really believe, that by my endeavours, it was finally rejected.   I am fully sensible that I staked every particle of Credit, I had in the World on this business, and have been successful.   But let me lay my Account never to be thought of, for it.   Be it so,   I have made Enemies of all the Secretaries & all their Tools. perhaps of the President of the United States, and of Boney Johney Adams.   For the Many Peices I have wrote, with all the pains I have taken to conceal myself. must have betr⟨a⟩y'd me in One Shape or other.   But I have no Enemy, in my own bosom.   Williamson coming in and One of his Colleagues had a Considerable Effect,   When the Whole of the North Carolina Delegation appeared it settled the Business.[2]   The Assumption would have compleated the Pretext, for seizing every resource of Government, and Subject of Taxation in the Union. so that even the civil list of the respective Governments would have depended on the fœderal Treasury. This was the common talk of the Secretary's Tools—   We could not resist the

---

[1]See Appendix B(8).

[2]Williamson was seated on 19 March and Ashe on 24 March. Bloodworth and Steele followed soon thereafter, taking their seats on 6 and 19 April respectively. The fifth North Carolina representative, Sevier, was not seated until 16 June.

pressing invitation of, Parker & some Virginians to dine with them on Turtle. All this is not worth a Note. But on the next page, are some Anecdotes of Genl. Washington.

No Virginian can talk on any Subject, but the perfections of Genl. Washington it Weaves itself into every conversation. Walker had called at his farm as he came thro' Virginia it consists of three divisions. the Whole contains some 10 or 15,000 Acres. It is under different overseers. Who may be stiled Generals—under Whom are Grades of Subordinate Appointments descending down thro Whites Mulattoes Negroes Horses Cows Sheep Hogs &ca. it was hinted that all were named. The Crops to be put into the different fields &ca. and the hands Horses Cattle &c. to be Used in Tillage pasturage &ca. are arranged in a Roster calculated for 10 Years. the Friday of every Week is appointed for the Overseers, or we will say Brigadier Generals to make up their returns. not a days Work, but is noted What, by Whom, and Where done, not a Cow calves or Ewe drops her lamb, but is registered. deaths &ca. Whether accidental or by the hands of the Butcher, all minuted. Thus the etiquette and arrangement of an army is preserved on his farm. This may be truly called Shandian. But is it not nature? When Once the human mind is penetrated, by any System, no Matter What. It never can disengage itself. Quere did not the roman poet Understand nature to perfection, who makes his heroes Marshal their Armies of Ghosts in the Elysian Fields. And Spirits imitate in Shadows the Copies of their former Occupations.[3]

Sunday, 2 May 1790

The forepart of this day was very pleasant   an east Wind blew up and deformed the Afternoon. I however Walked a good deal. I have drank Wine with the Speaker at the rate of about 3 Glasses ℔ day. and I really consider myself Worse for it. May be I am mistaken, I will observe for a day or Two longer. I bore this day with more impatience & have thought more about my family, than any day since I have been in New York. I wrote as usual to them, and Sundry other acquaintances.

Monday, 3 May 1790

There really was a considerable deal of Business done this day in Senate and would have been much more. had it not been. for an appeal that was made to the Chair for information respecting the Salary necessary for an Ambassador. full one half of our time was taken up in Two Speeches on the Subject of Etiquette. and expence attending and necessary to constitute the very Essence

---

[3]The reference is to the sixth book of Virgil's *Aeneid*.

of an Ambassador. the lowest farthing should be £3,000 Sterling ℔ ann. besides a Years Salary at setting out. much of What he said bore the Air of the Traveller. In fact I did not not believe him, and of Course voted in the face of all his information, A commitment of the bill was called for and I was contrary to my expectation put on it. another Short bill was committed. which I really Suspect, is a base Job, calculated to make a nest for an Individual.[4] The Spirit of the last Session really was to make Offices for Men. to provide for Individuals without regarding the public or Sparing Expence. I fear this Spirit is not Yet laid.

For Some time past the Philadelphians have been proposing a Weekly dinner. our former Meetings sunk into disuse. but they now are very Urgent. & this day We began the Business Judge Wilson being a Pennsylvanian was of Course invited. We soon relaxed into conviviality, & indeed something More. We expected something political would be proposed. And out it came. Fitzsimons. Gentlemen it is expected of Us that we should fix the Governor of Pennsylvania. I introduced some trivial remarks of the Weather &ca. and the thing was checked. for a time. Scott⟨,⟩ General Hiester and General Muhlenberg Went away. It was now Broatched seriously by Fitzsimons. Morris made a public declaration, That he was fully sensible of the honor done him in the Present Appointment. But if the Choice of Governor fell on him he would discharge it with impartiality. &c. &ca. That he considered the present Governor[5] as a very improper Man, & hoped they would unite in Opposition to him. The Speaker declared himself in Terms of a Similar nature. The Result was this that their Friends should determine, & that their interest should be united to keep out Mifflin— Mr. Morris by way of finishing the Business gave as his Toast. addressing himself to the Speaker. *May You or I be Governor*.

There is a Prospect of Tench Coxe Succeeding Duer in the Assistancy of the Treasury. his Character was spoke of with great Asperity, by Fitzsimons⟨,⟩ Morris & Wilson. Clymer rather Supported him.

We got on the Subject of the finances of Pennsylvania Fitzsimons, asserted that our State had drawn between Two and three Million of Dollars from the Continental Treasury, and that we had not more than four Millions Substantiated against the Union. I hinted to him That, from anything I had seen. We had not drawn more than about a Million. from the Continental Treasury. That Nicholson had rendered Accounts to the amount of 10 Millions, & had stated an unliquidated Charge at five Millions But I added, let the Accounts be settled fairly and if we really are in debt, let Us pay it. We sat too long & drank too much. But We seemed happy, and parted in great good humor.

---

[4] The Foreign Intercourse Act [HR-52] was the bill debated and committed. The individual who benefitted from the Salaries–Executive Act [HR-54] was Roger Alden. See n. 16.
[5] Thomas Mifflin.

Tuesday, 4 May 1790

I felt in some degree the effects of the bad Wine We had drank. for I had an head Ach. dressed however for the Levee I had a Card Yesterday to dine with the President on ~~Monda~~ Thursday. The Pet if he had any on him, is gone off. A great deal of Business was done this day in the Senate in the Way of passing & reading bills but no Debate of any Consequence. Elsworth manifested some strong Traits of Obstinacy. went to the Levee. made my bows, walked about, turned about, and came out.

Wednesday, 5 May 1790

A Considerable deal of Business was done in Senate but no debate was entered on the Rhode Island Committee reported. The amount of it was to put ~~them~~ that State in a kind of Commercial Coventry. to prevent all inter-course with them in the way of Trade. I think the Whole Business prema-ture. We adjourned early I went to call on R. H. Lee. and Mr. Langdon both of Whom are sick Mr. Hazard Whom I saw in the Street told me Langdon could not be seen I called on Lee. found him better. I now addressed myself to sift, the Merits of a bill referred to myself and others for the Allowance of 45 Doll. ℔ Month to a Col. Ely. Which by Attending to his Accounts in the Office of the Commissioner for Army Accounts I find to be a most Groundless & Unjust Charge.[6] A Petition of his was referred to the Secretary at War, and the Secretary at War reported in his favour. The great Pin on Which so much hung. the Assumption of the State Debts having failed. Every other thing that can be thought of, will be brought forward to encrease the Volume of the national debt. We already rejected in Senate. A bill which appeared to me of mischievous Consequences touching the Com-mutation half pay & Pensions of Officers. It is renewed and sent up to Us.[7] Baron Stuben,[8] is supported in a Demand of near 600 Guineas a Year. In fact

---

[6]John Ely (1737–1800), a doctor from Saybrook, Connecticut, petitioned for compensa-tion for services rendered to Revolutionary War prisoners. See also the petition volumes. (Samuel G. Goodrich, *Recollections of a Lifetime*, 2 vols. [New York, 1857], 1:533–36)

[7]On 23 April the Senate rejected the Officers Bill [HR-53] and on 4 May it received the Invalid Officers Bill [HR-59] from the House.

[8]Frederick William Augustus, Baron von Steuben (1730–94), had served as a captain in the Prussian army during the Seven Years War. Dismissed in 1763 under mysterious circum-stances, he spent several years attempting to secure a military commission with little success. In 1777 Benjamin Franklin recommended him to various Americans as a lieutenant general in the Prussian army, and a year later he was received with unusual honors by Congress. He agreed to serve for his expenses only until the American cause prevailed, at which time he would accept whatever pay Congress offered him. Appointed inspector general of the Continental army with the rank of major general by Washington, Steuben's most outstand-ing contributions were the creation of a manual of drill and field service regulations. Steuben

to overwhelm Us with Debt is the endeavour of Every Creature in Office, for fear, as there is likely to be no War, that if there should be no debt to be provided for, There would be no business for the General Government. with all their Train of Officers.   Henry of Maryland expressed himself in Words full up to the foregoing Ideas, to me a few days ago, but I spoiled his Communication by expressing a Wish of *the Sooner the better*.   It is remarkable to me at least, that he has since that time left his Usual seat, which Used to be Near, and commonly rambles from one empty seat to another on the Opposite side of the house.

The Secretaries have had a Clear Majority in the house of Representatives, on Every question save the adoption of the State Debts.   they carried this at first.   but some publications, reminded Gentlemen That there was an Election approaching.

Thursday, 6 May 1790

little was done this day in Senate   Two Bills came up agreed to from the House of Representatives.   The Rhode Island Committee. requested That they might have back their Report. to amend it.   this was comply'd with. Their amendment amounted to

An Adjournment was called, and I joined the Committee on the bill for the Salaries of Ministers Plenipotentiary Charges des Affaires &ca.[9]   I bore my most pointed Testimony, against all this Kind of Gentry.   declared I wished no political Connection Whatever with any other Country Whatever.   Our Commercial intercourse could be well regulated by Consuls and Consuls who would cost Us nothing.   All my discourse availed nothing.   the Whole Committee agreed with me that, they were Unnecessary.   Why then appoint any? or make ~~for~~ Provision for the appointment of any.   For so sure as we make a Nest for one. The President will be plagued till he fills it.   We agreed to the Bill as it stood. but I proposed Twice to strike out all about Ministers plenipotentiary.

Went to dine with the President, agreeable to invitation.   he seemed more in good humor than ever I saw him. Tho he was so deaf That I believe he heard little of the Conversation—   We had Ladies.   Mrs. Smith⟨,⟩ Mrs. Page & Mrs. White.[10]   their Husbands all with them.

settled in New York after the war and wrote an influential pamphlet on an established militia. See also the petition volumes.

[9]Foreign Intercourse Act [HR-52].

[10]Charlotte Izard (c. 1770–92), daughter of Senator Izard and Alice De Lancey, married Representative Smith of Charleston, South Carolina, in 1786. (George C. Rogers, *Evolution of a Federalist* [Columbia, S.C., 1962], pp. 129, 236)

Friday, 7 May 1790

the Ailment called the influenza rages to a great degree. all over the City.   I
feel a dryness and Soreness of my throat & a pain & heaviness in my head. and
flying pains all over my body, so that I had better be as attentive as possible to
my health.   No Business of Consequence done in the Senate   the Members
began to straggle about after the Minutes were read.   I called on the Committee who have Ely's bill.   We sent for Ely. and heard a Pack of Stuff from him,
too flimsy to impose even on Children.   he may have rendered Service to the
Sick on Long Island. but it appears that his own Emolument was his Object.
and he has had this and pretty compleatly answered already. by a generous
settlement with the State of Connecticut.   On my Return into the Senate
Chamber, One Member only remained, sitting in a State of ennui.   I have
remarked him for some Weeks past, and he really affords, a striking proof of
the inconveniency of being a fashionalist   he set up a Coach about a Month
ago. and of course must have it come for him. to the Hall.   But behold. how
he gets hobbled.   The Stated hour for Senate to break up is Three, but it
often happens, that Senate adjourn a little after Twelve, and here an healthy
Man must sit 2 or 3 for his Coach to take him 3 or 400 Yards.   this is highly
embarrassing. and some excuse must be formed for his staying for the Carriage.   and he is now lame. And stays alone till the Carriage comes for
him.[11]   Thus folly often fixes her Friends.
    Tench Coxe came this day to Town, in Order (as is said) to enter on the
Assistancy of the Treasury.   He is deeply affected with the literary itch. The
cacœthes Scribendi.[12]   he has persevering industry in an eminent degree.
These are the qualities That have recommended him to this appointment.
Hamilton sees that, the campaign will open against him, in the field of
publication, and he is providing himself with Gladiators of the quil, not only
for defense but attack.

Saturday, 8 May 1790

I felt myself rather indisposed and staid at home all this day,   drew a Report
on the affair of Col. Ely.   read and lounged away the day.

Margaret Lowther, daughter of the New York City merchant William Lowther, married
Representative Page in 1789.
    Elizabeth Wood White (b. 1739) was the daughter of Mary and James Wood, the founder
of Winchester, Virginia. She spent the second session of the FFC at New York with her
husband, Representative White, and their children. (*DGW* 6:36n)
    [11]Perhaps Izard, who owned a coach. (Izard to Tench Coxe, 26 October 1789, Coxe
Papers, PHi)
    [12]The irresistible urge to write.

Sunday, 9 May 1790

This day I employed as usual in Writing to my family.   I spend my time but miserably in Absence from them.   I will however endeavour to make out this Session.   Col. Hartley returned to Town this day,   What a Strange Peice of Pomposity this thing is grown.   he is if possible more affected and disgusting than ever.   he called to see Us. but took the Speaker Twice out and kept him out with him almost the Whole time he was on his Visit—   The State has really a poor bargain of him, and if she can dispose of him at the October Sales, she need not care at how low a rate.

Monday, 10 May 1790

Attended at the Hall at 10 OClock to hear Col. Ely's Witnesses.[13]   he failed in proving the points, he had alledged in his favour.   We spent some time while the Senate was engaged in Business   When we came in. We found them on the ~~Roh~~ Rhode Island Resolves   the Committee had been called on to give reasons ~~of their Cond~~ on which they founded their Resolutions.   Elsworth spoke with great deliberation, often and long. and Yet. I was not convinced by him.   I saw I must if I followed my Judgment Vote against both resolutions.   It was therefore incumbent, on me to give some reasons for my Vote.   I observed that the Business was under deliberation in Rhode Island.   That the Resolves carried on the face of them, a punishment. for rejection. On Supposition That they would ruin our Revenue.   let Us first establish the fact against them that an intercourse with them has ~~ruined~~ injured our revenue, before we punish them with a prohibition of all intercourse.   This Resolution I considered as premature.   The other for the demand of 27,000 doll. I considered as equally so.   let the Accounts be settled. & Rhode Island has a right to be charged with, & has a right to pay her proportion of the Price of Independence.   By the present Resolutions, the attack comes visibly from Us.   she is furnished with an Apology and will stand justifyed, to all the World, if she should enter into any foreign Engagements.

This was a day of Company at our Mess.   The Strangers were Capn. Barry⟨,⟩ Col. Moylan.[14] & Mr. Tench Coxe, now succeeded to the Assistancy of the Treasury.   I could not help thinking of last Monday, as he sat in One of

---

[13]WM chaired the select committee on the Ely Bill [HR-56].

[14]Stephen Moyland (1737–1811), an owner of merchant vessels, came to Philadelphia from Ireland in 1768 and quickly established himself both socially and economically. Upon recommendation of John Dickinson, Washington appointed Moyland muster master general of the Continental army in 1775. He subsequently held several other posts, including aide-de-camp to Washington, before being breveted brigadier general in 1783. (Martin Griffin, *Stephen Moyland* [Philadelphia, 1909])

the Seats from Whence, Censure had been thrown on him, a Week ago. I was too sick to enjoy the Company I could eat but little, and drink nothing.

Tuesday, 11 May 1790

the Morning or part of it spent on the troublesome affair of Col. Ely. The Rhode Island resolutions were taken up. I was twice up against these Resolutions. They admitted all hands That Rhode Island was independent. and did not deny that the Measures now taken were meant to force her into an adoption of the constitution of the United States. and founded their Arguments in our Strength and her Weakness. I could not help telling them plainly that this ~~way~~ was playing the Tyrant. to all intents & purposes. I was twice up and said a good deal, but it answered no purpose Whatever.

Wednesday, 12 May 1790

This day as chairman of the Committee on Col. Ely's bill I handed in the Report which was dead against Col. Ely. The Report Stated That Col. Ely had submitted his Case to the Legislature of Connecticut, that they had made him What they considered as ample Allowance. We had the Whole fire of New England on Us for this Step. but We Suppo⟨r⟩ted the attack & finally carried the business hollow.[15] I would now remark if I had not done it before that there is very little candour in New England Men. Mr. Morris was in most of the time. and shewed a disposition to make away from my side of the Question. Surely I had better keep Myself to myself ~~on this~~ with regard to him. Wingate tho of the Committee behaved dirty in one point, at least I thought so at the time. It is in vain to be wasting paper with this Subject. Doctor Johnson, certainly gave a most improper certificate on this Subject & One part of it was not True Viz. That the reason Col. Ely had not an Allowance in the old Congress was thise not having nine States, When there were Eleven at the time alluded to. I cannot keep some other Strange Opinions out of my head about him. and the Report which cannot now be found by Alden his Son in Law.[16]

money saved by rejecting this bill 2,025 doll. or thereabout.	Received 20 doll. of the Speaker in part of recd. more	50 −10
		20 due

---

[15]The word "hollow" is used here in its colloquial meaning of "completely."

[16]Roger Alden (1754–1836), who performed the clerical duties associated with the home or domestic functions of the department of state, was born in Lebanon, Connecticut, and graduated from Yale in 1773. He served in the American army from 1775 until 1781, when he began the study of law with William S. Johnson, whose daughter he married two years later.

This day exhibited a Grotesque Scene in the Streets of New York   being the old first of May the Sons of St. Tammany,[17] had a grand parade thro the Town in Indian dresses delivered a talk at one of the Meeting Houses—and went away to a dinner.   There seems to be some kind of Scheme laid, of erecting some kind of Order or Society Under this denomination, but it does not seem Well digested as Yet.   The expense of the dresses must have been considerable, and the Money laid out in cloathing might have dressed a Number of their ragged Beggars.   But the Weather is now, Warm.

Joseph Thomas[18] is the name of the Man Who has the Statutes at large, an unsaleable book.   it is found we may occasionally want such an One.   It is true that heretofore we used to be supply'd with this book When we wanted it, from Jay's[19] or some other library.   but it will soon be found convenient (for the Yorkers) that we should take every thing off their hands. that they cannot otherwise dispose of, even to their insolvent debts.

Thursday, 13 May 1790

This day was remarkably busy with me. & and some singular Occurrances happened.   as Chairman of the Comittee on the Baron Steubens Bill I had called on the Commissioner of Army Accounts.[20]   he had furnished me with all in his power. finding That a Resolve, had passed the old Congress on the

Shortly after her death in 1785, he was elected deputy secretary of the Confederation Congress, a position he held until its demise. Alden unsuccessfully sought appointment as secretary of the Senate in 1789. In July 1789, when Secretary of Congress Charles Thomson resigned, Washington appointed Alden custodian of the papers of the Continental and Confederation Congresses and the great seal of the United States. When the state department was created, he assumed his additional duties. The FFC, in its second session, authorized a temporary salary for Alden at his request. The Salaries–Executive Act [HR-54] made this salary permanent and authorized a second chief clerk in the state department. Shortly after this action was taken, Alden resigned and moved to northwestern Pennsylvania. (*Yale Graduates* 3:469–70; *PTJ* 17:347–49)

[17]Begun in 1789 by William Mooney as a social and patriotic organization, the Sons was named after the legendary North American Indian, Tamanend, a symbolic American hero of the 1770s and 1780s. The society consisted of about 250 members in 1790, the year in which it organized the first museum for the preservation of American history and antiquities. Its best-known activities were the parades in which the members marched, dressed as Indians. (*New York*, pp. 78–79; Gustavus Myers, *The History of Tammany Hall* [New York, 1917], chap. 1)

[18]Joseph Thomas was a Philadelphia attorney from whom the Senate was trying to purchase a ten volume set of the British *Statutes at Large, 1225–1785*. (Records of the Secretary: Publications, SR, DNA; *1790 Pennsylvania Census*, p. 239)

[19]John Jay had a small law library in New York City.

[20]Commissioner of Army Accounts Joseph Howell, Jr., of Pennsylvania (1750–98), served as a captain in the Continental army from 1776 to 1778 and as auditor of the army from 1779 to 1781. In 1783 Howell became deputy to John Pierce, paymaster general of the army and commissioner for settling army accounts. When Pierce died in 1788, Congress elected Howell to fill the post. (*PRM* 4:401n; *PJM* 13:337n)

27th of Sepr. 1785 giving him 7,000 doll. in full.[21]   I called on Mr. Nourse the Register[22] for the Receipts given by the Baron for this Sum. which were endorsed on the Warrants or Warrant given for it.   I had first transacted some Business of my own.   Mr. Nourse was extremely polite and attentive,   took the note or memorandum which I gave him.   Assured me my request should be comply'd with.   asked When I would have the papers   followed me to the head of the Stairs,   as I came down Stairs I told him I wished for them this day.   he said I should have them.   this was at 10 OClock.   I received between eleven and twelve at the Hall. a few lines from Mr. Nourse stating the Resolve of Congress.   That 3 Warrants had issued for the Payments   One for 4,000 the other for 2 and the last for 1,000 Doll.   That the Warrants themselves were deposited at the bank for Security among the Papers of the late Treasurer[23] for Security untill a Settlement would take place.   I thought there was evasion on the face of this Business.   But I concluded, That if Mr. Hillegas had lodged his papers at the bank the Key and Care of them must be with some person and off I went to the bank.   I received for answer that some books papers or property of that kind was lodged at the Bank by Mr. Hamilton, Who had the Keys and Care of them   I should have minuted that as I left the Hall. in Wall Street I passed the Baron[24] he on one side and I on the other.   I wished to make him a bow, as Usual. but such an Aspect he wore.   Nay if he had brought all the Gloom of the black forest from Germany, he could not have carried a more Sombl Sombre Countenance.   Just as I came out of the Bank door I met Hamilton and told him what I wanted.   he refused me in pretty stiff terms.   he could not answer for it to open any Gentlemen's Papers.   I told him I would take unexceptionable Characters with me. The Speaker of the Representatives.   That the papers I wanted belonged to the public & to no private Gentleman Whatever.   nor would it do for him to refuse information to a Committee of Congress.   he then said if there was a Vote of a Committee for it he would get the Papers.   I told him any Member of Congress, had a right to any Paper. in any Office Whatever.   That as Chairman of the Committee I had promised to procure What Papers were necessary.   I deemed this necessary. and of course called for it.   he begged for half an hour to [lined out] consider of it and he would write me a note on the Subject.   I parted with him telling him I should expect to hear from him in half an hour.   he said I

---

[21]The resolve is printed in *JCC* 29:774.

[22]Joseph Nourse (1754–1841) was born in London, England, and immigrated to Berkeley County, Virginia, with his parents in 1769. He served as a clerk and an official for the board of war from 1777 to 1778, as assistant auditor general of the treasury from 1779 to 1781, and as register of the Treasury from 1781 until removed by Andrew Jackson in 1829. (*PRM* 2:364n; *DGW* 6:57n)

[23]Michael Hillegas (1729–1804), treasurer of the United States from 1775 to 1789, was a Philadelphia-born sugar refiner and iron manufacturer who served in the assembly for a decade before his election as treasurer by Congress.

[24]Baron von Steuben.

should. this was before Twelve. [*lined out*] the Senate adjourned at One. I sat half an hour longer waiting for my note. but it came not. I went directly to the Treasury   the Warrant to draw my Indents was delivered to me with all the pomp of official ceremony.   I told Young Kuhn[25] That I had a further business with the Secretary.   That he had promised me a Note which was not come to my hands.   he returned to me. and desired me to Walk into the inner Room or rather to cross the Entry, into a room. in the other End of the house.   I did so. and after being admitted into the ~~holi~~ Sanctum Sanctorum, I told his Holiness, That he had been good enough to promise me a note which was not come to my hands.   he got up went out & left me alone for a Considerable time.   came in with Young Kuhn with him.   but now a new Scene opened.   Before he went out he said The Papers I wanted were here.   I said What here in this Office   he said Yes.   he now asked Kuhn before me. do You know of any Box desk or any Place Where ~~Where~~ Mr. Hillegas kept the Warrants.   the Young Man said Yes the ~~Box~~ Desk in the other room had them in it.   he added if I had them there was no Receipt on them   only *received the Contents—*   Hamilton said the desk was locked & bound round with tape and Mr. Hillegas had the Key in Philada.   I expressed great Surprize That Mr. Hillegas should lock puplic Papers belonging to the Treasury in his private desk.   Hamilton affected to believe I meant some censure on his Conduct.   I repeated What I said—and declared I thought it very strange of Mr. Hillegas to do so. and concluded.   I suppose then I must write to Mr. Hillegas for to send over the Key ~~before~~ before I could see the Papers.   he said I could not get them otherwise. and by way I believe of getting me out of the room told me to come and see the desk.   I walked into the room of the Assistant Secretary and he there shewed me the Desk as he said Which contained the Warrants.   I need make no comment on all this.   I think I have his History compleat.   A School Boy should be Whipped for such pitiful Evasions.   I went to see Mr. Meredith but he was out.   fell in with Mr. Fitzsimons   he talked familiarly with me.   L. L.[26]   I am tired of minuting any more for this day.   But I must note part of Mr. Fitzsimons's discourse. "these Southern People have a Matter much at heart & it is in *my power to oblige them*.   They fear a settlement,   they cannot bear it,   they have been negligent of their Accounts, and the eastern People have kept exact Accounts of every thing." (perhaps and more than every thing added I)   this Moment Heartly fine as a Lord met Us & broke off our discourse.   some Triffling Chat engaged Us for a few Moments. and Hartley parted from Us.   I waited for him to take up the discourse again but he did not.   We were approaching the Hall Where I knew we would part.   I began they will want You to support

---

[25]Henry Kuhl (1764–1856), a clerk in the treasury department, had performed similar functions for the board of treasury from 1785 to 1789. (PCC Index, p. 2801; *PAH* 7:101n; *PMHB* 33:66)

[26]See February 1790, n. 19.

them on the discrimination of Tonnage too, against the New England Men.[27]   But as they are the People Who keep Us here. by joining the New England & York Votes, I have no Objection to see them Whipped with their own rod—   He seemed to enjoy this thought and laughed heartily but the Hall was at hand & the old Subject lost.

Friday, 14 May 1790

The business of most importance agitated this day was the Rhode Island bill which must have had a first reading Yesterday While I was out.   I contented myself with giving my Nagative to every particle of it.   I knew I could gain no Proselites, and that as the bill could not be justifyed on the Principles of freedom law the Constitution or any other Mode Whatever. Argument could only end in Anger.   Mr. Morris was one of the Warmest Men for it altho' he knows well, That the only Views of the Yorkers are to get Two Senators more into the House on whose Votes They reckon, on the Question of residence. But he must think. the getting Rhode Island in Superior to all other Consider-ations.   The Yeas & nays were called.   and now after the Question was taken there seemed a disposition for Argument. and some very remarkable Expres-sions were Used.   Izard said *if gentlemen will show Us how we can accomplish our End by any means less arbitrary and Tyrannical I will agree to them.* when we were on the Clause for demanding 25,000 dollars, Mr. Morris said this is the most Arbitrary of the Whole of it—   The nays were Butler, Elmer, Gun, Henry, Maclay, Walker, Wyngate. 7   Yeas Basset⟨,⟩ Carrol⟨,⟩ Dalton⟨,⟩ Elsworth⟨,⟩ Johnson⟨,⟩ Johnston⟨,⟩ Izard⟨,⟩ King⟨,⟩ Langdon⟨,⟩ Mor-ris⟨,⟩ Strong⟨,⟩ Schyler⟨,⟩ Read.

This day, to my great Joy, a Statement of the Pennsylvania Accounts came forward   10,642,403⁴⁰/₉₀ Doll. Specie & 47,010,138 continental Money liqui-dated & charged against the United States, by our State and delivered in due time to Mr. White the General Agent,[28] and his receipt taken for it in due time. ~~Mr. Clymer⟨,⟩ Fitzsimons & Morris~~ besides an unliquidated Claim of 5 Millions Specie.   I understood this to be the State of our Accounts at the Begin⟨nin⟩g. of the session and so it seemed to be considered by all of Us. For Mr. Morris⟨,⟩ Mr. Clymer & Fitzsimons used to harrangue on this Subject.

---

[27]The House was considering the committee report of 16 April, which led to the Trade and Navigation Bill [HR-66].

[28]John White (c. 1754–90), commissioner for settling accounts between the United States and the states of Pennsylvania, Delaware, and Maryland, from 1787 to 1789, was from Connecticut. He became an auditor for the army in 1779 and at the end of the war was sent to Maryland to settle the accounts of its continental line. In November 1789 he replaced the very popular Mary Katherine Goddard as postmaster at Baltimore. (Joseph T. Wheeler, *The Maryland Press, 1777–1790* [Baltimore, 1938], pp. 14–15; [Baltimore] *Maryland Journal*, 21 May 1790; Series 7, GWP; *JCC* 28:20)

and cry up that so large an annual interest would be due to Pennsylvania, That she would draw Money enough from the Continent. to pay her Whole Civil list, make her roads build her bridges open her canals, I Knew that Hamilton was fool enough, at One time to think That he could make the State Governments dependent on the General Government for every shilling, I used to oppose all this dream of folly. But all at Once the State Debts must be assumed. It was demonstrable That this Measure would defeat all Settlement. ~~all at Once~~ Now the very Gentlemen who had promised Us such Revenues from the Union, cryed out. Burn the Books, no Settlement, Pennsylvania is in debt. she has drawn from the Continent between Two & three Million of good Doll. and has not substantiated, but between 4 & 5 Million against the Union. A mutilated Account of but about this Sum was actually exhibited and handed about by Clymer & Fitzsimons. and an Attack begun on the Comptroller[29] about the same time as if to anihilate his Reputation, and turn him out of all employment. as if it ~~was~~ had been foreseen that he was the only one could detect this Management, or obtain Justice for the State.

Saturday, 15 May 1790

devoted this day altho I was sick, to the Matter of removing to Philada. Mr. Morris entertained me with a long detail of the difficulties he met with in the Settlement of his Accounts. I believe the clamors against him, make the Officers inspect every thing with a jealous Eye. I really act rather improperly In ranging about so much this day in my bad State of health. should the Effects of my influenza encrease and I fall a Victim to my Zeal for serving the City of Philada. My Character would only suffer ridicule and my dear Family the loss of their head. I will however do What I think my Duty. called to see the President every Eye full of Tears. his life despaired of. Doctor Macknight told me he would Triffle neither with his own Character nor the public Expectation, his danger was iminent, and every reason to expect, That the Event of his disorder would be unfortunate.[30]

Sunday, 16 May 1790

I called on Mr. Morris to advise with him, in some points the little Scheme we laid, did not Succeed in bringing in Lee of Virginia to ~~support~~ make our Motion.[31] Mr. Morris proposed to me to call on Us, a⟨n⟩d walk out of Town

[29]John Nicholson.
[30]Washington's pneumonia, which he contracted on 9 May, passed the critical stage on this date, but his convalescence required several weeks. (*DGW* 6:76–77)
[31]At issue was the removal of Congress from New York to Philadelphia.

& catch a dinner.   We did so and the day was lost.   I had wrote to my family
in the forenoon.   I considered the day as lost.   not a Sentiment or an Expression all day that touched the Heart. or warmd the bosom with philanthropic
feelings or vibrated on the Strings of domestic Joy.   We dined at One Brannon's Where there was a Green house and some elegant improvements but all
Was a Meer flutter.

Monday, 17 May 1790

I was engaged this Morning getting documents & papers. respecting a bill,
for the granting the Baron Steuben 7,000 and an annuity of 2,000.   I really
never saw so Villanous an Attempt to rob the public. as the System which has
been brought forward by the Secretary of the Treasury.   The Baron's Whole
Accounts have been settled on a liberal Scale indeed,   An Office was created
in Addition to his rank as a Major General, for which he had additional pay &
emoluments.   7,000 doll. over and above were granted to him,   all these
payments he has received.   Invention has been tortured to put Money into his
hands.   The Secretary has however framed a System which has as the basis of
it. The allowing of him 580 Guineas a Year, over and above all his emoluments
both as a Major General and Inspector General of the Army, & interest calculated up in a Compound ratio on all the balances.   and after all he is not able
to raise a balance of more than about 7,000 doll. for the Baron.   But all this
without the Shadow of proof of the Baron ever having had any such offices or
Salaries.   however if he even had been possessed of them, he could not have
held them & served Us, both at the same time.   and since he chose our Service
and our pay, we are obliged to him. but we have no right to pay him. for What
he did not hold.   The Baron's papers kept Us of the Committee, Untill after
three O'Clock, And this being club day, I went to dine, with the Pennsylvania
Mess   We sat down to dinner half after 3   eating stopped our mouths Untill
about 4 & from that to near 9 I never heard such a Scene of Beastial Ba⟨w⟩dry
kept up in my life.   Mr. Morris is certainly the greatest Blackguard in that way
ever I heard open a Mouth.   But let me shut out the remembrance of it for
ever.

Tuesday, 18 May 1790

no debate of any Consequence arose this day. Untill the Rhode Island bill,
which had been recommitted, was reported   Mr. Lee opposed it in a long &
sensible speech   Butler blustered away but in a loose & desultory Manner.
King⟨,⟩ E⟨ll⟩sworth⟨,⟩ Strong⟨,⟩ Izard spouted out for it.   It was long
before there was a Slack.   As this was to be the last reading & as the Yeas and

nays would in my Opinion be called. I took What ~~in my Opinion~~ I thought was new Ground.　The bill had been assigned to Various Motives. self defense self preservation, self interest &ca.　I began with observing, that the Convention of Rhode-Island met in a Week.　that the design of this bill evidently, was to impress the People of Rhode Island, with Terror.　It was an Application to their fears, hoping to obtain from them, an Adoption of the Constitution, a thing despaired of, from their free Will or their Judgment.　That it was meant to be Used the same Way That a Robber does a dagger or a Highwayman a pistol. & to obtain the end desired by putting the party in fear.　That ~~were~~ where independence was the property of both sides. no End Whatever could justify the Use of such means, in the Aggressors.　I therefore was against the bill in every point of View &ca. &ca.　the debate was long　I was up a second time. but to no avail.　the Question was put at about 3 OClock and carried the Yeas & Nays were called & Stood nearly as before. With the addition of Mr. Lee to the negative—　I laboured hard to arrange affairs for bringing on our Question of removing to Philada. and cannot help remarking, that the Philadelphians, seemed the Slackest of any People concerned in the Business—　I appointed, warned or I know not well What to call it, a Meeting of the Delegation at Clymer & Fitzsimons lodgings.　Mr. Morris and the Speaker were all that met.　The Philadelphians really threw cold Water on the Business.　Mr. Morris Twice proposed that It should be the new Congress that was to meet in March next that, Should Assemble in Philada.　Once he got on the Subject of Trenton, here him & I rather clipped.　I proposed that We should all be busy in the Morning among the Members ~~in the M~~ I engaged to call on Gun⟨,⟩ Langdon & Basset. and set them to Work on others　The form of the Resolution was agreed to, but it all seemed up hill, or like a cold drag with the Philadelphians.　I hope One day to be independent of them. but this is a Matter I must consult, them in now.　L. L. & L. L.[32]

Wednesday, 19 May 1790

I run this Morning like a foot boy from Post to Pillar now to Gun's then Langdon's⟨,⟩ Bassets &ca.　Langdon refused to bring forward our Motion, And I then called on Basset.　he excused himself.　with much ado I got them to keep the Motion Which I put into their hands　neither of them would make the Motion.　Mr. Morris did not come near the Senate Chamber untill after 12 O'Clock.　I called him out　he said. It must be omitted this day.　I found I need not oppose him.　And we came into the Senate Chamber Langdon soon after came & told Us that Dalton objected to going to Philada. untill March next. and That we must alter the Resolution.　Mr. Morris &

---

[32]See February 1790, n. 19.

Dalton Went together, & Mr. Morris returned & told me he had agreed with Dalton that it should be the first of March next.   Thus it is That all our Measures are broken in Upon.   And after all the pains I have taken this Business will end in smoke.   The most Villanous & abandoned Speculation took place last Winter from the Treasury.   some Resolutions have passed the House of Representatives, and are come up to Us.[33]   King⟨,⟩ Dr. Johnson & Strong with Many others.   opposed these Resolutions, in an abandoned & shameless Manner   this engaged the House to 3 O'Clock   they were committed and the House adjourned—   Genl. Hiester & Mr. Buckley called on Us this Evening.   We talked, over the Affairs of the day,   Mr. Wynkoop came in,   and a kind of Agrement was made that the Pennsylvanians, should meet to Morrow at Clymers.

Thursday, 20 May 1790

I could not attend at Clymer's This Morning   I however saw the Speaker at the Hall.   some Strange maneuvers have taken place.   Jackson of the President's family has been both with Morris & Langdon.   Morris is set right & Dalton will agree with Us.   but new Mischeif has happened   Dr. Elmer is crossed to the Jerseys.   Patterson is not Yet come   Few & Gun are both absent, so that Two States are this day unrepresented.   I offered to make the Motion.   Mr. Morris however now makes a point of it doing it, but the thinness of the Senate seems a good reason for putting it off for this day.   I cannot account for Jackson having medled in this business.   or his knowing any thing of it. by any other Means than thro' Buckley.   however we have got the Errors of Yesterday corrected.   Mr. Morris was called out and came in, with a most joyous Countenance,   I was called out by Boudinot, said he, to make proposals to me from the New England Men in favour of Trenton.   I immediately told him You cannot possibly make any bargain by which You will not loose as much as you can gain.   a bargain with the eastern People, is to loose Maryland Virginia & all southward,   a southern bargain will on the contrary loose all the eastern interest.   We must be able to declare upon honor that we have no bargain.   he was a little hurt & said leave all that to me.   No Sir I will make no bargain.   if it is but suspected that we have a bargain we are ruind.   I was called out. & I took, That Opportunity, of calling out Mr. Fitzsimons. & told him of Boudinot being in Treaty with Mr. Morris and begged him to counteract, every thing of this kind.   He promised that he would.

the Senate got into a long debate on on the Resolves. relating to arrears of pay due to the Virginia and North Carolina lines of the Army, in 1782 & 1783. which have been made the Subject of an abandoned Speculation.   the Report

---

[33]The resolutions related to arrearages of pay due to soldiers of the Virginia, North Carolina, and South Carolina lines.

has an Addition of Elsworth's. calculated as much as possible to favour the Speculation. It was debated to 3 O'Clock and adjourned. Elsworth is really A Man of Abilities and it is ~~really~~ truly surprizing to see the pains that he will display to varnish over villany & to give roguery effect, without avowed licence. I can see him Warping over in the Case of the Baron. to get a Sum of Money on his Account, or rather only in his name. Which would sink immediately into the Jaws of Hamilton & his crew.

Friday, 21 May 1790

And now again Elmer is Absent. & Patterson is not returned, and Mr. Morris thinks the Motion had not best be made untill they return　so one day more is lost　I spent a good deal of time on the affair of Baron Steuben,　got the report agreed to.　And now the Debate of the day came on respecting the Resolutions. or rather the amendment offered. to the last One.　the Amendment was supported by King⟨,⟩ Elsworth⟨,⟩ Dr. Johnson⟨,⟩ Izard, and ~~some~~ others　Lee answered them.　towards the end of the debate I rose and explained the reasons of all the Resolves.　that they regarded the Sums due the Places in Which the payments were to be made, and What kind of transfers were to be considered as valid.　all this was directing to our own officer, and had nothing to do with the proceedings of Courts.　if Soldiers had entered into Contracts, the Resolves before the Chair neither defaced Writings nor tore the Seals from obligations. and the law was open.　The directions were moreover in conformity to the laws of north Carolina. One of the States Whose Citizens were were concerned.　That the present amendment was a modification of the Resolution. to protect the interest of the late Speculation.　The reason offered for it was that probably some innocent person might suffer.　I did not believe this was possible.　I would chearfully agree That it was better 10 guilty should escape than One innocent suffer. but no innocent Man was privy to this business.　The Soldiers knew nothing of the Matter.　The Speculators knew ~~nothing~~ & they only knew, in Whose hands the lists were lodged.　For the Soldiers having received their final Settlements, since the Service was performed concluded, that nothing more could remain due,　&c. &ca.　The Question was put on the Amendment & lost 10 for 12 against.
The Question was now put on the 3d Resolution, and carried 13 & 9.　King however & a number of Gentlemen called for the Yeas & Nays.　Yeas Basset⟨,⟩ *Butler*⟨,⟩ Carrol⟨,⟩ Few⟨,⟩ Gun⟨,⟩ Hawkins⟨,⟩ Johnston⟨,⟩ Henry⟨,⟩ Lee⟨,⟩ Maclay⟨,⟩ *Read*⟨,⟩ Walker⟨,⟩ Wingate.　Nays Dalton, Elsworth, Johnson, Izard⟨,⟩ King⟨,⟩ Langdon⟨,⟩ Morris⟨,⟩ Strong⟨,⟩ Schyler　Now a New Whim came into their heads and they would have the Yeas & nays. On the former Question.　they were told It was out of Order.　however

they had t them & Now Mr. Butler voted for the amendment. least he should loose his interest at the Treasury   & of course we were tyed II & II.   But for Once in my Opinion Our President Voted right & gave it against the Amendment.

Saturday, 22 May 1790

being Saturday & no Congress I got an horse & rode out.   came home about noon prodi⟨gi⟩ously tired indeed.   The little exercise I have taken for upwards of four Months makes me almost sink Under it.   I went to bed and slept about an hour & roose much refreshed.   In the evening a large number of Gentlemen called at our house.   My Barber had disappointed me in the Morning.   I was rather in deshabille but came down Stairs.   Altho' I am not in the least given to dress, Yet I found that I was on this Occasion below par. & to know that any point about One is deranged, or improperly adjusted, imparts an Aukward Air to One.   It is on this Account more than any other, That a propriety of dress should be attended to.   to suspect that Your Company believe anything Wrong about You, distresses a Modest Man.   of the Company was Mr. Fitzsimons.   he took me by the hand & said. tomorrow at 9 I wish to me⟨e⟩t with you and the Speaker.

Sunday, 23 May 1790

It was near 10 When I was called down on the coming of Fitzsimons.   he had been some time with the Speaker.   We had considerable loose talk on the Subject of the removal of Congress.   But Fitzsimons after some time declared, That was not the Business on which he came.   It was to settle something As to the Government of Pennsylvania.   Who should be run for the Chair of it at the next Election.   he spoke of the dignity of the speakers present place and the certainty of his continuance in it.   It was evident That he wished the Speaker to decline.   The Speaker said very well I will give You an answer tomorrow Morning—   nothing remarkable happened this day   I wrote to my dear Family as usual.

Monday, 24 May 1790

I dressed and went early to Work.   called on R. H. Lee of Virginia on Walker & Dr. Elmer.   after Senate met I reported the amendment on the Baron Steubens bill.   It was the Opinion of the Committee that he should have An Annuity of 1,000 dollars.   There never was so Vile and bare faced a business.

As this. it is well known That all he would get would immediately sink into the hands of Hamilton. it lay however over for tomorrow. Some Business came up from the Representatives. And now Mr. Morris rose. and made the long expected Motion. In the followg. Words, "Resolv'd That Congress shall meet & hold their next Session of in the City of Philada." Langdon seconded the Motion. a dead pause ensued; Our President asked if we were ready for the Question. Genl. Schyler got up and hoped not. As it was a Matter of great importance to move the Seat of Government. he moved a postponement. Mr. Morris said if the Gentleman would name tomorrow he had no Objection, and tomorrow was accordingly named for it. The House soon after adjourned. And now Izard⟨,⟩ Butler⟨,⟩ Dr. Johnson⟨,⟩ Schyler & King flew about. the People they mostly attacked were Govr. Johnston⟨,⟩ Hawkins and Gun. I soon left them and came home but this was Mess day and I went at half past 3 and found the Company already seated, and the dinner almost eat up. I could not stay very long. as We had an appointment with Jefferson the Secretary of State at 6 O'Clock. When I came to the Hall Jefferson and the rest of the Committee were there. Jefferson is a slender Man has rather the Air of Stiffness in his Air Manner. his cloaths seem too small for him. he sits in a lounging Manner on One hip, commonly, and with one of his shoulders elevated much above the other. his face has a scruny aspect his Whole figure has a loose shackling Air. he had a rambling Vacant look & nothing of that firm collected deportment which I expected would dignify the presence of a Secretary or Minister. I looked for gravity, but a laxity of Manner, seemd shed about him. he spoke almost without ceasing. but even his discourse partook of his personal demeanor. It was lax & rambling and Yet he scattered information wherever he went, and some even brilliant sentiments sparkled from him. The information which he gave Us respecting foreign Ministers &ca. was all high Spiced. he has been long enough abroad to catch the tone of European folly. he gave Us a sentiment which seemed to Savour rather of quaintness. "It is better to take the highest of the lowest, than the lowest of the highest" Translation. it is better to appoint A Chargé des affaires with an handsome Salary, than a Minister Plenipotentiary with a small One. he took his leave, and the Committee agreed to strike out, the Specific Sum to be given to any foreign appointment. leaving it to the President to account. and appropriated 30,000 doll. generally for the purpose.

Tuesday, 25 May 1790

this day again I was busy engaged in the main business. called on Sundry of the Members. The Yorkers are now busy in the scheme of bargaining with

the Virginians, offering the permanent Seat on the Potowmac, for the temporary One in New York.   Butler is their Chief Agent in this Business.   Walker,
a Weak Man seems taken off by it.   Patterson however is not Yet come.
Baron Steuben's Business was taken up.   The Committee were called on to
give the Reasons of their report   as I was Chairman, I had to take the lead,   I
knew there was, blame ready to fall on Us.   I however did not decline the
Business but laid down the outlines in as strong colours as I thought consistent
with Truth, That those Who came after me, might not be bashful and thus
taking Scope enough for them to act in.   I thought I took Many of the Senate
with me.   some I knew it was impossible   In fine I thought demonstration
was on our side.   That the Baron could demand nothing   Izard is certainly a
bad Man in Grain.   He drew conclusions that were obviously wrong indeed to
his own party.   Even Butler disavowed his reasons.   but he was for doing the
same thing without a reason.   Elsworth got up and spoke exceeding well for
more than an hour.   he was severe in some of his Strictures.   but I was
pleased to hear him.   The Debates lasted Untill past three O'Clock and an
adjournment took place without any Question.   One Object of the delay was
to put off our Question on the Residence.

Wednesday, 26 May 1790

This day may be considered by me as an unluckey One,   last night I rested
but poorly owing I believe to a Rheumatic fever.   my Short slumbers were
much interrupted, by fanciful appearances of Women passing by, in flights or
gliding along.   I really have no faith in dreams.   But ever since I was plagued
with this kind of fabling during my distresses on board the Sloop Swallow,[34] I
cannot help considering such illusions as unfortunate.   The Baron's bill as it
was called, was taken up.   Perversion of Reason perversion of Principle, The
World turned upside down. only could Justify the determinations.   But the
Cabals of the Secretary were successful. and the Baron's bill was ~~tran~~ triumphant.   I put a Question to myself Whether there was on the face of the Earth
a deliberative body. That could possibly depart further from the Principles of
Justice. and a regard to the public Wellfare.   none, none, answered every
faculty about me.   But the fact is, That every Officer of the Treasury has
embarked in this business with the Warmth of Solicitors.   John Adams gave
Twice the casting Vote in this business.   I really felt a disposition to take a
lamentation over human Frailties.
    But after this was done Mr. Morris called for his Motion.[35]   if he really
intended to loose it he could not possibly have taken a more certain Method.

---

[34]WM probably referred to a voyage to England.
[35]The motion was for the removal of Congress to Philadelphia.

he rose laughing heartily every time he got up. King laughed at him and he laughed back at King. and a number more joined in the laugh. This was truly ridiculous. Few⟨,⟩ King & Butler rose the amount of all they said was that a removal was inconvenient, that Philada. was not central if we once got into it we would be accomodated in such Manner That we never could leave it &ca. I reply'd That a removal was not called for immediately by the Resolution. That the next session of Congress was to meet in Philada. That altho' it was not central, it was more so than the place Where We now were That the Universal Consent of the Provinces before we were States and of the States since, was in favour of Philadelphia. this was veryfyed by every publick assembly Which had been called, from the Meeting of the first Congress, down to the late Meeting of the Cincinnati. That the Arguments drawn from the Conveniencies of Philada. and the insinuations, That if we were once there Nobody would ever think of going away from it. I thought were reasons which should induce Us to embrace this place which would come so compleatly up to our Wishes. I begged Gentlemen however to be easy on that Subject. Philada. Was a place they never could get as a permanent Residence. the Government neither would nor could part with it. It was nearly equal to one third of the State in Wealth & population. It was the only port belonging to the State. It was excepted by the ~~State~~ Government in her offers to the Congress. That in such a place. The deliberations of Congress on the Subject of the permanent Residence could be carried on to the greatest advantage &c. &ca. I was up a second time. But to no purpose, a postponement was moved by Butler and seconded by Gun. for the Question of postponement Strong⟨,⟩ Dalton, Johnson⟨,⟩ Elsworth, King⟨,⟩ Schyler, *Patterson*⟨,⟩ Hawkins⟨,⟩ Johnston, Butler⟨,⟩ Izard, Few⟨,⟩ Gun. 13. our side Langdon⟨,⟩ Wyngate, Elmer⟨,⟩ Morris⟨,⟩ Maclay⟨,⟩ Reed⟨,⟩ Basset, Carrol⟨,⟩ Henry⟨,⟩ Lee⟨,⟩ Walker.

Thursday, 27 May 1790

Mr. Morris went off Yesterday in Company with King, and I really thought there was too much levity in his ~~Chat~~ conduct all thro'. I really suspected that he did not treat the Matter with sufficient seriousness. This day he showed a violent disposition of anger cursed and Swore that he would go any where but insisted on withdrawing the Motion I could not readily agree with him as to the propriety of withdrawing the Motion. but he Swore he would. Butler rose & said he gave notice That he would bring in a bill on Monday next to establish the permanent Residence. Mr. Morris Jumped up in haste and moved for leave to withdraw his Motion Langdon agreed there was some demur but the Question was carried. Now the Baron's bill as we have called it was taken up. if the fate of the Union had depended on it. It could not have been more pertinaciously adhered to. Elsworth persevered, and cut King in Argument more severely than ever I heard any Member of the Senate, heretofore. King felt it. And I confess I enjoyed it. Butler by One of those excentric Motions Which he is remarkable for, flew his party & voted on our side. Good God What a Consternation! I observed him rising, and said aloud, it is carried. The Whole day was spent in a Contest, between the Secretary's Tools, & the independent part of the House. As the Arguments were nearly the same, on every Question it is in Vain to repeat them. Bonny Johney Adams took uncommon pains, to bias Us without effect. I voted uniformly against allowing him one farthing, as I was convinced nothing was due to him I cannot help noting John Adams's foolish speech. In extolling the Baron. he told Us that he (the Baron) had imported to Us the Arts & principles of War. learned by him, in the only school in the World where they were taught, by the great King of Prussia who had ~~learned~~ copied them from the antient greek and roman lessons. & in fine to these Arts & principles We owed our Independence. Childish Man to tell Us this, when Many of our Sharpest Conflicts, and most bloody engagements, had terminated fortunately, before ever we heard of the Baron.

Friday, 28 May 1790

this day we had expectations That the House of Representatives would have brought on the Vote for adjournment to Philada. But the day passed without anything being done. no debate of any Consequence in Senate. I felt exceedingly indisposed, in the forepart of the day, and dreaded going into Company. the Speaker entertained. I however joined them drank a few glasses and felt much better but I must note how my feelings will be tomorrow.

Saturday, 29 May 1790

cannot complain of my health. I staid in all day it was raw and inclining to rain. almost too cold to be without fire. I was dull & heavy in the Evening received a note to dine with Col. Gun tomorrow.

Sunday, 30 May 1790

I rested but badly last night, had Ugly dreams. am to dine out this day. I had best be attentive and careful— how Idle this Idea. dreams are but fallacious things.

I have dined out & have met with no disaster.   I had one Strange dream of seeing some Man fall from a place like a Saw Mill.   I thought the Mill was mine Yet, it differed, from my Mill at Sunbury.   What an heap of Idleness my head ached.   hence I suppose my dreams.   The Man was not killed.   A dead Child plagued me at another time.   I have really little to do, or I would not note all this down.

Last night Fitzsimons and Clymer called on Us.   They agreed to call on Goodhue⟨,⟩ Gilman⟨,⟩ Huntington and some other of the New England Men. and tell them plainly. that the Pennsylvanians, would not stay in New York.   That if they of New England would persist in voting for New York the Pennsylvanians would agree to any other place Whatever. & from here they would go.   Fitzsimons & Clymer were appointed for this service.   I readily agreed to join Mr. Morris in a similar Service, with respect to the Senate.

Monday, 31 May 1790

went early out to call on sundry Members, and try to prepare them for the grand Question.   came to the Hall at the Usual time.   The Bill for inter-course with foreign nations came up from the Representatives, with an ~~Assis~~ insistance   both ~~having~~ houses having insisted, it remained for us to recede, or call for a Conferrence.   It ended in a Conferrence.   a Considerable debate however. or rather delivery of Sentiments, took place.   Elsworth in a slow languid Manner said It was easy to see that the Representatives had in View some old regulations, by their insisting on the 9,000.   That formerly the Busi⟨ness⟩ had been done by some Gentlemen for about 6,000 doll. ℔ ann.

Mr. Adams Jumped up   said that could not be   that he had kept the Ac-counts with his own hand in Paris & they amounted to about 3,000 Guineas Yearly.   he had now a Vast deal to say   When he had done Elsworth took a small Paper out of his pocket.   said he was very Willing to Shew the docu-ments from Which he had Spoken.   here was an Abstract of the Accounts of the Honorable President While he was in Paris and all the particulars for 20 Months amounting to 9,800 doll. which was not more than at the rate of 6,000 ℔ ann.   Adams appeared cut   the fact was he was found lying as they all have been on this Subject.   Now Butler rose and had a good deal to say on the Merits of the permanent Residence. and concluded with asking leave to bring in a bill for the permanent & temporary Residence.   Lee made a long speech.   I felt so much interested, That I could not help rising,   I observed that fixing the permanent residence to a future period would work no relief of present inconveniencies,   That the complaints were felt & well founded, as to the place in Which we now Were.   That the Gentleman had given notice some days ago that he would offer a bill for the permanent Residence,   he now added the temporary Residence   &ca. &ca.   the End of the Matter was, that he delivered in his bill.   I could almost curse Mr. Morris for having left me at such a time.

June 1790

Tuesday, 1 June 1790

I called early this morning on Fitzsimons & Clymer. I told them that all things considered, I thought it best in me to endeavour a postpone Butler's Bill.[1] they both approved of it. I went to the Hall to observe the Members as they came in. Langdon was there he certainly manifested something which I thought singular in his Manner, if I had not had such strong proofs of him heretofore I would have suspected him. he desired me to assure the Two Members of Massachusetts, That there was no bargain with Virginia. I told him I would do anything he requested and I did so. The Senate met I considered myself as among Wolves. with only neutral Characters to support me. The President was hasty enough to take up Butler's bill. Butler absolutely spoke against taking it up at all, as he said he was afraid, of a difference arising between the Two houses. the Word agreed, agreed, was heard from different parts. of the house I really felt happy. a Message was received from the President, and some other triffling business done. there was some ~~Motions &~~ small ta⟨l⟩k and communications which I did not mind, but all at On⟨c⟩e the President began to read the bill. I wished much for somebody Else to begin an Opposition. and was determined to throw myself along with them, let them mold their attack as they would Mr. Reed. ⟨rose⟩ & spoke against proceeding on the bill but made no Motion. Butler got up & moved that the bill should be committed Gun seconded. Mr. Carrol said there could be no Use in committing it. I said the Honorable Gentleman had set out with declaring. That he wished to avoid any difference with the other House, There were none of Us could affect Ignorance of What had passed in the House of Representatives Yesterday. a vote had passed for the meeting of the next ~~Congress~~ Session at Philada. That we might every moment expect our door to be opened for the Receipt of such a Communication, for us therefore to adopt a different mode of treating the same subject. would have the appearance of court⟨in⟩g. a difference &c. &ca. Butler got up in reply and said every insulting thing in his power. I had concluded That I thought it best that the bill should lie on the Table, untill the Resolution came up & that they should be considered at the same time. This took place after a good deal

---

[1] Residence Act [S-12].

of talk.   It was remarkable That the Resolution came up Just as Butler began to rail at me.   The Senate adjourned early and soon after in came Mr. Morris covered with Sweat & Dust.

Wednesday, 2 June 1790

I went early this Morning to meet our delegation. & to inculcate this doctrine, on our Representatives, That in all Cases we should be prepared for the Worst.   & That we should now think of the next Step to be taken, in Case of the Worst. happening in our house.   That a conduct of this kind. would keep the Matter alive, keep his party collected & in Spirits. they admitted as well as The Principle but seemed at a loss for the Means.   I hinted the propriety of bringing forward a Resolution naming the *day* of adjournment, & the time of meeting.   Fitzsimons & Mr. Morris (all that were present) seemed to carp at it,   however I told them I only Urge You, to think of, & provide Your next Step.   In the Course of this short tete à tete Chat with them I had room to remark that I cannot be on Terms of Confidence with these People.   a hint was dropped that I had better be at the Hall.   I readily agreed. & went there.   I could see as the Members came in That We had nothing to expect from North Carolina South Carolina Georgia nor Massachusetts.   The Senate met, and waited and waited for Mr. Morris.   I never Wished for him more in my Life.   I saw now that Butlers bill would be committed, & I wished to arrange something of a Ticket for the Committee.   Several of the Senate asked why I did not send for him.   I went out and desired the door keeper to go for him.   Mather answered, I have sent for him Long ago.   It was past Twelve before he came. & Now We went, at the Business.   (I cannot help asking myself in this parenthesis what Mr. Morris could possibly Mean by this Conduct.   Indeed I may ask how he can account, for his going away last Week or many other parts of his Conduct,   it is most certainly his Interest to go take Congress to Philada.   is it possible That Hamilton can have any influence with him on this Subject?)   I could remark something of a partiality in Adams. at the setting out. The first Question for Commitment of Mr. Butler's bill.   It was moved to postpone this & take up the Resolution for adjournment holding the next session in Philada.   Senate divided 12 & 12   J. Adams gave it against postponement.   now on the Commitment 12 & 12   J. Adams gave It for it.   the division was by States on both these Questions or at le⟨a⟩st they divided so.   We had N. Hamshire Jersey, Pennsylva. Delaware Maryland Virginia.   the others against Us.   Now it was that I regretted Mr. Morris's absence   had he been here in time, I could have settled with him Who should have been the Committee   Now we could Communicate only with our our Friends on One side of the House.   The Committee rather unfavourable   Butler⟨,⟩ Dalton⟨,⟩ Lee⟨,⟩ Johnston⟨,⟩ Henry.   now it was moved to refer the Resolution to the same Committee.   the Senate divided equally but Dalton was against it & Patterson for it as they sat next each other.   I believe this was settled between them. and shews that Patterson is not to be depended on, and indeed I have long considered him, as a most despicable Character.

Thursday, 3 June 1790

Attended at the usual time at the Hall.   I determined to behave in personal Deportment, as nearly as I possibly could, to my former habits, and I believe I effected it.   of this however I could not Judge as well as perhaps others.   Mr. Morris came the last of any of the Members this day but nothing remarkably so.   much earlier than Yesterday.   I got into chat with him, and after some time remarked how unfortunate we had been Yesterday in not prearranging a Ticket for the Committee,   I said his Absence had been unluckey, but could not now be helped.   he said *his Accounts had engaged him so closely he could not come.*   I thought this Stranger than ever. That he should stay away on no other Excuse than his daily business.   Wyngate⟨,⟩ Elmer almost the Whole senate have taken notice of it,   how can I avoid observing it, for I have smarted under it.   No Business of Consequence took place this day.   the nominations for the Officers of the Army, had come in Yesterday. & were taken up this day.   I had made some Objections a few days ago, to giving my advice and Consent, to the appointments of Men of whom I knew nothing.   Izard now got on the same Subject & bounced a good deal.   however the thing was got over, by the Members rising and giving an Acct. of the Officers appointed, from the different States.   and all were agreed to[2]—   the funding bill which has engaged the Representatives almost the Whole Session came up Yesterday, was taken up this day, and Monday assigned for it.

Friday, 4 June 1790

This a day of small Consequence in the Senate   I had busied myself much last night & this Morning in arranging and disposing of Matters.   but Sundry pages would not contain the Whole of it, so I will minute only What happened in the Senate.   We called on the Committee to report   Butler excused himself & the bu⟨r⟩then of the excuse Was. That Govr. Johnston One of the Committee had fallen Sick   Mr. Morris Moved & was seconded by Lee to add another Member in his room.   this Occasioned considerable debate   Reed

---

[2] Both the receipt of the message of 2 June and actions on it on 3 June are recorded in the *SEJ*.

however declared against Us. and We lost the Question. Izard Manifested the most illiberal Spirit. asserted in Opposition to Lee, things that even his own party were ashamed off. I left the Senate Chamber this day compleatly sickened at the uncandid and ungentlemanly Conduct of the South Carolina Men. Few of Georgia said some improper things, but I this day was almost altogether an Hearer. There really was no serious debate, It was nothing but Snip Snap & Contradiction.

Saturday, 5 June 1790

This was a Slack day, I had promised Mrs. Bell to go with her to the Hall. and I called at about 10 for the purpose. Mrs. Bell however could not go this day, and I found her as finicking and fickle as the finest Lady among them. with a bunch of Bosom and bulk of Cotton, that never was warranted by any feminine appearance in nature. she had learned the New York Walk to a tittle. bent forward at the middle she Walked as they all do, just as if some disagreeable disorder prevented them from standing erect. is it ill nature or What? that inclines me to assign this fashion, to a Cause of this kind.

I went from her, called on Sundry People Went and sat a long time with Mr. Morris & repeated to him all the Arguments I had made Use of on Monday & Tuesday last When he was absent. One in particular he seemed pleased with, drawn from the difference of Mileage Which would arise to the Treasury of about 1,100 doll. in favour of a Residence in Philada. I desired him to get from the treasury an Account of the Expence of removing Congress from Princetown to New York,[3] he said he would do it— there seemed really to be more of cordiality in this Tete a Tete which I had with him, than any ever I had. I then called on Mr. Wynkoop. I chatted a good While with him. and had again occasion to observe the blind Obediance, which he pays to the Opinions of his Philada. Colleagues. came home read and lounged away the day.

Sunday, 6 June 1790

Five Months have I been in Town This day. devoted my time to think of my family Wrote letters read &ca. but did not stir out all day remarked something this day. General Muhlenberg talks of visiting Sunbury &ca. &ca. I received Yesterday a letter from George Logan he is greatly displeased about the Grant to Baron Steuben. This is really a Worthy Man. I think he holds the first place in point of integrity. he has invited me strongly to call and see

---

[3] A reference in the diary entry of 8 June indicates that WM was interested in the cost of the removal of Congress from Trenton, New Jersey, in December 1784.

him.   I believe I must do so.   this old Man the Baron it seems talks in the
most insulting Manner of the Grant which has been made to him. and tells
that he must and will have more When a new Congress Meets. &ca. &ca.   being at the Head of the Cincinnati makes him assume these Arrogant
Airs—   Tis probable the Whole Body of them will soon be demanding Pensions; to Support their Titles and dignity.

The funding bill, the basis on which Speculation has built all her Castles. is
now to come before Us. and Woe to him who says a Word in favour of the
Country,   load the Ass   make the beast of burthen, bear to the utmost of his
Abilities.   I am really convinced, that ma⟨n⟩y a Man has went into the
Martial Field, and acquitted himself with gallantry and honor, with less cour-
age and firmness than necessary to to attack this disposition in our Senate.

Monday, 7 June 1790

The funding Law under went some debate this day.   We adopted by a kind
of common consent. a mode somewhat different from former practice respecting it.   supposing ourselves in Committee of the Whole. a paragraph is read.
and the Members generally express their sentiments on it.   after every One
has given his Sentiments, it is passed by postponement. with a design to
commit it to a Special Committee.   we proceeded, about half way with the
bill in this way.   the Committee on the Bill for the permanent Residence &
the Resolution sent up from the Representatives, were called on to report and
Butler their Chairman did so.   he read the Report which was a Sleveless thing,
for the Potowmack to be the permanent Residence.   But alledged the ground
was too narrow to fix the temporary Residence.   Many desultory things were
said. and all Went off untill tomorrow.   This was Pennsylvania Mess day.   I
was so unwell That I first told Mr. Morris, I could not attend. but I afterwards
Went.   We here agreed to send for all the Senators Who were friends of
moving to Philada.   11 attended   Virginia Maryland Delaware Pennsylva.
Dr. Elmer from Jersey & New Hampshire.   much desultory discourse was
held.   Virginia & Maryland Manifested a predilection for the Potowmack.
But the final Resolutions in Which Virginia led the way were as follows—

That as the Business of a permanent Residence was brought forward by our
Enemies evidently with a design of dividing Us, We would Uniformly Vote
against every place named for the permanent Residence.   The Virginians &
Marylanders declared they would Vote against the Potowmack.   Mr. Morris
declared he would Vote against Germantown and the Falls of Delaware   the
Susquehannah was not publickly named, but of Course imply'd. for Mr.
Morris in enumerating the places to be Voted against, named Potowmack
Germantown Falls of Trenton.   the Line of proceeding of tomorrow was

agreed to.   Mr. Lee to Move & Langdon to second the Postponement of the permanent Seat in Order to take up the Resolution for the next session being held in Philada.   if all was lost let it go down to the House of Representatives. for them to originate new Measures on it.

Tuesday, 8 June 1790

How shall I describe this day of Confusion In the Senate?   Mr. Lee laid on the Table a Report of some additional Rules, relatative to the intercourse between the Two houses.   after this he moved that the bill for the permanent Residence of Congress should be postponed to take up the Resolution of the Representatives for adjourning to Philada.   now it was That Izard flamed and Butler bounced & both seemed to rage with madness.   Mr. Lee's Motion was in Writing, and they moved a postponement of it.   the division was 11 & 11 and the President gave it against Postponement.   Now all was hurry and Confusion.   Izard & Butler actually went & brought Governor Johns⟨t⟩on with his night Cap on, out of bed. and a bed with him,   the bed was deposited in the Committee room,   Johns⟨t⟩on was brought in a Sedan.   Few was Well enough to come without being carried.   and we waited half An hour. the Vote was taken   we had our 11 & they had 13 against the Resolution   I thought all was over now.   but no such thing.   they must carry their conquest farther.   In the Mean While a Mob and noise was about the Hall, as if it had been a fish Market.   the postponed bill and the report of the Committee on it was called for   the report was read.   The first clause of the report was a Resolution that The permanent Resolution [*Residence*] should be now fixed.   The Question was taken upon it, and it was negatived.   This threw them all in the dumps.   The Report was however lost.   But now they would have the bill.   They accordingly had it, for they had the Most Votes   And altho, the Senate had decided by a most unequivocal Vote, That the permanent Residence should not be taken into consideration. Yet they moved to fill the blank, with the Potowmack.   this was lost 15 & 9   much desultory discourse was now engaged in. & many Motions were made of postponement of the bill,   some of them actually carried and Yet they still Made new Motions for the blank to be filled   Baltimore was named.   this was lost 17 to 7—   Wilmington was named,   it had only 3 or 4—   a Motion was made to adjourn.   the first was lost.   a Motion was even made to pass the first clause of the bill with a blank, notwithstanding the absurdity of it. even in the face of a Vote that this was an improper time to fix the permanent Residence.   all in fact was confusion & irregularity.   a Second Vote of adjournment was called for & carryed   so ended the uproar of the day.   John Adams has neither Judgment firmness of mind nor respectability of deportment to fill the Chair of such an Assembly.   Gun had scolded out a good deal of Stuff.   Were for ever to be plagued with a removal &ca.   This I thought deserved some answer.   I went over all the disadvantages of New York contrasted with Philada. and concluded that such inconveniencies would always produce such complaints and Uneasiness, and could not be removed but by taking away the Cause   I was listened to, but made no Converts   I was a good While up as I went largely into The Business but I took the same Ground which I had before travelled over. the Notes of which I sent to Doctor Rush.[4]   Just before I rose I asked Mr. Morris for the estimate of removing Congress from Trenton which he had promised to procure.   had nothing of it.   I really communicated this Matter to him to enable him to make some figure in the debate. and if possible to bind him to me by this kind of confidential communication.   but I have another proof. That all advances on my part are in Vain.   I walked this Evening with Mr. Wynkoop   fell in Company with several of the Representatives.   exhorted them all to as much as I possibly could to unanimity & firmness & did not fail to recommend to Steady perseverance under this Assurance that ~~the~~ We would be Successful.

Wednesday, 9 June 1790

attended the Hall at the usual time.   The Rhode Island bill had a 3d reading and now the funding bill was taken up.   We had passed the Clause founding the old Continental Money and left a blank on Monday   I then called it, the Resurrection of a dead demand against the public   Mr. Morris seemed in Sentiment with me   King spoke against the Clause altogether. but now the Secretary's Report was the Text book. & it must be funded at 40 for 1   I called the Attention of the Senate to the Characters who now had this Money.   Many meritorious Persons received it as gold & Silver and still kept it, as the Monuments of the Sacrifices which they made for the liberties Made in the Cause of America.   would 75 for 1. 40 for 1. or 100 for 1. indemnify such Characters,   would it not be a mockery of their demands.   a time might come a Manner might be thought of for their relief but this was not perhaps the time, nor was it the Manner.

The other Class of Individuals Who were possessed of it, had collected it from holes & Corners after it had ceased to be an Object of Speculation. When it really was worth nothing. and Who neither gave Value for it. nor had any Merit in the Act of Collection.   ~~all the Continental~~ for these humble Speculators infinitely too much was done.   they had no claims in justice.   the Whole of the continental Money was sunk by depreciation, a most unequal

---

4 WM sent the notes in his letter of 5 June (Rush Papers, DLC). They were the basis for the newspaper piece that can be found in Appendix B(9). See n. 28.

mode of taxation truly but an effectual one.   he that touched it was taxed by it.   this was resting a claim.   a defunct demand was conjured up against the Union as if they feared the Mass of debt would be too small. tho' I feared they would find it much larger than we could discharge.   &c. &ca.   the Clause was passed and We went to the 4th.   Mr. Morris moved in a moment to strike out the Two first Alternatives & blazed away for 6 ℔ Cent. on the nominal amount. of all public Securitys.   Elsworth answered want of Ability.   Mr. Morris made nothing of the Whole of it   the Broadside of America, was able enough for it all   We had property enough and he was for a Land Tax. and if a Land Tax was laid there would be Money enough.   he said Many weak things, and was handled closely for them by Elsworth.   The debates loose indeed & desultory continued untill Three O'Clock   adjourned.

Thursday, 10 June 1790

attended at 9 O'Clock at the Hall on the bill for making Compensation to one John McCord,[5]   It was a painful Business,   His claims do not seem overly well founded in point of Law. or any act of Congress.   he is 79 Years old and appears to have suffered deeply, in the American cause.   We spent a Considerable time on his Business.   When We came into the House of Representatives.[6] the funding bill was under Consideration.   It was passed over without much debate in our cursatory Way.   But now rose Elsworth. and in a long elaborate discourse recommended the Assumption of the State Debts.   he concluded that he would read his Motion Which he said had the approbation of the Secretary of the Treasury.   It was verbatim One of Gerry's papers. Which had been moved and laid on the Speaker's Table in the house of Representatives about a Week ago.[7]   We had Speakers enough Now.   Dr. Johnson was somewhat singular in his Assertions   he deny'd there was any such thing as a State Debt.   they were all equally the debts of the United States.   the day was mostly spent in this Business.   I rose and took the Field which I had several times laboured in with my pen.   the old Acts of Congress. settle and Assume the balances &ca. &ca.   a Short publication Which ~~Which~~ I wrote and Which by one Means or other got into almost all the Newspapers was the basis of it.[8]   the Boston Men & King talked much of their fears, of the

---

[5] WM had been attending the select committee on the McCord Act [HR-70]. John McCord (b.c. 1711) of Quebec sought compensation for supplies he provided to the American army in Canada in 1775. See also the petition volumes.

[6] The Senate, not the House, was debating the Funding Act [HR-63].

[7] Gerry made his motion for the assumption of state debts in the committee of the whole House on 24 May. Boudinot reintroduced it in the House on 27 May, and it was printed. It was the latter version that Ellsworth moved in the Senate.

[8] See Appendix B(8).

Consequences &ca. &ca.   I objected Handcock's Speech[9] to one, and the
divided Votes of their Representatives to the other.   One of the Massachusetts
Men now produced Instructions from their Government. authorizing their
voting for the Measure.[10]   I alledged that if One state instructed all should
instruct. and perhaps this should be considered as a good reason of postponement Untill all had instructed on the Subject &ca. &ca.   The Consideration
was postponed, untill tomorrow.

Friday, 11 June 1790

attended the Hall on Mr. McCord's bill early[11]   Mr. Morris Joined Us.
Went in and attended the funding bill.   the clause for the Assumption of the
State debts.   Mr. Gerry's amendment was negatived   9 only rose for it.
The bill was now committed.   The only debate of any Consequence was
between Elsworth and myself.   he set forth in a Curious Argument. that the
debts contracted near the Seat of Congress were made federal that those at a
distance were made State debts. supposing that the Authority of Congress was
less efficacious.   There really was not a Shadow of truth in this.   he only
adapted his Argument to an accidental fact. South Carolina and Massachusetts
having the largest State debts.   I rose and Shewed that there really was nothing at all. in this Matter.   That the origin of some of the State debts. was their
adopting the debts due to individuals, Which they did by way of paying their
requisitions, and got Credit for them accordingly.   That this was the origin of
the Large State debt of one of them at least.   King was obliging enough to get
up and tell the House I meant, south Carolina &ca.   this brought up Butler &
Izard. with some degree of Warmth.   It was a good While before I could get
saying anything.   I however avowed and supported all I had said.   That the
fact was indubitably so.   That no censure was imply'd in any thing I had
said.   That south Carolina had assumed debts due to her Citizens to the
amount of 186,799 doll. and had Credit in full of her quota of the requisitions,
of 10th Sepr. 1782 on that account   that Pennsylvania had paid at the same
time 346,632 doll. & Massachusetts a large Sum. of the said Requisitions.
That Pennsylvania, might have brought forward her State Debt and had
Credit for it, in the requisitions but this she did not do, but remaind

---

[9]John Hancock (1737–93), governor of Massachusetts from 1780 to 1785 and from 1787 to
1793, was a Harvard educated merchant. He served in Congress from 1775 to 1780 and
became an Antifederalist. His widely reported speech of 1 June 1790 to the Massachusetts
legislature opposed assumption of the state's debt by the federal government unless the state
requested it or consented to it first and recommended that the legislature instruct its
congressional delegation on the matter. (*NYDA*, 10 June 1790)

[10]The Massachusetts instructions were adopted on 4 June and sent express to its senators.
(*Boston Gazette*, 7 June 1790)

[11]WM attended the select committee on the McCord Act [HR-70].

burthened with both her State debt & Requisitions and has done much towards payment of both. While S.C. had paid nothing to either. &ca. &ca. The Committee were Mr. Lee, Elsworth, Maclay⟨,⟩ King & Patterson. some little Council business was done.[12] and We adjourned. just as we adjourned. Butler wished Carrol Joy of a Vote being carried in the Representative Chamber for the Temporary ~~Vote~~ Residence to be in Baltimore.

There was some kind of entertainment. to which I heard Fitzsimons a few days ago inviting the Speaker, I thought he took him to the door to do. it. The Speaker asked me to go with him, I declined it as Well I might. after the Speaker came home I asked him, what he had heard Mr. Morris say of the Baltimore Vote. *He had not made up his mind.* I can find he is now scheming. and will not Vote for Baltimore. I have had a spell of fishing of which I was the Subject to know Whether I ~~will~~ would not oppose the Baltimore Vote. I saw clearly the person was set on to do it. and will report to his employers L. L.[13] I in all probability am come to the point, that will be seized to turn the Whole City of Philada. against me. but I trust no tint of dishonor~~able Conduct~~, will ever stain my Conduct. {As to consequences I care not.}

Saturday, 12 June 1790

A day of Storm and rain. I attended at the Hall at 11. on the funding bill. The alternatives (as they were called) ~~was~~ were the Chief Subject of discussion untill near three O'Clock.[14] Candor sit by me while I describe The Committee R. H. Lee, the Man Who gave Independence (in One Sense) to America. a Man of a clear head, and great experience in public business. certainly ambitious, and Vain glorious but his passions seek gratification, in serving the public. Elsworth a Man of great Faculties. and eloquent in debate, but he has taken too much on himself, he wishes to reconcile the Secretary's System to the public Opinion, and Wellfare but it is too much. he cannot retain the Confidence of the People & remain in the Good graces of the Secretary. he may loose both. King plausible & florid. Patterson more taciturn and lurking in his Manner. and Yet when he speaks, commits himself hastily. a Summum Jus, Man.[15] both Lawyers, and both equally retained by the Secretary. & now Billy What say you of Yourself. not over burthened either with Knowledge or Experience, but disposed to make the

---

[12]By "Council business" WM refers to the receipt of a message from the president, recorded in the *SEJ*.

[13]See February 1790, n. 19.

[14]Several funding alternatives were offered to holders of the public debt in section 4 of the Funding Act [HR-63]. This discussion occurred in the select committee. See *DHFFC* 5:914.

[15]A man who believes in the supreme rigor of the law and applies it without concern for justice.

best Use of Your tools.   I objected in general to the bill, disliked funding at all, was willing to pay as an interim 3 ℔ Cent. and place it on the footing of disability to do more.   I objected to funding the Interest, proposed to establish a Land Office to sink the interest now due. & that Indents should be given to all persons intitled to them receivable in that Office.   declared that even prodigals abhorred compound interest, that the bill went on this principle tho not in an annual Ratio.   It was however In vain altho I could perceive that I made an impression.   there were three Alternatives in the Secretarys Report.   The last was by Much the most favourable to the public.   This however really meant only to try the disposition of Congress, and Fitzsimons, when he took in his ~~amendments~~ Resolutions contrived to have this rejected and One Substituted vastly more favourable to the Subscribers,   a good Man could not have done this,   I found I could not effect anything on my own plan.   I therefore Watched and promoted. every favourite Sentence that fell from Lee & Elsworth.   The Result of all Was that We struck out. all the Alternatives, & voted a general fund of four ℔ Cent.   In the Evening came Mr. Wynkoop Heyday all Wrong. to go to Baltimore &ca. &ca. full charged with the permanent seat &ca. &ca.   I knew, he had not this of himself.   I however delivered myself with firmness on the Subject.   recapitulated the Conduct of the Yorkers. &c. &ca.   shewed him (as I thought) that to concur with the Baltimore Vote was politically right.   he found he could make no impression   It was nearly dark as he went away,   I followed to the door   he took the way of Queen Street & the Speaker Who was with me. said he is going to Fitzsimons.

{This day changed my last Bank bill of 50 dollars.}

Sunday, 13 June 1790

This day was very Wet,   I staid at home all day, in my usual occupation of writing to my dear family reading &ca.

Monday, 14 June 1790

I left home early and called on the Assistant of the Treasury, on McCord's affair.   He would not let me tell my business, so keen was he, on the Subject of proposing a bargain to me, Pennsylvania to have the ~~have the~~ permanent Residence ~~of~~ on the *Susquehannah*, and her delegation to vote for the Assumption,   I contained my indignation at this proposal, with much difficulty, within the bounds of decency, and the more so, as I knew that however it might be with him. Hamilton the Principal in this Business was not sincere.   I gave him such looks and answers, as put an End this business.   I then got my

Errand settled, ~~with~~   Went to Mr. Jefferson's Office, on Mr. Baily's Affair,[16]
arranged his affair, and went down Broadstreet,   here I met Mr. Lee.   spoke
a few Words with him And passed on to the lodgings of Mr. Carrol   my only
business with him was to forewarn him, That an Objection would be made to
Baltimore That there were no public buildings, and that he should be prepared on this Subject.   From here I went to Mr. Morris's lodging,   I found
him somewhat engaged.   But the moment he disposed of a small Matter of
business, he dismissed his Clerk[17]   told me he was just going to look for me,
and was fortunate in my Coming in.   said he had much to say, but some part
of it must be on the most intire confidence.   That on friday Jackson of the
President's Family. In whom he said he could not have Confidence had been at
Clymer's & Fitzsimons lodging   That Coxe likewise of the Treasury had been
there   that their Business was to negotiate a bargain.   the permanent Residence in Pennsylvania, for her Votes for the Assumption or at least as many
Votes as would do the needful.   The burthen of their business, seemed to be
to open the Conferrence, with Mr. Hamilton on this Subject.   Mr. Morris
continued.   I did not chuse to trust them but wrote a note to Col. Hamilton,
That "I would be walking early in the Morning on the Battery,[18] and if Col.
Hamilton had anything to propose to him, he might meet him there as if by
accident."   I went in the Morning there and found him on the *Sod before
me*.   Mr. Hamilton said he wanted One Vote in the Senate and five Votes in
the House of Representatives.   That he was willing and would agree, to place
the permanent Residence of Congress ~~on~~ at Germantown or the falls of Delaware, if he would procure him these Votes.   Mr. Morris owned that he comply'd on his part, so far as that he agreed to consult some of the Pennsylvania
Delegation (I abru⟨p⟩tly said You need not consult me). but proposed That
the Temporary Residence of Congress in Philada. should be the Price.   They
parted upon this, but were to communicate on the Subject again.   Mr. Morris
& Fitzsimons made a party out of Town and took Mr. Reed with them on
Yesterday as the Man Whose Vote they would engage.   (Let me here recollect
the Application made to me on Saturday night by Mr. Wynkoop.   I now
know that he was trying me on that Subject   and the Speaker was not much
out, When he said Wynkoop was gone to Fitzsimons's   he should have added

---

[16]WM saw Jefferson in regard to securing Francis Bailey a patent for his invention to
prevent counterfeiting. WM had been a member of the select committee on the Patents
Act [HR-41] which killed a bill specifically drafted to grant Bailey protection, the Bailey Bill
[HR-44].

[17]James Rees (1763–c. 1850) had been associated with Morris as a clerk since 1776, when he
began work for the firm of Willing and Morris. From 1781 to 1783 he assisted Morris in the
office of finance and after that with his personal affairs. (*PRM* 2:340n)

[18]The 1,450-foot-long Battery was an earthwork that ran approximately from what is now
Battery Place to Whitehall Street at the southern tip of Manhattan Island. It was being
extended into the harbor and converted into a public walk as part of New York's efforts to
make the city a more attractive residence for Congress. (*New York*, pp. 21–22; St. John de
Crevecoeur to William Short, [13?] July 1790, Short Papers, DLC)

and Morris's.)   Mr. Reed's answer was What Mr. Morris called polite.   *Gentlemen I am disposed to facilitate Your Wishes.*   But now this Morning says Mr. Morris I have received a Note from Col. Hamilton That he cannot think of negotiating about the temporary Residence.   That his Friends will not hear of it.   Mr. Morris added, I know, he has been able to manage the destruction of the Baltimore Vote without me. but I cannot Yet tell how.   I sent for Mr. Reed.   he says they have Accounts, That the Senators from Rhode Island are appointed, and expected every Moment.   But Mr. Morris added, I think he has some other Assurances.   I now parted with Mr. Morris and joined the Committee on the funding bill   The Senate were formed some time before.   We joined them, and after some of the ro⟨u⟩tine business of the day was done. th & the Baltimore Resolution handed in. it was called for.   Schuyler moved it should be postponed a fortnight.   Govr. Johns⟨t⟩on of N.C. seconded him.   Elsworth got up   said this Matter, mixed itself with all our affairs   there was a Secret Understanding a Bargaining, that ran thro' all our proceedings, and therefore it ought to be postponed.   I retorted his his *secret understanding bargaining*, &ca. on himself   as he knew there were such things he knew Where they arose. & if they mixed with and polluted our proceedings. it was time to put an End to them which could only be done, by deciding the the Matter.   &c. &ca.   The question was put & it was the old 11 & 13—   this Was Mess day   I did not join the Company untill about 5 O'Clock, and staid untill after 8   But Oh such noise & nonsense.   Fitzsimons railed out at One time against Pennsylvania interferences about the Assumption of the State debts.   had it not been for these, the funding System, would have been compleated Months ago.   he had received letters that Stones would be thrown at him in the Streets of Philada. if he were there   &c. &ca.

Tuesday, 15 June 1790

We finished our Observations on the funding bill[19] and reported,   the Whole day was spent in debate on it.   I have so often expressed my Sentiments respecting the Subject of this bill, That I need not set any of them down here.   I was not often up.   I took at one time some pains to explain the nature of facilities and Indents, but no Question was taken on any point   all was postponed.   Docr. Elmer told me as I left the Hall That he had something to impart to me.   Mr. Morris however called me aside, and told me that he had, a Communication from Mr. Jefferson. of a disposition of having the temporary Residence 15 Years in Philada. and the Permanent Residence at George Town on the Potowmack. and That, he (Mr. Morris) had called a

---

[19]This action occurred in the select committee on the Funding Act [HR-63].

Meeting of the delegation at 6 O'Clock this Evening at our lodging on the Business. I was really very unwell. and had to lie down the most of the Afternoon. the Delegation met at Six. I was called out. however When I came in What passed was repeated to me. Hamilton proposed to give the permanent Residence to Pennsylvania at Germantown or the falls of Delaware. on Condition of their Voting for the Assumption. In fact it was the Confidential Story of Yesterday. all over again. Mr. Morris, also repeated Mr. Jefferson's Story, but I certainly had misunderstood Mr. Morris at the Hall. For Jefferson Vouched for nothing. I have seen no prospect of fixing the permanent Residence of Congress in the proper place at the Present Session. and When ever it is Went into it will be involved in much difficulty. I have therefore declared uniformly against everything of the kind. but to continue the temporary Residence here, under a promise of the permanent Residence being in any part of Pennsylvania I considered as Madness. It was giving them time to fortify & entrench themselves with such Systematic arrangements That We never should get away. While the Law acted as a tie on Us and bound Us hand & foot, but gave them all the power and all the Opportunity of fixing Us permanently in this place. I would rather be under no obligation, and keep up an unremitted effort, to get away which I had no doubt would be crowned with Success. I know not Whether What I said was the reason of it. but these Sentiments seem to be adopted. As to the bargain proposed by Hamilton, I spoke of it with detestation. Mr. Morris now proposed that a paper should be drawn up with reasons of our Conduct. that they might not be able to brand Us with any neglect of the Interests of Pennsylvania. and A Committee for this purpose was appointed Mr. Morris⟨,⟩ Mr. Fitzsimons⟨,⟩ Mr. Hartley.

Wednesday, 16 June 1790

I called early this morning at Col. Hartley's lodgings, in Order to give him a Sketch of What I thought might be well enough, for Us to sign. he was gone but I fell in with him at the Hall, and delivered it to him. I sauntered about. till Congress formed. and now We got at the funding bill. here we had all the Stuff over again. of public Credit &ca. the great Question Was Whether the report of the Committee for 4 ℔ Cent. should be adopted. I soon committed myself in such Sort That I must expect all the public Creditors to be my Enemies. the great ground Which I took was that I did not believe We could impose any direct Taxes on our Constituents, for a purpose which they knew as well as I did— that the Holders of Certificates in Pennsylvania. had them funded When they were but 2/6 in the £. that 100:0:0 purchased 800: that they had drawn interest on the nominal amount for 4 Years = 192. Justice

and law allowed them but 124   hence they had £68 clear already and the
Certificates into the bargain.   &ca. &ca.   I was up a long time.   Mr. Morris
rose against the report.   his Cholor fairly choacked him.   he apologiz'd to
the House that his agitation had deprived him of his Recollection on the
Subject. and he sat down.   he rose again some little time before the Senate
adjourned,   mentioned his late confusion but declared it did not arise from
the personal Interest he had in public Securities,   That altho' he was possessed of some he was no Speculator &ca. &ca.   I wished he had not made this
last apology. for I fear it fixed the matter deeper on him.   We spent untill past
3 O'Clock, but took no Question. & indeed in seemed almost, agreed, that
that we would not, proceed without the other Bill.[20]

Thursday, 17 June 1790

Spent this morning before the Meeting of Senate in calling on Mr. Coxe &
For the papers in Case of McCord. and at the office of the Secretary of State on
Mr. Bailys Affair.   The Senate Met. and untill near Two O'Clock We were
engaged, on the Subject of Consuls & vice Consuls.   the grand question was
Whether Foreigners were eligible to those Offices.   It was admitted That they
Were. and a number accordingly appointd.[21]   When I came home at dinner
The Speaker told me That a bill was proposed in the House of Representatives
for giving them Salaries   Thus it is that we are led on by little and little to
encrease the civil list to increase the mass of public Debt. and of Course the
Taxes of the public.   This however is all of a piece with former pieces of Man-
agement from the Offices.

The funding bill was now called for.   Butler repeated the same things he
had said Yesterday.   But now up rose Patterson with a lode of Notes before
him.[22]   To follow him would be to write a pamplet. for he was up near an
hour.   near the begining he however put a kind of Question.   What Principle shall We adopt? to settle this business.   if we follow Justice *she says three ₱*
Cent. or even Two, is as much as the holders of Certificates can demand.   But
what says law   6 ₱ Cent.   and he was a Summum Jus Man[23] to the End of the
Chapter.   It was near three When he had done.   I felt an impatience to
attack him & Up I got   at first exploded a doctrine which he had stated of
Congress being One party and the Claimants another.   I Stated the People at

---

[20]The other bill was the Duties on Distilled Spirits Bill [HR-62]. Its rejection by the House
on 21 June made way for the Ways and Means Act [HR-83].

[21]The confirmation of individuals nominated as consuls and vice-consuls in Washington's
message of 4 June is recorded in the *SEJ*.

[22]A brief outline of what appears to be Paterson's speech of this day and a summary of the
subsequent speeches of WM and others can be found in Part II of this volume.

[23]A man who believes in the supreme rigor of the law and applies it without concern for
justice.

large as being the Debtors and the holders the Creditors & Congress the
Umpires   the Legislature between them   I then Stated his Two principles of
Justice & Law.   declared myself an adherent of the former.   Law was the Rule
for Courts ~~of Justice~~ and Magistrates in the Execution of their offices.   But
Justice was our guide.   and had been the guide of all Just legislation, from the
Jewish Jubilee[24] to the present day.   That ever in Law it was a Maxim that rigid
Law was rigid Injustice.   hence the necessity of Courts of Chancery, expressly
for mitigating the Severity of Unjust Contracts.   I repeated his own Words *of*
3 ⅌ *Cent. perhaps* 2 ⅌ *Cent.* being the Voice of Justice.   if then the point of
Justice stands at 3 ⅌ Cent. or if at 2 ⅌ Cent. all beyond that point is injustice,
and injustice to Whom?   To that very People whose interest it is our bounden
duty to support & protect.   &ca. &ca.   I rebrobated his Positions even with
acrimony As the Shylock Doctrine of my Bond my Bond.

Friday, 18 June 1790

went early to the Hall As I Was on Two Committees this Morning   the One
the Case of One Twining.[25]   the other McCords   We spent a Considerable
Space of Time on Twinings affair, which to me did not seem a just Subject of
legislation.   I then joined the Committee on McCord's Case.   This was truly
One in Which Compassion mingled herself with Justice.   The Generals
Thomson⟨ , ⟩[26] Irvine & others had received effects from him in Canada in the
Year 1776.   they gave him a bill Which was never paid.   The Auditor &
Comptroller settled the Sum due on this bill 809 Doll. 71 Cents.[27]   he had
suffered greatly in Canada.   had his house burn'd   took our continental

[24]The jubilee year in ancient Israel occurred every fifty years. At that time there was a
compulsory restoration of hereditary properties to their original owners or their legal heirs as
well as the emancipation of certain servants.

[25]Nathaniel Twining petitioned the FFC for relief for losses he had sustained as a result of a
federal mail contract. For the legislative history of the Twining Act [HR-72], see the petition
volumes.

[26]William Thompson (1736–81) emigrated from Ireland and settled near Carlisle before
the French and Indian War, in which he served. His military career during the War for
Independence began in 1775 and ceased a year later when, as a brigadier general, he was
taken prisoner in Canada.

[27]Oliver Wolcott, Jr. (1760–1833), auditor of the treasury from 1789 to 1791, was born to a
politically prominent family in Litchfield, Connecticut. He graduated from Yale in 1778,
joined the state bar, and participated briefly in the War for Independence. In 1784 he served
with Oliver Ellsworth as a commissioner for settling Connecticut's accounts with the United
States, and in 1788 he became comptroller of Connecticut.

Nicholas Eveleigh (c. 1748–91), comptroller of the treasury from 1789 until his death, was
born in Charleston, South Carolina. Raised and educated in England, he returned to
America in 1774 and served in the Continental army from 1775 to 1778. South Carolina
elected him to the Confederation Congress in 1780 and 1781, but he attended only from 1781
to 1782. See also *SEJ*, p. 543.

WM's reference may be to James Milligan, comptroller of the treasury under the Confederation, and any of several persons who held the office of auditor during that time.

Money to a Considerable amount as Specie. Which he produced to Us to the amount of 12 or 1,300 doll. advanced Money and goods to many People Who now refuse to pay him & Many of them, he cannot find. all these things, are indubitable. I had no difficulty of allowing him the 809 doll. 71 Cents in Ready Money in lieu of a Certificate but anything more. I seemed to feel a difficulty in. Lands had been set apart, by the old Congress. to make Compensation for Canadian Sufferers. We reported the Bill with the 809 Doll. 71 Cents & left a Blank for the Value of his Lands. the Senate filled the blank with 500 doll. my heart would not let me rise against this ~~Money~~. motion. Tho' it is a Triffle to his Sufferings. Yet how Many hundreds of our own People Suffer equal distress Up now came the funding Bill, Butler railed at Elsworth. Elsworth talked back. there really was no entertainment. no Man ever rambled or talked more at random ~~that~~ than Butler, he is ever ~~talk~~ quoting Authors on Trade finance &ca. ever repeating What he has seen in Europe. This day he asserted that the circulating Coin of great Britain was 300 Millions— Authors (if I remember right) place it at about 16. There really was nothing new. some were pressing for the Question. but it was postponed, Generally.

I received a letter from Dr. Rush, and a Newspaper, containing a mutilated publication of the ~~pee~~ peice which I sent to him on the Subject of the federal Residence.[28] he has left out, many of what I considered as the best arguments. and very improperly, reduced the Argument drawn from the Mileage one half by his miscalculation. But I really never was served otherwise.

This Evening Mr. Morris & Fitzsimons called ~~again~~ on Us. Hamilton has been with them again. never had a Man a greater propensity for bargaining than Mr. Morris Hamilton knows this, and is labouring to make a Tool of him. he affects to tell Mr. Morris, That the New-England Men will bargain to fix the permanent Seat at the Potowmac or at Baltimore. Mr. Fitzsimons counted all the Members, which it was likely would Vote for such a Measure. & The Conclusion was that no such Measure could be carried, by them.

Saturday, 19 June 1790

Attended at 10 OClock at the Hall on Mr. Mr. Twining's bill. The Committee heard all the Witnesses produced. We then Walked to View the domolitions of Fort George The leaden Coffins and remains of Lady ~~Thay~~ and & Lord Bellamont.[29] now exposed to the Sun after an interment of about

---

[28]The enclosed newspaper article, written by Rush from the notes WM sent him on 5 June, can be found in Appendix B(9).

[29]Fort George stood at the foot of Broad Way just below the Bowling Green and above the Battery. It was being levelled to construct a residence for the president of the United States. Richard Coote, Earl of Bellamont, the English governor of New England, 1697–1701, died in

90 Years.   They and Many more had been ~~been~~ deposited in Vaults in a Chappel which Once stood in the Fort.   The Chappel was burned down about 50 Years ago, and never rebuilt.   the levelling of the Fort, and digging away the foundations. have uncovered the Vaults.   The Talk of the day is the death of one Telfair from Georgia, Who this Morng. cut his throat with a Razor.[30]   a negro Boy who waited on him. has manifested marks of astonishing attachment.   'Tis said ~~the~~ he was seperated from the dead Body by force, and ~~was~~ restrained with difficulty from committing Violence on himself.

Sunday, 20 June 1790

I spent the most of this day at home,   finished some letters,   read occasionally.   In the Evening I went to see Mrs. Bell   she proposed to Walk, and offered to come and see Mrs. Muhlenberg.[31]   I set out with her. but she knew almost every Body We Met.   A Mrs. ~~Jason~~ somebody joined Us and made Us gad over almost the Whole Town, to visit somebody else.   We however parted with our adventitious comrade, and performed our first Tour.   this does not deserve mention. only for What, Mrs. Bell mentioned,   as the Subject of the removal of Congress. from this place. was her constant Theme.   She took occasion to tell me that Mr. Morris, was not sincerely attached to the Pennsylvania Interest. on that Subject.   That his commercial arrangements were calculated for this place.   That the Yorkers depended on him but were lately Staggered by an Oath which (it was said) he had Sworn. (~~as was said~~).   That he would have Congress away.   I endeavoured to perswade that Mr. Morris was now in earnest. and the Yorkers would find him so &c. &ca.   Yet I had my own thoughts on the Subject.   Mrs. Bell reply'd he may have good reason, now to wish for popularity in Pennsylvania.

Monday, 21 June 1790

attended at the Hall early on the Bill for remitting certain Penalties to one N. Twining.[32]   The Senate Met.   I observed a Strangeness of disposition in

---

office at New York. The *NYDA* of 17 June described the archeological discoveries. (*New York*, pp. 20–23)

[30]The victim was probably related to Edward Telfair, governor of Georgia during the FFC. Representative Theodore Sedgwick also mentioned the "servant's" attempts to kill himself. (To Pamela Sedgwick, 19 June, Sedgwick Papers, MHi)

[31]Either Catherine Schaeffer (Mrs. Frederick) Muhlenberg (1750–1835) or Hannah Meyer (Mrs. Peter) Muhlenberg (1751–1806). (Paul A. Wallace, *The Muhlenbergs of Pennsylvania* [Philadelphia, 1950])

[32]WM attended the select committee on the Twining Act [HR-72].

the House the Moment, or rather a few Moments after, the Minutes Were read.   Patterson moved to adjourn   Schuyler seconded.   this was lost.   It was now moved to take up the Vote of the House of Representatives. for fixing the Time of Adjournment,   this was agreed to, and Strong⟨,⟩ Basset & Walker appointed on our part to Confer.   Izard now rose   said there was something to put on the Minutes, and renewed the Motion for adjournment.   seconded by Patterson   This was lost and now the funding bill was taken up.   We had a great deal of the old Ground gone over again.   King received a note, rose & moved that the funding bill should be postponed as the House of Representatives had negatived the bill for the Ways and Means.[33]
he was seconded by Schuyler   We had now a long desultory kind of debate Whether the bill should be postponed   it was not postponed.   now the debates on the Merits of the bill.   the question was Whether all the alternatives should be struck out, and a fund of 4 ℔ Cent. adopted.   adopted 13 for, 10 against.   now the Question. on the Striking out of the Indents.   Elsworth & the New England Men know that Pennsylvania has a number of Indents. and the Invention of all of them is at work to turn it to her disadvantage.   The Vote was however carried to keep in the Indents. since the other back interest was to be funded.   I bore my Testimony in the Strongest Terms against funding any Interest. and proposed to open a Land-Office as a sinking fund for the Whole of the back interest including the Indents.   but I found no second.   The interest of the Whole was placed on one footing almost without a division.   now a long debate ensued about the Jersey ~~Money~~ Payments, and a proviso which had been inserted to favour them.[34]   no other Question was however taken, and the House adjourned a Quarter after 3. this was Mess or Club Day.   I went and staid till the fumigation began. alias Smoking of Sigars. a thing I never could bear.

Elsworth made a long Speech. amounting to this.   That since a general System of funding could not be obtained. Gentlemen would be against all funding. Whatever.   I placed his speech in as strong colors as I could. that since a party in Congress. could not build as they pleased. they would turn and pull all down.   There was a Majority against the Assumption of the State debts. & the minority, indignant at being controuled. since they could not rule would join the discontented part of ~~the~~ Congress & stop all Business. Adams affects to treat me with all the neglect he can While I am speaking by turning his head a different Way looking side ways &c. &ca.   But I care not. I will endeavour to bear it.

---

[33]Duties on Distilled Spirits Bill [HR-62].

[34]Boudinot had proposed a proviso that was inserted at the end of section 3 of the Funding Act [HR-63], covering cases in which a state had paid interest on certificates of the United States held by its citizens.

Tuesday, 22 June 1790

I called this Morning on Genl. Irwin who is one of the Commissioners for settling the Accounts between the United States and the individual States. For the amount of the Jersey Claim for interest paid by that State on the continental Certificates found it to be about half a Million. now attended the Committee on Twinings Case. Mr. Morris called me aside. (I had Yesterday expressed my indignation of the New England attempt upon Pennsylvania, in excluding or trying to exclude Those Indents which would pass into her hands, in Consequence of the late funding law, from being funded. had endeavoured to possess him of the Facts, to obtain his Assistance. and indeed expressed, perhaps unguarded solicitude on that Subject.) told me this is an important Affair respecting the Indents to Pennsylvania I would have You think Well of it. The New England-Men are determined to carry it against Us. The Assumption is the only Way We can rid ourselves of this thing. I would have you think of it—think of it— I had to say I will think of it. I felt a little disturbed. not if I know my own mind, with regard to the part I should act, but to think that everything should be set to sale. and that even just measures, could not be pursued but by Contract. and that men should be hunted into Measures. I have often thought myself deficient, in readiness of Judgment, or quickness of determination. perhaps any Man can think more, and better too, at Twice than at once. I however in a few minutes took my seat beside Mr. Morris. told him That I considered the Assumption so politically wrong. and productive of so much injustice That no offer could be made. Which would induce me to change my mind. I had however reasons of another nature. I could depend nothing on the promises of the New England Men, but further I had collected, That the State of New York was circumatedstanced nearly in the same way as Pennsylvania. with respect to indents. And I considered this as the Sure pledge, That we would not be pushed to extremities on that Ground. The result shewed That I was right for after a great deal of debate in the house. affairs settled nearly as I would have them. There is a lesson in the Matter. and I must be on my Guard with respect to my Colleague. Hamilton has him unhappily, in his power, with respect to these old Accounts. Which are still before the Treasury. The bill for Establishing the Post Office, was read for the first time We adjourned early. Mr. Fitzsimons called this afternoon. We had much loose conversation. on the Subject of Adjournment, I expressed a Wish the sooner the better. Fitzsimons said it never would do, to go away without funding the debts. Pennsylvania was too deeply interested She would draw *three millions* of dollars annually from the funds. I Stared as well I might. for at 4 ℔ Cent. she must possess more than the Whole of the continental Debt to do it. viz. 75 mill. he corrected himself and said, above 15 Millions would belong to her and her Citizens.   I said this might be.   he now got on the Subject of Pennsylvania paying her civil list &ca. &ca. with continental Revenue.   In fact this Man has no Rule of conduct, but convenience. and he shifts Opinions and Sentiments to answer Occasions.   The Speaker walked away with Mr. Fitzsimons.   When he returned I asked him to repeat What Mr. Fitzsimons had said.   he said Mr. Fitzsimons had explained himself in their Walk.   That the State of Pennsylvania possessed three Millions on Which she would draw interest & that the Citizens of that State possessed 15 Millions on Which they would draw interest.   There are More Turners than dish Makers— but in fact, None of these things deserved noting down.

Wednesday, 23 June 1790

This day could not be considered as very important in the Senate.   The funding bill was called, for and ~~negatived~~ postponed.   The intercourse bill. or that for appointing Ambassadors had been ~~committed~~ referred, to a Committee of Conferrence so long ago That I had forgot it.[35]   but the thing was neither dead nor sleeping.   It was only d dressing. and friends making ~~for it~~. The report encreased the Salaries. and added 10,000 dollars to the Appropriations.   I concluded they had secured Friends enough to support it. before they committed it to the House.   This turned out to be the case.   The Whole appropriation was 40,000 Doll. and they were voted with an air of perfect indifference. by the affirmants. altho' I consider the Money as Worse than thrown away.   For I know not of a Single thing, that we have for a single Minister to do at a Single Court in Europe.   indeed the less We have for them to do the better.   Our Business is to pay them What We owe and the less Political connection the better, with any European power.   It was well spoke against.   I voted against every part of it.   We received also, a bill for the Indian Trade.   read for the first time.   Mr. Morris was called often out; he at last came in and Whispered me. The Business is settled at last.   Hamilton gives up the temporary Residence.   I wrote on a ~~pi~~ Slip of paper (as We could not converse freely) *If Hamilton has his hand in the Residence now, he will have his Foot in it, before the End of the Session.*   I afterwards told Mr. Morris That this seeming Willingness of Hamilton proceeded from his knowledge ~~that~~ that the North Carolina Senators & Col. Gun could not be restrained from Voting for Baltimore, & that the present proposal, and bill (for a bill was shewed to me by Mr. Morris) were meant to divert the Southern Members from Baltimore. and they would finally destroy the bill—   I got Henry of Maryland into the Audience room. and gave him a detail of What was going on, and made the same reflections on it, to him.   I saw he believed the North Carolina

[35]The Senate referred the Foreign Intercourse Act [HR-52] to a conference committee on 31 May.

Men would vote for Baltimore. I find there is a ferment among them. and good may come of it— paid lodgings.

There is a Jockeying and bargaining going on respecting which I am not consulted, and which I hear of only by the by. the Temporary Residence in ~~the~~ Philada. for 15 Years and the permanent Residence on the Potowmack. A Solemn engagement has been entered into by Eleven Senators to push the Temporary Residence only. on this Ground we of Pennsylvania are perfectly safe, and our interest is to keep this contract alive if We go from this, the temporary Residence may remain in New York, and the permanent Residence to the Potowmack it is a Species of Robbery, to deprive Pennsylvania of the Residence. how can a Delegate reconcile himself to such a Vote Unless he confide in future contingency to repair his errors. which is neither safe nor honorable.

Thursday, 24 June 1790

This was a day of Small Business in the Senate. the report on a bill for remitting fines to one Twining was rejected and the Bill confirmed. contrary in my opinion to every Idea of Justice. for this Man had got already from the public upwards of 2,000 dollars without consideration; tho little Business was done in the Senate Yet I ought never to forget this day. In the Senate Chamber Mr. Walker told me that the Pennsylvania Delegation had in a general Meeting agreed to place the permanent Residence on the Potowmack, and the temporary residence to remain 10 Years in Philada. I answered I knew nothing of any such agreement. no truth was ever better founded. he said Scott had come from the Meeting to him. he seemed willing I should take a lead in the business. I heard nothing further on the business. Docr. Elmer & I called on Mr. Morris and here for the first time I heard him declare he was satisfyed with ten Years. he did not say much to me but the Moment I came home the Speaker attacked me. here You have been doing fine things, You have broke the bargain &ca. &ca. I deny'd I had broke any bargain. That I never knew of any bargain for ~~Six~~ Ten Years being made. did not Genl. Muhlenberg speak to You. Yes on monday last, he bid me tell Mr. Morris, That he thought Mathews, could not make them agree to more than 10 Years. I forgot to mention it to him then but mentioned it to him afterwards he said if ~~they~~ we agreed to 10 they would propose 7 &ca. and declared himself against listening to any such proposals. We however met in the Evening. Basset & Read of the Delaware State ~~were there~~ came with Mr. Morris Docr. Elmer came some time after. I now did the most foolish thing ever I did in my life. I declared that I considered the permanent Residence as a Matter that ought to belong to Pennsylvania, in What ever point of View it was considered geographically or politically.   That to deprive her of it, was in my Opinion a Species of Robbery.   *but since we came there to consult the public good, I was willing to be governed by republican principles, and would stand by the Vote of the Majority on this point as an House divided against itself, could not Stand.*   Mr. Morris now said that my Arguments were too late,   I should have made these Objections when the contract was made. for 15 Years Residence at Philada.   I very freely declared I never entered into any such contract.   Morris⟨,⟩ Fitzsimons and the Speaker declared that I did, and the Speaker reminded me that a Committee was appointed,   I agreed that a Committee was appointed But it was to draw up our reasons for rejecting Hamilton's Proposals.   and That I understood them so would be evident from my sentiments, which I had committed to paper at the time & which were now in the hands of Col. Hartley.   they all three persisted in the charge. Hartley however had Spirit enough to say there was no such Contract.   this seemed to cool them a little.   but after some time Scott came in.   the Matter was repeated to him.   he declared there was no number of Years mentioned at all, as any bargain. and of course no Contract.   This made them look a little blue.   I must note, that I read the Sketch which I gave to Hartley, to the Speaker. and That he approved of it, and I expressly mentioned both to him and Col. Hartley. That all we did respected only What was past.

I may write L. L.[36] to the end of the line,   But now the Speaker put the Question   shall we vote for a bill giving the Temporary residence 10 Years to Philada. and the permanent Residence to the Potowmack   they all said Yes, but myself.   I said no.   But unlu⟨c⟩kily am bound by my foolish declaration.   Good God deliver me this once.   {Fate familiar as her Garter undid the difficulty. but the Tale is long, and I had better begin the Business of the Day, on the next page.}

Friday, 25 June 1790

A day of excessive rain   I went to the Hall in the Speaker's Carriage, at an early hour to attend the Committee on the post Office Business.   I found Mr. Carrol there—   We had much lose talk   he told me his plan which was to take Butlers bill—amend it so that the Residence should be 10 Years in Philada. at the End of Which the permanent Residence should be on the Potowmack   The first Business was the Report on What was called Stephen Moore's bill.[37]   This man is the owner of the land on Which the old Fort of West point

[36]See February 1790, n. 19.
[37]West Point Act [HR-76]. Stephen Moore (1734–99) owned West Point on the Hudson and had petitioned the FFC for compensation for federal use of the land. For a legislative history of the act, see *DHFFC* 6:2059–62. (Hugh Lefler, ed., *Orange County, 1752–1952* [Chapel Hill, N.C., 1953], p. 335)

stands,   he is got in debt in Town to the amount of £2,000 or some such Sum.   he has nothing but the Rocks of West point   the Secretaries of War and Treasury &ca. and other influential Characters have interested themselves in getting this bill passed to buy the land from him, to pay his debts, under the notion that the ground is necessary for a fortress   barefaced as this business is, it was carried in the Senate by a great Majority.   Am I mistaken or is the Spirit of prodigality broke loose since Rhode Island came in.   Yesterday Twinings base business   this day Mo⟨o⟩re's Case. and a bill for Claims for One Gould[38] come up.   The ayes & noes are on the Journals and strange to tell for Once Mr. Morris was with me.   Mr. Carrol now rose and was seconded by Lee. Izard⟨,⟩ Few⟨,⟩ King, on one side, Carrol & Lee on the other.   Butler bounced between both, but declared for the bill and he would be for it &ca. the Motion was to take up the bill[39]   The President from the Chair with the most unparall⟨el⟩ed partiality. said *there has been a Motion for Postponement   I do not know Whether it has been seconded.*   no such thing had happened.   But the hint was soon after taken   all now was consternation and Commotion   out ran King⟨,⟩ Schuyler⟨,⟩ Izard and Sundry of the Eastern Gentry, and in Were Ushered the Senators from Rhode Island.   and now the hinted for postponement was called for, of the bill Which in fact, had not been taken up.   but the new members just Sworn & seated, did not get up   signs nods motions were ~~inf~~ ineffectual,   They kept their Seats.   and the bill of Course was taken up, or in parliamentary Stile not postponed. Izard begged leave to explain, or in other Words to tell, the new come Gentlemen. That they ought to have voted for the postponement.   Mr. Adams without any ceremony put the same Question over again.   King got on one side and Elsworth on the other of the New Members and up they got them. Butler too after all his declarations voted for the postponement,   it was 13 & 13 and Bonny Johney Voted the postponement.   & thus the Business of the day was got over. without much difficulty so far, or at least the knotty parts of it.   & thus my neck got out of the Noose—   Adjourned untill monday.

   I must note here. that a number of our own people were duped. in pushing the Rhode Island-bill.[40]   they are now paid for it.   I told them at the time, what was intended.   they must take what follows.

Saturday, 26 June 1790

Attended this day on the Committee, on the Post Office bill.   The Bill came up from the Representatives, with every post road described bothe main

---

[38]David Gould (d. 1781) was a surgeon in the Continental army whose heirs petitioned the FFC for settlement of his claims. For the legislative history of the Gould Bill [HR-79], see the petition volumes.
[39]Residence Act [S-12].
[40]Rhode Island Trade Bill [S-11].

and cross Roads.   Carrol & Strong were for blotting out every Word of description, and leaving all to the Postmaster Genl. & the President of the U.S.   I
proposed a different plan   That one great Post road should be described by
law. From Portland in N.H. to Augusta in Georgia.[41] passing thro' the Seats of
the different Governments. and That 2 Pos Cross roads only should be described, from New York to Canada, and from Philada. or some other proper
place to Fort Pitt. for the Accomodation of the Western Country.   The other,
or blank System prevailed.   but We are to meet again on Monday at 10
O'Clock.

Sunday, 27 June 1790

    called on Scott, this morning   went to Walk but the heat was as insupport-
able   returned to my lodgings.   spent the Residue of the day in writing
Letters reading &ca.

Monday, 28 June 1790

    met at 10 on the Post Office Committee, but such running and Caballing of
the Senators nothing could be done.   Stephen Moore's bill[42] the first Business   Izard made a long Speech, telling *how injurious it would be to this Man,
if the bill did not pass &c. &ca.* & would not let the Question be put untill the
senate was full.   It was carried.
    Now the Baltimore Vote was read.[43]   Carrol & Lee moved to postpone it,
it was postponed.   Carrol now moved to read some Representations from
Baltimore & George Town   this was comply'd with.   Carrol surprized me by
taking me out and requesting me to move the insertion of Baltimore for the
permanent Residence.   Said he wished it to be put and negatived.   This had
a crooked Aspect,   I declined it.   Izard however moved this very thing &
Walker told me it was expected That he would do it.   I called for the amendments that had been proposed on Friday. but Carrol got up and wished the
Vote on Baltimore   It was negatived.   Carrol now got up with the Amendments.   he surprized me with his slowness.   We wrangled on Untill near 3
O'Clock calling Yeas & nays on almost every Question.   but for these Vid. the
Minutes   When We came to the blank for the place of the Temporary Resi-
dence, and by the by there was no blank in the amendment which carrol read

---

[41]WM may have meant Portland, in the Massachusetts district of Maine, rather than
Portsmouth, New Hampshire's capital and only seaport.
    Augusta, on the Savannah River in Richmond County, was the capital of Georgia.
[42]West Point Act [HR-76].
[43]The Senate was considering the House resolution of 11 June, by which the FFC would
have adjourned to Baltimore at the close of the second session.

on Friday. but he now suffered Adams to proceed on the original bill.   he
evidently waited and paused, untill Izard moved to fill the blank with New
York,   now We had the Warmest debates of the day.   Mr. Morris took no part
Whatever   Langdon & myself were the Warmest.   The Question was put at 3
OClock and carried for New York 13 to 12.   Col. Gun has been Absent all this
day, designedly as is Supposed.

This day the Delegation had Invited the Vice President and the other
Officers of the General Government.   The Chief Justice[44] & V.P. did not
attend.   The three Secretaries Were with Us.   The Discourse before dinner
turned on the Manner of doing business in the Senate   it was remarked, that
as every Question of Moment was carried only by a Majority of one, or for the
Most part by the casting Vote of the President. It might be [*lined out*] as well to
Vest the Whole Senatorial power in the President of the Senate.   The fact
really is as it was stated   But they did not mention the loan   Hamilton and
his New York ~~interest~~ Junto do business on the Principles of Œconomy. and do
not put themselves to the Expence of hiring more than just the number
necessary to carry their point.   This is a deplorable Truth with respect, to our
Senate. and certainly is a foul evil at the Root of our legislation.   I could not
help making some remarks on our Three Secretaries.   Hamilton has a very
boyish giddy Manner.   our Scotch Irish People would call him a Skite.   Ŧ
Jefferson transgresses on the Extreme of Stiff Gentility, or lofty Gravity.   Knox
is the easiest Man, and the most dignity of Presence.   They retired at a decent
time. One after another   Knox staid longest. As indeed suited his Aspect
best. being more of a Bachanalian Figure.

Tuesday, 29 June 1790

The Tonnage bill was taken up & committed,   this bill Uses the same rates
of Tonnage as the old bill. and Why it was brought forward is more than I can
say unless it was solely to employ time.   A bill to make compensation to one
Gould was also committed.   And now the Residence bill was taken up   the
Joy of the Yorkers made them cry out for an adjournment. When they had
filled one of the blanks.   Now the other One was to be filled, with the time of
the temporary Residence   it was carried for 10 Years. and Carrol Voted for
it.   13 to 12.   but now the Question was taken on the Clause and the Whole
was rejected 16 to 9.   Now Izard and the adherents of New York, shewed
visible perturbation. and bounced at a Strange rate.   I looked at Carrol and
got him now to rise with his clause.   10 Years for Philada.   Why he kept it
back so long explains itself.   Schyler & King offered to amend it by dividing
the time 5 Years to each place   long debates here.   this Question was lost 13

---

[44]John Jay.

to 13   V.P. against.   they now moved Baltimore   lost it 10 to 16.   Butler
now moved to stay 2 Years in N. York   13 to 13   P. against.   the Question
put on Clause   13 to 13   P. against it.   so the Clause was lost.   the Question
was now put   shall the bill pass to a third reading.   the Noes certainly had it.
but the House did not divide.   And an adjournment obtained before anything more was finished.   In the Course of King's Speech, I noted down the
following Words *convulse the Union* &c. &ca.   This as he stated it, would be
the Effect of removing from New York.   In my Reply I mentioned the
Words   he denyed that he had used such Words.   Mr. Morris was the first
Man to cry out. That he did not Use any such Words.   From the Drift of Chaff
and feathers, it is seen how the Wind blows.   Mr. Morris has never rose this
day or Yesterday   I might speak or let it alone.   he has never said One Word.
except giving me the above contradiction—   {Mr. Wingate and Sundry other
Members declared he did Use them.   But As he chose to retract. I passed it by
As Words that had never been Spoken.}

Wednesday, 30 June 1790

I called early at the Hall.   Langdon only there,   went & paid off my bill for
monday   28/ the price of a Two days head Ach.   When I came to the Hall
Dr. Elmer told me That Carrol & Co. Were Using every endeavour to pass the
bill to a third reading without anything of the Temporary Residence.   here we
certainly had every right to leave them.   Yet Walker said they would drop
Philada. if We would not go with them.   I am fully satisfyed that they have
had an Under plot on hand all this time with the Yorkers.   Carrol finding the
bill would not be carried to a third reading, moved a Reconsideration of the
Philada. Clause.   but he was out of order not having been of the Majority.   I
passed the Word to get Butler to move as he had been of that side   he did so
after talking almost half an hour.   It was reconsidered and adopted 14 to 12
Butler changing his Ground.   Before We could get a Question on the paragraph. they Moved the question of 5 Years in New York and 5 in Philada.
lost 12 & 14.   then to stay 2 Years in New York   this Butler joined them in,
and the House stood 13 & 13.   The President gave Us a long Speech on the
Orderly decent behaviour of the Citizens of New York, expecially in the
Gallery of the other House   said no People in the World could behave
better.   I really thought he meant, this lavish praise as an indirect Censure on
the City of Philada. for the Papers have teemed with censorious Charges, of
their Rudeness to the Members of publick Bodies.[45]   Be that however as it
may He declared he would go to Philadelphia, without staying a single Hour,

---

[45]See, as examples, "June 1" in the *NYDA*, 3 June; "A Citizen of the Union," *NYP*,
12 June; and "Q.E.D.," *NYDA*, 29 June.

& gave Us his Vote. I think it was well he did not know all. for had he given this Vote. the other way the Whole Was lost. The Question on the paragraph was carried 14 to 12. Mr. Langdon now moved a Reconsideration to Strike out the Loan of the 100,000 a long debate ensued. It was evident his Vote would turn it this I mentioned to Walker. We told them however that We were with them. But they did What good Policy directed they gave the Matter up. and the Appropriation was Struck out. the Question on the bill passing to a third reading was now taken carried. 14 to 12. I am fully convinced Pennsylvania could do no better. The Matter could not be longer delayed. It is in fact the Interest of the President of the United States, that pushes the Potowmack, he by Means of Jefferson⟨,⟩ Madison⟨,⟩ Carrol & others Urges the Business. and if We had not closed with ~~him~~ these Terms a bargain would have been made, for the Temporary Residence in New York.

They have offered to support the Potowmack for three Years Temporary Residence. And I am very apprehensive they would have succeeded if it had not been for the Pennsylvania Threats that were thrown out. of stopping all Business, if an Attempt was made to rob them of both temporary, & permanent Residence.

July 1790

Thursday, 1 July 1790

knowing nothing of immediate consequence I attended the Hall early took a Seat in the Committee room, began An Examination of the Journals of the old Congress touching some Matters, before Us in Committee.[1] had thus an Opportunity of the Members as they came in. but Such runing and caballing of the New England Men and Yorkers. When the Minutes were read. King observed that the Yeas & nays were not inserted, on the Motion for Staying Two Years in New York. The President & Secretary both deny'd they had been taken But I believe they erred. This however I did not consider as much for them. We read the Rhode Island Enumeration bill. committed the Settlement bill, and the one for the Regulation of Seamen. and now came the Residence. Elsworth moved That the Extent on the Potowmack should be 30 miles above & 30 Miles below Hancock Town.[2] lost. second Motion to insert the first Monday in May instead of first Monday in Decemr. for removal. the Yeas and nays equal & now John Adams gave Us one of his pretty speeches, he mentioned Many of the Arguments for removal. and concluded That Justice Policy and even necessity called for it. Now King took up his Lamentation he sobbed Wiped his Eyes and scolded. & railed, and accused first every body and then nobody of bargaining contracting arrangements and engagements that would dissolve the Union. he was called on sharply. he begged pardon. and Blackguard like raild again Butler reply'd in a long unmeaning Talk repeated That he was sure the [Honorable] Gentleman did not mean him. And Yet if there [really] was any Person there to Whom Kings Mysterio[us] hints would apply. Butler's Strange conduc[t] marked him, as the most proper object for them. Talk followed Talk it was evident, that they meant to spend the day. Dr. Johnson cryed adjourn. Question Question reechoed from different Quarters of the House. Few begged leave to move an amendment. It was to restore the appropriation Clause. It was lost. And at last We got the Question on Transmitting the bill to the Representatives Yeas 14 Nays 12. as I came from the Chamber

---

[1]WM was a member of the committee on the Gould Bill [HR-79].
[2]Because western Maryland is only about three miles wide at Hancock, the location held out the enticement of placing the seat of the federal government in three states, Pennsylvania, Maryland, and Virginia.

King gave me a look.   I reply'd *King's lamentations* That Won't do. said he.   When We were down Stairs, he turned to me   said. let Us Now go and receive the Congratulations of the City for What We have done.   I had heard so much and so many Allusions to the Hospitality &ca. I thought it no bad time to give both him and them a Wipe.   "King for a session of near Six Months I have passed the threshold of no Citizen of New York,   I have no wish to commence acquaintance now"   he Uttered some ejaculation. and went off.   In truth I never Was in so inhospitable a place.   The above declaration I thought it not amiss to make. That they may Know, That I am not insensible, of their Rudeness. & further That I am, quite clear of any Obligations to them.

Friday, 2 July 1790

Attended the Committee on the affair of Gould's bill.   There did not appear much animation in the House,   that Keeness of look and preying eagerness which marked all our former looks had departed with the Residence.

Elsworth moved a Commitment of the Resolution with regard to the State Debts   I saw we were taken unawares on this Subject.   they carried the Commitment & and the Committee both against Us.   Carrol joined them. We got now at the indian bill.   it was committed.   and now We joined the Post Office bill & debated on it to the time of adjournment.   Wyngate told me this day of a Violent breach having happened between king and the Massachusets men,   they would not Vote for the Potowmack, as King wished them to do.   had they joined the Connecticut & York Votes. We would have obtained the Temporary Residence on Much Worse Terms.   This is a still further Proof of What I knew before, that there was an under plot. and a Negotiation still open, between the Potowmack and New York.

The Speaker told me this day that the Assumption would pass.   I heard him with Grief, and, trust I may Yet disbelieve him.   he dined with the President Yesterday.

Saturday, 3 July 1790

General Irwin called early on me this Morning.   It was to tell me That King & Lawrence had been asserting with great confidence That We had bargained to give the Assumption for the Residence &ca.   That I was to go away, and Carrol to Vote direct for it   &ca. &ca.   That a very great Hubbub was raised among the Southern Gentlemen &ca.   I could only tell him it was false and much indeed as I wished to see my family, That now home I would not go, That I would stay and he was at Liberty to say so.   I called on Williamson As I went to the Hall and on Hawkins & told them so.   These ⟨New⟩ Yorkers are

Political Cartoon on the Residence Act, July 1790. (Courtesy of the American Antiquarian Society.)

the Vilest of People.   Their Vices have not the palliation of being Manly,
they resemble bad Schoolboys, Who are Unfortunate at play,   they revenge
themselves by telling notorious thumpers.   Even the New England Men say,
that King's Character is detestable. a perfect Canvass for the Devil to paint on.
a ground Work void of Every Virtue.   Senate Sat untill three on the Post
Office bill. but the Debates Were unimportant.   When I came in the Speaker
told me, that the ⟨New⟩ York Malevolence was shewing itself, in curious
caricaturas in Ridicule of the Pennsylvanians—&ca. &ca.[3]

Sunday, 4 July 1790

being Sunday was celebrated only by the firing of Cannon about noon.   I
Walked to Scotts lodging   he came home with me.   he shewed a disposition
to go over all the Arguments Which I had Used in the Senate on that
Subject.   I did so with much chearfulness[4]   spent the rest of the day in
Writing Letters to my family and others.   I called this Morning on Mr. Lee and
shewed him plainly as I thought how We could by a side Wind in the bill for the
Settlement of Accounts give the Assumption a decided Stroke.   I promised. I
would see him again tomorrow.

Monday, 5 July 1790

I was detained long before I could get to see Mr. Lee.   he had consulted
Madison as he said, and had altered the amendment in point of form. but it
certainly was much more Obscure.   said he would second the Motion if I
made it.   The Post Office bill was taken Up and a long debate Whether the
Post Master should appoint the Post Roads, or the Congress declare them so by
Law.   It was carried in favour of the Post Master's doing it.   A motion was
made that Congress should adjourn, to Wait on the President with the Compliments of the Day.   negatived   a Second Motion to adjourn One hour for
the above purpose.   lost.   Some Business was done. and a second Motion for
adjournment was called.   all the Town was in Arms   Grenadiers ~~and~~ light
infantry & artillery passed the Hall. and the firing of Cannon and small arms
with beating of Drums kept all in uproar.   This motion carried & now all of Us
repaired to the President's.   We got Wine punch & Cakes. from hence We
Went to St. Paul's and heard the Anniversary of Independence pronounced by
a Mr. B. Livingston.[5]   The Church Was crouded   I could not hear him

---

[3] At least four political cartoons were hawked on the streets of New York about this time.
Further information on the engravings will be included with the July 1790 letters of congressmen in a later volume of the *DHFFC*. See *PTJ* 17:xxxiv–xxxvii.

[4] The reference is apparently to the location of the capital.

[5] Henry Brockholst Livingston (1757–1823), a prominent lawyer and civic leader, was a
native of New York City. He graduated from the College of New Jersey in 1774 and spent the

Well. some said it Was fine. I could not contradict them. I Was in the next pew to Genl. Washington part of his Family and Senators filled the Seats with Us. Was Warm & Sweated a good deal. Some say That the ⟨New⟩ Yorkers will make desperate Resistance. tomorrow. others say they will die soft. Jackson gave Me the Presidents Compliments & an invitation to dinner on Thursday.

Tuesday, 6 July 1790

was called on early this Morng. by Mr. Hanna of Harrisburgh.[6] a letter from Mr. Harris say's my family are Well. attended at the Hall. ~~the Commitments~~ after having paid some Visits. The Post Office bill was passed after some debate. Gould's bill was rejected, I had Occasion to be up on both these bills— Now came the settlement Bill— Mr. Lee had spoiled my amendment, or at least, greatly obscured it but if I stirred at all I must Use his Motion and great Man as he is there really was misspelling in it. the Ground I took was that the 5th section of the bill. laid down a ratio in Consequence of Which. there must in the nature of things be Creditor & Debtor States. the 6th Section told Us how the Creditor States were to be paid. but not One Word was said as to the Debtor States paying One Was as necessary as the other. Justice demanded it. Vid. my amendment,[7] I attacked, the Secretary's System of suppositious balances. as not only unjust, radically and a total departure from the Acts & requisitions of congress, but as going to lay great taxes and encrease the Volume of our Debt. Elsworth and Strong answered, King admitted every principle which I laid down, but wavered. Lee seconded and forsook me. the Child was none of his. I really thought I had the best of the arguments. Which grew bulkey and by degrees spread over all our field of finance. But on the Question I had but a small division in favour of the Motion. The true History of this bill is that it has been fabricated ~~in~~ by the Secretary's People particularly Fitzsimons. and is meant as a

---

years 1776–82 in the Continental army as an aide to General Philip Schuyler, attaining the rank of lieutenant colonel. From 1779 to 1782 he acted as private secretary to his brother-in-law, John Jay, during the latter's diplomatic mission to Spain. (*Princetonians, 1769–75,* pp. 397–406)

[6]John Andre Hanna (c. 1761–1805), a prominent Harrisburg lawyer and civic leader after 1785, graduated from the College of New Jersey in 1782. He married into the Harris family. A Dauphin County delegate to the ratification convention, he signed the dissent of the minority, and he served in 1788 as secretary of the Antifederalist Harrisburg Convention. See Appendix C. (*Princetonians, 1776–83,* pp. 363–66)

[7]WM wafered a copy of his amendment into the diary at this point. It reads:

And those States against Whom balances shall be found, shall have a portion of their State Debt, which shall have accrued as aforesaid, left charged upon them, equal to such deficient balance; and if it should so happen, That the Whole State Debt, of any particular State, shall fall Short of such balance, Such deficiency shall ~~be~~ remain charged against such State, on the books of the Treasury.

(To be added to the 6th Section)

meer delusion. or to amuse the publick. for they seriously never wish the accounts to be settled.   but a Shew must be kept up, of giving satisfaction on this point.

As to myself. I may draw a lesson from Lee's conduct. to bring forward my own Motions only.   I spoiled the amendment to obtain his support.   And he saw it perish with the indifference of a Stranger.

Wednesday, 7 July 1790

attended at the Hall.   every face wore the Marks of anxious expectation. Schyler came to me and owned the Bill for the Settlement of Accounts, was to the full as imperfect as I had stated it Yesterday. and shewed me a long amendment.   said the bill should be committed.   wished me to second him   I readily agreed to it & now We Went on the Subject of Debate.   I was not alone as Yesterday.   I supported My old System of ascertaining the Expences of the War. agreeing to the Ratio. and fixing the Quotas. giving certificates to the Cr. States. and leaving the State debts on ~~them~~ the Debtors respectively so far as to equalize the Accounts   Elsworth. certainly confused himself,   he wished to equalize the Accounts by Credits only, taking the lowest Exertion as the Basis and selling off to each State in proportion to it & funding all over it.   as the exertions of some of the States stood nearly at .o. this in fact would be nearly funding the Whole Expence of the War.   Butler had a third System, Viz. take no notice of any thing bygone. but divide the existing Debt among the States   I thought it Strange to hear My Colleague declare for this last Opinion.   After a very long debate the bill was committed.   The Secretary's People got the advantage of Us again.   A Bill which had disappeared a long While of the most futile nature with regard to relieving certain Officers from What they considered as a grievance was reported favourably. on but rejected.   This same bill or at least one Verbatim the same had been rejected by Us formerly.[8]   some other Triffling business was done. and We adjourned.   Sundry Questions were taken in the House of Representatives on the Residence bill.   the decisions have hitherto been favourable. but the question on the bill not Yet taken.

Thursday, 8 July 1790

This day was slack in the Senate Untill the Report came in on the bill for the settlement of the Accounts.   As might be expected their amendment fol-

---

[8]On 25 April the Senate rejected the Officers Bill [HR-53], and on 4 May it received the Invalid Officers Bill [HR-59] from the House. The second bill languished in committee from 5 May to 7 July.

lowed the Secretary's report. or nearly so.   It amounted to this. that the neat
advances of the States. should be made an aggregate of. and this aggregate
divided, by the Ratio of Population. which whould fix the Quotas   then the
Quotas compared with their respective advances. would determine the balances of Debt or Credit, or Turn out just equal.   and here it was agreed to
leave the Matter for the present.   As the bill respected, the ascertaining the
balances only. This wa and left the payment to the Cr. States, and the payment
from the Dr. States. to the future operations of the legislature.   all this was far
short of What I wanted. and indeed the bill will turn out as I fear a mere
delusion.   but under its present form the State debts must be embraced in
the Accounts. if the Commissioners do their duty.   and if so this will operate
as a reason Why they should not be assumed.   I was called out by Mr. Hanna.
who was just setting off home.   I wrote a hasty line by him, to Charles Biddle[9]
that the Votes stood this day 28 and 33 on the Residence   staid at the Hall
untill 4 O'Clock and Went to dine with the President.   It was a great dinner in
the Usual stile. without any remarkable occurrence.   Mrs. Washington was
the only Woman present.   I walked from the President's, with Mr. Fitzsimons
part of the Way to his lodgings,   he really seemed good humored, and as if he
wished to be on good Terms with me.   Clymer called on me at our lodgings
in the evening and seemed condescending & good humored in a remarkable degree.   But all in the dumps again about the Residence   only 30 real
Friends to the bill in the House &ca. &ca.

It is time indeed that this Business should be settled. for all our Affairs are
poisoned by it.   Nothing can be plainer than the simple Mode of D⟨ebto⟩r.
& C⟨redito⟩r. for the settlement of the public Accounts of the Union.   But
the State of South Carolina is most miserably in arrear And Wishes to avoid all
settlement. or to have such a partial one as will Screen her defects.   she has
been devoted to New York on the Subject of the Residence.   therefore New
York. (or I should rather write Hamilton) labours incessantly to confuse embarrass and confound all settlement.   the thing cannot be openly denyed,
But they will involve it in so many difficulties. as will either prevent it all
together, or render it Useless, if it should take place.

Friday, 9 July 1790

Attended the Hall at the Usual time.   There was much whispering of the
Members Elsworth⟨,⟩ Strong & Izard.   We had a bill for regulating the

[9]Charles Biddle (1745–1821), secretary of the Pennsylvania Supreme Executive Council
from 1787 to 1790, was born in Philadelphia. A merchant and military ship captain, he spent
most of the years between 1763 and 1784 at sea. He was elected to the Supreme Executive
Council the year he returned to his native city and served for three years. From 1785 to 1787 he
was vice president of Pennsylvania, a position that gave him significant power because of the
poor health of President Benjamin Franklin. (*Philadelphia Families* 1:165–67)

intercourse with the indians Which was passed, a Vile thing Which may be made the basis of much Expence. Superintendants are to be appointed, altho the Superintendance of the Indians in the Government N.W. of the Ohio is already vested in the Governor and so south of the Ohio. By & By we shall have a call for their Salaries. It really seems as if We were to go on making Offices untill all the Cincinnati are provided for. The settlement bill engaged Us Warmly. for the most of this day. The object was to fund the Balances due to the Creditor States & how. Ingenuity itself is tortured to find ways and means of increasing the public demands. and passing by & rendering the State Governments insignificant. I declared What I thought plainly on the Subject. That the bill was one for the Settlement but not the payments of the respective balances That the old confederation clearly contemplated. the payment of the balances from the delinquent States to the Creditor States. That every Act of the old Government carried this on the face of it. That altho' We could not lay unequal Taxes, Yet the adoption of the New Constitution did not go to the discharge of Just debts due from the States Which might be hereafter found Debtors. And that Congress certainly had the power of liquidating the balances, and making the demands from the Debtor States. The bill after a long debate passed on the Principle of a settlement bill only.

I find by Letters which I have received, That the public Creditors, are to be the Body Who are to rise in Judgment against me and try to expell me from the Senate. This is only What I expected. {Nor are they the Only Ones, The Adoption of the New Constitution raised A Singular ferment In the Minds of Men. Every One ill At ease In his Finances Every One Out at Elbows In his Circumstances, Every Ambitious Man every One desirous of a Short cut to Wealth & honors cast their Eyes on the New Constitution, As the Machine Which Could be Wrought to their Purposes, either in the funds of Speculation It Would afford the Offices it Would create. Or the Jobs to be obtained Under it. Not One of these has found a Patron in me In fact I have Generally set My face against Such Pretensions. As Such Men are generally Wantg. in Virtue, their Displeasure, Nay their resentment May be expected. Why *You Want nothing neither for Yourself nor Friends,* Said A Senator, One day, to Me, in some Surprize. It was somewhat Selfish, but I could not help Uttering a Wish, *That he could say so, With truth, of every One.*}

Saturday, 10 July 1790

being Saturday the Senate did not meet. But I went to the Hall by a kind of instinct created by Custom. something like a Stage Coach which always performs it⟨s⟩ Tour Whether full or empty. I met King & Langdon here, we spent an hour or Two in very familiar Chat, nothing worth noting. unless it was the declaration of King That a bargain was certainly made, on the Subject of the Residence, to obtain at least One Vote in the Room of his. as it was most likely he would vote against the Assumption, if the Residence went to Philada. I was astonished at King's owning this. Which in fact amounted to this. That he had engaged his Vote for the Assumption, if the Residence stayed in New York.

Sunday, 11 July 1790

Sunday the 11th was with me a very dull day I read at home wrote the usual letters to my family and other Correspondents. After dinner Walked alone out on the Commons beyond the Bowery Wherever I could find any Green Grass or get out of the dust which was very troublesome on the Roads.

Monday, 12 July 1790

Attended at the Hall at the usual time. We received Two Messages from the Representatives one of them contained the Residence bill. We had considerable Debate on the Post Office bill. insisted on our amendments and appointed a Committee to confer— insisted on our amendment to the indian intercourse bill And passed the Tonnage. This bill deserves a re-mark. the bill is in every respect the same as the old one bating the Remission of some unintentional severities which had fallen on some Fishermen & Coasters. Which were remitted. the taking all the time & passing all the forms of a New bill, would perhaps bear an interpretation as if We feared running out of Work. A Motion was made for taking up the funding bill but Withdrawn. no other Serious business was gone on. the House ad-journed. a number of Us ~~got~~ gathered in a knot and got on the Subject of the Assumption. the report on Which had been just handed in by Mr. Carrol. It is in favour of it. And now from Every appearance Hamilton has got his number made up. he wanted but one Vote long ago. The flexible *Reed* was bent for this purpose some time ago. and Carrol having joined, to make up the Defection of King. The mine is ready to be Sprung. Since I am obliged to give up Carrol's political Character. I am ready to say Who is the just Man that doeth right & sinneth not? The Sum they have reported to be assumed is Twenty One Millions of Dollars. This is most ~~indubiably~~ indubitably to cover the ~~Assump~~ Speculations That have been made in the State debts. This Assumption will immediately raise the Value of the State Securities and enable those People Who have plunged themselves over head and ears. in these Speculations to emerge from impending ruin. and secure them the

Wages of Speculation. The Report is Ordered to be printed. After dismissing this Subject We got on the ~~Subject~~ prospect of an approaching War between Spain and England. here was a large Field for conjecture and We indulged our Fancies on the Subject Untill near three O'Clock.

☛I will here note down an Observation which which, I wonder never made an impression on the Pennsylvanians. Every State is charged with having local Views designs &ca. could any motives of this kind be justly ~~charch~~ chargeable on our State in adopting the constitution by our impost we laid many of the neighbouring states under contribution. part of Jersey Delaware part of Virginia, and almost the whole of the Western Country. it appears One 4th of the Whole impost is received at Philada. This was a great Sacrifice. Quere did our Polititians ever think of this advantage?

Tuesday, 13 July 1790

I attended this day at the Hall at the usual time or rather Sooner General Schyler only was before me. Our President came next they sat opposite to me and we had a long Chat on Various Subjects. but nothing Very interesting Mr. Morris came at last. The Resolutions for the Assumption of 21,000,000 Millions of the State Debts was taken up. This was perhaps the most disorderly day ever We had in Senate. Butler was irregular beyond all bearing. Mr. Morris said openly before Senate was formed *I am for a 6 ⅌ Cent. fund on the Whole, and if Gentlemen will not vote for that I will vote against the Assumption.* I thought him only in Sport then. But he three times in Senate openly avowed the same thing. declaring he was in Judgment for the Assumption. But if Gentlemen would not vote for 6 ⅌ Cent. he would Vote against the Assumption. and the Whole funding bill. his adding the funding bill along with it, in the last instance, operated as some kind of palliative. But I really was struck with astonishment to hear him offer his Vote to sale in so unreserved a ~~Matt~~ Manner. Izard got up & attacked him with asperity. Mr. Morris rose in Opposition. Then Izard declared he did not mean Mr. Morris. so much did he fear the loss of his Vote. But his invective was inapplicable to any body Else. I was twice up and bore my most pointed testimony against the Assumption. It was incurring a certain debt on uncertain Principles. the certain effect was the incurring and encreasing our Debt by 21,000,000. by mere conjecture. this debt was already funded by the States and was in a Train of Payment. Why not settle, and let Us see how the Accounts stand before the States are discharged of their State Debts. I alledged the funds on which these debts were charged by the States, were those by which the States could pay with the greatest facility. as every State had facilities of this kind. the transferring the Debts to any general fund. would lose these local advantages.   it was dealing in the dark   we had no Authentic Evidence of these debts.   if it was meant as an experiment how far People would bear taxation, it was a dangerous one.   I had no notion of drilling People to a Service of this kind.   &ca. &ca.   But I cannot pretend to write all I said.   Mr. Morris has twice this day told me what Great disturbances there would be in Pennsylvania if 6℀ Cent. was not carried.   I consider these things as threats thrown out against my reappointment.   but be it so.   So healp me God, I mean not to alter One Tittle.   I am firmly determined to act without any regard to consequences of this kind.   every Legislator ought to regard himself as immortal.

Wednesday, 14 July 1790

This day the Resolutions on the Assumption were taken up   I am so sick and so Vexed with this angry subject that I hate to commit any thing to writing on the Subject respecting it.   I will however seal one of the copies of it in this book as a monument of political Absurdity.[10]   It had friends enough 14 to 12 so far but I am not without hopes of destroying it tomorrow.   I am now convinced That there must have been something in the Way of bargain as King alledged on Saturday   It must have been managed with Butler.   Elsworth at one time this day used the following Words.   *No Man contemplates a final liquidation of the Accounts between the U.S. and I⟨ndividual⟩ S⟨tates⟩ as practicable or probable*   I took them down and shewed them to Mr. Morris and Mr. Walker.   he observed me & after some time got up. and in the Course of speaking. said *a settlement was practicable and we must have it*.   He will absolutely say anything.   nor can I believe that he has a particle of Principle in his composition.   Mr. Morris⟨,⟩ Langdon & others moved to Strike out the 5th 3d section   We of the opposition Joined Elsworth & kept it in.   the State of Pennsylvania has not but about One Million of existing State Debt.   This Clause if the Vile bill must pass may be considered as in her favour. more especially if they prevail and prevent a Settlement of the Accounts   I saw Mr. Petett. Yesterday at the Levee and as. I was advised by letter that he was appointed Agent for the Settlement of the Pennsylvania Accounts with the Union. I waited on him. with great Joy hoping for much information on that Subject.   But What a disappointment?   he could tell me nothing about them. but was come here to gain information and return back again.   seemed to speak rather unfriendly of the Comptroller.[11] as to What he had done about the Accounts.   This surpriz'd me.   he quit the Subject with impatience & attacked me rather with rudeness on the subject of the public Debts.   I have

---

[10]WM wafered a printed copy of the committee report of 12 July into his diary at this point. For the text of the report, see *DHFFC* 5:923–26.
[11]John Nicholson.

heard him spoke of, as smoth artful & insinuating. he certainly displayed none of these Qualities And as to the public Accounts. he seems rather an Agent for the public Creditors. and talked of the Settlement as a very distant object— {He teized me to tell him Who Were the principal Holders of Certificates in Boston New Port New York &ca. declaring that he wished to correspond with them and Unite them in the common cause. I cannot help regarding him as the Curse of Pennsylvania. for some time After the War Certificates were sold as low as 9∂. in the £ John Ray my old Servt.[12] told me that he sold one of £80 for £3 & could get no more. But it appears by a Remonstrance of the Executive Council, to the Legislature of Pennsylvania, entered on their Minutes, that the Market price was 2/6 in the £ at the time of passing the funding Law, Yet by the instrumentality of this Man on a Weak (and in some cases interested) legislature. 6 ₩ Cent. was given on the Certificates or 48 ₩ Cent. on the real Specie Value. this Pennsyla. paid for 4 Years. As the Certificates were generally below 2/6 it is no exageration to say Every Speculator doubled his Money in 4 Years. And Still has the Certificates on Which he expects the 48 ₩ Cent. with respect to the Original Cost. thus 100 £ Specie bought £800 in Certificates (perhaps much more) these Certificates brought 48 £ ₩ Ann. for 4 Years = 192 £ and the Holders of Certificates remain as clamorous as ever.}

Thursday, 15 July 1790

The Business of the Senate was soon done this day. the President took up the funding bill without any call for it. Mr. Morris appeared in high good humor. asked if any body had taken me aside to communicate anything to me. I told him no. But it was easy to observe that something was going On. he said there was. but did not tell me What it was nor did he affect to know. I saw Carrol writing a Ticket with a number of names on it. Sand and put it by. In the Mean While Up rose Elsworth and moved that both the funding bill & the Resolutions for the Assumption should be referred to a Committee. he was seconded soon. Lee rose said. he knew no good could come from a committment Mr. Morris rose said he was for the Committment. That they might be made in one Law. and the Rate of interest fixed at 6 ₩ Cent. I rose said I know of but Two Ends generally proposed by committment, The One was to gain information the other to arrange principles agreed on the first was out of the Question the second only could be the object, but what were the materials to be arranged. a bill originated in

---

[12]John Ray, a former WM servant who resided at Chillisquaque near Sunbury, was with WM in December 1775 when he and other Pennsylvanians attacked the Connecticut settlers in the Wyoming Valley and in the autumn of 1785, when he delivered various goods to the Six Nations after the Treaty of Fort Stanwix. (*NCHSP* 2:58, 9:39, 11:196)

the other House and Resolves on the Assumption which had originated in this. I knew the Opinion of Many of the Representatives, was opposed to our powers of originating, any thing relating to the Subjects of the ~~deb~~ public Debts, taking Two so dissimilar Objects together, more especially if our powers were called in Question, was the way to loose both. Gentlemen hoped much good from the Measure. I wished they might not be disappointed. But I was not certain of anything but delay. which in our Present Circumstances I considered as an Evil &ca. &ca. Mr. President who was to appearance in the Secret seemed impatient untill I had done. and putting the Question it was carried. the Risers were all the 6 ₱ Cent. Men and all the Assumption Men. they carried the Committee all of their own number.
This done the Senate adjourned. Henry came and Sat beside me a good While. He told me That Carrol wrote his Ticket with the 7 names (that being the number of the Committee) before ~~a Word of~~ any Business Whatever was done. This I had observed in part myself. We did not need this demonstration. to prove that ~~that~~ the Whole Business was prearranged. {Nor can Any Person be now at a loss to discover That All the three Subjects Residence Assumption and funds equivalent to Six ₱ Cent Were all bargained & contracted for On the principles of Mutual Accomodation for Private Interest.
The President of the U.S. has (in my Opinion) had Great Influence in this Business. The Game Was played by him and his Adherents of Virginia & Maryland. between ⟨New⟩ York & Philada. to Give One of those places the Temporary Residence. But the permanent Residence on the Potowmack. I found a demonstration That this Was the Case And That ⟨New⟩ York Would have Accepted of the Temporary Residence if We did not. But I did not then see so clearly That the Abominations of the funding System and the Assumption Were so intimately connected With it. Alas! That the Affection nay Almost ~~Vene~~ Adoration of the People should meet so unworthy a return. here are their best Interests sacrificed to the Vain Whim of fixing Congress And a Great Commercial Town (so opposite to the Genius of ~~Suth~~ the Southern Planter) on the Potowmack. And the President has become in the hands of Hamilton The Dishclout of every dirty Speculation, as his name Goes to ~~cover everything~~ Wipe away blame and Silence all Murmuring.}

Friday, 16 July 1790

Senate had not been formed but a few minutes When a ~~bill~~ Message from the President of the U.S. was announced. It was Lear And the Communication the Signature of the President to the Residence bill was the Communication. The Pension Bill came up from the House of Representatives the Committee on the Indian Bill reported. that 20,000 doll. in addition to 7,000 in the hands of the Secretary of War and 6,000 in Georgia in goods should be granted for the holding Treaties with the Indians. and all this When there does not appear a Shadow of reason for holding a Treaty at all with any Indians Whatever. opposition was vain It was carried. now Mr. Morris came raging angry. said and Swore he would Vote against every thing, the Committee had agreed to the Secretarys 3d Alternative for the principal and 3 ℔ Cent on the Interest due. and he had left them. the Report[13] came in after some time and it was proceeded on. I wispered to Mr. Morris now we had got the Residence. It was our province to guard the Union and promote the Strength of the Union by every Means in our power. otherwise our prize would be a blank. I told him I would move a postponement of the Business, and I would wish a Meeting of the delegation this Evening he assented. a Vast deal was said on the Subject of the Contract and breach of Obligation When I rose I stated that I had no difficulty on that head. That we stood here as legislators, Judges and Executive officers were bound to observe Laws and Contracts. But Justice was the great Rule which we should Govern our Conduct by. the holder of the certificate called do me Justice. but the original holder performer of the Service, Who sold it for One eight⟨h⟩ part of the nominal Value. and on Whom the Tax, to make it good is about to fall. cries Do me Justice also. both sides of this picture ought to be viewed. and their relative numbers to each other. no guess could be made in this Matter. but by comparing the number of Speculators with the number of those Who had sold and perhaps the ratio would not be to 1 to 100. It was also true there were a Class of Men the Original holders Whom were not embraced in the above description. but if we cast our Eye over the Calamities of the late War, they would appear to be the fortunate Characters. all the others Who touched continental Money were taxed by it, and it finally sunk in their hands. the Original holders have at least if not the Whole Value at least something to Show &ca. &ca. I hoped for the progress of the public business. and that a Short postponement would perhaps bring Us nearer together and moved for tomorrow but it was not carried. the Report was pushed with Violence. and all carried. 20 members rising for it 4 only sat. 2 were out. the President said 20 for 4 against— When they came to the part for engrafting the Assumption Resolves on the bill Mr. Lee with what Assistance I gave him retarded the Business a little. When I spoke I endeavoured to narrow the Ground a little, and Spoke solely to the Question of combining the Assumption with the funding bill. the funding bill. was to provide for the Domestic debt which floated at large. and was at this time in no train of payment. the Propriety of paying the foreign and Domestic was admitted by every person It was really the Business which brought Us together. But here we must not

---

[13]The committee that reported, and on which Morris served, was appointed on 15 July to consider the Funding Act [HR-63] and the 12 July committee report on it.

pass it, unless we tack to it another which Which we consider as a political Absurdity. This was contradicting the Spirit of free legislation Every Subject ought to hang on its own merits. It was offering Violence to our Understandings. I said a good deal on the Subject. and could not restrain myself from going into the Merits of the Assumption but I might as well have poured out speech to senseless Stocks or Stones. It was carried against Us. 15 to 11. a Committee was immediately appointed to make the Arrangements. We adjourned. I came down Stairs and all the Speculators both of the Representatives and City were about the Iron Rails. Ames & Sedgwick were conspicuous among them. The Secretary & his group of Speculators, are at last in a degree triumphant. his Gladiators with the influence that has arisen from 6 doll. ℘ day, has wasted Us Months in this place. but I cannot see that I can do any further good here and I think I had better go home. {Every thing even to the Naming of A Committee is prearranged by Hamilton & his Group of Speculators, I cannot even find a Single Member to condole in sincerity with me, over the political Calamities of my Country. Let me deliver myself from the Society of Such Men, for I verily believe the Sun never shone upon a More abandoned Composition of Political Characters.}

Saturday, 17 July 1790

having some Leisure this Morning I called on Dr. Williamson. and told him my intention of going home. he got into a long tale of his settling his Children in Philada. and taking a More northern position for his Family than N. Carolina. &c. &ca. by the way would only remark he has one Child only born. but he has begotten another, as he says. but no Gray headed Man ever was fuller of future arrangements for a numerous progeny he went into the Hall and every body soon had it that I was going home &c. &ca. I went from here and called on Fitzsimons & Clymer told them I wished to go home, but had no Objection to take the Sense of the Delegation on the Measure. Fitzsimons said nothing but looked, *Go to the Devil,* as I thought. Clymer spoke most pointedly against my going. said We would lost 9 Votes south of Virginia. on a Postponement bill[14] which was going to be brought forward. By the by We never had but 7 from that Quarter. I told him. the Delegation were to dine together tomorrow. if it was their Opinion That I should Stay I would do so.

Attended at the Hall little was Done and We sat waiting an hour for the Committee to report the bill with amendments.[15] It was done an attempt

---

[14]On 5 August, the House rejected 35 to 23 a motion by Bloodworth that a bill be prepared postponing for a limited time the portion of the Residence Act [S-12] that mandated the removal of Congress to Philadelphia before the third session of the FFC.

[15]The Funding Act [HR-63] and the two committee reports on it had been recommitted on 16 July.

was made to pass it immediately by a third reading. down to the House of Representatives it was moved that it should be printed. this was opposed the President gave the History of both the Bill & Resolutions, with respect to Order he made this out to be third reading. and of Course the Question would be the sending it to the Representatives It was now proposed as an expedient that the Cl Secretary should read the bill from his desk for information of the members this obtained. and now behold to a great Many innovations and amendments a Whole New Clause Was added. There was something of unfairness in this. It was however Ordered to be printed for Monday. When I came down Stairs Mr. Clymer came to Where I stood with Genl. Irwin. We talked over the General belief That the Assumption was forced upon Us to favour the Vi⟨e⟩ws of Speculation Mr. Clymer mentioned One Contract on Which about 8/ in the pound had been cleared in £80,000. Genl. Irwin seemed to Scruple 8/ in the £. Mr. Clymer said he was not so sure of the rate Cleared, but the Sum Speculated on Was 80,000. Much of this Business is done in the Change Alley Way.[16] Constable however is known in the Spe Begining of the session to have cleared 35,000 doll. on a Contract for 70,000— The Whole Town almost has been busy at it & of Course all engaged in influencing the Measures of Congress— {Nor have the Members themselves kept their hands clean from this dirty work. from Wadsworth with his boatload of Money, down to the daily Six dollars, have they generally been at it. The Unexampled Success, has obliterated every Mark of reproach. and from henceforth we may consider Speculation As a congressional Employment. Nay all the Abomin⟨a⟩tions of the South Sea Bubble[17] are Outdone in this dirty Work Vile Business. in Wrath I wish the Same fate May attend the Projectors of both.}

Sunday, 18 July 1790

This day the Delegation dined at Brandon's. Mr. Morris [*lined out*] stated to the Representatives the Train the Business was in with the Senate. mentioned the importance of compleating the funding Law. particularly to Us Who now had the Residence of Congress before Us. That the Rising of Congress without funding might go to shake and injure the Government itself &ca. We had much talk but nothing was concluded, or any agreement entered into. Mr. Fitzsimons avowed in the most unequivocal Manner. the grand object of the Assumption to be *the collecting all the resources of the United States into One Treasury.* &ca. speaking of the State of Pennsylvania,

---

[16]The Change Alley was the location in London where stocks were sold.
[17]The South Sea Bubble was the name applied to the financial scheme by which the British South Sea Company attempted to buy up the national debt in 1720. The speculation collapsed, and its name became a symbol for the dangers of stock speculation.

he averred she would be a Debtor State to a large amount on the Settlement of the Accounts and the next moment said she would draw interest on 3,000,000 Doll. annually   It is not easy to reconcile his assertions on this Subject—   a great deal of loose talk passed among Us.   As I had the delegation together. I mentioned my intention of going home. and desired to know if any of them had any Objection.   the Discourse soon took a ludicrous turn but no Objection was made. and I believe I will set off tomorrow afternoon.

Monday, 19 July 1790

have made up my mind on the Subject of going home.   I cannot serve my country any thing by my staying longer here.   I will certainly feel ashamed to meet the face of any Pennsylvania⟨n⟩ Who shall put me to the Question What have You done for the publick Good   I can answer with Truth I have been trying the best in my Power.   settled with the Speaker   he would have nothing for any liquors but said his Boy had cost him 50 Doll. which he desired me to pay One third of.   I agreed.   he had about 40/ of my Money in his hands.   I owe him 4:6:3 Pennsylva.   I will recollect the Service of the Boy was mentioned, Who or at least all the services which I wanted in that way, when I agreed for my Boarding at 4 doll. ⅌ Week   I have drunk occasionally some of his Wine.   he said not amounting to more than a Bottle or Two.   I am convinced it would not amount to Gallons.   But I most chearfully agreed to pay What he proposed.

I attended the Hall at the Usual time.   And now the Material business of the day the consolidated funding bill and Assumption were taken up.   Mr. Morris shewed a Vindictive and ireful disposition from the very Start. and declared he would have the Yeas and nays on every Question   This in fact is declaring War against me only. as it is me only which they can affect in Pennsylvania.   I know they mean to slay me with the Sword of the public Creditors.   he was as good as his Word and moved every point, to increase the Demands against the publick and uniformly called Yeas and nays.   all the Motions were made for the augmentations by him⟨,⟩ Schyler & King.   Vid. the minutes for the Yeas and nays.   When he moved that 6 ⅌ Cent. should be paid on the back interest. as there were but 4 of them for it. and that enough did not rise for the Yeas and Nays. I told him I was sorry to see him in distress, and jumped up.   if I can turn these yeas and nays against him, the Act act will be a righteous one.

In the language and calculations of the Treasury. the first 3d alternative is actually Six ⅌ Cent. without taking in the advantage of Quarterly over annual Payments. grounded on the irredeemable Quality of the debt.   but I really Question if we shall ever see that Change Ally doctrine established here. which makes debt valuable in proportion to ~~the irredeemable~~ that qualification   it never can happen without a gradual fall of interest. which in this Country may be rather considered as improbable.

Before Congress met I walked a While cross the Chamber with Mr. Lee.   he lamented equally with me the baneful Effects, of the funding disease.   no nation ever has adopted it. without having either actually ~~having~~ Suffered Shipwreck~~ed~~, or being on a Voyage that must inevitably end in it.   the Separation from great Britain, seemed to assign Us a long run of political Existence.   but the management of the Secretary, will soon overwhelm Us with political ruin.   Schyler assigned a new kind of reason this day. for Taxation   3 Million & an half of doll. raised annually would be only One doll. ℔ head on an average.   It was nothing &ca.   It is true it is not an heavy tax. but it ought not to be imposed without necessity.   This Wretch is emaciated in person slovenly in dress. and rather aukward in address.   no Jew ever had a more Cent. ℔ Cent. aspect.   he seems the prototype of Covetousness.   nor is it possible to assign to his appearance, any other passion ~~affection~~ property or affection but the love of Money. and the concomitant Character of a Miser.

I cannot help noting something which maybe void of design.   Yesterday Two letters were shewed, at dinner, One by Mr. Morris to the Governor & Council. another by Clymer to the Mayor and corporation.[18]   It was agreed That the Senators should sign the one to the Governor and Council. and the Speaker in behalf of the Delegation, should sign the one to the Corporation.   I was much pleased with this arrangement for there was a Clause in Clymers letter, of advice to erect a new building for Congress, for the giving the State House to Congress. would furnish a reason for removing the Seat of Government Elsewhere.[19]   this day in Senate Mr. Morris produced this last letter to me. desiring me to sign it.   I declined it. telling him the Speaker was to sign that letter.   I could not help concluding there was design in this business.   there was a dinner this day, which I had no notice of, & never thought of such a thing.   in the Evening Mr. Rees Clk. to Mr. Morris called on me with the letter to Government.   this I readily signed but here comes. the Speaker with the other letter for me to sign.   all this does not look like accident,   I told the Speaker my Objections.   there is a Subject in that letter which I never have touched,   I will not touch it now.   I have already wrote fully to the Mayor[20] on the Subject.

---

[18]A copy of the letter from the Pennsylvania delegation to Mayor Samuel Miles, dated 19 July 1790, can be found in the Common Council Minutes, PHi.

[19]The question of moving the seat of the state government to a location west of Philadelphia was an important issue in Pennsylvania politics from 1783 to 1799. A major effort on behalf of Harrisburg failed in 1787. (*Counter Revolution*, pp. 149, 197)

[20]Samuel Powel (1739–93), member of the Pennsylvania Senate from Philadelphia City and County and Delaware County from 1790 until his death, was born in that city and graduated from the College of Philadelphia in 1759. Active in city politics, he served as mayor in 1775 and again in 1789–90, when the office was reinstituted. Powel and his wife,

Tuesday, 20 July 1790

We went this day at the funding system. and pursued it, with nearly the same temper that we did Yesterday   Mr. Morris had often declared himself That he would be for an Assumption equal to the Representation, and had calculated a Schedule for the purpose.   but all I could say to him he would not gratify me in moving it.   I knew there was no chance of carrying it.   But he levelled his Whole force against the 19th Section. which in fact is the only one favourable to our State.   for our existing State debt. cannot be much more than one Million.   I will refer to the minutes for the proceedings of the day.
Mr. Morris having often threatned that he would vote against the bill. at last made this remarkable Speech.   *half a Loaf is better than no bread.   I will consent to the bill on behalf of the public Creditors for whom I am interested* (I looked up at him and he added) *as well as for the rest of the Union.*   This last shed some palliation over his expressions.

I contended that the Speculators generally had dealt on the face of the Certificates, or if they dealt on the amount. it was always at an abated rate. clear proof they never expected the back interest to be funded.   by the ~~law~~ bill every hundred of principal draws 4 annually and as the back interest is about on an average equal to half the principal (at least it is so by the Secretary's report) this at 3 ℔ cent adds $1^1/_2$ more equal $5^1/_2$ ℔ Cent ℔ ann. for 10 Years & then the other third. (or what is equal to it in change Alley calculation) comes in at 6 ℔ Cent. which added gives about $7^1/_2$ ℔ Cent. on the face of the original certificate.

I have turned the leaf to note that I may consider myself as now having passed the Rubicon with the Philadelphians.   I saw Clymer through the Window of the Senate Chamber.   Morris was sent for and went out.   he came in with the same letter Which I had refused to sign Yesterday and asked me to sign it.   I refused and told him plainly, it touched a Subject which I never had touched, ~~now~~ nor would now.   he said no more.   Mr. Morris told me this day I must allow myself to get the lands of which he had spoke to me.
I told him all on my part was ready only, put the Warrants into my hands.   I however added We have ruined our Land Office by the Assumption.   the State Certificates, were the materials to buy lands with.   the offices will now be shut. for neither State Money nor Specie can be got. or spaired for it.   he was silent. and I really thought he looked as if he feared that his conduct. would be turned against him in ~~this business~~ In the public Eye.

After dinner this day, I read a letter to the Speaker, from John Montgomery of Carlisle[21] not. much in favour of Mr. Morris.   he then gave me the follow-

---

Elizabeth Willing Powel (1743–1830), were intimates of George and Martha Washington. (*Philadelphia Families* 1:111–12; *DGW* 4:210n)
    [21]John Montgomery (1722–1808), who represented Cumberland County in the 1790–91 Pennsylvania House of Representatives, arrived in Carlisle from northern Ireland about 1740

ing intelligence.   That Fitzsimons and Mr. Morris adherents, fearful. That he
could not be carried by a popular Election. were determined, to change the
mode to Electors, but all the difficulty was to know how Wilson could save his
Credit in Convention, and carry his party over with him. After What had
already happened.   this being one of the pillars on which his late popularity
was supported.   It is easy to see the reason of all this.   The mode of Electors,
admits of more cabal intreague &ca. &ca.[22]

Wednesday, 21 July 1790

King's motion of Yesterday for postponement,[23] And Sundry other Matters
which I had observed, made me fearful that Some Storm was gathering,   I
called on Mr. Morris and expressed my apprehension, and Proposed to him,
That if any Unexpected maneuvre should display itself, We should with the
Utmost apparent coolness call for a Concurrence of the Resolution for the
adjournmt. of on the 27th.   Attended at the Hall on the Affair of Donald
Campbell.[24] The most impudent & ill founded set of claims, ever I was Witness to.
    The first Business in the Senate was the new Bill of Ways and Means.   Com-
mitted.
    A Message with a bill respecting Consuls & Vice Consuls.   The bill for the
Military grants of Land to the Virginia Officers.   Committed.
    The Senate was now full and the funding Bill Was taken up for the last
time.   I made a dying a despairing Effort.   Having Almost Uniformly opposed the Measures of Congress during the present Session, some general
Declarations of my principles or Motives may be necessary, to prevent any
Suspicion of a disposition inimical to the Government itself.   first then I am
totally opposed to the practice of funding, upon republican as well as œco-
nomical principles.   I deny the power as well as Justice of the Present Generation charging debts more especially irredeemable Ones upon Posterity,   And
I am convinced that they will One day negative the legacy.   I will suppose
(Suppositions are common in this house) that not one Member of Congress,
has been influenced by any personal Motive Whatever in Arranging the Amer-

and established himself as a merchant. He served on various revolutionary committees at the
outset of the War for Independence, in the assembly from 1781 to 1782, and in Congress from
1782 to 1784.
    [22]A problem for those advocating the use of electors in the election for governor was how
to achieve this goal at the second sitting of the state constitutional convention in August,
since their ally, James Wilson, had been a strong proponent of popular election at the first
sitting. (*PBR*, pp. 290n–291n; *NQ*[3], pp. 3, 48)
    [23]King's motion was for the postponement of the Funding Act [HR-63].
    [24]WM was a member of the select committee on Campbell's petition. Donald Campbell
(c. 1740–1800) of New York petitioned the FFC for compensation for his services during the
War for Independence. See also the petition volumes.

ican funding System, Which now spins on the doubtful point of pass or not pass And As it falls may turn up Happiness or Misery for centuries to come No I will take Gentlemen at their Word, and believe that it is the Glare of British Grandeur, suppos'd to flow from her funds, That has influenced their Conduct, And that their intentions are pure Wishing to render America great & happy by a Similar System.   This will lead to an Inquiry into the Actual State of Brittain,   And here I trust we shall find All is not Gold that Glitters.

It is (if I mistake not) about a Century since the Commencement of the English funds or in other Words, since that Nation began to Mortgage the Industry of Posterity, to gratify the Ambition & Avarice of the then Government.   Since that period Wars have been Almost continual.   The pretexts have been ridiculous.   Balance of power, balance of Trade Honor of the Flag &ca. Sover⟨e⟩ignty at Sea &ca.   but the real Object was to fill the Treasury, to furnish Opportunity for royal peculation, Jobs & Contracts for needy Courtiers, to encrease the power of the Crown by the Multiplication of Revenue & military appointments, And the Servility of the funds; for every Stockholder is of Course a Courtier.   The effect of these Wars has been the Commotion of almost the Whole World, And the loss of Millions of lives, And the English Nation stands at this day charged with a debt of about 250 Millions Sterlg. the Annual interest of Which and Charges of Collecting in that Country is above 11 Millions annually And would be above 15 in this.   It has been been said that this is nothing in a National point of View, As the Nation Owes it to Individuals among themselves,   this is true only in part, as foreigners draw great Sums.   Yet it is believed that near half a Million of the Inhabitants of Great Brittain including Army Navy Revenue and Stockholders are supported from the Treasury, the Whole of them be the number What it may, must be considered As Unproductive Drones, Who are ever ready to support Administration be it ever so oppressive to their Fellow Citizens.   There is another Calcula-⟨tion⟩ said to be much more exact   Viz. that nea⟨r⟩ a Million of Paupers, reduced by exorbitant taxes below the power of house Keeping, are dependent on National Charity & the poor rates.   Great Cry has been made about Mr. Pitt, as the Political Savior of his Country, that he has paid part & will finally discharge the Whole of the National debt.   This is a Vile Deception—by some Management between him and the Stock-Jobbers   As he buys they raise the price of the remaining Stock—the Aggregate Value of which is now greater at Market price than When he began to purchase.   so that the nation instead of gain⟨in⟩g. is a looser by to the amount of the new duties imposed.   It is not likely That the trad⟨in⟩g. of Government in Stock or Certificates ever will have a different Effect.   There is another part of his Conduct for which I am ready to give him proper Credit,   He seems, by his Sham Armaments, to have hit on an Expedient to plunder the Nation without Bloodshed;   let him enjoy this praise in common with other English Robbers, Who (Unlike those of other

Nations) seldom accompany their depradations with Murder. It is in Vain to expect the payment of the British ~~national~~ debt, in any other way than by a National Bankruptcy And Revolution. Is this then the precipice to Which We would reduce the rising Nation of North America? It may be said none of Us Will live to see it, let Us, at least, ~~preserve~~ Guard our Memories, from the reproach of such Misconduct. It may be here Asked What then is to be done? Just What the public Expectation called for. The Western lands have been considered, from the begining of the late Contest, As the fund for discharging the Expences of the War, The old Congress made laudable Advances in this way. The present session has not passed without Applications on that Subject As well from Companies Among Ourselves, As Persons from Europe. We have now a Revenue far exceeding the limited 5 ₩ Cent. Which was the desideratum of the Old Congress And the Want of Which Occasioned the formation of our present Constitution, And fully Sufficient to discharge A Reasonable interest proportionate to the Market price of the public Debt, Untill the Whole is extinguished by the Western Sales. thus no One Will Sustain loss— Substantial Justice Will be done And the public Expectation will be fully satisfyed. But to bind down the public by an irredeemable debt. W~~hich~~ith such sources of payment in our power. is equally Absurd As shakling the hands & feet with fetters rather than walking at liberty.

The friends of the Bill paid no Attention Whatever to me & were but too Successful in engaging the Attention of others by nods Whispers engaging in Conversation &ca. Morris⟨,⟩ Dalton And some others Went out & staid for an Hour. they Carried the bill against Us 14 to 12 It is in Vain to dissemble the Chagrin, Which I have felt On this Occasion— We had a Resolution relating to Howel's Clerks.[25] Committed. I am of the Committee. Report of Joint Committee on Settlement bill read, for information but could not be Acted On As the bill is in the power of the lower House. I find I need be Under No Uneasiness About the Residence Bill.

Thursday, 22 July 1790

Attended the Hall this day a⟨s⟩ mu⟨ch⟩ to take the Wrinkles out of my face, which my Yesterdays disappointment, had placed in it as for anything Else, It is in Vain to think of changing a Vote Anyway A Majority are sold & Hamilton has bought them. I can be of no further Use And will Absolutely leave them. It is certainly a defect in my political Character That I cannot help embarking my passions, & Considering the interest of the public As my own It was so While I was at the Bar in respect of my Clients When I thought their Cause just Well be it so, it has it's inconveniencies & hurts my health

---

[25]The resolution that was committed related to the salaries of clerks in the office of the Commissioner of Army Accounts, Joseph Howell. See the petition volumes.

but I declare I never will endeavour to mend it.   Attended all the Committees ~~& Gave~~ On Which I was and Gave my Opinion As to the Reports &ca.

In Senate the Collection Bill was reported   Almost an intire new System or the old One so renovated As to make a Volume of New Work for Congress.   I listened an Hour to the Reading of It.   rose   bad⟨e⟩ a silent and lasting farewell to the Hall And went to my Lodgings for the purpose of packing.[26]

{And now at last we have taken leave of New York   It is natural to look at the prospect before Us.   The Citizens of Philada. (such is the Strange infatuation of self-love) believe That ten Years is Eternity to them with respect to the residence. ~~Th~~ & that Congress Will in That Time be so enamoured of them As never to leave them.   And all this with the recent example of New York before their Eyes.   Whose Allurements are More than Ten to Two compared with Philada.   to tell the Truth I know no so unsocial a City as Philada.   The Gloomy Severity of the Quakers has proscribed all fashionable dress and Amusement.   denying themselves these enjoyments they as much As in them lies endeavour to deprive others of them Also.   While at the same Time there are not in the World more scornful nor insolent Characters than the Wealthy among them.   Witness the Wartons⟨,⟩ Pembertons &ca.[27]   No these feeble expectations Will fail   go they Must.   Nay taking it in another point of View Political necessity Urges them; And a disruption of the Union Would be the consequence of a refusal.   There is however a further and more latent danger Which attends their going.   Fixed as congress Will be among Men of other Minds on the Potowmack, a new Influence Will in all probability take place.   And the Men of New England, Who have hitherto been held in check ~~only~~ by the Patronage & loaves & Fishes of the President, combined with a firm expectation that his resignation (which is expected) will throw all power into their hands. ~~Will~~ may become refractory and endeavour to Unhinge the Government.   For my knowlege of the Eastern Characters Warrants me in drawing this conclusion, that they Will cabal against And endeavour to subvert Any Government which they have not the Management of.

The Effect must be sensibly felt in Philada. Should a great commercial Town arise on the Potowmack.   She now supplies all the over hills Country And even the Frontiers of Virginia & other Southern States with Importations. this must cease, nor need she expect A Single Article of Country produc⟨e⟩, in return from the West side of Susquehannah.   It is true That the Genius of Virginia and Maryland too, is rather averse to extensive Commerce.   The Southern Planter situated on his extensive domain surrounded with his Slaves & dependants feels diminution and looses his consequence by being Jumbled

---

[26]WM later stated that his departure from New York was hastened by receipt of information that his wife's health was in a perilous condition. (To Rush, 30 July 1790, Rush Papers, DLC)

[27]The Whartons and the Pembertons were prominent Philadelphia Quaker merchant families whose members held political office. (*Philadelphia Families* 1:276–315, 531–45)

among Brokers & Factors.   And Yet We have seen What Baltimore has become in a few Years. From the Small beginings of a few Pennsylvanians at first
and afterwards by the Accession of other Strangers.   for Wherever the Carcase
of Commerce is, thither will the Eagles of Traffick be gathered.   For my own
part I would rather Wish That the Residence of Congress, should not be
Subject to commercial Influence.   too Much has that Influence, conducted
by the ~~Councils~~ Interest of New England Whose naval connections throws
them onto that Scale, governed, nay tyranniz'd in the Councils of the
Union.   My consolation for going to the Potowmack is that it may give a
preponderance to the Agricultural Interest.   dire indeed will be the contest
but I hope it Will prevail.   I cannot however help concluding that all this
~~Tings~~ Things would have been better on the Susquehannah.   But Quere, is
not this Selfish too?   Aye, But it May nevertheless be just.}

Miscellaneous Notes

Philada. August 27th[1]

Rascality personifyed in the conduct of the Two Blanks[2] my former Friends— from the Drift of Chaff & feathers is found how the Wind blows. the Catastrophe of the Catalogues. & concomitant circumstances nulla fides fronti, ang⟨e⟩lica,[3] political Air highly pestilential.

It is determined, by a several powerful parties to destroy me politically. Lewis & Peters have had their former resentments reinforced by Rawles indignation against my Brother on the Subject of the Comptroller[4] and the division of Dauphin County.[5] Lewis has roused the Bar against me Smith[6] in our own County. Ross[7] over the Alleganey Mountains Duncan[8] in Carlisle &ca. to this is joined the wi⟨sh⟩ for ~~these~~ the office Which I hold. But the unparalelled attempt of the Muhlenbergs is base beyond description. *If you wish to be served a dirty trick* said Zantzinger, *put it in the power of a Dutchman.* how often and how fully have I found this veryfyed— put him ⟨out⟩ say one party for he is a tool to Morris put him out say the other party, for he will not follow Morris. but put him out to make room. is the real Reason.

Sepr. 1st a coalition has taken place between the rump of the constitutionalists and the Germ⟨ans⟩ the price of the bargain is my office to be given to General Muhlenberg. the Whole System was developed, and communi-

---

[1]The notes for August and September 1790 appear on two pages at the end of volume 2 of the manuscript diary, after the December 1790 entries. With both the assembly and the constitutional convention in session, WM recognized the importance of visiting Philadelphia so that he could defend his record in the Senate. To refresh his memory, he brought along his diary. The last three notes may have been written either then or when WM returned to Philadelphia for the third session of the FFC.

[2]WM meant Representatives Frederick and Peter Muhlenberg, the Pennsylvania Germans or "Dutchmen" with whom he had resided during the second session of the FFC.

[3]There is no reliance on your angelic appearance.

[4]John Nicholson.

[5]Soon after Dauphin County was established in 1785, attempts were made to divide it. In 1813 its southeastern townships became Lebanon County. (Luther Kelker, *History of Dauphin County, Pennsylvania*, 3 vols. [New York, 1907], 1:chap. 3)

[6]WM probably meant Charles Smith (1765–1836), a lawyer who represented Northumberland County at the Lancaster Convention in 1788 and in the state constitutional convention of 1789–90. He was the son of Provost William Smith of the College of Philadelphia. (*PMHB* 4:380–81)

[7]James Ross (1762–1847), a delegate from Washington County to the 1789–90 state constitutional convention, was a lawyer.

[8]Stephen Duncan (c. 1729–94) was a Carlisle merchant and Cumberland County treasurer. (*NQ*[1898]:151)

cated to Fitzsimons   he said *as the reappointment of a Senator is connected
with the reelection of the Representatives. I will not intermeddle with it.*

Sepr. 1st 1790   let me remember That he expressed himself thus to me, at the
Corner of 2d and Walnut Streets.   he shewed a very different comprection
Yesterday.   Rush asked me a singular question this day.   Does Wilson of the
Council[9]   lodge with You?   this raised a Train of Ideas in my mind.

The Speaker desired to speak with me   he declared he knew nothing of his
Brothers attempt on my place as Senator.   I knew he lied, for he was with
Finley on the Evening of the meeting.   I told him, it was an ungenerous
attempt,   he said he thought so too.   A scholl boy ought to be whipped for
such lies as they both have told—
Memdm. a bargain was made between Charles Biddle Agent for Mifflin and
the Muhlenbergs,   Biddle to give his influence in favour of Peter for Senator,
by which was meant Mifflin's interest, in Consideration that Frederick would
not oppose Mifflin for Governor.   Mifflin in fact owned this to me, on the
morning when, it was reported that Fredk. would stand for the Government.   he stopped me,   said Peter has lost 4 or 5 Votes this Morning by
his Brother standing for the Government.   Charles Biddle will now oppose
him with all his might.   Dr. Edwards[10] however told me of it.   the Sur-
v⟨eyo⟩r. Gen⟨era⟩l.[11] told me such a bargain was made, but was cautious to
conceal the Consideration—   Edwards further told me on 3d. 7ber. that now
Fk. Muhlenberg would stand for the Government, since the Elections were to
be at different times—The disclosure of the Grand Trick having stopped all
business in the Assembly—

Moravian Minister lives in the Corner house of the Moravian Alley, in Race
Street, between second & third Street[12]—

Mr. Adlum receited a Warrt. to One Snell[13] for 20 acres of land, on the first
April 1789—Located on the Tract on which he lives, on the West side &
adjoining Tioga River.

Memorandum respecting Saml. Warton.[14]

[9]William Wilson (d.1813) represented Northumberland County at the ratification convention in 1787, at the Lancaster Convention in 1788, and on the Supreme Executive Council
during its last year of existence. A nephew of Samuel Hunter, he arrived in Northumberland
County from northern Ireland just before the War for Independence and served throughout
the conflict. (*NCHSP* 10:5–24)
[10]Dr. Enoch Edwards (1751–1802), delegate from Philadelphia County to the ratification
and state constitutional conventions, had practiced medicine briefly. (*PMHB* 11:74–75)
[11]Daniel Brodhead.
[12]The Moravian minister at Philadelphia from 1785 to 1799 was John Meder. (Scarf and
Westcott, *Philadelphia* 2:1326)
[13]Probably Jacob Snell of Luzerne County.
[14]Samuel Wharton (1732–1800) was a Philadelphia merchant and land speculator who
became an early advocate of the American cause against Great Britain. (*Philadelphia Families* 1:542)

THIRD SESSION

December 1790

Philadelphia   Wednesday, 1 December 1790

late in the Afternoon I arrived in Philada. in Order to attend Congress which is to meet on Monday next.   Saw nobody this afternoon nor Evening.

Thursday, 2 December 1790

dressed and called first on Genl. Mifflin.   he was abroad.   then on Mr. Morris Who rece⟨i⟩ved me with Frankness,   called on the President.[1] Clymer and at Fitzsimons,   the day soon grew rainy   came home.   heard from my Brother in the Evening That some attempt was making on the Sunbury Lands[2] by One Sewell and Hurst.   this has cut out Work for me in the Morning.

Friday, 3 December 1790

dressed and went early to the Governor's[3]   he was at Breakfast, and had four School boys about him, making them show him their latin Exercises, repeat their Lessons, tell what Books they were reading &ca. &ca.   so much does he love to be the Cock of the School. that he seems actually to court the Company of Children When he is sure he will meet with no contradiction.

---

[1]WM probably called on the president of the United States rather than the president of the Senate. In Philadelphia, Washington resided at 190 High Street (present day Market Street), a mansion built in 1772 and reconstructed in 1785 by its owner, Robert Morris. (Decatur, *Private Affairs of Washington*, p. 159)

[2]WM received a large grant of land near Sunbury from the Penn family as compensation for his work in the survey of the lands granted by the Penns to Pennsylvania officers in the French and Indian War. At one time he owned 2,400 acres in the area. (*NCHSP* 2:51; "William Maclay," *Now and Then* 9:217)

[3]Thomas Mifflin.

his Tongue ran like a Whirligig   there was no getting a Word in among the Children.   I had however considerable Attention paid to me by Two dogs who pawed me over.   I learned that no decision had been given by the board of Property,[4] in the Case of the Sunbury Lands.   took the first Opportunity, I possibly could of withdrawing.   No public Character ever appea⟨red⟩ to me more disgusting.   called on David Kenedy of the Land Office, and made What We thought the best arrangement. respecting the affair of Sunbury—   met with Mr. Langdon. and went a visiting. in which we spent the forenoon.   called in the Evening at McConnel's the Broker.[5]   He told me the public Creditors were very busy under their Chairman, Petitt, preparing petitions Memorials &ca. for Congress.   I made some remarks tending to shew that they were well enough For the purposes intended.   He readily joined me. and said it was carried on to answer electioneering purposes   That Petitt wanted to be in Congress &ca. &ca.   Petitt is my old Enemy, and will supplant me if he can.   {Agreed.}

Saturday, 4 December 1790

I have deliberated much on the Subject Whether I will call to see Bingham⟨,⟩ Powel and others.   I have called on Morris⟨,⟩ Clymer & Fitzsimons   Why not on them,   by the Rules of Etiquette perhaps, they should call on me   I have revolved all over in my mind, Jacta est Alea.[6] and I will go.   But as I went, I fell in with Mr. Clymer and away we went a visiting.   Clymer certainly means to be on good Terms with me.   We had Two long Visits.   I called at Binghams   found him at home and had a long Chat, took leave and left a Card ~~with~~ at Mr. Powel's   called at Mr. Chew's Who Urged me to stay for dinner   I accepted his invitation, For Two OClock and the rest of the day was accordingly disposed of. for it was past three before We sat down.   I called Twice this day at Doctor Rush's but saw him not.   saw the Speaker   the Skeaker said on the Authority of Doctor Rush That We would all be reelected.   {Believe it not.}

---

[4]The board of property, founded in colonial times and reestablished in 1782, settled land office disputes over titles and other issues related to Pennsylvania's vast public lands. It consisted of the president or vice president of the state and an additional member of the Supreme Executive Council (WM had occasionally been that member), the secretary of the land office, the receiver general, and the surveyor general. The board was reconstituted on 6 January 1791 to consist only of the latter three officials and the master of rolls. (*Pennsylvania Statutes* 10:408, 14:6–7)

[5]Mathew McConnell (c. 1743–1816), a Philadelphia merchant and stockbroker, was born in Chester County. In 1787, his *Essay on the Domestic Debts* (E-20470) was published at Philadelphia. (*PMHB* 46:362–63; *American Daily Advertiser*, 12 Nov. 1816; *DHROC* 2:132n)

[6]The die is cast.

Sunday, 5 December 1790

was sent for early by Mr. Morris on the Subject, of taking up Frontier Lands. I agreed to procure him a Draught of such parts of the State as had vacant Lands in them. no contract with him. I mean to have such a draught made for the Use of the Members of Assembly or at least for their information. pressed me to dine with him. did so. Mr. Powel returned my Visit. visited Langdon in the Evening.

Monday, 6 December 1790

My Brother informed me this Morning. That Chas. Thomson had apply'd to One Collins a Member from Berks.[7] for his interest to obtain my place as Senator. It comes very direct and was talked over Yesterday at Blair McClenachan's Where Mathew Irwin dined, from whom my Brother had it.[8] Out some of the Citizens would have me if they should put the Devil in my place. This is what I must expect of them.

Attended the Hall at Eleven,[9] A Senate was formed, but no business done

---

[7]James Collins represented Berks County in the Pennsylvania House of Representatives during the 1790–91 session.

[8]Blair McClenachan (d. 1812) represented Philadelphia County in the 1790–91 Pennsylvania House of Representatives. He arrived in Philadelphia from Ireland before 1762 and a decade later was one of the most successful merchant importers in the city. Although chairman of the 1788 Antifederalist Harrisburg Convention and an unsuccessful candidate for the FFC, McClenachan maintained close business ties with Robert Morris and had accumulated one of the largest holdings of the public debt in Pennsylvania. (*DHFFE* 1:420–21)

Matthew Irwin (c. 1740–1800) was the register of deeds for the City and County of Philadelphia as well as Master of Rolls for Pennsylvania, in which office he had responsibility for the enrollment of state laws. (*CRP* 16:113; *NQ* [1898]:172)

[9]Congress Hall stood on the northwest corner of State House Square, at Chestnut and Sixth streets. Although one Philadelphian had suggested erecting a new building with quiet, elegant, and garden-enhanced quarters west of Broad Street on one of the many still rural squares that William Penn had platted a century earlier, the state decided instead on the County Court House. Originally conceived in 1736, the Philadelphia County Court House was begun in 1787 and completed in March 1789. The brick building's dimensions, two stories approximately sixty-five feet in length by fifty feet in width, provided less than half the amount of floor space of Federal Hall. Between September and December 1790, it was remodeled slightly, primarily to accommodate a visitors' gallery on the first floor, and renamed Congress Hall. The building as it stands today reflects the major renovation of 1793, which included a twenty-eight foot extension to the south.

During the third session of the FFC, the first floor consisted of a ten foot wide vestibule off Chestnut Street and the House chamber itself. Two stairs in the vestibule provided access to the second floor and to the public gallery over the House chamber. From the vestibule one entered a twenty-two by forty-seven foot public standing area or loggia under the gallery. It was separated from the thirty by forty-seven foot carpeted House chamber by a railing. Mahogany desks and arm chairs for the members were arranged in rows and faced an eight foot deep bay on the south side of the building where the speaker presided from a dais. He sat behind a desk in an arm chair under a canopy with curtains. Below and in front of the

save the sending a Message by our Secretary to the Representatives That the Senate was ready to proceed to Business— spent the Rest of the day in Visits &ca.

Tuesday, 7 December 1790

went early this Morning to see if Mr. Montgomery of our County or Mr. White were come in.[10] found none of them. called at Mr. Finley's lodgings in my way home, he said he would call on Me in the Evening.

Col. Antis[11] spent some time this forenoon with me. attended at Eleven at the Hall. an house was formed by the Representatives on the 7th of Jany. last King had introduced, a new Record altogether on the Minutes, the intention of Which was, to secure the delivery of the Presidents Speech in the Senate Chamber. A Resolution Verbatim with the Entry of last Jany. was moved carried and Sent down for Concurrence. While this was done with Us, a Resolution passed the Representatives for a joint Committee waiting on

---

speaker, the clerk and perhaps one or more of his assistants occupied desks. Elsewhere in the chamber desks were provided for the newspaper reporters. Four fireplaces, each with a Franklin stove, provided heat. The windows had curtains and sunlight was controlled by venetian blinds; candles provided additional light when the House remained in session late in the day. Other accoutrements included spitting boxes and a table which held liquid refreshment, including rum, for the members. The office of the Clerk of the House and the House committee room were in the west wing of the State House, a few yards to the east.

The second floor consisted of the Senate chamber at the south end and two smaller rooms separated by a hall leading from the stairs at the north end of the building. The secretary of the Senate used one of the smaller rooms as an office and Senate committees used the other. The richly appointed chamber contained the portraits of the King and Queen of France and a brightly colored carpet with a large eagle and other American symbols. Mahogany desks and red leather arm chairs for the senators were arranged in semi-circles and faced the bay on the south end of the room. Vice President John Adams presided over the Senate from a desk and canopied arm chair on a dais in the bay. The Senate secretary sat at a desk below and in front of the vice president. The windows had venetian blinds and undoubtedly curtains, most likely crimson to match the canopy above the vice president's chair. Fireplaces provided heat and candles evening light. (*FG*, 26 July 1790; "Historic Structures Report," Part II, chap. 3, 1960, "Furnishing Plan for the First Floor of Congress Hall," 1961, Part C, "Furnishing Plan for the Second Floor of Congress Hall," 1963, Part C, PPIn)

[10]William Montgomery (1736–1816), senator from Northumberland, Luzerne, and Huntingdon counties in the 1790–91 Pennsylvania legislature, became a prominent landowner, merchant, and judge of Northumberland soon after moving to what is now the Danville area from his native Chester County in 1777. In 1783 he and WM were appointed commissioners to examine the navigation of the Susquehanna River and to determine what part of Lake Erie lay in Pennsylvania. Montgomery lost election to the FFC when he ran as an Antifederalist. (*DHFFE* 1:421; *Wilkes Barre* 3:1316n)

John White, with WM's brother Samuel, represented Northumberland County in the 1790–91 Pennsylvania House of Representatives.

[11]Frederick Antes (1730–1801), Antifederalist and treasurer of Northumberland County, left Philadelphia in 1779 and continued his career as a gunsmith and iron founder at Northumberland. He lost election to the assembly in the bitterly disputed 1783 contest in which WM was declared one of the winners but was elected the next year and served until 1787. (*Wilkes Barre* 3:1385; *Counter Revolution*, p. 145; *NQ* [1898]:244)

the President with information, That Quorums were formed in both Houses.   Our Secretary and the Clerk of the Representatives passed each other on the Stairs, with their respective Resolutions.   each House appointed Committees under their own Resolutions. and the Committees met.   The Representatives Urged that it was Idle to name any place to do business in, untill it was known whether any business would be done.   the Precedent, was in our Favour.   this silly thing kept Us talking an Hour and an half.   the Clk. of the Representatives announced the Non Concurrence of our Resolution this had like to have raised a flame   But a Motion was at length made & carried for the Concurrence of the Resolution, which came up   The Joint Committee now waited on the President Who charged them with information. That he would tomorrow at 12 O'Clock deliver his speech to both Houses in the *Senate Chamber*.   and so ended this arduous affair   The Senate adjourned.   The first Levee was held this day at Which I attended.

At about 7 O'Clock Mr. Findley called on me,   We had a long conversation, or at least a busy One for about an hour.   I must be blind indeed if I did not see, That he is doing every thing in his power to supplant me by way of preparing me for the part which he is about to act.   He first told me That Gurney[12] and him had some conversation, which would seem to import, That John Montgomery of Carlisle was the Man to supplant me.   I mentioned it as a Matter that would savour too strongly of cabal, to take one of the electing members.   this Threw him off his guard, and he spoke rather tartly of my remark. and alledged there could be nothing in it.   said *if I am elected I will serve, but I will take no part in the Matter, and I will give You leave to blame me if I do,*   this sentiment he reiterated more than once.   he kept looking at his Watch incessantly, and was in evident perturbation from the time I hinted the impropriety of one of the electing Members being chosen.   When I hinted that some complaints had been raised against my Brother he alledged it was so.   That I likewise had made proposals to Col. Smith,[13] which he insinuated had not been adhered to.   I told him what I recollected of the discourse between Col. Smith and myself. and ~~told him~~ Said I had entered into no engagements with him or any other One on the Occasion.

---

[12]Francis Gurney (1738-1815) was a Philadelphia County member of the 1790-91 Pennsylvania House of Representatives. (*DGW* 6:189n)

[13]The reference is probably to Abraham Smith (d. 1813), a state senator for Franklin and Bedford counties in the 1790-91 legislative session. He was a farmer who made his reputation as a militia colonel before the War for Independence. An Antifederalist, Smith served on the Supreme Executive Council from 1787 to 1790; part of his term coincided with WM's. His interest in land involved him in a dispute before the Board of Property in December 1790. (J. F. Richard, *History of Franklin County* [Chicago, 1887], p. 556; *Counter Revolution*, p. 206; *DHROC* 2:209n; *Pa. Ar.*[3] 1:721)

It is possible, however, that WM meant Col. Matthew Smith (1734-94), prothonotary of Northumberland County and its representative on the Pennsylvania Supreme Executive Council from 1780 to 1783, who earned the rank of colonel during the War for Independence. (*NCHSP* 12:35-54)

Wednesday, 8 December 1790

This was the day assigned for the President to deliver his Speech and was attended with all the Bustle and hurry usual on such Occasions   the President was dressed in black, and read his speech well enough, or at least tolerably   after he was gone and the senate only remained our President, seemed to take great pains to read it better,   if he had such a View he succeeded.   but the difference between them amounted to this   One might be considered as at home. and the other in a strange company.   the speech was committed.   I could not help taking some pains to counter act Mr. Finley.   But my situation is a critical one   I must stand with open breast to receive the wound inflicted by my adversaries, while the smallest endeavours on my part, either to obtain favour or to remove misrepresentation is called, begging of Votes, by my pretended tho false Friends   I will however do what I think proper, for to attempt pleasing every One would be to carry the Ass indeed.   {Finley drew away my Mind for a Moment.   Let me return to the President.   does he really look like a Man Who enters into the Spirit of his appointment, does he show That he receives it in Trust for the happiness of the People, And not a fee simple for his own emolument?   Time and practice will perhaps best elucidate this Point.}

Thursday, 9 December 1790

This day, in the Senate, afforded neither motion nor debate,   the Communications hinted at in the President's Speech were delivered to Us, and continued to be read untill past Two O'Clock When the Senate adjourned.

A War has been actually undertaken against the Wabash Indians,[14] without any Authority of Congress, and What is Worse so far as intelligence is come to hand, We have reason to believe it is unsuccessful.   Mind What comes of it. The Vice President⟨,⟩ Mr. Wyngate and some more of Us stood by the fire, Where the Affairs of France were talked.   I said the National Assembly had attacked Royalty Nobility Hierarchey and the Bastile alltogether, and seemed likely to demolish the Whole.   The V.P. said it was impossible to destroy Nobility, it was founded in nature.   Wyngate engaged.   the V.P. arguments were drawn from the Respect shewn to the Sons of eminent Men, altho vitious & undeserving.   When the parties had nearly exhausted themselves, I asked Whether our Indians might not be considered as having devised an excellent

---

[14]The loosely used term Wabash Indians referred to some or all of the tribes whose villages were situated in present-day Indiana, northwestern Ohio, and southern Michigan. Its most specific usage was for four tribes (Piankashaw, Kickapoo, Wea, Potawatomi) which resided along the Wabash River and its tributaries. In this instance the Miami Indians of northwestern Ohio are included. (Richard Kohn, *Eagle and Sword* [New York, 1975], pp. 92n, 112)

method of getting rid of this Prejudice, by rank⟨in⟩g. all the Children after the Mother. This sent off the Whole Matter in a smile. Adams, however, either never was cured, or is relapsed into his Nobilimania. After We were seated and a slack moment happened Mr. Morris drew his Chair near mine. and hinted to me That Binghams Unanimous Vote for the Speaker's Chair,[15] was the Price ~~of~~ for his his Vote & influence in favour of Finley. I said I thought it likely. But Bingham had obtain his End and might now lie on the other Tack.

Friday, 10 December 1790

This day was unimportant in the Senate. the Committee reported an answer to the President's Speech. the Echo was a good One, and adopted without any material amendment.

A Packet had arrived from France some time ago. directed to the President and Members of Congress. the President from Motives of delicacy would not open it, it came to the Senate and was sent back to the President. and now returned opened. it contained a number of Copies of the Eulogium delivered on Doctor Franklin by Order of the National Assembly. Our President looked over the letter some time and then began ~~telling Us~~ reading the additions that followed the Presidents name he was a Doctor of the Sorbonne &ca. &ca. to the number of 15 (as our President said) These appellatives of Office, he chose to call titles, and then said some sarcastic things against the National Assembly for abolishing Titles.[16]

I could not help remarking that this whole Matter was received and transacted with a coldness and apathy, That astonished me, & the letter and all the Pamphlets were *sent*. down to the Representatives, as if unworthy the attention, of ~~so~~ our body. I deliberated with myself Whether I should not rise & claim one of the Copies. in right of my being a Member. I would however only have got into a Wrangle by so doing. without working any change on my fellow Members. there might be others who indulged the same sentiments. But. 'Twas silence all.

Monday, 13 December 1790

The Senate having adjourned over from Friday to this day (Monday) nothing of public nature has taken place I was engaged Saturday and this Morn-

---

[15]Speaker of the Pennsylvania House of Representatives.

[16]Adams was interested enough in the titles of the president of the commonalty of Paris to write them out, possibly for inclusion in the *SLJ*. See *SLJ*, pp. 504n–505n.

ing in negotiating the sale of some Certificates which I compleated & placed the Money in the Bank.   The Minutes were read about half after Eleven & the Committee on the Business reported That the President had appointed 12 to receive our address.   12 soon came.   We went on this peice of formality which finished the Senatorial Business of the day.   {This day compleated the sale of Mr. Harris's Certificates at the most either Bobey or myself could make of them.   got a Check on the bank & put the Whole in post notes.}[17]

Tuesday, 14 December 1790

attended the Senate but no Business of Moment was transacted   Official information was communicated to the Senate of General Harmar's Expedition.[18]   The ill fortune of the Affair breaks thro' all the colouring that is given to it.   'tis said 100 Indians have been killed, but 200 of our own People have certainly perished in the Expedition   This was Levee day, and I accordingly dressed and did the needful.   It is an Idle thing but What is the life of Man but folly.   and this is perhaps as innocent as any of them.   {so far as respects the persons Acting; The practice however considered as a feature of Royalty, is certainly Antirepublican; this certainly escapes Nobody.   The Royalists glory in it as a point gained; the Republicans are borne down by fashion And a fear of being charged with a want of Respect to Genl. Washington.   If there is Treason in the Wish I retract it.   But would to God, this same Genl. Washington were in Heaven.   We would not then have him brought fo⟨r⟩ward as the constant cover to every Unconstitutional and irrepublican Act.}

Wednesday, 15 December 1790

This day was really a blank in the Senate   Two Petitions, were presented which being only counter parts of What were expected to be acted upon in the lower house, were laid on our Table.   Mr. Morris was called often out by our own Citizens.   the Door keeper named the People Who sent in for him.   P. Muhlenberg was One   Col. Hartley was another—   this day Certificates raised 4∂. in the pound.

---

[17]Post notes were issued by banks as part of the circulating medium. They were payable to order at a future specified date rather than to a particular bearer or on demand.

[18]Josiah Harmar (1753–1813), a brigadier general, commanded the United States army, or Old Establishment as it was known to the FFC, from 1784 to 1791. Born in Philadelphia, he served in the Continental army throughout the War for Independence. His defeat in October 1790 at the hands of the Miami Indians near present-day Fort Wayne, Indiana, was a major issue during the FFC's third session. See also *SEJ*, p. 534.

Thursday, 16 December 1790

I this day attended the Board of Property,   there never was a more Ground-less persecution Than has been set on foot against me and is now supported by One Rawle the same with whom my Brother quarrelled last Winter.   he seems determined to injure my Reputation if possible.   I had to oppose him. and there certainly never was a clearer case.   It was however agreed That my Brother's deposition should be taken. and the Board to meet tomorrow   I was taken away the Whole day by this Vile Business.

Friday, 17 December 1790

got my Brother's deposition and attended at the Board having first heard Prayers and sat an half hour at the Hall.   Rawle was at the Board, and display'd every petty fogging Shift and evasion,   he is really a Rascal.   and all this Matter is pushed by him, to injure me at my ensuing Election.   I have letters from home from my dear Chigld Johney[19] telling me That he had information of this kind.   I spent the Residue of the day in various other peices of Business.

Saturday, 18 December 1790

being saturday and excessive cold, staid at home all day.   was visited by Madison, Bishop White[20] and many other respectable Characters—   settled with Mr. Ogden[21]   his bill in full for the Carpet carriage Horse and lodging for Two Weeks, ending the 15th at night and all the Washing, heretofore done 4:7:7 paid off.   and he has 10 Dollars in his hands, to stand opposite fire-wood.   the rate of boarding 3 doll. ℔ week exclusive of firewood.   at least it is so by this bill—   This night reported that the 6 ℔ Cents were at par.

---

[19]John Harris Maclay (b. 1770), WM's oldest child, managed the family farm at Sunbury. In 1797 WM disinherited him for "disorderly conduct," and he disappeared from family history. See Appendix C. (William Maclay Will, 1797, Maclay Papers, Dauphin County Historical Society)

[20]William White (1748–1836), Episcopal bishop of Pennsylvania since 1787, was born in Philadelphia and graduated from the College of Philadelphia in 1765. He served as chaplain to Congress from 1777 to 1783 and for the decade during which Congress sat at Philadelphia. White was the brother-in-law of Senator Morris. (*Philadelphia Families* 2:1746–48)

[21]William Ogden (b. 1742) kept the tavern at 222 S. Second Street where WM resided during the third session of the FFC. (*PMHB* 47:373–74)

Sunday, 19 December 1790

the cold continued,   dined out with Mr. Powel,   spent the most of the day in writing letters home.

Monday, 20 December 1790

paid some. visits   attended at the Hall   congress were engaged untill almost 3 with the reading of a long and most impudent Memorial from the publick Creditors   paid visits &ca.   the Weather abated. and the Prospect of a thaw.

Tuesday, 21 December 1790

the Memorial and remonstrance of the publick Creditors engaged Us some time.   I saw or at least thought that I saw a Storm gathering in the Countenances of the Senators Yesterday, & moved an adjournment.   I told Mr. Morris of it.   he agreed it was so and for fear of this same storm he moved an adjournment this day.   but schuyler had a long Motion.   It concluded with the *danger* and *inexpediency* of any innovation in the funding.   a Variety of Opinions were now offered as to the time of proceeding   tomorrow, Monday, Friday and Thursday were all spoke off. and Thursday agreed to take it up. This day the Governor of our State[22] was proclaimed.   Mr. Morris spoke early to me,   his Words were. I expect every moment from the Delegation, who are now meeting, to fix a time to wait on the Governor, and I will let you know of it.   I ~~went~~ waited but heard nothing from him.

Wednesday, 22 December 1790

I called this morning on the Comptroller[23] and he was obliging enough to send for Mr. Smilie and did my character Justice in respect to Sundry Aspersions cast on it by Mr. Finley & family.   I came home was dressed and went out to visit about 10.   came to the Hall about Eleven   here Mr. Langdon told me that Mr. Morris & the Delegation were just gone to wait on the Governor.[24]   I posted after & thought to overtake them.   called on the Governor   was sure I would find them there.   It was not so.   was sure they would come in every moment.   they did not come in.   I returned to the Hall   found Mr. Morris. there.   he apologized.   said he got the notification Yesterday in

---

[22]Thomas Mifflin.
[23]John Nicholson.
[24]Thomas Mifflin.

Company,   the time was half after ten   he had sent his Servant up with a note to me.   I asked at my lodgings   no note was there nor had any body seen the Servant.   from the Drift of feathers & dust You see how the Wind blows—

paid my Boarding up to last night   3 dolls.

{I cannot help wishing myself honorably quit of this enviable Station. What an host of Enemies has it not raised about me, with calumny and detraction in every corner,   Fate but grant me this, That their dissentions and cabals may protract the Election Untill my period be expired, and if You find me in this City 24 hours longer, inflict what insult You please on me.   placed on an eminence, Slander & defamation are the hooks applyed to pull me down.   It is natural to make some efforts to dissengage one's self from such Graplings. ~~Which~~   yet every the Sligh⟨t⟩est endeaver of this kind, is reprobated As an attempt to procure Votes.   What a Set of Vipers.}

Thursday, 23 December 1790

Visited this Morning to near eleven   attended at the hall.   Mr. Morris was late in coming, and now the Resolution ~~of the pu~~ respecting the public Creditors. or rather in answer to their Memorial was taken up.   every mode was tryed to let them down easy, as the Phraze is.   great accomodation was tryed to get Mr. Morris to come into the Measure. and he really said more than once that he was satisfyed, with Elsworth's Modification of the Resolution.   King offered a second, or perhaps I might say a fourth One which was adopted. Mr. M⟨orris⟩. told me he would agree to it.   But a number rose for the Yeas and nays.   Mr. Munroe of Virginia desired to be excused and was so.   Mr. Morris was the only Nay.   I was in good humor myself altho' I considered the Vote of this day as wadging a War with the public Creditors in which I will most probably loose my Re Election, and was sorry to see my Colleague manifest such a degree of Obstinacy and peevishness.   he left the Senate Chamber immediately after the Vote.   {Vid. paper annex'd.}

{A Vote for the inexpediency of Altering the funding System at this time, from a person who uniformly opposed that System in its passage into a law. may seem to ~~need some~~ require some apology.   my Vote proceeds not from an Approbation of the funding System but from a total disapprobation of the memorial now before Us.   Upon republican principles I hold the Voice of the Majority to be Sacred,   that the funding Law has obtained that Majority is Undeniable, And Acquiescence is our duty, but I will never Subscribe to a blind and unalterable One.   the making debts irredeemable and perpetual is a power that I am convinced posterity will spurn at.   The Western lands are the natural fund for the redemption of our national debt.   it is now unproductive. perhaps the fault is ours that it is so. As soon as it is otherwise, I would be happy to see all Stocks made Strictly personal, unalienable and incapable of descent, or any negotiation save Commutation into lands. And let it die with the Obstinate Speculator Who refuses such Commutation. The Stock holder to any amount, is an Unproductive Character. Worse he is the tool of a bad administration. a Good One needs none. It is enough that we have seen one Generation of them. let Us not perpetuate the Breed. their Children cut off from such expectations, will be restored to Industry.}

It is a fact That the 6 ℔ Cents are now nearly at par. or at least this appearance is kept up among the Speculators. an Act passed hastily Just at the close of the last sessions directed the borrowing 2 millions of dollars with design of buying in the public debt & lessening it. the real Object was the encreasing it by raising the Value. Three Millions of Florins have been borrowed in pursuance of this law. the Board of Purchase[25] named in the law. compleated their purchases of Novr. at about 12/4∂ on the face and 7/3∂ arrears. It was natural to expect this would be about the stand⟨in⟩g. rate. but by one Effort of impudence Par was demanded, in 3 days, on the appearing of the Treasurer's[26] advertisements. All the Effect of preconcert.

Friday, 24 December 1790

the Papers full of advertisements this day of Stock of every kind for sale. and there is no doubt but ~~there will~~ the ~~appearance~~ Show of Sales, nearly at Par, will be kept up. in Order to save appearances, and cover the advanced Prices which are daily given, by the board of Purchases, thro' the Medium of the Treasury.

This Whole Matter of purchasing in Stock to sink the debt, ostensibly, has really no other object, but to raise the Value of it, & so to make immense fortunes to the Speculators who have amassed vast quantities of Certificates for little or nothing. I did not think it possible that mankind could be so easily duped. and Yet there never was a Vainer task than to attempt to undeceive them.

Very little done in the Senate this day sundry communications were made from the Representatives relating to the Settlements of Post St. Vincennes on the Wabash.[27] which were laid on our Table.

---

[25]On 21 December John Adams reported to the Senate for the board of purchase, which had been created by the Sinking Fund Act [HR-101]. The Board consisted of the vice president, the chief justice, the secretaries of state and treasury, and the attorney general.

[26]Samuel Meredith.

[27]St. Vincennes was located on the Wabash River 150 miles above its juncture with the Ohio in the Northwest Territory. Old Fort Knox was erected at the site in 1787. The Northwest Territory Act [S-17] resolved questions relating to land titles at Vincennes.

Yesterday the secretary's Report on the Subject of a National Bank was handed to Us. And I can de readily find that A Bank will be the Consequence. Considered As an Aristocratic engine I have no great predilection for Banks. they May be considered in some Measure as operating like a Tax in favor of the Rich against the poor, Tending to the Accumulating in a few hands, And Under this View may be regarded As opposed to republicanism. And Yet Stock Wealth Money or property of any kind Wherever Accumulated has a Similar effect. The power of incorporating may be inquired into. But the old Congress enjoyed it. Bank Bills are promisary Notes and of Course not Money. I see no Objection on this Quarter. The great point is, if possible, to prevent the making of it a Machine for the Mischievous purposes of bad Ministers, And this must depend more on the Vigilance of future legislators, than on either the Virtue or foresight of the present Ones.

Saturday, 25 December 1790

This being Christmass day, dined with Parson Ewing[28] and had the Task of hearing him rail almost all the time I was with him against Congress. He talked of demonstration and mathematical proof of the impositions which he had sustained. but he really did not understand the Law. I wa⟨i⟩ved all Altercation with him as much as I could, he had the Terms of Rogue and Cheat very familiarly at his finger Ends. or I should rather say at his Tongue's End. He however talked of selling out. I was this day assured that the Six ₽ Cents were above par. The law for purchases,[29] allows the overplus, Money in the Treasury after satisfying the Appropriations to be laid out in the purchase of Certificates, as well as the M Two Millions of dollars to be borrowed abroad. it was originated and passed after I left New York. and is certainly the most, impudent Transaction, That I ever knew in the political World. I regret my being absent When it passed. altho' my presence could have had no effect Whatever on it the progress of it further than I would have borne my testimony against it. This nominal Reduction is a Virtual raising of the Whole Value of the Debt. Something of this Kind I have heard is common in England When Government attempt a purchase of any kind of Stock, the Holders of that kind of Stock never fail to raise the Residue. Hamilton Must have known this Well. Our Speculators or Stock Holders know all this,

---

[28]John Ewing (1732–1802), Antifederalist and provost of the University of Pennsylvania from 1779 to 1802, was born in East Nottingham, Maryland, and graduated from the College of New Jersey in 1754. His daughter Elizabeth married WM's brother-in-law, Robert Harris, in May 1791. Their son, George Washington Harris (1798–1882), published an abridged edition of WM's diary in 1880. See Appendix C. (*Princetonians, 1748–68*, pp. 95–98; *DHROC* 2:728; *Commemorative Biographical Encyclopedia of Daupin County . . .* [Chambersburg, Pa., 1896], pp. 82–83)

[29]The act authorizing the foreign loan was the Sinking Fund Act [HR-101].

they have a general Communication with each other   they are actuated by One Spirit or I should rather say by Hamilton.   Nobody (generally speaking) but them, buys,   it is easy for them by preconcert to settle What proposals they will give in & these being filed, the Commissioners are justifyed in taking the lowest.   I cannot however help predicting that When the Florins are Out. there will be a Crash, And the Stocks will fall.

Sunday, 26 December 1790

being Sunday my Brother agreed with me that we would visit Docr. Logan.   This Man, has every Testimony both of practice and profession in favour of his Republicanism.   he has been in the Assembly of Pennsylvania. and then had it in his power to have formed a Coalition with the city Interest.   he has however continued firmly attached to the rural plans and arrangements of life, and the democratic System of Government.   his Motto is Vox Populi Vox Dei.[30]   but Mottos and professions now a days. are as the Idle wind which no One ought to regard, unless supported by practice.   and Scarce can You depend on Practice. Unless You see it contravene Interest. This has been in some degree his Case.   We had been but a little While here with him when we were joined by Judge Burke of South Carolina.   This is the very Man Who, while in New York, railed so tremendously against the Quakers and against Philada. and indeed all Pennsylvania for having Quakers. but behold a Wonder.   now he rails against Slavery, extols Quakers. and blazes against the Attentions shewed to General Washington. which he calls Idolatry. and That am a Party wh wish as much to make him a King as ever the Flatterers of Cromwell wished to raise him to that dignity.   Docr. Logan has Oswald's paper at his devotion, and I can foresee that Burke will discharge many of his Sentiments thro' this channel.   Burke said Many just things but he is too new a convert to merit confidence.   I find however on Examination, That this is the same Man Who wrote against the Cincinnati.[31]

Monday, 27 December 1790

I received just after Breakfast a letter from Mr. Harris, and spent the day mostly in buying things, which were to go by the Man who brought the letter, He being a Waggoner.   Just as I came out of the door of the Hall. Hartley had fallen and broke his Arm.   I was among the first to shew him every attention,

---

[30]The voice of the people is the voice of God.

[31]Representative Burke's anonymous *Considerations on the Society or Order of the Cincinnati* (E-17862–66) was published at Charleston in 1783 and reprinted at Newport, Hartford, New York, and Philadelphia the same year. See May 1789, n. 2.

that his situation required. and the more especially as I have reason to consider him as inimical to my reappointment, to the Senate of the United States.

This day produced nothing of Consequence in the Senate.   my attention to Hartley prevented my returning. into the Senate chamber.

Tuesday, 28 December 1790

attended the Senate as usual   a slight debate took place respecting a law for continuing the permission to the States of Rhode Island, Maryland and Georgia to levy certain duties of Tonnage for the purpose of repairs on their respective ports.[32]   the bill was recommitted. with Two additional Members, added to the Committee.   This being Levee day I attended in a new Suit.   This peice of duty I have not omitted since I came to Town. and if there is little harm in it, there cannot be much good.   Jackson looked Shyly at me this day.   I observed his Eye upon me. and it had in my Opinion something of the malignant in it.   but I never cared less, for Court favor.   I really feel a thirst to return to my family. and tho' I will feel the pang which the insult of being rejected will inflict, yet perhaps a reelection might be among my misfortunes.

Wednesday, 29 December 1790

this day a blank in the Senate with respect to any business of importance. Mr. Morris told me I was blamed for not going among the Members and Speaking to them &ca. &ca.   What a set of Vipers I have to deal with   One party watch and ridicule me, if I am seen speaking a Word to a Member.   in Order to avoid the censure of these. I have rather secreted myself from the Members and a fault is fixed on it.   Wm. Montgomery called this Evening to tell me that he must go home on Account of the Indisposition of his Wife.[33] This is, perhaps, a Vote out of Pocket, but cannot be helped.

I called this Evening at the lodging of some of the Members who were out of Fitzsimons had often said he was ~~in~~ at home in the Evenings and desired me to call.   I drank Tea. with him & the family.   sat a good While,   the Chat was various.   he did not touch the Subject of my reelection.   he did not come with me to the door When I took leave. as much as to say I want no private communication.   Be it so.   if I ~~need~~ want help I need not look to him for it.   Whatever is, is best. and I have little doubt, but my Rejection, if it takes place, will be best.   {The Character of Brakenridge[34] was introduced.   Fitz-

---

[32]Navigation Act [HR-103].

[33]Isabella Evans (1741–91), daughter of Robert and Margaret Evans of Chester County, married William Montgomery in 1772. (Septimus Niven, *Genealogies of Evans, Niven & Allied Families* [Philadelphia, 1930], pp. 152, 153)

[34]Hugh Henry Brackenridge (1748–1816), a Pittsburgh lawyer, came to Pennsylvania from

simons said He came down in the State Legislature Once.   We took Notice of him, And he imbark'd for Us like a Barrister thro' thick and thin, But he sold himself, by it ~~And~~ lost his popularity & we have never seen him since.   he accompanied this with a loud laugh, Which is uncommon with him, As his risibility seldom exceeds ~~the~~ a dry Smile or Sarcastic Grin.   Mrs. Fitzsimons[35] Cry'd out, How insufferably cruel is that my Dear.   You first Mislead the Man, and now ridicule him for the Consequence of his Mistakes.   she did not just say the Devil does so. but something not unlike it.   It gave my Friend Thomas the Flatts. for he hardly said a Word afterwards.}

Thursday, 30 December 1790

I called this day on Sundry Members of the Assembly.   as I came home I called at Boyd's[36] the place where all the plots are laid against me   Finley talked confidently.   Smiley and Boyd rather seemed to oppose him.   But I have a right to consider my self as among a Den of thieves.   I need never cross this Threshold again.   advances to them are Idle.   attended the Hall at the Usual time.   a Communication from the President respecting the Prisoners at Algiers 14 of Whom only are Alive, was delivered to the Senate, read & committed, to the Committee on the Mediterranian navigation.

did some business about the Offices.   called & sat a good part of the Evening with White Who had, 2 of the Lancaster Members with him. Carpenter & Brickbill,[37]   I need say nothing more to them, they now know me. {From White I had much information of the malignant Whispers Innuendoes and Malevolent Remarks Made respecting me   It Was painful; And I could not refrain demanding of him. What, or Whether Any charge, Was made Against me?   No?   No?   nothing in particular, But every Body says *the People don't like You* the People Wont hear of Your Reelection.   Who Are they that say so?   The *leading Members* of *the Assembly*, Officers of the Land Office. Citizens of Philada. & others.

Quere is not the Same Spirit that dictated the Ostracism At Athens, The

Scotland in 1753. Prior to graduating from the College of New Jersey in 1771, he began a long literary career as a poet, novelist, satirist, polemicist, and political propagandist. From 1786 to 1787, he represented Westmoreland County in the Pennsylvania Assembly, where he advocated ratification of the United States Constitution and other issues unpopular in the western counties. He thus lost his political base and was denied election to the state ratification convention in 1787. (*Princetonians, 1769–75*, pp. 138–46; *DHROC* 2:727)

[35]Catherine Meade (c. 1740–1810), daughter of Robert and Mary Meade of Philadelphia, married Thomas Fitzsimons in 1763. (*American Catholic Historical Researches* 5:2–27)

[36]Alexander Boyd, a minor local state official and political activist, ran a boarding house at 214 N. Second Street, which was popular with western Pennsylvania legislators. (*DHROC* 2:121–22; *CRP* 15:53)

[37]Abraham Carpenter (c. 1758–1815) and John Breckbill (1728–1813) of Strasburg Township represented Lancaster County in the Pennsylvania House of Representatives during the 1790–91 session. (Birth and death dates courtesy of the Lancaster County Historical Society.)

Petalism At Syracuse, And similar Measures in other places, Still prevalent in the human Mind & Character.   The ~~real~~ true Cause of these Banishments, Whether by the Oyster Shell, or Olive leaf.[38] Was really to remove, A blameless rival, out of the Way of less deserving Competitors for Office, by the Name And clamor of the People, When no other cause Could be alledged Against them.   In this Way, is there not in every Free Country, Where the Competition for Offices is laid Open, A Constant Ostracism, at Work, on the Character of Every Man Eminent for Worth or Talents?   These Arts Will no doubt prevail, on Many Occasions, But they Will not be Universally Successful; When they do, We must Submit to them As in some Measure inseperable from Republicanism.}

Friday, 31 December 1790

attended the Senate this day where nothing ~~of Consequence~~ was done of any consequence,   Sundry Papers relating to the Inhabitants of Post St. Vincent. or Vincennes on the Wabash were committed.   I was of the Committee.   I went a visiting with Langdon.   dined this day with Mr. Morris.   I can observe, in General rather a Coolness of the Citizens towards me.   be it so   I will endeavour not to vex myself much with them.

This is the last day of the Year and I have faithfully noted every political transaction, that has happened to me in it.   and of What avail has it been?   I thought it probable, That I would be called on with respect to the part I had acted in Senate by the Legislature of Pennsylvania, or at least by some of them.   But is there a Man of them, who has thought it Worth while to ask me a single Question?   No.   are they not every Man of them straining, after Offices, Posts and preferments. at least every One of them who has the smallest chance of Success.   Yes verily.   nor is there a Man who seems to care a farthing, how I acted.   But wish me out to make a Vacancy.   Reward from men it is in vain to look for.   It is however of some consequence to me, That I have nothing to charge my self with.

Having some leisure on hand I have looked over my Minutes for the last Month.   It is with shame & contrition that I find the Subject of my reelection has engaged so much or indeed any of my thoughts.   blessed with affluence, domestic in my habits & Manners, rather rigid and uncomplying in my temper. generally opposed in Sentiments to the preva⟨i⟩ling politicks of the times, no placeman Speculator Pensioner or Courtier. It is equally Absurd for

---

[38]Ostracism was the ancient Greek custom of banishing for five or ten years a person considered to be a danger to the state. Citizens used shells or similar objects on which they wrote the name of the person to be banished. Petalism was a five-year banishment from Syracuse effected by writing on an olive leaf.

me to Wish a continuance in Congress. As to desire to Walk among briars and Thorns, rather than on a beaten road.

It may be said a love for the Good of my Country should influence My Wishes. Let those care to Whom the trust is committed. but let me never beg for that trust When in my own Opinion I have been of so little Service, And have sacrificed both health and domestic happiness at the schrine of my Country. Nothing that I could do either by conversation or writing has been wanting to let ~~the People~~ Men see the danger which is before them. but seeing is not the Sense that will give them the Alarm, Feeling only will have this effect, and it is hard to say how callous even this may be. Yet When the seeds of the funding System ripen into taxation of every kind and upon every Article. When the General Judiciary like an enforcing Engine follows them, up, seizing and carrying Men from One Corner of a State to another and perhaps in time thro' different States, I should not at all be disappointed if A Commotion, like a popular Fever, should be excited and at least attempt to throw off these political Disorders. Ill however will that Government be Under Which an old Man cannot eke out 10 or a Dozn. Years of an unimportant life in quiet. And May God Grant Peace in my day.

But as to the point in hand let me now mark down some Rules for my future Conduct.

First then let me avoid anything that may seem to savour of singularity or innovation; call on & speak to my Acquaintances as formerly. but avoiding with the Utmost Care, the Subject of Senatorial election and every thing connected with it. if any other Person introduces it. he must be either a real or pretended Friend, hear him therefore with complacence and even with a thankful Air. Avoid every Wish, or Opinion of my own especially of the negative kind, for every thing of this ~~kind~~ sort will hazard my sincerity.

should An Election come on While I am in Town. Stay ~~at~~ in my ~~lodging~~ place during the Time of it. And if if it should be adverse, A thing I can Scarce doubt of. immediately send in my Resignation. As the appointment of another Person, must be considered As Unequivocal proof of my having lost the Confidence of the State. For this purpose let my letter of Resignation be ready all to the filling the Date, and revise it While I am cool. For it is not Unlikely that with so many Eyes Upon me, I may undergo some perturbation at the time. Lastly have my Mare in Readiness And let the first day of my Liberty, be employed in My Journey homewards. {A determination of this kind is certainly right, For I have tried and feel my own insignificance & total inability to give the Smallest Check to the torrent Which is pouring down Upon Us. A system is daily developing itself Which must Gradually Undermine And finally destroy Our so much boasted equality liberty & Republicanism. high Wages Ample Compensations Great Salaries to every Person connected with the Government of the U.S. The desired effect is Already produced   the frugal & parsimonious Appointments of the individual States are held in Contempt.   Men of Pride Ambition Talents All press forward to exhibit Their Abilities on the Theatre of the General Government.   This I think May be termed Grade the first.   And to a Miracle has it Succeeded—   The Second Grade or Stage is to create & multiply Offices and Appointments Under the General Government by every possible Means In the diplomacy Revenue Judiciary & Military,   This is called Giving the President a respectable *Patronage*   A Term, I confess, new to me in the Present Sense of it. Which I take to Mean neither more or less, Than that the President should Always have A number of Lucrative Places in his Gift, to reward those Members of Congress Who may promote his Views or Support his Measures, More especially if by such Conduct they Should forfeit the Esteem of their Constituents.   We talk of Corruption in Brittain.   I pray We may not have Occasion for complaints of a Similar Nature here.   Respice Finem,[39] As to the Third.}

[39]Regard the end.

January 1791

Saturday, 1 January 1791

Neither Congress nor the Legislature of the State met this day.   I went to settle some Business with the Comptroller of the State.[1] but he was equally complaisant to the day as the Government,   I determined to do something since I was out. and called on my Taylor. who took the amount of his bill freely   I then visited Hartley. Who lies ill with his broken Arm.   just as I passed the President's, Griffin called to me, and asked Whether I would not pay my respects to the President,   I was in Boots and had on my worst Cloaths,   I could not prevail on myself to go with him.   I had however passed him but a little way When Osgood the P.M.G. attacked me so warmly to go with him.   I was pushed forward by him, bolted into the Presence ~~Wished~~ paid the President the Compliments of the Season had an hearty Shake by the hand.   I was asked to partake of the punch & Cakes but declined it.   I sat down and we had some Chat. but the diplomatic Gentry and foreigners coming in.[2] I embraced the first vacancy to make my bow and Wish him a good Morning.   I called next on the Governor of the State[3] & paid my Compliments, and so came home to my dinner, and Thus have I commenced the Year 1791.

Sunday, 2 January 1791

being Sunday I staid at home in the Forenoon, and attended at Meeting in the Afternoon.   To worship once ~~a day~~, on the day devoted to the Deity, is as small a compliment, as Decency can pay to the Religion of any Country. and a Regard to health, will prefer the After to the forenoon Service. At this Season of the Year. as the fire in the Stoves, has had then time to produce a greater

---

[1]John Nicholson.

[2]The diplomatic representatives to the United States during the third session of the FFC were Franco Petrus van Berckel, minister from the Netherlands; Louis Guillaume Otto, chargé d'affaires from France; Charles Hellstedt, Swedish consul since 1784; José de Viar and José de Jaudenes, two attachés of former minister Gardoqui who acted as chargés for Spain; and Sir John Temple, consul general for Great Britain from 1785 to 1798. (*PTJ* 19:269–73; *PJM* 5:3–4, 8:426n)

[3]Thomas Mifflin.

Effect, in Warming the house.   I saw nobody this day. but received a letter
from home by Col. Cook.[4]

Monday, 3 January 1791

being monday I attended at the Hall early on a Committee respecting the
Settlers on the Wabash and Mississipi.[5]   The Business being tedious. the
Committee agreed to meet tomorrow at 10 O'Clock.   We had a Communication from the President, with some nominations[6] and One from the Representatives respecting the Algerines.   It was from Jefferson.   It held out, That we
must either go to War with these piratical States, compound and pay them an
annual Stipend, and ransom our Captives, or give up the Trade.   The report
seemed to Breath resentment, and abounded with martial Estimates in the
naval way.   we have now 14 unhappy Men in captivity at Algiers.   I wish we
had these released, and the Trade to the mediterranean, abandoned.   there
can be no chance of our wanting a Market for our Produce.   at least nothing of
the Kind has Yet happened.
    This day the Bank bill reported,   It is totally in Vain to oppose this bill.
the only Useful part I can Act is to try to make it of some Benefit to the public,
which reaps none from the existing Banks.

Tuesday, 4 January 1791

attended early on the Committee on the Wabash business.   I could not
help remarkg. the amazing predilection of the New England People for each
other.   There was no room for debate. but even good Sense. and even demonstration herself, if personifyed, would be disregarded by the wise Men of the
East, if she did not come from a New England Man.   several bills were read
this day, and business proceeded in the usual ro⟨u⟩tine, without any debate of
Consequence.   It was Levee day.   I dressed & did the duty of it.   handed a
Petition of Mr. Adlum's[7] to Major Jackson.   nothing else of Consequence
happened.   {This petition Business carried me there, & now I think unless I
am somehow called On I will never see them more.}

---

[4]William Cooke (d. 1804), a Northumberland County judge, had been a colonel in the
Continental army. Born in Lancaster County, he was elected Northumberland County's first
sheriff in 1772 and later represented it in the Pennsylvania constitutional convention of 1776
and the assembly of 1781–82. (*PMHB* 3:320–21)
    [5]WM was a member of the committee that reported the Northwest Territory Act [S-17] on
7 January.
    [6]Receipt of the president's message is recorded in the *SEJ*.
    [7]In his petition to Washington, Adlum asked to be appointed agent for Indian affairs in
the Northern Department. (Series 7, GWP)

Wednesday, 5 January 1791

attended early at the Hall, to meet the Committee,[8] but they let me sit an hour without attending me. Strong had not made his draught of a Report. and was busy at it in the Secretary's Office. & Elsworth would do nothing without him. but at last both draughts Strong's and mine were produced. I was ready to condemn my own, when there was a shadow of Objection. but even this conduct would not excite a particle of Candor, I however cared but little and was so well guarded, that the Smallest Semblance of discontent, did not escape me. Genl. Dickenson came in. he took me to One side. "You have" said he "Enemies in this place. I dined Yesterday with the Governor.[9] he is your Enemy. he said You would be hard run. and mentioned Smiley as being your competitor." I thanked him for the Communication, nor I could I do less. however indifferent I might be, as to the Event.

and now it is evident, What plan has been chalked out, at Boyd's— My Brother overheard, Mathew Irwin tell Finley, That he Finley could command anything in the power of the People. that another Man whom my Brother believed was Smily could not do it so certainly. therefore that Finly must depend on the People and the other One on the Legislature. Mr. Kenedy told my Brother that ~~Smiley~~ Maclane[10] ~~wanted~~ wanted much to be in the Representatives. and The arrangements of districts, which Finley read over at our lodgings, plainly pointed out a nest for McLane. Franklin⟨,⟩ Bedford⟨,⟩ Mifflin⟨,⟩ Huntington & Northumberland. Maclane is all powerful in Franklin and Bedford, and has a Son, living and a considerable party attached to him in Huntington. so that the Patriotism of all these three Champions for Liberty resolves itself into providing ~~themselves~~ places, for their accomodation. {I could add more names evidently actuated by the same principles. ~~The sh~~ But the shortest way of compleating the Catalogue, is by declaring the Rule general. for I candidly confess I know not an exception among the present political Figurants of Pennsylvania. Avarice & Ambition are the Motives, While the Cry of Patriotism and the interest of the People are used As the ways and Means of advancing their private ends. This political Malady is not peculiar to Pennsylvania It is the disease of all popular governments. Nor does the fault seem to be in Nature, she certainly at all times produces Store of Candid and ingenious Characters, but these generally modest and Unassuming, are passed by in the ferment of popular elections, While the fiery

---

[8]WM was a member of the committee that reported the Northwest Territory Act [S-17] on 7 January.

[9]Thomas Mifflin.

[10]James McLene (1730–1806), a member of the 1790–91 Pennsylvania House of Representatives, represented Franklin County in almost every statewide legislative and constitutional body that met between 1776 and 1790 except the ratification convention. He was an Antifederalist. (*DHROC* 2:730)

and forward declaim on general grievances, and pour forth their promises of Redress.   It is thus that Ambitious Men obtain the Management of Republicks,   And to this cause is perhaps owing their fall and declension throughout the World. For No selfish Ambitious Man ever was a Patriot.}

Thursday, 6 January 1791

Nothing of Consequence to the Continent, was transacted this day unless it was the Report, of the Committee on the Algerine business   The amount of it was first the Trade of the american States in the Mediterranean cannot be supported without an armed force and going to war with them.   2dly. this ought to be done as soon as the Treasury of the United States will admit of it.
It is evident that War has been engaged in with the Indians on the Frontiers, in rather an unadvised Manner.   And it is also evident That there is a Wish to engage Us in this distant War with those Pirates.   all this goes to encrease our Burthens & Taxes & these in a Debate of this day were called the only bonds of our Union.   I will certainly oppose all this.
Dined this day with Mr. Bingham.[11]   I cannot say barely that he affects to entertain in a Stile beyond every ~~body~~ thing in this place, or perhaps in America,   he really does so.   There is a propriety a neatness a Cleanliness that adds to the Splendor of his costly furniture, and elegant Apartments   I am told he is my Enemy.   I believe it, but let not malice harbour with me.   {It is not as Wm. Maclay that he opposes, and vilifies me. but as the Object that ~~opposes~~ stands in the way of his Wishes, and the dictates of his Ambition, and on this Principle he would oppose Perfection itself.}

Friday, 7 January 1791

Attended Senate as usual   we reported a bill, for the Wabash and Illionois donation,[12]   Sundry other things were done in the usual ro⟨u⟩tine of business.   the Kentuckey bill was taken up   I considered it as so imperfectly drawn with respect to What was to be the ~~new~~ Boundaries of the New State, That I opposed it, and there was much altercation on the Subject, but intirely in the Gentlemanly way.   It ended in a postponement, with the consent of the Virginia Member Mr. Munroe.   Mr. Morris staid out all the time of the debate.   when the senate adjourned he asked me to go and eat Pepper Pot

---

[11]Bingham, speaker of the state House of Representatives in 1790–91, and his wife Anne made their mansion at Spruce and Third streets the social center of the federal government after Congress moved to Philadelphia in 1790. For a description of the mansion, see Robert C. Alberts, *The Golden Voyage . . . William Bingham* (Boston, 1969), pp. 162–63. See August 1789, n. 13.
[12]Northwest Territory Act [S-17].

with him.   I agreed and accordingly dined with him en familie.   I cannot believe that he is my enemy with respect to my reelection,   the thing is impossible.

I chatted with the family till near dark and came home as I had an appointment with Mr. Hanna.

{The Human heart is really a Strange Machine.   I certainly have severely felt the inconvenience of being from home these 2 Years past, & my Judgment tells me plainly That I am wrong. in having submitted to it.   further I cannot help knowing That my reellection with no Friends and many Enemies is impossible,   And Yet Under all these Circumstances, The Man Who expresses favorable Wishes is by far the Most Acceptable to me.   But upon the Whole this is right   good will ought to beget Gratitude.   But oh, what a Recollection is it? That Under such Circumstances, I am independent, or in other Words, That my Manner of living, has always been within my means.}

Saturday, 8 January 1791

To Mr. Harris

Philada. 8th Jany. 1791

Dr. Sir.

Agreable to your request, I send you by Mr. Hanna 61:14:6 in State Money of 1785 & 3200 doll. in post Notes of 100 doll. each, being 1200£   the Whole amount which I received for your certificates was 1275:13:5.   the present remittance leaves a balance of 75:13:5 in my hands from which deduct 9:15:0 paid for a Carpet, and ten pound 15 / 11∂ paid for groceries

```
      9:15:0      75:13:5
     10:15:11     20:10:11
                  55: 2:6
```

this leaves a balance of 55:2:6 of your money in my hands. agreeable to an account current which I have inclosed.   this balance I will pay to your Order at anytime.   as for news papers and other occurrences I refer you to Mr. Hanna for them.   ~~I had the Groceries put~~ The bills are all i⟨n⟩closed to you and One which I paid to Edward Brooks, not put into my Acct. current, as you gave me 4 dols. for this purpose.

I am Sir with much regard your most
Obedt.& most Hble. Servt.
W.M.

I added a considerable deal more to my letter & sent the 3200 doll. and the State Money 61:14:6 along with Mr. Hanna. who set off on Sunday Morning.
{Monday I find that Mr. Hanna or I. made a mistake and he has a note of 1 doll.

70 ninetieths instead of One of 100 doll.   I have sent the note of 100 doll. by Bobey Harris.   this only lessens the Balance I owed Mr. Harris by the Value of the small note 13 / 6—

$$55{:}2{:}6$$
less   13:6
Bal.   £54:9:0}

Sunday, 9 January 1791

The most disagreeable of any day this year   I however went to meeting and the consequence was a Cold.   wrote letters to my family and spent the after-part of the day at home.

Monday, 10 January 1791

attended the Hall as usual   the Bank bill was the Order for this day,   I did not embark deeply, but was up Two or Three times.   the debates were conducted rather in a desultory Manner.   the Objectors were Izard⟨,⟩ Butler and Munroe.   a postponement took place.

Tuesday, 11 January 1791

the bank bill taken up & the debates became rather more close and interesting,   I was up several times but the debates rather on collateral points, than on the Substance of the bill.   The ostensible object held out by Butler & Izard were That the publick should have all the advantages of the bank.   But they shewed no foundation for this. no System no plan or Calculation.   they were called on to shew any any. and were promised support, if they could shew any practicability in their System.   till after 3 O'Clock was the Matter agitated. and a postponement broke up the business of the day.

Wednesday, 12 January 1791

The Bank was the business of this day, but Munroe called for a postponement of the Subject and Succeeded.   A bill was now called up respecting Consuls and Vice Consuls,   this bill was drawn and brought in by Elsworth and of Course he hung like a Cat to Every particle of it.   The first clause was a mere Chaos   preamble, Stile, preamble, and enacting Clause all jumbled together,   It was really unmendable   at least the Shortest way to amend it

was to bring in a new One.   This same Elsworth is a Striking instance how
powerful, a Man may be in some departments of the mind and defective in
others.   all powerful & eloquent in Debate he is notwithstanding, a miserable Draughtsman.   The habits of the bar, and the lists of litigation have
formed him to the former   the later is, in a great degree the Gift of nature.

I dined this day with Mr. Nicholson.   the Company Mr. Montgomery⟨,⟩
Smiley⟨,⟩ B. McClenachan⟨,⟩ T. Smith, Kittera⟨,⟩ Hamilton[13] & others.
desultory conversation. on a Variety of subjects.   {I left them soon, for from
some hints it seemed as if they meant to discourse of the appointment of a
Senator &ca.—& a thought passed my Mind That Nicholson, who has often
expressed approbation of my Conduct had some hand in it.   But I will not
disgrace myself in this Business.   circumstan⟨ced⟩ As I am all the caballing
and intreague I could exercise would not be effectual.   and suppose me
successful   What am I to gain?   pain remorse vexation and loss of health.
for I verily believe That my political Wrangles have affected my corporeal
Feelings so as to bring on in degree my rheumatic indisposition—   It is a
Melancholy Truth. but I see plainly That even the best Men Will not emerge to
Office in republicks without submitting either directly or indirectly to a degree
of intreague.   it is not perhaps so much the Case in Monarchies, for even
Tyrants Wish to be served with Fidelity.   sed Ubi plurima notent non ego
~~pauis~~ paucis offendar maculis—}[14]

Thursday, 13 January 1791

This day the Bank bill was debated, but in so desultory a Manner. as not to
merit the commitment of anything to paper.   This day I dined with General
Dickenson   as I went there I fell in with Mr. Morris.   he told me that
Bingham had informed him. That Great discontents prevailed in the ~~house~~
General Assembly. And that they were about to instruct their Senators.[15]   he

---

[13]WM probably meant Thomas Smith (1745–1809), president judge of a western Pennsylvania judicial district. In 1769, a year after his arrival from Scotland, he settled at Bedford and
was appointed deputy surveyor for that part of Pennsylvania lying southwest of the counties
in which WM held the same position. A lawyer, he served in a variety of local, state, and
federal legislative offices, including the Confederation Congress. Smith was the half brother
of William Smith, provost of the College of Philadelphia. (Burton A. Konkle, *The Life and
Times of Thomas Smith* . . . [Philadelphia, 1804])

John Wilkes Kittera (1752–1808) graduated from the College of New Jersey in 1776 and
practiced law in his native Lancaster County. (*Princetonians, 1776–1783*, pp. 59–61)

Hamilton, apparently a Pennsylvanian, could have been any one of several individuals
active in legal and political affairs.

[14]But where the majority should censure, I would not be offended by a few men.

[15]The three resolutions on the Duties on Distilled Spirits Act [HR-110] which were
adopted by the Pennsylvania House of Representatives on 22 January contained a "hope"
that the two Pennsylvania senators would oppose those parts of the bill "which shall militate
against the just rights and liberties of the people." On a 9–8 vote, the state senate refused to
concur with the resolutions.

added That he was sure that Bingham had an hand in it.   The dinner was a great One, and the Ladies 3 only of Whom attended were richly or at least fashionably drest.   nothing remarkable   I sat between Two Merchants of considerable note.   I broached the Subject of the Bank. and found them magnetically drawn to the Contemplation of the Monied Interest.

Friday, 14 January 1791

this day the Bank engaged Us to the Hour of adjournment,   It was limited to 20 Years   Mr. Morris had Yesterday declared that the Public Ought to subscribe on the same Terms as other individuals.   It was not so in the bill.   I shewed him an Amendment to this purpose. and asked him to Support me in it.   he said Schyler had told him that Hamilton said, it must not be altered. but concluded I will speak to Hamilton.   adjourned over untill Monday.

Saturday, 15 January 1791

This a very disagreeable day   I staid at home and read Price on Annuities.[16]   I find he establishes an Opinion which I had long entertained That Women are longer lived than Men.   This I used to charge to accidents and intemperance.   but he goes further & seems to place it in nature, as more Male than Females die in infancy.

Sunday, 16 January 1791

went to Meeting and caught some cold As Usual.   Spent the Residue of the day in Reading.

Monday, 17 January 1791

This day Mr. Morris stayed very late.   Langdon came and complained of him.   "this always his way,   he never will come When there is any debate"[17]   he however came.   I asked him Whether he had called on Hamilton.   No.   I said I had a mind to move a recommitment, That the Secretary of the Treasury might be consulted and furnish the Committee, with calculations. if on the Subject, as I had no doubt but he had such.   he said he would move such a thing. but he did not   the Question was put. on the Clause Several said Aye.   I got up spoke longer than I intended, and made such a

---

[16]Richard Price, *Observations on Reversionary Payments; on Schemes for Providing Annuities for Widows* . . . (London, 1771).

[17]The subject of the debate was the Bank Act [S-15].

Motion but my colleague did not second me.   I was seconded by Butler. and now such a Scene of confused Speeches followed as I have seldom heard before.   Every One affected to understand the Subject, and undervalue the Capacities of those Who differed from himself.   if my mental faculties, and Organs of hearing did not both deceive me. I really never heard such conclusions attempted to be drawn.   I wanted some advantage to the ~~Bank~~ United States   they were to subscribe Two Millions Specie.   Elsworth repeatedly said they were to do this only as a deposit & I am convinced he wanted to deprive the public of all advantage save that of safe Keeping and convenience in collecting, which they could derive from the banks in Existence as well as from any new Ones.   all other Persons had the power of Subscribing ³/₄th in public Securities.   It was contended that this was nothing against the Public altho' it was admitted on all hands. that the 6 ⅌ Cents were now at 16/ in the pound.   King⟨,⟩ Elsworth & Strong all harped on this String with the most bare faced Absurdity That I ever was Witness to in my life.   I am now more fully convinced than ever I have been of the propriety of Opening our doors. I am confident some Gentlemen would have been ashamed to have seen their Speeches of this day, reflected in a News paper of tomorrow.   We sat to a ¹/₄ after 3 and adjourned without any Question being put— {I know not Whether this fear of taking the Question did not arise from some pointed Expressions Which fell from me.   I told them plainly, That I was no Advocate for banking Systems.   That I considered them as Machines for promoting the profits of unproductive Men.   That the Business of the United States so far as respected deposits, could be done in the present Banks.   That the Whole profit of the Bank ought to belong to the publick provided it was possible to advance the Whole Stock on her Account.   I was sorry That this at present was not possible.   I would however take half, or I should rather in the present Case say ¹/₅ of the loaf rather than no bread.   But I must remark that the publick was grossly imposed on in the present instance,   While she advanced all Specie, individuals advanced ³/₄ Certificates Which were of no more Value in the Support of the Bank than so much Stubble.   to make this plain, suppose the Vaults empty & a Note presented for payment,   would the Bearer take Certificates as Specie.   No Verily.   Besides the Certificates were all Under interest Already & it was highly Unjust That other paper should be issued on their Credit, Which bore a premium & Operated as A further Tax on the Country.}

Tuesday, 18 January 1791

This day the Bank Bill was taken up again.   I feel much Reluctance, to minute anything on this Subject.   I never saw the Spirit of Speculation dis-

play itself in stronger colors.   indeed the Guise of Regard for the interest of
the public was not preserved   Two Millions of Specie is to ~~pu~~ be subscribed in
by the public.   This is to be the basis of the Bank.   and the other Subscribers
Who are to draw dividends according to their Subscriptions, are to pay three
fourths in certificates.   King evidently wanted by a side wind, to exclude the
public from any dividend, under an Idea which he strongly inculcated That
the Subscription of the public was to be over and above the Capital ~~of the Ba~~
10 Millions of the Bank, and was to be considered as deposit.   A position
which resolves it itself into this. That the public should find the Specie to
support the Bank, While the Speculators who subscribe almost Wholly in
Certificates receive the Profits of the dividends.   Morris gave me some marks
of his Malevolence.   While I was up and Speaking. and Saw well what I said.
he said loud enough to be heard over half the Chamber. That I was mistaken
I varied the Arguments a little.   Took new Ground and After placing them in
What I thought an incontrovertible light I concluded, here I am not
Mistaken   the point on Which my mistake was charged was my alledging
That the Bank of North America wrought but 750,000 Doll.   Genl. Dickenson sat by me. and was willing to be called on.   That they wrought but
740,000—10,000 less than I had mentioned.   He is however a very good
natured Man, and I would not call on him.   He whispered this day, The
Treasury will make another purchase, for Hamilton has drawn 15,000 doll.
from the Bank, in Order to buy, as I suppose.   What a damnable Villain!

Wednesday, 19 January 1791

My Brother ~~and~~ went with me to the lodgings of Mrs. Bell, last night, and
communicated to her, the the news of the death of her Father.[18]   she manifested the most unbounded Grief. so as to give distress to the Bystanders.
Death! Death! thou art a solemn Messenger. and will take Us all in Rotation.
But let me Pause   What art thou?   I have been so ill that I would have
swallowed thee in an Anodyne.   Yes   When our Joys leave Us. When pain
possesses all our feelings thou art the Grand Composer of all our Miseries. the

---

[18]William Plunket (c. 1720–91), WM's longtime friend and associate, was a member of a
landed family in northern Ireland. He settled on the Pennsylvania frontier about 1748 and
practiced medicine. A year later he married Esther Harris, the sister of John Harris, Jr., later
WM's father-in-law. He served with WM during the French and Indian War and later settled
on the military bounty lands that he received on the West Branch of the Susquehanna. With
the creation of Northumberland County in 1772, he became president judge. Plunket was a
vocal opponent of the Connecticut settlers in the county and led the December 1775 *posse
comitatus*, which attempted unsuccessfully to drive them out. His opposition to independence ended his political career. At the time of his death he was blind and residing in WM's
Sunbury home. WM's brother Samuel married one of Plunket's daughters. See Appendix
C. (*Genealogical and Biographical Annals of Northumberland County . . .* [Chicago, 1911],
p. 488; *Wilkes Barre*, pp. 858–59; *NCHSP* 5:153)

last potion in the Cup of life.   and surely it need not be called a bitter one, for none ever complained after swallowing the Draught.   how little of the Sweet, and how deeply dashed with ~~bitter~~ Gaul is the Diet of life?   passes there a day in which we taste not of it?

This day the Bank bill passed all thro'.   the last clause was cavilled at.   I supported it. on this Principle   That any law containing a Grant of any kind should be irrepealable.   Laws touching the *regulation* of Morals Manners or property are all made on the principles of experiment and accomodation to time and place, but when legislators make grants the Deed should remain inviolate.   Three Opinions prevailed in Senate respecting this bill or perhaps I should rather say 3 Motives of Action.   The most prevalent seemed to be, to accomodate it to the Views of the Stock holders, Who may Subscribe. ~~from~~ The Potowmack interest seemed to regard it as a Machine Which in the hands of the Philadelphians, might retard the removal of Congress.   the Destruction of it of Course was their Object.   I really wished to make it as subservient to the public Interest as possible.   tho' all professed this. Yet I thought ~~nobody would give~~ few gave themselves any Trouble to promote it— I cannot help adding a Sincere Wish That the Integrity of the directors may make amends for the Want of it in Many of the Legislators who enacted it.   For in the hands of bad Men it May be made a Most Mischievous engine of.   but indeed so may Any, even the best of human Institutions.

Thursday, 20 January 1791

The business of this day was the third reading of the Bank Bill.   the same Questions were agitated over again, but without heat.   it was moved to reduce the limitation to 10 Years.   I at one time thought this long enough. but I conversed on the Subject with every Money'd Man I could find. and they uniformly declared that they would not subscribe on so short a period.   and the Consequence would be that they would all join in supporting the old banks and bearing down the national One.   I sincerely wish to derive a Benefit to the public from the Bank, and considering that the public are in this respect in the hands of the monied interest, I thought it best to agree to such bargain as we could make and accordingly Voted against this Motion,   Accident threw me in Company with these men, but I abhor their design of destroying the bank altogether.   Mr. Morris came very late this day, indeed not untill all the Business was over.   but he desired leave to have his Vote inserted on the minutes which was granted to him.   Dined with the President this day.   Sundry Gentlemen met me at the Door. and tho' I rather declined they pushed me forward.   After I had made my bows and and was inclining towards a Vacant seat the President Who rose to receive me edged about on the Sofa as he sat down and said here is room. but I had put myself in Motion for another Vacant Seat, a true Courtier would have changed, but I am not one, and sat on the opposite Settee or Sofa. with some New England Men. at Dinner after my second Plate had been taken away, the President offered to help me to som part of a Dish which Stood before him. was ever anything so unluckey, I had just before declined being helped to anything more, with some expression that denoted my having made up my dinner. had of course for the sake of Consistency to thank him negatively. But When the desert came and he was distributing a pudding, he gave me a look of interrogation and I returned the thanks positive. he soon after asked me to drink a Glass of Wine withe him, this was readily accorded to. and What was remarkable, I did not observe him drink with any other Person during dinner—but I think this must have been owing to my inattention Giles the New Member from Virginia sat next me but One. I saw a Speech of his in the papers which read very Well, and they say he delivers himself handsomely. I was therefore very attentive to him. But the Frothy Manners of Virginia were ever uppermost. Canvasbacks ham & Chickens Old Madeira, the Glories of the Antient Dominion, all *amazing* fine, Where were his constant Themes. boasted of personal Prowess, *more manual Exercise than any Man in New England.* fast but fine living in his Country, Wine or Cherry bounce from from 12 O'Clock, to night, every day. he seemed to practice on these principles too, as often as the Bottle passed him. declared for the Assumption & Excise &ca. he is but a Young Man. and seems as if he always would be so. {But after this digression let me. turn to the Unexpected Incident of dining With the President & his Marked Attention to me. he knows the Weight of political Odium Under Which I labor. he knows That my Uniform Opposition to funding Systems (at least to Ours) Assumptions high Compensations And expensive Arrangements, have drawn on Me the Resentment of all the Speculators Public Creditors Expectants of Office And Courtiers. In the State. there is another Point, Which I presume he does not know Viz. That I will receive no Support from the Republican or Opposition party. for there is not A Man of them, Who is not Aiming At a Six Doll. Prize, And My Place is the best chance in the Wheel. But he knows enough, to satisfy him, That I will be no Senator After the 3d of March. And to the Score of his Good Nature Must I place these extra Attentions. Be it so It is at least One Amiable Treat in his Character. I have however now seen him for the last Time perhaps. let me take a review of him As he really is. In Stature about Six feet, with An Unexceptionable Make, but lax Appearance, his frame Would seem to Want filling Up. his Motions rather slow than lively, tho he showed no Signs of having suffered either by Gout or Rheumatism. his complexion pale Nay

Almost Cadaverous.   his Voice hollow and indistinct Owing As I believe to Artificial teeth before in his Upper Jaw. Which occasioned a flatness of } [19]

Friday, 21 January 1791

This was a day of no great Business in the Senate.   Col. Gun of Georgia wanted Copies of the Secret Journal.   much talk passed about his application   he was however gratifyed.   In fact we have never kept our Journal agreeable to the Constitution   all the Executive part has been kept Secret without any Vote for it.   A Committee is however appointed and the Matter will hereafter be under better regulation.   We received some lengthy communications from Captn. Obryan[20] and the Prisoners at Algiers.   A Committee of the Senate some time ago recommended a War with them.[21]   War is often entered into, to answer domestic not foreign Purposes.   I fear such was the design of the Present report,   It was even talked, how many Ships should be fitted out and of What force.   But Obrien seems to show plainly, That a Peace may be obtained on easy Terms, by furnishing them with naval Stores. We have it plainly also from his letters. That the French⟨,⟩ danes and above all the British have done Us all the injury in their power with the Algerines.   in fact all who are at Peace with them are decidedly against Us & have done Us all the disservice ~~in their Power~~ they could.   The former Report was recommitted and these Papers referr'd to them.   Mr. Morris came late and left Us soon   We adjourned at about half after 2 O'Clock.

{George Remsen One of the Clerks of the Treasury[22] returned from New York Where he had been sent by the Secretary,   among his letters he pointed to a packet and said it contained 90,000 doll.   How can I help believing, That Speculation, was the Object of his Journey?}

Saturday, 22 January 1791

The Speaker U.S. called on me Yesterday.   asked me to go and Visit with him this day.   I agreed and called at his House about 10   he was however

---

[19]WM wrote the remainder of his description of Washington on a separate sheet that he then wafered into the diary. This sheet was later removed or lost. George Washington Harris, the editor of the 1880 edition of WM's diary, indicated that the page was already "wanting."

[20]Richard O'Bryen (c. 1758–1824) of Maine was captain of the *Dauphin* at the time of its capture by the Algerians in 1785. He corresponded with the United States government as spokesman for himself and other captives. See also *SEJ*, pp. 425–49, and *PTJ* 18:369–445. (Dorothy Twohig, ed., *Journal of the Proceedings of the President, 1793–97*, [Charlottesville, Va., 1981], p. 55n)

[21]The Senate committee on Mediterranean trade reported on 6 January.

[22]George H. Remsen was a clerk in the treasury department during at least the second and third sessions of the FFC. He left the department before the summer of 1791. (*PAH* 13:107)

gone. his House sat this day. and this will be his Excuse. I went to the Chamber of the State Representatives   The Resolutions against the Excise were the Order of the day. and were passed by a great Majority.   The Arguments were not important nor Striking,   some ill nature was expressed by Mr. Finley against a Mr. Evans.[23]   I feel sincere pleasure that so much independence has been manifested by the Yeomanry of Pennsylvania.   Indeed I am fully satisfyed that if a Spirit of this kind was not manifested from some Quarter or other our liberties would soon be swallowed up.   I triffled away the rest of the day.   much as was said in the Chamber of Representatives. They seem totally ignorant of the principle which appears to actuate the Adherents of Hamilton.   Taxes originally flowed from necessity; ways and Means followed contracted or unavoidable Expence.   here the System seems reversed.   the ways and Means are obvious to every Reader of a Register of the European Taxes   We have heads   we have ~~have~~ lands Slaves & Cattle   And every Article of European and Assiatic Convenience or Luxury is used among Us.   the difficulty is to find plausable pretexts, for extending the Arm of Taxation, and ways and Means to consume the collected Treasures.   and the reighning party seem to consider themselves as wanting in Duty, if the Fiscal Rent Roll should fall Short of the Royal Revenues of England.

Sunday, 23 January 1791

I had firmly devoted this day to my family in the way of writing Letters. but Just as I had adopted this resolution. A Message was brought me from Govr. Langdon, to go with him to Meeting,   This I could not refuse,   before I was half dressed I received a polite note from Mr. Morris to be One of his Friends, at a family dinner and this I could not refuse.   and before I had quite dressed Langdon called on me.   We attended at Arch Street meeting[24]—   dined with Mr. Morris, the Company Judge Wilson⟨,⟩ Governor St. Clair⟨,⟩ Genl. Butler.   Genl. Irwin was expected but did not come.   We were sociable and I sat later than I usually do.   Mr. Wallis[25] came into Town this Evening but brought me no letters, and I now hear that Charles Smith set off this day for Sunbury without giving me an Opportunity of writing, or at least without my knowing of his departure.   it is not handsomely done of either of them.   But

[23]Cadwalader Evans represented Montgomery County in the 1790–91 Pennsylvania House of Representatives.

[24]The Second Presbyterian Church was located at Arch and Third streets. (Scharf and Westcott, *Philadelphia* 2:1266)

[25]Samuel Wallis (1736–98) was a Philadelphia merchant and land speculator with a home and extensive lands near Muncy, about 25 miles north of Sunbury on the West Branch of the Susquehanna. His contemporaries were unaware that he spied for the British during the War for Independence. (John Bakeless, *Turncoats, Traitors and Heroes* [Philadelphia, 1959], pp. 294–302; *NCHSP* 4:48–59)

somebody Else will do them a dirty trick. ~~but.~~ God forbid it should be my luck, to do it. I had told the Treasurer[26] some time ago that I wanted to sell him some Stock. When I came home from meeting I found a note from him, importing that he would ~~buy~~ buy tomorow. {This in a great Measure confirms my former Suspicions, with respect to the Treasury.}

Monday, 24 January 1791

This day voluminous communications were introduced by Secretary Lear. a Volume of a Letter from a Docr. Ofallen[27] to the President. avowing the raising a Vast Body of Men in the Kentuckey Country to force a settlement in the Yazou Country. the state of indian Affairs both in the southern and Government N.W. of the Ohio. the Translation of all Which was a Want of more Troops. But the most singular of all was a proclamation for running lines of Experiment for the Ten Miles Square   the Message accompanying the proclamation calls for an emendatory law, permitting the President. to locate lower down. and to lay half of the Square in Virginia,   This really seems like unsettling the Whole Affair. I really am surprized at the Conduct of the President. to bring it back at any rate before Congress is certainly the most imprudent of all Acts. to take on him to fix the Spot by his own Authority, When he might have placed the three Commissioners in the Post of Responsibility, was a thoughtless Act. I really think it not improbable, That Opposition may find a nest to lay her eggs in. from the unexpected Manner of Treating this Subject. the General Sense of Congress certainly was that the Commissioners should fix on the spot. and it may be a query Whether the Words of the Law will warrant a different construction   the Commissioners now are only Agents of Demarkation, mere Surveyors to run four lines of fixed Courses and distances.

sold my Stock 6 ℔ Cents at 17/4 deferred & 3 ℔ cents at 9/.

Tuesday, 25 January 1791

Had this day another hearing at the Board of Property. I really have suffered persecution on this affair. Rawle My Adversary did not appear. and

---

[26]Samuel Meredith.

[27]James O'Fallon (1749–c. 1794) of Ireland received medical training at the University of Edinburgh prior to his arrival in North Carolina in 1774. After a medical career in the army during the War for Independence, he settled in South Carolina at the encouragement of Pierce Butler and became general agent for that state's Yazoo Land Company. It was on company business that he went to Kentucky in 1790 to gain support for a colonizing scheme aimed in part at separating the territory south of the Ohio River from the United States. Washington's proclamation of 19 March 1791 warned westerners of O'Fallon's designs and authorized his prosecution by federal authorities. The letter is printed in *DHFFC* 5:1377–83. (*MVHR* 17:230–63)

Daniel Rees[28] called about dinner time to tell me That Roberts⟨,⟩ Vaux and Coats[29] had been told of my cheating a Man out of a Tract of land, after it had been surveyed to him.   I really have had my share of Trouble with this Business of Senator and it would be well for me if I was fairly & honorably shot of it.   Mr. Brown of Northampton[30] called on me and told me That ⟨Peter⟩ Muhlenberg was very busy in giving Oyster Suppers &ca. and seemed to think that I should go more among the Members. &ca.   I find I will offend him & some others if I do not, But it is a Vile commerce and I detest this beast Worshiping.   how Melancholy a thing is it, That the Liberties of Men should be in the hands of such Creatures,   I cannot call them men.   But Brown seemed to think that Muhlenberg had made an impression on the Germans or some of them.   {Be it so, such arts have prevailed & will prevail.   but the day of my deliverance draweth nigh.   the 4th of March is not distant   from the different schemes and parties that are formed, And the want of any fixed form or mode of election, I cannot think the Choice will be made before that time.   And let them affront me, if they find me here, afterwards.}

Wednesday, 26 January 1791

I never in my life had more distressing dreams than last night, but I received imaginary relief from my [*lined out*] visionary perplexity, and the emotion was so great as to awaken me.   the ~~emotion~~ agitation I underwent was so ~~great~~ extreme that my head ached for some time after I awoke   This I may charge to the Vexation of Yesterday   I went and called on a number of the Members of Assembly and Senate.   all seems fair and Smoth.   Some of them indeed said expressly. They would support me at the ensuing Election {believing That to be the Object of my Visit. As it in some Measure was.}   *sed nulla fides Fronti.*[31] may be applyed to ~~some~~ many of them.

The Bill regulating Consuls and Vice Consuls had the 2d Reading this day,   a Letter from the National Assembly of France on the Death of Doctor Franklin was communicated from them and Received with a Coldness, That was truly amazing.   I cannot help ~~figuring~~ painting to myself the disappointment that awaits the French Patriots.   While their warm fancies are figuring ~~to themselves~~ the raptures that we will be thrown into, on the Receipt of their letters, and the information of the honors which they have bestowed on our

---

[28]Daniel Rees was a resident of Northumberland County.

[29]Jonathan Roberts (1731–1812), James Vaux, and Lindsay Coats (1742–99) represented Montgomery County in the 1790–91 Pennsylvania legislature, the former two in the house of representatives and the latter in the senate. Coats's district also included Bucks and Chester counties.

[30]Robert Brown (1744–1823) represented Northampton County in the state senate during the 1790–91 session. He had been a member of the Pennsylvania Assembly from 1783 to 1787 and an Antifederalist. (*DHROC* 2:67)

[31]Yet there is no reliance on appearance.

Countrymen and anticipating the complimentary echos of our Answers. When they find that we cold as Clay, care not a fig about them Franklin or Freedom.   well. we deserve!   What do we deserve?   To be d....d.

Cures for the Rheumatism

A Tea Spoonful of the Flour of Brimston taken every Morning before Breakfast.   General St. Clair and Mr. Milligan both relieved by it.   Note they are both Scotchmen.

2d

Assa Fœtida laid on burning Coals and held to the Nose.   Mr. Todd greatly relieved by this.

3d

Cyder in Which an hot Iron has been Quenched   this has relieved many tho Cyder, is to many People very hurtful, in that disorder.

Thursday, 27 January 1791

This day communications were received from the P. of U.S. relating to indian depradations, a post on the Muskin-Gum, cut off.   The Wishes of many People are gratifyed. to involve Us in War, to involve Us in Expence at any rate seems the great Object of their desires.   It perhaps would be unjust, perhaps cruel to suppose it.   But had a System been needed to involve Us in the depth of difficulties with the Indians, none better could have been devised.   last Year at New York much Altercation happened Whether a discrimination in the Duties of Tonnage should not be made in favour of Foreign nations in Treaty with Us.   this measure was lost, altho in my Opinion a just One.   the Court of France remonstrate against ~~it~~ the duties, expecting favours as a nation in Treaty.   some Gentlemen on the receiving the Communications affected recantation publickly, and by these very Means obtained themselves to be put on the Committee.   this day they reported. directly against the claims of France.[32]   I have hitherto, attended only to the part acted by some Persons whose Conduct, from Appearances, is not very consistent.   I called on Otis for the Papers,[33]   he said Butler got them and had Given them to One of the Representatives, a minute after I saw them in the hands of Mr. Dalton.   But Otis is really so Stupid, That I know not Whether he lyed or Blundered.   When the Matter of no discrimination was carried in Congress, in our first Session, I could hardly suppress a thought, which I felt ready to spring up in my mind. That some Persons wished to destroy the Confidence between Us and France, and bring Us back to the Fish Potts of British dependence.   This I charged to the influence of the City of New

---

[32]This action is recorded in the *SEJ*.

[33]The papers, or French papers, to which WM refers here and elsewhere relate to tonnage duties on French vessels. They are printed in the *SEJ*, pp. 104–12, 389–423.

York. But Philada. has not altered the Tenor of their Political Conduct. Elsworth could not rest a Moment all this day. he was out & in, in and out, all on the figgets. Twice or Thrice was an adjournment hinted at. and as often did he request that it might be withdrawn, expecting the Excise Bill[34] to be taken up. but he had to bear his impatience. three O'Clock came before the Bill. I can see that he now will stand foremost in the Gladiatorial list.

Friday, 28 January 1791

Much crouded this Morning with People with Whom I had not much to do. had to call at the Board of Property. twas the Usual time before I went to the Hall. The Excise bill came up. But Oh! What a Mistake, it is only a bill for discontinuing certain duties and laying others in their Stead. the Odious name is omitted, but the thing is the same. It was read and ordered ~~for~~ to the press. I went to the Senate of the State to hear the Debates on the Resolutions. but they were postponed. returned to our Chamber and the Report of the Committee on the difference with the Court of France was taken up.[35] almost every Body gave it against the French demands. I differed from them in some points, but as I could not obtain a Sight of the papers I joined in the Motion for postponement which was carried.

Saturday, 29 January 1791

called twice this day at the office of our Secretary, to get the French Papers. Otis says Carrol took them away, but there is no believing a Word ~~which~~ that he says. went to hear the debates in the State Senate The Resolutions for instructing the Senators, had been postponed Yesterday, expressly ~~on this principle~~ for the purpose of obtaining a sight of the bill which is in its passage thro' Congress.[36] but the same Men pushed for a decision this day. The State has now an Opportunity of seeing the Benefit of Two houses. the division was 9 to 8 the Yeas and nays were called. Graff of Lancaster[37] was going home. this was the Reason of pushing the Vote this day. assembly-men and Senators may be equally considered as Representatives of the People, from the division of the Two houses, the Voice of the People appears to be unequivocally against an Excise.

---

[34]Duties on Distilled Spirits Act [HR-110].
[35]This action is recorded in the *SEJ*.
[36]Duties on Distilled Spirits Act [HR-110].
[37]Sebastian Graff (c. 1750–91) was a senator for York and Lancaster counties in the 1790–91 legislature. He had supported the Constitution at the state ratification convention in 1787 and served in the state constitutional convention in 1789–90. (*PMHB* 11:77–78)

Sunday, 30 January 1791

Not well this day and staid at home the most of the day.   went in the
Evening to the funeral of Judge Bryan.[38]   {This man rests from his labours,
but the Tongue of Malevolence resteth not.   so inhuman are many of the
Citizens of this place, as to speak of his discease with Joy.   but the Anodyne of
Death hath spread her Mantle over him.   he was said to be spiteful & revenge-
ful.   his Enemies were not less so, and he had the qualities of Industry and
love of freedom. which few of them can boast of.   he was the Father of the
Abolition Law.}

Monday, 31 January 1791

the excise Bill read a 2d time but the Bill not being in our hands. it was made
the Order of the day for Wednesday.   the affair of the French discontents
taken up.[39]   God forgive me if I wrong some People But there certainly have
been more censorious conclusions. than to charge some People with a design of
breaking our connection with France.   I called on Friday   I called Twice on
Saturday   Otis lyed basely about the papers and I have never got my Eyes on
them.

{When or how will all these Mad Measures lead Us.   We hear it ever in Our
Ears That the Present General Government (with respect to the Persons Who
compose it) contains the collected Wisdom and learning of the United
States.   It must be admitted that they have generally been selected on Ac-
count of their Reputation for knowledge, either legal political Mercantile
Historical &ca.   News papers are printed in every Corner.   In every Corner
Ambitious Men abound for Ignorance or Want of qualification is no bar to this
Vice.

Thus then the Tylers and Jack Straws[40] Will May come in play, & talents Experience And learning be considered As disqualifications for Office And thus
the Government be bandied About from One Set of Projectors to another. 'till
some One More Artfull than the rest to perpetuate their power Slip the Noose
of Despotism about our Necks.

'tis easy to say this can never happen Among a Virtuous People—   Aye
But We are not more Virtuous than the Nations That have gone before Us.}

---

[38]George Bryan (1731–91), a judge of the Pennsylvania Supreme Court since 1780, was a
leader in the Pennsylvania government during the War for Independence. While a member
of the assembly in 1780, he authored the act for the gradual abolition of slavery. Bryan was a
prominent Antifederalist.

[39]This action is recorded in the *SEJ*.

[40]Wat Tyler and Jack Straw were leaders of the Peasants' Revolt in southern England in
1381. Their names, particularly the latter, came to stand for worthless men of no substance.

February 1791

Tuesday, 1 February 1791

This day I had much to say against the Report of a Committee which went to declare War against the Algerines.   It is not suspicion. That the designs of the Court are to have a fleet and Army.   The Indian War is forced forward to Justify our having a standing Army.   and eleven unfortunate Men now in Slavery at Algiers is the pretext for fitting out a fleet, to go to War with them, While 14 of these Captives were alive the Barbarians asked about 35,000 doll. for them.   but it is Urged that we should expend half a Million of dollars rather than redeem these unhappy Men.   I vociferated against the Measure and I suppose offended my Colleague.   This thing of a fleet has been working among our members all the session   I have heard it break out often.[1]

Wednesday, 2 February 1791

the Excise bill read over and remarked on and committed to five Members.   I gave notice That I would endeavour to show that a much lower duty would answer the demand of the Secretary.   I spoke to sundry of the Members to second a General Postponement for the session. but not a Man approved of any such thing   dined this day with Mr. Burd.   Lewis was there   Rawle was there   Old Shippen was there.[2]   I endeavoured to be easy but could not be Sprightly.   From the circle of the Universe could not be collected a Group Who have manifested equal malignity to me personally as I have received from

---

[1]WM's comments of this day refer to action that is recorded in the *SEJ*. See March 1791, n. 2.

[2]The intermarried Shippen and Burd families had long been interested in the military, political, and land transactions of the Sunbury area. James Burd (1726–93), a resident of Dauphin County, used his political influence there to oppose the interests of John Harris, Jr. The dinner host was probably James's son Edward (1751–1833), prothonotary of the Pennsylvania Supreme Court and a resident of Philadelphia. Old Shippen was probably Joseph Shippen II (1706–93) rather than his nephew Joseph Shippen III (1732–1810). WM had made land surveys for the Shippens. (Randolph Klein, *Portrait of an Early American Family: The Shippens . . .* [Philadelphia, 1975]; Lewis B. Walker, *The Burd Papers* [n.p., 1899], preface, pp. 60–63; *NCHSP* 3:82–104, 4:113–29; WM to Edward Burd, 22 September 1786, Provincial Delegates, PHi; Joseph Shippen Letterbooks, 1767–69, PPAmP)

the above Characters.   May they never have it in their power to do unto others
as they have done unto me.

Thursday, 3 February 1791

This day was unimportant in the Senate   no debate of Consequence took
place.   I was called off the Street to dine with a Quaker. at about 2 OClock
as he seemed very Friendly I went and eat heartily of a good dinner. and was
perfectly easy. much more than I could say of the great dinners where the
Candles are ready to be brought in with the going out of the last dishes.   This
high life is really very distant from nature   all is Artificial.   I negotiated
sundry small Matters and went in the evening to the Meeting of a Society
formed lately for promoting the improvement of Roads and inland Communications.   Docr. Smith is at the bottom of this Business.   his Object is to
invalidate the report of the Commissioners who have lately viewed the Communications on the Susquehanna Juniata &ca. at least so far as to bring
forward, the Juniata only[3]   in this business Finley is joined with him. and a
dirty pair they are.   I attacked the proceedings of the Committee who drew
up the Memorial, with perhaps more eagerness than prudence.   I had however some Success.   My old Friend[4] shewed some Malignity.   From the drift
of Chaff and feathers, you know how the Wind blows says the Proverb   much
more if you see Ships sail or Trees Come down with the blast.   Yesterday
Ryerson the the devoted Creature of Mr. Morris, put up a nomination of Wm.
Finley for Senator in my room.   They will be easy when they get my place. and
I trust I will be easyer without it than with it.   What is the reason that I do not
hear a single Word from Harrisburgh.   not a Word from Davy   not a Word
from Bob.   not a Word from the old Man.[5]   I will give myself no trouble
about them, or as little as I can help.

Friday, 4 February 1791

This day we had a long report from the secretary of State, transmitted to Us
from the house of Representatives, respecting the Fisheries of New England.

---

[3]WM belonged to the Pennsylvania Society for Promoting the Improvement of Roads and
Inland Navigation, a Pennsylvania organization of almost 100 members established in 1789
to influence the state legislature. The meeting WM attended considered a memorial drafted
by a committee consisting of Rev. William Smith, Representative Clymer, Tench Coxe,
William Montgomery, John Adlum, and John Nicholson. It relied in part on the efforts of
John Adlum, Samuel Maclay, and Timothy Matlack, commissioners appointed by Pennsylvania in 1790 to study potential water transportation routes in the northwestern part of the
state. (*PMHB* 65:446–47; Wilkinson, *Land Policy,* pp. 102–3)
    [4]This is probably a reference to Rev. William Smith, whom WM despised. See December
1789–January 1790, n. 4.
    [5]WM referred to David, Robert, and John Harris, Jr., respectively.

The great object seems to be the making them a nursery for Seamen, That We like all the Nations of the Earth may also have a Navy. We hear every day distant hints of such things as these. in fact it seems we must soon forego our republican innocence. and like all other nations, set apart a portion of our Citizens for the purpose of inflicting Misery on our fellow Mortals. This practice is Felony to posterity. the Men so devoted are not only cut off. but a proportionate share of Women remain unmatched. had the Sums expended in War been laid out in meliorating the kingdom of England or any other modern Government, what delightful abodes might they have been made. Whereas War leaves only the Traces of desolation.

dined this day with Charles Biddle, he has some point to carry in the State Government, as I believe and the dinner may be on Account of my Brother the Company were mostly members of the legislature

I must here note of our President that he this day hurried the adjournment for for tomorrow at 11 OClock. all this is plain. he is deep in the cabals of the Secretary. the Secretary sat close with the Committee on the Excise bill. Every moment it was expected they would report. but so anxious are the Secretary's party to have it passed, That even John Adams, who used to show as much Joy on an adjournment from Friday to Monday as ever school boy did at the Sweet sound of Playtime. fixed the House to meet tomorrow.

Saturday, 5 February 1791

The Senate met. I found Hamilton with the Committee, who had the excise bill in their hands. We sat and sat and Sat. but no Report, I had busied myself in geting a Return of the number of Stills from the different Members of Assembly. I went to the door of the Committee room to Use it in argument with them. but finding Hamilton still with them I retired. Mr. Morris took the paper & went in. and I suppose no further Use was made of it. he however restored it again. The Report on the Fisheries by Jefferson was directed to be printed. No Report from the Committee. it was agreed to that the power of the inspectors should extend only to importations and distillation. but I find Hamilton will have it even this modifyed to his mind. nothing is done without him. {I have been troublesome in my speeches against the Excise; Upon general principles, It is equally exceptionable as a Poll Tax. ~~Welt~~ Wealth is not it's object. The Mouth of One Individual may be supposed to consume as much liquor as another, any difference is rather in favour of the Most costly imported liquors. it is a Tax Oral, and has only this advantage over the poll Tax. That You may refrain from using your mouth in drinking liquor. with some People this is {as} impossible} {as to do without an head.}

Sunday, 6 February 1791

attended meeting, and wrote letters to Harrisburgh and home to my family.   on the 3d of March Congress will rise.   I have wrote for my Mare to be here against that day.   and from deceit dissimulation and Ambition, from Mere artificial life from whence both Truth and sincerity are banished. I will go & meet nature love affection and sincerity in the embraces of my wife and dear Children.

Monday, 7 February 1791

Attended at the Hall   Mr. King made One of his curious Stretches,   he said the Minutes were wrong and he wished to correct them.   The Report which was ordered to be printed on Saturday. he wished to be postponed to the 28th of Decemr. next. and corrected the minutes of Saturday to read so.   This same King is a singular Man.   Under the Idea of correcting the Minutes he introduces matter totally new.   It is not correcting Matter of Form. but total Alteration, and adjection of New Matter.   I opposed him and certainly he ought to be ashamed of the Measure and Yet it was carried. but amended Afterwards and placed nearer the Truth.[6]

There certainly is a design of quarelling with France. and That Jefferson should seem to countenance this.   What can this Mean?   I am really astonished at all this.   I think I must be mistaken. and Yet to think so is to disbelieve my senses.   {And What can I do?   I have attempted everything And effected nothing Unless it be to render myself An Object of Aversion. For Well indeed Speaks the Poet—

Truths would You teach, or save a Sinking Land,
All fear, none Aid You & few Understand.}[7]

Tuesday, 8 February 1791

The Senate met and the appropriation bill had the last reading.   There was a pausing about taking up the Excise bill. like people pausing on the brink of a precipice. afraid to take the dangerous leap.   however it was at length attempted. and we blundered along to the 4th Section.   Objections had been made to this Section. and it was expected the Committee would alter it.   they have done so with a Vengeance.   it now runs that there shall be an Inspector General over a district.   The district to be divided into Surveys. and an

---

[6]Neither the rough nor smooth version of the *SLJ* reflects any correction to the minutes; nevertheless, Jefferson's report on the cod and whale fisheries was not considered until the Second Congress.
[7]Alexander Pope, "An Essay on Man."

Inspector to be set over each Survey who shall appoint People under him to do the business. as many of these to be appointed as the President shall think proper. and he shall pay them too. It is the most execrable System that ever was framed against the liberty of a People. This abominable clause was postponed the Members by degrees stole away. The Men who did it. shewed their disapprobation of it in their looks It is in vain our Government cannot stand.

All my Opposition has been considered as Vain babbling, but to get quit of it in some degree this business of committment has taken place, And Now the Majority have a kind of Scape Goat in the Committee, and a pretext for following them and disregarding Opposition, Under the Idle Idea. of their knowing best. having consulted Hamilton &c. &ca.— {How Abandoned is the conduct of these Men— Abuse, rail at, vilify and traduce the European Systems of Excise, As much as You will, demonstrate their Absurdity Villany & deplorable Effects on Society As much as You please. 'tis all right. they echo every Sentence; Ours is no such thing is their Language, quite innocent & harmless. Yet such is the indolence of Hamilton And his Adherents That they will not Use even the Guise of different Terms or words to conceal the Copy. Nor will they Stop 'till perhaps As in Britain, ten Men may be employed to Guard One Distillery.}

Wednesday, 9 February 1791

Attended the Hall this day and was perhaps never more vexed, were eloquence personifyed and Reason flowed from her Tongue. her Talents would be vain in our Assembly. or in any other Where all business is done in dark Cabal, on the principle of interested management. The Excise bill is passed and a pretty business it is. The Ministry fore see opposition and are preparing to resist it by a band, nay an host of Revenue Officers. it is put in the power of the President to make as many Districts, appoint as many General Surveyors & and as many Inspectors of Surveys as he pleases, and thus multiply force to bear all down before him War and bloodshed is the most likely consequence of all this.

Congress may go home Mr. Hamilton is all powerful and fails in nothing which he attempts. little avail As I was sure it would be. off of. I nevertheless endeavoured not to be wanting in my duty And told them plainly of the precipice Which I considered them as having approached. That the State Legislature of Pennsylvania had been obliged to wink at the Violation of her Excise laws,[8] in the western parts of State ever since the revolution. That in my Opinion, it could not be enforced by Collectors or Civil Officers of any kind

---

[8]Pennsylvania, following colonial precedent, adopted its excise law in February 1777 and modified it several times before repealing it in 1791.

be they ever so numerous.   And that nothing Short of a permanent Military force could effect it.   That this for Aught I knew, might be acceptable to some Characters.   I could only answer for myself, that I did not wish it, & would avoid every Measure that tended to make it necessary.

Thursday, 10 February 1791

I returned home this day from the Senate Chamber, more fretted, and really more off the center of good humor than I ever I did in my life.   I really was ready to pray Lord deliver Us from Rascals.   I cannot have Charity enough to believe That the prevailing party in our Senate are honest Men.   some letters however have come in since Yesterday from New England. and Strong was willing to move the Reductions which we wanted.   after the bill was read over and ready for the question. Foster from Rhode Island moved a Reduction of 3 Cents on the distillations from Molasses &ca.   I rose & seconded him on condition of his extending the Motion thro' all the distillations in the U.S. and a reduction to 40 Cents on the contents of Stills.   King objected to the lessening of the Ratios, ~~and~~ as productive of deficiencies in the Revenue demanded.   I shewed in answer that the importations into the port of Philada. & the Sum expected from Stills in this State would go a great way. towards raising one half of the ~~80026~~ 8 hundred 26 thousand dollars demanded by the Secretary   Elsworth answered with rudeness, That I was mistaken.   that the Secretary ~~waved~~ demanded a Million and half   I reply'd by reading part of the Secretary's report. which confirmed the position which I had made & repeated my other Arguments.   he did not reply.   This Man has abilities. but Abilities without candor and integrity, are characteristicks of the Devil. at half after 3 the question was ready to be put.   Henry of Maryland. told me he had a bet depending with Butler on the Division of the House. and desired the Yeas & nays.   I needed not this excuse. and called sharply for the Yeas and nays.   with all their strength they were startled.   and up got King. and round and round and about & about. one while commit the⟨n⟩ recommit then postpone.   Elsworth too had the world and all to say   and now in fact they are afraid of the figure they have raised—and the 4th Section was recommitted   This whole day Mr. Morris was dead against me. in the voting way, sat quite away back from me, but spoke none either way.

Friday, 11 February 1791

I find this day, that the Reason of recommitting the Excise bill Yesterday was to enable Hamilton to come forward with some new Schemes.   three new Clauses were brought forward and all of them from the Treasury.   the Obnoxious One (at least to me) was the putting it in the power of the President to form districts by cutting up the States, so as to pay no respect to their Boundaries. this was curiously worded. for fear of the little States taking any alarm. it stood by adding from the great to the lesser States. This they got adopted and having been successful so far King got up, and talked about it Goddess and about it. He wanted the United States divided into a number of Districts independent of any of the State Boundaries. Like an Indian at the War Post he wrought himself into a passion, declared the that *we had no right to pay any more attention to the State boundaries, than to the boundaries of the Cham of Tartary.*[9] When he had spent his Froth on this Subject. up Got Elsworth, and echoed most of What he said, but said he wished only three great districts and the President might subdivide each into Six. Whe⟨n⟩ he had done up Got Mr. Morris & declared himself in Sentiment with King. and spoke against the conveniency of the State Boundaries. King rose again repeated his old Arguments and wished for an Opportunity for taking a Question on the Principle of dividing the United States without any regard to their boundaries. pop at length out of his pocket comes a Resolution. It imported That the United States should be divided into Six Districts Two East of the Hudson Two from that to the Potowmack and Two from that Southwestward or Words to that import, and That the President should subdivide them into Surveys &ca. This pretty System was however after all negatived. Annihilation of the State Governments is undoubtedly the Object of these People. The late Conduct of our State legislature has provoked them beyond all bounds. they have created an indian War, that an Army may Spring out of it. and the Triffling Affair of our having 11 Captives at Algiers (who ought long ago to have been ransomed) is made the pretext for going to war with them and fitting out a fleet. with these Two engines, and the collateral aids derived from an host of Revenue Officers. farewell Freedom in America. {Gently indeed did I touch it in Argument. but is not a Motion for the destruction of the individuality of the States, treason against the duty of a Senator, Who from the nature of his Appointment Ought to be Guardian of the State Rights. The little I said however (I believe) raisd a Goblin that frightened them from the project, at least for this time.}

Saturday, 12 February 1791

This day we passed the Excise law, and a pretty piece of business it is. I found there was an unwillingness in many of the Members to have the Yeas and nays I however called them sharply and enough rose. and I had the

---

[9]The khanate of Tatar prospered as an independent nation for a century previous to its subjugation by Czar Ivan the Terrible in 1552. Despite popular uprisings over the course of two centuries, the policy of russification prevailed.

pleasure of giving my decided negative against what I consider the ~~Pandora~~
Box of Pandora with regard to the happiness of America. The Communications came in this Morning respecting the indian Affairs. and the bill was
ordered to be printed. As we came down Stairs Doctor Johnson spoke with
great Joy. now said he all is over the Business is compleat, we have a
Revenue that will support Government, and every necessary Measure of Government. We have now the necessary support for national Measures, &c.
&ca. I told him perhaps we might undo all. That the high demands we had
made, would raise opposition and That Opposition might endanger the Government. he seemed a little Struck I repeated that the Government might
& perhaps would fall by her over exertions to obtain Support. I called this
Evening at Boyd's. I found Gallatine and Beard and James Finley.[10] I told
them I wished to hear them speak freely on the defense of the Frontiers.
some desultory discourse passed, I sat a While and Dr. Hutchinson[11] came
in, greasy as a ~~bag~~ Skin of Oyle and puffing like a porpoise. This must certainly be a dirty fellow. if external appearances do not much belie mental
management, and internal intention. Fame fixes them on the same footing.
and I fancy for Once she has not sounded a false alarm. he had a pretty tale to
tattle, over quite new. quite, ~~a la Doctor~~. quite medical. Is the Town sickly
Doctor? No. No. Yes Yes. for the Season. Accidents Accidents. half of
a family Struck down Yesterday, they had feed on Pheasant, all Who had
eaten affected. all the Doctors called. discharged the offensive food, recovered. the Craws of the Pheasants examined, laurel leaves found in them.
The death of Judge Bryan explained. he and his wife eat Pheasant, both fell

---

[10] Albert Gallatin (1761–1849), a member of the 1790–91 Pennsylvania House of Representatives from Fayette County, came to the United States in 1780 from Switzerland. He was well
educated and had an aristocratic background. In the mid 1780s he settled in western Pennsylvania and entered politics. Gallatin was an influential member of the 1788 Antifederalist
Harrisburg Convention and also served in the 1789–90 Pennsylvania Constitutional Convention. As secretary of the treasury for presidents Jefferson and Madison, he made few changes
in the Hamiltonian financial system other than to reduce spending, particularly by the
military, and to advocate the elimination of the federal debt. He succeeded by 1811, but the
War of 1812 created a debt that was significantly larger than it had been when Jefferson took
office in 1801. (Marshall Smelser, *The Democratic Republic, 1801–1815* [New York, 1968], pp.
54–57)
    John Beard [Baird] (c. 1740–1800) represented Westmoreland County in the 1790–91
Pennsylvania House of Representatives. He had recently served on the Supreme Executive
Council and was a prominent Antifederalist in the Pennsylvania Ratification Convention.
(*PMHB* 10:449–50; *DHROC* 2:241n, 639)
    James Findley represented Fayette County in the 1790–91 Pennsylvania House of Repre-
sentatives.
    [11] James Hutchinson (1752–93), prominent Philadelphia physician and Antifederal polit-
ical leader, was born in Bucks County and graduated from the College of Philadelphia in
1774. He received further medical training in England and served as senior surgeon of the
middle department of the Continental army. (Whitfield J. Bell, "James Hutchinson . . .,"
Lloyd Stevenson and Robert Multhauf, eds., *Medicine, Science and Culture: Historical
Essays in Honor of Owsei Temkin* [Baltimore, 1968], pp. 256–83)

comatose, torpid, she evacuated, he died.   and thus were we entertained
with the belchings of this bag of blubber for half an hour   I took my hat and
left them.   I had come but a few Steps when I met Mr. W. Finley   told him I
had called to talk on the Subject of the Western War with the Indians.   That
altho the management would be in different hands. Yet as the means must be
furnished by Us, it was in some measure necessary to contemplate the mode.
he immediately quit the Subject & got at the Excise.   it must be submitted
to   great Credit due to the General Governments   very honorable management to raise the debts to their full Value &ca.   in Short I believe he forgot
himself or the company he was in,   I begged pardon for stopping him in the
Street, and left him.   he chose to let me know of his Communications with
General Knox & and other great Men &ca. &ca.

Sunday, 13 February 1791

I went to the Meeting of Market Street[12]   came home,   the day rather
disagreeable in the afternoon and I staid at home the Residue of the day.
{Had made a remark here Which I think it best to erase}   [erased] with the
Rheumatic affection in my hand and so spent the day {mostly} in
Reading—   {went however down stairs   found a large company   the Subject religion and most unmercifully Was it handled.   the point Which attempted to be established was, that the Whole was craft & imposition.   That
all our Objects were before Us   believe What You see.   Observe the fraud &
endless Mischiefs of Ecclesiasticks, in every Age &ca.   few of the Historic facts
Which they adduced could be refuted.   but by Way of ~~refutation~~ opposition
Luther's reformation Was mentioned.}   {It was easily Answer'd that had
there been no abuse there needed no reformation.   But a further remark was
suggested.   That Luther was a Mere political Machine in the hands of those
German princes Who could no longer bear to see their Subjects pillaged by
Roman rapacity.   The Doctrine was pay for indulgences & purchase Salvation
with good Works Alias Money.   the New Doctrine was faith is better than
Cash, only believe & save Your Money.   It ~~not~~ need not be doubted but the
New Doctrine Was on this Account more Acceptable to both Prince &
People   Luther however had the Scripture with him.   Another position I
thought still less tenable.   That Man was but the first Animal in nature, That
he became so by the feelings of his fingers. & hence all his faculties,   Give said
they only a hand to a Horse   he would rival all the human powers.   This I
know to be Groundless   The Possum from it's feeble harmless & helpless
faculties is almost extinct in Pennsylvania, And Yet one that I killed in the

---

[12]The First Presbyterian Church was located on Market Street between Second and Third.
(Scharf and Westcott, *Philadelphia* 2:1263, 1270)

Island at Juniata[13] had as compleat an hand with 4 fingers & a Thumb as one of the human Species.}

Monday, 14 February 1791

Tis done   I doubt no longer.   This day came in bulkey communications from the President.   The amount, was the Result of a Negotiation arrived on by his Order with the Court of Great Britain, ~~by~~ Thro' the Agency of Gouverneur Morris.[14]   From the letters from the President it appears, that the Vote ~~of~~ against discrimination which has involved Us in difficulties with France was the Work of the President {avowedly procured by his influence}. and that he did it to facilitate a Connection with Great Britain. thus offering direct offense to France and incurring the Contempt of Britain.   for ~~they have~~ she has spurned every ~~of~~ overture made to ~~them~~ her.   and now the Result is, (I suppose) a War with Great Britain.   at least these Troops are (as I suppose), meant to wrest the Posts from her   she will resist.   Reprisals at Sea will take place. and all the Calamities of War ~~follow~~ ensue   It is with difficulty that I refrain from giving the most severe language to some of our Senators   King this day vapoured at a most unaccountable rate

The Opponents to the Constitution, said he were blind, they did not see the Ground to attack it on.   I could have shewn them how to defeat it.   The most popular ground against it never was touched.   The Busines is now compleat.   we need not care for Opposition   Henry of Maryland joined with him,   said the Constitution of the U.S. implyed everything   it was a most admirable System.   Thus did these Heroes Vapour and boast of their address, in having cheated the People. and establishing a form of Government over them which none of them expected.   ☞ I will leave a blank here to copy Genl. Washington's letters[15] in   perhaps this is wrong for I never can contemplate the insult offered to France *to procure more agreeable arrangements* without feeling resentment. {☞The System laid down by these Gentlemen was avowed as follows. or rather the developement of the desi[gns] of a certain party.   The General Power to carry the Constitution into effect by a construc-

---

[13]WM probably referred to the island he owned in the Juniata River near present-day Mifflintown.

[14]Gouverneur Morris (1752–1816) was sent by Washington in 1790 on a special mission to Great Britain aimed at resolving differences between that nation and the United States. A member of a prominent New York family and a 1768 graduate of King's College, Morris became a lawyer and an early advocate of a strong central government. He represented New York in the Continental Congress and Pennsylvania in the Federal Convention, and from 1781 to 1785 he served as assistant secretary of finance under Robert Morris, to whom he was not related.

[15]WM did not insert Washington's two letters sent to the Senate on this date. One is printed in the *SEJ*, p. 116; the other in the *SLJ*, p. 608. The papers relating to commercial relations with Great Britain are printed in the *SEJ*, pp. 451–67.

tive interpretation. wou[l]d extend to every Case That Congress may deem necessar[y] or expedient.　should the very Worst Thing Supposab[le] happen Viz. the claim of any of the States to any of the powers exercised by the General Government such claim will be treated with contempt.　The laws of the U.S. Will be held paramount to [*lined out*] their Laws claims & even ~~for~~ Constitutions.　the Supreme power is with the General Governm[ent] to decide in this as in every thing Else.　for the States have neglected to Secure any Umpi[re] or mode of decision in Case of difference between　nor is there Any Point in the Constitution for them to rally Under.　They May Give An Opinion. but the Opinion of the General Government mu[st] prevail, &ca.　This open point this ungarded pass has rendered the General Government compleatly incontrolable,　with a fleet and Army wh[ich] the first War Must give Us, all future oppositi[on] will be chimerical—}　{I ventured to dissent from these political Heroes, by declaring that the People Themselves would Guard this pass. That The right of Judging with respect to encroachments still remained with the People,　it was originally wit[h] them and they never had divested themselves of it—　with all their Art however, since they now confess their Views, I think they have made but a bungling hand of it.　The Old Congress had no power over individuals.　And of Course no System of Consolidation could take place.　their legislative or recommendatory powers were over States only.　the new Constitution by the instrumentality of the Judiciary &ca. Aims at the Government of individuals,　And the States Unless as to the conceded points, and with regard to their individual Sovereignty and independence, are left Upon Stronger Ground than formerly.　And it can only ~~by~~ be by implication or inference That the General Government can exercise controul over them, as States; any direct & open Act would be termed Usurpation.　But Whether the Gradual influence and encroachments of the General Government may not gradually Swallow Up the State Governments, is another Matter.}

Tuesday, 15 February 1791

This day was rather unimportant in the Senate　General Dickenson and I had a long discourse in the Committee Room.　The subject was the Speculations of the Treasury. or I should rather say of Hamilton.　No Body can prove these things but every body knows them.　Mr. Morris laboured in private with me this day to get me to join in postponing the complaints of the French Court.　The President, altho' it is undeniable that it was thro' his instrumentality that the Offense was given to France, Yet now wishes all this done away, the Breach made up with France and the Resentment shewn to England—　the Measure is right, but his Motives wrong.　never should the paths of rectitude be forsaken, had the President left Congress to themselves, the discrimination would have obtained and as the discrimination had heretofore obtained by the State laws. England could have taken no Umbrage. & ~~France~~ we should have experienced no interrupting Harmony with France. The crooked policy of the President, has involved us in difficulty. unless we repeal the law, We loose for ever the Friendship of France. and even after repealing it the Confidence of France in Us will be impaired, as she may attribute ~~to~~ our first motives to ingratitude and our last to fear. continuing the Law will have no effect on Britain, as she has already treated Genl. Washingtons application with contempt but a repeal of it, will be followed with a burst of Resentment. This we will have to submit to. & ought not to regard. {King delivered An Opinion that Executive papers should be redelivered to the President's private Secretary.[16] it was evident he alluded to the Communications of Yesterday and to the Strictures I passed on them. No Vote was taken on the Subject. But I have hitherto been Unsuccessful in endeavouring to lay my hands on them.}

Wednesday, 16 February 1791

engaged in the Morning in unimportant matters about the Land Office and other places, after the Senate met. Mr. Carrol moved for leave to bring in a bill supplementory to the Residence bill. The Matter I believe stands thus in fact. Virginia is not fully satisfyed, without having half the 10 mile Square. she gives the 120,000 doll. perhaps on this very principle. of having Alexandria included. This cannot be done without the supplementory law, which is now apply'd for. I spoke to Mr. Morris, and gave him my thoughts on the Matter he made a just observation. there will be People enough to manage this Matter without our taking an Active part in it. The Rule demands one days notice to be given for bringing in a bill. Carrol withdrew his Motion on being told of this. but afterwards hoped the Senate would indulge him by common consent. Elsworth however said it had better lay over one day. my *Friend*[17] on the Subject of reelection told me That he had some Conversation on that Subject with the Speaker of the State Senate.[18] the Result was that they would soon elect. said he found him wavering but on the Whole considered him as friendly. I had business out. and called on Mr.

---

[16]Tobias Lear.

[17]This may be a reference to Benjamin Rush, whom WM had known since they were school boys together thirty-five years earlier. They corresponded regularly while the FFC was at New York City, yet Rush's name occurs only once in WM's diary during the third session. Rush paid close attention to the electioneering but was not always supportive of WM. See also June 1789, n. 27, and Appendix E. (Rush to Tench Coxe, 13 Sept. 1790, Coxe Papers, PHi)

[18]Richard Peters.

Montgomery,[19] told him That the agricultural interest of Pennsylvania ought to unite That it was the policy of the City to disunite Finley and myself and run in Bingham, at least this was the game he was playing. he agreed with me. Mr. Smiley soon after called on me. He spoke harder of Finley, particularly of his unsufferable Vanity than ever I had heard any one do before. he promised he would call on me. I returned to the Senate found the Draughts of General Harmar's Expedition before the Committee.[20] they look finely on paper, but were we to View the green bones, and scattered Fragments of our defeat on the Actual Field, It would leave very different Ideas. on our minds. This is a most Vile business—so far and meant to be much Viler. I believe I ought not to vote for any of the new bill.

Thursday, 17 February 1791

This day Mr. Carrol's motion for the emendatory Act respecting the Potowmack was to be taken up.[21] Mr. Morris was very late in coming. it is remarkably singular That I never knew him otherwise when a debate was expected. I however wish he had staid away for he voted for leave to bring in the bill, I confess, to my Astonishment. I saw him considerably embarrassed. how noble it is to be independent, leave was obtained and the bill read. The Military bill was reported with amendments much longer than itself. they were ordered to be printed. I shall most undoubtedly vote against the Augmentation of the Troops. The War is undertaken without the Shadow of Authority from Congress. and this War is the Pretext for raising an Army meant to awe our Citizens into Submission— Fitzsimons has been heard declaring that *1000* Men would revenge the insults offered to Congress. Where are these things to End. {By the insult offered to Congress is Meant The State deliberations &ca. respecting the Excise— But I can already plainly see, That all this Matter will vanish in Air. Finley⟨,⟩ Gallatin⟨,⟩ Smiley⟨,⟩ [*John*] Montgomery in fact all the Conductors of the Business having nothing further in View than the securing themselves Niches in the Six dollar Temple of Congress. And these popular Measures are only meant as the Step-lather to facilitate their ascent. I confess I have more than once been a little taken in with the Sunshine of some of their Speeches in my favor. but Actions are louder than Words. I have differed beyond the power of reconcil-

[19]WM probably talked to William Montgomery, who supported his reelection, and not John Montgomery, who sought the seat. Both men were in Philadelphia attending the state legislature.
[20]WM visited a meeting of the committee on the Military Establishment Act [HR-126A]. The papers regarding the Harmar expedition are printed in *DHFFC* 5:1358–65.
[21]The Residence Act [S-21] was supplemental to the Residence Act [S-12] adopted in the second session.

iation with the Citizens & high flying Federalists.   And Genuine Republicanism has been my Motive.   if the Old constitutional party were really
Patriots they would glory in taking me up.   this however is not the Case & I
am greatly Mistaken, if they do not lord it with as high an hand over the
People, should they get into Congress, As the Present Majority.   And perhaps
even then We May not hear a Word against the Excise.}
    {The Entry for the 18th, by Mistake, entered Two leaves back in a
blank which I had left to Copy Letters in.}

Friday, 18 February 1791

A number of Communications were handed in respecting the Appointment
of David Humphreys Resident at the Court of Portugal.   The President sends
first, and asks for our advice and consent after.[22]   Now Carroll's emendatory
bill.[23] was called up.   it was debated with temper. but a great deal of Triffling
discourse was had upon it.   I had determined to say nothing on the
Subject.   I however changed my mind and made the following remark.   "so
far as I had an Opportunity of knowing the public Mind. the Expectations of
People had been disappointed.   a belief had obtained That the President
would appoint three Commissioners who under his direction would lay out the
10 mile square,   I did not arraign his Authority, I did not call it in question,
but he had done himself what should have been done by others under his
direction.   I would neither pull down nor build up, let the Measure rest upon
the law.   if all was right it would support itself.   if wrong our mending it was
improper &ca. &ca."   Mr. Morris followed me   I could not well collect his
drift, but he said with pretty Strong emphasis, that if any one would move a
Postponement he would be for it.   This hint was laid hold of by Langdon and
Schyler and a postponement moved which was carried.   Mr. Morris sustained
a small attack from Gun. for this as an indirect way of getting rid of the
Measure   Twice however did Mr. Morris declare he would vote for the bill if
the Question was to be taken on it.   I think this kind of Conduct, ill Judged
for the Court will think as ill of him as they do of me who voted dead against
the Measure from the Begin⟨nin⟩g.
    Oh!   I should note that Mr. Jefferson with more than parisian politeness,
waited on me in my chamber this Morning.   he talked politicks mostly, the
French difference, and the Whale Fishery. but he touched the Potowmac too.
as much as to say there Oh there—

---

    [22]Washington's message on the appointment of Humphreys and documents relating to
Humphreys's confidential 1790 mission to establish a diplomatic exchange with Portugal are
printed in the *SEJ*, pp. 117–18, 469–73.
    [23]Residence Act [S-21].

Wednesday, 23 February 1791

I have in General been so closely engaged that That I have not had time to minute the dayly Transactions and indeed unless I wish gratification to myself there is no Use in it. for no Man has called on me for any information.   On Friday the emendatory Act was taken up and read and postponed for a Week.[24]   Mr. Morris⟨,⟩ Langdon & Schuyler. voted for the Postponement. they might as well have voted against the Bill. for the postponement is equally ungrateful at Court.   Saturday We had Communications from the President.[25] &ca. &ca.   a most Villa⟨i⟩nous bill (in my Opinion) was committed to Genl. Dickenson⟨,⟩ Wingate and myself.   It was for paying off at par, 186. thousand doll. due to foreign officers.   this was domestic debt beyond a Doubt.   the Bill went to pay it out of the funds appropriated for foreign debt.   Strip it however of all coloring it is to sanctify the most abandoned Speculation.   some say the Whole of it has already been bought up.   I set myself to defeat it and have happily succeeded.   The Consequence is That I have all the Secretary's Gladiators upon me.   I have already offended Knox and all his Military Arrangements   I have drowned Jefferson's regards in the Potowmac.   Hamilton with his Host of Speculators is upon me, and they are not Idle.   the City Hates me and I have offended Morris. And my place must go.   my peace of mind however shall not go.   and like a dying Man I will endeavour that my last Moments be well Spent.   Tuesday my report was read and Wednesday, It was agreed to. or at least the Resolution subjoined was adopted that the Bill should not pass to a third reading.[26]   Business crouded much and I have almost determined to pass all.   the difference however On the new impost law, between the Two Houses, explains so fully the Trim of the Senate. That I must leave a word or Two on the subject.   The Bill commonly called the *Excise* Law. tho the Term is carefully avoided in the Law. puts it in the power of the President to appoint as many Inspectors as he chuses and to pay them what he pleases so as he does not exceed 5 ⅌ Cent on the Whole Sum collected.   This Check is a mere nullity, and depends on a point arising posterior to the Appointments.   the Reason given for vesting this power in the President is the want of Knowledge of the Subject, how many what duties &ca. they will have to discharge.   The House of Representatives seem to say. Experience will dispel this Ignorance in Two Years. & therefore they ~~add a clause~~ amend limiting this power of ~~collecting~~ paying &ca. to Two Years. No say our Senate we will not Trust the new Congress &ca. &ca.   in fact the Object is to throw all possible power into the hands of the President even to the

---

[24]Residence Act [S-21].
[25]WM probably referred to Washington's three messages of Friday, 18 February.
[26]Foreign Officers Bill [HR-116].

stripping of the Senate, a Conferrence appointed— {It is believed That any Measure That can be fairly fixed On the President will be Submitted to by the People, thus making him the Scape Goat of Unconstitutio⟨na⟩l Measures, And leading Them by their Affection to him, into An Acquiescence in these Measures that Flow from him. to break down the boundaries of the States has been a desideratum. This was attempted, at the Time of the impost. The Geographical situation of Maryland with respect to the Chesapeack bay, afforded a Pretext, to do something of this kind Under the plea of Convenience, by adding the Eastern Shore to the State of Delaware. & indemnifying Maryland out of Virginia. Clouds of Letters reprobated the Measure. It would not do.[27] The President, is now put upon something of this kind. to Alter the Lines of States, by taking from the larger and adding to the smaller, in his arrangements for collecting the Excise. Will he really become the Tool of his own administration?}

Thursday, 24 February 1791

This day nothing of moment engaged the Senate, ~~unt~~ in the way of Debate untill The Virginia Senators moved a Resolution That the doors of the Senate Chamber should be opened, On the first day of the next session &ca. they mentioned their Instructions[28] This brought the Subject of instructions from the different legislatures into View Elsworth said they amounted to no more than a Wish. and ought to be no further regarded— Izard said no legislature had any right to instruct at all. any more than the Electors had a right to instruct the President of the United States. Mr. Morris followed, said Senators owed their Existence to the Constitution the legislatures were only the Machines to chuse them. and was more violently opposed to Instruction than any of them. We were Senators for the United States and had nothing to do with One State more than another. Mr. Morris Spoke with more Violence

---

[27]WM referred to the creation of collection districts by the Collection Act [HR-11].

[28]The Virginia instructions, adopted by the legislature on 27 November 1790, stated:

The General Assembly of Virginia considering it as one among the important privileges of the people, that they should have free admission to hear the debates of the Senate, as well as the House of Representatives, whenever they are exercising their legislative functions;

Resolved, therefore, nemine contradicente, that the Senators of this State in the Senate of the United States be instructed to use their utmost endeavours to procure the admission of the Citizens of the United States, to hear the debates of their House whenever they are sitting in their legislative capacity.

Resolved, nemine contradicente, That the Speakers of the two Houses of the General Assembly, be requested to inclose copies of the foregoing resolution, to the Legislatures of the several States in the Union, requesting their cooperation in similar instructions to their respective Senators.

The Senate doors were not opened to the public until the second session of the Third Congress.

than Usual. perhaps I may be considered as imprudent. but I thought I would be wanting in the duty I owed the public if I sat silent. and heard such doctrines without bearing my Testimony against them. I declared I knew but Two lines of Conduct for Legislators to move in. the one absolute Volition. the other responsibility. The first was ~~absolute~~ Tyranny. the other was inseperable from the Idea of Representation. were we chosen with dictatorial powers, or were we sent forward as servants of the public to do their business. the later clearly in my Opinion. the first Question then which presented itself was. were my Constituents here what would they do? the Answer if known was the Rule, for the Representative. Our Governments were avowedly republican. the Question now before Us had no respect to what was the best kind of Government but this I considered as genuine republicanism. As to the late conduct of the Legislature of Pennsylvania. I spoke with but few of them I had no Instructions from them. and all things considered I was happy That I had given my Voice on a former Occasion for it.[29] The Reasons which I gave then operated still in full force on my mind. The first was that I knew of no reason for keeping the doors of any legislative Assembly open, That did not apply with equal force to Us. The second was. That I thought it a Compliment due to the smallest [*largest*] state in the Union to indulge them in such request. the Objections against it. Viz. that the Members would make speeches for the Gallery and for the public Papers. would be the fault of the Members. if they waged war in Words. and oral Combats, if they pitted themselves like Cocks or play'd the Gladiator for the Amusement of the Idle & curious, the Fault was theirs. That let who would fill the Chairs of the Senate. I hoped discretion would mark their deportment. That they would rise to impart Knowledge & li⟨s⟩ten to obtain information. That while this line of Conduct marked their debates it was totally immaterial whether thousands attended or there were not a single Spectator.

{This day Butler handed forward a Resolution for augmenting the Salaries of all federal officers ~~th~~ of the different departments one fourth. It is a great Object to encrease the Federal Offices & Salaries as much as possible to make them marks for the ambitious to aim at. This single Stratagem, has carried the new Government on so far, with encreased rapidity.}

Friday, 25 February 1791

This was a busy day in Senate we had a Communication from the President[30] respecting the loan of three Millions of Florins. which it seems come at

---

[29]On 22 January 1791 the Pennsylvania House of Representatives adopted a resolution calling on the United States Senate to open its doors. On 25 February the state senate disagreed to the resolution by a vote of 8–7. See April 1790, n. 35, for WM's previous vote.

[30]The communication was a letter from the secretary of the treasury which is printed in the *SLJ*.

5¹/₄ ℔ Cent. the expence of negotiation being between 4 & 5 ℔ Cent.   up now
was taken a bill for altering the time of the meeting of Congress.   The title
was the same with that of a bill rejected the other day but the former had the
first monday in November³¹   this had the 4 monday in Oc⟨tobe⟩r.   The
President declared that as the day was different, the bill was a different bill
there might be as many different bills as days in the year.   it passed but I
confess I thought him wrong.   Mr. Morris's Vote carried this bill.   I spoke
against but without Effect.   now we had the Resolution for opening the
doors.   9 votes were given for it. and it was lost.   and now came the Potowmac emendatory Act.³²   a postponement was moved.   but Langdon⟨,⟩
Schyler⟨,⟩ Elmer⟨,⟩ Morris and Reed Voted against the Postponement and
finally for the bill.   this is astonishing indeed.   It is plain the President has
bought them.   I know not their price but That is immaterial.   I had a good
Opinion of Elmer Once.   it is with pain I retract it.   I think the City must see
Morris in a new point of View.   were I to give such a Vote I certainly dared not
walk the Streets.   {Mr. Morris wishes his Name Sake Governeur (now in
Europe selling lands for him) placed in Some conspicuous Station abroad;
he has acted in a Strange kind of Capacity half pimp half envoy, or perhaps
more properly a kind of Political Eavedropper about the British Court for some
time past.   Mark the End of it.   As to Langdon I am at no loss.   the appointment. of his Brother Woodberry³³ is sufficient explanation.   Schyler is
the supple Jack of his Son in law Hamilton.   of Elmer I know not What to
say.   I once thought him honest.   As to Reed I have heretofore known him to
have been shaken by something else beside the Wind.}

Saturday, 26 February 1791

The third reading was given this day to the detested bill of Yesterday, and
the last hand put to the still more detested excise law.³⁴   all these however
were considered as Triffles in political iniquity.   for Weeks has the Report of
the Committee on the French complaints lain dormant³⁵   shame I believe
had some hand in keeping them back but now a Steady Phalanx appeared to
support the Report   I opposed it what I could. & contended for the third

---

³¹Time of Meeting Act [HR-132]. The previous Time of Meeting Bill [HR-122] was
rejected by the Senate on 22 February.

³²Residence Act [S-21].

³³Woodbury Langdon (1739–1805), a merchant from Portsmouth, New Hampshire,
served in the Continental Congress and in the state legislature and judiciary. He had been
confirmed by the Senate on 24 December 1790 as one of the commissioners for settling
accounts between the United States and the individual states. See also *SEJ*, p. 516.

³⁴The Residence Act [S-21] and Duties on Distilled Spirits Act [HR-110].

³⁵The remainder of WM's entry for this date describes a debate on the committee report of
27 January which is recorded in the *SEJ*. Documents relating to the issue are printed in the
SEJ, pp. 389–423.

against the alternatives in the Report of the Secretary of State As ~~the least~~ exceptionable And opposed the Whole.   but all in Vain   the report with some Variation was adopted.   I was the only One who voted boldly and decidedly against it.   I have annexed the Alternatives proposed by Jefferson and the Resolutions of the Committee[36]

{On the Whole, if it be the Opinion, that the first construction is to be insisted on, as ours, in opposition to the 2d urged by the court of France, and that no relaxation is to be admitted, an answer shall be given to that Court, defending that Construction, and explaining in as friendly terms as possible the difficulties opposed to the Exemption they claim

2d if it be the Opinion that it is advantageous for Us to close with France, in her interpretation of a reciprocal and perpetual exemption from tonnage. a repeal of so much of the tonnage law will be the Answer.

3d if it be thought better to wave rigorous and nice ~~distinctions~~cussions of right, and to make the modification an Act of Friendship and of compensation for favours received the passage of such a bill will then be the answer

Arrets of 29th Decemr. 1787 and 7th Decemr. 1788

Resolved as the Opinion of the Senate That the 5th Article of the Treaty of Amity & commerce between the United States and his most Xtian Majesty, is merely an illustration of the 3d and fourth Articles of the same Treaty by an Application of the Principles comprized in in the last Mentioned Articles to the Case stated in the former

Resolv'd that the Senate do advise an Answer to be given to the Court of France defending this Construction in opposition, to that urged by the said Court. and at the same explaining in the most friendly Terms the difficulties opposed to the Exemptions they claim.}

{& some of my Observations in Opposition to Elsworth &ca.}[37]   they may afford me some amusement at a future day.   I will however call on Otis for a Certificate of my having voted against the Resolutions.   That there has been a design to sacrifice the French Interest as a Peace offering to the British Court I cannot doubt, but that this should be persisted in after the disappointment attending G. Morris's management is Strange indeed.   They however either hope or affect to hope to carry their point.   Mr. Morris a few days ago asserted that we would early this spring have a Minister from Great Britain and the Papers have many lying Accounts to the same purpose   there is a System pursuing the Depths of which I cannot well fathom.   but I see clearly that the Poor Goddess of liberty is likely to be hunted out of this Quarter as well as the

[36]Jefferson's alternatives were submitted to the Senate by Washington on 19 January, not 19 February as stated in the *SEJ*, p. 122, where the resolutions are printed. The arrets WM noted were included in the documents transmitted to the Senate by Washington and are printed in the *SEJ*, pp. 410–19.

[37]The sheet containing WM's observations in opposition to Ellsworth is no longer with the manuscript diary, although part of the wafer remains.

three other Quarters of the Globe.   I have deliberated much whether I should minute in any degree of Accuracy the proceedings of this day   hitherto delicacy has prevented me from keeping any Memorandums of the Executive or Secret Journal but if I am ever to give Any Account of my conduct to the State Government, there is perhaps no part to Which they will turn their Eye with More Attention.   I have another reason for Secrecy On this Subject, for I certainly never behaved so badly in my life—

Elsworth opened, hoped this Business would meet no further delay, as it had been long on the Table, And that the Resolution would be adopted—That the Members had full Time to make Up their Minds &ca.—

I declared That the Opportunity as well as Time was necessary   altho' the Time had been long some Members had not ~~the~~ had the Opportunity,   That I had called often for a sight of the papers but always experienced a disappointment   That I had indeed seen the Alternatives offered by the Secretary of State and no more.   That eminent as the Secretary was for Abilities I could not intirely approve of any of his alternatives (here I received a loud laug[h)] and of Course must be opposed to the Resolution which was engrafted on the first—   To suppose That after having framed the 3d & 4th Articles they were so Obscure As to require a 5th by way of illustration is an Absurd[ity] that cannot obtain belief[38]—   The Framers must have had a Seperate Object in View consistent ~~with~~ with their reputation as Men of Understanding   And so it clearly appeared to me.   to Justify The Construction I will read the Articles—(here read them[)]   The 3d Grants certain rights &ca. in Trade &ca. to the Subjects of the Christian King in the American ports with respect to *duties & imposts*   The 4th reciprocates these Rights &ca. to the People of the U.S. in the French ports—   here I take the Words *Duties And imposts* in the Strict and limited Sense As applying to the impositions charged On the Cargo and to no other.   The 5th Article has An imposition of another Kind for its Object Which evidently was not considered as falling within the purview of the 3d or 4th   Viz. Tonnage, A port Charge which is laid on in proportion to her Burthen independent of the Cargo & is charged Whether she comes loaded or in balast—   It is in fact the Machine by Which Commercial Nations encourage or discourage the Shipping of their Neighbours—   I am ready to admit that the poverty or rather the want of precision in Commercial Terms often confuses and confounds them together.   But with these ideas and Under this View of the Subject which I am satisfyed are correct let Us examine the 5th Article,   And the first feature That presents itself is a reciprocal design of Augmenting And favoring the Shipping of the Contracting parties.   Duties and imposts laid Upon Goods are Taxes paid by the Consumers   Tonnage is a Tax on the Ship   To lessen the Tax on Shipping or rather to do it away

---

[38]WM commented on the third, fourth, and fifth articles of the Treaty of Amity and Commerce between France and the United States, which was signed in 1778. It is printed in the *SEJ*, pp. 389–408.

altogether ~~with a~~ is in favor of naval property.   And in This Spirit run the Stipulations of the 5th Article.

But if Gentlemen will View them conjointly what Will be the effect— ~~certain~~ exemptions are generally stipulated between the contracting parties in the 3d & 4th Articles—   What says the 5th—"in the above exemption is particularly comprized the imposition of 100 Sols ℔ Ton &ca." with the exception of the Coasting Trade to French Vessels between their own ports, Which the Americans are allowed to balance with a similar ~~duty~~ Tonnage On French Vessels coasting in the American ports—and even this coasting Tonnage is not to continue longer than other   the most favoured Nations pay it.   Will any Man Undertake to say on seeing this Article That the French can legally charge the Tonnage of 100 Sols or any Greater or less Tonnage on American Vessels in their ports (~~others~~ Unless they become Coasters) consistent with Treaty.   I think not.   if the French then cannot, On the principles of Reciprocity We cannot.   What then is to be done.   ~~nearly What the~~   repeal the Law But upon a different principle from that held out by the Secretary either in his 2d or 3d Alternative.   The ~~first~~ 2d is Sordid As having Advantage for its Basis   the 3d ~~is insulting~~ carries something like an Air of insult, As much as to say we are right you are wrong   But take it our Good nature shall Yield to Your peevishness   The 2d Idea of Compensation for favors is Worse infinitely.   This is a Subject on Which the American [N]ation is and we[ll] must be Bankrupt,   to compensate the political salvation of America, France ought to be placed in the deplorable si[tua]tion which afflicted America, When rescued by ~~the~~ her helping ha[nd] ~~of France~~, And Ought to be relieved in Turn.   ~~Events~~ Statements tha[t] seem beyond the range of human Events.   Where would have been Our Washingtons and Patriots of every Grade had it not been for french interference.   When the Mildest Meek[est] And Most Gentlemanly of all the British Commanders ~~cou~~ would not associate ~~the name of~~ them with any other Idea than that of a Lord—   Not the Virtues of a Padilla[39] would have saved One of them.   No let Us do homage to the Spirit and letter of Treaty   Own our Mistake and repeal the Law.   I have ever thought that a liberal & Manly policy being most conformable to the Genius of the people was the surest method of engaging & preserving the Esteem of that Magnanimous nation   And the Alternative might be War & confusion.

A Burst of Abuse Was now poured forth against the French by Elsworth in the most vituperative Language that Fancy could invent—   Selfishness interested Views their Motive, to dismember the british Empire—   Divide et impera[40] their Motto   Nay slay british Subjects with the Sword of their Fellows,   no Gratitude in Nations   no Honor in Politicks.   none but a fool would expect it.   Ser[ve] Yourself, the first Article in the Creed of

---

[39]Juan Lopez de Padilla (1490–1521) was a Spanish insurrectionist who led a rebellion of the communes against absolutism in 1520.
[40]Divide and conquer.

Politi[cks]   no Return due to them   Ridicule not Thanks would attend Acknowledgements—   he seemed to have mistaken the w[ord] Genius which I
used for Genus and said some sarcastic Thing about Anim[als] which I could
not Well comprehend   The ~~Word~~ term Monkey was used—   it was meant in
[Ridi]cule of What I said,   he fell on me with the Most sar[cas]tic Severity
no confusion Any Where but in the Speak[er's] head—   Alas!   How shall I
write it,   I lost my Temper & find[ing] no protection from the Chair left the
Room.   A Mom[ent's] Reflection restored me.   I recollected That I had the
[Volume] of Congress of 1783 which I had looked Up for this Occasio[n] before
my seat.   Where the Greatest encomiums were bes[towed] on the
French—   I returned   King Was Up and alt[ho'] he was in the same Sentiments as Elsworth. he said Mr. Jay had Given a Similar construction with me,
or at least so Understood him ~~so~~.   I did not hear one of the Statem[ents]
which I made Answered or Attempted to be Answe[red]   I happened to turn
round and the Full length pi[ctures] of the King and Queen of France[41] caught
my Eye.   I really seemed to Think they would upbraid me if I was Silent.   I
knew the disad[vantage I laboured] Under.   But Up [I] got—   Nations being composed of individuals [the] Virtue character and reputation of the
Nation must depend [on] the Morals of individuals and could have no other
Basis—   [Gr]atitude Generosity sensibility of favors, Benignity & benefi-
cence had not Yet abandoned the Human breast,   in fact these Were the
Con[di]tions on Which the Human Race existed.   That these passions [s]o far
as they respected the French Nation were deeply engraved [on] the Bosom of
Every American Revolutionist.   I knew there were Characters of a different
Kind in America but for them we [ca]red not   That I was convinced the Sense
of America had [b]een fairly expressed by Congress on the Resignation of
Genl. Washington[42] When the Epithet of Magnanimous Nation was apply'd
to them.   What Were the Expressions of Congress as reported by a Committee some of Whom Are now ~~th~~ within my hearing, in the Year 1783—with
respect to That now vilifyed Nation—   *Exertions of Arms Succours of their
Treasury important Loans liberal Donations,* Magnanimity &ca.   Yess all this
And More for I have the book before me,   in fact language laboured and
seemed to fail in expressions of Gratitude to our Ally.   But here is a Reverse

---

[41]In 1779, Congress requested portraits of the King and Queen of France to hang in its
chamber. The approximately thirteen-by-six-foot formal portraits arrived at Philadelphia in
March 1784. A year later they were hung in Congress's chamber in New York City Hall, the
building that became Federal Hall. They were transported to Philadelphia when the government moved and hung in the Senate Chamber, which suggests that they may have been in
the Senate Chamber in Federal Hall as well. The originals have disappeared, but reproduc-
tions based on documentary descriptions now hang in Congress Hall, Philadelphia. These
were presented to the United States by France in 1976 as a bicentennial gift. (Charles Warren,
"What Has Become of the Portraits of Louis XVI and Marie Antoinette Belonging to
Congress," *Proceedings of the Massachusetts Historical Society* 59:67–71)
   [42]The address of Congress to Washington when he surrendered his commission on 23
December 1783 can be found in *JCC* 25:838.

indeed.   if right then, we must be Wrong now   And my heart tells me it is so.   Vituperation and Abuse more especially in the national Way, are of the reflective kind, and attach disgrace rather to the assailants than to the assailed—   Who ever believed That the Grins or dirty tricks of the ~~African~~ Baboon or Monkey in the african ~~forest~~ or american Wilds disgraced the Traveller that Walked be~~lowneath the african Forest~~low, Altho' they attached contempt to the Filthy animal Above.

Elsworth took a great deal of Snuff about this Time   he mumped and seemed to chew the cud of Vexation.   but he affected not to hear me.   and indeed they were all in knots talking and Whispering   Mr. Adams talked with Otis according to Custom.   The Committee Alluded to Were Madison⟨,⟩ Elsworth & Hamilton,[43]   I am too Sparing   I should have read ~~the Whole~~ that part of the report with their names &ca.   [1?]:8 pa:200.

I cannot help adding a remark or Two.   A War in some Shape or other seems to have been the Great Object with Hamilton's people.   At first they Would have war with the Southern indians,   that Failed,   they have succeeded in involving Us with the North Western Indians—   Britain at One time seemed their Object,   Great efforts were made to get a War with the Algerines,   that Failed.   Now it seems to be made a point of to differ with the French.   That lively Nation do not seem to have been aware that ours was really a Civil War with Britain.   And that the similarity of Language Manners & customs will in all probability restore Our old habits and intercourse and That this intercourse will revive, indeed I fear it has already revived our antient prejudices against France.   should we differ with France we are thrown inevitably into the hands of Britain.   and should France Give any Occasion— 1,000ds & tens of 1,000ds of Antirevolutionists ready to blow the coals of contention.

Sunday, 27 February 1791

This day made inquiry of George Remsen One of the Clerks. of Hamilton's Office. respecting a Story which is circulated with respect to Bingham having got 36,000 Dollars of counterfeit Certificates registered and a new Certificate for them.   he declares the fact is so.   these Counterfeits have been copied from Genuine Certificates.   the Counterfeits handed to the Auditor (Milligan)[44] passed by him to the Register (Nourse) and a new certificate given for the amount.   thus the Counterfeits being disposed off.   there could be no

---

[43]The report of the committee (Madison, Ellsworth, and Hamilton) on an address to the States is printed in *JCC* 24:277–83. Almost exclusively the work of Madison, it was agreed to on 26 April 1783.

[44]James Milligan (d. 1818) of Philadelphia served the Continental Congress as auditor of the treasury from 1779 to 1781 and the Confederation Congress as comptroller from 1781 to 1787. He had close ties to Robert Morris. (*PRM* 1:379n–380n; *DHROC* 16:583n)

Danger of detection ~~the~~ as the Genuine and counterfeit Ones could never meet.   Now the Genuine ones comining forward to be loaned the fraud is found out.   I dined this day with Doctor Ruston.   I mentioned this Circumstance.   a Gentleman of the name of Curry came in, While I talked of it with out mentioning names he said this must be Mr. Swanwick,[45]   he was asked. how large a Certificate Swanwick had founded in this way   he said only 20,000 doll.   Hell surely must have emptied her Rascals upon Us, or we never could have been served thus.   Remsen has promised to give me more information on this Subject.

Monday, 28 February 1791

This day I fell in discourse with Mr. Morris. and Mentioned the 36,000 Doll. Certificate in Possession of Bingham.   It seems it is the same which Swanwick had.   A Charles Young[46] owed Swanwick and was arrested in New York for the Debt on his return from Boston.   paid these Certificates to Swanwick, was discharged,   they were registered   Swanwick sold to Bingham for £1,200 knowing the State of the Registered Certificate.   this Cast an Air of innocence over the transaction   perhaps we shall hear more of it.   Schuylers bill[47] which went to make debts due to the United States be paid in certificates &ca. The object of which could not be well observed. and which truly might be called a Snake in the Grass was laid over to the next Session.   {I could not Ascertain the point in the Above Conversation Who obtained the Register of the above certificates.   And therefore have endeavoured to find from Mr. Morris. Who discovered the Cheat. At What Time, with respect to the Registering Viz. Whether before or after.   but he was Guarded And either Knew not or would not tell.   but he Admitted they were known to be Counterfeits At the Time of the Sale.   This in my Opinion involves both in Criminality.

Oh deluded Public little do You know of what Stuff the ~~publ~~ Federal debt is composed which You are daily discharging with Sorrow.}

---

[45]John Swanwick (1759–98), partner of Robert Morris and Thomas Willing in the import-export business since 1783 and a holder of substantial public securities, was born in Liverpool, England, and came to Philadelphia with his family just before the War for Independence. (*PMHB* 97:131–82)

[46]Charles Young was a Philadelphia speculator. (Charles Young to Tench Coxe, 8 Aug. 1788, Coxe Papers, PHi)

[47]Payment of Balances Bill [S-22].

March 1791

Tuesday, 1 March 1791

Attended this Morning the Eulogium in Honor of Docr. Franklin, pronounced by Do⟨cto⟩r. Smith.[1] People say much of it, I thought little of it. it was Trite & Triffling. perhaps I am censorious, I dispise Smith he certainly is a vile Character. much business was hurried thro' the Senate this day, now is the time for dark designing Men, to croud in and hurry thro' under some Specious ~~des~~ Pretext the deep laid plots of Speculation. the immature resolve, and ill digested Law often escape examination, while nothing but home Occupies the minds of the departing Members. Few days happen in which I do not meet with something to fret my political Temper. but this day I met with something that really roused every feeling of humanity about me. The President was directed some time ago to take Measures to to ransom eleven Americans who are slaves at Algiers, Money was appropriated for this purpose out of the Dutch Loan in 1788. The President however sent Us back ~~Word~~ a Message to appropriate Money for the purpose. And a Committee who had the African Business committed to them reported 20,000 Doll. to Treat with the Emperor of Morocco but not a Cent. for the poor Slaves.[2] hard was the heart that could do it. and Clay cold has the Conduct of the President been in the Business I said and did what I could, but all in vain. and we will not only confine to Slavery, but murder with the plagues of that deleterious Climate these Unhappy Men.

Izard came over made a long Complaint against Hamilton. here said he

[1]William Smith's eulogy was delivered at the German Lutheran Church at Fourth and Race streets on behalf of the American Philosophical Society. Members of both houses of Congress attended. (*PTJ* 19:100–101)

WM's regard for France and Franklin and his shock at the Senate's behavior on 26 January when it received a tribute to Franklin from the National Assembly of France may have resulted in some resolutions adopted by the Pennsylvania House of Representatives. Led by Samuel Maclay, the latter body called for Pennsylvania to acknowledge the French tribute. An argument has been made that the resulting address may have been drafted in part by WM. (*PTJ* 19:95, 96n)

[2]WM referred to the committee on Mediterranean trade, which reported the Moroccan Treaty Act [S-23] in legislative session. Senate authorization on 1 February for the president to spend up to $40,000 to redeem the American seamen held by Algeria and Washington's message of 22 February requesting a formal appropriation for the purpose are recorded in the *SEJ*, pp. 114–15, 118–19. In another executive session on 3 March the Senate suspended its 1 February resolution. Documents regarding the issue are printed in the *SEJ*, pp. 425–49.

have we been waiting No-Body knows how long and Hamilton has promised to send Us a bill for the Mint. and now at last he sends Us a Resolution to employ Workmen &ca. Two things are clear from this. That Hamilton prepares all Matters for his tools, (this I knew long ago), the other is that he has kept back this exceptionable business. 'till there would be no time to investigate it.

Basset this day laid on the Table a Resolution, for a Committee of both Houses to wait on ~~Congress~~ the President to request him to take Measures to procure peace with the Indians &ca. to a pretty pass of servility are we already arrived. it would be much more consonant to the dignity of Congress, to institute a spirited inquiry, how we came to be involved in a War. without the Authority of Congress, than to be begging our own Servants to spare the Effusion of human blood— {every Account of this ~~However~~ Kind, seems to be received. with an Air of Satisfaction by the Adherents of Administration, As if our military defeats were political Victories.}

Wednesday, 2 March 1791

O twas joyful News when I came home and found my Mare sent by Bob. Murdock[3] and had the pleasure to hear of the Wellfare of my Family More Business has been hurried this day thro the Senate than has been done, in a Month of of our former sessions at some other periods. The Secretary has bought the Present House and he wishes to have the Worth of his Money out of them. the Resolution of the Mint was foully smuggled thro, I hope somebody will take notice of it in the other House it is evident What System has been adopted by the Secretary. We used to canvass every Subject and dispute every inch of his Systems, and thus sometimes detached some of his party from him, and defeated him. to prevent this, all has been put off Untill this late Moment and now not a Word will be heard. the plea of want of time prevails. And every One that attempts to speak is Silenced with the Cry of the Question, And a mere insurrection of Members in Support of the demand. I am at no loss now to ascertain the Reasons Why the mint Business has been delayed, And finally came forward under the form of a Resolution rather than a bill, bills cannot be read Out of Order but by unanimous Consent. It was known that I had controverted sundry positions laid down by Hamilton in his report And had prepared myself on the Subject,[4] it was easy to call the question & silence debate but now the time was short And I still had a Veto, by refusing Consent to an irregular reading of a bill, this Rule did not extend to a common Resolution. King made A Motion by side Wind to

---

[3]Robert Augustus Murdock (c. 1772–1845), first white male born in Northumberland County, was the son of William Murdock, who assisted WM in the survey of Sunbury. (*Genealogical and Biographical Annals of Northumberland*, p. 350)

[4]WM wafered into his diary an article on the Mint from the *NYDA* of 19 February, which controverted Hamilton's report. It is printed as Appendix B(10).

bring in the Principle of the bill for paying off the foreign Officers but being Smoked he sneaked off,   this great Man is Miserably deficient in Candor. He is an active Member of the smuggling Committee,   It was to a bill for the protection of the Treasury[5] that he wished to attach his moved Amendment. This bill seemed in a peculiar Manner committed to his Care.   Two ~~bills~~ Laws impowered Government to borrow in Holland,   One was to pay the interest on the foreign debt.   The other was to reduce the domestic Debt. by buying in While it was Under par[6]   (this the ostensible reason, but the real One to make a Machine of this Money, for raising the Stocks)   The first was a Matter of necessity, as the interest fell due.   The second loan was expressly confined to be done at an interest of 5 ℗ Cent.   but it has been done at a Charge of 4¹/₂ ℗ Cent. or in other Words 95¹/₂ Only is received on which 5 is paid Annually as interest   Now a bill is silently passing along in the Mass of business to sanctify this Wilful deviation.   The thing is done,   the Money is received, brought over, and in part, at least, expended.   there was nobody to hear Speeches or attend to argument.   I could not however help condemning the Measure. the Duty of Government was to borrow at 5 ℗ Cent or let it alone.   But if the Treasury could Once Establish the practice of acting without, or Contrary to law. the Whole Freedom of the Government might be sapped by fiscal Arrangements, And the Congress of the U.S. might in Time become as in Great Brittain the Mere Tools of Ministerial Imposition and Taxation   It has been Usual with declamatory Gentlemen in their praises of the present Government. by way of Contrast, to paint the State of the Country Under the old Congress, As if neither Wood grew nor Water run in America, before the late happy Adoption of the New Constitution.   It would be well, for the future, in such Comparisons, to say nothing of National Credit, (which by the by, I never considered as dependant on the prices current of Certificates in the hands of Speculators) For the Loan of 1788 was done in Holland at 5 ℗ Cent. only   Postponed.

Thursday, 3 March 1791

As well might I write the Rambles of Harlequin Ranger,[7] or the Vagaries of a pantomine, as attempt to Minute the Business of this Morning.   What with the Exits And the entrances of our Otis. The Announcings the Advancings Speechings drawings & Withdrawings of Buckley & Lear And the comings & goings of our Committees of Enrollment &ca. And the consequent running of Doorkeepers opening and Slaming of doors the House ~~was~~ seemed in a continual ~~Tempest of Noise &~~ Hurricane.   Speaking would have been Idle. for

[5]Sinking Fund Act [HR-136].
[6]The two acts were Funding [HR-63] and Sinking Fund [HR-101], respectively.
[7]Henry Woodward's *Harlequin Ranger* was a pantomime performed in London between 1751 and 1762. (George W. Stone, Jr., ed., *The London Stage, 1600–1800, Part 4: 1747–1776,* 3 vols. [Carbondale, Ill., 1962], 1:280, 2:955)

nobody would or could hear.   had all the Business been previously digested, Matter of form would have been of little consequence.   this however was not the Case,   it was patching peicing altering & amending   And even originating new Business.   It was however only for Elsworth⟨,⟩ King or some of Hamilton's People to Rise and the thing was generally done.   But they had ~~however~~ overshot themselves for, owing to little unforeseen impediments there was no possibility of Working all thro';   And there was to be a great dinner, Which must Absolutely be attended to.   terrible indeed but no alternative.   the House must Meet at 6 'OClock.

In the Evening by Candle-light

When I saw the Merry mood in Which the senate Assembled I was ready to laugh,   When I considered the Occasion, I was almost disposed to give way to a very different emotion.   I did however, neither the One, nor the other. and feeling myself ~~as~~ of as little importance, As I had ever done in my life. I took Pen & paper and determined, if possible, to keep pace, with the Hurry of Business, as it passed, Which I expected would now be very rapid. as I had no doubt but Hamilton's Clerks, had put the last hand to ~~the Business~~ Every thing.

Mr. Buckly announced.

He brought, 1. a *New* Resolve for the safe keeping of Prisoners &ca.

2.   A bill for Compensation to Commissioners of Loans for Extra-Expences.

3.   A Salary bill for the Executive Officers, their Clerks & assistants.

4.   Resolve for the President, to lay before Congress an Estimate of lands, not claimed by Indians

5   The Mint Resolve.   These obtained the Signatures of ~~V. P.~~ of the Senate & were sent off for the deliberation & approbation of the President.

The Prisoner Resolve was agreed to & sent back to the Representatives, by Otis

Mr. Buckly 2d Message

6   A *New* bill to carry into Effect the Convention with the French &ca. This Business had been most Shamefully neglected,   I had often spoke on the Subject, but my influence was gone.   I had however spoke lately to Sundry Members of the House of Representatives, And even at this late Hour was happy to see the bill.   to speak in the present uproar of Business was like letting off a popgun in a Thunder Storm but this was the Merest Matter of form possible,   it was only giving the Authority of law to a Convention solemnly entered into with the French.   My Colleague cryed No. on a Second reading.   I called for the Yeas & Nays, not out of Resentment. but merely with an exculpatory View, if this Conduct should draw on Us the Resentment of France. for I consider it as disrespectfull (to say no worse) towards ~~them~~ her & dishonorable in Us.

Mr. Buckley 3d Message

7   with the pension Invalid Light House Bill.[8]

---

[8]Mitigation of Forfeitures Act [S-24].

The Committee reported the enrollment of the following Acts.

8   For the Continuance of the Post Office

9   For granting lands to the settlers at Vincennes ~~For granting &~~ Illionoiss[9]

10   Supplementary Act for reduction of the public debt[10]

11   For granting compensation to Judicial Officers Witnesses & Jurymen

These Bills received the Signature of the President of the Senate, after being brought Up by Mr. Buckley in his 4th Message

~~13~~ 12 Who brought at the same time a New bill for the Relief David Cook.[11] Twice heretofore has there been an Attempt, to Smuggle this bill thro' in the croud,   it happened however to be Smoked & rejected.

Mr. Buckley's 5th Message

~~14~~ 13 Brought A Bill making further provision for Collection of Duties on Teas &ca. which reced. the signature &ca.

14—   And an Enrolled Resolve which also reced. the Signature[12]—&ca.

There now was such confusion with Otis⟨,⟩ Buckley⟨,⟩ Lear⟨,⟩ our Committee of Enrollment &ca. that I confess I lost their Arrangement ~~if they had Any.~~ indeed I am apt to believe, if they had any, they lost it themselves. ~~I can~~ they all agreed, at last, that the Business was done; the Presidt. left the Chair And the Members scampered down Stairs. I staid A Moment to pack up my papers. Dalton Alone came to me, And said he supposed We Two, would not see each other Soon. We exchanged Wishes for Mutual Wellfare. As I left the Hall I gave it a look, with that kind of Satisfaction which A Man feels on leaving a place Where he has been ill at Ease. being fully satisfyed that many A Culprit, has served Two Years at the Wheel-Barrow, without feeling half the pain & mortification, that I experienced, in my honorable Station.[13]

---

[9]Northwest Territory Act [S-17].

[10]Sinking Fund Act [HR-136].

[11]David Cook (d. 1823) sought a modification of the requirement that invalid veteran officers return all of their commutation to the United States prior to being placed on the pension list. Commutation was the term given to the March 1783 decision by the Confederation Congress to commute the life pensions offered Continental army officers in March 1780 to full pay for five years. For the legislative history of the Cook Bill [HR-140], see the petition volumes.

[12]Resolution on Safekeeping of Prisoners.

[13]"Wheelbarrow" is an allusion to the Pennsylvania penal system established in 1786 and abolished in 1790. Work on public improvements rather than incarceration was a central feature. Prisoners were required to push a wheelbarrow when outside the jailhouse. (*Counter Revolution*, pp. 219–20)

Because of the bitterness of the political dispute over WM's replacement in the Senate, the Pennsylvania legislature elected no one to fill his seat until February 1793. WM was nominated but received no votes. The new senator, Albert Gallatin, served from December 1793 until February 1794 when the Senate declared the seat vacant on the grounds that Gallatin had not been a citizen for nine years prior to his election. James Ross was then elected and served from April 1794 to 1803. In 1802, with the triumph of Jefferson, the legislature chose WM's brother Samuel to fill the seat; eleven legislators voted for WM at that time.

APPENDIXES

Appendix A
Miscellaneous Diary Documents

The preceding text is a complete transcription of the diary with only a few exceptions. Maclay began his diary in his letterbook for 1789. The retained copies of his letters will be printed with the letters of the members of Congress in later volumes of the *Documentary History of the First Federal Congress*. A list of them appears in Appendix D. On two occasions Maclay placed in his diary printed copies of official documents of the First Congress. Instead of reprinting them, the editors have indicated where they may be found in earlier volumes of the *Documentary History of the First Federal Congress*. Maclay usually noted in the text of his diary that he had added, or planned to add, supplemental manuscript material. Thus it was usually not difficult for the editors to place this material within the text of the diary. The three exceptions to this make up Appendix A.

WILLIAM MACLAY'S PROPOSED SENATE RULES

Each House may determine, *the Rules of its proceedings*, punish its members for disorderly behavior and with the Concurrence of two thirds, expel a Member   2d. Clause 5th Sect. 1st Art. Constitun. United States—

Rule 1st. The President shall [be in] the Chair, within half an hour, of the time to which the Senate stands, adjourned; and the Senators, shall immediately take their seats in circular order, those from New Hampshire occupying the right of the Chair, and those of Georgia the left.

2d   The minutes of the preceeding day shall be read before any other business is entered upon; inaccuracies or inelegancies may be corrected or amended; but no reconsideration as to Matter of Substance, shall take place, on such reading.

3d   Every Senator presenting a Petition memorial or other writing, shall briefly state the import of the same.   and every such paper after being read, shall be deemed to lie on the Table. unless the

same is dismissed upon special motion, for impropriety or want
of decency—

4th   Every Motion made and seconded shall be repeated aloud from
the Chair, and shall then be open to discussio[n.]   the Motion
if verbal shall be put in Writing, at the request of the President
or any Two Senators—

5th   Adoption, Rejection, Amendment, commitment or postponement, shall be considered as proper modes of treating business;
and in all Cases, (Treaties returned bills &ca. and the expulsion
of a Member excepted,) a Majority of Votes shall govern.

6th   Every Senator when speaking, shall address himself to the
Chair.   No Senator shall be named in debate, but may be
referred to, by mentioning the State he represents, or by allud-
ing to his place in the House.

7th   In Case of a debate becoming tedious, four Senators may call for
the question; or the same number may at any time move for the
previous question, Viz. ["Shall] the main question be now put"

8th   priority of speaking and all questions of Order, shall be decided
by the President, But either party may appeal to a Vote of the
House

9th   The name of the Senator making, and of the One Who seconds a
Motion, shall be entered [on] the Journals of the House—

10th   No Senator shall speak more than twice on the same subject,
without leave obtained of the Chair.

11th   Inviolable Secrecy shall be observed with respect, to all Matte[rs
trans]acted in the Senate, While the doors are shut, or as often as
the same is enjoined from the Chair.

12th   Every Member of a Committee shall attend the same at the time
appointed by the Chairman, who shall be the Senator of the
most northerly State of those, from Whom the Committee is
taken.

13th   When a commitment is agreed upon, the President shall take
the Sense of the Senate, as to the Manner of appointing the
Committee, Whether by Motion from the Senators, nomination from the Chair or by ballot. which shall take place accordingly

14th   The files of the House shall remain open for the inspection of all
the Senators But &ca. No original paper shall be removed from
the House without leave obtained for that purpose by the Senate—

15th   The Yeas and nays, on any question, shall be entered on the
Journals, at the desire of one fifth of the Senators present.

16th These Rules shall be engrossed on parchment, and hung up in some conspicuous ~~place~~ part, of the Senate Chamber. And — ~~the name of~~ every Senator, Who shall neglect attendance during a session; absent himself without leave, or withdraw for more than a quarter of an hour, without permission, after a quorum is formed, shall be deemed guilty of disorderly behaviour; and his name together with the nature of his transgression, shall be wrote on a slip of paper and annexed to the bottom of the Rules; there to remain untill the Senate, on his application or otherwise, shall take order on the same.

Maclay wrote these rules in the first volume of the manuscript before the earliest diary entry. He was a member of the Senate select committee on rules, and these are apparently his proposals. They are very similar in order, content, and tone to those of the highly democratic Pennsylvania Assembly when he was a member. Of particular interest are the seating arrangement, the manner of naming the chairmen of committees, the emphasis on duty and decorum, and WM's support for keeping the Senate doors open whenever possible.

MEMORANDA

On the Subject of funding—Domestic Debt Justice. with regard to the Soldier.

The continen[tal] Bill given to a Soldier for his Monthly pay, bore the nominal amount on the face of it. in as ample manner as possible.   he got but little for it (say 1/8)   all the World allowed him the loss so sustained, and he got a Certificate of depreciation accordingly.   This Measure was called Justice, at the time.   Necessity ever pursues a Soldier.   the same Necessity. which obliged him to take What he could get for the continental bill, obliged him to take 1/8 of the nominal amount for his certificates.   is not the Voice of Justice the same in both cases?   The Soldier must sell, and they are worth no more. let Us apply.

Justice to the Buyer.   can he plead that he has given valuable consideration. so as to intitle him to 20/ when he has given but 2/6?   certainly not. Want of Consideration, is a good plea against any demand.   dealing in certificates is in the nature of Money Contracts.   Six ℔ Cent. is the highest interest known to the law.   is not the Contract which gives a Man 48 ℔ Cent. highly usurious and illegal.

But to reduce a Case to actual Practice.   let a Speculator bring his action for damages. on his certificates. ~~demanding~~ laying them at 20/—when he bought at 2/6.   suppose him a Pennsylvanian Who has drawn 4 years full interest on the nominal amount. which will yield £192 for every original hundred laid out. an unbiassed Jury could not be empannelled in the United States that would give him one farthing.

Manuscript, volume 2 of the diary of William Maclay, DLC. The editors believe this may have been a draft of a newspaper article.

[OBJECTIONS]

first Objection, not an Echo—yess—
2d the Word Trust—conveys Mistrust
if The Gentleman meant to Convey the Idea of Mistrust in the Amendment. he has been very unfortunate in using a Term. which means directly the Reverse—
had rather this Motion had not been made—
but since it is—I shall vote for it—
some say there are none—therefore Useless
others say there are /

Manuscript, glued into the blank pages in the back of volume 3 of the diary.

Appendix B
Newspaper Pieces

Existing evidence indicates that WM was the most prolific writer of newspaper pieces among members of the First Federal Congress. With the exception of item (10) on the Mint, the pieces included in this appendix can be documented as his work. He may have written others as well.

(1)
FOR THE DAILY ADVERTISER

Messrs. PRINTERS,

IT seems generally agreed, that the Susquehannah is the nearest to the center of wealth, territory, and population, taking our view of the United States on the Atlantic side. So far, no doubt is raised against it. The objection most strongly urged against this river, is the connection with the western waters. The western country is a large field—some point must be taken as a center. Fort Pitt has been called the Key of this country—let then our arguments point to this object.

From the tide water on the Potowmack to Fort Pitt, following the usual calculation, the distance is 304 miles. From the tide water on Potowmac to Fort Cumberland 200, portage to the three Forks of Turkey Foot 30, water carriage 8, portage at the Falls of Yohiogena 1, down the Yohiogena to Monongahela

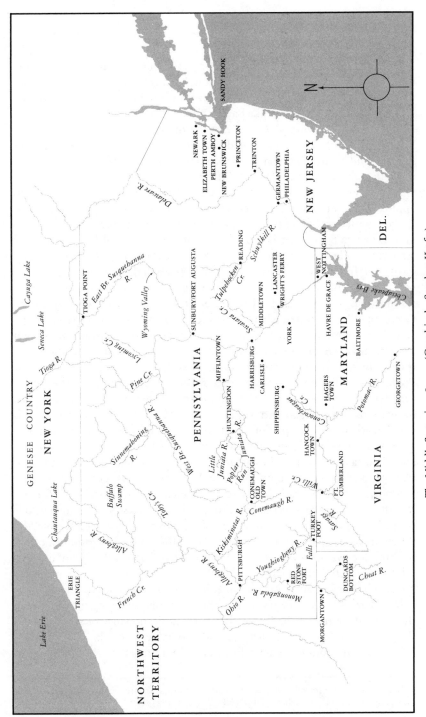

The Middle States in 1789–91. (Graphics by Stephen Kraft.)

50, to Fort Pitt 15—in all 304 miles. The rout by the way of Cheat River, between the same places is 360 miles.

From the tide water on the Susquehannah to Fort Pitt, following also the usual calculation, which is certainly best in both cases, as all new calculations may be more liable to suspicion. The distance is 276 miles, viz. from Havre de Grace at the head of Chesapeake Bay, to Wright's Ferry [*Columbia, Pa.*] 40, to Harris's Ferry [*Harrisburg, Pa.*] 26, to the mouth of Juniata 15, up Juniata River to Standing Stone, now called Huntington, 75, from thence to Cohnimaugh, Old Town 36, down the Kiskemenetas to the Ohio [*Allegheny*] 60, down the Ohio [*Allegheny*] to Fort Pitt 30—in all 276.

It is allowed by all competent judges, that there are not two rivers which approach nearer to each other in circumstances of size, than the Potowmac and Juniata, with this difference, that Juniata having a more northern situation, is known to retain its water better. The Potowmac, it is well known, is made serviceable only by great expence and labor. The Juniata in its natural state, is navigated, from Huntington downwards, by boats of the burthen of from 1000 to 600 bushels of wheat; from Huntington up to Poplar Run, by boats of about the burthen of 400 bushels. The present portage from Poplar Run to the Connemaugh is 23 miles, where a good road is now made. This pass over the Allegany Mountains used to be the most frequented of any by the old Indian traders, and is still declared to be the easiest that can be found any where over these ridges. The latest observations however assure us, that the waters of Poplar run, and Connemaugh approach within 40 perches of each other, are of sufficient size for supplying canals; and that they may be connected by a lock navigation. The navigation down the Connimaugh to the Kiskemenetas, is equal in goodness to the part of Juniata between Poplar Run and Huntington. That of the Kiskemetas and the Allegany, down to Fort Pitt, is unexceptionable. The navigation of the Juniata is no matter of speculation—it is a thing of daily practice. A second communication between the Susquehannah and the Allegany, is by the heads of the West Branch and Toby's Creek [*Clarion River*]—This is not so direct to Fort Pitt, nor has it been so well examined, but by the Indian accounts it may in some respects be considered as preferable, the different waters approaching very near each other in the low grounds, called the Buffaloe swamp; a well attested fact will place this in a clear point of view. John Hart,[1] an Indian trader, was taken dangerously ill on the Allegany; he was brought by two Indians in a canoe up Toby's Creek, and down the Susquehannah to Harris's Ferry—the Indians carrying him, and dragging the canoe over the necessary portage in half a day. This communication may be serviceable to the parts of the Allegany in the neighborhood of French creek.

The Sinnemononing, or north fork of the West Branch, has but a portage of

---

[1]John Hart, a trader who was active in Pennsylvania as late as the early 1760s, was considered by the Indians to be a friend. (*PMHB* 37:37, 183)

11 miles to good navigation on the head of the Allegany River; from here by the way of the Chittockyay [*Chatauqua*] Lake there is a portage of 7 miles only to Lake Erie. This communication is almost direct, and has been lately well explored. The east branch of the Susquehannah affords a still more enlarged navigation extending upwards of 300 miles from the Forks at Sunbury. Boats have been repeatedly hauled into it, from the Mohawk River in the State of New York. It was thus that General Clinton transported his whole army in the year 1779, descending the Susquehannah to the forks of the river at the Tioga Point, and then ascending the Tioga [*Chemung River*] on his way to the Genisee country.

From the main branch of the Tioga, a portage of 18 miles connects the navigation with the Cannodasago [*Seneca*] lake. This is in fact connecting it with lake Ontario. Thus taking the connections of the Susquehannah, we find a double one with the Allegany or Western Waters, that by the Juniata superior to the Potowmac connections, both in distance and convenience. The one by the west branch and Toby's creek, more circuitous to Fort Pitt, but better adapted to the upper parts of the Allegany. The connections with lake Erie is unrivalled in point of convenience; and the northern communications with the waters of Ontario, and all the western waters of New-York, so far as respects the Potowmac are exclusively connected with the Susquehannah. In those quarters, it seems highly probable, that new regions will one day be opened to commerce. The lands watered by the Susquehannah have been estimated at forty thousand square miles. This whole extent of country, the small parts hitherto cultivated excepted, is cloathed with the finest timber. Iron ore, limestone and stone coal are found in abundance, the soil in every place where it has been essayed, has not disappointed the husbandman. It is found adapted to the winter grains, as well as the summer crops. And the new settlements are at this time proceeding with great rapidity.

It may however, be worth while to pause a moment, and ask, for what purposes the federal town is to be seated on a river? the answer is plain and obvious. For the more easy supplying the inhabitants with provisions, materials of building, fewel, &c.

Has there during all the time of the high price of wheat, flour, &c. in the Atlantic states, a single boat been loaded with these articles at Fort Pitt, and ascended the Monongohela or any other stream, so that these same articles reached the mouth of Potowmack? The answer must be, no. Have not boats without number, been loaded at Fort Pitt, with provisions, &c. to take their chance of the Mississippi market at 2000 miles distance? the answer must be yes. This precludes all speculation on the subject. The commerce of the western waters, so far as respects the carrying out of country produce has made, its elegit, and the reason is obvious. Boats with country produce, to neat any thing worth while, must be heavily loaded, such cannot ascend streams with ease if the water is high; oars will not do, and the bottom cannot be purchased with setting poles. If shallow, they cannot proceed for want of water; critical times only will suit, and even then the labor of the boatmen is extreme. Hence country produce will always descend the full stream, be the prospect of the market ever so distant. Thus it is plain, that the Atlantic rivers never can supply any town on their banks with provisions or any heavy articles, but those which are produced on their own lands.

Let applications of these principles be made to the Potowmac and the Susquehannah. State the whole produce of the Potowmac, be it what it may, as 1. The Juniata is allowed by men of candor who know both rivers, to be quite equal to the Potowmac, with, perhaps, generally speaking, a more productive country in grain, on its banks. It will therefore stand as 1. But the Juniata is not equal to one fifth part of the whole waters of the Susquehannah; it is not half so large as the west branch, and bears a still less proportion to the east branch. As to what respects air, climate, soil, &c. the difference is trifling; the 2 branches then being rated as 4. the clear result is, that the advantages to a city situated on the Susquehannah with respect to the navigation will be as 5 to 1, compared with the Potowmac.

But if connections with the Western Waters, must still be attended to, and considered as a fundamental principle, it is plain that the Susquehannah possesses them, in a greater degree than the Potowmac, and is besides intimately connected with the northern waters, and great lakes; advantages which the Potowmac cannot pretend to.

NYDA, 17 Sept. 1789. The present names of rivers and towns have been included in brackets when they differ significantly from WM's usage.

(2)
POLITICAL
THE BUDGET OPENED
OBJECTS

1st.   *Extending the powers and influence of the Treasury.*

2d.   *Establishing the permanent residence of Court and Congress in New-York.*

3d.   *Securing the revenues of the Union, to the inhabitants of that city.*

WAYS AND MEANS

ENCREASE the public debt by every possible method—admit all accounts *authorised* and *unauthorised*—blend the state debts with those of the Union, that thus a pretext may be afforded, to seize all the sources of revenue, and depress the state governments; for without reducing them to insignificance, a pompous Court cannot be established; and without such a Court, as a proper machine, no government can be properly managed; or in other words, the people will be meddling with serious matters, unless you amuse them with trifles. Fund all demands indiscriminately in the highest interest possible; but previous to this communicate the grand secret to all the monied interest of New-York, and to as many influential characters in Congress as may ensure the success of the project; that they may, by an united effort of speculation, secure all the certificates. Thus the whole Union will be subsidized to the city of New-York. The revenues of the United States will flow entire into the hands of her citizens. Thus possessed of the wealth of the Union, she will govern the Councils of the Empire, secure the residence of the Court and Congress, and grow in power, splendor and population, while there is room left on the island to build another house. The idle and affluent will croud to her from all the new world, as well as many adventurers from the old. New loans must be opened on every pretext, in Holland and elsewhere; for the greater the mass of public debt, the greater will be the influence of the Treasury, which has the management of it, and all this will redound to the emolument of the favored city. Thus shall the capital of the United States in a few years equal London or Paris in population, extent, expence and dissipation, while for the aggrandisement of one spot, and one set of men, the national debt shall tower aloft to hundreds of millions.

Independent Gazetteer, 6 Feb. 1790. The manuscript version and the unsigned covering letter to John Nicholson dated 30 January are in Miscellaneous Manuscripts, DLC.

(3)
FOR THE INDEPENDENT GAZETTEER

MR. PRINTER,

I AM an old soldier, and an Irishman. This I tell you at once by way of subscribing my letter; for by letting you know before who I am, you may soon guess what I will be after.

I followed the fortunes of the great Washington thro' all the wars; and hearing of his glory in New-York—heaven be praised, for she has a knack of doing things handsomely—aye, in New-York, where he used to be cursed regimentally, and on field-days, by whole brigades, that there his honors should be shed upon him. To New-York, however, I came; and the first thing I wanted to see, was some of the laws made by my old General; for as I had been long under his command, I did not want to disobey orders now. I soon got one of them, but could not understand it well—There was a string of names at the end of it, and among the rest, one *Vice*. Now I knew *Vice* in camp to be, drunkenness, swearing and some other things, which used to befall us when we happened to be well fed for a day or two, and had nothing else to do. But cousin Patrick coming by told me, that this *Vice* never was in camp, but that it was a man that took the room or place of my General, who they now call President. What! and before his face too? says I. Where was the man to take his place when our frost-bitten toes looked thro' our ragged shoes—in the Jersies, or at Brandywine, or Germantown, or Monmouth, or York-Town? He for a—I was just going to curse, and call names, but Pat stopped me; and it was a thousand pities, for I never was in a finer humor for it. Well, Pat, says I, coming a little to myself, how shall I contrive to see him? And will there ever any thing more be done for us, poor soldiers? As to seeing him, says Pat, I believe that must be out of the question. He is now in the hands of fine folks, who do not like to admit any body who has not new shoes, and is not as neat about the heels as a pin; and I doubt, in your present trim, you would not pass muster. But then brave times are coming on: the certificates will all be paid off at there full amount; and money will be so plenty, expecially among those who have taken care to provide themselves well with them, at a proper time, that they will be able to live at their ease, and give generous prices to you, and to every body else that will work for them. And as for the trifle of taxes that will fall to the share of any individual man, to make them up, a clever fellow would not have his name told for it. Pat, says I, these fine folks would spoil our General if they could. He never was a greater man, than when he rode among us with his dusty boots. They may hide him from us, but they never can make him hate or despise us, though we may have a patched shoe, or a ragged stocking. As to other matters, Pat, you must have your finger in the pie, or you never would talk so. If our earnings are to procure ease and affluence to any, it ought to be to ourselves. To work for our money a second time, and pay taxes a third time for it, won't do, Pat. No, no, Pat, it never will do. I guessed you meant some mischief, when you, and a set of rooks, used to be following us, poor soldiers, like a pack of wolves, or a flight of ravens, to prey up our distresses. Was it for this you used to give us such friendly advice—O, take any thing for your certificates; they'll follow the continental money—they'll not be worth a farthing—And now to be served such a dog's trick—to be told to work and pay taxes for them, Pat—by—But I believe, Mr. Printer, it would not do to swear in a newspaper—and I'm not a fine writer, and can't give you a whole chapter on my feelings. Pat surely had some feelings too; for I did not know that I had got my stick elevated a tone or too higher than a presented musket, till I saw him edging off to get out of the reach of it.

Now, Mr. Printer, to have lost my youth, my health, my strength and pay— to have become the heir of aches and pains, hunger and nakedness, would not grieve me. A belief, that the virtues and sufferings of the American army would be had in grateful rememberance, should have been my consolation; but to see luxury and riot rise on our hard earnings, while misery is our lot—a brave heart cannot bear the contrast! Farewell! But if there be a word of truth in what Pat says, you Congress, and all the world, shall hear from me.

Independent Gazetteer, 20 Feb. 1790. WM's letter to John Nicholson of 8 February enclosing the piece for publication is in the Gratz Collection, PHi.

(4)
For the Independent Gazetteer

MR. PRINTER,

It cannot have escaped an attentive observer, that some individuals have endeavored to model the Constitution of the United States to the standard of the British monarchy. This is a matter far from being impossible—it needs but the overcharging of some features, and the lessening or obscuring of others. The first step to a work of this kind, would be, to swallow up the state Legislatures in the federal Government. The Judiciary of the United States is considered, by some, as capable of producing a like effect, with regard to the state Judiciaries. The Report from the Treasury, on the subject of finance, copies after a British nation, and if pursued in its full extent, cannot fail of soon overwhelming us with masses of irredeemable debt. Men, who lay it down as a maxim, that England is the happiest and best governed spot on the globe, will not consider themselves as criminal in endeavoring to place their country in the same situation. Doing it, however, by indirect means, seems to need an apology—Nor will it do to tell enlightened Americans, that thus children are beguiled into health, by imposing physic upon them instead of food. Such state physicians will always be suspected of having an eye to the loaves and fishes, which are generally dealt out with a bountiful hand in royal governments. The cost, however, should be well counted, before systems of such magnitude are attempted. Several serious questions will arise—for instance— Are we able to support a civil list of a million sterling a year? Can, or will we bear the exactions of the miriads of retainers to the law, and the protractions of causes for ages, that attend the practice in England? Her criminal jurisprudence, indeed, never should be mentioned without a tribute of praise to its excellence. Shall we, in our infancy, adopt a system of finance, which will at one stroke reduce us to the beggary of borrowing every shilling we may want on any emergency, while our whole resources are mortgaged to a set of speculators, for the support of riot and dissipation?

Public faith—public credit—inviolable observation of contracts—the fairest names in the social catalogue—have in all ages been brought forward to cover the grossest enormities; thereby verifying what has been said of rigid law, SUMMUM JUS, SUMMA INJURIA;[1] and have ever called for the interposition of the

---

[1] Rigorous application of the law causes rigorous injustice.

supreme power, as a correcting chancery, to remedy the evils which have been engrafted by accidents and artifices upon them.

The Jewish jubilee,[2] of divine origin, had this for its object. The Roman secession to the Aventine mount,[3] gives us a clear example of it. But to descend to modern times—The Legislature of Great-Britain, in the present century, deranged the course of the law respecting contracts, in the affair of the South Sea Company. Debts were discharged, on payment of ten per cent. Sureties acquitted, and law-suits discontinued, by act of Parliament. And perhaps no occasion ever existed, that would more fully justify the exercise of such chancery in government, as the present one in the United States.

Whether a splendid government, with all the retainers to, and trappings of, royalty, be for the advantage of the governed, is a question which ought be fully settled, before any imitations or innovations take place. Men, who have given grave opinions on the prosperity of nations, seem to refer the whole to the mass of productive labor carried on among any people. Whether a court, such as the head of a great empire is generally surrounded with, is a likely place to produce such qualifications, may justly be doubted. In such places, men sacrifice every thing to appearance: they soar above common life; and the domestic habits of industry and frugality are forgotten. Examples from such high sources cannot fail of imitation; and the contagion may be spread far a wide.

Should, however, such a misfortune ever befall America, we have a sure resource in the different state Legislatures. Here the seeds of genuine republicanism have flourished, and brought forth fruit—and here they are still cherished. Let not, however, the different state governments be wanting to themselves, but fill, with firmness and decision, the stations assigned them in the general arrangement of the empire. For this purpose, let them instruct and direct the conduct of their Senators, in the Senate of the United States.

Thus will the confidence of the people, in the federal government, receive additional strength, and the interests of republicanism a further security and support.

Independent Gazetteer, 20 Feb. 1790. WM's letter to John Nicholson of 8 February enclosing the piece for publication is in the Gratz Collection, PHi.

[2]See June 1790, n. 24, in Part I of this volume.
[3]The secession occurred when, in order to force Rome to accept their views, the plebians left public and political life and withdrew to Aventine, one of the seven hills outside of the city.

(5)
FOR THE INDEPENDENT GAZETTEER

MR. PRINTER,

As the assumption of the state debts, by the general government, is now a common subject of conversation, permit me, through the channel of your paper, to offer to the public, some observations on the debt of Pennsylvania, which has been incurred in the general defence, and which, as far as I have been able to learn, is comprised under the following heads.

		DOLLARS.
1st.	Certificates of depreciation granted to the army, hospital, &c. about	1,403,793
2d.	Certificates for supplies for the army, by act of June, 1780, about	34,583
3d.	Certificates for horses for the army, in the year 1780, about	90,336
4th.	Certificates for the residue of the state debt, funded on interest, about	478,351
		2,007,063

One third of the depreciation debt, in the hands of original holders, was paid off in the money of 1781. The interest of the other two thirds was funded on the state excise. The depreciation lands, and confiscated estates, were appropriated, as a sinking fund for the whole.

The certificates mentioned under the second and third heads, were receivable in taxes at the time of issuing, and have generally been paid off, or continue to be paid, at the Treasury, in bills of 1781.

The interest on those, under the fourth head, is paid at the Treasury, out of the arrears of taxes, imposts, &c.

All the foregoing certificates are receivable in the Land-Office of the state, and it is reasonable to suppose that nearly one half of them are already taken up by the sale of lands, city lots, confiscated estates, payments of arrears of purchase money, &c.

The whole mass of state debts proposed, to be assumed by Congress, is stated by the Secretary at twenty five millions of dollars: but throw off one million, for that part of the state debt of Pennsylvania which is already paid, and suppose the whole to stand at twenty-four millions; one million[1] of which belongs to Pennsylvania. Now by the effect of the federal impost, it appears that the port of Philadelphia, pays one fourth of the present revenue of the union. Six millions then of the newly assumed debt (on the principle of impost) must be provided for by that port. Had Pennsylvania been among the debtor states, there would not perhaps be cause of complaint, but she has ever been considered as a creditor to a great amount.

It may be said all this can be adjusted by a final settlement. There is but a distant prospect of such settlement; and many say it never will, nor can take place. But the settlement, can equally take place after each state has paid her

---

[1] At this point WM's manuscript includes the word "only."

own debt; and there is no doubt but the balances of both debt and credit, would be lessened by postponing it to that period, or by, what amounts to the same thing, giving each state credit in the general account for the amount of her own state debt. The effect of the assumption proposed is virtually (so far as respects Pennsylvania) the assuming to pay six millions of dollars, in order to get rid of the payment of one.

The payment of the state debt of Pennsylvania, in its present form, by receiving the certificates in the Land-Office, may be considered as an accommodation to the landed interest, and will not be attended with new taxes. By the proposed assumption, the debt will not only be increased in the proportion of six to one; but the payment must be in cash, raised by new federal taxes. The payments also, to the Land-Office of the state, must in future be in money, instead of certificates.

A PENNSYLVANIAN

Independent Gazetteer, 27 March 1790. The manuscript of this piece is in the John Nicholson Papers, PHarH.

(6)

From a Philadelphia paper
INTELLIGENCE EXTRAORDINARY

Hamiltonople, March 18

WE hear, that two chosen Janissaries[1] have been dispatched by the Grand Vizir,[2] about 100 miles south of this capital, to take off the heads of certain malcontents, who have dared to whisper dissatisfaction at the present measures of government.[3] Should success attend this undertaking, there is no doubt but the first honors of the state, will reward the enterprise, though in the opinion of the impartial, it justly merits a bow-string. In the mean while, the deliberations of the Divan[4] are suspended, or diverted, to some petty regulations about the slaves, for the double purpose of attending to the secret expedition and waiting the return of their celebrated partizans, whose voices in council are equally necessary with their customs abroad.

Independent Gazetteer, 27 March 1790. This piece was reprinted in the *NYJ* on 1 April.

---

[1]Thomas Fitzsimons and George Clymer. Janissaries were a class of Turkish soldier-slaves which accepted absolute obedience to the sultan.

[2]The secretary of the treasury. The Grand Visir was the chief minister of the Sultan of Turkey.

[3]Report on the public credit.

[4]Congress. The divan was the privy council of Turkey.

(7)
POLITICAL
FOR THE INDEPENDENT GAZETTEER

Mr. PRINTER,

I AM a poor distressed woman,[1] who for the thirteen or fourteen years since I kept house, have had as great a variety of fortune as ever beset any female. Glorious gleams of sunshine indeed have I had, and happiness ever seemed in my reach; yet by the mismanagement of servants, in brakeing cups and saucers, spoiling provisions, &c. I think I am likely to be ruined. A few days ago I expected to put an end to all my troubles, by sending for a worthy gentleman,[2] who had often taken me out of the gutter, when I considered myself as irretrievably fallen. Hearing he was at hand, I requested my neighbour[3] (as good a man I thought as could be) to brush the furniture, and sweep the house, where I used to lodge my best friends.[4] Now could you think it, Sir? Off he runs, and buys such an heap of pots and pans, and dishes and ladles, as run me to ten or twelve pounds of expence. Good Lord! and all this after my being so much in debt already. I determined not to pay him. But what of that? *Sawny*[5] the servant, who had the keeping of the trifle of cash I was possessed of, the moment my back was turned, gave him the money. Was there ever such a trick? People tell me the Grand Jury[6] should indict him; but la Sir, the Jury know all about it, and I am afraid will take no notice of him, but lye by, till it suits them too, to get a slap at me.

Mr. Printer, I think I am not deficient in the qualities of my head; my heart I know to be possessed of the principles of rectitude. Is it not dreadful that my concerns should be knocked about at this rate, every body doing what they please with me? After describing my situation, you cannot expect me to tell my name, but pray publish my case, which is a plain one. Perhaps some humane person may direct me how to get out of my difficulties.

Independent Gazetteer, 27 March 1790. The manuscript of this piece, which WM sent to John Nicholson on 14 February, is in Miscellaneous Manuscripts, DLC.

---

[1] The United States of America.
[2] George Washington.
[3] Samuel Osgood.
[4] Osgood's house at 3 Cherry Street had been the residence of the presidents of the Confederation Congress.
[5] Alexander Hamilton. Sawny is a play on words. While it is a nickname for Alexander, its colloquial meaning is "fool."
[6] Congress.

(8)

FOR THE DAILY ADVERTISER

Messrs. PRINTERS,

whoever will pay attention to the acts of the old Congress, both during the war and since the peace, will find, that the public demands, for the exigencies of the general government, were managed by requisitions, charged on the different states, in a ratio, that was supposed to bear proportion to their abilities, for the time being, carrying on the face of each requisition, an express reference to a final settlement, and a direct assumption of any balance which an individual state might advance, more than her proportion should be found to be, on a general adjustment of the accounts.

As all debts contracted and engagements entered into, under the confederation, were confirmed by the new constitution, it may be justly demanded, by what authority, any *ex post facto* law can now be passed, altering the arrangement for settlement, or in any wise impairing the force or effect of former engagements? The hope and firm belief of a final settlement, when ample justice would be done to the advancing states, gave confidence to the exertions of the union. The state debts which stand charged on the funds of individual states, are the most effectual pledges to secure this settlement. For should the general assumption of the state debts take place, agreeable to some late proposals, the debtor states, which are believed to be, by much, the most numerous, would check every motion for settlement, as it must be contrary to their interest. We are informed that this was actually the case in Holland, and that the city of Amsterdam never was reimbursed the sums which she advanced, beyond her proportion, during the revolution of the United Provinces.

The states being charged with their respective debts, may be regarded as a fortunate circumstance in facilitating a final settlement, and equalizing the accounts—thus when any state is deficient in her requisitions, let a portion of her state debt remain upon her, equal to such deficiency; in this manner the general burthen will be distributed agreeable to the principles on which the debt was contracted. Innovation will be avoided. and the public expectation complied with. Whereas a general assumption of the state debts, would deprive Congress of a simple and easy mode of obliging the delinquent states to make up their deficiencies and have a direct tendency to prevent all settlement whatever. The evident consequence of which, would be, the punishment of the creditor states for their superior exertions, and the rewarding the deficient ones for their delinquency.

April 28.

NYDA, 28 April 1790; reprinted in *FG* on 4 May. The piece was also printed in the *Freeman's Journal* on 28 April. WM asked Benjamin Rush to get it published in the

Pennsylvania Packet or any other newspaper he thought proper. (To Rush, 24 April 1790, Rush Papers, DLC)

(9)
Philadelphia, 16 June

The question concerning the temporary residence of Congress has been viewed in different lights. While some consider it as of the utmost importance, others conceive it to be a matter of total indifference. Perhaps a medium between the two will be right. That the seat of government should be near the centre is on all hands admitted. No one wishes Congress to remove to Savannah or the province of Maine. But whether they should sit at New-York, Philadelphia or Baltimore, is a point upon which we cannot so readily agree. That Philadelphia is nearer the centre of population than either New-York or Baltimore can easily be shewn. On each side of it the number of senators is equal. The representatives from the eastward are 27, those from the southward are 30. To the eastward of New-York there are but 8 senators and 17 representatives, while to the southward there are 16 senators and 42 representatives. To the north and east of Baltimore there are 16 senators and 36 representatives, to the southward but 8 senators and 23 representatives. As representation is in proportion to population Philadelphia appears to be the most central situation. But if it can be shewn that a residence at Philadelphia will be less expensive to the union, it will be a more powerful argument in favour of this city. From New-York and beyond it the number of members which will come to this city is 33. The mileage from New-York to Philadelphia will be 30 dollars to each member every session. This will amount to 990 dollars. But on the other hand mileage of 30 dollars each will be deducted from 52 members to the southward, which will be 1560 dollars. Deduct from this 990 dollars and the remainder is 570 dollars saved to the union every session by a residence in Philadelphia. Allowing two sessions per annum, the annual saving will be 1140 dollars. Upon a comparison with Baltimore it will appear that the annual saving will be 720 dollars.

There is another circumstance worthy of notice. A number of our citizens from different parts of the states are obliged to visit the seat of federal government, to transact business of different kinds to attend the federal court; to solicit a mitigation of fines and forfeitures; to apply for patents for useful inventions; to make applications for different appointments under the general government; or to transact business at the treasury or in the war office. A central situation will be found most eligible on this account. New-York is too near to the northern extremity. The interest of the southern states requires the seat of government to be removed further south; and at the same time it is the interest of the eastern states that it should not be removed as far as Baltimore.

Philadelphia is the medium which will suit the interests of both extremities of the union.

A want of confidence in Congress will be the certain consequence of staying, in an improper place; as it will be apparent, that this must be the fruit of undue influence, and if such influence is successful in a case of such moment, it may be expected to govern in every one.

Affecting to establish the permanent residence at a future day, does not go to remedy present inconveniences. It is saying to the sick man, wait two or three years and you shall be cured, to the hungry man, next year I will give you bread.

The inconveniences exist, and a free legislature ought to remedy them.

To fix the permanent residence by contract is unjustifiable in every point of view. It is treating the public like an unhappy person, locked up in a spunging-house;[1] stay here six or seven years, and consent to let us pillage you, or you shall not get away at all. Is this language fit for, or treatment proper to be offered to freemen?

The intercourse between New-York and the United States, is principally by water. All connection with the agricultural interest of the union is cut off, or nearly so. The inhabitants are merchants, or very generally engaged in some kind of speculation or other. If the members of Congress are to go by sea to the Federal residence, and be cooped up in an island, perhaps Bermudas will be found to be a more eligible situation than New-York. The members of Congress ought to travel to the federal residence by land. Thus they would become possessed of a knowledge, not only of their own state, but of the United States in general. And the residence should be fixed in a central position, to promote and facilitate this object.

FG, 16 June 1790. This piece was composed by Benjamin Rush from WM's notes. (To Rush, 5, 18 June 1790, Rush Papers, DLC)

---

[1]A spunging house is a place where people are robbed.

(10)
FOR THE DAILY ADVERTISER

THOUGHTS on COINAGE, and the establishment of a MINT, submitted to the consideration of those Statesmen only, who dare to quit the *beaten path*.

It has often been predicted that our emancipation from the yoke of Britain would deliver us all from European prejudice, that liberal and new ideas would characterize the American revolution.

In some points, this prediction has been verified; in others (and those of no small importance) it has been too fatally contradicted. I pass them by without observation, because my praise or censure would be of very little amount, and confine myself to a single proof of the influence of old modes of thinking. European nations have their mints; they are adapted to the circumstances of many of them, and so must we, though in no sort necessary to us. Europe debases its money by alloys that deceive no body; and only render it easier to counterfeit their coin. America catches the idea, borrows their calculations and their reasoning, and sets seriously about making an adulterated coin. Such is the force of prejudice, that I have never heard the propriety of these measures doubted. The idea has been early imbibed. We do not remember how we admitted it, and so familiarized by long habit, that the propriety of retaining it, is never questioned. It may be worth while however on so important a subject, to awaken inquiry; it may lead to conclusions which we have never attended to. Money was originally introduced to facilitate the exchange of commodities. He that gave ten shillings for a sheep to one who wishes to employ it in the purchase of two bushels of wheat, gives (in the estimation of the seller) two bushels of wheat. This substitute of a portable commodity, which should represent every saleable article, was early adopted. And the precious metals for obvious reasons, became the common standard with most nations. These however, passed originally by weight; but as people found it advantageous to go to market, without being loaded with commodities, it was natural for them to wish also to be disburdened of their weights and scales. A mark descriptive of the weight and fineness of the metals was affixed by persons of established credit, and character, and ultimately by the sovereign, this converted the metals into coins, the circulation of which, was coextensive with the authority of the sovereign, beyond this, the mark was not acknowledged; and the metals were received by *weight* only. As the affixing of this mark was attended with some expence, the sovereign compensated himself by adulterating the coin, while the intercourse of nations with each other, was inconsiderable. No great evil arose from this fraud, for while coin is confined to one state, and no ballances are to be paid to another, it derives its value from the authority of the sovereign, or the tacit consent of the people, and it is therefore a matter of indifference to the individual of what materials it is composed. We accordingly find that leather, red feathers, beads, shells, iron, &c. have been the current money of nations, whose commerce was circumscribed by the limits of their territories. Coin then may be considered as the money of the *nation by which it is emitted*, but *pure silver or gold only* as the money of the *world*. If payments are to be made by one nation to another, those payments must be made in gold or silver, and not in coin as coin, but in bullion or coin, at the rate of bullion, that is, in proportion to the quantity of gold or silver, that it contains. As nations become commercial, they have refined their coins, that of England and Holland being among the purest we know: And thus, upon principles which have not been sufficiently attended to, or understood, which indeed, I never remember to have seen properly explained. That nation is richest with respect to other nations which possesses and retains the greatest quantity of the money of the *world*, that is of pure gold or silver. If the coins of a country were of copper only, gold and silver would be a commodity of which no more would be received from one nation, than could be passed off to another, and whenever the ballance of trade was in favour of such nation, both would fall in their price, and be purchased by foreigners, below their value, when; against the country, they would rise beyond their first price.

The trade of such country would fluctuate in extremes—nor would any more specie ever remain in it than would just suffice for the annual demand of foreigners—such a nation would be incapable of great or sudden exertions, even its trade would be limitted from the uncertainty of its remittances. Every well policied and commercial nation has therefore deemed it expedient to devise means for retaining a considerable quantity of specie in their country, beyond what is necessary to discharge an unexpected ballance; and in proportion as they have succeeded in this, is the equality of their markets and their power of exertion. The best and most effectual of these expedients is to compose the circulating money of the country of the precious metals—by rendering them necessary to every body, every body endeavours to retain a part of them, they diffuse themselves thro' the whole community instead of being confined to the warehouse of the merchant; in this case the ballances paid or received in any one year become trifling compared to the general mass of wealth, and of course their fluctuations are less felt. If then this reasoning is just, it must follow that in proportion as any other substance which does not compose the *money of the world* is introduced into circulation and made the *money of the country* in the same proportion, less of that money will be retained. If copper supplying the place of silver would diminish the quantity of silver, it must follow, that copper combined with silver will have exactly the same effect, thus an alloy composed of one twelfth copper will unavoidably render a country one twelfth poorer with respect to foreign nations who only receive coin as bullion, and give no credit either for the stamp or the alloy. In proportion therefore as nations become enlightened and understand their true interests they purify their coins; none of them have indeed yet freed their money from alloy—first, because it is extremely difficult to get rid of old prejudices, and second, because the re-coinage of their alloyed metals would put them to expence; and as ministers are generally the people of a day they do not wish to purchase the greatest permanent advantage by a temporary inconvenience. I confess I should feel a pride in thinking that America had set an example on the occasion and had contrived (if she might coin) to render her coins the money of the world. Let her free them from alloy; foreigners will then acknowledge her mint; when she is compelled to ship them she will do it with less loss; and her Eagles will soar where the Princes and Potentates of Europe will not dare to shew their brazen faces. If the alloy was taken from a guinea it would certainly pass in France for at least as much as it does now, nor would it be diminished in value in England, since the present value is set by the Sovereign, it would be just as easy for him to say that the gold it contained should pass for 21/, as that a base metal should pass for gold—What then is the effect of alloy? 1st, It renders the nation which uses it as much poorer than it would otherwise be as the proportion of alloy in its circulating money is to the precious metal it contains.

2d. It defeats one of the great purposes for which money was designed, and converts gold and silver from the money of all countries into the coin of one.

3. It occasions an actual loss by the value of all the metal of which the alloy is composed.

4th. It renders the precious metals they contain intrinsically worse by the whole value of the expence of refining it.

5th. It occasions an additional expence in compounding them.

6th. It renders it easier to counterfeit, for as all counterfeits must be composed of base metals, the more alloy the coin contains the nearer it approaches the counterfeit.

7th. It affords the Sovereign a temptation to defraud his subjects, and his servants the means of defrauding him.

The reasons for alloy arising from the expence of refining and the necessity of rendering the metals harder, have long since been charged to the account of fraud and ignorance, and refuted by the slightest knowledge of chymistry and the nature of metals.

Previous to declaring *how* we should coin, it might perhaps have been proper to ask *why* we should coin? Our commerce already supplies us with a medium which will receive no addition from a coinage. If the ballance of trade is in our favour, the coin of other nations will multiply upon us—If the ballance is against us, our coin will leave us, nor shall we receive any compensation for the coinage.

It is said that some standard is necessary by which to regulate contracts, and to prevent deceptions in the receipts of foreign coin—The reasoning is just, and were there no other way of effecting this than thro' the medium of a mint, I should (notwithstanding its inconveniencies,) subscribe to the measure— The true standard of value is *pure silver* (for even gold is less so, for reasons which it would lead me into too great length to detail here) this may be applied equally to ascertain the value of merchandize in every commercial nation; why then should we look for any other? The mint can only declare the quantity contained in our own coins, and this too very imperfectly, for after an Eagle has passed from hand to hand it contains less gold than it originally did, will sell for less at foreign markets, and of course is worth less at home—and yet this standard, imperfect as it is, cannot be purchased but at very considerable expence—while an unalterable one may be attained not only without expence, but with proper attention may be rendered in some sort profitable to the community: I shall now endeavour to trace the outlines of a plan which may, I conceive, operate these effects. The good sense of those who may approve it will easily discover the necessary details, should it ever be carried into effect—Let the money unit, or dollar be equal in value to the quantity of pure silver, contained in the dollar now in common circulation, let this be divided into as many decimal parts as may be deemed best; let the proportion of gold to silver, be as 1 to 15; let an office be established to assay the coins of those nations with whom we have a common intercourse and to publish every three months their value in dimes, cents &c. Let Banks of deposit [or the National Bank, if deemed best,] receive all coins, so estimated, and give Bank notes for them, which shall express the species of money lodged and its value in units, dimes, cents, &c., as thus "the Bank is indebted to the bearer 10 Spanish milled dollars of the emission 1776, valued at   units &c.   " The Bearer of this certificate may be entitled on demand to receive the amount in the very species of money lodged, paying a small agio on depositing and drawing out his money.

Let these Bank notes be the only legal tender in all money transactions above the value of five pounds.

The advantages resulting from this plan would be

1st. That it affords the standard sought by a mint.

2d. That this standard would be invariable and not affected by the wearing of money, since coins, which fell perceptibly below the standard published by the Assay office should not be received.

3d. That the expence of coinage would be saved, which may at a very moderate calculation including the expence of officers &c. on the coinage of silver, be rated at seven per cent. independent of the risk from frauds &c.

4th. The loss occasioned by the wearing of the metals would be saved, which in a course of years would be so considerable, as to render a re-coinage as necessary, which would be attended with great loss to the public since the deficient weights must be supplied by the mint.

5th. The stagnation of trade, manufactures, and the fall of lands, which is an obvious consequence of drawing out of circulation all the foreign coins before their place is supplied, and the impossibility of supplying their place in a short period, without an expence to government which is ill adapted to their present circumstances, would be prevented.

6th. The convenience which foreigners would find in trading with a Nation in which their money was not only known and received, but where it may at all times be purchased at a cheaper rate than at home.

7th. The introduction of paper, the most convenient money for the payment of large sums without precluding the circulation of foreign coins, for the convenience of change while the expence of the wear would be borne by nations that coined them, since when too light to be received at the Bank they would naturally go back to their old masters.

8th. The variety of coins in circulation, reduced to our own standard, would facilitate the gradual introduction of the money of account, and the calculation by decimals, an invention, that I consider as one of the most honorable of our improvements.

9th. It would afford us advantages in the payment of ballances to foreigners, which no other nation enjoys. The existence of money in a country, supposes a favorable ballance on the general amount, of its commerce, this ballance may be favorable with one nation, and disadvantageous with another, it may sometimes fluctuate with the same nation—when a ballance is to be paid, it can only be in bullion, for as no nation acknowledges the mark which designates the fineness and weight of foreign coin, the primitive custom of taking money by weight, and not by tale, still exists in every money'd transaction between the subjects of different states. But as gold or silver are seldom to be purchased in considerable quantities, the coin of the country, paying the ballance, supplies its place, and is received as bullion, after deducting the alloy and the expence of coinage. If this money, so brought into a country, cannot circulate as money, but must be recoined, if this coinage is free, the public is put to expence in affixing its mark. If the coinage is not free, the loss falls on the individual—and when the money is reshipped, to pay the ballance which may be due to a foreign nation, will be received by them as bullion, and the expence of the coinage is lost, whereas, by the expedient proposed, the coins of foreign nations, circulating with us only at the rate of bullion, they will be received from foreigners, at that rate; but when a ballance is to be paid to the same nation, which often happens, where trade is upon an equal footing, the circulating note will be carried to the bank, and the money of the state to which the ballance is to be paid, will be reshipped and received at the current tale, in such state, by which means we shall gain the whole profit of the difference between bullion and coin. Even if the ballance should be uniformly in our favor with one nation, and against us with another; so that we are compelled to send the coin of one country to another, yet, in that case, we sell it as we received it, without any loss: whereas, by shipping our own coin, we experience a certain loss. Nor will it be thought a matter of little moment to a merchant, that coins of other nations, no sooner enter the country, than they become circulating money, without waiting for the operations of a mint, and the opportunity of vending to render them such.

10th. Some revenue may be made to arise to the public, from their operation. A bank being established, it will certainly find it very important to be the general depository of all the specie of the nation, since it renders it absolutely safe against every attack, and enables it to derive no small profit from paying in notes, which circulating as money, must be liable to casualties; and this, without any charge since a very trifling agio repays the expence. The bank, therefore, deriving such advantages from this operation, may easily afford a revenue to the public, or what, perhaps will be still more advantageous to both, may agree to discount at a lower interest, in consideration of being rendered the national bank of deposit.

But should this plan be rejected as too complex, it may be simplified, though not with equal advantage, merely by establishing an office for assaying all foreign coins, and publishing their value in money of account of the United States; this will still permit foreign coins to circulate, furnish a national standard, and save the expense of coinage.

NYDA, 19 Feb. 1791. No evidence exists to prove that WM authored this piece. It is printed here because he wafered it into volume 3 of his manuscript diary.

Appendix C
Maclay-Harris-Plunket Connections Related to the Diary

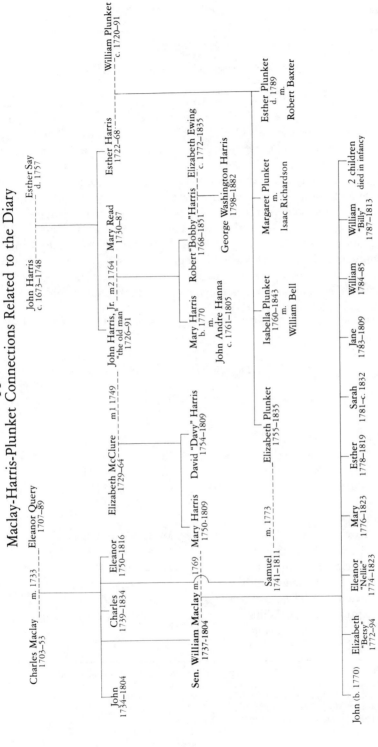

Graphics by Stephen Kraft.

Appendix D
The First Federal Congress Correspondence of William Maclay

When William Maclay died in April 1804 his estate paid $3.75 to build a trunk to hold his papers.[1] With the exception of the three volume diary of his Senate term, the contents of that trunk have disappeared. Thus his letterbooks—except for part of 1789 in volume 1 of the manuscript diary—and the letters he received during the First Congress are not extant. On the other hand, a significant body of letters he wrote during the First Congress has survived, although many of the most revealing have been alienated from the recipients' papers. To supplement the manuscript diary it had just purchased, the Library of Congress secured all but three of his letters to Benjamin Rush when they were auctioned in 1943 and 1944. Maclay's letters to John Nicholson and the manuscripts of several of his newspaper pieces enclosed in them were included in Nicholson's papers when the state sequestered them in the 1790s. Almost a century later many were stolen from the Pennsylvania Capitol, sold at auction, and were widely scattered.

The following is a list of all extant letters written by Maclay during the First Congress.

LETTERS FROM MACLAY

Date	Recipient	Location
	1789	
6 March	Thomas Mifflin	RG 27, PHarH
6 March	Benjamin Rush	Rush Papers, DLC
12 March	Richard Peters	Dreer Coll., PHi; Maclay Diary, DLC[2]
[post 12] March	Richard Peters	Maclay Diary, DLC[3]
13 March	Jasper Yeates	*Historical Register* 2:301
19 March	Benjamin Rush	Rush Papers, DLC
26 March	Benjamin Rush	Ibid.
30 March	Tench Coxe	Coxe Papers, PHi
2 April	Richard Willing	Maclay Diary, DLC
3 April	Edward Hand	Ibid.[4]
3 April	Joseph Ogdon	Ibid.[5]

[1]Receipt, 28 May 1804, Maclay Papers, Dauphin County Historical Society.
[2]Robert Morris also signed this letter.
[3]Robert Morris also signed this letter.
[4]Robert Morris also signed this letter.
[5]This is only a summary of the letter's contents.

7 April	Benjamin Rush	Rush Papers, DLC
15 April	Tench Coxe	Coxe Papers, DLC
16 April	Richard Peters	Maclay Diary, DLC
23 April	Benjamin Rush	Rush Papers, DLC
25 April	Alexander Todd	Maclay Diary, DLC
25 April	A Westmoreland Co. correspondent	Ibid.
25 April	A Northumberland Co. correspondent	Ibid.
25 April	George Ross	Ibid.
6 May	Andrew Ellicott	Ibid.
6 May	Benjamin Rush	Rush Papers, DLC
11 May	Richard Peters	Maclay Diary, DLC
13 May	Samuel Meredith	Ibid.
16 May	Tench Coxe	Ibid.; Coxe Papers, PHi
18 May	Benjamin Rush	Ibid.; Rush Papers, DLC
30 May	Richard Peters	Maclay Diary, DLC
30 May	Tench Coxe	Coxe Papers, DLC
3 June	Charles Biddle	Maclay Diary, DLC[6]
3 June	Tench Coxe	Coxe Papers, PHi
16 June	Tench Coxe	Ibid.
16 June	Thomas Mifflin	*PaAr*(1) 2:590–91
22 June	Benjamin Rush	Rush Papers, DLC
4 July	Benjamin Rush	Ibid.
4 July	Tench Coxe	Coxe Papers, PHi
4 July	Jared Ingersol	Maclay Diary, DLC
20 July	George Washington	GWP; Maclay Diary entry, 14 Feb. 1791, DLC
1 Sept.	John Adams	Hull Coll., DSI[7]
18 Oct.	Benjamin Rush	Rush Papers, PHi
18 Oct.	Tench Coxe	Coxe Papers, PHi

1790

9 Jan.	Thomas Ruston	Coxe Papers, PHi
15 Jan.	John Nicholson	Autograph Coll., Morristown National Military Park
16 Jan.	Benjamin Rush	Misc. Manuscripts, NjP
30 Jan.	Thomas Ruston	Coxe Papers, PHi
30 Jan.	John Nicholson	Misc. Mss., DLC

[6]Ibid.

[7]The paucity of Maclay's letters during the last two months of the first session of the FFC is due to his absence from New York and his illness when he returned to the seat of government.

2 Feb.	John Nicholson	Gratz Coll., PHi
8 Feb.	John Nicholson	Ibid.
9 Feb.	John Nicholson	Stack Autograph Coll., OMC
14 Feb.	[John Nicholson] enclosure to above	*Argosy Cat.* 448, item 377; Misc. Mss., DLC
18 Feb.	John Nicholson	*Henkels Cat.* 946, item 225; 1057, item 352
19 Feb.	John Nicholson	Gratz Coll., PHi
7 March	Benjamin Rush	Rush Papers, DLC
11 March	John Nicholson	Gratz Coll., PHi
14 March	Benjamin Rush	Rush Papers, DLC
20 March	Robert Morris	Maclay Diary entry for 20 March 1790, DLC
27 March	Benjamin Rush	Rush Papers, DLC
27 March	Benjamin Rush	Rush Papers, DLC
28 March	John Nicholson	Gratz Coll., PHi
30 March	Benjamin Rush	Rush Papers, DLC
2 April	Benjamin Rush	Ibid.
10 April	Benjamin Rush	Ibid.
10 April	John Nicholson	Gratz Coll., PHi
12 April	John Nicholson	Gratz Coll., PHi
12 April	Benjamin Rush	Rush Papers, DLC
24 April	Benjamin Rush	Ibid.
25 April	George Logan	Logan Papers, PHi
27 April	John Nicholson	Gratz Coll., PHi
30 April	Tench Coxe	Coxe Papers, PHi
2 May	John Harris Maclay	Dreer Coll., PHi
7 May	Benjamin Rush	Rush Papers, DLC
12 May	Benjamin Rush	Ibid.
23 May	Benjamin Rush	Ibid.
5 June	Benjamin Rush	Ibid.
18 June	Benjamin Rush	Ibid.
26 June	Benjamin Rush	*Parke-Bernet Cat.* 484, item 194; *Carnegie Book Shop Cat.* 312, item 302
1 July	Benjamin Rush	*Parke-Bernet Cat.* 484, item 194; *Carnegie Book Shop Cat.* 312, item 303
7 July	John Nicholson	Nicholson Papers, PHarH
10 July	Benjamin Rush	Rush Papers, DLC
16 July	Benjamin Rush	Ibid.
30 July	Benjamin Rush	Ibid.

1791

| 8 Jan. | John Harris, Jr. | Maclay Diary entry for 8 Jan. 1791, DLC |
| 15 Jan. | Francis Alison | Gratz Coll., PHi |

LETTERS TO MACLAY

1789

17 March	Edward Hand[8]	Petitions, SR, DNA
23 March	Jasper Yeates	*Historical Register* 2:305
13 July	Benjamin Rush	*Scheuer Cat.* 4, item 1834

1790

[28 Jan.]	John Nicholson	[Philadelphia] *Freeman's Journal*, 3 Feb. 1790[9]
29 Jan.	John Nicholson	Ibid.[10]
8 Feb.	John Nicholson	Ibid., 10, 17 Feb. 1790[11]
24 Aug.	David Mead	RG 59, DNA

[8]This letter is also addressed to Robert Morris.
[9]A draft of this letter is in the Nicholson Papers, PHarH.
[10]Ibid.
[11]Ibid.

Appendix E
Biography of William Maclay

William Maclay was born on 20 July 1737, at New Garden Township, Chester County, Pennsylvania, the son of Charles and Eleanor Query Maclay, who had emigrated from Lurgan in County Antrim, Ireland, three years earlier. The Maclay family had lived in Ireland for a century following its decision to leave County Ross, in the north of Scotland. Both moves were part of a large migration of Scots seeking a better life. In 1742 the family joined yet another migration when social conflict between the so-called Scotch-Irish settlers and the more established Quakers and Germans in eastern Pennsylvania led the colony to encourage the former to settle on the frontiers. Many crossed the Susquehanna River to the Conococheague Valley, in what eventually became Lurgan Township in Franklin County.

Charles and Eleanor soon became prominent in a farming community three miles northwest of Shippensburg. The Middle Springs Presbyterian Church provided the social center for the community, and its minister, John Blair, presided over an academy at which William began his formal education. To further his studies he was later sent to Samuel Finley's academy at West Nottingham in Chester County (Cecil County, Maryland, after the Mason and Dixon survey), where he studied history, geography, geometry, logic, natural philosophy, and Latin. He may also have gained here his appreciation for English literature and a love of reading. The exact years of Maclay's tenure at the academy are uncertain, but they probably ended by 1755.[1]

Unlike many of his schoolmates, who made their way after graduation to the College of New Jersey at Princeton, the ambitious young man returned to central Pennsylvania, anxious to be "brought forward." Maclay had two advantages over the men with whom he associated. Few were as well educated; even fewer could boast of his imposing six-foot-three-inch height. Like the early career of the equally imposing but less well educated George Washington, Maclay's rise to prominence included military service in the western Pennsylvania theater of the French and Indian War, surveying, and land speculation and depended on the patronage of a colonial proprietary family.

Maclay may have begun his military career as early as 1755 as an ensign with responsibilities for enlistment. In May 1758 he was commissioned a lieutenant in the third Pennsylvania battalion and served under General John Forbes in his successful campaign to establish British control over the forks of the Ohio River. The six-month-long operation was slow, methodical, and almost devoid of military action. Instead, it entailed surveying and clearing a road across the mountains and constructing supply depots and forts along a route from Raystown on the Juniata to the forks. It was probably during this time that Maclay learned the fundamentals of surveying, the profession on which he would ultimately settle and from which he made his fortune. After the Forbes campaign Maclay studied law, probably at York, where he was admitted to the county bar in 1760. Soon thereafter he settled at Carlisle, the seat of Cumberland County. There he practiced law, assisted both the county prothonotary and the deputy land surveyor, and made the acquaintance of Dr. William Plunket, his close friend for the next thirty years.

Maclay returned to active military duty during Pontiac's Rebellion in July 1763, marching west with Lieutenant Henry Bouquet to relieve Fort Pitt at the forks of the Ohio. Less than a month later at Bushy Run, in the foothills twenty miles east of the fort, Maclay saw action in an unusual encounter between British and Indians, a two-day pitched battle made particularly horrible by the

---

[1]WM to Rush, 2 March 1783, Rush Papers, PHi; *PMHB* 70:85. Edgar S. Maclay, *The Maclays of Lurgan* (Brooklyn, N.Y., 1889), details the family's European background and provides short sketches of each member through the nineteenth century. The best and most complete account of WM's life is Heber G. Gearhart, "The Life of William Maclay," *NCHSP* 2:46–73. Others are E. S. Maclay's introduction to the 1890 edition of WM's diary (reprinted in the Charles Beard edition of 1928); Lewis R. Harley's pamphlet, *William Maclay, United States Senator from Pennsylvania, 1789–1791* ([Philadelphia?], 1909); and Mary Beard's sketch in the *Dictionary of American Biography*.

scarcity of water, the howling of the Indians at night, and the cries of wounded friends and horses. Although Bouquet's superior strategy resulted in victory, he was again required to go west to subdue the Ohio Valley Indians in the autumn of 1764. This time, however, Maclay was stationed at one of the supply depots on the road he had helped to blaze in 1758. Between the 1763 and 1764 campaigns Maclay traveled to London to visit Thomas Penn, proprietor of Pennsylvania. Armed with an introduction from William Allen, an influential leader of the colony's proprietary party, Maclay so impressed Penn that he employed Maclay professionally as a surveyor and provided him with political protection. Most importantly, Penn told his nephew, Governor John Penn, to appoint Maclay as a deputy land surveyor in Cumberland County.[2] The twenty-six-year-old had succeeded in being "brought forward" and suffered no setbacks until the temporary ones he met in seeking elective political office after the Revolutionary War.

Maclay received his surveyor's commission in 1764 and ceased the practice of law. His survey district lay in Cumberland County north of the Juniata River. Under the colony's land system, deputy surveyors retained two thirds of the fee they received for each tract surveyed, often accepting land in lieu of money. In part because of the influence of the Penns, Maclay's clients soon included many of the well to do families and politicians of eastern Pennsylvania. For them and the fees they paid, he undertook long trips into the wilderness in search of tracts that were well situated and/or particularly rich in soil or timber.   By 1765 he owned 600 acres in the county. He surveyed almost 600 tracts during the years 1767 and 1768 and was so busy that Surveyor General John Lukens reprimanded him for delays. His surveys prior to 1769 included the sites of Lewistown, Millerstown, Thompsontown, Bellefonte, and Sellingsgrove as well as manors for the Penns near Potter's Mills and Spring Mills. Maclay's relationship with Lukens was uncomfortable and caused him many problems, but his connection to the Penn family protected him, in part because Proprietor Thomas Penn considered Lukens ill tempered, while Governor John Penn described him as a low-life drunk. By the time Maclay ceased surveying in the 1790s, his surveys had become the basis for land titles in a half dozen of Pennsylvania's present-day counties. His own extensive landholdings and financial independence resulted primarily from his work during the decade preceding the War for Independence.[3]

In 1768 the Penns purchased a huge tract of land from the Indians and

---

[2]*PaAr*(2) 2:484; *PaAr*(5)1:184, 335; Dale Van Every, *Forth to the Wilderness* (New York, 1977), chaps. 5, 9; Thomas Penn to John Penn (2 letters), 8 Oct. 1763, Thomas Penn Papers, PHi.

[3]*PaAr*(3) 24:714; Thomas Penn to John Penn, 8 Oct. 1763, John Penn to Thomas Penn, 16 June 1764, Thomas Penn to James Tilghman, 12 Sept. 1766, Thomas Penn Papers, PHi. WM's letters to James Tilghman, secretary to the Pennsylvania land office, written between 1766 and 1774, describe his difficulties as a deputy land surveyor. They are in RG 17, PHarH. WM's surveying career is detailed in Heber G. Gearhart, "William Maclay, the Surveyor,"

employed Maclay to deliver payment for it. The area included that sought as bounties by Pennsylvania's officers, and they received 24,000 acres near the confluence of the east and west branches of the Susquehanna. Maclay's share included land on the Penn Manor of Pomfret at the confluence. In 1769, his survey district was expanded northward to include the land granted to the officers; the Pennsylvania Assembly appointed him as one of the commissioners to extend the county lines of central Pennsylvania westward. He surveyed the site of Lewisburg and, assisted by his younger brother Samuel, surveyed the officers' tracts.[4]

Despite the pressure of business, Maclay took time out from his surveying trips to court Mary Harris, the eldest daughter of John Harris, Jr. One of the most influential families in central Pennsylvania, the Harrises had resided on the Susquehanna since 1705. By mid-century they owned hundreds of acres on the river as well as one of its major ferries. Maclay probably became acquainted with the family through his friend William Plunket, who was married to a sister of John Harris, Jr. Thirty-two-year-old William married nineteen-year-old Mary in April 1769 and took his wife to reside at Content, a 275-acre tract he had surveyed and purchased at the site of Mifflintown on the Juniata River. Their first child, John Harris Maclay, was born there in 1770. Maclay continued his surveying activities, and the family resided at Content until 1772. In that year they moved to Fort Augusta near his Pomfret lands in newly created Northumberland County, a situation that offered new opportunities to Maclay, particularly because of Thomas Penn's interest in the area.

Northumberland County remained Maclay's home and political base for the next twenty years. Soon after his arrival he participated in the survey of Sunbury, the county seat, and was hired by the Penns to sell town lots and tracts for them in the adjacent Pomfret Manor. Plunket and Maclay bought lots near each other in Sunbury. On his, Maclay built the stone house beside the river on Front Street which, although substantially altered, still stands. On his Pomfret lands he erected a grist and saw mill that provided a constant source of income from the expanding community.

County government consisted of twelve appointed justices and from 1772 until 1786, except when he represented the county in the assembly, Maclay held one of these positions. Presided over at first by Plunket, the justices performed legislative, judicial, and executive functions, including the creation of townships, the granting of liquor licenses, and the punishment of law breakers. Maclay surely participated in the decision to place the town's stocks and pillories across the street from his home. In addition, he served as prothonotary, register, recorder, and clerk of the county court, lucrative offices

---

NCHSP 9:20–43. See Burton Konkle, *Thomas Smith* (Philadelphia, 1904) for an account of the activities of a Pennsylvania land surveyor.

[4]NCHSP 9:22, 25–30, 33; James Sullivan et al., eds., *The Papers of Sir William Johnson*, 14 vols. (Albany, N.Y., 1921–65), 6:562, 595.

that he received in 1772 and held for several years. In 1774 the assembly appointed him as one of the commissioners for erecting the county's public buildings.[5]

Maclay's move to Northumberland County involved him in a controversy that was not to be resolved during his lifetime and that deeply influenced his attitude toward New Englanders. Connecticut claimed jurisdiction over a large area of northern Pennsylvania. Its Susquehanna Company had attempted to settle the Wyoming Valley on the east branch of the Susquehanna during the 1760s, but Indians or armed Pennsylvanians had twice driven the settlers out. The return of these settlers in 1771 stimulated the assembly to move swiftly to create Northumberland County. With the full backing of their government, some Connecticut citizens moved from the Wyoming Valley in 1774 and established themselves on the West Branch. Maclay undoubtedly spoke for many Pennsylvanians who, like himself, held title to these lands from Pennsylvania when he complained that "there surely never was so great a pest in any civilized country." He considered it villainous "to carry this intestine dispute to the length of hostilities and bloodshed at this day of American distress" with England; nevertheless, he participated in military action against the Connecticut settlers. In September 1775, Sheriff Plunket attacked the West Branch settlements, imprisoning the men at Sunbury and returning their families to Wyoming. Backed by a posse of 500 men including Maclay, Plunket attacked Wyoming in December but was repulsed. Connecticut and Pennsylvania agreed to preserve the status quo during the Revolutionary War, and early in 1783 Congress awarded jurisdiction of the disputed area to Pennsylvania. The problem of conflicting land titles remained a divisive issue in Pennsylvania politics into the nineteenth century, and Maclay participated in several unsuccessful legislative efforts to resolve the issue.[6]

A supporter of the Declaration of Independence, Maclay served on the Northumberland Committee of Safety for six months after its adoption. In addition, he offered to assist in the manufacture of flints from Penn's Creek should the continental war office be interested. Two years later the war reached Northumberland County when the Senecas, allies of the British, destroyed the Connecticut enclave at Wyoming. Within days, the entire county was evacuated, except for the military garrison at Sunbury. Maclay, his pregnant wife, and their four children joined the "great runaway," traveling down river to her family at Harris's Ferry. Flooding the Pennsylvania government with information, Maclay urged military action. Colonel Thomas Hartley was sent to Sunbury with reinforcements and stockaded Maclay's stone house for use as a storehouse for supplies and arms. Early in 1779 Maclay became an assistant

[5]*CRP* 9:187; *NCHSP* 1:15–29, 3:3–27, 5:150; Joseph Shippen to WM, 11 Sept. 1772, Shippen Letterbook, PPAmP.
[6]*NCHSP* 14:91–94, 20:21–23, 52–55; WM to James Tilghman, 8 April 1774, RG 17, PHarH; ibid., 16 June 1775, Gratz, PHi; *Counter Revolution*.

commissary for purchase and spent a year procuring such supplies for the army as shad, wheat, pork, and liquor. He was particularly active in supplying General John Sullivan's successful expedition against the Iroquois in July 1779, after which the Northumberland County residents were able to return to their homes. In 1782 he performed similar functions for the state.

Although Maclay did not participate in any military engagements during the War for Independence, he did devote some thought to strategy. His interest in history included knowledge of the use of dogs by the Spaniards against the South American Indians, and, despite ridicule from his friends, he submitted the idea to the Pennsylvania government, which transmitted it to Commander in Chief George Washington. The letter remains in the Washington Papers, endorsed as from "a person of note in Northumberland." With the exception of an occasional Indian attack, the war did not directly affect central Pennsylvania after 1779, and Maclay turned his attention to other pursuits. He became increasingly convinced of the viability of the idea of an American nation. In 1780 he described Northumberland County as a place where "Whig Tory, Yankey, Pennamite Dutch Irish and English Influence are strangely blended. I must confess I begin to be national too and most sincerely believe every publick Interest of America, will be safer in the Hands of Americans, than with any others."[7]

William Maclay spent fifteen of the last twenty-five years of his life as an elected member of a legislative body, attempting to implement his concept of the public interest. His independent-mindedness caused him to associate himself with the minority during most of his legislative career. Maclay differed with the majority of his constituents in supporting the Pennsylvania Republican or Anti-Constitutionalist party and showing great sympathy for Philadelphia and its interests. This made his reelection difficult on more than one occasion during the 1780s.

First elected to the assembly in October 1781, Maclay was reelected in 1782. A disputed election in 1783 was resolved in his favor by the assembly. It is likely he ran for reelection in 1784 and lost. The next year Northumberland County submitted two sets of returns to the politically divided assembly, which held public hearings and appointed a committee to make a report. The committee recommended that the three Constitutionalist candidates be seated, but Maclay's friend and fellow Anti-Constitutionalist, Anthony Wayne, moved to strike one of the three and insert Maclay's name instead. Speaker Thomas Mifflin broke a tie in the assembly by casting the decisive vote in favor of Maclay. Three of Maclay's future colleagues in the First Federal Congress,

---

[7] Item 34, p. 149, item 69, 2:409, item 165, p. 412, RG 360, DNA; *CRP* 12:371; *PaAr*(1) 6:634, 7:192, 586, 590-93, 597-98, 623, 8:156 (quoted), 172; WM to Ephraim Blaine, 3 April, 4, 13, 20 Dec. 1779, Blaine Papers, DLC; ibid., 12 April 1779, Gratz Papers, PHi. The William Maclay who served in the Pennsylvania militia at Trenton and Princeton was a Philadelphian by the same name.

Robert Morris, Thomas Fitzsimons, and George Clymer, also gave him their support. Not surprisingly, the proud man refused to assume his seat. In the spring of 1786, however, he presented himself as a duly elected member from Westmoreland County. Led by Constitutionalist John Smilie, who claimed that Maclay was disqualified by virtue of his office as a deputy surveyor, the Constitutionalists prevented him from assuming the seat.[8]

In October 1786, Maclay was elected to represent Northumberland and adjoining counties for a three-year term on the supreme executive council. Restricted mainly to routine business, that body occasionally became involved in heated political issues such as the Wyoming Controversy. While a member of the Council, Maclay served at various times as its representative on the board of property, on the committee to instruct the commissioners appointed to purchase the Erie Triangle, on the committee to decide what action to take when Thomas Scott declined his election to the first United States House of Representatives, and on the committee to certify the results of the popular election for presidential electors in 1789. Maclay's last major involvement in state politics before assuming his seat in the United States Senate was in launching a petition drive to call a convention to draft a new constitution. The constitutionally mandated council of censors, for which he had been an unsuccessful candidate, was controlled by the Constitutionalists and had refused to call a convention in 1783. The petition campaign was the idea of a group of Anti-Constitutionalists, including Maclay and Thomas Fitzsimons, who met at the home of Benjamin Rush during Maclay's final days on the supreme executive council.[9] The effort proved successful and the convention, which met late in 1789 and again in 1790, agreed to a Constitution with a popularly elected governor and a bicameral legislature.

Maclay's public life during the 1780s was not limited to popularly elected office. Pennsylvania frequently turned to him to fulfil a variety of special commissions. In 1783, the assembly renewed his 1771 commission to superintend clearing the Susquehanna River and some of its tributaries above Wright's Ferry for navigation. He was appointed a commissioner to determine what part, if any, of Lake Erie lay within Pennsylvania, which of the rivers of western Pennsylvania might be navigable, and what was the precise location of the state's boundary with New York. The supreme executive council appointed him one of the commissioners at the October 1784 Treaty of Fort Stanwix, at which Pennsylvania purchased the remaining Iroquois claim to the northwestern part of the state. Subsequently, it elected him to deliver a variety of goods promised to the Iroquois by the treaty, and he performed this service

---

[8]*Counter Revolution; Minutes of the . . . General Assembly of the Commonwealth of Pennsylvania, 1781–82,* esp. pp. 513, 522, 524; ibid., *1782–1783;* ibid., *1783–84,* esp. pp. 45–46, 131; ibid., *1785–86,* esp. pp. 47–58, 213.

[9]*CRP* 15, esp. pp. 266, 279–80, 310, 380, 553–55, 665; ibid. 16, esp. p. 3; *PBR,* p. 509–10; *PaAr*(6) II:286.

in the autumn of 1785. His absence from the Treaty of Fort McIntosh in January 1785 lends credence to the story that he traveled to England in that year to meet with the Penn Family, for whom he continued to act as an agent.

Professionally, Maclay continued to survey, purchase, and sell land for himself, employers, and associates such as Benjamin Rush. In 1785 he was appointed deputy surveyor for a new district north of Sunbury and later received special commissions from the assembly to survey the land with which the state had endowed Dickinson and Franklin (later Franklin and Marshall) colleges. Between 1783 and 1785 Maclay assisted his father-in-law in the creation of Dauphin County and the establishment of Harrisburg as its seat. He was a member of the assembly committee that first reported in favor of the new county early in 1784. After the assembly established the county in 1785, Maclay platted Harrisburg for his father-in-law. At the same time he platted Maclaysburg on part of a 200-acre tract on the northern border of Harrisburg which he had bought years earlier from William Plunket. Both developers set aside land to be purchased by Pennsylvania should it decide to move its capital from Philadelphia to Harrisburg.[10]

Although Maclay was in Philadelphia attending the Supreme Executive Council during much of the meeting of the Federal Convention, he seems to have had little social interaction with the members, twenty of whom later became his colleagues in the First Congress. Maclay became a Federalist, although his activities on behalf of the ratification of the Constitution are unknown. He was actively involved in organizing the Lancaster Convention, which recommended a slate of Federalists for election to the first United States House of Representatives, and chaired the meeting that selected Northumberland County's delegates. When members of the assembly considered candidates for Pennsylvania's two seats in the United States Senate, it was clear that Robert Morris would be one. Some assemblymen who hoped to elect two Philadelphians supported either George Clymer or William Bingham. Political reality, however, demanded someone from central or western Pennsylvania. Maclay was the early favorite, in part because he could ably represent the landed interest of the state while at the same time showing sympathy for Philadelphia's interests. Many Federalists, however, switched their support to John Armstrong, Jr., of Carlisle, former secretary of the Supreme Executive Council and a member of Congress. At a Federalist caucus on 29 September, it became clear that Maclay had more votes than Armstrong because of his age

    [10]WM to Samuel Purviance, 8 Sept. 1785, Purviance Family Papers, NcD; WM to Benjamin Rush, 2 March 1783, Rush Papers, PHi; Charles C. Sellers, *Dickinson College* (Middletown, Conn., 1973), p. 483; James T. Mitchell et al., eds., *Statutes at Large of Pennsylvania from 1682 to 1801* (Harrisburg, 1896–1908), 8:37; *PaAr*(1) 10:129–30, 265, 510; *CRP* 14:40, 485, 15:140, 657; *Minutes of the . . . General Assembly, 1783–84,* pp. 175–77; Gearhart, "Surveyor," pp. 41–42; A. Boyd Hamilton, "William Maclay, City Planner," *NCHSP* 9:12–15; Harrisburg Tract Survey, Maclay Papers, PHi; *SEJ*, p. 143.

and steadiness, as contrasted with the latter's youth and inexperience. The next day the whole sixty-seven member assembly, with the exception of Thomas Mifflin, voted for Maclay, because the Antifederalists, unable to elect one of their own, considered him to be the best of the candidates.[11]

Maclay's term in the Senate from March 1789 to March 1791 is discussed in the introduction to this edition of the diary, a document that allows us great insight not only into the First Federal Congress but also into the personality of the man who kept it.

The years immediately after this, from 1791 to 1795, must have been very special for the Maclay family, for its head remained at home instead of spending months attending legislative sessions at distant New York or Philadelphia as he had during the previous decade. Sometime in 1791, perhaps about the time John Harris, Jr., died in July, the family moved to Maclaysburg, just north of bustling Harrisburg. There Maclay built the elegant mansion on the banks of the Susquehanna which, now greatly enlarged, still stands on the river at Front and South streets in Harrisburg. William and Mary had eleven children, all but three of whom survived the perils of an eighteenth-century infancy. Seven of the eight resided at home in 1791, ranging in age from four-year-old William to nineteen-year-old Elizabeth. Twenty-one-year-old John managed the family farm at Sunbury. Tragedy struck the family in the mid-1790s when Elizabeth died after a long illness and John disgraced his father, apparently by fathering a child out of wedlock. Despite the demands on his time and energy of a new home and a large family, Maclay found time to establish a ferry on the Susquehanna and to serve as a trustee of both Harrisburg Academy and Dickinson College at nearby Carlisle, a position he held from 1783 to 1796.[12]

As pleasant as life must have been for the retired Senator, domesticity did not satisfy all his needs. Whether it was the desire to serve society, to bask in the warmth of public adulation, or a combination of the two, Maclay still craved political involvement. When the Second Congress confirmed his early fears for the new government, Maclay joined the emerging Democratic-Republican party, gradually making political peace with many old Constitutionalists who dominated the party in Pennsylvania. In the spring of 1792, friends proposed him as a candidate for the third United States House of Representatives. Some of his former political enemies, led by James Hutchinson, refused to support him on the grounds that the ticket already contained too many men from the western counties and that Maclay's interest lay with western Pennsylvania, even though he resided on the east bank of the Susquehanna. Maclay badly wanted to return to Congress and complained to John Nicholson that the basest means were employed to defeat him. On election day he received fewer

---

[11]*DHFFE* 1:232–33, 272, 289–97, 306, 314–15.
[12]Hamilton, "William Maclay, City Planner," pp. 15–18; Will of WM, 1797, Dauphin County Historical Society. David Harris to Tench Coxe, 14 March 1791, Coxe Papers, PHi, confirms that WM had not yet moved to Harrisburg.

than 1,000 votes, while the winners totalled as much as 21,000. In February 1793, the Dauphin County members of the legislature nominated him to fill the United States Senate seat that had remained vacant since his term expired in March 1791, but he received no votes.[13]

In October 1795 Dauphin County sent Maclay to the Pennsylvania House of Representatives, reelecting him in 1796 and 1797. Despite Federalist control, the Pennsylvania legislature recognized and relied on his expertise in land matters and the Wyoming issue, as it had a decade earlier. Maclay also devoted considerable energy to repeated but unsuccessful attempts to move the state capital to either Lancaster or Harrisburg. Less controversial were his activities on behalf of dozens of internal improvement bills to aid the growing population in the area where he had been a wilderness surveyor thirty years earlier. Since both Congress and the Pennsylvania legislature held their sessions on State House Square in Philadelphia, he must often have seen colleagues from the First Congress, half of whom continued as members of Congress.

The Pennsylvania legislature did not ignore national issues. In his first term, Maclay voted in favor of considering amendments to the United States Constitution proposed by Virginia which would limit senators to a three-year term and remove impeachment trials from the Senate. In his next term he cast his vote against an address expressing regret at the retirement of Washington. Recognized as a spokesman for the Democratic-Republican party, he served as a presidential elector in 1796 and cast his vote for Thomas Jefferson and against the victorious John Adams. Maclay's most controversial action as a member of the Pennsylvania House of Representatives was introducing a resolution in March 1798 which declared the state's opposition to war, particularly with France, which had so recently been our ally, except in cases of invasion. Attacks on his unsuccessful resolution began almost immediately in the Harrisburg press, and the anti-French hysteria of 1798 cost him reelection to the assembly that fall by 90 votes.[14]

Between 1798 and 1803 Maclay held only Dauphin County judicial offices.[15] In October 1803 Dauphin sent him back to the Pennsylvania House of Representatives. For the first time since the 1780s, he found himself among the majority in a legislative body, and the Democratic-Republican members gave

---

[13]WM to John Nicholson, 24 Sept. 1792, Stan V. Henkels, *Sale Catalog No. 1074 pt. 1* (Dec. 1912), item 379; James Hutchinson to Albert Gallatin, 19 Aug., 14 Sept. 1792, Alexander Addison to Gallatin, 11 Oct. 1792, Gallatin Papers, NHi; [Philadelphia] *Independent Gazetteer*, 20, 27 Oct. 1792; *Journal of the . . . Third House of Representatives of the Commonwealth of Pennsylvania, 1792–93*, pp. 213, 217–21.

[14]*Journal of the . . . Sixth House of Representatives, 1795–96*, esp. pp. 77, 85, 163–69, 183, 270–73; *Journal of the . . . Seventh House of Representatives, 1796–97*, esp. pp. 127, 155–57; *Journal of the . . . Eighth House of Representatives, 1797–98*, esp. pp. 250, 306, 311, 319–39; WM to Tench Coxe, 19 Jan. 1801, Coxe Papers, PHi; [Harrisburg] *Oracle of Dauphin*, 28 March, 26 Sept., 17 Oct. 1798.

[15]Shouffler vs. Streby, 23 May 1801, Elder Family Papers, PHarH, indicates that WM was Dauphin County prothonotary.

him, their senior statesman, a variety of ceremonial appointments. In addition, he served on many committees, often reporting for them. The most important of these reports called for the impeachment of Pennsylvania Chief Justice Edward Shippen. Although the state capital had been moved to Lancaster during Maclay's absence from the legislature, many western Pennsylvanians wanted to move it another thirty miles further west to Harrisburg. Maclay was deeply involved in this unsuccessful effort, which had begun in 1787, and both political friends and enemies believed he had returned to the legislature solely for that purpose. He wrote a letter to the speaker donating five acres of land in Maclaysburg to the state and offering to sell it an additional one hundred acres if the state capital came to Harrisburg.

Maclay did not live until 1810 when the state accepted his donation. He died on 16 April 1804, two weeks after returning home from the legislature. A lifelong Presbyterian, William Maclay was buried in the churchyard of Paxtang Church at Harrisburg, under an impressive monument declaring, "to an enlarged and superior mind he added the strictest morality and . . . is now gone to receive a glorious reward for a life spent in Honour and unsullied by a crime."[16]

---

[16]*Journal of the . . . Thirteenth House of Representatives, 1802–3*, pp. 40–45; *Journal of the . . . Fourteenth House of Representatives, 1803–4*, esp. pp. 9, 13, 37, 235, 242, 646; Jasper Yeates to Edward Shippen, 4 April 1804, Shippen Family Papers, Nathaniel Boileau to Jonathan Roberts, 10 Dec. 1803, Roberts Papers, PHi; WM to Simon Snyder, 18 Jan. 1804, Maclay Papers, Dauphin County Historical Society; James M. Mast, "William Findley's Attempt to Move the State Capital to Harrisburg in 1787," *Western Pennsylvania Historical Magazine* 39:163–73.

PART II

Other Notes on Senate Debates

John Adams
Pierce Butler
William Samuel Johnson
Rufus King
William Paterson
Paine Wingate

The Notes of John Adams

Debate on the Foreign Affairs Act [HR-8]
Can the president remove federal officeholders?
[15 July 1789]

Mr. Carrol.   The Executive Power is commensurate with the Legislative and Judicial powers.

The Rule of Construction of Treaties, Statutes and deeds.

The Same Power which creates must annihilate.   This true w⟨he⟩r⟨e⟩. the Power is Simple, but when compound not.

if a Minister is suspected to betray Secrets to an Ennemy, the Senate not Sitting, cannot the President displace, nor Suspend.

The States General of France, demanded that offices should be during good behaviour.

It is improbable that a bad President should be chosen.   but may not bad Senators be chosen.

Is there a due ballance of Power between the Executive & Legislative, either in the General Govt. or State Governments.

Montesquieu.   English Liberty will be lost, when the Legislative shall be more corrupt, than the Executive.   have We not been witnesses of corrupt Acts of Legislatures, making depredations?   Rhode Island yet perseveres.[1]

Mr. Elsworth.   We are Sworn to Support the Constitution.

There is an explicit grant of Power to the President, which contains the power of Removal.   The Executive Power is granted—not the Executive Powers herein after enumerated and explained.

The President—not the Senate appoint—the⟨y⟩ only Consent, and advise—

The Senate is not an Executive Council—has no Executive Power.

The Grant to the President express, not by Implication.

Mr. Butler.   This Power of Removal would be unhinging the Equilibrium of Power in the Constitution.

---

[1]Rhode Island's legislature had passed a law requiring citizens to accept the state's paper money or be disenfranchised. This was widely viewed as an infringement of property rights.

The Statholder witheld the fleet from going out, to the Annoyance of the Ennemies of the nation.

in Treaties, all Powers not expressly given are reserved.

Treaties to be gone over, Clause by Clause, by the president and Senate together, and modelled.

The other Branches are imbecil

disgust and alarm

The President not sovereign.   The U.S. sovereign, or People, or Congress sovereign.

The House of Reps. wd. not be induced to depart, so well Satisfied of the Grounds.

[15 or 16 July 1789]

Elsworth.   The Powers, of this Constitution are all vested.   parted from the People, from the States, and vested not in Congress but in the President.

The Word Sovereignty is introduced without determinate Ideas.   Power in the last Resort.   in this sense the Sovereign Executive is in the president.

The U.S. will be Parties to 1000 Suits—shall Proscess issue in their Name vs. or for themselves.

The President it is Said, may be put to Gaol for Debt.

Lee.   U.S. merely figurative meaning the People.

Grayson.   The President is not above the Law.   an absurdity to admit this Idea into our Government.   not improbable that the President may be Sued.   Christina Q. of Sweeden[2] committed Murder—France excused her.

The Jurors of our Lord the President, present that the President committed Murder.

a Monarchy by a Sidewind.   you make him Vindex Injuriarum.[3]   The People will not like, The Jurors of our Ld. the President—nor the Peace of our Ld. the President, nor his Dignity.   his Crown will be left out.   do not wish to make the Constitution a more unnatural monstrous Production than it is.

The British Constn. a three legged Stool.   if one legg is longer than another, the stool will not stand.   unpallatable.   The removal of Officers not palatable.   We shd. not risk any Thing for nothing.   come forward like Men, and reason openly, and the People will hear more quickly than if you attempt side Winds.   This Measure will do no good and will disgust.

---

[2]Christina (1626–89) was queen of Sweden from 1644 until her abdication in 1654. While a resident of France she ordered the execution of a high-ranking attendant and refused to defend the action beyond insisting on her royal authority.

[3]Protected from unlawful conduct.

[16 July 1789]

Mr. Lee.   The Danger to liberty greater from the disunited opinions and jarring Plans of many, than from the energetic operations of one,   Marius, Sylla⟨,⟩ Cæsar, Cromwell trampled on Liberty with Armies.

The Power of Pardon—of adjourning the Legislature.

Power of Revision, Sufficient to defend himself.   he would be Supported by the People.

Patronage.   gives great Influence.   The Interference more nominal than real.

The greater Part of Power of making Treaties in the President.

The greatest Power is in the President.   the less in the Senate.

cannot see Responsibility, in the President or the great officers of State.

a masqued Battery of constructive Powers would compleat the destruction of Liberty.

Can the Executive lay Embargoes, establish Fairs, Tolls &c.?

The fœderal Govt. is limited.   the Legislative Power of it is limited, and therefore the Executive and judicial must be limited.

The Executive not punishable but by universal Convulsion, as Charles 1st.

The Legislative in England not so corrupt as the Executive.

There is no Responsibility, in the President, or Ministry.

Blackstone.   the Liberties of England owing to Juries.   The greatness of England owing to the genius of that People.

The Crown of England can do wt. it pleases, nearly.

There is no ballance in America, to such an Executive as that in England.

does the Executive Arm, mean a standing Army?

Willing to make a Law, that the President, if he sees gross misconduct may Suspend pro tempore.

Mr. Patterson.

laments that We are obliged to discuss this question.   of great Importance and much difficulty.

The Executive co extensive with the Legislative.   had the Clause Stood alone, would not there have been a devolution of all Executive Power?   Exceptions are to be construed strictly.   This is an invariable Rule.

Mr. Grayson

The P. has not a continental Interest, but is a Citizen of a particular State.   a K⟨ing⟩. of E⟨ngland⟩. otherwise.   K. of E. counteracted by a large powerful rich and hereditary aristocracy.   Hyperion to a satyr.[4]

---

[4] In Greek mythology, Hyperion was one of the giants or Titans, while satyrs were woodland deities fond of revelry.

Wr. there are not intermediate Powers, an alteration of the Govt. must be to despotism.

Powers ought not to be inconsiderately given to the Executive, without proper ballances.

triennial and septenial Parliaments made by Corruption of the Executive.

Bowstring.   General Lally.   Brutus's Power to put his sons to death.[5]

The Power creating shall have that of uncreating.   The Minister is to hold at Pleasure of the appointor.

if it is in the Constitution, why insert it, in the Law?   brought in by a Sidewind, inferentially.

There will be every endeavour to increase the consolidatory Powers.   to weaken the Senate, and Strengthen the President.

No Evil in the Senates participating with the P. in Removal.

Mr. Reed.

P. is to take care that the Laws be faithfully executed.   he is responsible.   how can he do his duty or be responsible, if he cannot remove his Instruments.

it is not an equal sharing of the Power of Appointment between the President & senate.

The Senate are only a check to prevent Impositions of the President.

The Minister an Agent a Deputy to the great Executive.

difficult to bring great Character to Punishment or Tryal.

Power of Suspension.

Mr. Johnson.   Gentn. convince themselves that it is best the President Shd. have the Power, and then Study for Arguments.

Exceptions.

Not a Grant.   Vested in the President, would be void for Uncertainty.   Executive Power is uncertain.   Powers are moral, mechanical natural.   which of these Powers.   wt. Executive Power?   The Land—The Money. conveys nothing.   wt. Land? wt. Money.

Unumquoque dissolvitur, eodem modo, quo ligatur.[6]

meddles not with the question of Expediency.

The Executive wants Power, by its duration and its want of a Negative, & Power to ballance.

Fœderalist.

---

[5]Thomas-Arthur Comte de Lally (1702–66), French general in the Seven Years War, was beheaded by order of the Parlement de Paris for treason and cowardice.

Lucius Junius Brutus, Roman consul of the sixth century B.C., who, according to legend, took part in the expulsion of the Tarquins and sentenced his own two sons to death for conspiring to restore them.

[6]Every obligation is dissolved by the same method with which it is created.

Mr. Elsworth.   Wt. is the difference between a Grant and a Partition.

Mr. Izard.   Cujus est instituere ejus abrogare.[7]

Debate on the Seat of Government Bill [HR-25]
Shall the bill be postponed until the second session?
22 September 1789

Mr. Grayson.   No Census yet taken, by which the Center of Population.

We have Markets, Archives, Houses Lodgings.   extreamly hurt at wt. has passed in the House of Reps.   The Money.   is your Army paid?   Virginia offered £100,000. towards the federal Buildings.   The Buildings may be erected without Expence to the Union.   Lands may be granted—these Lands laid out in Lots and Sold to Adventurers.

Mr. Butler.   The recent Instance in France Shews that an Attempt to establish a Govt. vs. the Justice and the Will of the People is vain and idle, and chimerical.

Shall section 1 and part of section 2 be postponed?
23 September 1789

Mr. Lee.   Navigation of the Susquehannah.

Mr. Grayson.   Antwerp and the Scheld.[8]   Reasons of State have influenced the Pensilvanians to prevent the navigation from being opened—The limiting the Seat of Empire to the State of Pen. on the delaware is a characteristic Mark of partiality.   The Union will think that Pen. governs the Union, and that the general Interest is Sacrificed to that of one State.
The Czar Peter took time to enquire and deliberate before he fixed a Place to found his City.[9]

---

[7]Whose right it is to institute, his right it is to abrogate.

[8]By 1560 Antwerp had superseded Venice as the first city of European commerce, but the treaty of Münster in 1648, recognizing the independence of the United Provinces, stipulated that the Scheldt River be closed to navigation. It was not reopened until 1795.

[9]During the 1690s Peter the Great contemplated establishing his capital on the Black Sea, but after his victory over Sweden he located St. Petersburg on the Baltic Sea in 1703.

We are about founding a City which will be one of the first in the World.   and
We are governed by local and partial Motives.

Mr. Morris moves to expunge the Proviso [*in section* 2].

Mr. Carrol.   against the Motion to expunge the Proviso.   considers the Western Country of great Importance.   some Gentn. in both houses Seem to
undervalue the Western Country or despair of commanding it.   Govt. on the
Potowmack would Secure it.

Mr. Butler.   The question is not whether Pensilvania or Mayryland Shall be
benefited.   but how are the United States benefited or injured.

Mr. Macclay.   Pensilvania has altered the Law this month respecting the navi-
gat. of the susquehannah.[10]

24 September 1789

Mr. Grayson moves to Strike out the Words, "in the State of Pensilvania" [*in
section* 1].

Mr. Butler.   The Center of Population the best Criterion   the Center of
Wealth and the Center of Territory.

Mr. Lee.   The Center of Territory is the only permanent Center.

Mr. Macclay.   See his minutes.[11]

Debate on the Report of the Joint Committee
on Unfinished Business
25 January 1790

It was not the Sense of either House, or of any member of either, that the
Business pending at the Adjournment Should be lost.
Where is the Œconomy of repeating the Expense of Time?
Can this opinion be founded on the Law of Parliament?   The K. can
prorogue the Parliament.   But there is no such Power here.

---

[10]See September 1789, n. 22 in Part I of this volume.
[11]Adams here refers to the daily notes that WM took on the Senate floor and then rewrote
as his diary. WM regularly destroyed these notes, except those he took on 24 September 1789
and later wafered into the diary.

The Rule of Parliament that Business once acted on, and rejected shall not be brought on again, the Same session, is a good Rule, but not applicable to this Case.

Mr. Elsworth—in Legislative Assemblies, more to be apprehended from precipitation than from ~~the~~ Delay.

D/JA/46, Adams Papers, Microfilms, Reel 2, MHi. Charles Francis Adams assembled the loose sheets of paper on which his grandfather made the notes of these three debates with other fragments as addenda to the earlier, lengthy diaries.

The Notes of Pierce Butler

Debate on the Impost Bill [HR-2]
Shall the report of the committee appointed
on 8 June be adopted?
9 June 1789

Mr. Elsworth—

———

Mr. Morace—
The only way to promote a Competition is to Grant an Exclusive right—If they buy the Goods they cant keep them on hand   sell them   they must pray may they not burn them as in the Case of the Ginseng—
He says American Vessels make three Voyages where others make two—& that my motion held but an Invitation to European Vessels to come here—
So long as they Consume Teas it will be best to get them that way provided they come Cheaper
Monopoly—He fited out a Ship alone   does this prove the General Utility—
No—It proves more strongly what I have said.

Mr. Landon
The freights to Europe can ~~not~~ never pay the Expense unless they can get some freight back—
Shall We not Encourage the Shiping of Our Masts &ca.

Debate during the third reading of the bill
10 June 1789

Mr. M.
Says that in Great Britain they will not Suffer the materials for Manufacturing any of their Staple Articles

Elsworth
There never can be a Monopoly of Cardmaking—There never can be a Monopoly

Mr. Morace—
This Bill was Intended to Levy on the Consumers—
Value of Imports in Pensilva. amt. £750,000 in 1789—

Mr. Carrol
foreign Tonage 160,000 Tons   He says it may be reduced to half—But the
price of the Article will be Affected by the price of the freight—

Patterson
that they ought to Transport their own Article to A foreign Markett—Encourage yes but not at the Expence of Citizens   We may regulate the freight   We
can not regulate it—
It will regulate   He comes to Advance the Interest of the whole but surely not
at the Expence of a part   that is Unequaly taking from One part more than
another

Agriculture We are told by the Best writers is the Organical part—Anything
that difficulties Agriculture Affects every part of Your Government—
Draw backs were considered wise because it they Encouraged Vessels to come
into Our Ports—and every Vessel that comes leaves some Money among Us
Drawback of ten per Cent on Goods in American Bottoms is allowed as an
Encouragement

Mr. Langdon
says that all other Nations make a discrimination   He says Massachusets Exports are Equal to those of Virginia

Elsworth
wishes We may lay aside local Ideas.   See I am constrained by the partiality of
the proposition to be local   the Example is Set me And sundrey gentlemen
disposed to lay a difficulty on a part that trusted Us with their Interests & equal
rights Wen when We see them likely to be Injured We must attend to them

Mr. Dalton
He says the fishing Vessels return in Winter—We want Shipping just at that
time—Petitions from So. Carolina respecting Ship Building—

Elsworth—
Carolina Sent them powder by land & Rice—

Pierce Butler Papers, PHi. The editors believe that Butler took these notes for the purpose
of responding to individual senators. It is not always clear which of the remarks in the notes
were made by the senators named and which were made by Butler. The lines between
speeches may indicate a change of speaker, that Butler spoke, or that he stopped taking
notes.

Debate on the Judiciary Act [S-1]
Motion by Lee to limit lower federal courts
to admiralty jurisdiction
22 June 1789

Elsworth on the Judiciary Says that there will be Attacks on the General Government that will go to the Very Vitals of it—Who then are to support the General Law　Surely it must be the people of the State—He tells You that Judges may Swerve—

Strong
One State saying that their officers shall not take Cognisance of the Cause of the Federal Governmt.　Whether all the Advantages of a Nisi prius Court— He says those who Apply must be draged up to the Supreme Court—He Argues against Article—

Mr. E.　Asks if You will trust the life of a Man to One Judge　No　He tells You the people will not Submit to　He says You must Associate other Judges　Yes the Assize Judges[1]—
He tells Us in Order to Encourage Us to Agree, that it will be Confined to the Sea Board—

Patterson
Says We have not the force of Monarchys—Of Course We shoud be more Careful how We proceed on their ridged Maxims—
he objects to the Bill because it not Strong Enough.

Elsworth
Says He Scarce knows any Country where two powers do not Legislate—This Doctrine I suppose may go so far as to prove, because fiscall Courts, Mayoralty Courts[2] &ca. are exercised　therefore this Complex System can be as Easily carried into practice—

Mr. Lee
Wants a final Judgement in the first Court.　Sec⟨ondary⟩ Appeals are Considered as Additional of case[?].

[23 June 1789]

Mr. Elsworth
Says that the General Law of England in some Instances found inapplicable to the Circumstances of some of the States—

---

[1] Assize judges met in the English shires for the trial of matters of fact in civil and criminal cases.

[2] Fiscal and mayoralty courts are executive courts.

Patterson

In the Chancery in England the Determination is the opinion of the Court and not the Law of the Land Shapen as the Court may please.

Section 1: Structure of the Supreme Court

Mr. Strong

Says in the manner We Vote there is no Responsibility   true—Neither was it intended We have no Affirmative No Nomination   therefore shoud not be responsible when We only express our Approbation—If We Actualy Named the Man We ought be answerable—The President ought to be responsible for he Selects the Man—Perhaps if the Senate the might had the Nomination they might Name Another though they dont altogether disapprove of the Man Named—

Pierce Butler Papers, PHi. The editors believe that Butler took these notes for the purpose of responding to individual senators. It is not always clear which of the remarks in the notes were made by the senators named and which were made by Butler.

Shall the bill pass?
[17 July 1789]

[Butler]

It may be well Sir before We Send this Judiciary Bill down to the House of Representatives to allow Ourselves to reflect one moment on the Ultimate tendency of it, which manifestly will be to destroy, to Cut up at the Root not only the State Judiciaries but to and to Anhialate their whole system of Jurisprudence & and but finaly to Swallow up every distinguishing Mark of a Distinct Governmt. now equal to the purposes of Civil society.

It is a Singular and Strange effect if it shall result—It is to me a Phenominon if it shall result in tracing from things A Posteriori from effect to Cause to find that the result of Success, in contending for rights the most precious shall be more destructive of those rights than the System against which We Contended against, and finaly successfully overturnd—

If the People of America Shall be Subject to two Systems of Jurisprudence to the Passions and Caprices of two Sets of Judges or Rulers their Situation is not bettered by their Success; and they have been Contending for a Phantom—That this will be the Case if the presen Bill before you is adopted in its present State can not well be denied—The District Courts and Still more the Circuit Courts are paramount to the Laws of the Individual States and of Course to the Courts that are to Administer those Laws—I may Shall be told Sir that this

System does not interfere between Citizen And Citizen—true Sir—But this is not the most Important object—If in all Civil or Criminal Causes it shall opperate on a Ci against a Citizen of any Individual State while He is bound down by the Laws of His that State in all Concerns Civil or Criminal with the Citizens of His own State—His Situation is more precarious than it was under any System of British Jurisprudence heretofore Established in America.

I shall be told Gentlemen perhaps will say that this Centricaling power in the General Judiciary is Essential for the preservation of the Supremacy of the General Governmt.   I differ from those who think so.   But I contend Sir in such a Wide Extended Republick it can not opperate an hour longer than it has the intire Approbation And Confidence of Every State; nay of the influential Men of [lined out] Every State.

The moment that Men find that One System restrains them while another leaves them open to other they will Combine to Counter Act and finaly oppose that System that Exposes them to Injury or inconvenience while they are in many, perhaps to them the most important Cases, precluded from the like benefit that is given to their opponent Adversary.

Perhaps some Gentlemen will tell me that my objections extend to destroy all Centricaling power in the General Judiciary—I answer No—I woud give them Appellate Jurisdiction in all Cases, And Original in Admiralty or Maritime Cases And in whatever related to the Collection of the Revenue of General Government—Everything beyond this will on trial be found delusive   time will Call it a wanton Exercise of power in Order to try what Men may be brought to bear—The Seldomer the Main Spring is Exerted to its utmost power the longer will it retain its original Strength.

Possibly It may be asked said—What word What! woud the Gentleman then destroy this System after all the time We have taken up in Debating it! To this I answer Our time is the property of those who Sent Us here—that it is better to Sacrifise a little time than to send out a System that will Create Discord—Sow the Seeds of Jealousy & destroy that Confidence that at present the People of America are well disposed to place in Us.

Sir I think We are obliged to the Gentlemen who Arranged the Bill before Us—If the Principle is just the Bill is Well Executed but it is the principle I contend against—Against all power but Appellate Powers Except in Admiralty or Revenue Cases   I shall be under the Necessity of Entering my protest if the present Measure shoud be insisted on—But I have reliance on the Wisdom & prudence of this House to take from Me that the painful Necessity of entering my a protest, By Confining the Bill to the Exercise only of Such powers as [illegible interlineation] are Sufficient for the preservation of General Justice, peace and Good National Governmt.

Pierce Butler Papers, PHi.

Debate on the Method of Senate Consent to Treaties[3]
[22 August 1789]

Mr. Elsworth—

All the power necessary to carry the Legislative measure into Effect are given to the President only—In all Grants Treatise all are given that are not especialy reserved   all that are not Expressed in Treatise Civilians Say are reserved— They that make Treatise only can Construe them—The Gentleman asks in Order to Enforce his Argument is it Judiciary & [*illegible*]—No he says it is Executive & that all Executive power Vests in the President—He says the President must not take no ask our Advice in Anything   pray how is he to make Treaties   If powers are to be Exercised by Implication surely it makes as Strong for the Exercise of this power ~~as for the president~~—in the Senate as the President—He says the President is to direct Him therefore it is the President himself—If this reasoning is good the President must Appoint Him, but that is not the Case—

The Gentleman Prophesies about what may herafter happen to the Execu- tive   as I am no Prophet I will not follow him here

In Order to Secure Tranquility You must make a Tyrant   He says the people are dissatisfied at the small, Executive power Vested in the Senate   Yet in the former part of His Argumt. He says all Executive is Vested in the President.

Pierce Butler Papers, PHi. The editors believe that Butler took these notes for the purpose of responding to individual senators. It is not always clear which of the remarks in the notes were made by the senators named and which were made by Butler.

Debate on the Treaty of Fort Harmar
with the Six Nations[4]
[22 September 1789]

[Butler]

No province while Under the British Government was allowed to purchase Lands from the Indians   No objection was made by Massachusets and new york to that treaty—therefore the desire of postponement is not well- founded   though the territory might be said to be in an Individual State yet the Governors of those States were never permited to Grant the Lands held or possess'd by the Indians—Mr. King says that Genl. Sintclair exceeded His Powers—He asks if the Six Nations have fomented hostilities   he himself

---

[3]This debate is recorded in the *SEJ*; the related document is printed in the *SEJ*, pp. 353–57.

[4]This debate is recorded in the *SEJ*; related documents are printed in the *SEJ*, pp. 3–6, 40–41, 160–63. General Arthur St. Clair, governor of the Northwest Territory, negotiated the treaty on the part of the United States.

answers No—There is then the Greater obligation to faithfully observe the treaty

Debate on the Seat of Government Bill [HR-25]
Shall section 1 and part of section 2 be postponed?
[23 September 1789]

[*Butler*]
Mr. Morace
says that this business has had a full discussion in the other House—
He is regardless of threats held out by Virginia—Yet He says there will be no peace in Israel—He believes Pensilvania will give the money—I believe not otherwise they woud not have offered the Buildings of Philada.   he hopes as the Publick mind is alarmed We shall take it up
He says he will attend to those who threaten Us with a Consumption of time—

Pierce Butler Papers, PHi.

Debate on the Rhode Island Trade Bill [S-11]
[11, 14, 18 May 1790]

[*Butler*]
It is no infringement on Her Sovereignty to withdraw Your Trade—Civilized Countrys call this a declaration of War   opposition to Boston Port Bill[5] was Natural right   Pray what is this—It is hard that so Small a part shoud have any power as it were to put a Veto on the Interests of the whole   Granted—Mr. Izard says thire little State is brought into Compact with the other States.

Pierce Butler Papers, PHi.

Debate on the Residence Act S-12
Comments when introducing the bill
[7 June 1790]

[*Butler*]
I have said before that when We formed this Confederacy We did it under the Strongest Conviction of equality   I mean equality of advantages that the

---

[5]The first of Parliament's Coercive Acts against Massachusetts, passed in 1774 after the Boston Tea Party, the Boston Port Bill closed the port of Boston to trade and prohibited the loading or unloading of ships in Boston harbor.

State of Del. shoud have an equal Title to the ~~advantages~~ benefits flowing from the Union as V⟨irginia⟩. or M⟨aryland⟩.

No honest Man coud think otherwise

No Candid Man Advocate the contrary   It woud be a sentiment too humiliating—to have admission &ca.

I need no better evidence of Advantages resulting &ca.

If the Conveniencies and benefits are greater &ca.

the Inconveniencies and &ca. equaly   It shoud then be so Centricaly placed &c.

If the direct Rays cannot

Whether We shoud gratify Philad. or N.Y. is not I conceive &ca.

but where shall &ca.

that & that only ought to be our Object

Where is that proper point

If We run a line—

that is the Centre of Territory so far as regards the Sea Coast   this We will agree ought to be One leading object to fix our Judgement

But if We carry our idea of Territory farther We shall find that the Southern States have Stronger Claims   take all the Country East & No. E. of the Del.

If Resourse is an object &ca.

Half the Wealth is South of Susquehanna—The true Criterion of Wealth ~~is~~ are exports—Say the best Writers on Finance—I believe the position to be a Just One   how do We stand in this point

Exports before the War three Million—Suppose now four

Georgia	150,000
So. Carolina	700,000
No. Car.	300,000
Virgini	800,000
Maryland	400,000
	2,350,000

here We See Clearly that Wealth and Extent of Territory is in favour of the Southern States and woud warrant a much more southern position

If Population be taken into View and

but allowing for a progress of 20 Years I think the Centre &ca.

but if it were reasonable to suppose it woud yet the other two objects Territory & Wealth warrant a more southardly position—So that the So. States will be Considered as not Claiming the whole of their right in trying to fix Congress on the East Bank of Patomack

With respect to the position we shall find it desireable on more points than One   It is not only Centrical or nearly so as to Territory but it is on a Navigable River looking to a preservation of the Union with the Western Territory—It may be placed in a healthy, Rich & fertile Country.

If Navigation for Sea Vessels is Covited Georgetown is a very desirable position. the Tide flows about 5 Miles higher   If Gentlemen wishes to go higher Up I shoud Suppose the Next best Station woud be some where about the Mouth of Connegogig [*Conococheague Creek*] which is about fifty or fifty 3 Miles above Georgetown or 80 by Water—from Connegogig to Fort Cumberland is 54 Miles in a direct Line or 78 by Water—from Connegogig to the Mouth of Savage River the head of Navigation is 57 Miles from there to Cheat River 33 Miles or 38 by the present road—Any Batteaux may Navigate from that part of Cheat River where the road Strikes it at Duncards bottom to Fort Pitt 79 Miles in a right Line

From Duncards bottom on Cheat River to Morgans town [*Morgantown, W. Va.*] on the Mohongahely [*Monongahela River*] is 22 Miles by the Road—

from Fort Cumberland to Red Stone fort [*Brownsville, Pa.*] on Mohungahelee is a Portage of 60 Miles from there to Fort Pitt 40 Miles—

From the Mouth of Connegogig to the Pensylvania line is 9 Miles   from Hancock town [*Hancock, Md.*] to the Line is 1 Mile & 3/4   from Hancock Town to Connegogig is 19 1/2 Miles

I mention these distances to shew that the Pensylvanians have no right to object to this Situation as the Seat of Government will then be nearer them than to the other 10 States.

The Country about Hagars town [*Hagerstown, Md.*] is rich Level and highly Cultivated—In Short I think that God & Nature intended this Situation as the Bond of Our Union

Pierce Butler Papers, PHi.

Debate on the Funding Act [HR-63]
Shall the report of the committee appointed on 11 June be adopted?
[18? June 1790]

[*Butler*]
Mr. Elsworth

Says You throw 15 or twenty Millions into the Markett to be Speculated on— What ever You do have no dead Stock   have live Stock that a poor Man may hold His Stock as well as a rich Man—Are You to Adopt a System for which You must Mortgage everything   Where then is Your resourse—You must run to Europe to borrow Money like England   You must borrow for every trifle— did ever a Nation to go to War for Instance with its own Capital—He says that the Creditors will be satisfied   I say no—but if they were we are not Justified in doing it   there is no Compulsion he says—Is it not Compulsion when You give the first Tax to the Subscribers—

fund at what rate You please the Speculation will be the same   then His former Argument falls to the ground about dead Stock

he wishes every holder may know the Value of His property So he will in 3 Months on the Dead Stock—He says every Man knows the Value of His Land— he may know his own Estimation but the Value must depend on the Nature of the Government

Pierce Butler Papers, PHi.

Shall the report of the committee appointed on 15 July be adopted?
[19? July 1790]

[*Butler*]

1st. Article—Not practicable this Year as the Impost are not payd ad Valorem—If they were the Lands woud be rated lower than their *real* Value to avoid pressing hard upon such as might lose part of the product of the Land by rains or other Accidents.   I conceive a just Appraismt. *on Oath* by three Independent Gentlemen Certified through all the forms by Notary, State Secretary & the Governor with the seal of the State woud answer the above purpose just as well—

[Art.] 7 Shall not be held to furnish more than the Eight ℔ Ct. of their Quota of the Loan or Capital borrowed for any longer term than 27 or 28 Years

A. 9   Quere   Reserving to themselves the right of being Reimbursed by the Proprietors of the Landed Estates so far as relates to the Capitals redeemed by the One ℔ Ct. sinking fund which was always intended as a Reserve to make good Eventual Losses—By this Article it is meant and intended that if any subsequent Loss shd. contrary to probability happen to an Amt. greater than the 1 ℔ Ct. fund of the Year the Capitals redeemed in the preceding Years by the 1 pr. Ct. shall be liable to such losses as may happen in any subsequent Year Not intending by this Article however to invalidate that part of the 7th. article that obliges the borrowers to furnish no more than Eight ℔ Centum on their Quota of the Loan or Capital for a term not Exceeding 27 or 28 Years—

Article 21   So long as the whole of Each borrowers ~~Loan~~ Capital shall not be redeemed the whole property Mortgaged shall remain bound Agreeable to the regulations in the 7th. 8th. & 9th. Articles

Pierce Butler Papers, PHi.

Debate on the Report on the National Bank
and the Bank Act [S-15]
[23 December 1790]

[Butler]

I do not rise to find fault with the Secretarys Report but to offer my Sentiments to Senate on the Establishmt. of a Bank on a Construction some what differing from the proposed Plan—

The Secretarys own Report proves in different places that the benefits will be local and partial

[23 December 1790, 10–20 January 1791]

[Butler]

Influence of Wealth on Individuals   how much more in Bodies politick Country Men Can not discount Notes without a resident Endorses—hence the Landed Interests made Dependent on the Commercial   destructive of Order   It ought to be Constructed to facilitate the payment of the Taxes Say the Excise as well as the Imposts—It is Calculated for Commerce not to Encourage Agriculture   might in the moment of any temporary disorder be a dangerous Instrument for the Executive to Court & Use—Interest on the Lodgement of Publick Securities—Where there Are wrong Ballances it will facilitate the Draining of Specie to the Centre

Pierce Butler Papers, PHi.

[23 December 1790, 10–20 January 1791]

[Butler]

Principles seem to teach Us, that Commerce should rather be the Consequence of Agriculture, Arts, and Manufactures than the means of them.   Agriculture being the Basis All the rest follow of Course, and progressively in their Order: But to begin with Commerce, and so in an reverse method, through the medium of Arts and Manufactures to arrive at the Culture of Land, is a reversal of All Order in the œconomy of things, and Constitutes their retrogade Motion—The progress to refinement in Bodies Political as well as Natural should be by degrees, not hasty Stride   By the Union is it meant that We shall plunge into all the refinements of the British System however dissemal Our Situation   England adva[nced] by Degrees to Her Commercial

Greatness—She proportiond means to Ends—She prudently made Agriculture the foundation of Her Wealth and Consequence

Pierce Butler Papers, PHi.

Debate on the Resolution for Open Sessions of the Senate
[24 or 25 February 1791]

Combinations of Men
the simple Yeas and Nays do not Elucidate Mens Sentiments—prevents Members from Justifying themselves out of Doors by publick Appeals   Measures
Carrid by a very bear Majority are at a distance often Submited to under an
Apprehension of its being a more general opinion

Mr. Izard
says the privileges granted to the House of Lords was for the good of the people
not on their own acct.
Nothing Spoken in Congress Shall be questiond else where   this was to prevent Individuals insulting Members for anything they have Spoken

Mr. Morace
Shoud the Doors be opend there will not be the same Decorum—

has not pride of Character an Influence on Our Conduct   Has not then
publick opinion an Effect on Our Conduct

Pierce Butler Papers, PHi. The editors believe that Butler often took notes for the purpose
of responding to individual senators. It is not always clear which of the remarks in the notes
were made by the senators named and which were made by Butler.

Debate on the Sinking Fund Act [HR-136]
[2 or 3 March 1791]

Mr. Elsworth
that it Carries with it Jealousy & mistrust   We shoud be free from Jealousy &
Mistrust   preposession is Wrong because of Impeachmt.   If We Entertain a
Distrust We ought to be peculiarly Cautious how We Express it

He says the Loan is not objectionable on acct. of the Sum—the Interest is
small—You do not Encrease Debt   He says as it is only An Anticipation—Is

there any probability of it's being Wanted—Have You a Sufficiency without it
He asks & Ansrs. No

    200,000   to   Bank

    700,112[?]   Dolrs. Interest
      150   Civil List
      200   War Department

Will any Gentleman Suppose a Quarter Revenue will [*illegible*]   He lays
foreign Loans out of the question   Why because it makes against Him
The Revenues Cant be Collected within ~~now~~ one or two Million this Quarter
Is it not he asks Demonstrable that this Loan is necessary   the Money on the
Bills is for foreign Loans

Pierce Butler Papers, PHi. The editors believe that Butler often took notes for the purpose
of responding to individual senators. It is not always clear which of the remarks in the notes
were made by the senators named and which were made by Butler. The lines between
speeches may indicate a change of speaker, that Butler spoke, or that he stopped taking
notes.

The Notes of William Samuel Johnson

Debate on the Foreign Affairs Act [HR-8]
Can the president remove federal officeholders?
[14 July 1789]

[*Johnson*]

1 Had formd. no Opin⟨io⟩n. (& am sorry could not have Credit) as believing that the Sen⟨at⟩e. wd. inst⟨antl⟩y. reject it coming in so Quest⟨ionabl⟩e. a shape.

2. Yet through out some tho'⟨ugh⟩ts. of the grounds of doubt which taken as Artful Argum⟨en⟩t. I defendd. it not but cooly attended the Arg⟨umen⟩t. on the other side willing to be convinced, but own the more I hear the better am satisfyd. that those who hold that the Presid⟨en⟩t. has this Power by the Const⟨itutio⟩n. are wrong.   I cannot find it there—Believe it is not there.

3. There is but one Arg⟨umen⟩t. which all repeat.   That it is exped⟨ien⟩t. & best the Presid⟨en⟩t. shoud have this power—Then they argue The 1st. Clause is a Grant of all power—The subseq⟨uen⟩t. Except⟨io⟩ns. to be taken strictly, & leaving this in the Presid⟨en⟩t.

4ly. I think they are mislead as many good Men have been in Divin⟨it⟩y. They 1st. Form their plan, then seek for Texts of Script⟨u⟩r⟨e⟩. to supp⟨or⟩t. it.   so here 1st think it best then find it in the Constit⟨utio⟩n.   Wrong end.   But examine it striped of the Ornam⟨en⟩t.

5ly. This a Grant, & compared to Grant of Land.   It is not a Grant, but a Repartit⟨io⟩n. of the Powers or if a Grant poss'⟨esse⟩s nothing so Vague & inde⟨finit⟩e.   consider it by itself—*The Execut⟨iv⟩e. shall be Vested* What is execut⟨iv⟩e.?   Gent⟨leme⟩n. have shewn one thing here an-o⟨the⟩r. there.   Supp⟨os⟩e. this all   could you have said what it was?   The Leg⟨islativ⟩e. Jud⟨icia⟩l. same   could you have made anything of it. No.   The Land shall be Vested—The Money shall be Vested   What a Grant!   Nothing.   My Colleag⟨ue'⟩s. Grant of 10 Acr⟨es⟩. 20 Acr⟨es⟩. &ca.   Right.   but how unlike this.   toto Colo Differt.[1]   This misleads you—Thus apply Rules improperly.

---

[1]Diametrically opposed.

6ly. But look to Const⟨itutio⟩n.   The People speak—This Peop⟨l⟩e.   Thus Circumstancd. as State Govern⟨men⟩ts.   Federal Govt.—We Grant— You are to find them in the grant or necess⟨aril⟩y. implied or they are not The 1st. Not a Grant only a Repartition.   They then go on to Define—None here that Rule that particulars contr⟨o⟩l. the General if not repugn⟨an⟩t. even if a Grant which it is not—As Release.

7ly. Consid⟨e⟩r. then the partic⟨ular⟩s.—Here the first Gr⟨an⟩t. of Power. The last but one a very compreh⟨ensiv⟩e. one but not that convey this power. 8ly. See then if not Grantd. by necess⟨ar⟩y. Implicat⟨io⟩n. in that Grant of App⟨ointmen⟩t.—It is from Nat⟨ur⟩e. of thing as Ten⟨an⟩ts. at Will, A joint Will—2ly. As universal Constr⟨uctio⟩n. & Practice.   Unumquod-q⟨ue⟩ dis⟨s⟩olv⟨itu⟩r. eod⟨e⟩m. mo⟨d⟩o. ⟨quo ligatur⟩[2] can you show example to contrary?   Is not this the case throug⟨hou⟩t. the world?   In all the States—They found on double Implicat⟨io⟩n.   1st. of a Grant where none—2ly. Against an Act⟨ua⟩l. Power which clearly con[veys] it where no exception—So of Treat⟨ie⟩s.   can Pr⟨e⟩s⟨iden⟩t. [do aught with⟨ou⟩t the Senate]?[3] Treat⟨ie⟩s. may be dissolvd. by Agree⟨men⟩t.   can he Agree alone.   They may be Declared Null when one party Violates—Can he de-clare—It is indeed an execut⟨iv⟩e. Power but vested in Presid⟨en⟩t. & Sen-⟨at⟩e. by Vesting the App⟨ointmen⟩t. to which it is necessarily inciden⟨ta⟩l.   This Const⟨ructio⟩n. might place it any where   supp⟨os⟩e. had given it to Legis⟨latur⟩e. or to Sen⟨at⟩e. by ad⟨vic⟩e. of Repr⟨esenta-tive⟩s. or even in Sup⟨rem⟩e. C⟨our⟩t.   Co⟨u⟩ld Presid⟨en⟩t. dismiss. They Presid⟨en⟩ts app⟨ointmen⟩ts.   Is it not taught of Thos. Aquinas.

I medd⟨l⟩e. not with exped⟨ienc⟩y. It depends. on the Con-⟨stitutio⟩n.   We sit not here to make a Const⟨itutio⟩n. but to execute the one we have.   It is theref⟨or⟩e. a waste of time to talk of it.   I want no Powers.   I will usurp none.   but I will renounce none that are given.   I wd. perhaps willingly have taken more.

Let me however just observe That the weakness of the Grant so Conferred lies not there—but in his want of durat⟨io⟩n.—& ~~not particip~~ [*blotted out*] not participat⟨in⟩g more conclusively in the Legislat⟨iv⟩e. so as to hold firmly the Bal⟨anc⟩e. between Sen⟨at⟩e. and Rep⟨resentative⟩s. [*blotted out*] To Defend himself ag⟨ains⟩t. both.

What I chiefly regret is the Decept⟨io⟩n. we are putting upon the People.   We all know That the Const⟨itutio⟩n. in this point was defendd. on the ground I contend for.   That excel⟨len⟩t. Fed⟨eratio⟩n. defendd. on this

---

[2] Every obligation is dissolved by the same means with which it is created.
[3] The words "do aught" through "Senate" are no longer visible in the manuscript. We have taken them from a transcription made in 1936 and kept with the document.

gr⟨oun⟩d. We all did so. No sooner met, without a reason or Motive change our ground, & by a forced const⟨ructio⟩n. give this power. What will People say wantonly insult their Underst⟨anding⟩? Where is our Prudence & Policy—

William Samuel Johnson Papers, DLC. The manuscript is annotated "Draft Sp⟨eech⟩" by Johnson.

The Notes of Rufus King

Debate on the Seat of Government Bill [HR-25][1]
Shall the bill be postponed until the second session?
22 September 1789

Butler—I am opposed to this bill—suitable buildings may be obtained with out public Expence, it is therefore Unnecessary to borrow a large sum of money for that object—I move to postpone the consideration until the next session—

Grayson I second the motion from So. Carolina—The bill is exceptionable—it is a problematical what rule shd. be chosen to decide this question—some say population, some wealth, and others Territory—besides the expence is an objection.   Virga. has by law offered £100,000, provided the Congress will reside in that State—Pensa. ought to do the same—Lands and money shd. be offered by the State which solicits the residence.   In addition to this, we shd. wait till a new Census, & until No. Carolina & R. Island are in union—we are well accomodated here, and are un[*der*] no necessity to remove to Cabbins & a place of general inconvenience—

Morris I presume that a postponement will not obtain—the objection from the appropriation of money is not of importance—I think that the 100,000 Dollars will be loaned in Pen.   nay the State will give the Land, and pay to the amount of 100,000 Dollars towards erecting the buildings—I cannot speak with positiveness concerning the Legislature of Pensa. but if they do not I am certain that Individuals will do all that is necessary—and if the Law passes, I doubt not but that the Delegates of Pensa. will come forward at the next session with a proposition offering free of Expence to the U.S. a suitable District and monies to a considerable amount to erect the buildings for the accomodation of Congress—

Lee—I concur with my Colleague—we are well situated here, and shd. remain here until we obtain farther information concerning the proper place for a permanent Residence—

---

[1]In 1789 and 1790 King made notes about the off-the-floor politics of the location of the capital. They will appear chronologically with the correspondence and miscellaneous papers of the members in later volumes of the *DHFFC*.

Shall section 1 and part of section 2 be postponed?
23 September 1789

Mr. Morris—proposed and the senate agreed to postpone the preceeding part of the Bill establishing the permanent Residence of Cong. in order to take into consideration his motion to strike out the proviso, which requires the prerequisite of Laws passed by Maryland & Pennsylvania consenting to the removal of the obstructions to the navigation of the susquehannah—he observed that pensylvania would not gratify maryland by consenting to open this navigation, until Maryland would gratify Pennsyl. by consenting to the opening a canal communication between Chesapeak & Delaware Bays—that the proviso compelled Pensyl. to consent to the opening the navigation as a condition to have the federal town, & thereby deprives her of a consideration which wd. induce maryland to agree to the canal between Chesapeak & Delaware—besides he observed that Maryland might desire the permanent Residence to be fixed on the Potomoc, if so, the proviso requiring the consent of maryland to the opening the navigation of the susquehannah, she might decline giving her Consent and thereby defeat the bill—certain it is that many Gentlemen opposed to the Bill voted in favor of the proviso in hopes of thereby procuring the rejection of the bill—

Mr. Carrol—Maryland has incorporated a company who have power to open the navigation of the susquehannah within the state of maryland. that company has already expended many thousands to affect the navigation—this remark answers the objection that maryland might defeat the bill by witholding her consent that the navigation shd. be opened—Maryland has consented and the consent being in nature of a Contract cannot be revoked—as to the Canal between Ches. & Del. Pennsyla. has proposed the subject to Maryland, and Maryl. has appointed Comrs. to confer with those of Pensa. I think that Maryland will not object—one of the Comrs. has informed me that he has no objection, and if there is any objection, I think it must be in Delaware & not in Maryland—I prefer the Potomoc to the susquehannah, but if the proviso is retained and the potomoc cannot be carried I shall vote for the bill, if the proviso is lost I must vote against the bill—

Maclay. Pensylvania is not disposed to obstruct the navigation of the Susquehannah—the business of opening the Canal has languished—and by a late law passed on the 12 instant by Pensyl. the susquehannah is declared to be a common high way through the state of pensyl. and Commissioners are appointed to remove the obstruction—Pensyl. therefore has expressed her consent to the opening the navigation, and the proviso meets the opinion of the State as expressed by this law—I know & can speak with Confidence concerning the navigation of the susqueh.—all the supplies for Genl. Sullivan's Army passed through my hands[2]—Until Harvest or the last of Augt. there is water enough—the boats pass freely   they carry 60 Bll. of flour or 40 Blls. of Beef— Genl. Clinton drew his boats across from the Mohawk to the Head of the susquehannah and descended to the falls.[3]

Rufus King Papers, NHi.

Debate on the Residence Act [S-12]
Shall the bill be postponed?
8 June 1790

Mr. Lee moved to postpone the Bill introduced by Majr. Butler for the establishment of both permanent & temporary residence, to take up a resolution sent from the house that the next Session of Cong. shd. be in Philadelphia—a motion was made to postpone the whole subject till tomorrow—the Senate being equally divided (Mr. Johns⟨t⟩on & Mr. Few being both absent,) The Vice president voted against the postponement—Mr. Johns⟨t⟩on & Mr. Few being notified of the question, attended—Mr. Johns⟨t⟩on came with his night cap and wrapped in many Garments, attended by Doctrs. Bard & Romaine,[4] and having a Cot with a Matras in the antichamber to repose on— by general consent the resolution was taken up—and negatived 13. to 11—the report of the Committee was afterwards taken up & the first clause, which asserted the propriety of fixing the permanent residence at this time, was negatived by the voice of the vice president—the report being laid aside a motion was made to fill the blank in the Bill with Potomack as the permanent Residence—this was negatived as were also Baltimore and Wilmington—a motion to postpone the bill a fortnight, as also another motion to postpone it indeffinitely, were negatived—finally congress adjourned—previous to negativing the Resolution Mr. Butler told me that Mr. Schuyler & myself must vote to fill the Blank in the Bill with potomack, as they cd. not vote against the Resolution—I agreed so to vote—and finally voted accordingly—

Rufus King Papers, NHi.

[2]As an assistant commissary for purchase, WM was responsible for gathering supplies for Major General John Sullivan's expedition against the Iroquois in 1779.

[3]During the summer of 1779, General James Clinton dragged his bateaux across a twenty-mile portage from the Mohawk River to Lake Otsego. To transport the boats down the narrow creek that connected the lake to the East Branch of the Susquehanna, he dammed the mouth of the lake, cleared the creek of obstructions, and then broke the dam and floated down on the flood to the junction of the Tioga and Susquehanna rivers.

[4]King probably referred to Samuel Bard (1742–1821) rather than his father, John Bard (1716–99), who opened a medical practice in New York City with Samuel in 1767. Nicholas Romaine, a Columbia College professor of medicine, had an office at 156 Queen Street. (*New York*, pp. 93–94)

Debate on the Funding Act [HR-63]
[7 June 1790]

Sec. 1. [*Lee*]	By the appropriation of the duties arising from the existing impost & tonnage laws the government is precluded from altering these laws—commercial Laws and treaties may require alteration—Lee ~~And the~~
[*Morris*]	The savings from the *civil* list are appropriated to the foreign Debt. this is unnecessary; it will embarras the accounts & is unimportant, Morris
Sect. 2d. [*Butler*]	the Secn. shd. be amended by giving the Creditors on the new loans a right of refusing payment of any part of the Capital in less than 15 years. *Butler*

Shall the first two alternatives of section 4 be struck?
[9 June 1790][5]

Morris

I propose to strike out the 2 first alternatives because I object to a sale of the western Lands as proposed—the Lands will be of no value—the rights will depreciate like soldiers Rights, and will depreciate the residue of the public Lands—Let the Western Lands be appropriated sold & the money employed in purchasing the public Debt—I contend for Six ℈ Cent that is the Contr.

Elsworth

1	the quality of the Debt $^2/_3$ of real money wd. have answered the purpose of the whole Debt—there is therefore $^1/_3$ alloy
3d.[6]	the situation of the Debt as it relates to Purchasers—no discrimination can take place. but the public will never see with equal satisfaction a provision for speculators as if made for the or⟨i⟩g⟨inal⟩. Cred⟨ito⟩rs. others did not do so well with that money
4[7]	When we fund we must provide for extinguishing the capital—the western territory must be resorted to—these Lands must not not be given away according to the first alternative—
1.	the abilities of the government to raise the taxes for a full provision is doubtful—the loan will be voluntary. it will be called a *four per Cent*

---

[5]King used his notes on the speeches of Morris and Ellsworth as the basis for part of the next document.

[6]King wrote "3" over "2".

[7]King wrote "4" over "3".

loan. we shall have no credit for the Lands—they will in fact be given away—

let the alternatives be expunged, and a clause inserted to pay four per cent and no more—

Rufus King Papers, NHi.

[9 June 1790]

Wingate—I wish the alternatives expunged—and that we shd. lay taxes and pay the Creditors as much as they will produce—I would proceed in this way until I fully complied with the public Engagements—

Morris—I propose to expunge the two first alternatives; because I disapprove of a sale of the western Lands in the manner therein proposed—I think the Lands will in consequence thereof be of small, or no value; the rights or Certificates will depreciate as the soldiers Rights formerly depreciated and the residue of the public Lands will sink with the value of the Certificates—My wish is that the western Lands may be appropriated as a sinking fund, that they shd. be sold for money, and the money employed in the purchase of Stock—

Elsworth. We must proceed with deliberation—I am willing to strike out the first and third alternatives and to modify the second—We cannot pay six per Cent our abilities are not equal to it—so much of the alternatives as relate to Lands I wish expunged—I am willing because I suppose the public able to pay four per Cent—as the alternatives stand, the loan is called a four per Cent, and we shall waste an immense quantity of property by the Grants of Land without gaining any Credit—

In addition to the inability of the country I add, that there ought to be satisfaction among the Creditors by payment of 4 p. Ct.—because there is great alloy in the Debt—from the necessities of government, and other considerations the Debt is one third beyound what the services & supplies could have been procured for in ready money—

and because the certificates have changed hands—I do not desire a discrimination, but the purchasers came easily by their Property, and the public will not see a full provision for the Debt thus situated with as much pleasure as though the Debts had not passed from the hands of those who earned them—

and because, ~~under any~~ The public Creditors will be better situated with 4. pr. Ct. than any other description of Citizens those who put their Confidence in Govt. will be in a better Condition than, the merchant who has sunk his capital [or?] the purchasor of Lands which have depreciated in astonishing manner

One other Objection to the system is that the Lands shd. be sacredly preserved as a sinking fund—

Debate on the Residence Act [S-12]
Shall Congress establish no permanent residence
at this time?
29 June [1790]

Elsworth.

Being charged by majr. Butler with having deceived him when I said a few moments since, that I had given my Votes under a conviction that the permanent Residence could not now be established, and with a hope that the Bill wd. fail—I explain, I did tell that Gentleman that I wd. agree to Baltimore as the permanent Residence—I voted in conformity wt. this decision, and with a sincere wish & hope that my vote would succeed—that having failed, & the Potomack having been established, from that moment I hoped the bill would fail.

I am now convinced that the permanent Residence cannot be established— and am willing to pass a Bill giving a short Residence to N. York and then remove to Philada.

Rufus King Papers, NHi.

The Notes of William Paterson

Debate on the Impost Act [HR-2]
Drawbacks in sections 4 and 5
[11 June 1789]

Am⟨eric⟩a a Govt. sui Generis.

Drawbacks a Premium to smuggle. Established in comm⟨ercia⟩l. Nations—Will import no more than for the Home Consumpt. if no Drawbacks; otherwise if Drawbacks—There will be more revenue. Send out Rum & bring back Articles, that will bear the Duty—No Rum on Speculation—

2 Kinds of Drawbacks—

1. On Home Manufacture. 2. on foreign—the first right because of Industry & Wealth. No such Thing in this Country.

On foreign Manufacture—1. Tobacco. 2. Sugars—This is right.

Not on wrought Silks—nor on French Cambricks or Lawns—nor Calicoes printed, dyed, &c.

Easy to mix, modify, and confound N. England and W. India Rum; so as to export the latter under such Disguise—We are not a thorough Fare, as they are in Europe—

To what Country shall we export Rum—

The Dutch allow no Drawbacks—their Duties are very low—

An armed Force the only Way to prevent Smuggling, and may be the Foundation of a Marine—

The Principle of Drawbacks is, that we have no Right to tax a foreign Consumer—

An armed Force will not prevent smuggling out—

Gin is imported from Holland in Order to export to the East Indias, where it is used and drank when mixed with Water—So as to Brandy.

West Inda. Rum exported to Africa, to Asia, to the Baltic, ~~up the Straits~~ to Gibrlr.—

The People of this Country not worse than elsewhere—Export Teneriffe;[1] Sherry, & Claret to the East Indias—

Paterson Papers, NjR. Paterson took these notes without indicating who was speaking. By

---

[1] Teneriffe was a white wine from the Canary Islands.

comparing them with Maclay's account of the same debate, it becomes evident that some of the remarks Paterson recorded were made by Grayson, Ellsworth, and perhaps Maclay.

Debate on the Judiciary Act [S-1]
Motion by Lee to limit lower federal courts
to Admiralty jurisdiction
[22 June 1789]

[Lee and/or Grayson]

The amendmt. proposed by the Convention of Virginia—that there shall be no subordinate federal Courts except Admiralty.

1. A Stigma upon State Courts; that they will not do what is right—&c.
2. There may be an appeal from the State Courts to the federal—
3. Circuit Courts cannot pervade so extensive a Country, as this.   The Idea taken from the Mother-Country—

How then as to appeals—
England—Scotland—
Nisi Prius Courts.
Mass of people if corrupt no Laws can effect—
They operate on the same Objects—
2 Supreme Legislatures, omnipotent—
No Proof that the Debt is due—☞
No Time to study—
Abolition of State Legr.—

Paterson's Notes for his reply on 23 June 1789

Objects different—
Self-Preservation—As to Crimes—as to Revenue—Judges annually appointed—Sheriffs—regrs.
Why Admiralty Jurisdn.—
When & how are the Facts to be tried—
How as to Appeals—
Bring Law Home—meet every Citizen in his own State—not drag him 800 miles upon an appeal—The silent operation of Law—or by Force—An appeal from Scotland to England—No appeal in criminal Cases—Sup. Court cannot go into each State—
The Necessity—Utility—Policy of federal Courts—they grow out of the Nature of the Thing—
A number of Republics confederated.
Why call upon other Tribunals—

Clashing of Jurisdn.—will destroy their Respectability—
Uniformity of Decision.

A Beauty—if the Bill presents—
I consider federal Courts as inevitable—the Necessity.
Who are we—
United we have a Head—separately we have a Head, each operating upon different Objects—
When we act in Union—
The States in their federal Capacity have an Ex—have a Leg—and who shall adjudicate—Judges chosen by the Union—no—Judges &c.   They legislate upon different Objects, their should be other Judges to decide upon them—It grows up out of the very Nature of the Thing.
The State Tribunals consist, &c.   The Union has no Vote in their Election, &c.
Consider how appointed—some annually, &c.
Their Salary—how paid—They become your Judges—fixed upon you during good Behaviour—entitled to a permanent Salary—and therefore if the State refuses to elect them the year following, the Union will be saddled with the Expence of 3 or 4 Judges in a State instead of one—Or if your Judges no longer than they are State Judges then you make them entirely dependant upon the State.   Is this an elegible Situation—
Ap. of casting a Stigma, &c.   fear their Virtue—
We have as Men individually our Interests, &c.   So as to States—
Shall we suffer Men so situated to mingle in our federal Admn.—
Their Interests—
    1. Different Objects—therefore different Tribunals—
    2. Situation of the State Judicatures—

Again—Consider over what the Dist. Court is to exercise Jurisdn.
    1. Adml.   2. Crimes of a certain Grade.   3. Revenue—
The first conceded.

    2. as to Crimes—an axiom, that every Com⟨munit⟩y. ought to have within itself & to retain in its own Hands the Powers of self preservation.
Offenses will arise, &c.—Your Existence depends upon their Punishment   if committed, will you put it in the Power of S⟨tate⟩. J⟨udges⟩. to decide upon them—&c.—you put your Life in their Hands—you present with a Sword to destroy yourself—
    No Appeal.
    3. Revenue—Do not give up the Power of collecting your own Revenue—you will collect Nothing—The State Officers will feel it their Interest to consult the Temper of the People of the State in which they live rather than that of the Union—

4. Become one People.   We must have Tribunals of our own pervading every State, operating upon every Object of a national Kind.

Hence Uniformity of Decision—

Hence we shall approximate to each other gradually—

Hence we shall be assimilated in Manner, in Laws, in Customs—

Local Prejudices will be removed—State Passions & views will be done away—the Mind expands—it will embrace the Union; we shall think, and feel, & act as one People—

Circt. Courts—Mistaken Notions of them—Not in the Nature of Nisi prius.   Courts of origl. Jurisdn.—you carry Law to their Homes, to their very Doors—

meets every Citizen in his own State—

Not many appeals—if q⟨uestio⟩n. intricate, adj⟨ourne⟩d. till next Term & take the Opinion of the Judges.   appeals from the State Tribunals—monstrous—you make them expensive & oppressive.

Cirt. Courts cannot pervade the Country—too extensive.   Silent operation of Laws.

The Laws should be more wisely framed—judiciously expounded, & vigorously executed in Republics than in Monarchies—

England—Scotland—

Two omnipotent Bodies—Aversion of People to strange Judicatures—Pope's authority; & King's.

England.   Scotland—An appeal from Scotland to England—

Some Courts are appointed by the People—limited by age—some during Pleasure—

Cannot compel them to act—or to become our Officers—

How as to Jayls—what Power over Sheriffs—Gov. of Laws.

When a Crime is created, who shall have Jurisdn. of it—you must enlarge the Jurisdn. of a State Court.

The Constn. points out a Number of Articles, which the federal Courts must take up.

The objects are not different—they legislate upon Persons and Things—

Corporations shew the actual Existence of distinct Jurisdns.—

The Constn. has made the Judges of the several States the Judges of the Union; because they have taken an Oath to observe the Constn.—

This proves too much—

Instance the State Legislatures.

The Oath is in Nature of an Oath of Allegiance, and not an Oath of Office—

Transcript, Bancroft Papers, NN.

[23 June 1789]

[*Paterson*]

The Proposition now before the House has undergone a very able Discussion. It ~~is a~~ involves Question of Magnitude; and no Doubt will receive the most dispassionate Investigation. What Objects shall the Jurisdn. of your Dist. Court ~~shall~~ embrace, what Qn. of Power shall be attached to it. ~~It~~ This is the Qn. & it is proper to consider it with a critical Eye—Gent. yesterday took a large Field—they viewed the whole System—they took it in Connection—~~this perhaps they considered~~ this perhaps was right. A Beauty frequently results from a View of the whole ~~System~~, which is lost when garbled, or taken by Piecemeal. If the Bill presents a System properly founded, the more thoroughly it is examined the ~~better~~ brighter it will appear the more it will please; if bad, if radically defective, the sooner it tumbles to the Ground the better. ~~Let me consider it~~ Ever since the Adoption of the Constn. I have considered federal Courts of subordinate Jurisdn. and detached from State Tribunals as inevitable—The Necessity, the Utility, the Policy of them strikes my mind in the most forcible Manner—The Arguments made Use of Yesterday must carry Conviction—Who are we—how compounded—of what Materials do we consist—We are a Combination of Republics—a Number of free States confederated together, & forming a social League—United we have a Head—separately we have a Head—each ~~acting~~ operating upon different Objects—When we act in Union we move in one Sphere, when we act in our individual Capacity, we move in another. Totally different, & altogether detached from each other—God grant they may remain so—Contemplate the States in their federal Capacity. they have an Executive—they have a Legislature consisting of two Houses to frame Laws for the Weal and Salvation of the Union—And who are to adjudicate upon these Laws—Judges chosen by the Union—No—A new Era indeed—Judges chosen by the respective States; in whose Election the Union has no Voice, and over whom they have little or no Control. This is a Solecism in Politicks—a Novelty in Govt.—The State-Tribunals consist of Judges elected by the States in their separate Capacity to decide upon State Laws and State Objects; they are not elected to decide upon ~~St~~ national Objects or Laws, except as they may come in incidentally in a Cause. The Union has no Vote in their Election, no Voice in their Appointment—they are Strangers—Creatures of the State—dependant upon the State for their very Subsistance—

Consider how appointed—In some States annually—in some States for a Term of Years—in some during good Behaviour—In most they depend ~~upon~~ for their Salary upon the Legr. from Year to Year—It is reducible to this Dilemma—either they become your Judges & so fixed upon you during good Behaviour & entitled to a permanent Salary, and therefore if the State refuses to choose them the Year following, the Union will be saddled with the Expence of both of them in a State because they are they have become your Judges—or if your Judges no longer than they are State Judges then you make entirely dependant upon the State—Is this an eligible Situation—

It is said, that it has the Ap. of casting a Stigma upon State Courts; that you fear their Virtue—that they will not do what is right—I do not think it should be viewed in that Light—It is a proper Precaution agt. dependant Men— However I may value a Man, yet if he be dependant upon another, I should not like to submit to his Decision a Dispute in which that other is concerned—We have as Men individually our Interests, Connections, & Ambition—So as to States—Shall we suffer Men so situated to mingle in ~~the~~ federal Adm. their Interests—Virtue—Vice—

1. Different Objects—different Judicatures—2. Situation of the State Tribunals—

The Objects—1. Admy. 2. Crimes of a certain Grade 3. Revenue

The first conceded—but why—cannot the State Tribunals decide upon Mari⟨time⟩. Causes subject to an Appeal as well as upon others—

2. As to Crimes—It is an Axiom, That every ~~Sta~~ Com⟨munit⟩y. ought to retain in its own Hands the Means of Self-Preservation—If Offences be committed agt. the Union, will you put it in the Power of State Judges to decide Thereupon—to acquit or to condemn—I hope not—You put your Life in their Hands—you present them with a Sword ~~wherewith~~ to destroy yourself—Suppose New Jersey was to make such a Req⟨ues⟩t. of Virginia—

No Appeal—

3. As to the revenue—~~repeat not~~ do not give up the Power of collecting your own Revenue—How is to be done—you will collect Nothing—The state Officers will feel it their Interest to consult the temper of the People of the State in which they live rather than that of the Union—

There must therefore be Distt. Judges of more extent of Jurisdn. than maritime Causes—

4. To become one People—We must have one common national Tribunal— hence Uniformity of Decision—hence a band of Union—we shall approximate to each other gradually—be assimilated in Manners, in Laws, in Customs—

Circuit Courts—State Tribs. keep up local Prejudices, &c. Mistaken Notions of them—not in the Nature of Nisi Prius—They are Courts of original Jurisdn.—you carry Law to their Homes, Courts to their Doors—meet every Citizen in his own State—not many Appeals—if Q⟨uestio⟩n. is intricate, adjn. till next Term & take the Opn. of the Judges—

Appeals from the State Tribunals—Monstrous—you will make it expensive & oppressive—
Circuit Courts cannot pervade a Country so extensive as this—Silent operation of Laws—The Laws should be more wisely framed, judiciously expounded, & promptly executed in Republics than in Monarchies—

England—Scotland

Paterson Papers, NjR.

Section 1: Structure of the Supreme Court
[23 June 1789]

The Number of Judges not sufficient—Life, Liberty, and Property.   House of Lords in England—Sessions in Scotland 13 or 15—No Appeal from them—

———

Too few, if Circuit Courts—too great, if no Circuit Courts—

———

The Powers of the S. Court are great—they are to check the Excess of Legislation—
The State-Courts will take up the great Mass of Business.
Difficult to get Judges enough
Numbers no Security agt. Corruption—

———

Sections 4–14: Structure, jurisdiction,
and procedures of federal courts
[24–27 June 1789]

Saving of Expence in Nisi Prius Courts—as to W⟨itnesse⟩s.
Arguments more solemn when at Bar—
Difficult for Parties to attend at the Sup. Court.
Extent of the Country—Great Labour & Expence—
Counsel—two Sets of them—
New Trials—
Gaol Delivery—Jury of Assize to ascertain the Fact.

Equity Cases should be reserved for Ch⟨ancer⟩y.—they should not be blended. Ld. Mansfield.[2] Equitising—keep them distinct—

Hab. Corpus & Sovereignty of the State—

Germany like America—Russians & Peter the Great.

People in the Extremity bold, enterprising, &c. not cringing, and courting Offices as about the Court—Must have Nisi Prius Courts, & not circuits—

Must trust a great Deal to State-Courts—

Advantages of Nisi Prius
1. Uniformity of decision.
2. Maturity of Judgment.
Comm⟨unicatio⟩n. swift, easy, and direct.

None—except as to a new Trial—

Ex con⟨tinenti⟩.[3] Affidavits—Cases.
Nisi Prius.

Why should not the Jurisdn. of the Distr. Court be complete & extend to all Cases at Law & in Equity, with an Appeal, limiting the same—

If a small Sum, it may involve a Question of Law of great Importance, and should be liable to be removed.—

Hambden—his a Cause of 20/[4]

_____

Sum of 500 D⟨ollar⟩s. small enough—General Intercourse—

No Complaint as to the Admn. of Justice—2. Sheriffs.

Dep⟨osition⟩s.—but how as to the Pl⟨ainti⟩ff. Concurrent Jurisdns.—

Pervade the Union—

More Satisfn. to the Parties—The Farmers in the New England States not worth more than 1,000 Ds. on an Average—

Money—Merchandize—Land bought and sold—

Suppose 2 District Courts in a large Distr.—

Where Titles are held under different States, each State will endeavor to protect its own Grant—they should be tried in the federal Court.

_____

[2]William Murray, first Earl of Mansfield (1705–93), was England's Lord Chief Justice from 1756 to 1788. Part of his published work became authoritative during his lifetime, especially in the area of commercial law.

[3]A term of the civil law meaning immediately without any interval or delay.

[4]The reference is to the refusal of John Hampden (1594–1643) to pay his share of the ship money levied as a tax by Charles I in 1636 without the consent of Parliament. The judges found for the king in *Rex v. Hampden*, but Parliament declared the levying of ship money illegal in 1641.

Section 15: Federal court procedures
[29 June 1789]

May compel a Man to disclose on Oath in one Side of the Court & not on the
other—Stranger—
No Ground for the Distinction.
More within the reach of Juries—Juries can judge of evidence—
Uncertain—Too common—better a particular Mischief than a general Incon-
venience—
Judges cannot infer a Fact from a Fact—
A Witness may testify agt. his Interest—
May in Com⟨mon⟩. Law Courts admit a Party's Oath by Consent—
Cannot compel a Man to discover a Fraud—A Factor—

Here ~~both~~ the Court possesses the same Jurisdn. both Law and Equity—
Cheaper swearing in one Court than the other—
An interested Person may swear in his own Behalf—
Less Delay, & less Expence in taking the evidence at Com. Law, than in
Equity—
Equity has swallowed up the Com. Law Courts—

In Delaware they have double Jurisdn.—much Confusion—
House of Lords take up Appeals from Equity—
Motion, that Clause be amended by swearing the Pl⟨ainti⟩ff.—
1. The same Judges here exercise both.   This perhaps an Imperf⟨ectio⟩n.—
impracticable—
2. Eq⟨uity⟩. has swallowed up the Com. Law—overleaped her Bounds.
How as to the Com. Law Courts.   Too strait laced—
3. Whether viva Voce Testimony preferable to written—not the Question—
No Interrogt. no Ex⟨aminatio⟩n. before the Judge or Exn.   The Answer—
~~Too sh~~
4. Why not swear in one Court as well as in the other—
Cheaper in one than the other—Make Oaths cheap—
An interested Person may swear at Com. Law—[5]
Both Plff. and Def⟨endan⟩t. ought to swear—
Novel Idea—
The Remedy is not reciprocal at Com. Law, it should be mutual—both
swear—

---

[5] The words "1. The same Judges" through "Com. Law—" appear to be notes Paterson
made for a reply to the remarks beginning "Here both the Court" through "by swearing
the Pl⟨ainti⟩ff—", which appear opposite them on the manuscript.

[30 June 1789]

Mode of Proof the same in the Bill in both Courts.

Provide for Mortgages; and then Equity will have Nothing to do—

Why have not the Com⟨mon⟩. Law Courts in England this Power—Parliament sits frequently—it is improper—

If the Judges thought with Blackstone, a Bill would have been brought forward—

A Witness interested may be sworn—

The Parties by mutual Consent may swear—

The Law—Wager—simple Contract Debt—but not tried by a Jury—

Ans. Auditors—the Parties there swear before the Auditors.   Lord Mansfield's Decisions generally followed—

Trial by Battle.

It will narrow the Court of Equity—

To try the credibility of W⟨itnesse⟩s.   To try a Question at Law—Very tedious—very expensive—and then an Arb⟨itratio⟩n. advised—

Paterson Papers, NjR. Paterson took these notes without indicating who was speaking. By comparing them with Maclay's account of the same debates, it becomes evident that some of the remarks Paterson recorded on 23 June were made by Maclay, Strong, Ellsworth, and perhaps Grayson; on 29 June by Ellsworth and Read or Bassett; and on 30 June by Ellsworth and Strong. The lines between speeches may indicate a change of speaker or that Paterson stopped taking notes.

Debate on the Foreign Affairs Act [HR-8]
Can the president remove federal officeholders?
[14 July 1789]

Maclay.   Impeachments confined to the removal from office—no other way of excluding from office—hold their offices during good behaviour—a presidt. should not turn out at his pleasure; it is a stigma; no man of abilities will submit to it.   The constn. contemplated offices to be held during good behaviour, & to be turned out by impeachmt. only   If at pleasure, it creates servility—which will lead to despotism—

It strikes at the very power of the senate—chief clerk.   Moves to strike out the whole Clause—not seconded.

_____

[*Langdon*]

Moved, that the words, *by the president of the U.S.,* be struck out,   it was seconded.

Elsworth.

3 powers—legislative, judicial, and executive—distinct—should be placed in different hands.   To turn a man out of office is neither legislative or judiciary power—

The ex., without any Thing more, has a right to make appointmts.—Certain restrictions in certain Cases—The president eventually appoints—

The rest⟨rictio⟩n. is as to the appointmt. and not as to the removal—Impeachment.

If no term annexed, every appointmt. is at will—

The president is the responsible person—responsibility rests in one—his reputn. his honor at stake—

If presid. impeaches and does not succeed, there will be a variance—he may have evidence in his own bosom—

If you strike it out, the impl⟨icatio⟩n. will be, that the presidt. has not the right.   It will create a Doubt instead of removing one—

Butler.

It takes away the Power from the senate—

The Senate has a certain Portion of the executive—

The Officer if good will check the Presidt. and do Nothing but what he ought to do—

Why not a check upon the legislature itself—

The judiciary is to determine the question—how get it there—

Presidt. cannot apoint without the senate—

The Senate a Check upon the Presidt.

Izard.

the power of appointmt. implies that of removal—

Can the Presidt. alone abrogate a treaty—

The King of England is part of the Legislature—he is the executive—Part of the executive vested in the Senate.   The Senate to protect the officer, if he behaves well—responsible—when—to whom—how—if he removes, you cannot impeach him—So as to the Senate—

A great Officer of State is not to do an uncons⟨titutiona⟩l. Act; if he does, tho' at the Command of the President, he will be liable to Impeachment—

The Presidt. will have a privy Council of some kind or other—Shall it be the Senate or others of his own choosing—

The Heads of Departmts.—only as to their Departmts.   besides, they are dependant.

Strong.

Senate has no active power; the moving principle

Johnson.

The Judiciary should decide—

No Distribn. of Powers in the Constn. as to Offices—Must not be construed as a Deed—All sub Modo[6]—Officers—at whose will—as much at the Will of the Senate as that of the Presidt.—two wills necessary to appoint, so to remove—This is a Principle; he who appoints, ~~be~~ must displace—

Lee—

It is only by inference in the Presidts.—what is meant by executive Power—

In England, the ex. possesses absolute Perfection—it is not the executive power of England, France, Holland, &c.

It refers to the Powers enumerated in the Constn.—

When the legislative Powers are mentioned, it is said all the legislative Powers herein granted—So it must be as to executive—

Perhaps removeable only by Impeachment.

The Ground of holding at Will is too precarious—

The Judges shall hold their Offices during good Behaviour—the Impl⟨ica-tio⟩n. that others should not—

The Presidt. if vicious may have a private Council to direct him—

The chief clerk—

Responsibility in the Presidt. is a mere Chimæra—can you bring him to justice—

Presidt. should have a public Council, who should sign the Advice they give, and then would be responsible.

Should lose Sight of bringing such a Person as the Presidt. to Punishmt.—

Let the Presidt. suspend pro Temp. till the Senate meets—

[15 July 1789]

Carroll—

The Presidt. to exercise the powers expressly given or necessarily implied—

Every particular ex. power is not enumerated—

The ex. commensurate with the leg. & jud. powers.

Must take Care, that the Laws of the U.S. are duly executed—

The power of Suspension is not in the Constn.

States-General in France in 14 [7] cited by Mr. Lee—

Atrocious Assumptions of Power in the Legislature—

Elsworth—

The words omitted on Purpose as to the executive.

---

[6]Subject to restriction.

[7]The reference is to the Estates General of 1484 at which certain members attempted to establish its right to control the membership of the King's Council. (J. Russell Major, *Representative Institutions in Renaissance France, 1421–1559*[Madison, Wis., 1960], pp. 80–94).

As to the Leg. 2 objects. 1. positive. 2. restrictive upon the states.

The ex. & jud. are co-extensive with the leg.—The ex. to carry into effect all the Laws, &c. of the Govt.—

The Enumeration does not go to all the powers of the ex.—an enumn. of part⟨icula⟩r. powers does not exclude others—Then the sweeping words—to see all the laws carried into effect.

No Implic⟨atio⟩n. it is express—

The Maxim, he that creates can destroy, does not apply; an inherent right—

The Presidt. appoints—The Advice of the Senate does not make the Appointmt.—

The Senate not a Council to the Presidt.—

The President's Power is not to be extended by Impl⟨icatio⟩n.—This false in Principle—

1. If not in the presidt. by Impln. it is not in the Senate.

2. It wants no Impln.—it passes by the Grant; it is like a Tree growing upon Land granted.

Dangerous to the Constn.—

The Officers should be attentive to the Presidt.

No Compl⟨aint⟩. agt. the Powers of the executive in England—The Leg. powers sufficiently extensive—~~tto~~ goes to all points—A Presidt., without a standing force, 4 yrs. in Existence, a qualified Neg. on the Laws—

Do you wish to embarrass the Presidt.—that he should decide upon a doubtful Question—

Izard.

Butler.

House of Commons. The Leg. is supreme. Blackstone.

Paterson Papers, NjR. The lines between speeches may indicate a change of speaker or that Paterson stopped taking notes.

[15–16 July 1789]

Suppose the Presidt. should desire him to do an improper Thing—
Jure divino[8]—

———

[16 July 1789]

Grayson
Must exclude the Clause in Question—

---

[8]By divine right.

The Presidt. is a State-Being, subject to local & state prejudices—

The King of England has a national Interest—has no Preference or attachmt. There a powerful nobility to counteract him—

This constn. nothing like that of England. it feeble Representn. of the people in the senate—*No intermediate powers here to stop the progress of the Presidt.*

4 Years with an Army is enough—Cæsar had but 5 years. The Senate is not amenable—The senate had a voice in the appointmt. and therefore the officer is under their Protection. The Genl. who arrests an officer has prejudged the Cause. Lord George Germain[9]—

The Inconvenience arises from the Nature of the Thing—

Triennial & septennial parl⟨iaments⟩. the work of the ex⟨ecutive⟩. who had corrupted the Parliamts.

The paper-Money of New York—

All leg. powers herein granted—The Expr. with respect to the ex.—a relative Expression—

Things not described will not pass—no ex. powers pass but what are mentioned—

Tenancy at Will. Presidt. & Senate Tenants in Comn. and a Body-politick—

Coparceners, Joint-Tenants, and Tenants in Com.—

The Leg. ought not to be limited; but the Ex. ought—

The Heads of the Departments ought to have some will of their own—they are to give their Opinions—Why so, if under the Subjection of the Executive—They are the officers of the nation, & not of the Presidt.—

If the Thing is in the Constn. why insert it in the Law; if it is not in the Constn. then give it, if necessary.

There will be every Attempt at Consolidation—the Senate will be weakened—because they are representatives of the State—throw more power into the Presidt.—[10]

Wingate—

If in the Constn. then unnecessary—it makes agt. the Presidt. unless the same Expressions are inserted in every Bill—Let us stand upon constitutional Ground—if not, you take nothing from the President—

Reed.

It being a supreme Legr. it was necessary to fix its Bounds. The Ex⟨ecutive⟩. admits of more general Expression to describe it than the Legislature.

---

[9]George Germain (1716-85), Lord George Sackville, was removed from military command for alleged disobedience to his commander in 1759. The court martial he demanded found him guilty and unfit to serve in any military capacity. The sentence, with a short commentary, was ordered read to British troops in every quarter of the globe.

[10]At this point Paterson delivered the speech that follows this document.

The appointmt. of officers is a Property of the executive—

The Senate can give him infn. respecting proper Characters for office—their approbn. necessary, he being a local man—not so as to removeability—

Responsibility of Character at Large—

The Legisl. must pay the Troops—they cannot be kept up without their Consent.   This a Check upon the Executive.

If lodged in the Senate, we should consider ourselves as watchmen over the executive, and responsible for them—Can we exercise this Duty?

Dalton.

Thinks the removeability belongs to the Executive—The Senate ought not to participate—

Izard.

The Gen⟨tlema⟩n. from Jersey has reviled all the Legislatures—
Establish a Tyranny—

Morris.

The ap. of an assumption of power will hurt the Senate.

Transcript, Bancroft Papers, NN. The line between speeches may indicate a change of speaker or that Paterson stopped taking notes.

[16 July 1789]

[*Paterson*]

In the present constn. the powers of governmt. are distributed into three branches, the leg. the ex. and the judiciary—It has been asked, what do you mean by the ex. Powers of Govt. under the federal Constn.—Is it like the ex. of England.   I answer, no.   In England the King is supposed to possess all possible Perfection in the scale of political Existence.   He can do no wrong; of course he cannot constitutionally be impeached, and tried—there is no responsibility.   Our Constn. views the Presidt. as a man, liable to Error, and capable of malversation—He is amenable to Justice, he may be impeached; if found guilty, he will be removed from office—Hence his responsibility—Resp. then is not that Chimera which some honble. gentn. suppose—Besides Resp. to the Tribunal of Justice, there is a Responsibility to the Opinion, & Sentiments of his fellow-citizens—his honor is concerned, his reputation is at stake; all the fine and aggrandizing Passions are in motion & tremblingly alive—4 years only in office—The same honble. gentn. has said, that the Presidt. should have a public Council, who should sign the advice they give, & who would be responsible—In answer—We are not to enquire, whether the Constn. is wisely framed or not; we have it—and it is our Rule to walk by—if open to discussion, I am at present opposed to a standing Council, because

destitute of secrecy, dispatch, energy, and responsibility—The mingling of
the ex. and senate has been esteemed by some as a very exceptionable Part of
the Constn.   The more the three great governmental powers are kept separate
the better—It is said, that the King of England is part of the Legr. & yet is the
supreme executive.   True—and this is right. 1. for the sake of preserving that
balance in governmt. which wise men think necessary—2. for the preservation
of the executive itself, otherwise he might be annihilated by the other two
branches of the Legr.—his Ex. depends upon his own will—It has been further
said, that there is no Distribn. of Powers in the Constn. as to Offices—this
leads to the true Point before the Senate—Suppose the Constn. had said, that
all the ex. powers of govt. should be vested in a Presidt. and nothing more—
would not the presidt. have the right of appointing all the Officers—It is a
right incidental to the executive, inseparably connected with it, that grows up
naturally and unavoidably out of the Thing itself—it is necessarily involved in
it—and what is necessarily implied is as strong as if expressly mentioned—
Such is the principle of Constn.—It is so with respect to Deeds, and Grants—
admitted by Dr. Johnston [*Johnson*]—but then it is said, that the Constn.
must not be construed as a Grant—Why not as to the Principle just laid
down—It is true, that the appt. of certain officers is sub modo—is qualified,
and restrained—and therefore in those Instances there is a Departure from the
general rule—How far—only as to the appointmt. itself—it is modified in that
particular and no other—It is Implicn. in both cases—if the Senate has the
Power of rem. jointly with the Presidt. it arises from Implicn.—from the
assumed Principle, that they who appoint must displace—and which Implicn.
is the most natural—

>It must be somewhere—
>Impeachmt.   Except where the constn. hath expressly laid down
>some Boundary or Exception—
>Strife—if he can procure a Majority of the Senate, he is fixed for-
>ever—
>Suppose Incapacity arising from a fit of Sickness—
>Suspension—no Suspension in the Constn.   A caballing Spirit.

Unanimity
Strength.
Dispatch
1. Bl. 250.
com. subordn.
he is not only the chief, but the sole mag. of the nation[11]—

Transcript, Bancroft Papers, NN. The manuscript was in private hands in 1942. (William
Paterson Case file, DLC)

[11]Blackstone 1:250 states that the executive is placed in a single hand for the sake of

Debate on ratification of the
1788 Consular Convention with France[12]
[22 July 1789]

1782. Jany. 6th. Article—Depended till 14 Novr. 1784. Feby. 1785 Letter from Doctr. Franklin.

1. The Scheme. Jany. 25th. 1782.
2. The Convention signed by Doctr. Franklin 29th. July, 1784.
3. The Convention signed by Mr. Jefferson—14 Novr. 1788.

a. not to trade.
b. as to chapels—funeral rites—

Octr. 3d. 1786—resolution of Congress upon the Report of the Secretary of foreign Affairs—and the Letter thereupon to ~~Dr. Franklin~~—Mr. Jefferson—

4 Art. Laws of Nations given to the Consuls—J⟨efferson⟩. Omitted—

7. 8. 10. 14.

Debate on the Collection Act [HR-11]
Shall oaths be required of shipmasters?
[23 July 1789]

Custom-House Oaths.
1. Unnecessary—the provisions in the bill sufficient—the same penalties.
2. Pernicious—has no effect on the bad—binds only the good—loosens the bands of society—their frequency will induce perjury. A snare for conscience.

The Checks in the Bill will do for Citizens, but not for Foreigners, without the Oath be retained—

The Impost will not be productive; people will say, because we have introduced smuggling, by omitting, the Oath—

Swear the Master where not interested—and the Mate also where not interested—

As the Consignee is to make Oath, it will check the Master—

The Master does not generally receive the Goods on Board, but the Mate, the former swears only as to his own knowlege—

"unanimity, strength, and dispatch" and that all others act "by commission from, and in due subordination" to the sole magistrate.

[12]This debate is recorded in the *SEJ*; the related documents mentioned here are printed in the *SEJ*, pp. 251–351.

Many honest Men distinguish between Malum in se and malum prohibitum[13]—the latter, they think, contains no moral turpitude—

Paterson Papers, NjP.

Debate on the Seat of Government Bill [HR-25]
Shall section 1 and part of section 2 be postponed?
[23 September 1789]

Seat of Governmt.
Greayson. Certain Points established by the House of Representatives—
1. Commerce—
2. Western Territory.
3. Access to the Atlantick—

———

No Fuel or Coal unless the River be[?] opened—Coal on the Banks of the Susquehannah—Arts, Sciences, &c. must have Water—

Morris—
Moves to have the Proviso-Clause expunged—Navigation of the Susqh. good above the Spot where the Town will be fixed—

Carrol.
The Potomack the proper Place for the Seat of the Govt.; it connects the Western Territory with us—Susquehannah the next best Place—If ~~struck~~ the Proviso be struck out he shall vote agt. the Bill.

McClay—
Act of Pennsylva. of 12th of Sepr., 1785 for clearing the Obstructions of the Susqh. from the Maryland Line upwards—

Shall the permanent seat of government be on the Potomac?
[24 September 1789]

Lee.
3 Things.
1. Extent of Territory.
2. Fertility of Soil.

---

[13]The former is a wrong in itself, illegal from the nature of the transaction, while the latter is illegal because it is prohibited by law.

3. Goodness of Climate—
Potomack will in some Time be the Centre of Population—
The Western Waters point to the Potomack—

Maclay.
  1. Actual Number of Inhabitants.
  2. Number of Representatives—
  3. Requisitions of Congress to shew Wealth—

Paterson Papers, NjP. The line between speeches may indicate a change of speaker or that Paterson stopped taking notes.

Debate on the North Carolina Cession Act [S-7]
[18, 22 February, 3–5 March 1790]

Bassett.
Want of Inf⟨ormatio⟩n.   Conditions—
Want of Certainty—   Right of Occupancy—
                                          —of Entry—   Non-residents—
                                          Completion of Titles in the Govm.—
                                          no Control over him—
Sentiments in the act of Cession impliedly agt. the Constn.   When Cession is completed or accepted then the Frontiers under the Protection of Congress. Be a Barrier for N. Carolina—

Wingate—wishes it delayed.

Few—agt. Delay—30,000 out of Jurisdn.

Langdon—for Delay—100 Miles beyond Sunset.

Elsworth—About 20,000,000 M⟨illion⟩s. of Acres—18 of which will be clear of all Claims—Some of the Grants not completed; want the Signature of the Gov⟨erno⟩r.—
Cond⟨itio⟩n. with Respect to Slaves—
Temporary Governmt. must be instituted—
People on the Frontiers already under the Protection of the Union—
    Can better manage the Indians when the Land is under Congress; than under a States—Can conduct Settlements better—prevent people going t in their a scattered Manner to their Injury and that of the Union—

Johnston.   N. Ca⟨rolina⟩.—The people there had rather be under Con-g⟨r⟩ess than the State—they live at a Distance—Qy. of Land not less than 16 Miln. of Acres.   No Entries in the pe Land Office since May 1784, when Armstrong's Office was shut[14]—No Returns of some Surveys made to the Secretary; who must transmit them to the Gov⟨erno⟩r. for Grants—Most of the Grants are completed—

Bassett.
The Title of Occupancy does not depend upon any Thing in Writing.

~~Hawkins~~
Wingate.
    N. Ca⟨rolina⟩. to have Credit for all they have paid—hereafter to be charged distinct from the Cession—the latter Congress must take—The Sum uncertain—$1/6$ of the people in the Cession—Congress must assume that $1/6$—

Docr. Johnson.
Every right to be determined according to the rule at the Time when the Right accrued.   As to Indians only a right of Pre-emption—as between Citizens an absolute right.
    a. Conveyance to Individuals, or Corporations.
    b. Such parts as belonged to the Crown
If Patent good for one part it is good for the whole.
Whether the Title of the Crown be by usurpation or Conquest is immaterial—Lex postlimini[15]—
Congress conquered for each individual State—
    Patent of Virginia vacated in 1624.   In Consequence the Crown was reinstated in its right, and actually exercised its right 'till the Revolution—Q⟨uestio⟩n. whether properly vacated—
Patent of North Cara. surrendered to the Crown—Did that revest the Property, or only the Jurisdn.—Georgia different.   A Settlemt. made by the crown, its Creature—A re-conquest by the U. States.

Few
Congress a right to control and govern the Indians.   The State of Georgia the right of Pre-emption to the Indian Lands.

Paterson Papers, NjP. The line between speeches may indicate a change of speaker or that Paterson stopped taking notes.

---

[14]In 1783 North Carolina established an office for the sale of its western lands with John Armstrong as entry taker. By the time the office was closed in 1784, when the state first decided to cede what became Tennessee to the federal government, three million acres had been entered, primarily by speculators. (Sam B. Smith and Harriet Owsley, eds., *Papers of Andrew Jackson* [Knoxville, Tenn., 1980], 1:37n)
    [15]The recapture of property taken by an enemy and restored to its original owner; restoration of the status quo.

Debate on the Naturalization Act [HR-40]
[8–9, 15–18 March 1790]

Tenure and protection of property belong to each state—The right of things—

An alien can acquire political rights only under Congress, as electing & being elected; the right of holding property belongs to the State—

———

No one can remove Disability as to holding Lands except he has the Power of Naturalizn.—

———

Denization—it does not flow from naturaln.—If to hold Property, why not to regulate its rules—

Who has power to enable an alien not residing here to hold Lands—Mortgages—

Every greater includes a less—if I empower a man to sell land, he cannot lease it—

The Constn. of delegated Powers.

The right to hold Land follows from Citizenship.   We can make a Citizen; we cannot do less—when a Citizen, the right to hold Lands follows—it is the effect of Citizenship and not of Naturalizn.

[*illegible*] Ju⟨d⟩g⟨men⟩ts.   Escheats.[16]

Naturalizn. includes both political rights and rights of Property—A foreigner has no rights—

Transcript, Bancroft Papers, NN. The debate is similar to that recorded by William Maclay on 17 March 1790. The lines between speeches may indicate a change of speaker or that Paterson stopped taking notes.

Debate on the Funding Act [HR-63]
Shall the first two alternatives in section 4 be struck?
[9 June 1790]

Motion to strike out 1 & 2 Alternatives.

Ellsworth.   agt. 1. and 3. and for retaining the 2d. or opening a Loan at 4 per Cent.   saying nothing about Land.   For money only.

---

[16]The reversion of land to the state; for example, when its heir is not legally entitled to hold it.

1. Will satisfy & make whole the Creditors; they will subscribe.

2. Two Classes—Creditors & Debtors.   Deprecn. & Doubt entered into the Loan; if hard Money, Supplies for $^1/_3$ less.   Will satisfy the public Mind at Large.

3. The Creditor could not make more than 4 per Cent. of his Money.   If he let it out, it depreciated—If in Trade, pretty generally lost.

If in Land, it does not net more than 4 per Cent.

Morris.   Not optional but compulsive—for the 6 per Cent—borrowing the Certificates and paying money.   Land to be omitted.   A Deception—It will lessen the value of the residue—make Land low at Market.

Butler—It is optional—must preserve Credit.   G. Britain.   No Violation in the first Instance—otherwise we can procure no Loans in Europe.   Much of the Debt in Hand of Foreigners; bought up—they will by Law of Nations compel the Payment.   Lands will sell in Europe.

Morris—The 3 alternative to be modified so as to pay 6 per Cent. for the whole—raise a Tax on Land—for the residue—

Ellsworth—Cannot raise 6 per Cent.   The Creditor more secure under 4 than 6—must consider the resources.

Dalton.   The Promise to remain at 6 per Cent; to raise 4 at present; or more or less according to our ability.

Dr. Johnson.   For 6 per Cent. pursue the nature of the origl. Contract—Much will depend upon the Skill & managemt. of Governmt. and the Opinion of the People—Consolidate the Western Land & the Proceeds of the Revenue.

Shall the state debts be assumed?
[10 June 1790]

Ellsworth.   State Debts for common Defence.   The Duty of the Union to provide for that defence.   at a Distance from Congress—Deficiency of Money & Credit in the Union—States mere Agents.

It will simplify the Business—have but one Set of Collectors—

Creditors will stand not on the same footing, unless the Debt be consolidated—Some fully pd., some half, &c.

Excise will be unequal; some States will draw a revenue from others—

The Influence of every Class of Credrs. should be united; it will make the fund productive—if different funds, a Clashing of Interest—If no assumption, the the Revenue Laws will not be carried into effect—

Obj⟨ec⟩t⟨ion⟩s. The assumption will render unequal Justice to the States; some have made greater Exertions than others.

1. Exertions nearly equal both in War & Peace—considering the ability & natural advantages of each State.

2. It will not prevent a final Liquidation.

Moves to assume the State Debts—

Lee   agt. Assumption—

A Violation of the Constn.   must not originate Money Bills, but may amend.   It is originating a vast Debt on the States.

Several of the States have paid their Debts.

Exertions unequal with respect to the Paymt. of Debt since Peace—

Make the Debt too much; cannot get through with it—unpopular.

Ellsworth.   This not a Money Bill—it may lay a foundn. for a Money Bill—if a Money bill, still may amend—Connectt. has sunk 1¹/₂ M⟨illion⟩s. of D⟨ollar⟩s. of her Capital since the Peace.

Strong.   Obj⟨ec⟩t⟨ion⟩s.   The States have given Certifs. and therefore the Union exonerated.

1. No general Govt. at the Commencemt. of the war.

2. After Confedn. little or no Credit; and therefore

3 The States called upon to give their Credit.   Requisitions made by Congress.

Unequal advances, because War unequal.

Impost taken away.

Carroll.   Not a Money Bill—may originate a Bill for the Purpose.

The other House will not pass it as an amendmt.

The public Mind should be informed.   The Union will manage the Resources arising from Revenue better than the States individually—Direct Taxes would give great Umbrage, especially to Virginia—

Doctr. Johnson.   Now the Time—The Bill is for funding the Debts of the U.S.—War of the Union—Debt contracted by Order of Congress or for their Use—To fund Part & not all is absurd.

Lee.   Had Govt. before Confedn.—look at the Powers given to the Members of Congress—A Combin⟨atio⟩n. of Council, purse, & Force—

Dist⟨inctio⟩n. clear between Continental and State Debts—Accts. not settled; do not know what Debts were contracted by Order of Congress and what not.

Langdon.   The assumption ought not to be connected with this Bill.

King.   They should be connected—

Morris. Wished the Bill had coupled them together—he will not risk it in the present bill, as it will be lost. He is in favor of the Assumption—

Ellsworth. 4 per Cent. cannot be raised without an Excise or direct Tax; neither of these can be collected unless we assume.

Transcript, Bancroft Papers, NN.

Shall the report of the committee appointed on 11 June be adopted?
[17 or 18 June 1790]

[Paterson's Notes for a Speech]

1. Just.
2. Inability to pay.
   Taxes in Europe.
   Funding—
   Depopulation.
   Direct Taxes—
   Do not the States lay them—
   Deprec⟨iatio⟩n. of Certificates.
   Optional—Contract to remain—
   Alloy. 2/ or 3/ in the Pound.

If funded agreeably to the 3d. Prop⟨ositio⟩n. and not paid will there not be a Breach of faith—

Clause in Act as to Contract—

[17 June 1790]

Maclay. Congress not concerned. The Public concerned.

[17–18 June 1790]

Lee. Hard Money lent by the Hollanders. Not the Case with the domestic Creditors. The latter shared the Blessings in Common.
   Equity to mitigate Law.

[18 June 1790]

Elsworth. Constn. does not contain any new Oblign.—
They stand precisely on the same Ground aft. this Govermt. or aft. the former.

A Gen⟨tlema⟩n. of S.C. laughed at the Idea of the Debt ever having been paid.　If a Loss to be confined to the domestic Creditors, & not to Foreigners.

Hard Money—

The foreign Debt on a governmental footing.　It is said, that Ability should be put out of the Question.　6 per Cent. beyond our Ability.

Houses—Coaches—

The Parson and the Devil.[17]

Ought not to make a new Promise beyond our Ability.

Contract—Every continental Bill carries a Contract on its Face—why not observe it—

4 per cent. with irredemiable Quality & Quarter Payments equal to $4^{1}/_{2}$ at least, perhaps 5 per Cent.　Besides Governmt. Security.

Strong.　In Trover for Certificates when Damages assessed at about 3/ in the Pound.

Congress not in Fault; the states not in Fault.　Deprecn. happened through Necessity—The Nation a Bankrupt.　Contract on Contl. Bills of Credit.

Congress represents both Credr. & Debtor; and to do Justice between them—

Bassett.

The Credrs. before the present Governmt. would have been contented ⟨to⟩ have $^{1}/_{2}$ a Cent ⟨per cent⟩.

Contl. Bills 100 for 1—Widows & Orphans.

Paterson Papers, NjR. William Paterson's papers were in a state of disorganization when Parke-Bernet put them up for auction in 1938. His Senate notes appeared in various lots at that auction and were sold to several collectors and libraries. In those cases when the location of the original manuscript is unknown to the editors, we are printing the high quality transcriptions that form part of the Bancroft Collection at the New York Public Library. These transcriptions were made for the historian George Bancroft as early as the winter of 1879–80, when William Paterson of Perth Amboy, N.J., allowed access to his grandfather's papers. (Emily King Paterson to J. Franklin Jameson, [1902?], Jameson Papers, DLC; George Bancroft to William Paterson, 10, 30 Dec. 1779, 11 Feb. 1880, Paterson Papers, NjR; *Parke-Bernet Catalog No. 40* [11 May 1938], pp. 38–41)

---

[17]The context suggests that Ellsworth illustrated his point with one of many stories based on the Faust legend.

The Notes of Paine Wingate

Debate on the Foreign Affairs Act [HR-8]
Can the president remove federal officeholders?
[16 July 1789]

[*Wingate?*]

[*advi*]ce & consent of senate a part of legislative or judicial
[*?*] at will; at whose will?
[*no?*]t responsible—Responsponsible for what?
nt responsible for the misconduct of his officers—
[*he?*] may not—
powers not clearly given by the constitution

When provision is made "that this officer is removeable by the President," may not be supposed that when like provision is not made in other bills that the officer is not removeable

When a President shall dye or go out of office will not his instructions cease of course?   And will the Secretary of foreign affairs have any power to do the business of that office until he shall receive instructions from his successor?

The question before the house is simply this, Shall the clause be struck out?

A long train of arguments have been adduced to prove that the const⟨it⟩ution vests this power in the President.   The hon. Gen. from Connec. & N. Jersies have imagined that it is clear to demonstration that this is in the constitution why then in such an agony for the clause—are they jealous that the president did not discern his power

Why not the ~~respective~~ Representatives of the respective [*?*] to appointment— Why not to be consulted before the nomination

Annotations on a copy of the 2 June 1789 printing of the Foreign Affairs Act [HR-8] (E-45654), Paine Wingate Papers, NhD. Words are missing where the imprint has been cut. Wingate also listed here the names of the senators who voted on 16 July against striking from the bill the language authorizing the president to remove officeholders without the consent of the Senate. See July 1789, n. 19, in Part I of this volume.

KF
350
D 63
1972
vol.9

297458

DATE DUE

MADELEINE CLARK WALLACE LIBRARY

WHEATON COLLEGE

NORTON, MA 02766

(617) 285-7722